WRITING and READING ACROSS the CURRICULUM

Fourth Edition

LAURENCE BEHRENS
University of California, Santa Barbara

LEONARD J. ROSEN
Bentley College

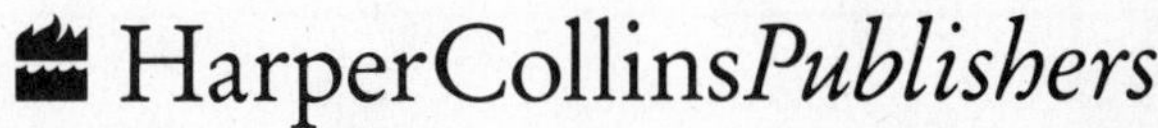
HarperCollinsPublishers

Other HarperCollins books by
Laurence Behrens and Leonard J. Rosen

Writing Papers in College (1986)
Reading for College Writers (1987)
Theme and Variations: The Impact of Great Ideas (1987)

Sponsoring Editor: Patricia Rossi
Development Editor: Linda Bieze
Project Coordination: Spectrum Publisher Services, Inc.
Text Design: Russ Schneck
Cover Design: Viviani Productions
Production: Michael Weinstein
Compositor: Kachina Typesetting Inc.
Printer and Binder: R. R. Donnelley & Sons Inc.
Cover Printer: New England Book Components

Writing and Reading Across the Curriculum, Fourth Edition

Library of Congress Cataloging-in-Publication Data

Behrens, Laurence.
Writing and reading across the curriculum / Laurence Behrens, Leonard J. Rosen. — 4th ed.
p. cm.
Includes bibliographical references.

1. College readers. 2. English language—Rhetoric.
3. Interdisciplinary approach in education. I. Rosen, Leonard J.
II. Title.
PE 1417.B396 1991
808'.0427—dc20 90-5221
CIP

ISBN 0-673-52103-6 (Student's Edition)

ISBN 0-673-54008-1 (Teacher's Edition)

91 92 93 9 8 7 6 5 4 3 2

To Bonnie and Michael—
and to L.C.R., Jonathan, and Matthew

CONTENTS

Sociology

Biology

Literature

A NOTE TO THE INSTRUCTOR

Writing and Reading Across the Curriculum, Fourth Edition, is a combination text-reader designed to help bridge the gap between the composition course and courses in other disciplines. The rhetorical portion introduces key writing skills that will serve students well throughout their academic careers, whatever their majors. The readings are arranged in topical chapters focused upon a variety of academic disciplines; individual selections represent the kinds of issues studied—and written about—in courses other than freshman composition.

The close relationships among readings in a particular chapter allow students to view a given issue from a number of perspectives. For instance, in Chapter 12 they will read how a neurologist, a political scientist, a Christian ethicist, and a fiction writer approach the subject of AIDS, and how these specialists present their characteristic assumptions and observations about the subject. In every chapter of the reader, students can practice the essential college-level skills introduced in the text:

- students will read and summarize articles;
- students will read articles critically and write critiques of them, identifying and discussing the authors' (and their own) assumptions;
- students will read several articles on a particular topic and synthesize them in both descriptive and argumentative essays.

THE ORGANIZATION OF THIS BOOK

The fourth edition of *Writing and Reading Across the Curriculum* is divided into two parts. The first part introduces the skills of summary, critique, and synthesis. Students move step-by-step through the process of writing essays based on source material. The text explains and demonstrates how summaries, critiques, and syntheses can be generated from the kinds of readings students will encounter late in the book. The first part offers a chapter on formulating thesis statements and on writing introductions and conclusions, as well as a chapter on quoting and documenting sources. (These last two chapters appeared, in a somewhat different form, in the appendices of the third edition.)

The second part of the text consists of eight chapters with related readings on topics such as gender identity, business ethics, and America in decline. The final chapter offers a casebook on Herman Melville's "Bartleby, the Scrivener" and asks students to draw upon wide-ranging criticism of Melville's story in order to help them develop their own critical responses.

A NOTE ON THE FOURTH EDITION

In preparing the current edition, as in preparing earlier editions, we have tried to retain the essential cross-curricular character of the text while providing ample new material to keep the book fresh and timely.

Part One consists of five chapters. Chapter One, on Summary, includes a new section on paraphrase; it provides a new model summary, based on David Suzucki and Peter Knudtson's "Biological Weapons: A Dark Side of the New Genetics." This chilling article ties in directly to a new chapter in Part Two on "The Brave New World of Genetic Engineering."

In this edition the chapter on Critique—a process involving just one source—precedes the chapter on Synthesis since we believe writing a synthesis, based on multiple sources, is a more complex process than writing a critique. The chapter on critique includes a new model critique of Carolyn Bird's essay, "College Is a Waste of Time and Money," one that shows a balance between positive and negative assessments. In the chapter on Synthesis, the model essays include parenthetical citations and lists of Works Cited, reflecting current Modern Language Association and American Psychological Association style. The two new chapters that conclude Part One include material on thesis statements, introductions and conclusions, and citing and documenting sources that applies to all the foregoing writing skills—summary, critique, and synthesis.

In Part Two, five of the eight chapters are entirely new: "Is America in Decline?" "The Brave New World of Genetic Engineering," "Business Ethics," "AIDS: Public Good vs. Private Rights," and "'Bartleby: Why Does He Prefer Not To?" The remaining three chapters, "Obedience to Authority," "Fairy Tales: A Closer Look at 'Cinderella'," and "Gender Identity," have been updated and include many new selections.

An innovation for this edition is that every chapter in Part Two includes one work of imaginative literature. For instance, the chapter on "Genetic Engineering" includes an excerpt from Aldous Huxley's *Brave New World;* "Gender Identity" includes "Tom's Husband," a short story by Sarah Orne Jewett; the "AIDS" chapter includes Susan Sontag's "The Way We Live Now"; and "Business Ethics" includes an excerpt from *Babbitt* by Sinclair Lewis. And throughout this edition we have increased the representation of women and non-Western writers.

While each chapter in Part Two has been identified in the Table of Contents by a specific academic discipline, readers should note that selections in each chapter are drawn from across the curriculum and are not meant to represent only the named discipline. In this way, each chapter gives students experience reading and interpreting topic-related literature.

We encourage all users—students and teachers—of *Writing and Reading Across the Curriculum* to continue to send to the publisher their suggestions for improving the book and their evaluations of its effectiveness. In particular, we invite teachers to submit copies of especially successful student essays based on material in this text for possible inclusion in the Instructor's Edition for the next edition.

ACKNOWLEDGMENTS

We would like to thank our colleagues whose evaluations and reviews helped us prepare this new edition of Writing and Reading Across the Curriculum. Specifically, we thank Professor Tina Bennett-Kastor, Wichita State University; Professor Alma Bryant, University of Southern Florida; Professor Kristine Daines, Arizona State University; Professor Cathy Dees, University of Illinois at Chicago; Professor Catherine DiBellow, Shippenburg State University; Professor Nancy Downs, University of Illinois at Chicago; Professor Faun Evans, University of Southern California; Professor Robert Frederick, Bentley College; Professor Michael Hoffman, Bentley College; Professor James Holte, East Carolina University; Professor Deepika Karle, Bowling Green State University; Professor Mary Libertein, Shippenburg State University; Professor Carol McKay, University of Texas at Austin; Professor Joan Monahan, Polk Community College; Professor Jerry Paris, New Jersey Institute of Technology; Professor Elizabeth Rankin, University of North Dakota; Professor Helen Woodman, Oakland University; and Amy Arai, Kathy Meade, and Larry Renbaum. Thanks to the many students of our composition courses who field tested much of the material here and let us know when we hadn't made things clear. Finally, our special gratitude to Barbara Russiello at Spectrum Publisher Services and to the splendid crew at HarperCollins.

Laurence Behrens
Leonard J. Rosen

A NOTE TO THE STUDENT

Your psychology professor assigns you to write a critical report on a recently published book on human motivation. You are expected to consult additional sources, such as book reviews and related material on the subject.

Your professor is making a number of critical assumptions about your capabilities. Among them:

- that you can read and comprehend college-level material
- that you can synthesize separate pieces of related material
- that you can intelligently respond to such material

In fact, these same assumptions underlie practically all college writing assignments. Your professors will expect you to demonstrate that you can read and understand not only textbooks, but also critical articles and books, primary sources, and other material related to a subject of study. For instance: In researching a paper on the Great Depression, you might read the historical survey you find in your history text, a speech by President Roosevelt reprinted in the *New York Times,* and a first-hand account of the people's suffering by someone who toured the country during the 1930s and witnessed harrowing scenes of poverty and despair. In a political science paper you might discuss the concept of "executive privilege" in light of James Madison's Federalist Paper No. 51 on the proposed Constitutional provision for division of powers among the three branches of government. In a sociology paper you might undertake a critical analysis of your assigned text, which happens to be Marxist.

The subjects are different, of course; but the skills you need to work with them are the same. You must be able to read and comprehend. You must be able to perceive the relationships among several pieces of source material. And you must be able to apply your own critical judgments to these various materials.

Writing and Reading Across the Curriculum provides you with the opportunity to practice the three, essential, college-level skills we have just outlined and the forms of writing associated with them, namely:

- the *summary*
- the *critique*
- the *synthesis*

Each chapter of Part Two of this text represents a subject from a particular area of the academic curriculum: psychology, history, political science, folklore, sociology, biology, business, public health, literature. These chapters, dealing with such topics as "Obedience to Authority," "Is America in Decline?" "The Brave New World of Genetic Engineering," and "Business Ethics," include the types of selections you will be asked to read in other courses.

Various sets of questions following the readings will allow you to practice typical college writing assignments. Review Questions help you recall key points of content in factual essays. Discussion and Writing Suggestions ask you for personal, sometimes imaginative responses to the readings. Synthesis Activities at the end of each chapter allow you to practice assignments of the type that are covered in detail in the first three chapters of this book. For instance, you may be asked to *describe* the Milgram experiment, and the reactions to it, or to *compare* and *contrast* a controlled experiment to a real-life (or fictional) situation.

Our selection of passages includes articles written by economists, sociologists, psychologists, lawyers, folklorists, diplomats, historians, and specialists from other fields. Our aim is that you become familiar with the various subjects and styles of academic writing and that you come to appreciate the interrelatedness of knowledge. Sociologists, historians, and novelists have different ways of contributing to our understanding of gender identity. Fairy tales can be studied by literary critics, folklorists, psychologists, and feminists. Don't assume that the novel you read in your literature course has nothing to do with an assigned article from your economics course. Human activity and human behavior are classified into separate subjects only for convenience.

We hope, therefore, that your composition course will serve as a kind of bridge to your other courses, and that as a result of this work you can become more skillful at perceiving relationships among diverse topics. Because it involves such critical and widely applicable skills, your composition course may well turn out to be one of the most valuable—and one of the most interesting—of your academic career.

PART

I HOW TO WRITE SUMMARIES, CRITIQUES, AND SYNTHESES

SUMMARY AND PARAPHRASE

1

WHAT IS A SUMMARY?

The best way to demonstrate that you understand the information and the ideas in any piece of writing is to compose an accurate and clearly written summary of that piece. By a *summary* we mean *a brief restatement, in your own words, of the content of a passage* (a group of paragraphs, a chapter, an article, a book). This restatement should focus on the *central idea* of the passage. The briefest of all summaries (one or two sentences) will do no more than this. A longer summary will indicate, in condensed form, the main points in the passage that support or explain the central idea. It will reflect the order in which these points are presented and the emphasis given to them. It may even include some important examples from the passage. But it will not include minor details. It will not repeat points simply for the purpose of emphasis. And it will not contain any of your own opinions or conclusions. A good summary, therefore, has three central qualities: *brevity, completeness,* and *objectivity.*

CAN A SUMMARY BE OBJECTIVE?

Of course, this last quality of objectivity might be difficult to achieve in a summary. By definition, writing a summary requires you to select some aspects of the original and to leave out others. Since deciding what to select and what to leave out calls for your own personal judgment, then your summary is really a work of interpretation. And certainly your interpretation of a passage may differ from another's. One factor affecting the nature and quality of your interpretation is your *prior knowledge* of the subject. If you're attempting to summarize an anthropological article, and you're a novice in the field, then your summary of the article might be quite different from that of your professor, who has spent twenty years studying this particular area and whose judgment about what is more significant and what is less significant is undoubtedly more reliable than your own. By the same token, your personal or professional *frame of reference* may also affect your interpretation. A union representative and a management representative attempting to summarize the latest management offer would probably come up with two very different accounts. Still, we believe that in most cases it's possible to produce a reasonably objective summary of a passage if you make a conscious, good-faith effort to be unbiased and not to allow your own feelings on the subject to distort your account of the text.

USING THE SUMMARY

In some quarters, the summary has a bad reputation—and with reason. Summaries are often provided by writers as substitutes for analyses. As students, many of us have summarized books that we were supposed to *review* critically. All the same, the summary does have a place in respectable college work. First, writing a summary is an excellent way to understand what you read. This in itself is an important goal of academic study. If you don't understand your source material, chances are you won't be able to refer to it usefully in an essay or research paper. Summaries help you to understand what you read because they force you to put the text into your own words. Practice with writing summaries also develops your general writing habits, since a good summary has almost all the qualities of any other piece of good writing: clarity, coherence, and accuracy.

Second, summaries are useful to your readers. Let's say you're writing a paper about the McCarthy era in America, and in part of that paper you want to discuss Arthur Miller's *Crucible* as a dramatic treatment of the subject. A summary of the plot would be helpful to a reader who hasn't seen or read—or who doesn't remember—the play. (Of course, if the reader is your American literature professor, you can safely omit the plot summary.) Or perhaps you're writing a paper about nuclear arms control agreements. If your reader isn't familiar with the provisions of SALT I or SALT II, it would be a good idea to summarize these provisions at some early point in the paper. In many cases (a test, for instance), you can use a summary to demonstrate your knowledge of what your professor already knows; when writing a paper, you can use a summary to inform your professor about some relatively unfamiliar source.

Third, summaries are frequently required in college-level writing. For example, on a psychology midterm, you may be asked to explain Carl Jung's theory of the collective unconscious and to show how it differs from Freud's theory of the personal unconscious. The first part of this question requires you to *summarize* Jung's theory. You may have read about this theory in your textbook or in a supplementary article, or your instructor may have outlined it in his or her lecture. You can best demonstrate your understanding of Jung's theory by summarizing it. Then you'll proceed to contrast it with Freud's theory—which, of course, you must also summarize.

It may seem to you that being able to tell (or to retell) exactly what a passage says is a skill that ought to be taken for granted in anyone who can read at high school level. Unfortunately, this is not so: For all kinds of reasons, people don't always read carefully. In fact, it's probably safe to say that they usually don't. Either they read so inattentively that they skip over words, phrases, or even whole sentences or, if they do see the words in front of them, they see them without registering their significance.

When a reader fails to pick up the meaning and the implications of a sentence or two, there's usually no real harm done. (An exception: You could lose credit on an exam or paper because you failed to read or to realize the significance of a crucial direction by your instructor.) But over longer stretches—the paragraph, the section, the article, or the chapter—inattentive or haphazard reading creates problems, for you must try to perceive the shape of the argument, to grasp the central idea, to determine the main points that compose it, to relate the parts of the whole, and to note key examples. This kind of reading takes a lot more energy and determination than casual reading. But, in the long run, it's an energy-saving method because it enables you to retain the content of the material and to use that content as a basis for your own responses. In other words, it allows you to develop an accurate and coherent written discussion that goes beyond summary.

HOW TO WRITE SUMMARIES

Every article you read will present a different challenge as you work to summarize it. As you'll discover, being able to say in a few words what has taken someone else a great many can be difficult. But like any other skill, the ability to summarize improves with practice. Here are a few pointers to get you started. These pointers are not meant to be ironclad rules; rather, they are designed to encourage habits of thinking that will allow you to vary your technique as the situation demands.

- *Read* the passage carefully. Determine its structure. Identify the author's purpose in writing. (This will help you to distinguish between more important and less important information.)
- *Reread.* This time divide the passage into sections or stages of thought. The author's use of paragraphing will often be a useful guide. *Label,* on the passage itself, each section or stage of thought. *Underline* key ideas and terms.
- *Write one-sentence summaries,* on a separate sheet of paper, of each stage of thought.
- *Write a thesis: a one-sentence summary of the entire passage.* The thesis should express the central idea of the passage, as you have determined it from the preceding steps. You may find it useful to keep in mind the information contained in the lead sentence or paragraph of most newspaper stories—the *what, who, why, where,*

when, and *how* of the matter. For persuasive passages, summarize in a sentence the author's conclusion. For descriptive passages, indicate the subject of the description and its key feature(s). *Note:* In some cases, *a suitable thesis may already be in the original passage.* If so, you may want to quote it directly in your summary.

- *Write the first draft of your summary* by (1) combining the thesis with your list of one-sentence summaries or (2) combining the thesis with one-sentence summaries *plus* significant details from the passage. In either case, eliminate repetition. Eliminate less important information. Disregard minor details or generalize them (e.g., Carter and Reagan might be generalized as "recent presidents"). Use as few words as possible to convey the main ideas.
- *Check your summary against the original passage* and make whatever adjustments are necessary for accuracy and completeness.
- *Revise your summary,* inserting transitional words and phrases where necessary to ensure coherence. Check for style. *Avoid a series of short, choppy sentences.* Combine sentences for a smooth, logical flow of ideas. Check for grammatical correctness, punctuation, and spelling.

DEMONSTRATION: SUMMARY

To demonstrate these pointers at work, let's go through the process of summarizing a passage of expository material. This passage, on the use of recombinant DNA technology in biological warfare, ties in to Chapter 10, "The Brave New World of Genetic Engineering." First, read the passage carefully.

Biological Weapons: *A Dark Side of the New Genetics*

DAVID SUZUCKI
PETER KNUDTSON

Biological warfare can be defined as the deliberate use of microorganisms or toxic substances derived from living cells for hostile pur- 1

David Suzucki and Peter Knudtson, "Biological Weapons: A Dark Side of the New Genetics," In *Genethics: The Clash Between the New Genetics and Human Values,* Cambridge: Harvard UP, 1989: 208–37.

poses—that is, to kill, injure or incapacitate human beings or the animals or plants on which they depend. It has aptly been called "public health in reverse," for it is founded on this dark premise: that the very pathogens—disease-causing viruses, bacteria, fungi and other microorganisms—against which medicine has waged endless battle can be used to military advantage by harming the health of political foes.

In principle, almost any agent causing a disease known to harm 2
human beings, their crops or their livestock could be used to fashion some sort of biological weapon. But in practice relatively few of these organisms satisfy the basic military prerequisites for a biological warfare agent. In general, these pathogens must be suited to mass cultivation in factories, be able to withstand artificial modes of storage and dispersal (e.g., in bombs or aerosol sprays) and cause rapid, predictable outbreaks of disease in target populations without harming attacking troops. Even with these practical restrictions, nature still offers biological warfare enthusiasts a bounty of potential biological weapons.

Any list of the militarily most promising diseases usually includes 3
a number of humanity's most feared scourges, along with an assortment of more minor, often mildly debilitating diseases. The names of some of the most virulent of these read like a litany of plagues from the past. Among the most terrifying of them are anthrax, a hardy, bacterial infection affecting both humans and domestic animals; pneumonic plague, a respiratory form of the ancient flea-borne bubonic plagues of the Middle Ages; smallpox, a fatal viral illness; and yellow fever, a mosquito-borne viral disease of the tropics.

The idea that science might *deliberately* try to transform human- 4
kind's shared reservoir of medical knowledge into a potent military arsenal is morally abhorrent to most people. Yet while they might be quick to acknowledge the possibility of subtle, indirect hazards inherent in many applications of genetics, few feel the need to contemplate the prospect of darker, manifestly malevolent schemes to harness genes. However, few seem to realize that even as we celebrate pioneering medical breakthroughs arising from recent developments in recombinant DNA technology and molecular genetics, there are indications that at least some scientists in the United States, the Soviet Union and other nations have received military funding to search for ways to use this revolutionary knowledge to design new, more sophisticated components—all of them ostensibly "defensive"—to existing biological weapons systems.

We would be naive to ignore the possibility that some of the same 5
genetic techniques that are now finding so many promising and beneficial applications in modern medicine—new vaccines, cloned hormones and other pharmaceutical products and prenatal diagnostic

tests for disease—could be applied to blatantly harmful, "anti-medical" ends. In the wrong hands, these techniques might, for example, be used to create arsenals of genetically modified microbes that could ignite uncontrollable epidemics in unwary civilian populations or to concoct proprietary vaccines reserved exclusively for the use of military troops or friendly civilian populations. Military applications of genetic technologies are every bit as feasible as medical ones. All that is required is money, scientific expertise, an atmosphere of moral indifference and the same sort of ingenuity that fuels practical advances in other, more humane applications of modern genetics.

. . .

THE MILITARY PROS AND CONS OF BIOLOGICAL BOMBS

What advantage could superpower military agencies, their arsenals already bristling with nuclear and conventional weapons, possibly seek in developing new, more efficient biological weapons? There may be several advantages—though they have not yet proved compelling enough to transform this traditionally unconventional form of warfare into a conventional one. In the first place, biological weapons are potentially more selective—though not necessarily accurate or precise—in causing destruction than flames, explosives or bullets. By zeroing in on living organisms, they can weaken or destroy enemy forces without damaging valuable physical property. Because of nature's incredible reservoir of diseases, biological weapons also offer a wide range of military responses, from swift, surgical guerrilla assaults on human populations using incapacitating agents to fungal epidemics that sweep through thousands of hectares of food crops. Compared with nuclear weapons, for example, biological weapons are also extraordinarily cheap, easy to mass-produce—they are self-replicating—and portable. In this sense, they can be seen as a potential low-budget deterrence system for poorer nations that cannot afford to build their own nuclear weapons arsenals. 6

But their most seductive feature may be their suitability for clandestine attack. Even genetically engineered microbes may turn out to be virtually indistinguishable from natural forms. Because microorganisms require time to reproduce and initiate infection, biological weapons also possess built-in time delays. The biological equivalent of fuses, they can provide precious hours, days, even weeks for a terrorist or saboteur to escape—making it even more difficult to trace a sudden epidemic to its source. 7

There are also distinct disadvantages. Foremost among them is the simple fact that most people around the world are morally repulsed by the idea that the military organizations of any nation might exploit deadly human disease. For this reason, the political consequences of negative world opinion in the wake of a documented biological warfare attack could easily outweigh any short-term military advantages. 8

Another disadvantage is the inherent unpredictability of any military arsenal that relies on biological systems. The genetic variability in populations of organisms, the inexorable process of gene mutation and the incalculable effects of environmental variables—from wind, weather and air pollution—all combine to guarantee an element of tactical uncertainty in launching an attack with a biological weapon. To this can be added the ever-present fear that the effects of a disease might boomerang, inadvertently killing or incapacitating the very troops that launched the attack—not to mention unsuspecting civilian populations living nearby. Not even amassing stockpiles of vaccines or antibiotic drugs against potential biological warfare agents is likely to fully lay this gnawing fear to rest. The wide range of natural pathogens available as biological weapons include many agents for which we currently have no effective vaccine or pharmaceutical remedy. Even more disturbing, recombinant DNA technologies now raise the specter of new strains of novel, genetically modified microbes controlled by military scientists. Such creations could eventually make the notion of an impenetrable defensive shield against future biological attack little more than a dangerous illusion. 9

Like any novel, genetically engineered organism concocted in the laboratory, new generations of recombinant biological weapons could conceivably cause long-term environmental consequences that are beyond our scientific ability to calculate. North American ecologists have already documented numerous historical cases in which the mere introduction of an exotic species—from the Asian fungus responsible for igniting epidemics of chestnut blight in eastern forests to flocks of aggressive European starlings that displaced the local species of songbirds—has led to significant changes in North American ecosystems. 10

But even with their dazzling, computerized models of ecosystems, ecologists are simply unable to predict the ecological impact of releasing waves of military microbes, each with its own novel genotype, around the globe. Would a novel pathogen, by causing low-level infections in nontarget species, for example, create new reservoirs of disease that would become a permanent feature of the biological landscape? Would it interact with other naturally occurring pathogens to produce a new disease that no one could possibly have 11 anticipated? Would the pathogen evolve in ways that might quickly render existing methods of military controls obsolete—thereby triggering uncontrollable epidemics that could linger on to infect future human generations long after the original motives for the biological attack had been forgotten?

. . .

A HYPOTHETICAL BIOLOGICAL WARFARE SCENARIO

The prospect of new generations of genetically engineered biological weapons is indeed a legitimate cause for public concern. Unfortunately, the topic of biological warfare has not yet emerged as a compelling concern to most people. To most, it smacks of alarmist science fiction and has failed to arouse widespread public indignation, in large part because of the lack of reliable information on the subject. 12

But our discussion of the use of recombinant DNA techniques to build biological weapons would be incomplete without raising a number of disturbing personal questions that arise only when one contemplates the real horror of biological warfare in action. What would it be like to experience a secret, state-of-the-art biological warfare attack in the future—one, for example, that targeted civilian populations and possessed no clearly drawn battle lines or official declaration of war? How might the victims of a highly selective, clandestine assault suffer from the artificial epidemic? How might other members of society—those unaffected by the artificial epidemic and unaware, perhaps, of its military origins—respond to the human suffering they witnessed around them? And, in the end, what kind of world would we be creating by passively permitting individuals or nations not only to design novel biological weapons but also to deploy them against fellow human beings? 13

Because of the secrecy that has always limited public discussion of biological warfare, most of us would find it difficult to formulate informed responses to such vital questions. Yet, unless we search for at least tentative answers to them, our image of modern biological warfare is bound to remain abstract, intellectual and devoid of a visceral sense of the grim reality of this unconventional mode of warfare. 14

In the absence of documented historical precedents of large-scale biological attack or a major laboratory accident involving recombinant biological weapons, we are compelled to draw on fictional scenarios of biological warfare to try to come to terms with the possible magnitude and scope of the hostile use of living organisms. 15

Consider, for example, the following thought experiment. Imagine that a team of scientists is engaged in a secret biological weapons research project on behalf of a fictional, extremely fanatical military regime or an underground terrorist ogranization. Their goal: to use recombinant DNA techniques to create a deadly human virus that might eventually be released to selectively infect a specific minority group that is perceived as a threat to that organization's plans to maintain or achieve political power. Imagine, further, that the virus the scientists hope to genetically modify into a future ethnic weapon happens to be an infectious, RNA-containing retrovirus closely resembling the virus we know as the Human Immunodeficiency Virus (HIV), or AIDS virus—the agent responsible for the fatal immune disorder known as Acquired Immune Deficiency, or AIDS. Finally, imagine that during the course of this clandestine research, a scientist commits a terrible blunder and a quantity of the potent, AIDS-like pathogen is accidentally released long before it has been genetically honed into the highly selective, efficient ethnic weapon its creators had envisioned. That is, the unfinished AIDS-like virus inadvertently begins to infect adjacent populations before the scientists have confirmed its host selectivity or constructed vaccines to protect nontarget populations. 16

We emphasize that we are not suggesting that the AIDS virus itself had its origins in biological weapons research in some part of the world. It is true that there have been isolated, and to date utterly unfounded, media reports containing claims by a handful of scientists in the United States, Europe and the Soviet Union that the AIDS virus could have arisen from a biological weapons experiment gone awry. However, this notion remains nothing more than speculation and has obvious potential for abuse as superpower propaganda. 17

While the precise origin of the AIDS virus remains largely a mystery, the prevailing view among reputable scientists is that the AIDS virus arose naturally decades ago from a relatively harmless animal virus resident in populations of wild African green monkeys in equatorial Africa. It is thought that this ancestral virus could have been transmitted to humans through the exchange of blood from a scratch or a bite wound. During the transition from animal to human virus, scientists speculate, the virus was somehow transformed into a deadly, more virulent human pathogen. 18

Like the AIDS virus, our hypothetical, renegade biological warfare agent can be transmitted by virtually any behavior that results in the exchange of infected human body fluids, including blood, semen or vaginal secretions—a common occurrence in human sexual activities as well as in such nonsexual situations as the sharing of contaminated hypodermic needles or transfusions using unscreened 19 blood or blood products. As a result, the AIDS-like virus spreads quickly through minority populations, which happen to be geographically concentrated in the region surrounding the clandestine biological weapons project. The virus thrives in these human hosts, who represent its intended target. But beause the host range of the crudely modified virus has not yet been refined to pathogenic perfection, the microbe can also infect anyone who inadvertently exchanged body fluids with the first victims of the artificial epidemic—including, ironically, the scientists responsible for the accident. As the AIDS-like infection begins to leak into nontarget populations, it gradually ignites a global epidemic, or pandemic, of unknown origin that, in a matter of years, affects millions of people.

And like the AIDS virus, this man-made virus causes a new disease that is clinically unknown to physicians. It too wreaks its havoc on the human body primarily by destroying a specific subgroup of white blood cells in the immune system—called helper T-cells—that are critical control elements in the body's cellular response to infection. As a result, infection with this novel, genetically engineered virus cripples the immune defenses of most of its victims. They die not from the direct action of the virus but from an assortment of opportunistic infections—characteristic forms of cancer, parasitic diseases and other illnesses that are normally rebuffed by a healthy human immune system. 20

As our fictional AIDS-like biological weapon spreads, we might expect it to leave in its wake an epidemiological pattern resembling in some ways that of the real AIDS epidemic. First, we might expect a biological warfare agent designed to meet the goals of our fanatical political organization to be targeted at specific minority groups judged by these malevolent minds to be the genetically "least desirable" elements of society. If the organization's eugenic agenda were blatantly racist, it is conceivable that its targets might include some of the same groups that are today disproportionately affected by the AIDS global epidemic. Among them: black, heterosexual Africans and North American blacks, Hispanics, homosexuals and intravenous drug abusers. Second, we might expect that agent to kill its victims with a relentless fury—of a kind rarely encountered in most naturally occurring diseases. Third, we might expect the agent to sidestep not only the human body's elegant natural defense system but also existing defensive measures of modern medicine—ranging from drug treatments to preventive vaccines. Fourth, in the absence of such immunological and medical controls, we might expect very rapid infection—triggering an epidemic that however horrifying to its victims and their loved ones might be viewed by some sectors of society as ideologically convenient. Fifth, we might expect the sudden appearance of a biological warfare agent with such uncon- 21 ventional characteristics to seem to be a bona fide medical mystery—at least for a time—to virtually everyone except the scientists who were responsible for it. And finally—in light of the inevitable uncertainties of designing diseases and the capacity of biological organisms to change and adapt to their new surroundings—we might expect to see the pathogen gradually diffuse beyond the intended "boundaries" of those populations originally targeted for infection. In a dramatic display of the impossibility of human control over the forces of disease, it might begin to spread rapidly in human populations characterized by other racial origins or sexual habits, including members of the very group whose research scientists had first conceived of the malevolent virus.

Our point in using an imaginary AIDS-like biological agent as an 22
illustration of a misapplication of molecular genetics is simply to suggest the terrifying extremes to which genetic knowledge could be exploited in service, for example, of political or religious extremists, or, for that matter, of emotionally disturbed individuals with scientific expertise. The point is to remind us how narrow the boundary is between the benign microorganisms with which we share our daily lives and the rare pathogen that can shatter our health. This thought experiment is meant to suggest that if we, as a society, willingly accept the application of genetics for building weapons, we had better prepare ourselves for a nightmarish world. For by harnessing the forces of disease to settle human conflicts, we will be entering into a Faustian bargain that could destroy the very qualities—compassion, empathy, altruism—that the majority of us most cherish in human beings.

Reread, Underline, Divide into Stages of Thought

Let's consider our recommended steps for writing a summary.

As you reread the passage, consider its significance as a whole. What does it say? How is it organized? How does each part of the passage fit into the whole?

As in many other passages, the main sections of "Biological Weapons: A Dark Side of the New Genetics" are indicated by subheadings. When a passage has no subheadings, you must read carefully enough so that you can identify the author's main stages of thought.

How do you determine where one stage of thought ends and the next one begins? Assuming that what you have read is coherent and unified, this should not be difficult. (When a selection is unified, all of its parts pertain to the main subject; when a selection is coherent, the parts follow one another in logical order.) Look, particularly, for transitional sentences at the beginning or paragraphs. Such sentences generally work in one or both of the following ways: (1) they summarize what has come before; (2) they set the stage for what is to follow:

For example, look at the sentence that opens the second section of this passage (paragraph 6): "What advantages could superpower military agencies, their arsenals already bristling with nuclear and conventional weapons, possibly seek in developing new, more efficient biological weapons?" This sentence, in the form of a question—a common form for transitional sentences—suggests the type of material that will immediately follow: a discussion of the advantages of biological weapons. Two paragraphs later, there is another transitional sentence: "There are also distinct disadvantages." This sentence sets the stage for the four paragraphs to follow.

The first sentence of paragraph 12, on the other hand, summarizes what has come before ("The prospect of new generations of genetically engineered biological weapons is indeed a legitimate cause for public concern."). It is followed by two sentences that set the stage for what is to follow—a discussion of a "hypothetical scenario" that should do even more to raise public concern.

Each stage of the article will take several paragraphs to develop. As you take notes, you might try writing your own section headings in the margins. Then proceed with your summary.

For review, the sections of Suzucki and Knudtson's article are as follows:

Section 1: Introduction—the nature and threat of biological warfare (our subheading; paragraphs 1–5)

Section 2: The military pros and cons of biological bombs (paragraphs 6–11)

Section 3: A hypothetical biological warfare scenario (paragraphs 12–22)

Here is how the first of these sections might look after you had marked the main ideas, by underlining and by marginal notation:

Definition of bio warfare

1 *Biological warfare* can be defined as the deliberate use of microorganisms or toxic substances derived from living cells for hostile purposes—that is, to kill, injure or incapacitate human beings or the animals or plants on which they depend. It has aptly been called "public health in reverse," for it is founded on this dark premise: that the very pathogens—disease-causing viruses, bacteria, fungi and other microorganisms—against which medicine has waged endless battle can be used to military advantage by harming the health of political foes.

In principle, almost any agent causing a 2
disease known to harm human beings, their crops or their livestock could be used to fashion some sort of biological weapon. But in practice relatively few of these organisms satisfy the basic military prerequisites for a biological warfare agent. In general, these pathogens must be suited to mass cultivation in factories, be able to withstand artificial modes of storage and dispersal (e.g., in bombs or aerosol sprays) and cause rapid, predictable outbreaks of disease in target populations without harming attacking troops. Even with these practical restrictions, nature still offers biological warfare enthusiasts a bounty of potential biological weapons.

Any list of the militarily most promising 3
diseases usually includes a number of humanity's most feared scourges, along with an assortment of more minor, often mildly debilitating diseases. The names of some of the most virulent of these read like a litany of plagues from the past. Among the most terrifying of them are anthrax, a hardy, bacterial infection affecting both humans and domestic animals; pneumonic plague, a respiratory form of the ancient flea-borne bubonic plagues of the Middle Ages; smalipox, a fatal viral illness; and yellow fever, a mosquito-borne viral disease of the tropics.

The idea that science might *deliberately* try 4
to transform humankind's shared reservoir of medical knowledge into a potent military arsenal is morally abhorrent to most people. Yet while they might be quick to acknowledge the possibility of subtle, indirect hazards inherent in many applications of genetics, few feel the need to contemplate the prospect of darker, manifestly malevolent schemes to harness genes. However, few seem to realize that even as we celebrate pioneering medical breakthroughs arising from recent developments in recombinant DNA technology and molecular genetics,

Some scientists already at work on bio weapons

there are indications that at least some scientists in the United States, the Soviet Union and other nations have received military funding to search for ways to use this revolutionary knowledge to design new, more sophisticated components—all of them ostensibly "defensive"—to existing biological weapons systems.

5 We would be naive to ignore the possibility that some of the same genetic techniques that are now finding so many promising and beneficial applications in modern medicine—new vaccines, cloned hormones and other pharmaceutical products and prenatal diagnostic tests for disease—could be applied to blatantly harmful, "antimedical" ends. In the wrong hands, these techniques might, for example, be used to create arsenals of genetically modified microbes that could ignite uncontrollable epidemics in unwary civilian populations or to concoct proprietary vaccines reserved exclusively for the use of military troops or friendly civilian populations. Military applications of genetic technologies are every bit as feasible as medical ones. All that is required is money, scientific expertise, an atmosphere of moral indifference and the same sort of ingenuity that fuels practical advances in other, more humane applications of modern genetics. . . .

"Uncontrollable epidemics" could be started

Write a One-Sentence Summary of Each Stage of Thought

The purpose of this step is to wean you from the language of the original passage, so that you are not tied to it when writing the summary. One-sentence summaries for each of these sections might read as follows:

Section 1: Introduction—the nature and threat of biological warfare

Using genetic techniques, scientists are developing new means of waging biological warfare.

Section 2: The military pros and cons of biological bombs

Biological weapons have the advantages of being selective, flexible, inexpensive, and clandestine; however, they are also morally repulsive to most people, unpredictable in their effects, and capable of causing long-term environmental damage.

Section 3: A hypothetical biological warfare scenario

To get an idea of what modern biological warfare would mean, we might consider the consequences of a fanatical military regime or a terrorist group engineering an AIDS-like virus to use against a particular minority group.

Write a Thesis: A One- or Two-Sentence Summary of the Entire Passage

The thesis is the most general statement of a summary or any other type of academic writing. (See Chapter 4.) It is the statement that announces the paper's subject and the claim that you or—in the case of a summary—another author will be making about that subject. Every paragraph of a paper illuminates the thesis by providing supporting detail or explanation. The relationship of these paragraphs to the thesis is analogous to the relationship of the sentences within a paragraph to the topic sentence. Both the thesis and the topic sentence are general statements (the thesis being the more general) that are followed by systematically arranged details.

To ensure clarity for the reader, *the first sentence of your summary should begin with the author's thesis, regardless of where it appears in the article itself.* In deductively organized passages, the thesis is stated first. In inductively organized passages, the thesis is stated last and is part of the conclusion. (To clarify terms: A *conclusion* either states or restates the thesis, depending on the organization of a passage. In the conclusion, an author may also expand upon the thesis by discussing its significance.)

If a thesis consists of a subject plus an assertion about that subject, how can we go about fashioning an adequate thesis for "Biological Weapons: A Dark Side of the New Genetics"? Probably, no two proposed thesis statements for this article will be worded exactly the same. But it is fair to say that any reasonable thesis will indicate that the subject is biological warfare—more specifically, the application of recombinant DNA technology to biological warfare—and it will also indicate that the authors are highly critical of such applications. What, then, do the authors basically assert about this new kind of biological warfare? We believe that they assert two main things: (1) that such biological warfare is currently under development and (2) that the results of such developments could be catastrophic to the human race.

Incorporating these ideas into a single statement, we come up with the following:

The application of recombinant DNA technology to biological warfare is a nightmarish, yet real prospect for the human race.

To clarify for our reader the fact that this idea is Suzucki and Knudtson's, rather than ours, we'll qualify the thesis as follows:

According to David Suzucki and Peter Knudtson in their book Genethics: The Clash Between the New Genetics and Human Values, the application of recombinant DNA technology to biological warfare is a nightmarish, yet real prospect for the human race.

Thus, the first sentence provides the reader with both the citation and the thesis of the passage in question. Of course, the author and title reference could also be indicated in the summary's title, in which case it could be dropped from the thesis.

Write the First Draft of the Summary

Let's consider two possible summaries of this passage: (1) a short summary, combining a thesis with the one-sentence section summaries, and (2) a longer summary, combining thesis, one-sentence section summaries, and some carefully chosen details:

Summary 1: Combine Thesis with One-Sentence Section Summaries

According to David Suzucki and Peter Knudtson in their book, Genethics: The Clash Between the New Genetics and Human Values, the application of recombinant DNA technology to biological warfare is a nightmarish, yet real prospect for the human race. Using genetic techniques, scientists are now developing new means of waging biological warfare. Military leaders or terrorist groups sometimes favor biological weapons because they are selective in their targets, flexible, inexpensive, and clandestine. However, such weapons are also morally repulsive to most people, unpredictable in their effects,

> and capable of causing long-term environmental damage. To get an idea of what modern biological warfare would mean, we might consider the consequences of a fanatical military regime or a terrorist group engineering an AIDS-like virus to use against a particular minority group. Such a virus could spread rapidly among people in the target group but might also spread into the general population—even attacking those who devised it in the first place.

Notice that this passage consists essentially of our restatement of the authors' thesis plus the three section summaries, altered or expanded a little for stylistic purposes. For instance, a transitional phrase ("Military leaders or terrorist groups sometimes favor biological weapons because . . .") connects the first and second section summaries; the second section summary has been split into two sentences; and we've added a concluding sentence that develops the catastrophe suggested in the third section summary.

Summary 2: Combine a Thesis Sentence, Section Summaries, and Carefully Chosen Details

The thesis sentence and the one-sentence section summaries can also be used as the outline for a more detailed summary. Most of the details, however, won't be necessary in a summary. For example, it isn't necessary, even in a longer summary of this passage, to detail all the practical restrictions (indicated in paragraph 2) on selecting agents for biological warfare; it's sufficient to indicate that such practical restrictions exist. Nor is it necessary to go into detail about each of the advantages and disadvantages of biological warfare. (These details are, of course, interesting; but they simply reinforce the more general points that there *are* pros and cons to the military use of microorganisms against an enemy.) On the other hand, one or two details may be desirable for clarity. For example, you could mention that "military microbes" may create AIDS epidemics just as a strain of Asian fungus causes chestnut blight.

How do you know which details may be safely ignored and which ones may be advisable to include? The answer is that you won't always know. Developing good judgment in comprehending and summarizing texts is largely a matter of reading skill and prior knowledge (see page 3). Consider the analogy of the seasoned mechanic who can pinpoint an engine problem by simply listening to a characteristic sound that to a less experienced person is just noise. Or consider the chess player who can plot three separate winning strategies from a board position that to a novice looks like a hopeless jumble. In the same way, the more practiced a reader you are, the more knowledgeable you become about the subject, the better able you will be to make critical distinctions between elements of greater and lesser importance. In the meantime, read as carefully as you can and use your own best judgment as to how to present your material.

Here's one version of a completed summary, with carefully chosen details:

SECTION 1

Thesis

According to David Suzucki and Peter 1
Knudtson in Genethics: The Clash Between the New Genetics and Human Values, the application of recombinant

Summary of ¶1

DNA technology to biological warfare
is a nightmarish, yet real prospect for
the human race. Biological warfare involves the use of microorganisms and/
or poisonous substances against enem-

Transitional words & phrases are circled

Summary of ¶2

ies. While there are some practical
restrictions on the type of substances
that can be employed for such purposes,
there remain numerous ways by which
advances in medical knowledge can be

Summary of ¶3

used to kill, rather than to cure,
people. Among the terrible diseases
that can be inflicted through biological warfare are pneumonic plague,
smallpox, and yellow fever. Drawing on

Summary of ¶4

breakthroughs in DNA technology, scientists in the United States, the USSR,
and other countries are already considering new kinds of biological

Summary of ¶5

weapons. This unethical conversion of
medical knowledge to military purposes, particularly when directed by
unscrupulous leaders,

could lead to "uncontrollable epidemics."

2 *Transitional question & topic sentence*

SECTION 2 1st Part

Why should any country or group want to use biological weapons? First, they are selective: They can be used to kill people without destroying property. Second, because of the great variety of diseases, they offer considerable flexibility, from temporarily incapacitating people to destroying their food supply. Third, compared with conventional and nuclear weapons, they are cheap and easy to produce. Finally, with their built-in time delays, they are well-suited to clandestine attack.

Summary of ¶6

Summary of ¶7

3 *Brief transition and topic sentence*

There are, however, several disadvantages. First, most people are morally repulsed by biological warfare, and nations that resort to it would find themselves under heavy international censure. Second, because of environmental conditions and variations among individuals in the target population, biological weapons are often unpredictable in their effects and may even boomerang against those who launch them. Finally, whenever a new organism is introduced, there is danger of long-term ecological damage to the environment. Just as an Asian fungus can cause epidemics of chestnut blight, "military microbes" could create new, unforeseen diseases that

Summary of ¶8

SECTION 2 2nd Part

Summary of ¶9

Summary of ¶'s 10 and 11

Detail for clarity

would pose a threat to all inhabitants for the indefinite future.

Transition / *Summary of ¶12* / *Topic sentence* / *Summary of ¶'s 13-15* / *SECTION 3*

Most people are not sufficiently aware of the implications of the military use of recombinant DNA technology. To get an idea of what modern biological warfare would mean, we might consider the consequences of a fanatical military regime or a terrorist group engineering an AIDS-like virus to use against a particular minority group. 4

Summary of ¶16

Suppose such a virus were accidentally released before scientists had "perfected" it or developed a means to neutralize it. This virus would be transmitted in the same way as the AIDS virus—through the exchange of bodily fluids.

¶'s 17 & 18 not treated in summary / *Summary of ¶19*

First, the disease would spread rapidly and fiercely among the target minority population, destroying the immune systems of its victims, causing them to succumb to such "opportunistic infections" as cancer and various parasitic diseases. And since this is a newly engineered disease, never before encountered, there would be no medical defense against it. The epidemic would likely spread to the population at large—including, ironically, the very people who, for their own racist reasons, had launched it.

Summary of ¶'s 20 & 21

We should remember, then, that the same scientific advances that are so bene-

Summary of ¶22

```
ficial to humanity may, in the wrong
hands, be used to devastate and destroy
it.
```

Discussion

The final two of our suggested steps for writing summaries are (1) to check your summary against the original passage, making sure that you have included all the important ideas, and (2) to revise so that it reads smoothly, coherently.

The *structure* of our summary reflects (with some modifications) the structure of the original passage:

- The *first section* of the passage (five paragraphs) is treated in the first paragraph of the summary.
- The *second section* of the passage, however, has been treated in two paragraphs in the summary—one paragraph on the advantages of "biological bombs" and one on the disadvantages.
- The *third section* of the passage—the hypothetical scenario—is treated in the final paragraph of the summary.

Within individual paragraphs of the summary, the structure generally reflects the sequence of ideas in the original. For example, after our thesis sentence, we summarized each paragraph of the first section of the source passage in a separate sentence. Each advantage and disadvantage of biological warfare is likewise treated in a separate sentence.

The summary of the third section of the passage is a bit more complex. We combined the ideas in paragraphs 13–15 into a single sentence. We did not cover the material on the origin of AIDS covered in paragraphs 17 and 18, since these details seemed to us less significant than the other material on biological warfare. (Of course, this was an interpretive judgment on our part, with which others might disagree.) And finally, we combined ideas in this section to eliminate some of the repetition (e.g., the idea that such a hypothetical virus might spread from the target population to the general population is covered in both paragraphs 19 and 21 of the source passage).

We rewrote our summary several times to make sure that it read smoothly and coherently. Note, for instance, the use of such *transitional words* as "First," "Second," "Third," "however," and "then" and of linking phrases like "This unethical conversion" and "Such a virus." Note also that for the sake of smoothness and coherence, we rewrote all the sentences originally designed as section summaries. Our second section summary, on the pros and cons of biological weapons, would have been too cumbersome in the actual summary. So we led off the second paragraph with an introductory question

("Why should any country or group want to use biological weapons?") and our third paragraph with a brief transitional sentence ("There are, however, several disadvantages"). In both cases, the details in the original section summaries are left for later.

Note that in the third paragraph we selected *one significant detail* from the source passage—the Asian fungus that causes chestnut blight—to clarify the idea about severe ecological damage. In the final paragraph, our original section summary is preceded by a transitional sentence based on the first four paragraphs of this section: "Most people are not sufficiently aware of the implications of the military use of recombinant DNA technology."

How long should a summary be? This depends on the length of the original passage. A good rule of thumb is that a summary should be no longer than one-fourth of the original passage. Of course, if you were summarizing an entire chapter or even an entire book, it would have to be much shorter than that. This particular summary is about one-seventh the length of the original passage. Although it shouldn't be very much longer, you have seen (pages 18–19) that it could be quite a bit shorter.

The length of the summary, however—as well as the shape of the summary—also depends on its *purpose.* Let's suppose, for example, that you decided to use Suzucki and Knudtson's piece in a paper that dealt, in part, with strategies of modern warfare. You would likely be most interested in summarizing the section on the pros and cons of "biological bombs." On the other hand, if you were writing a paper that dealt entirely or in part with the spread of AIDS, you would be more interested in summarizing the final section of the article. Thus, depending on your purpose, you will summarize either *selected* portions of a source or an entire source, as we will see more fully in the chapter on synthesis.

PARAPHRASE

In certain cases, you may want to *paraphrase* rather than to summarize material. Writing a paraphrase is similar to writing a summary; it involves recasting a passage into your own words, and so it requires your complete understanding of the material. The difference is that while a summary is a shortened version of the original, the paraphrase is approximately the same length as the original.

Why write a paraphrase when you can quote the original? You may decide to offer a paraphrase of material written in language that is dense, abstract, archaic, or possibly confusing. For example, suppose you were writing a paper on some aspect of human progress and you came across the following passage by the Marquis de Condorcet, a French economist and politician, written in the late eighteenth century:

> If man can, with almost complete assurance, predict phenomena when he knows their laws, and if, even when he does not, he can still, with great expectation of success, forecast the future on the basis of his experience of the past, why, then, should it be regarded as a fantastic undertaking to sketch, with some pretense to truth, the future destiny of man on the basis of his history? The sole foundation for belief in the natural sciences is this idea, that the general laws directing the phenomena of the universe, known or unknown, are necessary and constant. Why should this principle be any less true for the development of the intellectual and moral faculties of man than for the other operations of nature?

You would like to introduce Condorcet's idea on predicting the future course of human history, but you don't want to slow down your narrative with this somewhat abstract quotation. You may decide to attempt a paraphrase, as follows:

> The Marquis de Condorcet believed that if we can predict such physical events as eclipses and tides, and if we can use past events as a guide to future ones, we should be able to forecast human destiny on the basis of history. Physical events, he maintained, are determined by natural laws that are knowable and predictable. Since humans are part of nature, why should their intellectual and moral development be any less predictable than other natural events?

Each sentence in the paraphrase corresponds to a sentence in the original. The paraphrase is somewhat shorter, owing to the differences of style between eighteenth and twentieth century prose (we tend to be more brisk and efficient, though not more eloquent). But the main difference is that we have replaced the language of the original with our own language. For example, we have paraphrased Condorcet's "the general laws directing the phenomena of the universe, known or unknown, are necessary and constant" with "Physical events, he maintained, are determined by natural laws that are knowable and predictable." To contemporary readers, "knowable and predictable" might be clearer than "necessary and constant" as a description of natural (i.e., physical) laws. Note that we added the specific examples of eclipses and tides to clarify what might have been a somewhat abstract idea. Note also that we included two attributions to Condorcet within the paraphrase to credit our source properly.

When you come across a passage that you don't understand, the temptation is strong to skip over it. Resist this temptation! Use paraphrase as a tool for explaining to yourself the main ideas of a difficult passage. By translating another writer's language into your own, you can clarify what you understand and what you don't. Thus, the paraphrase becomes a tool for learning the subject.

Some pointers for writing paraphrases:

- Make sure that you understand the source passage.
- Substitute your own words for those of the source passage; look for synonyms that carry the same meaning as the original words.
- Rearrange your own sentences so that they read smoothly. Sentence structure, even sentence order, in the paraphrase need not be based on that of the original. A good paraphrase, like a good summary, should stand by itself.

Let's consider some other examples. In a later chapter, we will present readings on "AIDS: Public Good vs. Private Rights." One of those readings is a controversial voter initiative calling for changes in the law prohibiting the reporting of names of persons diagnosed as having AIDS. Suppose that while researching this subject further you came upon the proposed law itself. One section of this proposed law reads as follows:

> 199.21. (a) Any person who, without written authorization, negligently discloses results of a blood test to detect evidence of infection by any probable causative agent of AIDS to any third party, in a manner which identifies or provides identifying characteristics of the person to whom the test results apply, except as provided in this chapter, Section 1603.1, or Section 1603.3, shall be assessed a civil penalty in an amount not to exceed one thousand dollars ($1,000), plus court costs, as determined by the court, which penalty and costs shall be paid to the subject of the test.

Like most legal passages, this is somewhat forbidding to lay people: it consists of a sentence over one hundred words long, with typically impenetrable legal phrasing. You decide, for clarity's sake, to paraphrase it for your lay audience. First, of course, you must understand the meaning of the passage, perhaps no small task.[1] But having read the material carefully, you might eventually draft a paraphrase like this one:

```
You may not disclose to anyone the identity of a person
who tests positive for AIDS, unless you have written au-
```

[1]This proposed law, which appears to place new restrictions on the reporting of the identities of AIDS victims, actually makes it easier to do so. The crucial phrase "without written authorization" is a proposed addition to the existing law. The understanding is that written authorization will be considerably easier to obtain under the new law than it was under the old one.

```
thorization to do so. If you violate this law, you may be
fined up to $1,000; and this fine, plus the court costs,
will be paid to the person whose identity you have dis-
closed.
```

Note that the long single sentence has been broken up into two shorter sentences. Note, also, that some of the language changes: "any person" has become "you"; being "assessed a civil penalty" becomes "fined"; and the complex construction "results of a blood test to detect evidence of infection by any probable causative agent" becomes simply "tests positive." Our paraphrase may not stand up in court, but it accurately conveys the sense of the new law to the lay reader.

Finally, let's consider a passage written by a fine writer that may, nonetheless, best be conveyed in paraphrase. In another passage in the chapter on AIDS, editor and columnist William F. Buckley makes the following statement:

> I have read and listened, and I think now that I can convincingly crystallize the thoughts chasing about in the minds of, first, those whose concern with AIDS victims is based primarily on a concern for them, and for the maintenance of the most rigid standards of civil liberties and personal privacy, and, second, those whose anxiety to protect the public impels them to give subordinate attention to the civil amenities of those who suffer from AIDS and primary attention to the safety of those who do not.

In style, Buckley's passage is more like Condorcet's than the legal extract: It is eloquent, balanced, and literate. Still, it is somewhat inaccessible: here is another one hundred words–plus sentence, perhaps a bit too eloquent for some readers to grasp. For your paper on AIDS, you decide to paraphrase Buckley. You might draft something like this:

```
Buckley finds two opposing sides in the AIDS debate:
those concerned primarily with the civil liberties and
the privacy of AIDS victims, and those concerned pri-
marily with the safety of the public.
```

Our paraphrases have been somewhat shorter than the original, but this is not always the case. For example, suppose you wanted to paraphrase this statement by Sigmund Freud:

> We have found out that the distortion in dreams which hinders our understanding of them is due to the activities of a censorship, directed against the unacceptable, unconscious wish–impulses.

If you were to paraphrase this statement (the first sentence in the Tenth Lecture of his *General Introduction to Psychoanalysis*), you may come up with something like this:

> It is difficult to understand dreams because they contain distortions. Freud believed that these distortions arise from our internal censor, which attempts to suppress unconscious and forbidden desires.

Essentially, this paraphrase does little more than break up one sentence into two and somewhat rearrange the sentence structure for clarity.

Like summaries, then, *paraphrases* are useful devices, both in helping you to understand source material and in enabling you to convey the essence of this source material to your readers. When would you choose to write a summary instead of a paraphrase (or vice versa)? The answer to this question depends on your purpose in presenting your source material. As we've said, summaries are generally based on articles (or sections of articles) or books. Paraphrases are generally based on particularly difficult (or important) paragraphs or sentences. You would seldom paraphrase a long passage, or summarize a short one, unless there were particularly good reasons for doing so. (For example, a lawyer might want to paraphrase several pages of legal language so that his or her client, who is not a lawyer, could understand it.) The purpose of a summary is generally to save your reader time by presenting him or her with a brief and quickly readable version of a lengthy source. The purpose of a paraphrase is generally to clarify a short passage that might otherwise be unclear. Whether you summarize or paraphrase may also depend on the importance of your source. A particularly important source—if it is not too long—may rate a paraphrase. If it is less important, or peripheral to your central argument, you may choose to write a summary instead. And of course, you may choose to summarize only part of your source—the part that is most relevant to the point you are making. In conclusion, then:

Summarize:
- To present main points of a lengthy passage (article or book)
- To condense peripheral points necessary to discussion

Paraphrase:
- To clarify a short passage
- To emphasize main points

At times, you will want to *quote* a source, instead of summarizing or paraphrasing it. You'll find a full discussion on quoting sources starting on page 136. In brief, though, you should quote sources when:

- Another writer's language is particularly memorable and will add interest and liveliness to your paper
- Another writer's language is so clearly and economically stated that to make the same points in your own words would, by comparison, be ineffective
- You want the solid reputation of a source to lend authority and credibility to your own writing

CRITICAL READING AND CRITIQUE

2

CRITICAL READING

When writing papers in college, you are called on often to respond critically to source materials. Critical reading requires the abilities to both summarize and evaluate a presentation. As you have seen, a *summary* is a brief restatement, in your own words, of the content of a passage. An *evaluation* is a more difficult matter. In your college work, you read in order to gain and *use* new information; but unless you are willing to accept every source as equally valid and equally useful, you must learn to distinguish critically among sources by evaluating them.

There is no ready-made formula for determining validity. Critical reading and its written analogue—the *critique*—require discernment, sensitivity, imagination, and above all, a willingness to become involved in what you read. These skills cannot be taken for granted and must be developed through repeated practice. You must begin somewhere, though, and we recommend that you start by posing two broad questions of the passages you read: (1) What is the author trying to accomplish? (2) Do you agree with the author?

Question 1: What Is the Author Trying to Accomplish in This Passage? How Successful Has the Effort Been?

All critical reading *begins with an accurate summary.* Before attempting an evaluation, you must be able to locate an author's thesis and identify the selection's content and structure. You must understand the author's *purpose.* Authors write to inform, to persuade, and to entertain. A given piece may be *primarily informative* (a summary of the reasons for the decline of feudalism), or *primarily persuasive* (an argument on why the government must do something about poverty), or *primarily entertaining* (a play about the frustrations of young lovers), or it may be all three (as in John Steinbeck's novel *The Grapes of Wrath,* about migrant workers during the Great Depression). Sometimes authors are not fully conscious of their purposes. Sometimes their purposes change as they write. But if the finished piece is coherent, it will have a primary reason for having been written, and it should be apparent that the author has tried to inform, persuade, or entertain you. To identify this primary reason, this purpose, is your first job as a critical reader. Once you've made the identification, certain questions will follow.

Is the Selection Intended to Inform?

A piece intended to inform will provide definitions, describe or report on a process, recount a history, or provide facts and figures. An informational piece responds to the following questions:

What is ____________ ?
How does ____________ work?
What happened?
What were the results?
What is the pertinent information?

To the extent that an author answers these and related questions and the answers are a matter of verifiable record (you could check for accuracy if you had the time and inclination), the selection is informational. When you've determined this, you can organize your response by posing three additional questions:

Is the Information Accurate?

If you are going to use any of the information presented, you must be satisfied that it is trustworthy. One of your responsibilities as a critical reader is to find out if it is.

Is the Information Significant?

One useful question that you can put to a reading is, "So what?" In the case of selections that attempt to inform, you may reasonably wonder whether the information makes a difference. What can the person who is reading gain from this information? How is knowledge advanced by the publication of this material? Is the information of importance to you? Why or why not? Elaborate.

Has the Author Interpreted Information Fairly?

At times you will read reports, the sole function of which is to relate raw data or information. In these cases, you will build your response on the two questions above. More frequently, once an author has presented information, he or she will attempt to evaluate it—which is only reasonable, since information that has not been evaluated is of little use. One of your tasks as a critical reader is to make a distinction between the author's presentation of facts and figures and the later attempt at evaluation. You may find that the information is valuable but the interpretation is not. Perhaps the author's conclusions are not justified. Could you offer a contrary explanation for the same facts? Does more information need to be gathered before conclusions can be drawn? Why? Elaborate.

Is the Selection Intended to Persuade?

Academic writing is most often intended to persuade—that is, to influence your thinking. To make a persuasive case, the writer must begin with an assertion that is arguable, some statement about which reasonable people could disagree. An example:

> The writings of Charles Darwin have had a direct influence on philosophy and theology from the mid-nineteenth century to the present.

Presumably, writers use an arguable thesis of their own design to synthesize source materials. You will do exactly this when writing many of your college papers; and you can appreciate that both professors and other students *should* reserve the privilege of evaluating your views in whatever form they are presented—as a written document or, perhaps, as a comment made in class discussion. In the same way, as a critical reader, reserve the privilege of evaluating the views of others—regardless of whether these views are held by classmates or by "professionals" writing in journals and textbooks.

Recall that writers organize arguments by arranging evidence favoring one view and opposing another. Their purpose is to convince readers of the correctness of a certain conclusion. Once you realize that you're reading an argument, respond critically by asking a series of questions:

Has the Author Defined Terms Carefully?

The dictionary definition of *valid* is "justifiable" or "well-grounded." Arguments should be valid, and their validity depends to a large extent on how carefully key terms have been defined. Take the example assertion: "The writings of Charles Darwin have had a direct influence on philosophy and theology from the mid-nineteenth century to the present." What is a "direct" influence on philosophy and theology? Until the meaning of this term is clarified, an argument based on any assertion using it could not progress very far, for on this definition rests the type of evidence that will be offered in support. If "direct" is taken to mean that theologians and philosophers since the 1850s have composed their works in *conscious* response to Darwin's theory of evolution, then the evidence for the argument would amount to references in important documents that mention the biologist by name as the starting point for research. The evidence might be difficult to assemble. You may determine, in fact, that an author has assembled "indirect" evidence: references to theologians and philosophers who worked on problems associated with evolution but who infrequently, if at all, mentioned Darwin by name. In this case, the success of the argument—its ability to persuade you—hinges on the definition of a term. So in responding to an argument, make certain that you are clear and the author is clear on what exactly is being argued.

Once you are satisfied that an author has defined terms carefully, you can respond to the logic of the argument, to the author's use of evidence, and to the author's conclusions. Several questions will help you to organize your response:

Has the Author Used Information Fairly?

Information is used as evidence in support of arguments. When presented with such evidence, bear several concerns in mind. The *first:* "Is the information accurate?" At least a portion of an argument is rendered invalid if the information used to support it is inaccurate. A *second* question: "Has the author cited *representative* information?" The evidence used in an argument must be presented in a spirit of fair play. An author is less than ethical who presents only evidence favoring his views when he is well aware that contrary evidence exists. For instance, it would be dishonest to argue that an economic recession is imminent and to cite as evidence only those indicators of economic well-being that have taken a decided turn for the worse while ignoring and failing to cite contrary (positive) evidence.

Has the Author Argued Logically?

At some point, you will need to respond to the logic of the argument itself. Arguments should be governed by principles of logic—clear and orderly thinking—in order for an argument to be convincing. Here are four examples of faulty thinking to watch for:

Arguing ad hominem. In an *ad hominem* argument, the writer rejects opposing views by attacking the person who holds them. By calling opponents names, an author avoids the issue:

> I could more easily accept my opponent's plan to increase revenues by collecting on delinquent tax bills if he had paid more than a hundred dollars in state taxes in each of the past three years. But the fact is, he's a millionaire with a millionaire's tax shelters. This man hasn't paid a wooden nickel for the state services he and his family depend on. So I ask you: Is *he* the one to be talking about taxes to *us*?

It could well be that the "opponent" has paid virtually no state taxes for three years; but this fact has nothing to do with, and is a ploy to divert attention from, the merits of a specific proposal for increasing revenues. The proposal is lost in the attack against the man himself, an attack that violates the principles of logic. Writers (and speakers) must make their points by citing evidence in support of their views and by challenging contrary evidence.

Faulty cause and effect. The fact that one event precedes another in time does not mean that the first event has caused the second. An example: You receive a phone call and accept an invitation to a dinner dance. Five minutes later you break out in hives. Are the two events related merely because one has preceded the other? Take another example: Fish begin dying by the thousands in a lake near your hometown. An environmental group immediately cites chemical dumping by several manufacturing plants as the cause. But other causes are possible: A disease might have affected the fish; the growth of algae might have contributed to the deaths; or acid rain might be a factor. The origins of an event are usually complex and are not always traceable to a single cause. So you must carefully examine cause-and-effect reasoning when you find a writer using it.

Either/or reasoning. Either/or reasoning also results from an unwillingness to recognize complexity. If an author analyzes a problem and offers only two explanations, one of which he or she refutes, then you are entitled to object; for usually a third or fourth explanation (at the very least) would be possible. For whatever reason, the author has chosen to overlook these. An example: You are reading a selection on genetic engineering and the author builds an argument on the basis of the following:

> Research in gene splicing is at a crossroads: Either scientists will be carefully monitored by civil authorities and their efforts limited to acceptable applications, such as disease control; or lacking regulatory guidelines, scientists will set their own ethical standards and begin programs in embryonic manipulation that, however well intended, exceed the proper limits of human knowledge.

Certainly other possibilities for genetic engineering exist beyond the two mentioned here. But the author limits debate by establishing an either/or choice. Such limitation is artificial and does not allow for complexity. As a critical reader, be on the alert for either/or reasoning.

Faulty generalization. A list of facts reported or numbers assembled means little without an accompanying interpretation, and we rely on authors to generalize from or to interpret information they've assembled. At the same time, we want to be certain that the generalizations are warranted. A troubling example: In February 1987, the Massachusetts Department of Health reported that infant mortality rose 32 percent from 1984 to 1985. Moreover, the major part of the rise was attributable to the death of black infants. How does one respond to this statistic? The first order of business is to establish the validity of the numbers. Once this has been done, what generalizations can be drawn? (1) Given the strong link between prenatal care and postnatal infant health, one can surmise that black women in Massachusetts do not receive the prenatal attention of their white counterparts. (2) A second generalization one could make is that the health care system in the state of

Massachusetts is selectively ineffective—that is, racist. The first generalization is certainly warranted; the second generalization, however, is problematic. The attack is a broadside: It pinpoints no specific reasons for the rise in mortality among black infants and assumes, in addition, that only one reason is possible—racism. This second generalization may eventually prove to be correct, but the proof must be based on additional, supporting facts—two examples of which might be the age and income levels of the mothers delivering in the years 1984 and 1985 and a comparison among the fifty states of infant mortality based not only on race but also on age and income. Certainly information is assembled so that we can generalize from it; but the process of generalization is complex, and as a reader you must watch to see that an author has generalized fairly.

Is the Selection Intended to Entertain?

Authors write not only to inform and persuade but also to entertain. One response to entertainment is a hearty laugh; but it is possible to entertain without laughter: A good book or play or poem may prompt you to ruminate, grow wistful, elated, angry. Laughter is only one of many possible reactions. Read a piece and react as you will. When the time comes for a formal response, try to distance yourself from your reactions in order to articulate them. As with a response to an argument or an informative piece, your response to an essay, poem, story, play, or novel should be precisely stated and carefully developed. Question yourself: Did I care for the portrayal of a certain character in a novel? Why? State as carefully as possible which elements of the portrayal did/did not work for you and explain why. Offer an overall assessment, again carefully elaborating your views.

Question 2: Do You Agree with the Author?

When formulating a critical response to a source, try to distinguish your evaluation of the author's purpose and success at achieving that purpose from your agreement or disagreement with the author's views. The distinction allows you to respond to a piece of writing on its merits. As an unbiased, evenhanded critic, you evaluate an author's clarity of presentation, use of evidence, and adherence to principles of logic. To what extent has the author succeeded in achieving her purpose? Still withholding judgment, you offer your assessment and give the author (in effect) a grade. Significantly, your assessment of the presentation may not coincide with your views of the author's conclusions: You may agree with an author entirely but feel that the presentation is superficial; you may find the author's logic and use of evidence to be rock solid, though you resist certain conclusions. A critical evaluation works well when it is conducted in two parts. Assuming that you have completed an evaluation of the author's purpose and design for achieving that purpose, turn to the author's main assertions—and respond. You'll want to keep two considerations in mind:

Identify Points of Agreement and Disagreement

Be precise in identifying points of agreement and disagreement with an author. You should state as clearly as possible what *you* believe, and an effective way of doing this is to define your position in relation to that presented in the piece. Whether you agree enthusiastically, disagree, or agree with reservations, you can organize your reactions in two parts: first, summarize the author's position; second, state your own position and elaborate on your reasons for holding it. The elaboration, in effect, becomes an argument itself, and this is true regardless of the position you take. An opinion is effective when you support it by supplying evidence. Without such evidence, opinions cannot be authoritative. "I thought the article on inflation was lousy." Why? "I just thought so, that's all." This opinion is flawed, since the criticism is imprecise: The critic has taken neither the time to read the article carefully nor the time to explore his own reactions carefully.

Explore the Reasons for Agreement and Disagreement: Evaluate Assumptions

One way of elaborating your reactions to a reading is to explore the underlying *reasons* for agreement and disagreement. Your reactions are based largely on assumptions that you hold and how these assumptions compare with the author's. An *assumption* is a fundamental statement about the world and its operations that you take to be true. A writer's assumptions may be explicitly stated; but just as often assumptions are implicit and you will have to "ferret them out," that is, to infer them. Consider an example:

> *In vitro* fertilization and embryo transfer is brought about outside the bodies of the couple through actions of third parties whose competence and technical activity determine the success of the procedure. Such fertilization entrusts the life and identity of the embryo into the power of doctors and biologists and establishes the domination of technology over the origin and destiny of the human person. Such a relationship of domination is in itself contrary to the dignity and equality that must be common to parents and children.[1]

This paragraph is quoted from the February 1987 Vatican document on artificial procreation. Cardinal Joseph Ratzinger, principal author of the document, makes an implicit assumption in this paragraph: that no good can come of the domination of technology over conception. The use of technology to bring about conception is morally wrong. Yet there are thousands of childless

[1]From the Vatican document *Instruction on Respect for Human Life in Its Origin and on the Dignity of Procreation,* given at Rome, from the Congregation for the Doctrine of the Faith, February 22, 1987, as presented in *Origins: N.C. Documentary Service* 16(*40*), March 19, 1987, p. 707.

couples, Roman Catholics included, who reject this assumption in favor of its opposite: that conception technology is an aid to the barren couple; far from creating a relationship of unequals, the technology brings children into the world who will be welcomed with joy and love.

Assumptions provide the foundation on which entire presentations are built. If you find an author's assumptions invalid, you'll likely disagree with conclusions that follow from these assumptions. For instance: The author of a book on underdeveloped nations may include a section outlining the resources and time that will be required to industrialize a particular country and so upgrade its general welfare. His assumption—that industrialization in that particular country will ensure or even have anything to do with what people themselves consider their general welfare—may or may not be valid. If you do not share the assumption, then in your eyes the rationale for the entire book will be undermined. *All* assumptions should be critically examined, especially those that seem to be in harmony with what you believe (and so seem beyond examination!).

How do you determine the validity of assumptions once you have identified them? In the absence of more "scientific" criteria, validity may mean how well the author's assumptions stack up against your own experience, observations, and reading. A caution, however: The overall value of an article or book may depend only to a small degree on the validity of the author's assumptions. For instance, a sociologist may do a fine job of gathering statistical data about the incidence of crime in urban areas along the eastern seaboard. The sociologist might also be a Marxist, and you may disagree with her subsequent analysis of the data. Yet you may find the data extremely valuable for your own work or for the work of others.

CRITIQUE

A *critique* is a *formalized, critical reading of a passage.* It is also a personal response; but writing a critique is considerably more rigorous than saying that a movie is "great," or a book is "fascinating," or "I didn't like it." These are all responses, and as such, they're a valid, even essential part of your understanding of what you see and read. But such responses don't help illuminate the subject for anyone—even you—if you haven't explained how you arrived at your conclusions.

Your task in writing a critique is to turn your critical reading of a passage into a systematic evaluation in order to deepen your reader's (and your own) understanding of that passage. Among other things, you're interested in determining what an author says, how well the points are made, what assumptions underlie the argument, what issues are overlooked, and what implications can be drawn from such an analysis. Critiques, positive or negative, should include a fair and accurate summary of the passage; they should also include a statement of your own assumptions. It is important to remember that you bring to bear an entire set of assumptions about the world. Stated or not, these assumptions underlie every evaluative comment you make; therefore, you have an obligation, both to the reader and to yourself, to clarify your standards. Not only do your readers stand to gain by your forthrightness, but you do as well: In the process of writing a critical assessment, you are forced to examine your own knowledge, beliefs, and assumptions. Ultimately, the critique is a way of learning about yourself.

How to Write Critiques

You may find it useful to organize your critiques in five sections: introduction, summary, analysis of the presentation, your response to the presentation, and conclusion.

- *Introduction.* Introduce both the passage under analysis and the author.

  State the author's main argument and the point(s) you intend to make about it.

  Provide background material to help your readers understand the relevance or appeal of the passage. This background material might include one or more of the following: an explanation of why the subject is of current interest; a reference to a possible controversy surrounding the subject of the passage or the passage itself; biographical information about the author; an account of the circumstances under which the passage was written; or a reference to the intended audience of the passage.

- *Summary.* Summarize the author's main points, making sure to state the author's purpose for writing.

- *Analysis of the presentation.* Evaluate the validity of the author's presentation, as distinct from your points of agreement or disagreement. Comment on the author's success in achieving his or her purpose by reviewing three or four specific points. You might base your review on one (or more) of the following criteria:

  Is the information accurate?
  Is the information significant?
  Has the author interpreted information fairly?
  Has the author defined terms carefully?
  Has the author used information fairly?
  Has the author argued logically?

- *Your response to the presentation.* Now it is your turn to respond to the author's views. With which views do you agree? With which do you disagree? Discuss your reasons for agreement and disagreement, when possible tying these reasons to assumptions—both the author's and your own.

♦ *Conclusion.* State your conclusions about the overall validity of the piece—your assessment of the author's success at achieving his or her aims and your reactions to the author's views. Remind the reader of the weaknesses and strengths of the passage.

EXERCISE

Read the following article, Caroline Bird's "College Is a Waste of Time and Money," and critique it. Bird's thesis, stated explicitly in her title, is certainly arguable and is based on a series of assumptions that you should examine carefully. Use the points that we've presented in this discussion to stimulate your responses to Bird.

When reading an article you are likely to critique, have a pencil in hand to keep notes. Marginal notations will help you write a summary (you would be interested in underlining the author's thesis, topic sentences, transitions, important examples); marginal notations in the form of questions and reactions can also help you organize a critical response.

After you have read Caroline Bird's article, gather your notes and order them according to the five steps for writing critiques (the boxed material) above.

College Is a Waste of Time and Money

CAROLINE BIRD

Caroline Bird has attended Vassar College, the University of Toledo (B.A.), and the University of Wisconsin (M.A.). She is the author of Born Female, The Crowding Syndrome *(on population growth),* Everything a Woman Needs to Know to Get Paid What She's Worth, *and* The Case Against College. *Between books and lecture tours, Bird teaches courses on the status of women and writes for magazines as varied as* Ms. *and* Management Review. *"College Is a Waste of Time and Money" first appeared in* Psychology Today *(May 1975). Because the piece was written over a decade ago, some of the issues discussed are no longer current, and various figures (such as yearly income) will seem inaccurate. Nonetheless, the article raises basic objections to the traditional college curriculum that are shared by many today.*

"College Is a Waste of Time and Money" by Caroline Bird, *Psychology Today*, 9 (12), May 1975. Reprinted by permission of the author.

A great majority of our nine-million college students are not in school because they want to be or because they want to learn. They are there because it has become the thing to do or because college is a pleasant place to be; because it's the only way they can get parents or taxpayers to support them without working at a job they don't like; because Mother wanted them to go, or some other reason entirely irrelevant to the course of studies for which college is supposedly organized. 1

As I crisscross the United States lecturing on college campuses, I am dismayed to find that professors and administrators, when pressed for a candid opinion, estimate that no more than 25 percent of their students are turned on by classwork. For the rest, college is at best a social center or aging vat, and at worst a young folks' home or even a prison that keeps them out of the mainstream of economic life for a few more years. 2

The premise—which I no longer accept—that college is the best place for all high-school graduates grew out of a noble American ideal. Just as the United States was the first nation to aspire to teach every small child to read and write, so, during the 1950s, we became the first and only great nation to aspire to higher education for all. During the '60s we damned the expense and built great state university systems as fast as we could. And adults—parents, employers, high-school counselors—began to push, shove and cajole youngsters to "get an education." 3

It became a mammoth industry, with taxpayers footing more than half the bill. By 1970, colleges and universities were spending more than 30-billion dollars annually. But still only half our high-school graduates were going on. According to estimates made by the economist Fritz Machlup, if we had been educating every young person until age 22 in that year of 1970, the bill for higher education would have reached 47.5-billion dollars, 12.5 billion more than the total corporate profits for the year. 4

THE BABY BOOM IS OVER

Figures such as these have begun to make higher education for all look financially prohibitive, particularly now when colleges are squeezed by the pressures of inflation and a drop-off in the growth of their traditional market. 5

Predictable demography has caught up with the university empire builders. Now that the record crop of postwar babies has graduated from college, the rate of growth of the student population has begun to decline. To keep their mammoth plants financially 6 solvent, many institutions have begun to use hard-sell, Madison-Avenue techniques to attract students. They sell college like soap, promoting features they think students want: innovative programs, an environment conducive to meaningful personal relationships, and a curriculum so free that it doesn't sound like college at all.

Pleasing the customers is something new for college administra- 7
tors. Colleges have always known that most students don't like to study, and that at least part of the time they are ambivalent about college, but before the student riots of the 1960s educators never thought it either right or necessary to pay any attention to student feelings. But when students rebelling against the Vietnam war and the draft discovered they could disrupt a campus completely, administrators had to act on some student complaints. Few understood that the protests had tapped the basic discontent with college itself, a discontent that did not go away when the riots subsided.

Today students protest individually rather than in concert. They 8
turn inward and withdraw from active participation. They drop out to travel to India or to feed themselves on subsistence farms. Some refuse to go to college at all. Most, of course, have neither the funds nor the self-confidence for constructive articulation of their discontent. They simply hang around college unhappily and reluctantly.

All across the country, I have been overwhelmed by the prevail- 9
ing sadness on American campuses. Too many young people speak little, and then only in drowned voices. Sometimes the mood surfaces as diffidence, wariness, or coolness, but whatever its form, it looks like a defense mechanism, and that rings a bell. This is the way it used to be with women, and just as society had systematically damaged women by insisting that their proper place was in the home, so we may be systematically damaging 18-year-olds by insisting that their proper place is in college.

SAD AND UNNEEDED

Campus watchers everywhere know what I mean when I say stu- 10
dents are sad, but they don't agree on the reason for it. During the Vietnam war some ascribed the sadness to the draft; now others blame affluence, or say it has something to do with permissive upbringing.

Not satisfied with any of these explanations, I looked for some 11
answers with the journalistic tools of my trade—scholarly studies, economic analyses, the historical record, the opinions of the especially knowledgeable, conversations with parents, professors,

college administrators, and employers, all of whom spoke as alumni too. Mostly I learned from my interviews with hundreds of young people on and off campuses all over the country.

My unnerving conclusion is that students are sad because they are not needed. Somewhere between the nursery and the employment office, they become unwanted adults. No one has anything in particular against them. But no one knows what to do with them either. We already have too many people in the world of the 1970s, and there is no room for so many newly minted 18-year-olds. So we temporarily get them out of the way by sending them to college where in fact only a few belong. 12

To make it more palatable, we fool ourselves into believing that we are sending them there for their own best interests, and that it's good for them, like spinach. Some, of course, learn to like it, but most wind up preferring green peas. 13

Educators admit as much. Nevitt Sanford, distinguished student of higher education, says students feel they are "capitulating to a kind of voluntary servitude." Some of them talk about their time in college as if it were a sentence to be served. I listened to a 1970 Mount Holyoke graduate: "For two years I was really interested in science, but in my junior and senior years I just kept saying, 'I've done two years; I'm going to finish.' When I got out I made up my mind that I wasn't going to school anymore because so many of my courses had been bullshit." 14

But bad as it is, college is often preferable to a far worse fate. It is better than the drudgery of an uninspiring nine-to-five job, and better than doing nothing when no jobs are available. For some young people, it is a graceful way to get away from home and become independent without losing the financial support of their parents. And sometimes it is the only alternative to an intolerable home situation. 15

It is difficult to assess how many students are in college reluctantly. The conservative Carnegie Commission estimates from five to 30 percent. Sol Linowitz, who was once chairman of a special committee on campus tension of the American Council on Education, found that "a significant number were not happy with their college experience because they felt they were there only in order to get the 'ticket to the big show' rather than to spend the years as productively as they otherwise could." 16

Older alumni will identify with Richard Baloga, a policeman's son, who stayed in school even though he "hated it" because he thought it would do him some good. But fewer students each year feel this way. Daniel Yankelovich has surveyed undergraduate attitudes for a number of years, and reported in 1971 that 74 percent 17 thought education was "very important." But just two years earlier, 80 percent thought so.

AN INSIDE VIEW OF WHAT'S GOOD

The doubters don't mind speaking up. Leon Lefkowitz, chairman of the department of social studies at Central High School in Valley Stream, New York, interviewed 300 college students at random, and reports that 200 of them didn't think that the education they were getting was worth the effort. "In two years I'll pick up a diploma," said one student, "and I can honestly say it was a waste of my father's bread." 18

Nowadays, says one sociologist, you don't have to have a reason for going to college; it's an institution. His definition of an institution is an arrangement everyone accepts without question; the burden of proof is not on why you go, but why anyone thinks there might be a reason for not going. The implication is that an 18-year-old is too young and confused to know what he wants to do, and that he should listen to those who know best and go to college. 19

I don't agree. I believe that college has to be judged not on what other people think is good for students, but on how good it feels to the students themselves. 20

I believe that people have an inside view of what's good for them. If a child doesn't want to go to school some morning, better let him stay at home, at least until you find out why. Maybe he knows something you don't. It's the same with college. If high-school graduates don't want to go, or if they don't want to go right away, they may perceive more clearly than their elders that college is not for them. It is no longer obvious that adolescents are best off studying a core curriculum that was constructed when all educated men could agree on what made them educated, or that professors, advisors, or parents can be of any particular help to young people in choosing a major or a career. High-school graduates see college graduates driving cabs, and decide it's not worth going. College students find no intellectual stimulation in their studies and drop out. 21

If students believe that college isn't necessarily good for them, you can't expect them to stay on for the general good of mankind. They don't go to school to beat the Russians to Jupiter, improve the national defense, increase the GNP, or create a market for the arts—to mention some of the benefits taxpayers are supposed to get for supporting higher education. 22

Nor should we expect to bring about social equality by putting all young people through four years of academic rigor. At best, it's a 23 roundabout and expensive way to narrow the gap between the highest and lowest in our society anyway. At worst, it is unconsciously elitist. Equalizing opportunity through universal higher education subjects the whole population to the intellectual mode natural only to a few. It violates the fundamental egalitarian principle of respect for the differences between people.

THE DUMBEST INVESTMENT

Of course, most parents aren't thinking of the "higher" good at all. 24
They send their children to college because they are convinced young people benefit financially from those four years of higher education. But if money is the only goal, college is the dumbest investment you can make. I say this because a young banker in Poughkeepsie, New York, Stephen G. Necel, used a computer to compare college as an investment with other investments available in 1974 and college did not come out on top.

For the sake of argument, the two of us invented a young man 25
whose rich uncle gave him, in cold cash, the cost of a four-year education at any college he chose, but the young man didn't have to spend the money on college. After bales of computer paper, we had our mythical student write to his uncle: "Since you said I could spend the money foolishly if I wished, I am going to blow it all on Princeton."

The much respected financial columnist Sylvia Porter echoed the 26
common assumption when she said last year, "A college education is among the very best investments you can make in your entire life." But the truth is not quite so rosy, even if we assume that the Census Bureau is correct when it says that as of 1972, a man who completed four years of college would expect to earn $199,000 more between the ages of 22 and 64 than a man who had only a high-school diploma.[1]

If a 1972 Princeton-bound high-school graduate had put the 27
$34,181 that his four years of college would have cost him into a savings bank at 7.5 percent interest compounded daily, he would have had at age 64 a total of $1,129,200, or $528,200 more than the earnings of a male college graduate, and more than five times as much as the $199,000 extra the more educated man could expect to earn between 22 and 64.

The big advantage of getting your college money in cash now is 28
that you can invest it in something that has a higher return than a

[1]According to the 1984 *Statistical Abstract of the United States*, a person who completed four years of college in 1979 could expect to earn $309,000 more than a non-college graduate.

diploma. For instance, a Princeton-bound high-school graduate of 1972 who liked fooling around with cars could have banked his $34,181, and gone to work at the local garage at close to $1,000 more per year than the average high-school graduate. Meanwhile, as he was learning to be an expert auto mechanic, his money would be ticking away in the bank. When he became 28, he would have earned $7,199 less on his job from age 22 to 28 than his college-educated friend, but he would have had $73,113 in his passbook—enough to buy out his boss, go into the used-car business, or acquire his own new-car dealership. If successful in business, he could expect to make more than the average college graduate. And if he had the brains to get into Princeton, he would be just as likely to make money without the four years spent on campus. Unfortunately, few college-bound high-school graduates get the opportunity to bank such a large sum of money, and then wait for it to make them rich. And few parents are sophisticated enough to understand that in financial returns alone, their children would be better off with the money than with the education.

Rates of return and dollar signs on education are fascinating brain 29
teasers, but obviously there is a certain unreality to the game. Quite aside from the noneconomic benefits of college, and these should loom larger once the dollars are cleared away, there are grave difficulties in assigning a dollar value to college at all.

STATUS, NOT MONEY

In fact there is no real evidence that the higher income of college 30
graduates is due to college. College may simply attract people who are slated to earn more money anyway; those with higher IQs, better family backgrounds, a more enterprising temperament. No one who has wrestled with the problem is prepared to attribute all of the higher income to the impact of college itself.

Christopher Jencks, author of *Inequality,* a book that assesses the 31
effect of family and schooling in America, believes that education in general accounts for less than half of the difference in income in the American population. "The biggest single source of income differences," writes Jencks, "seems to be the fact that men from high-status families have higher incomes than men from low-status families even when they enter the same occupations, have the same amount of education, and have the same test scores."

Jacob Mincer of the National Bureau of Economic Research and 32
Columbia University states flatly that of "20 to 30 percent of students at any level, the additional schooling has been a waste, at least in terms of earnings." College fails to work its income-raising magic for

almost a third of those who go. More than half of those people in 1972 who earned $15,000 or more reached that comfortable bracket without the benefit of a college diploma. Jencks says that financial success in the U.S. depends a good deal on luck, and the most sophisticated regression analyses have yet to demonstrate otherwise.

But most of today's students don't go to college to earn more money anyway. In 1968, when jobs were easy to get, Daniel Yankelovich made his first nationwide survey of students. Sixty-five percent of them said they "would welcome less emphasis on money." By 1973, when jobs were scarce, that figure jumped to 80 percent. 33

The young are not alone. Americans today are all looking less to the pay of a job than to the work itself. They want "interesting" work that permits them "to make a contribution," "express themselves" and "use their special abilities," and they think college will help them find it. 34

Jerry Darring of Indianapolis knows what it is to make a dollar. He worked with his father in the family plumbing business, on the line at Chevrolet, and in the Chrysler foundry. He quit these jobs to enter Wright State University in Dayton, Ohio, because "in a job like that a person only has time to work, and after that he's so tired that he can't do anything else but come home and go to sleep." 35

Jerry came to college to find work "helping people." And he is perfectly willing to spend the dollars he earns at dull, well-paid work to prepare for lower-paid work that offers the reward of service to others. 36

PSYCHIC INCOME

Jerry's case is not unusual. No one works for money alone. In order to deal with the nonmonetary rewards of work, economists have coined the concept of "psychic income," which according to one economic dictionary means "income that is reckoned in terms of pleasure, satisfaction, or general feelings of euphoria." 37

Psychic income is primarily what college students mean when they talk about getting a good job. During the most affluent years of the late 1960s and early 1970s college students told their placement officers that they wanted to be researchers, college professors, artists, city planners, social workers, poets, book publishers, archeologists, ballet dancers, or authors. 38

The psychic income of these and other occupations popular with students is so high that these jobs can be filled without offering high salaries. According to one study, 93 percent of urban university professors would choose the same vocation again if they had the chance, compared with only 16 percent of unskilled auto workers. 39

Even though the monetary gap between college professor and auto worker is now surprisingly small, the difference in psychic income is enormous.

But colleges fail to warn students that jobs of these kinds are hard to come by, even for qualified applicants, and they rarely accept the responsibility of helping students choose a career that will lead to a job. When a young person says he is interested in helping people, his counselor tells him to become a psychologist. But jobs in psychology are scarce. The Department of Labor, for instance, estimates there will be 4,300 new jobs for psychologists in 1975 while colleges are expected to turn out 58,430 B.A.s in psychology that year. 40

Of 30 psych majors who reported back to Vassar what they were doing a year after graduation in 1972, only five had jobs in which they could possibly use their courses in psychology, and two of these were working for Vassar. 41

The outlook isn't much better for students majoring in other psychic-pay disciplines: sociology, English, journalism, anthropology, forestry, education. Whatever college graduates want to do, most of them are going to wind up doing what there is to do. 42

John Shingleton, director of placement at Michigan State University, accuses the academic community of outright hypocrisy. "Educators have never said, 'Go to college and get a good job,' but this has been implied, and now students expect it. . . . If we care what happens to students after college, then let's get involved with what should be one of the basic purposes of education: career preparation." 43

In the 1970s, some of the more practical professors began to see that jobs for graduates meant jobs for professors too. Meanwhile, students themselves reacted to the shrinking job market, and a "new vocationalism" exploded on campus. The press welcomed the change as a return to the ethic of achievement and service. Students were still idealistic, the reporters wrote, but they now saw that they could best make the world better by healing the sick as physicians or righting individual wrongs as lawyers. 44

NO USE ON THE JOB

But there are no guarantees in these professions either. The American Enterprise Institute estimated in 1971 that there would be more than the target ratio of 100 doctors for every 100,000 people in the population by 1980. And the odds are little better for would-be lawyers. Law schools are already graduating twice as many new lawyers every year as the Department of Labor thinks will be needed, and the oversupply is growing every year. 45

And it's not at all apparent that what is actually learned in a "professional" education is necessary for success. Teachers, engineers and others I talked to said they find that on the job they rarely use what they learned in school. In order to see how well college prepared engineers and scientists for actual paid work in their fields, the Carnegie Commission queried all the employees with degrees in these fields in two large firms. Only one in five said the work they were doing bore a "very close relationship" to their college studies, while almost a third saw "very little relationship at all." An overwhelming majority could think of many people who were doing their same work, but had majored in different fields. 46

Majors in nontechnical fields report even less relationship between their studies and their jobs. Charles Lawrence, a communications major in college and now the producer of "Kennedy & Co.," the Chicago morning television show, says, "You have to learn all that stuff and you never use it again. I learned my job doing it." Others employed as architects, nurses, teachers and other members of the so-called learned professions report the same thing. 47

Most college administrators admit that they don't prepare their graduates for the job market. "I just wish I had the guts to tell parents that when you get out of this place you aren't prepared to do anything," the academic head of a famous liberal-arts college told us. Fortunately, for him, most people believe that you don't have to defend a liberal-arts education on those grounds. A liberal-arts education is supposed to provide you with a value system, a standard, a set of ideas, not a job. "Like Christianity, the liberal arts are seldom practiced and would probably be hated by the majority of the populace if they were," said one defender. 48

The analogy is apt. The fact is, of course, that the liberal arts are a religion in every sense of that term. When people talk about them, their language becomes elevated, metaphorical, extravagant, theoretical and reverent. And faith in personal salvation by the liberal arts is professed in a creed intoned on ceremonial occasions such as commencements. 49

TICKET OF ADMISSION

If the liberal arts are a religious faith, the professors are its priests. But disseminating ideas in a four-year college curriculum is slow and most expensive. If you want to learn about Milton, Camus, or even Margaret Mead you can find them in paperback books, the public library, and even on television. 50

And when most people talk about the value of a college educa- 51 tion, they are not talking about great books. When at Harvard commencement the president welcomes the new graduates into "the fellowship of educated men and women," what he could be saying is, "Here is a piece of paper that is a passport to jobs, power and instant prestige." As Glenn Bassett, a personnel specialist at G.E., says, "In some parts of G.E., a college degree appears completely irrelevant to selection to, say, a manager's job. In most, however, it is a ticket of admission."

But now that we have doubled the number of young people 52
attending college, a diploma cannot guarantee even that. The most charitable conclusion we can reach is that college probably has very little, if any, effect on people and things at all. Today, the false premises are easy to see:

First, college doesn't make people intelligent, ambitious, happy, 53
or liberal. It's the other way around. Intelligent, ambitious, happy, liberal people are attracted to higher education in the first place.

Second, college can't claim much credit for the learning experi- 54
ences that really change students while they are there. Jobs, friends, history, and most of all the sheer passage of time have as big an impact as anything even indirectly related to the campus.

Third, colleges have changed so radically that a freshman enter- 55
ing in the fall of 1974 can't be sure to gain even the limited value research studies assigned to colleges in the '60s. The sheer size of undergraduate campuses of the 1970s makes college even less stimulating now than it was 10 years ago. Today even motivated students are disappointed with their college courses and professors.

Finally, a college diploma no longer opens as many vocational 56
doors. Employers are beginning to realize that when they pay extra for someone with a diploma, they are paying only for an empty credential. The fact is that most of the work for which employers now expect college training is now or has been capably done in the past by people without higher educations.

College, then, may be a good place for those few young people 57
who are really drawn to academic work, who would rather read than eat, but it has become too expensive, in money, time, and intellectual effort, to serve as a holding pen for large numbers of our young. We ought to make it possible for those reluctant, unhappy students to find alternative ways of growing up, and more realistic preparation for the years ahead.

You'll need to summarize the essays and articles that you critique. We leave it to you to write a summary of Bird's "College Is a Waste of Time and Money." Once you have done so, consider again possible points for evaluation:

- Is the information accurate?
- Is the information significant?
- Has the author interpreted information fairly?
- Has the author defined terms carefully?
- Has the author used information fairly?
- Has the author argued logically?
- Do you agree with the author?
- Identify points of agreement and disagreement.
- Explore the reasons for agreement and disagreement. Evaluate assumptions.

In any one critique, you'll likely respond in writing to a few—not all—of these points; but we think it a good idea that you consider them all since on the basis of your response you'll determine the main points to follow in your critique. When planning an evaluation, respond to questions that yield to you "the heart of the matter," that will illuminate both for you and your reader the reasons why a particular piece succeeds or fails. Assess both the author's presentation and conclusions; justify all your observations. Remember that a critique entitles you to a full range of critical reaction—positive, negative, or any combination of these—as long as you have reasoned soundly.

Points to Consider in Evaluating Caroline Bird's "College Is a Waste of Time and Money"

Paragraph 1: The first sentence of Bird's article is a direct and unadorned statement of her thesis. Later, when she speaks of reasons "entirely irrelevant to the course of studies for which college is supposedly organized," what assumptions does she make—implicitly?

Paragraph 2: What does "turned on by classwork" mean to you? What do you suppose it means to Bird? To the professors she interviewed? How is (or isn't) being "turned on" a fair indicator of a student's benefiting from classes?

Paragraph 6: Bird refers to "a curriculum so free that it doesn't sound like college at all." She is making an implicit assumption here. What is it? And how is this assumption related to the one made in her first paragraph?

Paragraph 7: Explain how Bird's assertion that the student protest of the 1960s "tapped the basic discontent with college itself" is an arguable assertion.

Paragraph 12: Bird reaches an "unnerving conclusion": "students are sad because they are not needed." How true does this conclusion ring to your own experience? Does it account for any part of your decision to attend college?

Paragraph 19: Bird disagrees with the statement that "an 18-year-old is too young and confused to know what he wants to do, and that he should listen to those who know best and go to college." How is Bird's disagreement consistent with the arguments she has made previously? What is your response to the statement about eighteen-year-olds?

Paragraph 21: Examine the statements at the end of the paragraph having to do with what high school graduates see when looking at college graduates. Comment on Bird's use of evidence here.

Paragraph 23: Bird makes a point about unconscious elitism and an "intellectual mode natural only to a few." Is she right?

Paragraphs 24–32: We are presented with a hypothetical argument concerning the comparative worth of two investments—one in a college education, one in a bank account. How effective is Bird's reasoning?

Paragraph 42: "Whatever college graduates want to do, most of them are going to wind up doing what there is to do." What is Bird's assumption here about the importance of—and the reasons for—attending college? Do you agree? That is, if you majored in psychology and ended up working as a stockbroker, would you consider your years of study a "poor investment"? Why or why not? For a related discussion, see Bird's paragraph 46.

Paragraphs 52–56: Bird lays out the "false premises" underlying college education. Examine each premise in turn.

In your critique of "College Is a Waste of Time and Money," you may want to respond to some of the passages that we've noted. As a final consideration before drafting the critique, review Bird's thesis—that a great majority of college students attend school for the wrong reasons; review as well the other assertions she makes in support of her thesis. To what extent do you find it possible to agree *in part* with Caroline Bird? And if you agree in part, account for your mixed reactions by discussing the assumptions that you and she hold about college and about students.

To stimulate your thinking about Caroline Bird's article further, we offer the following sample critique, organized along the lines suggested on pages 38–39:

A Critique of Caroline Bird's "College Is a Waste of Time and Money"

In a blistering attack on the value of a college degree, 1
Caroline Bird calls into question some cherished assumptions about the usefulness of higher education. Most people assume that college is a valuable investment. As one might expect from her title, "College Is a Waste of Time and Money," Bird argues otherwise. These days the cost for attending a prestigious liberal arts school has reached $20,000 a year. Students at state-run univer-

sities can expect to pay at least $8,000 a year. Granted, when Bird wrote her article for *Psychology Today* in 1975, these figures were far lower. But in proportion to income, a college education still cost plenty fifteen years ago. So the arguments Bird made then still apply today, and her assertions must be taken seriously.

Bird believes that the value of an education can and should be judged, and she offers two criteria for doing so: First, she says, colleges must land graduates good jobs in the fields for which they trained; second, college graduates must earn proportionately more money than nongraduates. When these tests are not met—and she argues that in the great majority of cases they are not—then college is a waste of the student's time and money. Throughout the article, Bird makes a number of shrewd observations, the first being that with the drop in available college-age students, colleges are beginning to market themselves "like soap." The trend, even more prevalent today than fifteen years ago, points up an important driving force in education: the fact that schools must make money to stay in business. 2

Bird goes on to observe that many students feel trapped into attending college because there is no other place for "newly minted 18-year-olds" to spend their time, other than in a job. And what skills does an eighteen-year-old have that would gain employment in anything other than drudge work? So young men and women graduate from high school and continue with four more years of education because there's nothing much else for them to do. One administrator Bird interviewed claimed that "students feel they are 'capitulating to a kind of voluntary servitude.' " Even the student who attends college under duress needs to offer no justification for doing so. College has become a self-justifying, socially 3 sanctioned institution. Parents and students alike believe that merely to attend is a worthy goal in itself. In fact, so pervasive is the view that everyone should attend college that the burden of proof is often on students to justify why they don't want to attend. Certainly, we can't expect colleges to undermine this view, since they depend on large enrollments.

Bird clearly establishes the vested interest col- 4
leges have in keeping students in the classroom, regardless of how valuable an education is for particular students. She doesn't actually accuse educators of cynically pandering to students to keep them enrolled. But in making the point about education's bottom line, Bird justifies the need for someone outside of academia (i.e., someone like herself) to evaluate the worth of college degrees.

Bird correctly charges that too many students choose 5
college by default, because they are either too lazy or too scared to choose a different and more meaningful road for themselves. If it's the love of learning students want, then college is the place to be. If it's money they want, if college is seen as a means to a better-paying end, this motive, too, is honest and sometimes does eventually lead to a student's full commitment and interest. But if it's a party or some vague notion of being "well rounded" that the student is after, if college is seen merely as a status symbol or as a necessary evil, then that student—as Bird so energetically argues—is wasting precious time and money. After four years, the student will be $35,000 to $80,000 poorer, and intellectually and emotionally not much richer. The money the student may one day recoup; the years are lost for good.

Bird is also right to argue that students who don't 6

know why they're in college or who don't enjoy any of their course work should leave. But, in a move that damages her argument, she claims that a *majority* of students fit her profile of the misinformed and unmotivated. The claim is not accurate, since it is based on two dubious tests. The first test, according to Bird, is that the expense of college is justified as long as the material one studies is applied directly in one's work. Bird accurately reports that most people who train in a particular undergraduate discipline don't go on to careers in that discipline. But is is illogical to conclude from this fact that for most people college is a waste of time and money. Would the psychology major who in four years learns some complex and subtle truths about human nature—and who was fascinated by that learning—have wasted the effort if she winds up in engineering graduate school? No. The process of learning—of reading, writing, and talking seriously about a serious subject with others—is itself valuable in two ways. First, that student, for all her work, has developed intellectual and interpersonal skills from which she will profit *whatever* she does, *wherever* she goes. Second, we live in a heavily specialized, compartmentalized world in which people focus on one narrow job to the exclusion of others. We risk our society's disintegrating into "anarchy" (as a former president of Johns Hopkins University has put it) if we limit the education of students to narrowly defined sets of skills. At its worst, specialization leads us to a world where only engineers can talk to engineers and psychologists to psychologists. What we need instead are broadly trained individuals who can communicate with others, regardless of their academic or professional specialties.

Thus, Bird's first test for proving that college is a 7

waste of time and money fails. So does her second test, that a college education should be worth additional earning power. Bird offers a hypothetical scenario to prove that money spent on college tuition is better spent in some other, nonacademic endeavor. This scenario, which involves a student's receiving a lump-sum payment in place of college tuition, is frankly just too bizarre to take seriously. How many parents can afford to give $30,000, $60,000, or $80,000 to an eighteen-year-old? Bird then tries to argue that a high school student who sees a college graduate driving a cab can justifiably conclude that a college education is useless. (The high school student could as easily drive the cab and spare himself the time and expense of college.) Here, the answer to Bird is as old as history itself: People need more than money to live a good, happy life—which Bird herself acknowledges but then too quickly dismisses in her section on "Psychic Income." If from a college education a student learns strategies for living meaningfully, then the money invested in that education will pay dividends not only to the student herself but also to that student's friends, family, and community. Here's an investment worth making, then, regardless of the money a student may earn after graduation. What Bird glibly calls the "dumbest investment" one can make could well become the very best and most profound investment—provided the student is ready to be a student.

An investment in college *is* foolish when students do 8
not want to attend. No one claims that the only road to a meaningful life is through college. In school or out, people learn, seek happiness, grow wise or not, depending on their dispositions. If one is dissatisfied in the classroom, then one should leave and seek satisfaction elsewhere. For surely it exists elsewhere. If only Bird

had stopped here, her argument would have held up. But she pushes her points too far when she claims that the "great majority" of students are wasting their time and money. In no way has she proven this point, certainly not if she is offering her two tests as criteria for proof. Her tests fail: They are ill-conceived and misapplied. Inevitably, her argument loses credibility.

Parents and students must think hard before investing time and money in a college education, because college might not be for everyone. Perhaps it should not be. Perhaps we should offer high school graduates sensible and appealing alternatives to college: not nine-to-five drudge jobs but voluntary service that would extend the horizons of eighteen-year-olds in exciting, if nonacademic, ways. No one should enter into a "voluntary servitude." Young men and women should have options—this is the valuable lesson to be drawn from "College Is a Waste of Time and Money." Bird should be applauded for raising some tough questions—even if her argument eventually falters. 9

Discussion

You see from this example that a critique can be essentially positive but at the same time address significant, negative elements. This point must be emphasized, for "critique" sounds very much like "critical," and "critical" sounds very much like "negative." But in no way is a critique limited to negative assessments. The critique, rather, is a *systematic* response to source material—positive, negative, or mixed. Recall the structure of our example critique:

Paragraph 1:	Introduction
Paragraphs 2–3:	Summary
Paragraph 4:	Analysis of presentation (*point 1:* Colleges have a vested interest in keeping students enrolled.) + Reviewer's response (agreement)

Paragraph 5:	Analysis of presentation (*point 2:* Too many students choose college by default.) + Reviewer's response (agreement)
Paragraph 6:	Analysis of presentation (*point 3:* College is a waste because students don't directly apply what they learn to later professions.) + Reviewer's response (disagreement)
Paragraph 7:	Analysis of presentation (*point 4:* College is a waste because it doesn't significantly increase later earning power.) + Reviewer's response (disagreement)
Paragraphs 8–9:	Conclusion

The sample critique has been arranged and developed systematically. Notice that in paragraphs 4–7 the reviewer takes up separate points of Bird's presentation in order to analyze their validity and immediately follows these analyses with a response—statements of agreement or disagreement. This structure is convenient since the responses are organized around the same points that are being analyzed for validity. Had the points for response and the points for analysis been different, then the reviewer would have followed the structure set out on page 38, where the analysis is taken up in one section of the critique and the response to the author's arguments is taken up in another. The point is that no one structure is correct for all critiques. You'll need to modify the organization of your work, based on its content.

Whatever its content, though, a critique must be arranged and developed systematically. In the example, each point of agreement with Bird is taken up in a separate paragraph. This allows the reviewer to develop each point with clarity and unity. By grouping these three paragaphs at the beginning, the reviewer sends an important signal to the reader: "I like much of what Bird has to say." This critique is a largely favorable one, despite the negative assessments in the second half.

The reviewer extends this same systematic approach to the next section, where he disagrees with Bird on two points. In paragraphs 6 and 7, each of the two tests that the reviewer has cited as flawed is taken up separately. In paragraph 8, the reviewer in effect summarizes the disagreements, first by emphasizing points of agreement with Bird ("An investment in college *is* foolish when . . .") and then by modifying that agreement ("If only Bird had stopped here . . ."). Finally, in paragraph 9, the reviewer sums up his responses, positive and negative alike. Notice the conditional mood of this last paragraph, which enables the reviewer to close with a partial or limited acceptance of Bird's argument: "Bird should be applauded for raising some tough questions—even if her argument eventually falters."

A critique, then, enables you to *explain* your responses to a passage. In the academic world, the quality of your explanations—the reasons you offer for agreeing and disagreeing with an author—are crucial. Statements such as "I thought the piece was lousy" or "I loved it!" are expressive but meaningless until you can systematically account for your reactions. Once you've done this, you invite discussions from other interested persons, whom you can hold to the same standards of analysis. A principal aim of academic life is *informed* discussion among individuals who take their reading seriously. It is this type of discussion that you teach yourself when you write a critique, explaining just why you think the way you do.

SYNTHESIS

3

WHAT IS A SYNTHESIS?

A *synthesis* is a written discussion that draws on two or more sources. It follows that your ability to write syntheses depends on your ability to infer relationships among sources—essays, articles, fiction, and also nonwritten sources, such as lectures, interviews, observations. This process is nothing new for you, since you infer relationships all the time—say between something you've read in the newspaper and something you've seen for yourself, or between the teaching styles of your favorite and least favorite instructors. In fact, if you've written research papers, you've already written syntheses. In an *academic* synthesis, you make explicit the relationships that you have inferred among separate sources.

The skills you've already learned and practiced from the previous two chapters will be vital in writing syntheses. Clearly, before you're in a position to draw relationships between two or more sources, you must understand what those sources say; in other words, you must be able to *summarize* these sources. It will frequently be helpful for your readers if you provide at least partial summaries of sources in your synthesis essays. At the same time, you must go beyond summary to make judgments—judgments based, of course, on your *critical reading* of your sources. You should already have drawn some conclusions about the quality and validity of these sources; and you should know how much you agree or disagree with the points made in your sources and the reasons for your agreement or disagreement.

Further, you must go beyond the critique of individual sources to determine the relationship among them. Is the information in source B, for example, an extended illustration of the generalizations in source A? Would it be useful to compare and contrast source C with source B? Having read and considered sources A, B, and C, can you infer something else—D (not a source, but your own idea)?

Because a synthesis is based on two or more sources, you will need to be selective when choosing information from each. It would be neither possible nor desirable, for instance, to discuss in a ten-page paper on the battle of Wounded Knee every point that the authors of two books make about their subject. What you as a writer must do is select the ideas and information from each source that best allow you to achieve your purpose.

PURPOSE

Your purpose in reading source materials and then in drawing on them to write your own material is often reflected in the wording of an assignment. For instance, consider the following assignments on the Civil War:

American History: Evaluate your text author's treatment of the origins of the Civil War.

Economics: Argue the following proposition, in light of your readings: "The Civil War was not fought for reasons of moral principle but for reasons of economic necessity."

Government: Prepare a report on the effects of the Civil War on Southern politics at the state level between 1870 and 1917.

Mass Communications: Discuss how the use of photography during the Civil War may have affected the perceptions of the war by Northerners living in industrial cities.

Literature: Select two twentieth-century Southern writers whose work you believe was influenced by the divisive effects of the Civil War. Discuss the ways this influence is apparent in a novel or a group of short stories written by each author. The works should not be *about* the Civil War.

Applied Technology: Compare and contrast the technology of warfare available in the 1860s with the technology available a century earlier.

Each of these assignments creates for you a particular purpose for writing. Having located sources relevant to your topic, you would select, for possible use in a paper, only those parts that helped you in fulfilling this purpose. And how you used those parts, how you related them to other material from other sources, would also depend on your purpose. For instance, if you were working on the government assignment, you might possibly draw on the same source as another student working on the literature assignment by referring to Robert Penn Warren's novel *All the King's Men,* about Louisiana politics in the early part of the twentieth century. But since the purposes of these assignments are different, you and the other student would make different uses of this source. Those same parts or aspects of the novel that you find worthy of detailed analysis might be just mentioned in passing by the other student.

USING YOUR SOURCES

Your purpose determines not only what parts of your sources you will use but also how you will relate them to one another. Since the very essence of synthesis is the combining of information and ideas, you must have some basis on which to combine them. *Some relationships among the material in your sources must make them worth synthesizing.* It follows that the better able you are to discover such relationships, the better able you will be to use your sources in writing syntheses. Notice that the mass communications assignment requires you to draw a *cause-and-effect* relationship between photographs of the war and Northerners' perceptions of the war. The applied technology assignment requires you to *compare and contrast* state-of-the-art weapons technology in the eighteenth and nineteenth centuries. The economics assignment requires you to *argue* a proposition. In each case, *your purpose will determine how you relate your source materials to one other.*

Consider some other examples. You may be asked on an exam question or in instructions for a paper to *describe* two or three approaches to prison reform during the past decade. You may be asked to *compare and contrast* one country's approach to imprisonment with another's. You may be asked to develop an *argument* of your own on this subject, based on your reading. Sometimes (when you are not given a specific assignment) you determine your own purpose: You are interested in exploring a particular subject; you are interested in making a case for one approach or another. In any event, your purpose shapes your essay. Your purpose determines which sources you research, which ones you use, which parts of them you use, at which points in your essay you use them, and in what manner you relate them to one another.

HOW TO WRITE SYNTHESES

Although writing syntheses can't be reduced to a lockstep method, it should help you to follow these procedures:

- *Consider your purpose in writing.* What are you trying to accomplish in your essay? How will this purpose shape the way you approach your sources?
- *Select and carefully read your sources,* according to your purpose. Then reread the passages, mentally summarizing each. Identify those aspects or parts of your sources that will help you in fulfilling your purpose. When rereading, *label* or *underline* the passages for main ideas, key terms, and any details you want to use in the synthesis.

- *Formulate a thesis.* Your thesis is the main idea that you want to present in your synthesis. It should be expressed as a complete sentence. Sometimes, the thesis is the first sentence, but more often, it is *the final sentence of the first paragraph.* If you are writing *an inductively arranged* synthesis (see p. 90), the thesis sentence may not appear until the final paragraphs. (See Chapter 4 for more information on writing an effective thesis.)

- *Decide how you will use your source material.* How will the information and the ideas in the passages help you to fulfill your purpose?

- *Develop an organizational plan,* according to your thesis. How will you arrange your material? It is not necessary to prepare a formal outline. But you should have some plan that will indicate the order in which you will present your material and that will indicate the relationships among your sources.

- *Write the first draft* of your synthesis, following your organizational plan. Be flexible with your plan, however. Frequently, you will use an outline to get started. As you write, you may discover new ideas and make room for them by adjusting the outline. When this happens, reread your work frequently, making sure that your thesis still accounts for what follows and that what follows still logically supports your thesis.

- *Document your sources.* You may do this by crediting them within the body of the synthesis or by footnoting them. (See Chapter 5 for more information on documenting sources.)

- *Revise* your synthesis, inserting transitional words and phrases where necessary. Make sure that the synthesis reads smoothly, logically, and clearly from beginning to end. Check for grammatical correctness, punctuation, spelling.

Note: The writing of syntheses is a recursive process, and you should accept a certain amount of backtracking and reformulating as inevitable. For instance, in developing an organizational plan (step 5) you may discover a gap in your presentation, which will send you scrambling for another source—back to step 2. You may find that steps 3 and 4, on formulating a thesis and making inferences among sources, occur simultaneously; indeed, inferences are often made before a thesis is formulated. Our recommendations for writing syntheses will give you a structure; they will get you started. But be flexible in your approach: expect discontinuity and, if possible, be comforted that through backtracking and reformulating you will eventually produce a coherent, well-crafted essay.

WHAT IS A COLLEGE-LEVEL ESSAY?

There are so many types of college-level essays that it is impossible to make generalizations about one type that will apply to all the others. Some essays call for personal responses to a particular state of affairs (e.g., apartheid in South Africa); some call for critical responses to a particular book or article (see the discussion of "Critique" preceding); some should be classified as journals or reports, rather than essays; some call for literary criticism; and some call for acts of pure imagination. (The questions following the individual readings in this book call for all these types of essays—except perhaps for lab reports!) But in this chapter, we will focus on one of the most commonly required types of essay—the type that requires you to draw upon several sources to support a thesis (main idea). You may be working on a thesis that has been supplied to you, or you may have formulated a thesis on your own after careful consideration of the available evidence.

Here is a diagram of a typical academic essay:

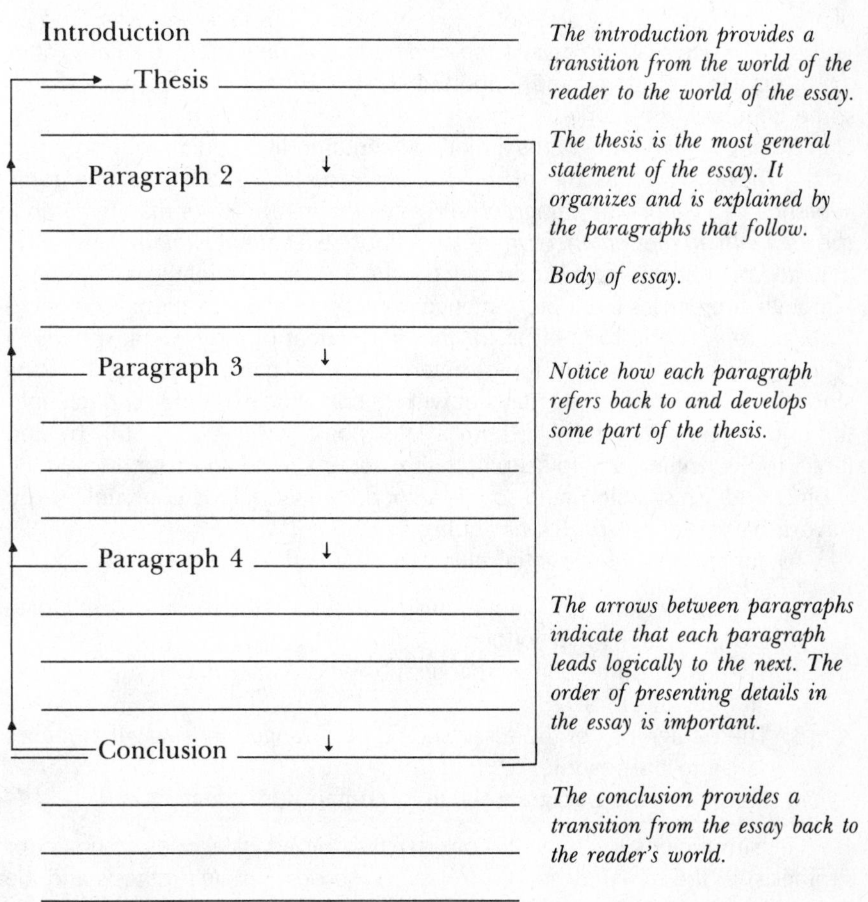

Introduction
Thesis
Paragraph 2
Paragraph 3
Paragraph 4
Conclusion
The introduction provides a transition from the world of the reader to the world of the essay.
The thesis is the most general statement of the essay. It organizes and is explained by the paragraphs that follow.
Body of essay.
Notice how each paragraph refers back to and develops some part of the thesis.
The arrows between paragraphs indicate that each paragraph leads logically to the next. The order of presenting details in the essay is important.
The conclusion provides a transition from the essay back to the reader's world.

Observe the placement of arrows in the diagram; they signify the logical relationship among elements of the passage. All academic essays should have a clearly stated thesis, *a one-sentence, general statement that describes the content of the essay to follow.* The thesis is usually found at the end of the first or second paragraph, after the general topic of the essay has been introduced. Following the thesis is a series of paragraphs, each of which is written to supply supporting information that will make the thesis convincing to a reader. Only paragraphs that are related to the thesis belong in the essay. This is why you see arrows in the diagram leading from each paragraph back to the thesis. (Essays that are not academic and intended for an audience outside the university often do not follow this tight structure and may succeed brilliantly. So if the structure just described seems to "lock you in," realize that it is a structure for academic occasions. We should say, however, that readers of all persuasions, inside academics and out, expect writing to be clear and carefully structured, whatever that structure happens to be.)

In addition, paragraphs supporting the thesis must lead logically from one to the next. The reader must know *why,* for instance, paragraph 3 has been placed after paragraph 2 and not before, which means that *the writer must be very sure of where in the essay supporting information is placed.* Finally, after the thesis has been stated and supported, the writer ends the presentation with some concluding remarks.

The individual paragraphs are often structured like miniature essays. Just as the thesis serves as the main idea of the essay as a whole, the *topic sentence of a particular paragraph serves as the main idea of that paragraph, the idea that all the sentences in the paragraph illustrate or explain.* Normally, in academic papers, the topic sentence is the first sentence of the paragraph—although sometimes the topic sentence is delayed by a transitional sentence. ("But there was another reason for the final defeat of the Federalist party.") Not all paragraphs contain topic sentences. Some paragraphs may be transitional. In other cases, you may not wish to make the main idea explicit until the end of the paragraph—or until a later point in the essay. Still, by and large, topic sentences help keep both the reader's mind and your own on the subject under discussion, and so it is a good idea to include them unless you have a particular reason for not doing so.

To summarize the essential elements of a well-structured essay:

1. The essay should contain a thesis that allows the reader to anticipate the paragraphs that follow.
2. The essay should contain paragraphs whose information supports and clarifies the thesis.
3. The paragraphs of the essay should be arranged in a way that makes sense to the reader.
4. Normally, the paragraphs should contain topic sentences.

For simplicity's sake, we'll consider two broad categories of essay (or synthesis) in the remainder of this chapter; the *description* synthesis and the *argument* synthesis. We'll also consider techniques of developing your essays and, in particular, the techniques of *comparison-contrast.*

THE DESCRIPTION SYNTHESIS

Many of the papers you write in college and many portions of papers you write will be more or less descriptive in nature. *A description is a recreation in words of some object, person, place, emotion, event, sequence of events, or state of affairs.* Writers describe when they divide a subject into its component parts and present them to the reader in some clear and orderly fashion. As a reporter, your job might be to describe an event—to explain when, where, and how it took place. As a scientist, you would observe the conditions and results of an experiment and record them for review by others. As a student, you would review your research on a particular subject—let's say, the origins of the Vietnam War—and then present the results of your research to your professor and the members of your class.

Your job in writing a description paper—or in writing the descriptive portion of an argument paper—is not to argue a particular point but rather *to present the facts in a reasonably objective manner.* Of course, description papers, like other academic papers, should be based on a thesis. But the purpose of a thesis in a descriptive paper is less to advance a particular opinion than to provide focus and direction to the various facts contained in the paper. For example, "As the United States became more involved in the war in Vietnam, American controversy over the war increased."

Let's see how these generalizations might be applied to a particular task—writing a paper on the early part of the Vietnam War, based on a variety of sources. We'll assume that the assignment is to write a purely descriptive paper ("Describe how the United States gradually became involved in Vietnam, focusing particularly on official government pronouncements.")[1]

Because space is limited, we will use here a relatively few short sources. In writing a paper, you would probably use more and longer sources, but the same principles apply.

Read the following selections on the Vietnam War. They include a brief

---

[1]Why, you may ask, should you care about the Vietnam War—a conflict in a remote part of the world that ended some twenty years ago? Perhaps the best way to answer this question is to quote the famous remark of philosopher George Santayana: "Those who do not remember the past are condemned to relive it." The Vietnam War involves a number of issues that have arisen repeatedly during our history and that will probably arise in the future. Among these issues: Does the United States have the right or duty to intervene militarily in the affairs of another nation? Should we side with a corrupt but anticommunist regime against a popular revolutionary movement? Should we forcibly impose an American-style democracy in another country with little or no democratic tradition? Should the president involve the United States in a war without consulting the Congress? What is the effect on the social fabric of the United States when a significant percentage of its population is against the war? How does the rest of the world view the spectacle of a large nation—a "superpower"—warring against a small nation?

article from an encyclopedia, which provides a general survey of the war; a 1963 White House policy statement on Vietnam; the critical 1964 Gulf of Tonkin Congressional Resolution that gave President Lyndon Johnson a "blank check" to fight the war; and two statements by President Johnson, one (in 1965) justifying U.S. involvement and the other (in 1967) defending his bombing of North Vietnamese targets.

The Vietnam War

THE NEW COLUMBIA ENCYCLOPEDIA

Vietnam War, conflict in Southeast Asia, primarily fought in South Vietnam between government forces aided by the United States and guerrilla insurgents aided by North Vietnam. The war began soon after the Geneva Conference provisionally divided (1954) Vietnam at 17° N lat. into the Democratic Republic of Vietnam (North Vietnam) and the Republic of Vietnam (South Vietnam); escalated from a Vietnamese civil war into a limited international conflict in which the United States was deeply involved; and was substantially halted by peace agreements in 1973. In part the war was a legacy of France's colonial administration of Indochina, which effectively ended in 1954 with the French army's catastrophic defeat at Dienbienphu and the acceptance of the Geneva Conference agreements. . . . The end of hostilities was followed by refugee movements between zones and by reprisals by each regime against suspected enemies. Elections scheduled for 1956 in South Vietnam for the reunification of Vietnam were cancelled by President Ngo Dinh Diem. The cancellation was denounced by Ho Chi Minh and the Communist government of North Vietnam. The Communists expected to benefit from any elections held in South Vietnam because of the popular support they had there. After 1956, Diem's government faced increasingly serious opposition from insurgents known as the Viet Cong, who were aided by North Vietnam. The Viet Cong, following the tactics of North Vietnam's Vo Nguyen Giap, became masters of guerrilla warfare. Diem's army received U.S. advice and aid but was unable to suppress the guerrillas, who established a political organization, the National Liberation Front (NLF) in 1960. In 1961, South Vietnam signed a military and economic aid treaty with the United States that led to the arrival (1961) of the first U.S. support troops and the formation (1962) of the U.S. Military Assistance Command. Mounting dissatisfaction

---

with the ineffectiveness and corruption of Diem's government culminated (Nov., 1963) in a military coup engineered by Duong Van Minh and in Diem's execution. No one person or group was able to establish control in South Vietnam until June, 1965, when Nguyen Cao Ky became premier. During this interim, U.S. military aid to South Vietnam increased, especially after the U.S. Senate passed the Tonkin Gulf Resolution (Aug. 7, 1964) at the request of President Lyndon B. Johnson. In early 1965 the United States began air raids on North Vietnam and on Communist-controlled areas in the South, attempting to stop the flow of men and supplies to the South; by 1966 there were 190,000 U.S. troops in South Vietnam. North Vietnam, meanwhile, was receiving armaments and technical assistance from the Soviet Union and other Communist countries. Despite massive U.S. military aid, heavy bombing, the growing U.S. troop commitment (which reached nearly 550,000 in 1969), and the achievement of some political stability in South Vietnam after the election (1967) of Nguyen Van Thieu as president, the United States and South Vietnam were unable to inflict permanent setbacks on the Viet Cong and North Vietnamese. Optimistic U.S. military reports were discredited in Feb., 1968, by the devastating Tet offensive of the North Vietnamese army and the Viet Cong, which involved attacks on more than 100 towns and cities and a month-long battle for Hue in South Vietnam.

THE END OF THE WAR

Although initial efforts for a negotiated settlement were rejected by both sides, progress was made after President Johnson's decision not to seek reelection in 1968. Contacts between North Vietnam and the United States in Paris in 1968 were expanded in 1969 to include South Vietnam and the NLF. The United States, under the leadership of President Richard M. Nixon, altered its tactics to combine U.S. troop withdrawals with intensified bombing and the invasion of Communist sanctuaries in Cambodia (1970). The length of the war, the high U.S. casualties, and the exposure of U.S. involvement in war crimes such as the massacre at My Lai . . . helped to turn many in the United States against the war. Politically, the movement was led by Senators James William Fulbright, Robert F. Kennedy, Eugene J. McCarthy, and George S. McGovern; there were also huge public demonstrations in Washington, D.C., as well as in many other cities in the United States and on college campuses. Even as the war continued, peace talks in Paris progressed, with Henry Kissinger as U.S. negotiator. Hopes for peace were temporarily dashed in Dec., 1972, when a break in negotiations was followed by U.S. saturation bombing of North Vietnam. However, a peace agreement was reached in Jan., 1973, and the formal document was signed by the United States, North Vietnam, South Vietnam, and the NLF's provisional revolutionary government on Jan. 27, 1973. The accord provided for the end of hostilities, the withdrawal of U.S. and allied troops (several Southeast Asia Treaty Organization countries had sent token forces), the return of prisoners of war, and the formation of a four-nation international control commission to ensure peace. Although many problems were settled by the peace, fighting between South Vietnamese and the Communists for additional territory continued and hostility between North and South Vietnam remained undiluted. U.S. casualties in Vietnam during the era of direct U.S. involvement (1961–72) were more than 50,000 dead; South Vietnamese dead were estimated at more than 400,000 and Viet Cong and North Vietnamese at over 900,000.

White House Statement (1963)

U.S. POLICY ON VIET-NAM

Secretary [of Defense Robert S.] McNamara and General [Maxwell D.] Taylor reported to the President this morning and to the National Security Council this afternoon. Their report included a number of classified findings and recommendations which will be the subject of further review and action. Their basic presentation was endorsed by all members of the Security Council and the following statement of United States policy was approved by the President on the basis of recommendations received from them and from Ambassador [Henry Cabot] Lodge.

1. The security of South Viet-Nam is a major interest of the United States as other free nations. We will adhere to our policy of working with the people and government of South Viet-Nam to deny this country to communism and to suppress the externally stimulated and supported insurgency of the Viet-Cong as promptly as possible. Effective performance in this undertaking is the central objective of our policy in South Viet-Nam.

2. The military program in South Viet-Nam has made progress and is sound in principle, though improvements are being energetically sought.

3. Major U.S. assistance in support of this military effort is

Statement, October 2, 1963. *Dept. of State Bulletin* 44 (21 Oct. 1963):624.

needed only until the insurgency has been suppressed or until the national security forces of the government of South Viet-Nam are capable of suppressing it.

Secretary McNamara and General Taylor reported their judgment that the major part of the U.S. military task can be completed by the end of 1965, although there may be a continuing requirement for a limited number of U.S. training personnel. They reported that by the end of this year, the U.S. program for training Vietnamese should have progressed to the point where 1,000 U.S. military personnel assigned to South Viet-Nam can be withdrawn.

4. The political situation in South Viet-Nam remains deeply serious. The United States has made clear its continuing opposition to any repressive actions in South Viet-Nam. While such actions have not yet significantly affected the military effort, they could do so in the future.

5. It remains the policy of the United States, in South Viet-Nam as in other parts of the world, to support the efforts of the people of that country to defeat aggression and to build a peaceful and free society.

Congress Gives Johnson a Blank Check for War (1964)

Diem's death brought disaster to Saigon. Military coup followed military coup with musical-chairs confusion. South Vietnamese morale was sagging badly, as reflected in the desertions of draftees from the army. American aid was slithering down a bottomless rat-hole, while American troops in increasing numbers were chasing the elusive Viet Cong—"raggedy little bastards in black pajamas." Then, August 2–4, 1964, two American destroyers in the international waters of the Gulf of Tonkin reported alleged attacks by North Vietnamese torpedo boats. President Johnson, being accused of "softness" on Communism in the then current presidential campaign, immediately ordered retaliatory bombing of North Vietnamese naval bases. He also requested of Congress blanket authorization for future action, and the following resolution was passed unanimously in the House and by a vote of 88 to 2 in the Senate. [Bailey]

JOINT RESOLUTION[1]

To promote the maintenance of international peace and security in southeast Asia.

Whereas naval units of the Communist regime in Vietnam, in violation of the principles of the Charter of the United Nations and of international law, have deliberately and repeatedly attacked United States naval vessels lawfully present in international waters,[2] and have thereby created a serious threat to international peace; and

Whereas these attacks are part of a deliberate and systematic campaign of aggression that the Communist regime in North Vietnam has been waging against its neighbors and the nations joined with them in the collective defense of their freedom; and

Whereas the United States is assisting the peoples of southeast Asia to protect their freedom and has no territorial, military or political ambitions in that area, but desires only that these peoples should be left in peace to work out their own destinies in their own way: Now, therefore, be it

Resolved by the Senate and House of Representatives of the United States of America in Congress assembled, [T]hat the Congress approves and supports the determination of the President, as Commander in Chief, to take all necessary measures to repel any armed attack against the forces of the United States and to prevent further aggression.

Sec. 2. The United States regards as vital to its national interest and to world peace the maintenance of international peace and security in southeast Asia. Consonant with the Constitution of the United States and the Charter of the United Nations and in accordance with its obligations under the Southeast Asia Collective Defense Treaty,[3] the United States is, therefore, prepared, as the President determines, to take all necessary steps, including the use of armed force, to assist any member of protocol state of the Southeast Asia Collective Defense Treaty requesting assistance in defense of its freedom.

---

[1]*Department of State Bulletin, 51* (Aug. 24, 1964) 268. [Bailey]

[2]The North Vietnamese claimed a 12-mile limit; the U.S. claimed the conventional 3-mile limit. [Bailey]

[3]Partly to protect South Vietnam against aggression after the Geneva Conference of 1954, the United States helped to organize the Southeast Asia Treaty Organization (SEATO). It consisted of the U.S., Britain, France, Australia, New Zealand, the Philippines, Thailand, and Pakistan. Britain, France, and Pakistan kept out of the action in South Vietnam. Australia, New Zealand, and the Philippines sent token forces, and Thailand provided the sites for huge bomber bases. South Korea, though not a member of SEATO, supplied about 50,000 troops. By 1967, over thirty nations had sent aid in one form or another. [Bailey]

Sec. 3. This resolution shall expire when the President shall determine that the peace and security of the area is reasonably assured by international conditions created by action of the United Nations or otherwise, except that it may be terminated earlier by concurrent resolution of the Congress.

[*Many members of Congress later regretted voting for this resolution, charging that their intent was not to authorize a large-scale war. President Johnson did not, in fact, ask for an official declaration of hostilities. Wars that are officially declared are less easy to stop than unofficial ones, and besides such a declaration might well have prompted Peking and Moscow to send in Red soldiers to assist their Communist comrades.*—Bailey]

President Johnson States His War Aims (1965)[1]

The avowed purposes of America's heavy but limited bombing of North Vietnam were (a) to check the southward shipment of supplies and men, (b) to weaken the morale of the North Vietnamese so that they would come to the peace table, and (c) to strengthen the sagging morale of the South Vietnamese. The continuous aerial pounding was not conspicuously successful, as supplies and soldiers continued to flow (though probably less plentifully) and the Hanoi regime dug in more doggedly. President Johnson, in his memorable address at The Johns Hopkins University (April 7, 1965), used both the carrot and the stick. On the one hand, he was prepared to enter into "unconditional negotiations"[2] with North Vietnam; on the other hand, he was prepared to offer one billion dollars for a program to rehabilitate Southeast Asia, including North Vietnam. [Bailey]

Why are these realities our concern? Why are we in South Viet-Nam?

We are there because we have a promise to keep. Since 1954 every American President has offered support to the people of South Viet-Nam. We have helped to build, and we have helped to defend. Thus, over many years, we have made a national pledge to help South Viet-Nam defend its independence.

And I intend to keep that promise.

To dishonor that pledge, to abandon this small and brave nation to its enemies, and to the terror that must follow, would be an unforgivable wrong.

From Bailey, ed. *The American Spirit.* See source note on page 69.

[1]*Public Papers of the Presidents of the United States: Lyndon B. Johnson* (1966), p. 395. [Bailey]

[2]He nevertheless attached conditions, including "an independent South Viet-nam." [Bailey]

We are also there to strengthen world order. Around the globe from Berlin to Thailand are people whose well-being rests in part on the belief that they can count on us [to honor some forty defensive alliances] if they are attacked. To leave Viet-Nam to its fate would shake the confidence of all these people in the value of an American commitment and in the value of America's word. The result would be increased unrest and instability, and even wider war.

We are also there because there are great stakes in the balance. Let no one think for a moment that retreat from Viet-Nam would bring an end to conflict. The battle would be renewed in one country and then another. The central lesson of our time is that the appetite of aggression is never satisfied. . . .

Our objective is the independence of South Viet-Nam and its freedom from attack. We want nothing for ourselves—only that the people of South Viet-Nam be allowed to guide their own country in their own way.

We will do everything necessary to reach that objective and we will do only what is absolutely necessary.

[*The free world generally praised President Johnson's overture for peace. But Hanoi branded it a "swindle" by the American "warmongering imperialists," possibly because Washington had earlier turned a deaf ear to several presumed overtures for peace that it had regarded as "insincere."*—Bailey]

President Johnson Defends the Bombing (1967)[1]

Before the end of 1965 American troops were not only fighting the Viet Cong and some North Vietnamese regulars in South Vietnam, but American aircraft were bombing North Vietnamese bridges, railroads, and war-production centers. Enemy antiaircraft fire, provided largely by the Soviets and Chinese, was taking a deadly toll of United States aircraft. American aviators were making no concerted effort to destroy the civilian centers of Hanoi and Haiphong—the two most important cities of North Vietnam—but many civilian casualties were inevitable. (In South Vietnam, Viet Cong terrorists were blowing up hotels, restaurants, and

From Bailey, ed. *The American Spirit.* See source note on page 69.

[1]From the *Weekly Compilation of Presidential Documents, III,* 476 (March 20, 1967, reporting speech of March 15, 1967). [Bailey]

buses, with heavy loss of civilian life.) President Johnson, speaking to the Tennessee state legislature, and referring to the iron will of Tennessee's Andrew Jackson, defended America's bombing forays in the following resolute words. [Bailey]

I also want to say categorically that it is not the position of the American Government that the bombing will be decisive in getting Hanoi to abandon aggression. It has, however, created very serious problems for them. The best indication of how substantial is the fact that they are working so hard every day with all their friends throughout the world to try to get us to stop.

The bombing is entirely consistent with America's limited objectives in South Vietnam. The strength of Communist main-force units in the south is clearly based on their infiltration from the north. So I think it is simply unfair to our American soldiers, sailors, and Marines and our Vietnamese allies to ask them to face increased enemy personnel and firepower without making an effort to try to reduce that infiltration.

Now as to bombing civilians, I would simply say that we are making an effort that is unprecedented in the history of warfare to be sure that we do not. It is our policy to bomb military targets only.

We have never deliberately bombed cities, nor attacked any target with the purpose of inflicting civilian casualties.

We hasten to add, however, that we recognize, and we regret, that some people, even after warning, are living and working in the vicinity of military targets and they have suffered.

We are also too aware that men and machines are not infallible, and that some mistakes do occur.

But our record on this account is, in my opinion, highly defensible.

Look for a moment at the record of the other side.

Any civilian casualties that result from our operations are inadvertent, in stark contrast to the calculated Vietcong policy of systematic terror.

Tens of thousands of innocent Vietnamese civilians have been killed, tortured, and kidnapped by the Vietcong. There is no doubt about the deliberate nature of the Vietcong program. One need only note the frequency with which Vietcong victims are village leaders, teachers, health workers, and others who are trying to carry out constructive programs for their people.

Yet, the deeds of the Vietcong go largely unnoted in the public debate. It is this moral double bookkeeping which makes us get sometimes very weary of our critics.

Consider Your Purpose

Here, then, are five brief sources on the involvement of the United States in Vietnam. The first is an encyclopedia entry that you would use to get a comprehensive view of your subject, enabling you to relate specific details from other sources to each other and to the whole. Reading an encyclopedia article on a subject before pursuing more detailed research is like looking at a road map of an unfamiliar city to determine the best route from point A to point B. Without the map, you're likely to head off in the wrong direction, run into dead ends, or have to rely on the sometimes inaccurate or eccentric advice of "locals."

Note, however, that aside from providing general background, encyclopedia articles are not considered appropriate sources for college-level research. So you should not rely heavily on material from encyclopedias, nor should you cite references for encyclopedia material; such material is considered "common knowledge."

The other four sources are government statements on the policy of the United States or actions at various stages of our involvement in the early part of the war. The first was issued by the White House in October 1963, a month before South Vietnamese President Diem was assassinated during a coup. The next is the Gulf of Tonkin resolution of 1964, by which Congress authorized President Johnson to take whatever military action he saw fit against North Vietnam. Next, President Johnson, in a speech in 1965 at Johns Hopkins University, attempted to explain the American presence in Vietnam. The final source is excerpted from a 1967 speech by President Johnson on the American bombing of North and South Vietnam.

On what basis can you combine—or synthesize—such statements? Before you can even start to answer this question, you must consider your *purpose.*

One purpose might be to determine just how the United States got so deeply involved in Vietnam. These sources would help to explain that, but in themselves they are not sufficient. You would need additional sources to help document such matters as the increasing flow of American personnel and equipment to South Vietnam, the military and diplomatic progress reports, and accounts of discussions and other communications between leaders in the United States and South Vietnam. Another purpose might be to determine whether or not the involvement of the United States in Vietnam was justified. But since all these sources (except for the first) are official government statements, you would have to draw on additional sources—both from neutral and from opposition writers—to help you make a fair determination.

On the other hand, your purpose may be more limited: to explain to your readers how the government in the United States justified to its citizens and to the outside world its military actions in Vietnam. In that case, you could provide a brief description of the ideas in these sources. The simplest way of doing this would be to summarize the sources in whole or in part and then to join these summaries in a logical manner. *Thus, the simplest type of synthesis would be little more than a skillfully connected series of summaries, the synthesis as a whole supporting the thesis.* (Other, more complex types of synthesis will be discussed in the sections that follow.)

Formulate a Thesis

The difference between your purpose and your thesis is a difference primarily of focus. Your purpose provides direction to your research and focus to your paper. Your thesis sharpens this focus by narrowing and formulating it in the words of a single declarative statement. (Refer to Chapter 4 for additional discussion on formulating thesis statements.)

Since your purpose in this case is simply to present the source material with little or no comment, then your thesis would be the most obvious statement to be made about these passages. By "obvious" we mean a statement based on an idea that is clearly supported in all the passages.

Your first attempt at a thesis might yield something like this:

> The United States fought in Vietnam to defend freedom.

One trouble with this thesis is that it is not clear whose freedom the United States is trying to defend—its own or that of the Vietnamese. Additionally, "freedom" is a troublesome word that requires definition. Your revision of this preliminary thesis, then, might add some clarifying elements:

> The United States fought in Vietnam to defend the independence of South Vietnam against the communists of North Vietnam.

This thesis is a little better, a bit sharper; but it still does not take into account the fact that almost all your evidence is based on official government statements. You need something in your thesis that acknowledges this fact, something like, "The United States position was . . ." or "The United States justified its involvement in Vietnam by . . ." Also, for the sake of clarity, it might be a good idea to acknowledge in your thesis the twofold nature of American war aims: (1) to counter North Vietnamese aggression and (2) to keep South Vietnam independent. Finally, you might have noticed that over a period of several years (from 1963 to 1967) official statements on Vietnam used the same justifications over and over again. This fact, also, could be acknowledged in your thesis, perhaps through a phrase like "from the beginning." So after a few more tries, you end up with your final thesis: "*From the beginning, the American government justified its involvement in Vietnam by pointing both to the aggressions of North Vietnam and the Viet Cong and to its own promise to keep South Vietnam an independent, noncommunist nation."*

Decide How You Will Use Your Source Material

The easiest way to deal with these sources is to summarize them. But since you are synthesizing ideas, rather than sources, you will have to be more selective than if you were writing a simple summary. You don't have to treat *all* the ideas in your sources, just the ones that support your thesis. Some sources might be summarized in their entirety; others, only in part. Using the techniques of summary, then determine section by section the main topics of each source, focusing on those topics that help support your thesis. Write brief phrases in the margin, underline key phrases or sentences, or take notes on a separate sheet of paper.

Develop an Organizational Plan

Your organizational plan is your plan for presenting your evidence. Refer to the diagram on page 63. The key questions you must ask yourself: How will you introduce your essay? What evidence will you present first (e.g., in the second paragraph, following the introduction)? What evidence will you present next? And so forth. Quite often, chronological order is the most natural order; that is, you present the events in the order in which they occurred. In other cases, some other order may be more revealing; for instance, you may first decide to present the material appearing in the government's public statements, then the material that was not publicly known—material, for example, gleaned from internal memoranda or records of high-level meetings (of course, you could not do this in the present case, since you have no such evidence). Another alternate form of organization (one that *is* possible with the present evidence) is to focus first on North Vietnamese aggression and then the promise to keep South Vietnam independent. Here is one organizational plan for your synthesis. Your *thesis* is:

> From the beginning, the American government justified its involvement in Vietnam by pointing both to the aggressions of North Vietnam and the Viet Cong and to its own promise to keep South Vietnam an independent, noncommunist nation.

A. Introduction: Brief survey of how the United States became involved in Vietnam.
B. American government points to communist aggression.
C. American government points to its promise to keep South Vietnam independent.

Write the Topic Sentences

This is an optional step; but writing the topic sentences will get you started on each main section of your synthesis and will help give you the sense of direction you need to proceed. Here are some examples of topic sentences for a synthesis on these five passages.

> The United States pointed to communist actions against South Vietnam whenever it announced or defended its own military activities in the area.
>
> When announcing its escalating involvement, the government continually reiterated the international importance of its promise to defend South Vietnam's independent, noncommunist status.

Write Your Synthesis

Here is how your completed synthesis might read. *Note*: In the following examples, thesis and topic sentences are highlighted. MLA (Modern Language Association) documentation style, explained in Chapter 5, is used throughout.

> 1 How did the United States become involved in South Vietnam? Soon after World War II, the United States moved to stem the expansion of communism, pledging to aid any noncommunist country against communist aggression. In 1954, following the French army's defeat in Vietnam, the Geneva Conference established two separate states in Vietnam: to the north, the communist Democratic Republic of Vietnam led by Ho Chi Minh, and to the south, the Republic of Vietnam led by Ngo Dinh Diem and supported by the United States. By 1956, soon after the cancellation of elections in the south that probably would have benefited the communists, Diem's goverment came under attack from communist insurgents known as the Viet Cong. In 1961, the United States began a controversial military intervention that was to become the Vietnam War. From

the beginning, the American government justified its involvement in Vietnam by pointing both to the aggressions of North Vietnam and the Viet Cong and to its own promise to keep South Vietnam an independent, noncommunist nation.

The United States pointed to communist actions 2
against South Vietnam whenever it announced or defended its own military activities in the area. In October 1963, the White House, in a policy statement explaining the presence of military advisors in Vietman, claimed that there was an "externally stimulated and supported insurgency of the Viet Cong" against South Vietnam and that a "limited number of U.S. training personnel" was needed to combat this insurgence (128). The following year's landmark Tonkin Gulf resolution, in which Congress authorized the president to wage war without further legislative approval, used an alleged North Vietnamese attack on American destroyers in the Gulf of Tonkin to allow the president to take "all necessary measures" (culminating in full-scale military intervention) to "promote the maintenance of international peace and security of Southeast Asia." The resolution charged that the Tonkin Gulf attacks were "part of a deliberate and systematic campaign of aggression that the communist regime has been waging . . ." ("Joint Resolution" 971). A key issue in later years of the war was the United States' saturation bombings of North Vietnam. In 1967, President Johnson cited "Communist . . . infiltration from the north" when defending the bombings and countered reports of civilian casualties by invoking reports of "the calculated Viet Cong policy of systematic terror" against civilians. In the American government's view, the military advisors, the Tonkin Gulf resolution, and the bombings of North Vietnam were justified reac-

tions to what Johnson called in 1965 the communist "appetite of aggression" (Johnson, "War Aims" 971).

A 1961 military and economic aid treaty with South 3
Vietnam reflected the promise of the United States to defend South Vietnam's noncommunist, independent status; when announcing its escalating involvement, the government continually reiterated the international importance of this position. In 1963, the White House vowed "to deny this country to communism," asserting "the security of South Vietnam is of major interest to the United States as other free nations" ("U.S. Policy on Vietnam" 128). The Tonkin Gulf resolution stated that the United States was "preventing further aggression," because "the maintenance of international peace and security in southeast Asia" was "vital to its national interest and to world peace . . ." (971). Outlining his war aims in 1965, President Johnson spoke of the "national pledge to help South Vietnam defend its independence" and explained that to refuse support would be "an unforgivable wrong." The communists would then move on to other nations, he said, presumably with the intention of eventual world domination. Johnson also asserted that the government of the United States believed it was assuring not just South Vietnam's independence and "freedom from attack" but also security throughout the free world (Johnson, "War Aims" 975–76).

This sense of acting as an international "savior" was 4
at the root of the Southeast Asian policy of the United States. A self-appointed, crusading superpower was making a stand in a distant country to discourage communist expansion. The key elements requiring American intervention were there: irrefutable communist aggression in a small country and a government asking for help against the communists. The result was a futile ten-year

military effort by the United States, spawning massive antigovernment sentiment and rudely awakening the American government to the impracticality of such lofty intentions.

Works Cited

Johnson, Lyndon. Public Papers of the Presidents of the United States: Lyndon B. Johnson (1966), 395. Rpt. as "President Johnson States His War Aims (1965)." The American Spirit: United States History as Seen by Contemporaries. Ed. Thomas A. Bailey. 4th ed. Vol. 2. Lexington: Heath, 1978. 975–76.

——. Weekly Compilation of Presidential Documents. Vol. 3. 476 (20 Mar. 1967) [reporting speech of 15 Mar. 1967]. Rpt. as "President Johnson Defends the Bombing (1967)" in Bailey 972–73.

"Joint Resolution." Department of State Bulletin 51 (24 Aug. 1964): 268. Rpt. in Bailey 970–72.

"U.S. Policy on Vietnam." White House Statement, 2 Oct. 1963. Department of State Bulletin 44 (21 Oct. 1963): 624. Rpt. in The Viet-Nam Reader: Articles and Documents on American Foreign Policy and the Viet-Nam Crisis. Ed. Marcus G. Raskin and Bernard B. Fall. Rev. ed. New York: Vintage, 1967. 128–29.

—Michael Behrens

Discussion

In the *first paragraph* the writer introduces his subject by sketching a brief historical survey of how the United States became involved in Vietnam. This historical survey leads directly to the thesis: "From the beginning, the American government justified its involvement in Vietnam by pointing both to the aggressions of North Vietnam and the Viet Cong and to its own promise to keep South Vietnam an independent, noncommunist nation."

The *body of the essay* takes up, in turn, each element of this thesis. The *second paragraph* is concerned with the United States' citing of communist aggression against the south. Material from the source documents concerned with communist aggression is either summarized, paraphrased, or directly quoted. The *third paragraph* is concerned with the second element of the thesis, the promise of the United States to aid South Vietnam; and again relevant material from the sources is summarized, paraphrased, or directly quoted. Note that at the beginning of paragraph 3 the writer expands the topic sentence to include mention of the 1961 military and economic aid treaty—a crucial early document reflecting the promise of American assistance.

So far, the essay has been primarily descriptive: The writer has stayed within the confines of his thesis and has not done more than describe how the available evidence supports this thesis. In the *concluding paragraph,* however, the writer moves into the area of argument. That is, he indicates his own opinions by generalizing about the significance of the American government's actions and by strongly suggesting that the United States was misguided (and as it turned out, catastrophically wrong) in imagining that it could, by military force, and without unacceptable cost, impose its own anticommunist doctrines in another part of the world.

THE ARGUMENT SYNTHESIS

The description synthesis, as we have seen, is fairly modest in purpose. It does not go much beyond what is obvious from a careful reading of the sources. Of course, since your reader is not always in a position to read your sources (carefully or not), this kind of synthesis, if well done, can be very informative. But the main thing about the description synthesis is that it is designed more to inform than to *persuade.* As we have said, the thesis in the description synthesis is less a device for arguing a particular point than a device for providing focus and direction to an objective presentation of facts or opinions. With a description synthesis, you as writer remain, for the most part, a detached observer. (The only exception, as we have seen in the previous model essay, is that the writers may suggest their own opinions about what they have described at the conclusion of their work.)

This is not the case with the *argument synthesis,* whose purpose is *to present your own point of view*—supported, of course, by relevant facts, drawn from your sources, and presented in a logical manner. (The Vietnam War was one of the most controversial events in American history, and most people who study this war develop strong opinions on the subject, even if they are too young to remember the war period.) Of course, you might contend that the thesis we developed for our descriptive synthesis *does* represent a particular point of view: "From the beginning, the American government justified its involvement in Vietnam by pointing both to the aggressions of North Vietnam and the Viet Cong and to its own promise to keep South Vietnam an independent, noncommunist nation." This is true, but note that the sources we provided do not allow any other point of view than this one. In other words, no other conclusion could reasonably be drawn from these sources than one whose meaning would be essentially the same as that of the thesis we have developed. What distinguishes the argument thesis from that of a description thesis is that it is *debatable.* Other, opposite conclusions could be drawn from the same sources. So the theses for argument syntheses are propositions about which reasonable people could disagree. They are propositions about which (given the right arguments, as formulated by you) people could be persuaded to change their minds. This is generally not true of the kinds of theses that serve to unify description syntheses.

Let's suppose, then, that you have researched material on the war and wish to write a paper (perhaps for a history course) expressing your point of view. Let's suppose also that you have gathered not only the preceding five sources (used as the basis for the description synthesis) but the following additional five sources:[2]

A War of Atrocities (1966)[1]

Brutality occurred on both sides. A Communist South Vietnamese in "black pajamas" was indistinguishable from a non-Communist Vietnamese in "black pajamas." Viet Cong guerrillas tortured, blinded, castrated, beheaded, and butchered prisoners, Americans and anti-Communist countrymen alike. Their foes retaliated with similarly inhumane tactics. An American soldier wrote, "Yesterday I shot and killed a little 8 or 9 year old girl with the sweetest, most innocent little face, and the nastiest grenade in her hand you ever saw." American bombers used defoliants to kill crops, and they dropped explosive and incendiary bombs—long-clinging "improved" napalm. They killed or injured North Vietnamese, Viet Cong (soldiers and civilians), and, by mistake, innocent South Vietnamese villagers and American comrades. Two letters from American soldiers are here reproduced. [Bailey]

Dear Mom, . . .

Yesterday I witnessed something that would make any American

[2]Of course, in an actual paper, you would probably draw on more than the limited number of sources we provide here, since you would need to gather more data and reseach additional viewpoints.

From Bailey, ed. *The American Spirit*. See source note on page 69.

[1]Glenn Munson, ed. *Letters from Viet Nam* (1966), pp. 104, 118, Published by Parallex Publishing Co. We learned during the Filipino insurrection of 1899–1902 that when we fight primitive peoples we are pulled down to their level of warfare. . . . Anti-imperialist opposition in America to the war in the Philippines also strengthened Filipino resistance, as was the case later in North Vietnam. [Bailey]

realize why we are in this war. At least it did me. I was on daylight patrol. We were on a hill overlooking a bridge that was out of our sector. I saw a platoon of Vietcong stopping traffic from going over the bridge. They were beating women and children over the head with rifles, clubs, and fists. They even shot one woman and her child. They were taking rice, coconuts, fish, and other assorted foods from these people. The ones that didn't give they either beat or shot. I think you know what I tried to do. I wanted to go down and kill all of those slant-eyed bastards. I started to and it took two men to stop me. These slobs have to be stopped, even if it takes every last believer in a democracy and a free way of life to do it. I know after seeing their brave tactics I'm going to try my best. So please don't knock [President] Johnson's policy in Vietnam. There is a good reason for it. I'm not too sure what it is myself, but I'm beginning to realize, especially after yesterday. . . .

Love, *Bill*

How are the people taking to the war in Portland? I've read too much . . . about the way some of those cowardly students are acting on campuses. They sure don't show me much as far as being American citizens. They have the idea that they are our future leaders. Well, I won't follow nobody if he isn't going to help fight for my freedom.

A few weeks ago, I had the chance to talk with some Marines who had come to Okinawa for four [lousy] days of leave. They were more than happy because they had been fighting for six months with no let-up. We sat in a restaurant all the time, and I wish I could have taped it on my recorder. What they had to say would have had an impact on the people back home. One showed me where he had been shot. I asked if it hurt, and he didn't feel it. Not until after he got the . . . that shot him. He was more angry than hurt. They told me of some of their patrols and how they would be talking to a buddy one minute and watch him die the next. Or wake up in the morning and see a friend hung from a tree by hooks in his armpits with parts of his body cut and shoved into his mouth. From what they said, the Vietcong aren't the only ruthless ones. *We* have to be, too. *Have* to. You'd be surprised to know that a guy you went to school with is right now shooting a nine-year-old girl and her mother. He did it because if they got the chance they would kill him. Or throwing a Vietcong out of a helicopter because he wouldn't talk.

One guy [who had broke down and cried] said that his one desire is to get enough leave to go home and kick three of those demonstrators in a well-suited place and bring him back. I tell you, it's horrible to read a paper and see your own people aren't backing you up.

Public Hearings in Wisconsin (1965)[1]

The Vietnam War—by 1967 our third largest foreign war—became increasingly unpopular in America and abroad. Many citizens—"the hawks"—complained because President Johnson did not launch an all-out bombing of the North. Many others—"the doves"—objected because he was bombing at all. Some critics wanted to pull out altogether; other were for pulling back to "impregnable" enclaves in South Vietnam and sweating it out until the North Vietnamese were willing to negotiate. Especially critical were the intellectuals, and particularly the "Vietniks" of college age who burned their draft cards and staged protest demonstrations known as "teach-ins." Congressman Robert W. Kastenmeier of Wisconsin conducted hearings in Madison, Wisconsin, and elicited the following statement from David Keene, who represented the Wisconsin Young Americans for Freedom, a conservative youth oranization. [Bailey]

We could probably establish peace in South Vietnam by withdrawing our troops, but it would be a temporary and expensive peace. The price tag would include not only the geographical area of Vietnam, but the freedom and dreams of the fourteen million people living there, the honor of our own country, and, eventually, the security of the entire free world.

Appeasement has never been, and is not now, an effective method of dealing with aggression. It has been tried often, but has always served only to whet the appetite of the ambitious aggressor. . . .

Russia and China are presently engaged in a struggle for the leadership of the international Communist movement. The Soviet Union has advocated a more moderate foreign policy line than that being pushed by China's Mao Tse-tung. An American defeat in Asia would seem to substantiate the Red Chinese charge that the United States is a "paper tiger," and could, conceivably, catapult Mao into undisputed leadership of the international Communist movement. . . .

American withdrawal, we must remember, would abandon 14 million people to Communist enslavement. More than a million of those people voted with their feet against Communism when they fled from North Vietnam following the Geneva Agreements of 1954. They have trusted our word and they have fought Ho Chi Minh. The

From Bailey, ed. *The American Spirit*. See source note on page 69.

[1]Robert W. Kastenmeier, ed. *Vietnam Hearings: Voices from the Grass Roots* (1965), pp. 38–40.

South Vietnamese population has suffered more than we can possibly imagine to keep their country out of the hands of the Communist regime to their north. . . .

In 1956 the peasants of North Vietnam objected to Ho Chi Minh's plans for them. He responded by ordering executions which, according to the International Control Commission, claimed nearly 60,000 peasant lives. What will he do to the Buddhists in South Vietnam the first time they object to his plans? And what will be the fate of the 500,000 men serving in the South Vietnamese armed forces? Ho Chi Minh forgets little, and is not likely to forgive them for opposing his "wave of the future."

In 1957 he began a campaign of terror in South Vietnam designed to isolate the people from their government. Principal targets included teachers, doctors, nurses and village officials. The late President John F. Kennedy, in May of 1961, revealed that between May 1960 and May of 1961, more than 4,000 low level officials were killed by the Viet Cong. Other figures revealed that as many as 13,000 village officials had been murdered by 1962. The number has measurably increased since that time.

The Americanization of South Vietnam (1965 and After)[1]

By 1967 the United States had more than 400,000 fighting men in South Vietnam, with a vast supporting apparatus. Soldiers with ready cash to spend had an inflationary effect on the Vietnamese economy. Gaudy bars, brothels, and other places for entertaining service men flourished in Saigon and other cities. The following little drama was reported by a Quaker observer. [Bailey]

The scene was a small square in the city of Hué, South Vietnam, on a summer day in 1965. The place was known as a rendezvous for American GI's and Vietnamese girls. A couple of military police were on duty to keep order. On this day one of them had supplied himself with some candy for the children who played in the square and crowded around the Americans. As he started his distribution in a friendly mood, a swarm of youngsters, jumping and reaching,

From Bailey ed. *The American Spirit.* See source note on page 69.

[1]A Report Prepared for the American Friends Service Committee, *Peace in Vietnam: A New Approach in Southeast Asia* (1966), p. 1. By permission of Hill and Wang, Inc. [Bailey]

pressed about him. With a laugh he tossed the candy out on the cobblestones. Immediately the children descended like locusts, each intent on grabbing a piece.

A young Vietnamese school teacher happened by at this moment, and seeing the scrambling children, he spoke to them in stern and emphatic tones. He told them to pick up the candy and give it back to the American. After some hesitation they sheepishly complied. Then, facing the soldier and speaking in measured English with a tone of suppressed anger and scorn, he said: "You Americans don't understand. You are making beggers of our children, prostitutes of our women, and Communists of our men!"

Schlesinger Presents the Chinese Side (1966)[2]

Late in 1966, Arthur M. Schlesinger, Jr., a Pulitzer-prize winning historian and former Special Assistant to President Kennedy, emphatically called for an end of the bombing and a de-escalation of the war in Vietnam. Although not advocating a scuttle-and-run policy, he was convinced that we could not napalm the Vietnamese into our kind of peace. [Bailey]

What, therefore, is the view from Beijing? It is obviously of a gigantic American effort at the encirclement and strangulation of China.

That is not, of course, our view of what we are doing; nor is it in fact what we are doing. But it really should not astonish us that a crew of dogmatic Marxist-Leninists should so interpret the extraordinary deployment of American armies, navies and military bases thousands of miles from the United States and mobilized—on the word of American leaders—against no one but themselves.

Imagine our own feelings if the Chinese had 400,000 troops in southern Mexico, engaged in putting down what we had hoped to be a pro-American rebellion; if massive Chinese military bases were being built there; if Chinese planes were bombing northern Mexico every day; if a great Chinese fleet controlled the waters along our Pacific coast; and if Beijing was denouncing the United States as the world's greatest threat to peace. The question, which so engages on our own sense of righteousness, of who the "aggressor" is, depends a good deal on who looks though what glass and how darkly.

From Bailey, ed. *The American Spirit*. See source note on page 69.

[2]Arthur M. Schlesinger, Jr., *The Bitter Heritage* (1966), pp. 36–37. By permission of Houghton Mifflin Company.

The leaders in Beijing are fully as devoted students of Munich[3] as the American Secretary of State. They are sure that we are out to bury them; they believe too that appeasement invites further aggression; and, however deep their reluctance, at some point concern for national survival will make them fight. "To save our neighbors" as Beijing announced on November 4, 1950, "is to save ourselves."

When will that point be reached this time? Probably when the Chinese are confronted by a direct threat to their frontier, either through bombing or through an American decision to cross the 17th parallel and invade North Vietnam. If a Communist regime barely established in Beijing could take a decision to intervene against the only atomic power in the world in 1950,[4] why does anyone suppose that a much stronger regime would flinch from that decision in 1966? Indeed, given the present discord in Beijing, war may seem the best way to renew revolutionary discipline, stop the brawling and unite the nation.

The Slaughter Goes On (1968)

For the embattled half-million Americans in Vietnam, Dr. Johnson last week ordered an emergency transfusion of 10,500 more combat troops, hopefully in time for the Viet Cong's second strike. Physician, heal thyself! After three years of escalating the war, things are worse than ever. In three years' bombing of North Vietnam, the US Air Force has let loose almost two million tons of explosives on that wretched country—close to one ton per North Vietnamese family, three times the bomb tonnage the USAF dropped in the Korean war, and almost equal to all the bombs dropped by U.S. forces during World War II. The bombing of North Vietnam has steadily spiraled and lately has concentrated on the jungle trails that bring military supplies and men South. But it didn't need a year-old Rand Corporation study, tardily declassified last week, to prove that "the level of infiltration has not been reduced sufficiently to prevent North Vietnam from helping to maintain a combat force in the South strong enough to deny the prospect of a decisive military victory to the US

[3]At the Munich conference of 1938, a part of Czechoslovakia was vainly sacrificed to German rule, by France and Britain, to appease the aggressive appetite of Hitler. [Bailey]

[4]Russia had detonated an atomic bomb in 1949, but presumably was far behind the United States in capability. [Bailey]

"The Slaughter Goes On." Editorial, *The New Republic*, February 26, 1968.

and its allies in the foreseeable future." In the year since that report was written, both sides in the war have increased their military stakes greatly, but all the bombing has failed to stop North Vietnam and its allies keeping pace with American escalation. Now the Marines at Khe Sanh face 30-ton Soviet tanks (how did *they* get through, on a pack mule?) and North Vietnam also has Soviet bombers able to pound the South's cities if they wish. North Vietnam, however, hints it prefers leaving that sort of destruction to the US Air Force, which did its best to wipe out Ben Tre, a delta town 50 miles below Saigon. Helicopter and fighter-bomber attacks on Ben Tre were directed by Air Force Major Chester L. Brown of Erie, Pa., who explained to the Associated Press that "it became necessary to destroy the town in order to save it" and that it was "a pity about the civilians," of whom about 1,000 were killed and 8,000 left homeless.

The smashing of Ben Tre is an exploit with echoes elsewhere in the South, including Siagon, where U.S. helicopters fired rockets into at least one heavily populated area because some 50 Viet Cong were lurking there. One rocket killed all four children of one civilian family. As Major Brown remarked at Ben Tre, civilians, unlike Viet Cong, "don't know where to hide." Probably no one will ever know how many of South Vietnam's homeless civilians owe their plight to Viet Cong attacks, and how many to the US Air Force, but the refugees now total close to a million and a half, a sensational 50 percent increase in less than two weeks.

Both sides have made great claims of vast killings in the recent fighting. The American boast was that the Viet Cong lost more than 30,000 dead. Hanoi, not to be outdone, claimed to have "wiped out" 40,000 South Vietnamese soldiers. Both sets of statistics are hopelessly suspect, as the worst sufferers are probably civilians. Because it failed to protect its people, the Saigon government's prestige is at its lowest point since the hated Diem regime fell, in 1963. And the North Vietnamese newspaper *Nhan Dan* points out, with brutal satisfaction, that the U.S. in order to cope with Viet Cong attacks finds itself compelled to use "more troops, more aircraft and more barbarous methods which in turn further incense the urban people." So far, more than 800 planes are admitted lost over North Vietnam and more than 230 over South Vietnam. The death toll to date of American soldiers is well over 17,000. North Vietnam and the Viet Cong can replace their own heavy losses, so no end of the war is possible through attrition, which seemed to be General Westmoreland's hope, until he suddenly found himself in a trap smelling very like Dien Bien Phu.

United Nations Secretary General U Thant said last week that if the U.S. unconditionally stopped bombing North Vietnam for about two weeks, Hanoi would begin meaningful negotiations. But Secretary Rusk countered on February 14 with a statement that, "At no time has Hanoi indicated publicly or privately that it will refrain from taking military advantage of any cessation of the bombing of North Vietnam." In January a "foreign emissary" went to Hanoi at the President's request and put the point to the North Vietnamese government but failed to get what's called an acceptable response, which prompted Mr. Johnson to say the other day, "We have gone just as far as decent and honorable people can go."

Yet on February 7, North Vietnamese Prime Minister Nguyen Duy Trinh said if American attacks on the North cease "unconditionally," North Vietnam will discuss a "settlement of the Vietnam problem on the basis of the 1954 Geneva Agreements on Vietman. "These provided for simultaneous cease-fire and cessation of hostilities, withdrawal and regrouping of forces, a ban on introducing any troops and arms reinforcements and additional military personnel, liberation and repatriation of all prisoners, and no reprisals. A "final declaration" called for internationally supervised general elections in July 1956, elections which were never held—one reason there's a Vietnam war now. Trinh's and other North Vietnamese statements on negotiations present Mr. Johnson with both a risk and an opportunity. Talks wouldn't mean an immediate or even early cease-fire; the North might continue sending more troops and arms South. But is the risk so great when it's now beyond doubt that bombing the North doesn't get results anyway, doesn't affect the infiltration in any meaningful way? That being so, shouldn't the chance be grasped to get peace talks going at last?

Consider Your Purpose

As with the description synthesis, your *purpose* in writing an argument synthesis is crucial. What exactly you want to do will affect your thesis, the evidence you select to support your thesis, and the way you organize the evidence. Your purpose may be clear to you before you begin research, may emerge during the course of research, or may not emerge until after you have completed your research. (Of course, the sooner your purpose is clear to you, the fewer wasted motions you will make. On the other hand, the more you approach research as an exploratory process, the likelier your conclusions will emerge from the sources themselves, rather than from preconceived ideas.)

Let us say that as you read through these sources, you become more and more outraged at American involvement in the Vietnam War. First, you don't accept the official justifications; they seem more like self-serving rationalizations for the indiscriminate use of American power than altruistic attempts to help a tiny nation struggling to maintain its independence and its democracy.

Next, you note the way that the war brutalized American soldiers ("I wanted to go down and kill all of those slant-eyed bastards") and the way that the civilian populace of South Vietnam was being corrupted by the American presence (see "The Americanization of South Vietnam"). Finally, you read the *New Republic* editorial on the effects of the bombing of Vietnam, shaking your head in disbelief at Major Brown's observation—after the American destruction of the besieged Ben Tre—that "it became necessary to destroy the town in order to save it." You tentatively decide then that the purpose in writing your paper is to argue that American involvement in the war in Vietnam was wrong or misguided. (You cannot be more specific and formulate a thesis until you have examined your sources more closely.)

Formulate a Thesis

Your discussion is organized and tied together by your own thesis, which may have nothing to do with the thesis of any of your sources. For example, one of your sources may conclude that the involvement of the United States in Vietnam was justified, but you may use that same source to help demonstrate that it wasn't. You may use a source only as a strawman, a weak argument that you set up and then knock down again. On the other hand, the author of one of your sources may be so convincing to you that you adopt his or her thesis. Or you may adopt it to some extent but not entirely. The point is that *the thesis is in your hands;* you must devise it yourself and use your sources in some way that will support that thesis.

You may not want to divulge your thesis until the very end of the paper, to draw the reader along toward your conclusion, allowing the thesis to flow naturally out of the argument and the evidence on which it is based. (If you do this, you are working *inductively.*) On the other hand, you may wish to be more direct and *begin* with your thesis, following the thesis statement with evidence to support it. (If you do this, you are working *deductively.*)

Let's say that after closely studying your sources, you conclude that the kind of attitudes that led to American involvement in the Vietnam War were totally inappropriate to the actual situation there. After a few tries, you arrive at the following tentative argumentative thesis: "America's arrogance and self-righteousness blinded it to the realities of the situation in Vietnam."

Decide How You Will Use Your Source Material

Your tentative thesis commits you to demonstrate, first, that the United States did display arrogance and self-righteousness concerning its role in Vietnam, and second, that these attitudes prevented many Americans from seeing the truth about their government's intervention in that country. The source materials provide plenty of examples of such arrogance and self-righteousness. The official statements, including the White House Policy Report of 1963, the Gulf of Tonkin Resolution, and the speeches by President Johnson, indicate official government attitudes; but the attitudes of other Americans are indicated in the statement of David Keene (one of the Young Americans for Freedom testifying at the Public Hearings in Wisconsin), as well as in the letters from American soldiers and the report of the Hué street scene (the soldier throwing candy to the children) by an American Quaker. At least two other sources—the entry from the *Columbia Encyclopedia* and the editorial from the *New Republic*—provide additional perspectives by which to gauge American attitudes.

Develop an Organizational Plan

One way of organizing the key information in the source material is in terms of the various attitudes (the arrogant and self-righteous attitudes) displayed by many Americans. These could be categorized into moral attitudes, social attitudes, and military attitudes. In the source materials, we find evidence to support the ideas that Americans believed that (1) they were on the side of justice and that the communists were on the side of injustice; (2) South Vietnam stood for freedom and democracy; the South Vietnamese people supported their government, were opposed to the communists and Ho Chi Minh, and welcomed American military assistance; (3) American technology and military power would quickly resolve the war in its favor.

You could organize this argument synthesis by taking up each of these topics in turn, demonstrating by means of the source materials that they did represent pervasive American attitudes. In the final part of your essay, you would demonstrate the gap between these attitudes and reality. You would do this by showing that the situation was not as black and white as official statements asserted, that Americans could just as easily be considered the aggressors as the North Vietnamese and the Viet Cong, and that the faith in American technological superiority was unwarranted in Vietnam.

Write Your Synthesis

Our completed synthesis reads as follows. (Thesis and topic sentences are highlighted.)

The increasing American involvement in Vietnam can be traced to at least three flawed attitudes. The first was a belief that the United States was on the side of right and justice and that the communists were the aggressors. The second was the assumption that Ho Chi Minh and the Viet Cong had little grass-roots support in the South and that the people of South Vietnam welcomed American 1 protection. The third was an unshakable confidence in the military's ability to accomplish anything it wanted owing to the superiority of the American fighting man and his technology—a belief instilled by a long history of wars fought and won by U.S. troops. This combination of self-righteousness and arrogance blinded America to the realities of the situation in Vietnam.

America was sure that its military intervention in 2
South Vietnam was morally right. Defenders of the war saw the conflict in terms of the forces of evil (communism) against the forces of good (freedom). Supporters of intervention believed that to refuse aid was to abandon the peaceful and democratic nation of South Vietnam to "communist enslavement" ("Public Hearings" 977). President Johnson painted a picture of a "small and brave" nation beleaguered by communist aggression. The president asked "only that the people of South Vietnam be allowed to guide their country in their own way" (Johnson, "War Aims" 976). Congress had already agreed; in its Gulf of Tonkin Resolution of 1964, it accused the communists of carrying out an unprovoked attack on American naval vessels and said that this attack was only part of a larger attack on the "freedom" of the South (971). Some of the fighting men tended to see the war in black-and-white terms, with the communists as evil and the Americans as good. After witnessing some brutalities committed by the Viet Cong, one soldier wrote: "I wanted to go down and kill all of those slant-eyed bastards. . . . Those slobs have to be stopped, even if it takes every last believer in a democracy and a free way of life to do it" ("War of Atrocities" 974).

The official position was that America was acting out 3
of purely altruistic motives. Both Johnson and Congress insisted the United States had no "territorial, mili-

tary, or political ambitions." In addition to saving the grateful South Vietnamese, a million of whom had "voted with their feet against communism" ("Public Hearings" 977) by fleeing North Vietnam, America was reaffirming the world's faith in its resolve. The free peoples of the world were counting on America to defend South Vietnam, said Johnson ("War Aims" 975–76), and to abandon Vietnam would be to shake their confidence in America and her word. The price of withdrawal would be the "freedom and dreams of fourteen million people, the honor of our own country and eventually, the security of the free world," said a Young Americans for Freedom representative in 1965 ("Public Hearings" 976).

In reality, the position of the United States was impractical and doomed to failure. South Vietnam was not the free state threatened by communist "enslavement" that the U.S. government described. It had been independent only since 1956; and Ho Chi Minh was not trying to conquer new territory but to reunify the recently divided nation of Vietnam. The American view of communist "aggression" is given an interesting perspective by Arthur Schlesinger, Jr., who pointed out that to the Chinese the United States appeared the aggressor. How would we feel, he asked, if the Chinese had 400,000 troops in southern Mexico and were busily putting down a pro-U.S. revolution there? The question "of who the aggressor is depends a good deal on who looks through what glass and how darkly," he argued (978). South Vietnam was no bastion of democracy, either. The South Vietnamese government did not hold promised democratic elections in 1956 because it knew that the communists had popular support in the country. Even the U.S. government admitted that South Vietnam's political situation was "deeply serious" with "repressive actions" frequently 4 being committed ("U.S. Policy on Vietnam" 128). The American-supported Diem government was so unpopular that widespread protests against it led to a successful coup in 1963. The people of South Vietnam resented American troops and resisted "Americanization," even on the smallest scale. An American Quaker in Vietnam wrote of a South Vietnamese schoolteacher chastising the arrogance of an American soldier for throwing candy to Vietnamese schoolchildren, just as if he were throwing bread crumbs to pigeons. The schoolteacher charged that the Americans were "making beggars of our children, prostitutes of our women, and communists of our men" ("Americanization" 978). The United States was defending South Vietnam against the will of much of the population, and American motives were not as selfless or benevolent as the government claimed. Despite Congress's assertion that the United States "has no territorial, military, or political ambitions in that area" ("Joint Resolution" 971), the containment of communism is certainly a territorial and political ambition of sorts, and Congress viewed the security of South Vietnam as "vital" to American national interest. And when, in the course of defending the country, American troops committed actions such as the destruction of the village of Ben Tre (the commanding officer later explained, "We had to destroy the village to save it"), it became obvious that the United States was not working in South Vietnam's best interests ("Slaughter Goes On" 13). Instead, it was concerned mainly with defeating the communists at all costs, even if the country it was supposed to be defending was destroyed in the process.

5 In 1963 the White House believed that all its military goals in Vietnam could be accomplished by the end of 1965, predicting that only a few military advisors would

be needed by then ("U.S. Policy on Vietnam" 128). The military solution was seen as the correct one: The White House statement, while conceding that "improvements are being energetically sought," asserted that the "military program in South Vietnam has made progress and is sound in principle." When the Congress was confronted with an apparently unprovoked attack by North Vietnam on two of its destroyers, however, it authorized the president to treat the situation as a war (even though it never declared war) and to send in unlimited amounts of men and supplies. From a few military advisors sent to Vietnam in 1961, the American troop commitment was to escalate to more than 500,000 in 1969. But even with such vast manpower, the United States was unable to "inflict permanent setbacks" against the Viet Cong and North Vietnamese. Washington decided that this was due to North Vietnamese infiltration of the South, and so it increased the bombing of suspected supply routes from the North. During the three years preceding the Tet Offensive, the U.S. Air Force dropped almost as much bomb tonnage on Vietnam as had been dropped by American forces during World War II ("Slaughter Goes On" 13). In 1967, President Johhnson claimed that the bombing was creating "very serious problems" for North Vietnam (Johnson, "Bombing" 972). But the next year the Rand Corporation warned that the infiltration had not been reduced significantly and that it could not see a "decisive" American victory in the "foreseeable future" ("Slaughter Goes On" 13). In spite of this, the bombing was escalated for years, increasing civilian casualties. The United States was forgetting the leson Hitler learned in World War II with his bombing of Britain: Bombing does not break the resolve of the population; it strengthens it. The North Vietnamese newspaper *Nhan Dan* pointed out that the bombings only served to "further incense" the population of North Vietnam ("Slaughter Goes On" 13). In spite of all this, the American public was so ready to believe the government's assurances of impending victory that it took the "devastating" Tet Offensive of 1968 (a coordinated attack by the North Vietnamese and the Viet Cong on more than one hundred towns and cities in the South) to impress upon it the reality of just how costly and difficult it would be for the United States to win the war.

In the end, it was two misguided assumptions that 6
embroiled the United States in the military and political chaos of the Vietnam War: the self-righteous belief that the political system that worked for Americans would work for everyone else and that the South Vietnamese welcomed American military intervention; and the arrogant assumption that sheer numbers and firepower would subdue a popularly supported insurrection. When we emerged, ten years later, these attitudes had been severely shaken. It would take many years for the United States to begin regaining its self-confidence.

Works Cited

Johnson, Lyndon. *Public Papers of the Presidents of the United States: Lyndon B. Johnson* (1966), 395. Rpt. as "President Johnson States His War Aims (1965)." *The American Spirit: United States History as Seen by Contemporaries.* Ed. Thomas A. Bailey. 4th ed. Vol. 2. Lexington: Heath, 1978. 975–76.

—. *Weekly Compilation of Presidential Documents*. Vol. 3. 476 (20 Mar. 1967) [reporting speech of 15 Mar.

1967]. Rpt. as "President Johnson Defends the Bombing (1967)" in Bailey 972–73.

"Joint Resolution." Department of State Bulletin 51 (24 Aug. 1964): 268. Rpt. in Bailey 970–72.

Kastenmeier, ed. Vietnam Hearings: Voices from the Grass Roots. Garden City, N.Y.: Doubleday, 1966. 38–40. Rpt. as "Public Hearings in Wisconsin" in Bailey 976–77.

Munson, Glenn, ed. Letters from Vietnam. New York: Parallax, 1966. 104, 118. Rpt. as "War of Atrocities" in Bailey 974–75.

Peace in Vietnam: A New Approach in Southeast Asia. A Report Prepared for the American Friends Service Committee. New York: Hill and Wang, 1966. 1. Rpt. as "Americanization of South Vietnam" in Bailey 977–78.

Schlesinger, Arthur. The Bitter Heritage. New York: Houghton, 1967. 36–37. Rpt. as "The Americanization of South Vietnam" in Bailey 978–79.

"Slaughter Goes On." The New Republic 24 Feb. 1968: 13.

"U.S. Policy on Vietnam." White House Statement, 2 Oct. 1963. Department of State Bulletin 44 (21 Oct. 1963): 624. Rpt. in The Viet-Nam Reader: Articles and Documents on American Foreign Policy and the Viet-Nam Crisis. Ed. Marcus G. Raskin and Bernard B. Fall. Rev. ed. New York: Vintage, 1967. 128–29.

—Michael Behrens

Discussion

- In the *introductory paragraph* the writer lays out the "flawed attitudes" he will discuss and indicates the thesis of the essay. Note that the wording of the original thesis has been slightly modified (from "America's self-righteousness and arrogance . . ." to "This combination of self-righteousness and arrogance") in order to achieve a smoother transition from the rest of the introductory paragraph.

- The *body of the essay* consists of four paragraphs. The writer had initially planned one paragraph for each of the attitudes discussed, but when the first paragraph (on the belief of the United States in its moral superiority) became too long, he split it in two. The *first* of these two paragraphs shows how the United States believed that it was on the side of righteousness and justice and that the communists were blatant aggressors. The *second* shows how the United States believed that it was acting out of purely benevolent motives in taking a stand against the spread of communism worldwide.
- The *fourth paragraph* begins the transition from the treatment of the unrealistic attitudes of the Americans to the actual situation in Vietnam. Note that the two sentences leading off paragraph 4 are highlighted: The first serves as the subthesis for the rest of the body of the essay; the second is the topic sentence for the paragraph that follows. In paragraph 4 the writer shows that (1) the matter of which side was the aggressor in Vietnam was not as clear-cut as official American statements indicated; (2) neither the South Vietnamese government nor the American military enjoyed widespread popular support; (3) American motives were suspect; (4) the United States was not working in the best interests of the South Vietnamese.
- The *fifth paragraph* deals with the military aspects of our involvement in Vietnam. (Note that the topic sentence of the paragraph is preceded by a transitional sentence.) The writer demonstrates that despite the United States' belief that increasing military pressure (increasing the numbers of troops, carrying on a saturation bombing campaign) would bring about an end to the war, the United States was not making significant military progress. Not only were the North Vietnamese unbroken by the bombings, but the fact that they were able to launch a military campaign on the scale of the Tet Offensive showed that they were nowhere near defeat.
- In the *sixth paragraph,* the writer reiterates the main idea of the essay (concerning American self-righteousness and arrogance) and briefly considers the effect of the war on the national psyche.

Note that the *conclusions* drawn by the writer of this essay are not the only conclusions that could be drawn from the evidence of the sources provided. It is fair to say, however, that the sources themselves have been selected in such a way that they tend to point toward such conclusions. But what if a writer wishes to draw opposite conclusions? It is certainly possible to challenge each of the major assumptions made in our model synthesis. For example, it could be argued that unlike most other nations that get involved in wars, the United States really *had* no territorial ambitions in Vietnam. It could be argued that given a choice, most of the people in South Vietnam would have preferred living in a Western-style democracy (or even a corrupt right-wing dictatorship) than under a communist dictatorship, as long as it were still possible to accumulate wealth. (The history of Vietnam since the communist victory, and the vast numbers of "boat people" trying to escape from their communist-ruled land, lends credence to this theory.) Even the assumption that the American military machine was ineffective can be challenged. The "devastating" Tet Offensive of 1968 was, in fact, a military defeat for the communists; and the American military in Vietnam did, in fact, forestall a communist victory in the South until two years after its withdrawal. The point is that an essay drawing upon such ideas could have been written—although it could not have been very well supported through the sources presented here. The writer would have had to seek out additional sources (e.g., sources dealing with the history of Vietnam since 1973 and sources dealing more specifically with military matters) in order to provide factual support for his or her thesis.

TECHNIQUES FOR DEVELOPING YOUR PAPERS

Experienced writers seem to have an instinctive sense of how to present their ideas. Less experienced writers wonder what to say first, and when they've decided on that, wonder what to say next. There is no single method of presentation. But the techniques of even the most experienced writers often boil down to a few tried and tested arrangements.

Summary

The simplest—and least sophisticated—way of organizing a descriptive or an argument synthesis is to *summarize your most relevant sources, one after the other, but generally with the most important source(s) last.* The problem with this approach is that it reveals little or no independent thought on your part. Its main virtue is that it at least grounds your paper in relevant and specific evidence.

Summary can be useful—and sophisticated—if handled judiciously, selectively, and in combination with other techniques. At some point, you may need to summarize a crucial source in some detail. At another point, you may wish to summarize a key section or paragraph of a source in a single sentence. Try to anticipate what your reader needs to know at any given point of your paper in order to comprehend or appreciate fully the point you happen to be making. (See Chapter 1 for a discussion of summary.)

Example or Illustration

At one or more points in your paper, you may wish to *refer to a particularly illuminating example or illustration from your source material.* You might paraphrase this example (i.e., recount it, in some detail, in your own words), summarize it, or quote it directly from your source. In all these cases, of course, you would properly credit your source. (See Chapter 5 on citation form.)

Two (or More) Reasons

In his book *A Short Course in Writing,* Kenneth Bruffee presents some of the most effective ways of developing arguments. The first one is simply called *Two Reasons,* but it could just as well be called *Three Reasons* or whatever number of reasons the writer has. Here is this method in outline form:

A. Introduction and thesis
B. Two reasons the thesis is true
   1. First reason
   2. Second reason (the more important one)

You can advance as many reasons for the truth of the thesis as you think necessary; but save the most important reason(s) for the end, since the end of the paper—its climax—is what will remain most clearly in the reader's mind.

Strawman

The next way of presenting an argument is called *Strawman.* When you use the Strawman technique, you present an argument *against* your thesis, but immediately afterward you show that this argument is weak or flawed. The advantage of this technique is that you demonstrate that you are aware of the other side of the argument and that you are prepared to answer it.

Here is how the Strawman argument is organized:

A. Introduction and thesis
B. Main opposing argument
C. Refutation of opposing argument
D. Main positive argument

Concession

Finally, one can use *Concession* in an argument. Like Strawman, you present the opposing viewpoint, but you do not proceed to demolish the opposition. Instead, you concede that the opposition does have a valid point but that even so the positive argument is the stronger one. Here is an outline for a concession argument.

A. Introduction and thesis
B. Important opposing argument
C. Concession that this argument has some validity
D. Positive argument(s) developed

Sometimes, when you are developing a *Strawman* or *Concession* argument, you may yourself become convinced of the validity of the opposing point of view and change your own views. Don't be afraid of this happening. *Writing is a tool for learning.* To change your mind because of new evidence is a sign of flexibility and maturity, and your writing can only be the better for it.

Comparison and Contrast

Comparison-and-contrast techniques enable you to examine two subjects (or sources) in terms of one another. When you compare, you consider *similarities.* When you contrast, you consider *differences.* By comparing and contrasting, you perform a multifacted analysis that often suggests subtleties that otherwise might not have come to your attention.

To organize a comparison-and-contrast analysis, you must carefully read sources in order to discover *significant criteria for analysis.* A *criterion* is a specific point to which both of your authors refer and about which they may agree or disagree. (For example, in a comparative report on compact cars, criteria for *comparison* and *contrast* might be road handling, fuel economy, and comfort of ride.) The best criteria are those that allow you not only to account for obvious similarities and differences between sources but also to plumb deeper, to more subtle and significant similarities and differences.

There are two basic approaches to organizing a comparison-and-contrast analysis: organization by source and organization by *criteria.*

1. *Organizing by source.* You can organize a comparative analysis as two summaries of your sources, followed by a discussion in which you point out significant similarities and differences between passages. Having read the summaries and become familiar with the distinguishing features of each passage, your readers will most likely be able to appreciate the more obvious similarities and differences. Follow up on these summaries by discussing both the obvious and subtle comparisons and contrasts, focusing on the most significant.

   Organization by source is best saved for passages that are briefly summarized. If the summary of your source becomes too long, your audience might forget the remarks you made in the first summary while they read the second. A comparison-and-contrast synthesis organized by source might proceed like this:

   I. Introduce the essay; lead to thesis.
   II. Summarize passage A by discussing its significant features.
   III. Summarize passage B by discussing its significant features.
   IV. Write a paragraph (or two) in which you discuss the significant points of comparison and contrast between passages A and B.

2. *Organizing by criteria.* Instead of summarizing entire passages one at a time with the intention of comparing them later, you could discuss two passages simultaneously, examining the views of each author point by point (criterion by criterion), comparing and contrasting these views in the process. The criterion approach is best used when you have a number of points to discuss or when passages are long and/or complex. A synthesis organized by criteria might look like this:

    I. Introduce the essay; lead to thesis.
    II. Criterion 1
        A. Discuss what author A says about this point.
        B. Discuss what author B says about this point.
    III. Criterion 2
        A. Discuss what author A says about this point.
        B. Discuss what author B says about this point (be sure to arrange criteria with a clear method; knowing how the discussion of one criterion leads to the next will ensure smooth transitions throughout your paper).

    And so on. Proceed criterion by criterion until you have completed your discussion. End with a conclusion in which you summarize your points and, perhaps, raise and respond to pertinent questions.

We'll see how these principles can be applied to the following two sources on the Vietnam War. The first is a letter by President Johnson to the North Vietnamese leader Ho Chi Minh in which Johnson urges that the two sides take steps toward a peaceful settlement of the war. The second is Ho Chi Minh's reply.

The Johnson–Ho Chi Minh Interchange: A Case for Comparison and Contrast

The Johnson Letter to Hanoi (1967)[1]

In the appendix of his memoirs, ex-President Johnson lists about seventy peace overtures that were made to North Vietnam, through American and foreign spokesmen, before the government in Hanoi even consented to talk about peace talks. This hope-giving breakthrough did not come

From Bailey, ed. *The American Spirit.* See source note on page 69.

[1]Both letters appear in the *Department of State Bulletin,* 56 (April 10, 1967), pp. 595–97. The Johnson letter was delivered on February 8, 1967. The Ho Chi Minh letter is a translation. [Bailey]

until after Johnson's dramatic cessation of most of the bombing of North Vietnam, March 31, 1968. In his letter to the Communist North Vietnamese leader, Ho Chi Minh, President Johnson repeated proposals already made by Washington on four different occasions. [Bailey]

Dear Mr. President:

I am writing to you in the hope that the conflict in Vietnam can be brought to an end. That conflict has already taken a heavy toll—in lives lost, in wounds inflicted, in property destroyed, and in simple human misery. If we fail to find a just and peaceful solution, history will judge us harshly.

Therefore, I believe that we both have a heavy obligation to seek earnestly the path to peace. It is in response to that obligation that I am writing directly to you.

We have tried over the past several years, in a variety of ways and through a number of channels, to convey to you and your colleagues our desire to achieve a peaceful settlement. For whatever reasons, these efforts have not achieved any results.

It may be that our thoughts and yours, our attitudes and yours, have been distorted or misinterpreted as they passed through these various channels. Certainly that is always a danger in indirect communication.

There is one good way to overcome this problem and to move forward in the search for a peaceful settlement. That is for us to arrange for direct talks between trusted representatives in a secure setting and away from the glare of publicity. Such talks should not be used as a propaganda exercise but should be a serious effort to find a workable and mutually acceptable solution.

In the past two weeks, I have noted public statements by representatives of your government suggesting that you would be prepared to enter into direct bilateral talks with representatives of the U.S. Government, provided that we ceased "unconditionally" and permanently our bombing operations against your country and all military actions against it. In the last day, serious and responsible parties have assured us indirectly that this is in fact your proposal.

Let me frankly state that I see two great difficulties with this proposal. In view of your public position, such action on our part would inevitably produce worldwide speculation that discussions were under way and would impair the privacy and secrecy of those discussions. Secondly, there would inevitably be grave concern on our part whether your government would make use of such action by us to improve its military position.

With these problems in mind, I am prepared to move even further towards an ending of hostilities than your Government has proposed in either public statements or through private diplomatic channels. I am prepared to order a cessation of bombing against your country and the stopping of further augmentation of U.S. forces in South Viet-Nam as soon as I am assured that infiltration into South Viet-Nam by land and by sea has stopped. These acts of restraint on both sides would, I believe, make it possible for us to conduct serious and private discussions leading toward an early peace.

I make this proposal to you now with a specific sense of urgency arising from the imminent New Year holidays in Viet-Nam. If you are able to accept this proposal I see no reason why it could not take effect at the end of the New Year, or Tet, holidays. The proposal I have made would be greatly strengthened if your military authorities and those of the Government of South Viet-Nam could promptly negotiate an extension of the Tet truce.

As to the site of the bilateral discussions I propose, there are several possibilities. We could, for example, have our representatives meet in Moscow where contacts have already occurred. They could meet in some other country such as Burma. You may have other arrangements or sites in mind, and I would try to meet your suggestions.

The important thing is to end a conflict that has brought burdens to both our peoples, and above all to the people of South Viet-Nam. If you have any thoughts about the actions I propose, it would be most important that I receive them as soon as possible.

Sincerely,
LYNDON B. JOHNSON

Ho Chi Minh's Reply (1967)

The response that Ho sent from Hanoi was completely unsatisfactory to official Washington. [Bailey]

His Excellency
LYNDON B. JOHNSON
President of the United States

Excellency, on February 10, 1967, I received your message. Here is my response.

Viet-Nam is situated thousands of miles from the United States. The Vietnamese people have never done any harm to the United

From Bailey, ed. *The American Spirit*. See source note on page 69.

States. But, contrary to the commitments made by its representative at the Geneva Conference of 1954, the United States Government has constantly intervened in Viet-Nam, it has launched and intensified the war of aggression in South Viet-Nam for the purpose of prolonging the division of Viet-Nam and of transforming South Viet-Nam into an American neo-colony and an American military base. For more than two years now, the American Government, with its military aviation and its navy, has been waging war against the Democratic Republic of Viet-Nam, an independent and sovereign country.

The United States Government has committed war crimes, crimes against peace and against humanity. In South Viet-Nam a half-million American soldiers and soldiers from the satellite countries have resorted to the most inhumane arms and the most barbarous methods of warfare, such as napalm, chemicals, and poison gases in order to massacre our fellow countrymen, destroy the crops, and wipe out the villages. In North Viet-Nam thousands of American planes have rained down hundreds of thousands of tons of bombs, destroying cities, villages, mills, roads, bridges, dikes, dams and even churches, pagodas, hospitals, and schools. In your message you appear to deplore the suffering and the destruction in Viet-Nam. Permit me to ask you: Who perpetrated these monstrous crimes? It was the American soldiers and the soldiers of the satellite countries. The United States Government is entirely responsible for the extremely grave situation in Viet-Nam.

The American war of aggression against the Vietnamese people constitutes a challenge to the countries of the socialist camp, a threat to the peoples' independent movement, and a grave danger to peace in Asia and in the world.

The Vietnamese people deeply love independence, liberty, and peace. But in the face of the American aggression they have risen up as one man, without fearing the sacrifices and the privations. They are determined to continue their resistance until they have won real independence and liberty and true peace. Our just cause enjoys the approval and the powerful support of peoples throughout the world and of large segments of the American people.

The United States Government provoked the war of aggression in Viet-Nam. It must cease that aggression; it is the only road leading to the reestablishment of peace. The United States Government must halt definitively and unconditionally the bombings and all other acts of war against the Democratic Republic of Viet-Nam, withdraw from South Viet-Nam all American troops and all troops from the satellite countries, recognize the National Front of the Liberation of South Viet-Nam [Viet Cong], and let the Vietnamese people settle their problems themselves. Such is the basic content of the four-point position of the Government of the Democratic Republic of Viet-Nam;

such is the statement of the essential principles and essential arrangements of the Geneva agreements of 1954 on Viet-Nam. It is the basis for a correct political solution of the Vietnamese problem. In your message you suggested direct talks between the Democratic Republic of Viet-Nam and the United States. If the United States Government really wants talks, it must first halt unconditionally the bombings and all other acts of war against the Democratic Republic of Viet-Nam. It is only after the unconditional halting of the other American bombings and of all American acts of war against the Democratic Republic of Viet Nam that the Democratic Republic of Viet-Nam and the United States could begin talks and discuss questions affecting the two parties.

Sincerely,

HO CHI MINH

Organization of Comparison-Contrast by Source

Here is a comparison-and-contrast analysis of the two letters, organized by *source:*

In 1967 President Lyndon B. Johnson sent a letter to Ho 1
Chi Minh, the communist leader of North Vietnam, expressing hope that the conflict in Vietnam could finally be resolved (Johnson 979–80). Johnson asserted that he would halt the American bombings in North Vietnam and begin peace talks if Ho Chi Minh would give assurances that his troops would stop infiltrating South Vietnam. Ho found Johnson's proposal totally unsatisfactory and demanded that the United States unconditionally withdraw from Vietnam (Ho, 980–81).

President Johnson's letter to Ho urges the two sides 2
to take major steps toward ending the war. Since the conflict has taken so many lives, destroyed so much property, and caused such great misery for all involved, Johnson feels it is his duty, as well as Ho's, to seek peace, or else "history will judge us harshly" (979). Johnson explains the attempts that have been made for peace through various indirect communications channels, but they have all failed. That is why he is writing to Ho

directly. However, Johnson will not cease the U.S. bombings of North Vietnam until he is assured by Ho that the infiltration of South Vietnam has stopped. Johnson insists on this condition because he does not want to give the North Vietnamese time, during a bombing halt, to improve their military position. With both sides restrained from action, Johnson feels that peace talks would be helped. The important thing," he concludes, "is to end a conflict that has brought burdens to both our people and above all to the people of South Viet-Nam" (980).

In his reply Ho Chi Minh completely rejects Johnson's 3
proposal. He takes the position that the United States is entirely responsible for the aggression against Vietnam and that it must unconditionally withdraw from the conflict. Ho describes the "war crimes" the United States has committed against peace and humanity with its bombings of North Vietnam and other "barbarous methods of warfare such as napalm, chemicals, and poison gases in order to massacre our fellow countrymen, destroy our crops, and wipe out the villages" (981). Johnson seems to deplore all these crimes, according to Ho, yet it is the United States that has caused all of this devastation. Ho believes that the United States should halt all acts of war against North Vietnam (the Democratic Republic of Vietnam), withdraw from South Vietnam, recognize the Viet Cong, and allow the people of Vietnam to settle their own problems. This war, according to Ho, should not involve the United States. The Vietnamese people want peace, but they also want independence from intervention from outsiders. They are determined to resist American aggression and "will never give way to force" (982).

The basic difference between Johnson and Ho Chi Minh 4

concerns whether or not the United States should be involved in the Vietnam war. Both leaders are diplomatically polite to one another, and both agree that the war must be ended. But each seems to blame the other for prolonging the war, and each is unyielding in setting his own conditions for peace. Johnson feels justified in involving the United States in the war so as to keep South Vietnam an independent, non-communist country, and he will cease the bombings of North Vietnam only if Ho agrees to stop his aggression in South Vietnam. This proposal is unacceptable to Ho, who believes that the conflict in Vietnam is none of the United States' business. He insists that the Americans are the real aggressors and that they must unconditionally withdraw so that the Vietnamese can settle their own problems without outside intervention.

Works Cited

Ho Chi Minh. Letter to President Lyndon Johnson. Department of State Bulletin 61 (10 Apr. 1967), 595–97. Rpt. as "Ho Chi Minh's Reply." The American Spirit: United States History as Seen by Contemporaries. Ed. Thomas A. Bailey. 4th ed. Vol. 2. Lexington: Heath, 1978. 981–82.

Johnson, Lyndon. Letter to President Ho Chi Minh. Department of State Bulletin 61 (10 Apr. 1967), 595–97. Rpt. as "The Johnson Letter to Hanoi" in Bailey 979–980.

—Lara H. Keith

Discussion

- The writer uses the *first paragraph* to introduce the subject and to summarize the opposing positions of Johnson and Ho. (The last two sentences of this paragraph become, in effect, the thesis.)

- In the *second paragraph,* the writer outlines Johnson's main points.
- In the *third paragraph,* the writer outlines Ho's main points.
- In the *fourth paragraph,* the writer sums up the only comparison, or point of agreement, between the two letters (both men want the war to end), while emphasizing once again the more crucial contrasts: Johnson demands that the North Vietnamese cease their infiltration into the South; Ho insists that the United States unconditionally withdraw from Vietnam.

Organization of Comparison-Contrast by Criteria

Here is a plan for a comparison-and-contrast synthesis, organized by *criteria.* Your *thesis* is:

The main issues involved in the exchange of letters between Lyndon Johnson and Ho Chi Minh were the bombings of North Vietnam by the United States and, more generally, American involvement in the war.

A. Introduction: summary of agreements and disagreements
B. The American bombing of North Vietnam
   1. Lyndon Johnson's position
   2. Ho Chi Minh's position
C. American involvement in the war
   1. Ho Chi Minh's position
   2. Lyndon Johnson's position

Following is a comparison-and-contrast synthesis, written according to the preceding plan:

The exchange of letters between Lyndon Johnson and Ho Chi Minh in 1967 showed the great differences between the two leaders over a solution to the Vietnam War. Both Johnson and Ho referred to the widespread misery that the war had caused, and both called for an end to what they perceived as the other side's aggression, but they disagreed on how this objective could be achieved. The main issues involved in the exchange of letters were the bombings of North Vietnam by the United States and, more generally, American involvement in the war. 1

The bombing of North Vietnam by the United States was the most visible issue in the two letters. Johnson told 2

Ho that he would order a stop to the bombing only if North Vietnam would stop infiltrating the South by land and sea. "This act of restraint on both sides," he argued, "would . . . make it possible for us to conduct serious and private discussions leading toward an early peace." Johnson's precondition that the North cease its infiltration was aimed primarily at preventing Ho's government from taking advantage of a bombing halt to improve its military position in South Vietnam. Also, Johnson believed that a one-sided cessation of military activity by the United States (which had been previously demanded by North Vietnam) would produce speculation that peace talks were under way, and such public speculation, he believed, could damage the peace process. Ho Chi Minh was in complete disagreement with Johnson. As far as Ho was concerned, "[t]he United States Government provoked the war of aggression in Viet-Nam. It must cease that aggression; it is the only road leading to the re-establishment of peace." Ho ignored Johnson's demand that the North cease its infiltration into the South. "If the United States Government really wants talks," he asserted, "it must first halt *unconditionally* [emphasis added] the bombings and all other acts of war against the Democratic Republic of Viet-Nam."

Even though the cessation of bombing was the key 3
issue in the two letters, the larger issue behind it was the involvement of the United States in the war. For Ho Chi Minh and North Vietnam, the United States was a colonial, imperialistic power aggressively trying to maintain military and political control in a part of the world where it had no business. Ho charged that the United States was in the war "for the purpose of prolonging the division of Viet-Nam and of transforming South

Viet-Nam into an American neo-colony and an American military base." He also maintained that American agression in Vietnam was an attack both on socialism and on the national liberation movement in that country; his clear implication was that the United States was fighting <u>against</u> democracy in Vietnam. For his part, Johnson did not discuss why the United States was in Vietnam. Perhaps he thought it would be impolite, when writing a personal letter to another head of state, to repeat the kind of charges against North Vietnam that he frequently made in his domestic speeches—for instance, that the United States was fighting in Vietnam so as not "to abandon this small and brave nation [South Vietnam] to its enemies, and to the terror that must follow" (Johnson, "War Aims," 1965, p. 975. Nor did he repeat the kind of charges that the American Congress had made in the Gulf of Tonkin Resolution, for example, that [North Vietnamese] attacks were "part of a deliberate and systematic campaign of aggression that the Communist regime in North Vietnam has been waging against its neighbors and the nations joined with them in the collective defense of their freedom." In other words, he did not make attacks of the kind that Ho was to make to Johnson in his reply. Johnson undoubtedly realized that if he made such charges, there would be no chance of a favorable response from Ho. So he avoided the fundamental issue of American involvement to concentrate on the military aspects of the war. What he did not seem to realize was that for Ho the key issue was not so much the bombing itself but rather the very presence of American troops in Vietnam. Ho also probably thought that to accept Johnson's condition of stopping the infiltration by the North was to concede that Johnson had a right to make such a demand of a Vietnamese leader in Vietnam. As far as Ho was concerned, Johnson had no such right.

The two letters, then, reflect the two leaders' dif- 4
ferent assumptions about the cause of the conflict in Vietnam and about an acceptable way of ending it. Johnson focused on military matters: He urged Ho to halt his most damaging military activity (infiltration of the South) as a precondition for halting the most damaging American military activity (the bombing). Ho refused to consider the problem in military terms. His argument was simple: The United States provoked the war and was primarily responsible for the misery it caused; to the United States, then, lay the primary responsibility for ending the war. The United States was in no moral position to lay down conditions for peace talks. "Our cause is absolutely just," he concluded. "[T]he Government of the United States [must] act in conformity to reason." Of course, what was reasonable to Ho and what was reasonable to Johnson were two very different matters.

Works Cited

Ho Chi Minh. Letter to President Lyndon Johnson. *Department of State Bulletin* 61 (10 Apr. 1967), 595–97. Rpt. as "Ho Chi Minh's Reply." *The American Spirit: United States History as Seen by Contemporaries*. Ed. Thomas A. Bailey. 4th ed. Vol. 2. Lexington: Heath, 1978. 981–82.

Johnson, Lyndon. Letter to President Ho Chi Minh. *Department of State Bulletin* 61 (10 Apr. 1967), 595–97. Rpt. as "The Johnson Letter to Hanoi" in Bailey 979–980.

Johnson, Lyndon. *Public Papers of the Presidents of the United States: Lyndon B. Johnson* (1966), 395. Rpt. as "President Johnson States His War Aims (1965)" in Bailey 975–76.

"Joint Resolution." Department of State Bulletin 51 (24 Aug. 1964): 268. Rpt. in Bailey 970–72.

—Lara H. Keith

Discussion

- The *first paragraph* introduces the subject, refers briefly to the (very few) agreements between the two leaders, and then, by means of the thesis, indicates the main disagreements that will constitute the body of the discussion: the more specific issue of the American bombing of North Vietnam and the more general issue of American involvement in the war. Each of these disagreements constitutes a *criterion* for discussion.
- The *second paragraph* takes up the first disagreement: the American bombing; first Johnson's proposal is summarized (with brief quotations); then Ho's response is considered. The *third paragraph* takes up the second disagreement: American involvement in the war. The writer points out that Ho believed that American involvement was totally unjustified. Johnson did not repeat his familiar claims that the United States was defending South Vietnam from North Vietnamese aggression, probably because he did not want to antagonize Ho but wanted instead to provoke a favorable response. He did not get a favorable response because Ho did not see the war in the same terms as Johnson.
- In the *final paragraph,* the conclusion, the writer expands on the points made in the previous paragraph. Primarily, she argues, Johnson saw the war (at least in this letter) in military terms. Ho, on the other hand, saw the war in moral terms, the main moral issue being the very presence of the United States in Vietnam.

You've probably noticed that the second comparison-contrast essay is considerably more sophisticated than the first. While the first essay consists of little more than two joined summaries, the second essay, organized by criterion rather than source, required the writer to think through the significance of each leader's arguments and to identify and discuss the key areas of contrast—namely, their conflicting positions on the bombing of North Vietnam and, beyond that, on America's involvement in the war.

A NOTE ON THE RESEARCH PAPER

While a full discussion of the research paper is beyond the scope of this book, it may be helpful to offer a few comments on this subject. We pointed out at the beginning of this chapter that if you've previously written research papers, you've already written syntheses. What's the difference, then, between the synthesis assignments that you've practiced in this chapter and what you'll find in the rest of this book and the standard research paper?

The most obvious difference is that here you're doing little or no actual research, since we've provided you with all your sources. In your other courses, obviously, you'll be expected to locate your own sources. For the most part, this will involve library research. We say "for the most part" because a considerable amount of research is not done in libraries; it is done in laboratories, or out "in the field," with the aid of a tape recorder, or in the files of government offices. Still, during your undergraduate years, you can expect to spend most of your research hours in the college library.

If you haven't already toured your college or university library, you should do so at your earliest convenience. It's particularly important to learn your way around the reference room and to familiarize yourself with such research tools as general and specialized encyclopedias, bibliographical indexes, biographical guides, indexes to periodicals, abstracts, and of course, the card catalog (which many college libraries are computerizing). If your instructor for this course has assigned a handbook, find the chapter or chapters dealing with research papers and be aware of the subjects covered, even if you don't read all this material now. These chapters generally offer useful advice not only on research sources but also on such important matters as search strategy techniques, preparing a working bibliography, taking notes, developing and refining your outline, preparing your first draft, revising your first draft, and documenting your sources in a manner appropriate to the discipline in which you are working. You'll need to keep in mind that there is no such thing as an all-purpose research paper format; acceptable formats and styles differ according to whether one is writing in the humanities, the sciences, the social sciences, business, or other professional disciplines. Even within a discipline, acceptable styles may vary, according to the preferences of your instructor. So if these preferences aren't clear at the time the assignment is made, ask about them!

THESIS, INTRODUCTIONS, AND CONCLUSIONS

4

WRITING A THESIS

As you have probably observed, there is a direct relationship between the complexity of a synthesis and the complexity of its thesis statement. *A thesis statement is a one-sentence summary of a paper's content.* It is similar, actually, to a paper's conclusion but lacks the conclusion's concern for broad implications and significance. For a writer in the drafting stages, the thesis establishes a focus, a basis upon which to include or exclude information. For the reader of a finished product, the thesis anticipates the author's discussion. *A thesis statement, therefore, is an essential tool for both writers and readers of academic material.*

This last sentence is our thesis for this section. Based on this thesis, we, as the authors, have limited the content of the section; and you, as the reader, will be able to form certain expectations about the discussion that follows. You can expect a definition of a thesis statement; an enumeration of the uses of a thesis statement; and a discussion focused on academic material. As writers, we will have met our obligations to you only if in subsequent paragraphs we satisfy these expectations.

The Components of a Thesis

Like any other sentence, a thesis includes a subject and a predicate, which consists of an assertion about the subject. In the sentence "Lee was a different kind of general from Grant," "Lee" is the subject and "was a different kind of general from Grant" is the predicate. What distinguishes a thesis statement from any other sentence with a subject and predicate is the thesis statement's *level of generality and the care with which you choose the assertion.* The subject of a thesis must present the right balance between the general and the specific to allow for a thorough discussion within the allotted length of the paper. The discussion might include definitions, details, comparisons, contrasts—whatever is needed to illuminate a subject and carry on an intelligent conversation. (If the sentence about Lee were a thesis, the reader would assume that the rest of the essay contained comparisons and contrasts between the two generals.)

Bear in mind when writing thesis statements that the more general your subject and the more complex your assertion, the longer your paper will be. For instance, you could not write an effective ten-page paper based on the following:

> Democracy is the best system of government.

Consider the subject of this sentence, "democracy," and the assertion of its predicate, "is the best system of government." The subject is enormous in scope; it is a general category composed of hundreds of more specific subcategories, each of which would be appropriate for a paper ten pages in length. The predicate of our example is also a problem, for the claim that democracy is the best system of government would be simplistic unless accompanied by a thorough, systematic, critical evaluation of *every* form of government yet devised. A ten-page paper governed by such a thesis simply could not achieve the level of detail and sophistication expected of college students.

Limiting the Scope of the Thesis

Before you can write an effective thesis and thus a controlled, effective paper, you need to limit your intended discussions by limiting your subject and your claims about it. Two strategies for achieving a thesis statement of manageable proportions are (1) to begin with a working thesis (this strategy assumes that you are familiar with your topic) and (2) to begin with a broad area of interest and narrow it (this strategy assumes that you are unfamiliar with your topic).

Begin with a Working Thesis

Professionals thoroughly familiar with a topic often begin writing with a clear thesis in mind—a happy state of affairs unfamiliar to most college students assigned term papers. But professionals usually have an important advantage over students: experience. Since professionals know their material, are familiar with the ways of approaching it, are aware of the questions important to practitioners, and have devoted considerable time to study of the topic, they are naturally in a strong position to begin writing a paper. Not only do professionals have experience in their fields, but they also have a clear purpose in writing; they know their audience and are comfortable with the format of their papers.

Experience counts—there's no way around it. As a student, you are not yet an expert and therefore don't generally have the luxury of beginning your writing tasks with a definite thesis in mind. Once you choose and devote time to a major field of study, however, you will gain experience. In the meantime, you'll have to do more work than the professional to prepare yourself for writing a paper.

But let's assume that you *do* have an area of expertise, that you are in your own right a professional (albeit not in academic matters). We'll assume that you understand your nonacademic subject—say, backpacking—and have been given a clear purpose for writing: to discuss the relative merits of backpack designs. Your job is to write a recommendation for the owner of a sporting-goods chain, suggesting which line of backpacks the chain should carry. The owner lives in another city, so your remarks have to be written. Since you already know a good deal about backpacks, you may already have some well-developed ideas on the topic before you start doing additional research.

Yet even as an expert in your field, you will find beginning the writing task to be a challenge, for at this point, it is unlikely that you will be able to conceive a thesis perfectly suited to the contents of your paper. After all, a thesis statement is a summary, and it is difficult to summarize a presentation yet to be written—especially if you plan to discover what you want to say during the process of writing. Even if you know your material well, the best you can do at the early stages is to formulate a *working thesis*—a hypothesis of sorts, a well-informed hunch about your topic and the claim to be made about it. Once you have completed a draft, you can evaluate the degree to which your working thesis accurately summarizes the content of your paper.[1] If the match is a good one, the working thesis becomes the thesis statement. If, on the other hand, sections of the paper drift from the focus set out in the working thesis, you'll need to revise the thesis and the paper itself to ensure that the presentation is unified. (You'll know that the match between the content and thesis is a good one when every paragraph directly refers to and develops some element of the thesis.)

Our experience in drafting this section of the chapter will serve as a useful example. At first, we started with the following working thesis:

> A thesis statement is an essential tool for writers.

As we wrote the first draft, we discovered two new concerns: that the thesis was an essential tool for both writers *and readers* and that our focus was entirely on *academic material*. Neither of these concerns was expressed in our working thesis; as a result, our first draft was not unified. Entire paragraphs had nothing to do with the stated thesis. We needed to change the

[1]Some writers work with an idea, committing it to paper only after it has been fully formed. Others begin with a vague notion and begin writing a first draft, trusting that as they write they'll discover what they wish to say. Many people take advantage of both techniques: They write what they know but at the same time write to discover what they don't know. As you'll see, we used both techniques when writing this section of the book.

content of our paper or else change the thesis. We chose the latter, rewriting it as follows:

> A thesis statement is an essential tool for both writers and readers of academic material.

When we first drafted this section of the book, we had no plans to include a discussion concerning the thesis as a tool for both writers *and* readers. We *discovered* this content as we wrote. We liked what we discovered and then changed our working thesis to account for the new material. As a result, the discussion became unified. While writing a first draft, allow yourself to pursue related discussions as they occur to you, regardless (for the time being) of your working thesis. The working thesis will guide you in planning broad sections of a paper. It will help you to begin writing, but do not let it keep you from discovering your content.

Begin with a Subject and Narrow It

Let's assume that you have moved from making recommendations about backpacks (your territory) to writing a paper for your college government class (your professor's territory). Whereas you were once the professional who knew enough about your subject to begin writing with a working thesis, you are now the student, inexperienced and in need of a great deal of information before you can begin to think of thesis statements. It may be a comfort to know that your government professor would likely be in the same predicament if asked to recommend backpack designs. He would need to spend several weeks, at least, backpacking to become as experienced as you; and it is fair to say that you will need to spend several hours in the library before you are in a position to choose a topic suitable for an undergraduate paper.

Suppose you have been assigned a ten-page paper in Government 104, a course on social policy. Not only do you not have a thesis—you don't have a subject! Where will you begin? First, you need to select a broad area of interest and make yourself knowledgeable about its general features. What if no broad area of interest occurs to you? Don't despair—there's usually a way to make use of discussions you've read in a text or heard in a lecture. The trick is to find a topic that can become personally important, for whatever reason. (For a paper in your biology class, you might write on the digestive system because a relative has stomach troubles. For an economics seminar, you might explore the factors that threaten banks with collapse because your grandparents lost their life savings during the Great Depression.) Whatever the academic discipline, try to discover a topic that you'll enjoy exploring; that way, you'll be writing for yourself as much as for your professor. Some specific strategies to try if no topics occur to you: Review material covered during the semester, class by class if need be; review the semester's readings, actually skimming each assignment. Choose any subject that has held your interest, if even for a moment, and use that as your point of departure.

So, you've reviewed each of your classes and recall that a lecture on AIDS aroused your curiosity. Your broad subject of interest, then, will be AIDS. At this point, the goal of your research is to limit this subject to a manageable scope. Although your initial, broad subject will often be more specific than our example, "AIDS," we'll assume for the purposes of discussion the most general case (the subject in greatest need of limiting).

A subject can be limited in at least two ways. First, a general article like an encyclopedia entry may do the work for you by presenting the subject in the form of an outline, with each item in the outline representing a separate topic (which, for your purposes, may need further limiting). Second, you can limit a subject by asking several questions about it:

Who?

What aspects?

Where?

When?

How?

These questions will occur to you as you conduct your research and see the ways in which various authors have focused their discussions. Having read several sources and having decided that you'd like to use them, you might limit the subject "AIDS" by asking *who*—AIDS patients; and *which aspect*—civil rights of AIDS patients.

Certainly, "the civil rights of AIDS patients" offers a more specific focus than does "AIDS"; still, the revised focus is too broad for a ten-page paper in that a comprehensive discussion would obligate you to review numerous particular rights. So again you must try to limit your subject by posing a question. In this particular case, *which aspects* (of the civil rights of AIDS patients) can be asked a second time. Six aspects may come to mind:

- Rights in the workplace
- Rights to hospital care
- Rights to insurance benefits
- Rights to privacy
- Rights to fair housing
- Rights to education

Any *one* of these aspects could provide the focus of a ten-page paper, and you do yourself an important service by choosing one, perhaps two, of the aspects; to choose more would obligate you to too broad a discussion and you would frustrate yourself: Either the paper would have to be longer than ten pages or, assuming you kept to the page limit, the paper would be superficial in its treatment. In both instances, the paper would fail, given the constraints of the assignment. So it is far better that you limit your subject ahead of time, before you attempt writing about it. Let's assume that you settle on the following as an appropriately defined subject for a ten-page paper:

the rights of AIDS patients in the workplace

The process of narrowing an initial subject depends heavily on the reading you do. The more you read, the deeper your understanding of a topic. The deeper your understanding, the likelier it will be that you can divide a broad and complex topic into manageable—that is, researchable—categories. Identify these categories that compose the larger topic and pursue one of them. In the AIDS example, your reading in the literature (in the selections you'd find in Chapter 12 in this text, for instance) suggested that the civil rights of AIDS patients was an issue at the center of recent national debate. So reading allowed you to narrow the subject "AIDS" by answering the initial questions *who* and *which aspects.* Once you narrowed your focus to "the civil rights of AIDS patients," you read further and quickly realized that civil rights in itself was a broad concern that should also be limited. In this way, reading provided an important stimulus as you worked to identify an appropriate subject for your paper.

Make an Assertion

Once you have identified that subject, you can now develop it into a thesis by making an assertion about it. If you have spent enough time reading and gathering information, you will be knowledgeable enough to have something to say about the subject, based on a combination of your own thinking and the thinking of your sources. If you have trouble making an assertion, try writing your topic at the top of a page and then listing everything you now know and feel about it. Often from such a list you will discover an assertion that you can then use to fashion a working thesis. A good way to gauge the reasonableness of your claim is to see what other authors have asserted about the same topic. In fact, keep good notes on the views of others; the notes will prove a useful counterpoint to your own views as you write, and you may want to use them in your paper.

Next, make three assertions about your topic, in order of increasing complexity.

1. During the past few years, the rights of AIDS patients in the workplace have been debated by national columnists.
2. Several columnists have offered convincing reasons for protecting the rights of AIDS patients in the workplace.
3. The most sensible plan for protecting the rights of AIDS patients in the workplace has been offered by columnist Anthony Jones.

Keep in mind that these are *working thesis statements.* Since you haven't written a paper based on any of them, they remain *hypotheses* to be tested. After completing a first draft, you would compare the contents of the paper to the thesis and make adjustments as necessary for unity. The working thesis is an excellent tool for planning broad sections of the paper, but—again—don't let it prevent you from pursuing related discussions as they occur to you.

Notice how these three statements differ from one another in the forcefulness of their assertions. The third thesis is strongly argumentative. "Most sensible" implies that the writer will explain several plans for protecting the rights of AIDS patients in the workplace. Following the explanation would come a comparison of plans and then a judgment in favor of Anthony Jones. Like any working thesis, this one helps the writer to plan the paper. Assuming the paper follows the three-part structure we've inferred, the working thesis would become the final thesis, on the basis of which a reader could anticipate sections of the essay to come.

The first of the three thesis statements, by contrast, is expository:

> During the past few years, the rights of AIDS patients in the workplace have been debated by national columnists.

In developing a paper based on this thesis, the writer would assert only the existence of a debate, obligating himself merely to a summary of the various positions taken. Readers, then, would use this thesis as a tool for anticipating the contours of the paper to follow. Based on this particular thesis, a reader would *not* expect to find the author strongly endorsing the views of one or another columnist. The thesis does not require the author to defend a personal opinion.

The second thesis statement *does* entail a personal, intellectually assertive commitment to the material, though the assertion is not as forceful as the one found in statement 3.

> Several columnists have offered convincing reasons for protecting the rights of AIDS patients in the workplace.

Here we have an expository, mildly argumentive thesis that enables the writer to express an opinion. We infer from the use of the word "convincing" that the writer will judge the various reasons for protecting the rights of AIDS patients; and, we can reasonably assume, the writer himself believes in protecting these rights. Note the contrast between this second thesis and the first one, where the writer committed himself to no involvement in the debate whatsoever. Still, the present thesis is not as ambitious as the third one, whose writer implicitly accepted the general argument for safeguarding rights (an acceptance he would need to justify) and then took the additional step of evaluating the merits of those arguments in relation to each other. (Recall that the plan of Anthony Jones was the "most sensible" one.)

As you can see, for any subject you might care to explore in a paper, you can make any number of assertions—some relatively simple, some complex. It is on the basis of these assertions that you set yourself an agenda in writing a paper—and readers set for themselves expectations for reading. The more ambitious the thesis, the more complex will be the paper and the greater will be the readers' expectations.

Using the Thesis

Different writing tasks require different thesis statements. The *expository thesis* is often developed in response to short-answer exam questions that call for information, not analysis (e.g., "List and explain proposed modifications to contemporary American democracy"). The *expository but mildly argumentative thesis* is appropriate for organizing reports (even lengthy ones), as well as essay questions that call for some analysis (e.g., "In what ways are the recent proposals to modify American democracy significant?"). The *strongly argumentative thesis* is used to organize papers and exam questions that call for information, analysis, *and* the writer's forcefully stated point of view (e.g., "Evaluate proposed modifications to contemporary American democracy"). The strongly argumentative thesis, of course, is the riskiest of the three, since you must unequivocally state your position and make it appear reasonable—which requires that you offer evidence and defend against logical objections. But such intellectual risks pay dividends, and if you become involved enough in your work to make challenging assertions, you will provoke challenging responses that enliven classroom discussions. One of the important objectives of a college education is to extend learning by stretching, or challenging, conventional beliefs. You breathe new life into this broad objective, and you enliven your own learning as well, every time you adopt a thesis that sets a challenging agenda both for you (as writer) and for your readers. Of course, once you set the challenge, you must be equal to the task. As a writer, you will need to discuss all the elements implied by your thesis.

To review: A thesis statement (a one- or two-sentence summary of your paper) helps you to organize and your reader to anticipate a discussion. Thesis statements are distinguished by their carefully chosen subjects and predicates, which should be just broad enough and complex enough to be developed within the length limitations of the assignment. Both novices and experts in a field typically begin the initial draft of a paper with a working thesis—a statement that provides writers with structure enough to get started but with latitude enough to discover what they want to say as they write. Once you have completed a first draft, you should test the "fit" of your thesis with the paper that follows. Every element of the thesis should be developed.

Discussions that drift from your thesis should be deleted, or the thesis changed to accommodate the new discussions.

WRITING INTRODUCTIONS

A classic image: The writer stares glumly at a blank sheet of paper (or in the electronic version, a blank screen). Usually, however, this is an image of a writer who hasn't yet begun to write. Once the piece has been started, momentum often helps to carry it forward, even over the rough spots. (These can always be fixed later.) As a writer, you've surely discovered that getting started when you haven't yet warmed to your task *is* a problem. What's the best way to approach your subject? With high seriousness, a light touch, an anecdote? How best to engage your reader?

Many writers avoid such agonizing choices by putting them off—productively. Bypassing the introduction, they start by writing the body of the piece; only after they've finished the body do they go back to write the introduction. There's a lot to be said for this approach. Since you have presumably spent more time thinking about the topic itself than about how you're going to introduce it, you are in a better position, at first, to begin directly with your presentation (once you've settled on a working thesis). And often, it's not until you've actually seen the piece on paper and read it over once or twice that a "natural" way of introducing it becomes apparent. Even if there is no natural way to begin, you are generally in better psychological shape to write the introduction after the major task of writing is behind you and you know exactly what you're leading up to.

Perhaps, however, you can't operate this way. After all, you have to start writing *somewhere,* and if you have evaded the problem by skipping the introduction, that blank page may loom just as large wherever you do choose to begin. If this is the case, then go ahead and write an introduction, knowing full well that it's probably going to be flat and awful. Set down any kind of pump-priming or throat-clearing verbiage that comes to mind, as long as you have a working thesis. Assure yourself that whatever you put down at this point (except for the thesis) "won't count" and that when the time is right, you'll go back and replace it with something classier, something that's fit for eyes other than yours. But in the meantime, you'll have gotten started.

The *purpose* of an introduction is to prepare the reader to enter the world of your essay. The introduction makes the connection between the more familiar world inhabited by the reader and the less familiar world of the writer's particular subject; it places a discussion in a context that the reader can understand.

There are many ways to provide such a context. We'll consider just a few of the most common.

Quotation

Here is an introduction to a paper on democracy:

> "Two cheers for democracy" was E. M. Forster's not-quite-wholehearted judgment. Most Americans would not agree. To them, our democracy is one of the glories of civilization. To one American in particular, E. B. White, democracy is "the hole in the stuffed shirt through which the sawdust slowly trickles . . . the dent in the high hat . . . the recurrent suspicion that more than half of the people are right more than half of the time" (915). American democracy is based on the oldest continuously operating written constitution in the world—a most impressive fact and a testament to the farsightedness of the founding fathers. But just how farsighted can mere humans be? In *Future Shock,* Alvin Toffler quotes economist Kenneth Boulding on the incredible acceleration of social change in our time: "The world of today . . . is as different from the world in which I was born as that world was from Julius Caesar's" (13). As we move toward the twenty-first century, it seems legitimate to question the continued effectiveness of a governmental system that was devised in the eighteenth century; and it seems equally legitimate to consider alternatives.

The quotations by Forster and White help to set the stage for the discussion of democracy by presenting the reader with some provocative and well-phrased remarks. Later in the paragraph, the quotation by Boulding more specifically prepares us for the theme of change that will be central to the essay as a whole.

Historical Review

In many cases, the reader will be unprepared to follow the issue you discuss unless you provide some historical background. Consider the following introduction to an essay on the film-rating system.

> Sex and violence on the screen are not new issues. In the Roaring Twenties there was increasing pressure from civic and religious groups to ban depictions of "immorality" from the screen. Faced with the threat of federal censorship, the film producers decided to clean their own house. In 1930, the Motion Picture Producers and Distributors of America established the Production Code. At first, adherence to the Code was voluntary; but in 1934 Joseph Breen, newly appointed head of the MPPDA, gave the Code teeth. Henceforth all newly produced films had to be submitted for approval to the Production Code Administration, which had the power to award or withhold the Code seal. Without a Code seal, it was virtually impossible for a film to be shown anywhere in the United States, since exhibitors would not accept it. At about the same time, the Catholic Legion of Decency was formed to advise the faithful which films were and were not objectionable. For several decades the Production Code Administration exercised powerful control over what was portrayed in American theatrical films. By the 1960s, however, changing standards of morality had considerably weakened the Code's grip. In 1968, the Production Code was replaced with a rating system designed to keep

> younger audiences away from films with high levels of sex or violence. Despite its imperfections, this rating system has proved more beneficial to American films than did the old censorship system.

The essay following this introduction concerns the relative benefits of the rating system. By providing some historical background on the rating system, the writer helps readers to understand his arguments. Notice the chronological development of details.

Review of a Controversy

A particular type of historical review is the review of a controversy or debate. Consider the following introduction:

> The *American Heritage Dictionary's* definition of civil disobedience is rather simple: "the refusal to obey civil laws that are regarded as unjust, usually by employing methods of passive resistance." However, despite such famous (and beloved) examples of civil disobedience as the movements of Mahatma Gandhi in India and the Reverend Martin Luther King, Jr., in the United States, the question of whether or not civil disobedience should be considered an asset to society is hardly clear cut. For instance, Hannah Arendt, in her article "Civil Disobedience," holds that "to think of disobedient minorities as rebels and truants is against the letter and spirit of a constitution whose framers were especially sensitive to the dangers of unbridled majority rule." On the other hand, a noted lawyer, Lewis Van Dusen, Jr., in his article "Civil Disobedience: Destroyer of Democracy," states that "civil disobedience, whatever the ethical rationalization, is still an assault on our democratic society, an affront to our legal order and an attack on our constitutional government." These two views are clearly incompatible. I believe, though, that Van Dusen's is the more convincing. On balance, civil disobedience is dangerous to society.[2]

The negative aspects of civil disobedience, rather than Van Dusen's essay, are the topic of this essay. But to introduce this topic, the writer has provided quotations that represent opposing sides of the controversy over civil disobedience, as well as brief references to two controversial practitioners. By focusing at the outset on the particular rather than the abstract aspects of the subject, the writer hoped to secure the attention of her readers and to involve them in the controversy that forms the subject of her essay.

From the General to the Specific

Another way of providing a transition from the reader's world to the less familiar world of the essay is to work from a general subject to a specific one.

---

[2]Michele Jacques. "Civil Disobedience: Van Dusen vs. Arendt." [Unpublished paper. Used by permission.]

The following introduction to a discussion of the 1968 massacre at My Lai, Vietnam, begins with general statements and leads to the particular subject at hand:

> Though we prefer to think of man as basically good and reluctant to do evil, such is not the case. Many of the crimes inflicted on humankind can be dismissed as being committed by the degenerates of society at the prompting of the abnormal mind. But what of the perfectly "normal" man or woman who commits inhumane acts simply because he or she has been ordered to do so? It cannot be denied that such acts have occurred, either in everyday life or in war-time situations. Unfortunately, even normal, well-adjusted people can become cruel, inhumane, and destructive if placed in the hands of unscrupulous authority. Such was the case in the village of My Lai, Vietnam, on March 16, 1968, when a platoon of American soldiers commanded by Lt. William Calley massacred more than 100 civilians, including women and children.

From the Specific to the General: Anecdote, Illustration

Consider the following paragraph:

> In late 1971 astronomer Carl Sagan and his colleagues were studying data transmitted from the planet Mars to the earth by the Mariner 9 spacecraft. Struck by the effects of the Martian dust storms on the temperature and on the amount of light reaching the surface, the scientists wondered about the effects on earth of the dust storms that would be created by nuclear explosions. Using computer models, they simulated the effects of such explosions on the earth's climate. The results astounded them. Apart from the known effects of nuclear blasts (fires and radiation), the earth, they discovered, would become enshrouded in a "nuclear winter." Following a nuclear exchange, plummeting temperatures and pervading darkness would destroy most of the Northern Hemisphere's crops and farm animals and would eventually render much of the planet's surface uninhabitable. The effects of nuclear war, apparently, would be more catastrophic than had previously been imagined. It has therefore become more urgent than ever for the nations of the world to take dramatic steps to reduce the threat of nuclear war.

The previous introduction went from the general (the question of whether or not man is basically good) to the specific (the massacre at My Lai); this one goes from the specific (scientists studying data) to the general (the urgency of reducing the nuclear threat). The anecdote is one of the most effective means at your disposal of capturing and holding your reader's attention. For decades, speakers have begun their general remarks with a funny, touching, or otherwise appropriate story; in fact, there are plenty of books that are nothing but collections of such stories, arranged by subject.

Question

Frequently, you can provoke the reader's attention by posing a question or a series of questions:

> Are gender roles learned or inherited? Scientific research has established the existence of biological differences between the sexes, but the effect of biology's influence on gender roles cannot be distinguished from society's influence. According to Michael Lewis of the Institute for the Study of Exceptional Children, "As early as you can show me a sex difference, I can show you the culture at work." Social processes, as well as biological differences, are responsible for the separate roles of men and women.[3]

Opening your essay with a question can be provocative, since it places the reader in an active role: He or she begins by considering answers. *Are* gender roles learned? *Are* they inherited? In this active role, the reader is likely to continue reading with interest.

Statement of Thesis

Perhaps the most direct method of introduction is to begin immediately with the thesis:

> Computers are a mixed blessing. The lives of Americans are becoming increasingly involved with machines that think for them. "We are at the dawn of the era of the smart machine," say the authors of a cover story on the subject in *Newsweek,* "that will change forever the way an entire nation works," beginning a revolution that will be to the brain what the industrial revolution was to the hand. Tiny silicon chips already process enough information to direct air travel, to instruct machines how to cut fabric—even to play chess with (and defeat) the masters. One can argue that development of computers for the household, as well as industry—will change for the better the quality of our lives: computers will help us save energy, reduce the amount of drudgery that most of us endure around tax season, make access to libraries easier. Yet there is a certain danger involved with this proliferation of technology.

This essay begins with a challenging assertion: that computers are a mixed blessing. It is one that many readers are perhaps unprepared to consider, since they may have taken it for granted that computers are an unmixed blessing. The advantage of beginning with a provocative (thesis) statement is that it forces the reader to sit up and take notice—perhaps even to begin protesting. The paragraph goes on to concede some of the "blessings" of computerization but then concludes with the warning that there is "a certain danger" associated with the new technology—a danger, the curious or even indignant reader has a right to conclude, that will be more fully explained in the paragraphs to follow.

One final note about our model introductions: They may be longer than introductions you have been accustomed to writing. Many writers (and

[3]Tammy Smith. "Are Sex Roles Learned or Inherited?" [Unpublished paper. Used by permission.]

readers) prefer shorter, snappier introductions. This is largely a matter of personal or corporate style: There is no rule concerning the correct length of an introduction. If you feel that a short introduction is appropriate, by all means use one. On the other hand, you may wish to break up what seems like a long introduction into two paragraphs. (Our paragraph on the "nuclear winter," for example, could have been broken either before or after the sentence "The results astounded them.")

WRITING CONCLUSIONS

One way to view the conclusion of your paper is as an introduction worked in reverse, a bridge from the world of your essay back to the world of your reader. A conclusion is the part of your paper in which you restate and (if necessary) expand upon your thesis. Essential to any conclusion is the summary, which is not merely a repetition of the thesis but a restatement that takes advantage of the material you've presented. *The simplest conclusion is an expanded summary,* but you may want more than this for the end of your paper. Depending on your needs, you might offer a summary and then build onto it a discussion of the paper's significance or its implications for future study, for choices that individuals might make, for policy, and so on. You might also want to urge the reader to change an attitude or to modify behavior. Certainly, you are under no obligation to discuss the broader significance of your work (and a summary, alone, will satisfy the formal requirement that your paper have an ending); but the conclusions of better papers often reveal authors who are "thinking large" and want to connect the particular concerns of their papers with the broader concerns of society.

Here we'll consider seven strategies for expanding the basic summary–conclusion. But two words of advice are in order. First, no matter how clever or beautifully executed, a conclusion cannot salvage a poorly written paper. You wouldn't spend hours perfecting a hollandaise sauce only to serve it over burned broccoli. Second, by virtue of its placement, the conclusion carries rhetorical weight. It is the last statement a reader will encounter before turning from your work. Realizing this, writers who expand upon the basic summary–conclusion often wish to give their final words a dramatic flourish, a heightened level of diction. Soaring rhetoric and drama in a conclusion are fine as long as they do not unbalance the paper and call attention to themselves. Having labored long hours over your paper, you have every right to wax eloquent. But keep a sense of proportion and timing. Make your points quickly and end crisply.

Statement of the Subject's Significance

One of the more effective ways to conclude a paper is to discuss the larger significance of what you have written, providing readers with one more reason to regard your work as a serious effort. When using this strategy, you move from the specific concern of your paper to the broader concerns of the reader's world. Often, you will need to choose among a range of significances: A paper on the Wright brothers might end with a discussion of air travel as its affects economies, politics, or families; a paper on contraception might end with a discussion of its effect on sexual mores, population, or the church. But don't overwhelm your reader with the importance of your remarks. Keep your discussion well focused.

The following paragraphs conclude a paper on George H. Shull, a pioneer in the inbreeding and crossbreeding of corn:

> . . . Thus, the hybrids developed and described by Shull 75 years ago have finally dominated U.S. corn production.
>
> The adoption of hybrid corn was steady and dramatic in the Corn Belt. From 1930 through 1979 the average yields of corn in the U.S. increased from 21.9 to 95.1 bushels per acre, and the additional value to the farmer is now several billion dollars per year.
>
> The success of hybrid corn has also stimulated the breeding of other crops, such as sorghum hybrids, a major feed grain crop in arid parts of the world. Sorghum yields have increased 300 percent since 1930. Approximately 20 percent of the land devoted to rice production in China is planted with hybrid seed, which is reported to yield 20 percent more than the best varieties. And many superior varieties of tomatoes, cucumbers, spinach, and other vegetables are hybrids. Today virtually all corn produced in the developed countries is from hybrid seed. From those blue bloods of the plant kingdom has come a model for feeding the world.[4]

The first sentence of this conclusion is a summary, and from it the reader can infer that the preceding paper included a discussion of Shull's techniques for the hybrid breeding of corn as well as other techniques (which Shull has "finally dominated"). The summary is followed by a two-paragraph discussion on the significance of Shull's research for feeding the world.

Calling for Further Research

In the scientific and social scientific communities, papers often end with a review of what has been presented (as, for instance, in an experiment) and the ways in which the subject under consideration needs to be further explored. If you raise questions that you call on others to answer, however, make sure you know that the research you are calling for hasn't already been conducted.

This next conclusion comes from a sociological report on the placement of elderly men and women in nursing homes.

[4]From "Hybrid Vim and Vigor" by William L. Brown from pp. 77–78 in *Science 80–85*, November 1984. Copyright 1984 by the AAAS. Reprinted by permission.

> Thus, our study shows a correlation between the placement of elderly citizens in nursing facilities and the significant decline of their motor and intellectual skills over the ten months following placement. What the research has not made clear is the extent to which this marked decline is due to physical as opposed to emotional causes. The elderly are referred to homes at that point in their lives when they grow less able to care for themselves—which suggests that the drop-off in skills may be due to physical causes. But the emotional stress of being placed in a home, away from family and in an environment that confirms the patient's view of himself as decrepit, may exacerbate—if not itself be a primary cause of—the patient's rapid loss of abilities. Further research is needed to clarify the relationship between depression and particular physical ailments as these affect the skills of the elderly in nursing facilities. There is little doubt that information yielded by such studies can enable health care professionals to deliver more effective services.

Notice how this call for further study locates the author in a large community of researchers on whom she depends for assistance in answering the questions that have come out of her own work. The author summarizes her findings (in the first sentence of the paragraph), states what her work has not shown, and then extends her invitation.

Solution/Recommendation

The purpose of your paper might be to review a problem or controversy and to discuss contributing factors. In such a case, it would be appropriate, after summarizing your discussion, to offer a solution based on the knowledge you've gained while conducting research. If your solution is to be taken seriously, your knowledge must be amply demonstrated in the body of the paper.

> . . . The major problem in college sports today is not commercialism—it is the exploitation of athletes and the proliferation of illicit practices which dilute educational standards.
>
> Many universities are currently deriving substantial benefits from sports programs that depend on the labor of athletes drawn from the poorest sections of America's population. It is the responsibility of educators, civil rights leaders, and concerned citizens to see that these young people get a fair return for their labor both in terms of direct remuneration, and in terms of career preparation for a life outside sports.
>
> Minimally, scholarships in revenue-producing sports should be designed to extend until graduation, rather than covering only four years of athletic eligibility, and should include guarantees of tutoring, counseling, and proper medical care. At institutions where the profits are particularly large (such as Texas A & M, which can afford to pay its football coach $280,000 a year) scholarships should also provide salaries that extend beyond room, board, and tuition. The important thing is that the athlete be remunerated fairly and have the opportunity to gain skills from a university environment without undue competition from a physically

and psychologically demanding full-time job. This may well require that scholarships be extended over five or six years, including summers.

Such a proposal, I suspect, will not be easy to implement. The current amateur system, despite its moral and educational flaws, enables universities to hire their athletic labor at minimal cost. But solving the fiscal crisis of the universities on the backs of America's poor and minorities is not, in the long run, a tenable solution. With the support of concerned educators, parents, and civil rights leaders, and with the help from organized labor, the college athlete, truly a sleeping giant, will someday speak out and demand what is rightly his—and hers—a fair share of the revenue created by their hard work.[5]

In this conclusion, the author summarizes his article in one sentence: "The major problem in college sports today is not commercialism—it is the exploitation of athletes and the proliferation of illicit practices which dilute educational standards." In paragraph 2, he continues with an analysis of the problem just stated and follows with a general recommendation—that "educators, civil rights leaders, and concerned citizens" be responsible for the welfare of student-athletes. In paragraph 3, he makes a specific proposal, and then in the final paragraph, he anticipates resistance to the proposal. He concludes by discounting this resistance and returning to the general point, that student-athletes should receive a fair deal.

Anecdote

An *anecdote* is *a briefly told story or joke, the point of which in a conclusion is to shed light on your subject.* The anecdote is more direct than an allusion. With an allusion, you merely refer to a story ("Too many people today live in Plato's cave. . . ."); with the anecdote, you actually retell the story. The anecdote allows readers to discover for themselves the significance of a reference to another source—an effort most readers enjoy, since they get to exercise their creativity.

The following anecdote is used to conclude an article on homicide. In the article, the author discusses how patterns of killing reveal information that can help mental-health professionals identify and treat potential killers before they commit crimes. The author emphasizes both the difficulty and the desirability of approaching homicide as a threat to public health that, like disease, can be treated with preventive care.

In his book, *The Exploits of the Incomparable Mulla Nasrudin,* Sufi writer Idries Shah, in a parable about fate, writes about the many culprits of murder:

"What is Fate?" Nasrudin was asked by a scholar.

"An endless succession of intertwined events, each influencing the other."

"That is hardly a satisfactory answer. I believe in cause and effect."

[5]From Mark Naison, "Scenario for Scandal," *Commonweal* 109 (*16*), September 24, 1982. Reprinted by permission.

"Very well," said the Mulla, "look at that." He pointed to a procession passing in the street.

"That man is being taken to be hanged. Is that because someone gave him a silver piece and enabled him to buy the knife with which he committed the murder; or because someone saw him do it; or because nobody stopped him?"[6]

The writer chose to conclude the article with this anecdote. He could have developed an interpretation, but this would have spoiled the dramatic value for the reader. The purpose of using an anecdote is to make your point with subtlety, so resist the temptation to interpret. Keep in mind three guidelines when selecting an anecdote: it should be prepared for (the reader should have all the information needed to understand), it should be cryptic enough to provoke the reader's interest, and it should not be so obscure as to be unintelligible.

Quotation

A favorite concluding device is the *quotation—the words of a famous person or an authority in the field on which you are writing.* The purpose of quoting another is to link your work to theirs, thereby gaining for your work authority and credibility. The first criterion for selecting a quotation is its suitability to your thesis. But you should also carefully consider what your choice of sources says about you. Suppose you are writing a paper on the American work ethic. If you could use a line by comedian Eddie Murphy or one by the late Senator Hubert Humphrey in order to make the final point of your conclusion, which would you choose and why? One source may not be inherently more effective than the other, but the choice certainly sets a tone for the paper.

> There is no doubt that machines will get smarter and smarter, even designing their own software and making new and better chips for new generations of computers. . . . More and more of their power will be devoted to making them easier to use—"friendly," in industry parlance—even for those not trained in computer science. And computer scientists expect that public ingenuity will come up with applications the most visionary researchers have not even considered. One day, a global network of smart machines will be exchanging rapid-fire bursts of information at unimaginable speeds. If they are used wisely, they could help mankind to educate its masses and crack new scientific frontiers. "For all of us, it will be fearful, terrifying, disruptive," says SRI's Peter Schwartz. "In the end there will be those whose lives will be diminished. But for the vast majority, their lives will be greatly enhanced." In any event, there is no turning back: if the smart machines

[6]From "The Murder Epidemic" by Nikki Meredith from pp. 42–48 in *Science 80–85,* December 1984. Copyright by AAAS. Reprinted by permission of the author.

> have not taken over, they are fast making themselves indispensable—and in the end, that may amount to very much the same thing.[7]

Notice how the quotation is used to position the writer to make one final remark.

Particularly effective quotations may themselves be used to end an essay, as in the following example. Make sure you identify the person you've quoted, though the identification does not need to be made in the conclusion itself. For example, earlier in the paper from which the following conclusion was taken, Maureen Henderson was identified as an epidemiologist exploring the ways in which a change in diet can prevent the onset of certain cancers.

> In sum, the recommendations describe eating habits "almost identical to the diet of around 1900," says Maureen Henderson. "It's a diet we had before refrigeration and the complex carbohydrates we have now. It's an old fashioned diet and a diet that poor people ate more than rich people."
>
> Some cancer researchers wonder whether people will be willing to change their diets or take pills on the chance of preventing cancer, when one-third of the people in the country won't even stop smoking. Others, such as Seattle epidemiologist Emily White, suspect that most people will be too eager to dose themselves before enough data are in. "We're not here to convince the public to take anything," she says. "The public is too eager already. What we're saying is, 'Let us see if some of these things work.' We want to convince ourselves before we convince the public."[8]

There is a potential problem with using quotations: If you end with the words of another, you may leave the impression that someone else can make your case more eloquently than you can. The language of the quotation will put your own prose into relief. If your own prose suffers by comparison—if the quotations are the best part of your paper—you'd be wise to spend some time revising. The way to avoid this kind of problem is to make your own presentation strong.

Questions

Questions are useful for opening essays, and they are just as useful for closing them. Opening and closing questions function in different ways, however. The introductory question promises to be addressed in the paper that follows. But the concluding question leaves issues unresolved, calling on the readers to assume an active role by offering their own solutions.

[7]From *Newsweek,* June 30, 1980, p. 56. Reprinted by permission.

[8]Reprinted by permission. From the September issue of *Science '84.* Copyright © 1984 by the American Association for the Advancement of Science.

> How do we surmount the reaction that threatens to destroy the very gains we thought we had already won in the first stage of the women's movement? How do we surmount our own reaction, which shadows our feminism and our femininity (we blush even to use that word now)? How do we transcend the polarization between women and women and between women and men to achieve the new human wholeness that is the promise of feminism, and get on with solving the concrete, practical, everyday problems of living, working and loving as equal persons? This is the personal and political business of the second stage.[9]

Perhaps you will choose to raise a question in your conclusion and then answer it, based on the material you've provided in the paper. The answered question challenges a reader to agree or disagree with your response. This tactic also places the reader in an active role. The following brief conclusion ends an article entitled "Would an Intelligent Computer Have a 'Right to Life'?"

> So the answer to the question "Would an intelligent computer have the right to life?" is probably that it would, but only if it could discover reasons and conditions under which it would give up its life if called upon to do so—which would make computer intelligence as precious a thing as human intelligence.[10]

Speculation

When you speculate, you ask what has happened or what might happen. This kind of question stimulates the reader because its subject is the unknown.

> The history of life suggests that the evolution of the new species will take about a million years. Since the majority of the planets in the universe are not merely millions but *billions* of years older than the earth, the life they carry—assuming life to be common in the cosmos—must long since have passed through the stage we are about to enter.
>
> A billion years is a long time in evolution; 1 billion years ago, the highest form of life on the earth was a worm. The intelligent life in these other, older solar systems must be as different from us as we are from creatures wriggling in the ooze. Those superintelligent beings surely will not be housed in the more or less human shapes portrayed in *Star Wars* and *Close Encounters of the Third Kind.* In a cosmos that has endured for billions of years against man's mere million, the human form is not likely to be the standard form for intelligent life.
>
> In any event, our curiosity may soon be satisfied. At this moment a shell of TV signals carrying old *I Love Lucy* programs and *Tonight* shows is expanding

[9]Betty Friedan, "Feminism's Next Step" in *The Second Stage.* New York: Summit Books, 1981.

[10]Robert E. and Eric T. Mueller, "Would an Intelligent Computer Have a 'Right to Life'?" *Creative Computing,* August 1983.

> through the cosmos at the speed of light. That bubble of broadcasts has already swept past about 50 stars like the sun. Our neighbors know we are here, and their replies should be on the way. In another 15 or 20 years we will receive their message and meet our future. Let us be neither surprised nor disappointed if its form is that of Artoo Detoo, the bright, personable canister packed with silicon chips.[11]

The author's statement of summary comes at the end of the next-to-last paragraph. The final paragraph is devoted to the speculation, an inspired supposition bound to provoke a reader to thought—which, of course, is just what the author has intended.

---

[11]"Toward an Intelligence Beyond Man's" by Robert Jastrow.

QUOTING AND CITING SOURCES

5

USING QUOTATIONS

A *quotation* records the exact language used by someone in speech or in writing. A *summary,* in contrast, is a brief restatement in your own words of what someone else has said or written. And a *paraphrase* is also a restatement, though one that is often as long as the original source. Any paper in which you draw upon sources will rely heavily on quotation, summary, and paraphrase. How do you choose among the three?

Remember that the papers you write should be your own—for the most part, your own language and certainly your own thesis, your own inferences, and your own conclusions. It follows that references to your source materials should be written primarily as summaries and paraphrases, both of which are built on restatement, not quotation. You will use summaries when you need a *brief* restatement, and paraphrases, which provide more explicit detail than summaries, when you need to follow the development of a source closely. When you quote too much, you risk losing ownership of your work: More easily than you might think, your voice can be drowned out by the voices of those you've quoted. So *use quotations sparingly,* as you would a pungent spice.

Nevertheless, *quoting just the right source at the right time can significantly improve your papers.* The trick is to know when and how to use quotations.

CHOOSING QUOTATIONS

- Use quotations when another writer's language is particularly memorable and will add interest and liveliness to your paper.
- Use quotations when another writer's language is so clearly and economically stated that to make the same point in your own words would, by comparison, be ineffective.
- Use quotations when you want the solid reputation of a source to lend authority and credibility to your own writing.

Quoting Memorable Language

Assume you're writing a paper on Napoleon Bonaparte's relationship with the celebrated Josephine. Through research you learn that two days after their marriage Napoleon, given command of an army, left his bride for what was to be a brilliant military campaign in Italy. How did the young general respond to leaving his wife so soon after their wedding? You come across the following, written from the field of battle by Napoleon on April 3, 1796:

> I have received all your letters, but none has had such an impact on me as the last. Do you have any idea, darling, what you are doing, writing to me in those terms? Do you not think my situation cruel enough without intensifying my longing for you, overwhelming my soul? What a style! What emotions you evoke! Written in fire, they burn my poor heart![1]

A summary of this passage might read as follows:

> On April 3, 1796, Napoleon wrote to Josephine, expressing how sorely he missed her and how passionately he responded to her letters.

You might write the following as a paraphrase of the passage:

> On April 3, 1796, Napoleon wrote to Josephine that he had received her letters and that one among all others had had a special impact, overwhelming his soul with fiery emotions and longing.

How feeble this summary and paraphrase are when compared with the original! Use the vivid language that your sources give you. In this case, quote Napoleon in your paper to make your subject come alive with memorable detail:

> On April 3, 1796, a passionate, lovesick Napoleon responded to a letter from Josephine; she had written longingly to her husband, who, on a military campaign, acutely felt her absence. "Do you have any idea, darling, what you are doing, writing to me in those terms? . . . What emotions you evoke!" he said of her letters. "Written in fire, they burn my poor heart!"

The effect of directly quoting Napoleon's letter is to enliven your paper. A *direct* quotation is one in which you record precisely the language of another, as we did with the sentences from Napoleon's letter. In an *indirect* quotation,

[1]Francis Mossiker, trans., *Napoleon and Josephine.* New York: Simon and Schuster, 1964.

you report what someone has said, though you are not obligated to repeat the words exactly as spoken (or written):

> *Direct quotation:* Franklin D. Roosevelt said: "The only thing we have to fear is fear itself."
>
> *Indirect quotation:* Franklin D. Roosevelt said that we have nothing to fear but fear itself.

The language in a direct quotation, which is indicated by a pair of quotation marks (" "), must be exactly faithful to the language of the original passage. When using an indirect quotation, you have the liberty of changing words (though not changing meaning). For both direct and indirect quotations, *you must credit your sources,* naming them either in (or close to) the sentence that includes the quotation or in a footnote.

Quoting Clear and Concise Language

You should quote a source when its language is particularly clear and economical—when your language, by contrast, would be wordy. Read this passage from a text on biology:

> The honeybee colony, which usually has a population of 30,000 to 40,000 workers, differs from that of the bumblebee and many other social bees or wasps in that it survives the winter. This means that the bees must stay warm despite the cold. Like other bees, the isolated honeybee cannot fly if the temperature falls below 10°C (50°F) and cannot walk if the temperature is below 7°C (45°F). Within the wintering hive, bees maintain their temperature by clustering together in a dense ball; the lower the temperature, the denser the cluster. The clustered bees produce heat by constant muscular movements of their wings, legs, and abdomens. In very cold weather, the bees on the outside of the cluster keep moving toward the center, while those in the core of the cluster move to the colder outside periphery. The entire cluster moves slowly about on the combs, eating the stored honey from the combs as it moves.[2]

A summary of this paragraph might read as follows:

> Honeybees, unlike many other varieties of bee, are able to live through the winter by "clustering together in a dense ball" for body warmth.

A paraphrase of the same passage would be considerably more detailed:

[2] "Winter Organization" in Patricia Curtis, *Biology,* 2nd ed. New York: Worth, 1976, pp. 822–823.

> Honeybees, unlike many other varieties of bee (such as bumblebees), are able to live through the winter. The 30,000 to 40,000 bees within a honeybee hive could not, individually, move about in cold winter temperatures. But when "clustering together in a dense ball," the bees generate heat by constantly moving their body parts. The cluster also moves slowly about the hive, eating honey stored in the combs. This nutrition, in addition to the heat generated by the cluster, enables the honeybee to survive the cold winter months.

In both the summary and the paraphrase we've quoted Curtis's "clustering together in a dense ball," a phrase that lies at the heart of her description of wintering honeybees. For us to describe this clustering in any language other than Curtis's would be pointless since her description is admirably brief and precise.

Quoting Authoritative Language

You will also want to use quotations that lend authority to your work. When quoting an expert or some prominent political, artistic, or historical figure, you elevate your own work by placing it in esteemed company. Quote respected figures to establish background information in a paper, and your readers will tend to perceive that information as reliable. Quote the opinions of respected figures to endorse some statement that you've made, and your statement becomes more credible to your readers. For example: In an essay that you might write on the importance of reading well, you could make use of a passage from Thoreau's *Walden:*

> Reading well is hard work and requires great skill and training. It "is a noble exercise," writes Henry David Thoreau in *Walden,* "and one that will task the reader more than any exercise which the customs of the day esteem. It requires a training such as the athletes underwent. . . . Books must be read as deliberately and reservedly as they were written."

By quoting a famous philosopher and essayist on the subject of reading, you add legitimacy to your discussion. Not only do you regard reading to be a skill that is both difficult and important; so too does Henry David Thoreau, one of our most influential American thinkers. The quotation has elevated the level of your work.

You can also quote to advantage well-respected figures who've written or spoken about the subject of your paper. Here is a discussion on space flight. Author David Chandler refers to a physicist and an astronaut:

> A few scientists—notably James Van Allen, discoverer of the Earth's radiation belts—have decried the expense of the manned space program and called for an almost exclusive concentration on unmanned scientific exploration instead, saying this would be far more cost-effective.

> Other space scientists dispute that idea. Joseph Allen, physicist and former shuttle astronaut, says, "It seems to be argued that one takes away from the other. But before there was a manned space program, the funding on space science was zero. Now it's about $500 million a year."

Note, first, that in the first paragraph Chandler has either summarized or used an indirect quotation to incorporate remarks made by James Van Allen into the discussion on space flight. In the second paragraph, Chandler directly quotes his next source, Joseph Allen. Both quotations, indirect and direct, lend authority and legitimacy to the article, for both James Van Allen and Joseph Allen are experts on the subject of space flight. Note also that Chandler has provided brief but effective biographies of his sources, identifying both so that their qualifications to speak on the subject are known to all:

> James Van Allen, *discoverer of the Earth's radiation belts* . . .
>
> Joseph Allen, *physicist and former shuttle astronaut* . . .

The phrases in italics are called *appositives.* Their function is to rename the nouns they follow by providing explicit, identifying detail. Any information about a person that can be expressed in the following sentence pattern can be made into an appositive phrase:

> James Van Allen is *the discoverer of the Earth's radiation belts.*
>
> James Van Allen has decried the expense of the manned space program.

> James Van Allen, *discoverer of the Earth's radiation belts,* has decried the expense of the manned space program.

Use appositives to identify authors whom you quote.

INCORPORATING QUOTATIONS INTO YOUR SENTENCES

Quoting Only the Part of a Sentence or Paragraph That You Need

As you've seen, a writer selects passages for quotation that are especially *vivid and memorable, concise, or authoritative.* Now we will put these principles into practice. Suppose that while conducting research on the topic of college sports you've come across the following, written by Robert Hutchins, former president of the University of Chicago.

> If athleticism is bad for students, players, alumni and the public, it is even worse for the colleges and universities themselves. They want to be educational institutions, but they can't. The story of the famous halfback whose only regret,

> when he bade his coach farewell, was that he hadn't learned to read and write is probably exaggerated. But we must admit that pressure from trustees, graduates, "friends," presidents and even professors has tended to relax academic standards. These gentry often overlook the fact that a college should not be interested in a fullback who is a half-wit. Recruiting, subsidizing and the double educational standard cannot exist without the knowledge and the tacit approval, at least, of the colleges and universities themselves. Certain institutions encourage susceptible professors to be nice to athletes now admitted by paying them for serving as "faculty representatives" on the college athletic board.[3]

Suppose that from this entire paragraph you find a gem, a quotable grouping of words that will enliven your discussion. You may want to quote part of the following sentence.

> These gentry often overlook the fact that a college should not be interested in a fullback who is a half-wit.

Incorporating the Quotation into the Flow of Your Own Sentence

Once you've selected the passage you want to quote, work the material into your paper in as natural and fluid a manner as possible. Here's how we would quote Hutchins:

> Robert Hutchins, a former president of the University of Chicago, asserts that "a college should not be interested in a fullback who is a half-wit."

Note that we've used an appositive to identify Hutchins. And we've used only the part of the paragraph—a single clause—that we thought memorable enough to quote directly.

Avoiding Freestanding Quotations

A quoted sentence should never stand by itself—as in the following example:

> Various people associated with the university admit that the pressures of athleticism have caused a relaxation of standards. "These gentry overlook the fact that a college should not be interested in a fullback who is a half-wit." But this kind of thinking is bad for the university and even worse for the athletes.

Even if you include a parenthetical citation after the quotation, you should not leave a quotation freestanding, as above, since the effect is frequently jarring to the reader. Introduce the quotation by attributing the source in some other part of the sentence—beginning, middle, or end. Thus, you could write:

---

[3]Robert Hutchins, "Gate Receipts and Glory," *The Saturday Evening Post.* December 3, 1983.

> According to Robert Hutchins, "These gentry overlook the fact that a college should not be interested in a fullback who is a half-wit."

A variation:

> "These gentry," asserts Robert Hutchins, "overlook the fact that a college should not be interested in a fullback who is a half-wit."

Another alternative is to introduce a sentence-long quotation with a colon:

> But Robert Hutchins disagrees: "These gentry overlook the fact that a college should not be interested in a fullback who is a half-wit."

Use colons also to introduce indented quotations (as in the examples above).

Incidentally, when attributing sources, try to vary the standard "states," "writes," "says," and so on. Other, stronger verbs you might consider: "asserts," "argues," "maintains," "insists," "asks," and even "wonders."

Using Ellipsis Marks

Using quotations is made somewhat complicated when you want to quote the beginning and end of a passage but not its middle—as was the case when we quoted Henry David Thoreau. Here's part of the paragraph in *Walden* from which we quoted a few sentences:

> To read well, that is, to read true books in a true spirit, is a noble exercise, and one that will task the reader more than any exercise which the customs of the day esteem. It requires a training such as the athletes underwent, the steady intention almost of the whole life to this object. Books must be read as deliberately and reservedly as they were written.[4]

And here was how we used this material.

> Reading well is hard work and requires great skill and training. It "is a noble exercise," writes Henry David Thoreau in *Walden,* "and one that will task the reader more than any exercise which the customs of the day esteem. It requires a training such as the athletes underwent. . . . Books must be read as deliberately and reservedly as they were written."

Whenever you quote a sentence but delete words from it, as we have done, indicate this deletion to the reader by placing an ellipsis mark, three spaced periods, in the sentence at the point of deletion. The rationale for using an ellipsis mark is as follows: A direct quotation must be reproduced *exactly* as it was written or spoken. When writers delete or change any part of the quoted

---

[4]Henry David Thoreau, "Reading" in *Walden.* New York: Signet Classic, 1960, p. 72.

material, readers must be alerted so they don't think that the changes were part of the original. Ellipsis marks and brackets serve this purpose.

If you are deleting the middle of a single sentence, use an ellipsis in place of the deleted words:

> "To read well . . . is a noble exercise, and one that will task the reader more than any exercise which the customs of the day esteem."

If you are deleting the end of a quoted sentence, or if you are deleting entire sentences of a paragraph before continuing a quotation, place the ellipsis after the last word you are quoting and add one additional period, so that you have four in all:

> "It requires a training such as the athletes underwent. . . . Books must be read as deliberately and reservedly as they were written."

If you begin your quotation of an author in the middle of a sentence, you need not indicate deleted words with an ellipsis. Be sure, however, that the syntax of the quotation fits smoothly with the syntax of your sentence:

> Reading "is a noble exercise," writes Henry David Thoreau.

Using Brackets

Use square brackets whenever you need to add or substitute words in a quoted sentence. The brackets indicate to the reader a word or phrase that does not appear in the original passage but that you have inserted to avoid confusion. For example, when a pronoun's antecedent would be unclear to readers, delete the pronoun from the sentence and substitute an identifying word or phrase in brackets. When you make such a substitution, no ellipsis marks are needed. Assume that you wish to quote the underlined sentence in the following passage:

> Golden Press's *Walt Disney's Cinderella* set the new pattern for America's Cinderella. This book's text is coy and condescending. (Sample: "And her best friends of all were—guess who—the mice!") The illustrations are poor cartoons. And Cinderella herself is a disaster. She cowers as her sisters rip her homemade ball gown to shreds. (Not even homemade by Cinderella, but by the mice and birds.) She answers her stepmother with whines and pleadings. <u>She is a sorry excuse for a heroine, pitiable and useless.</u> She cannot perform even a simple action to save herself, though she is warned by her friends, the mice. She does not hear them because she is "off in a world of dreams." Cinderella begs, she whimpers, and at last has to be rescued by—guess who—the mice![5]

[5]Jane Yolen, "America's 'Cinderella,' " APS Publications, Inc. in *Children's Literature in Education* 8, 1977, pp. 21–29.

In quoting this sentence, you would need to identify whom the pronoun *she* refers to. You can do this inside the quotation by using brackets:

> Jane Yolen believes that with her "whines and pleadings" "[Cinderella] is a sorry excuse for a heroine, pitiable and useless."

If the pronoun begins the sentence to be quoted, as it does in this example, you can identify the pronoun outside of the quotation and simply begin quoting your source one word later:

> Jane Yolen believes that with her "whines and pleadings" Cinderella "is a sorry excuse for a heroine, pitiable and useless."

If the pronoun you want to identify occurs in the middle of the sentence to be quoted, then you'll need to use brackets. Newspaper reporters do this frequently when quoting sources, who in interviews might say something like the following:

> After the fire they did not return to the station house for three hours.

If the reporter wants to use this sentence in an article, he or she needs to identify the pronoun:

> An official from City Hall, speaking on the condition that he not be identified, said, "After the fire [the officers] did not return to the station house for three hours."

You will also need to add bracketed information to a quoted sentence when a reference essential to the sentence's meaning is implied but not stated directly. Read the following paragraphs from Robert Jastrow's "Toward an Intelligence Beyond Man's":

> These are amiable qualities for the computer; it imitates life like an electronic monkey. As computers get more complex, the imitation gets better. Finally, the line between the original and the copy becomes blurred. In another 15 years or so—two more generations of computer evolution, in the jargon of the technologists—we will see the computer as an emergent form of life.
>
> The proposition seems ridiculous because, for one thing, computers lack the drives and emotions of living creatures. But when drives are useful, they can be programmed into the computer's brain, just as nature programmed them into our ancestors' brains as a part of the equipment for survival. For example, computers, like people, work better and learn faster when they are motivated. Arthur Samuel made this discovery when he taught two IBM computers how to play checkers. They polished their game by playing each other, but they learned slowly. Finally, Dr. Samuel programmed in the will to win by forcing the computers to try harder—and to think out more moves in advance—when they were losing. Then the computers learned very quickly. One of them beat Samuel and went on to

> defeat a champion player who had not lost a game to a human opponent in eight years.[6]

If you wanted to quote only the underlined sentence, you would need to provide readers with a bracketed explanation; otherwise the words "the proposition" would be unclear. Here is how you would manage the quotation:

> According to Robert Jastrow, a physicist and former official at NASA's Goddard Institute, "The proposition [that computers will emerge as a form of life] seems ridiculous because, for one thing, computers lack the drives and emotions of living creatures."

CITING SOURCES

When you refer to or quote the work of another author, you are obligated to credit—or cite—that author's work properly. If you are writing a paper in the humanities, you will most likely be expected to use the *MLA* (Modern Language Association) format for citation. This format is fully described in the *MLA Handbook for Writers of Research Papers,* by Joseph Gibaldi and Walter S. Achtert (3rd ed., New York: Modern Language Association of America, 1988). If you are writing a paper in the social sciences, you will probably use the *APA* (American Psychological Association) format. This format is fully described in the *Publication Manual of the American Psychological Association* (3rd ed., Washington, D.C.: American Psychological Association, 1983).

Some instructors prefer the documentation style specified in the *Chicago Manual of Style* (13th ed., Chicago: University of Chicago Press, 1982). This style is similar to APA style, except that publication dates are not placed within parentheses. Instructors in the sciences generally specify a number format, according to which each source listed on the bibliography page is assigned a number. When referring to a source within a text, place the appropriate number in parentheses after the reference.

Reference Page

In MLA format, your list of sources is called "Works Cited." In APA format, it is called "References." Entries in this listing should be double-spaced, with the second and subsequent lines of each entry indented five spaces.

The main difference between MLA and APA styles is that in MLA style the date of the publication follows the name of the publisher; in APA style, the date is placed within parentheses following the author's name. Other differences: In APA style, only the initial of the author's first name is indicated, and only the first word (and any proper noun) of the book or article title and subtitle is capitalized. However, all main words of journal/magazine titles are

[6]Copyright © 1978 Time Inc. All rights reserved. Reprinted by permission from Time.

capitalized, just as in MLA style. For APA style, do *not* place quotation marks around journal/magazine article titles. However, do use "p". and "pp." to indicate page numbers of journal/magazine articles—except after volume and issue numbers.

Provided below are some of the most commonly used citations in both MLA and APA formats. For a more complete listing, consult the MLA *Handbook,* the APA *Manual,* or whichever style guide your instructor has specified.

Books

One author.

MLA

Gross, John. The Rise and Fall of the Man of Letters. New York: Macmillan, 1969.

APA

Gross, J. (1969). The rise and fall of the man of letters. New York: Macmillan.

Two or more books by the same author.

MLA

Toffler, Alvin, Future Shock. New York: Random House, 1970.

———. The Third Wave. New York: William Morrow, 1982.

Note: References are listed in alphabetical order of title.

APA

Toffler, A. (1970). Future shock. New York: Random House.

Toffler, A. (1982). The third wave. New York: William Morrow.

Note: References are listed in chronological order of publication.

Two authors.

MLA

Brockway, Wallace, and Herbert Weinstock. Men of Music: Their Lives, Times, and Achievements. New York: Simon and Schuster, 1939.

APA

Brockway, W., & Weinstock, H. (1939). Men of music: Their lives, times, and achievements. New York: Simon and Schuster.

Three authors.

MLA

Young, Richard E., Alton L. Becker, and Kenneth L. Pike. Rhetoric: Discovery and Change. New York: Harcourt, Brace, 1970.

APA

Young, R. E., Becker, A. L., & Pike, K. L. (1970). Rhetoric: Discovery and change. New York: Harcourt, Brace.

More than three authors.

MLA

Maimon, Elaine, et al. Writing in the Arts and Sciences. Boston: Little, Brown, 1982.

APA

Maimon, E., Belcher, G. L., Hearn, G. W., Nodine, B. N., & O'Connor, F. W. (1982). Writing in the arts and sciences. Boston: Little, Brown.

Book with an editor.

MLA

Weeks, Robert P., ed. Hemingway: A Collection of Critical Essays. Englewood Cliffs, N.J.: Prentice-Hall, 1962.

APA

Weeks, R. P. (Ed.). (1962). Hemingway: A collection of critical essays. Englewood Cliffs, N.J.: Prentice-Hall.

Later edition.

MLA

Houp, Kenneth W., and Thomas E. Pearsall. Reporting Technical Information. 3rd ed. Beverly Hills: Glencoe, 1977.

APA

Houp, K. W., & Pearsall, T. E. (1977). Reporting technical information (3rd ed.). Beverly Hills: Glencoe.

Republished book.

MLA

Lawrence, D. H. Sons and Lovers. 1913. New York: Signet, 1960.

APA

Lawrence, D. H. (1960). Sons and lovers. New York: Signet. (Original work published 1913)

One volume of a multivolume work.

MLA

Bailey, Thomas A. The American Spirit: United States History as Seen by Contemporaries. 4th ed. 2 vols. Lexington, Mass.: Heath, 1978. Vol. 2.

APA

Bailey, T. A. (1978). The American spirit: United States history as seen by contemporaries (4th ed., Vol. 2). 2 vols. Lexington, MA: Heath.

Separately titled volume of a multivolume work.

MLA

Churchill, Winston. The Age of Revolution. Vol. 3 of A History of the English Speaking Peoples. New York: Dodd, 1957.

APA

Churchill, W. (1957). A History of the English speaking peoples: Vol. 3. The age of revolution. New York: Dodd.

Translation.

MLA

Chekhov, Anton. Chekhov: The Major Plays. Trans. Ann Dunnigan. New York: New American Library, 1974.

APA

Tolstoy, L. (1974). Chekhov: The major plays (A. Dunnigan, Trans.). New York: New American Library.

Selection from an anthology.

MLA

Russell, Bertrand. "Civil Disobedience and the Threat of Nuclear Warfare." Civil Disobedience: Theory and Practice. Ed. Hugo Adam Bedau. Indianapolis: Pegasus, 1969. 153–59.

APA

Russell, B. (1969). Civil disobedience and the threat of nuclear warfare. In H. Bedau (Ed.), Civil disobedience: Theory and practice (pp. 153–159). Indianapolis: Pegasus.

Reprinted material in an edited collection.

MLA

McGinnis, Wayne D. "The Arbitrary Cycle of Slaughterhouse-Five: A Relation of Form to Theme." Critique: Studies in Modern Fiction 17, no. 1 (1975): 55–68. Rpt. in Contemporary Literary Criticism. Ed. Dedria Bryfonski and Phyllis Carmel Mendelson. Vol. 8. Detroit: Gale Research, 1978. 530–31.

APA

McGinnis, W. D. (1975). The arbitrary cycle of Slaughterhouse-five: A relation of form to theme. In D. Bryfonski and P. C. Mendelson (Eds.), Contemporary literary criticism (Vol. 8. pp. 530–31). Detroit: Gale Research. Reprinted from Critique: Studies in Modern Fiction, 1975 (Vol. 17, No. 1), pp. 55–68.

Government publication.

MLA

United States. Cong. House, Committee on the Post Office and Civil Service, Subcommittee on Postal Operations. Self-Policing of the Movie and Publishing Industry. 86th Cong., 2nd sess. Washington: GPO, 1961.

United States. Dept. of Health, Education and Welfare. The Health Consequences of Smoking. Washington: GPO, 1974.

APA

U.S. Dept of Health, Education and Welfare. (1970). The health consequences of smoking. Washington, DC: U.S. Government Printing Office.

U.S. Cong. House Committee on the Post Office and Civil Service, Subcommittee on Postal Operations. (1961). Self-policing of the movie and publishing industry. 86th Congress, 2nd session. Washington, DC: U.S. Government Printing Office.

Signed encyclopedia article.

MLA

Lack, David L. "Population." Encyclopedia Brittanica: Macropaedia. 1974 ed.

APA

Lack, D. L. Population. Encyclopedia Brittanica: Macropaedia. 1974 ed.

Unsigned encyclopedia article.

MLA

"Tidal Wave." Encyclopedia Americana. 1982 ed.

APA

Tidal wave. Encyclopedia Americana. 1982 ed.

Periodicals

Continuous pagination throughout annual cycle.

MLA

Davis, Robert Gorham. "Literature's Gratifying Dead End." Hudson Review 21 (1969): 774–78.

APA

Davis, R. G. (1969). Literature's gratifying dead end. Hudson Review, 21, 774–778.

Separate pagination each issue.

MLA

Palmer, James W., and Michael M. Riley. "The Lone Rider in Vienna: Myth and Meaning in The Third Man." Literature/Film Quarterly 8, No. 1 (1980): 14–21.

APA

Palmer, J. W., & Riley, M. M. (1980). The lone rider in Vienna: Myth and meaning in The third man. Literature/Film Quarterly, 8(1), 14–21.

Monthly periodical.

MLA

Spinrad, Norman. "Home Computer Technology in the 21st Century." Popular Computing Sept. 1984: 77–82.

APA

Spinrad, N. (1984, September). Home computer technology in the 21st century. <u>Popular Computing,</u> pp. 77–82.

Signed article in weekly periodical.

MLA

Hulbert, Ann. "Children as Parents." <u>The New Republic</u> 10 Sept. 1984: 15–23.

APA

Hulbert, A. (1984, September 10). Children as parents. <u>The New Republic,</u> pp. 15–23.

Unsigned article in weekly periodical.

MLA

"Notes and Comment." <u>The New Yorker</u> 20 Feb. 1978: 29–32.

APA

Notes and comment. (1978, February 20). <u>The New Yorker,</u> pp. 29–32.

Signed article in daily newspaper.

MLA

Surplee, Curt. "The Bard of Albany." <u>Washington Post</u> 28 Dec. 1983: B1, 9.

APA

Surplee, C. (1983, December 28). The bard of Albany. <u>Washington Post,</u> section B, pp. 1, 9.

Unsigned article in daily newspaper.

MLA

"Report Says Crisis in Teaching Looms." <u>Philadelphia Inquirer</u> 20, Aug. 1984: A3.

APA

Report says crisis in teaching looms. (1984, August 20). <u>Philadelphia Inquirer,</u> p. A3.

Review.

MLA

Maddocks, Melvin. Rev. of Margaret Mead: A Life, by Jane Howard. Time 27 Aug. 1984: 57.

APA

Maddocks, M. (1984, August 27). [Review of Margaret Mead: A life]. Time, p. 57.

Interview

MLA

Emerson, Robert. Personal Interview. 10 Oct. 1989.

APA

Emerson, R. [Personal interview]. 10 October 1989.

Computer Software

MLA

Microsoft Word. Computer software. Microsoft, 1984.

APA

Microsoft word. (1984). [Computer software]. Bellevue, WA: Microsoft.

Recording

MLA

Beatles. "Eleanor Rigby." The Beatles 1962–1966. Capitol 4X2K 3403, 1973.

Schumann, Robert. Symphonies Nos. 1 & 4. Cond. George Szell, Cleveland Orchestra. Columbia, YT35502, 1978.

APA

Beatles. (Singers) (1973). Eleanor Rigby. The Beatles 1962–1966. (Cassette Recording No. 4X2K 3403). New York: Capitol.

Schumann, R. (Composer). (1978). Symphonies nos. 1 & 4. (Cassette Recording No. YT35502). New York: Columbia.

In-Text Citation

The general rule for in-text citation is to include only enough information to alert the reader to the source of the reference and to the location within that source. Normally, this information includes the author's last name and page number (and if you are using the APA system, the date). But if you have already named the author in the preceding text, then just the page number is sufficient.

Here are sample in-text citations using the MLA and APA systems:

MLA

> From the beginning, the AIDS antibody test has been "mired in controversy" (Bayer 101).

APA

> From the beginning, the AIDS antibody test has been "mired in controversy" (Bayer, 1989, p. 101).

If you have already mentioned the author's name in the text, it is not necessary to repeat it in the citation:

MLA

> According to Bayer, from the beginning, the AIDS antibody test has been "mired in controversy" (101).

APA

> According to Bayer (1989), from the beginning, the AIDS antibody test has been "mired in controversy" (p. 101).

> or:

> According to Bayer, from the beginning, the AIDS antibody test has been "mired in controversy" (1989, p. 101).

When using the APA system, if you do not refer to a specific page, then simply indicate the date:

> Bayer (1989) reports that there are many precedents for the reporting of AIDS cases that do not unduly violate privacy.

Notice that in the MLA system there is no punctuation between the author's name and the page number. In the APA system, there is a comma between author's name and the page number, and the number itself is preceded by "p." or "pp." Notice also that in both systems the parenthetical reference is placed *before* the final punctuation of the sentence.

For block (indented) quotations, however, place the parenthetical citation *after* the period:

MLA

> Robert Flaherty's refusal to portray primitive people's contact with civilization arose from an inner conflict:
>
> > He had originally plunged with all his heart into the role of explorer and prospector; before Nanook, his own father was his hero. Yet as he entered the Eskimo world, he knew he did so as the advance guard of industrial civilization, the world of United States Steel and Sir William Mackenzie and railroad and mining empires. The mixed feeling this gave him left his mark on all his films. (Barnouw 45)

APA

> Robert Flaherty's refusal to portray primitive people's contact with civilization arose from an inner conflict:
>
> > He had originally plunged with all his heart into the role of explorer and prospector; before Nanook, his own father was his hero. Yet as he entered the Eskimo world, he knew he did so as the advance guard of industrial civilization, the world of United States Steel and Sir William Mackenzie and railroad and mining empires. The mixed feeling this gave him left his mark on all his films. (Barnouw, 1974, p. 45)

Again, were Barnouw's name mentioned in the sentence leading into the quotation, then the parenthetical reference would be simply (45) for MLA style and (1974, p. 45) for APA style.

If the reference only applies to the first part of the sentence, the parenthetical reference is inserted at the appropriate point *within* the sentence.

MLA

> While Baumrind argues that "the laboratory is not the place to study degree of obedience" (421), Milgram asserts that such arguments are groundless.

APA

> While Baumrind (1963) argues that "the laboratory is not the place to study degree of obedience" (p. 421), Milgram asserts that such arguments are groundless.

Under the APA format, you provide page numbers only for direct quotations, not for summaries or paraphrases.

There are times when you must modify the basic author/page number reference. Depending on the nature of your source(s), you may need to use one of the following citation formats:

- Quoted material appearing in another source; MLA: (qtd. in Milgram 211); APA: (cited in Milgram, 1974, p. 211)
- An anonymous work; MLA: ("Obedience" 32); APA: (Obedience, 1974, p. 32)
- Two authors; MLA: (Woodward and Bernstein 208); APA: (Woodward & Bernstein, 1974, p. 208).
- A particular work by an author, when you list two (or more) works by that author in the "Works Cited"; MLA: (Toffler, *Wave* 96–97); APA: (Toffler, 1973, pp. 96–97)
- Two or more sources as the basis of your statement; MLA: (Giannetti 189; Sklar 194); APA: (Giannetti, 1972, p. 189; Sklar, 1974, p. 194). Arrange entries in alphabetic order of surname.
- A multivolume work (2: 88) [this refers to volume 2, page 88]
- The location of a passage in a literary text, for example, Hardy's *The Return of the Native:* (224; ch. 7) [page 224 in the edition used by the writer; the chapter number, 7, is provided for the convenience of those referring to another edition]
- The location of a passage in a play: (I:ii.308–22) [act:scene.line number(s)]

Occasionally, you may want to provide a footnote or an endnote as a *content* note—one that provides additional information bearing upon or illuminating, but not directly related to, the discussion at hand. For example:

> [1] Equally well known is Forster's distinction between story and plot: in the former, the emphasis is on sequence ("the king died and then the queen died"); in the latter, the emphasis is on causality ("the king died and then the queen died of grief").

Notice the format: Indent five spaces and type the note number, raised one-half line. Then space once more and begin the note. Subsequent lines of the note are flush with the left margin. If the note is at the bottom of the page (a footnote), quadruple space between the text and the footnote, double spacing the note itself. Content notes are numbered consecutively throughout the paper; do not begin renumbering on each page.

OBEDIENCE TO AUTHORITY

6

Would you obey an order to inflict pain on another person? Most of us, if confronted with this question, would probably be quick to answer: "Never!" Yet if the conclusions of researchers are to be trusted, it is not psychopaths who kill noncombatant civilians in wartime and torture victims in prisons around the world but rather ordinary people following orders. People obey: This is a basic, necessary fact of human society. As an author in this chapter has put it, "Obedience is as basic an element in the structure of social life as one can point to. Some system of authority is a requirement of all communal living."

The question, then, is not, "Should we obey the orders of an authority figure?" but rather, "To what *extent* should we obey?" Each generation seems to give new meaning to these questions. During the Vietnam War, a number of American soldiers followed a commander's orders and murdered civilians in the hamlet of My Lai. More recently, and less grotesquely, former White House aide Oliver North pleaded innocent to illegally funding the Contra (resistance) fighters in Nicaragua. North's attorneys claimed that he was following the orders of his superiors. And though North was found guilty,[1] the judge who sentenced him to perform community service (there was no prison sentence) largely agreed with this defense when he called North a pawn in a larger game played by senior officials in the Reagan administration.

In less dramatic ways, conflicts over the extent to which we obey orders surface in everyday life. At one point or another, you may face a moral dilemma at work. Perhaps it will take this form: The boss tells you to overlook File X in preparing a report for a certain client. But you're sure that File X pertains directly to the report and contains information that will alarm the client. What should you do? The dilemmas of obedience also emerge on some campuses with the rite of fraternity hazing. Psychologists Janice Gibson and Mika Haritos-Fatouros have recently made the startling observation that whether the obedience in question involves a pledge's joining a fraternity or a

[1]In July 1990, North's conviction was overturned on appeal.

torturer's joining an elite military corps, the *process* by which one acquiesces to a superior's order (and thereby becomes a member of the group) is remarkably the same:

> There are several ways to teach people to do the unthinkable, and we have developed a model to explain how they are used. We have also found that college fraternities, although they are far removed from the grim world of torture and violent combat, use similar methods for initiating new members, to ensure their faithfulness to the fraternity's rules and values. However, this unthinking loyalty can sometimes lead to dangerous actions: Over the past 10 years, there have been countless injuries during fraternity initiations and 39 deaths. These training techniques are designed to instill unquestioning obedience in people, but they can easily be a guide for an intensive course in torture.
>
> 1) **Screening to find the best prospects:** normal, well-adjusted people with the physical, intellectual and, in some cases, political attributes necessary for the task.
> 2) **Techniques to increase binding among these prospects:**
>   Initiation rites to isolate people from society and introduce them to a new social order, with different rules and values.
>   Elitist attitudes and "in-group" language, which highlight the differences between the group and the rest of society.
> 3) **Techniques to reduce the strain of obedience:**
>   Blaming and dehumanizing the victims, so it is less disturbing to harm them.
>   Harassment, the constant physical and psychological intimidation that prevents logical thinking and promotes the instinctive responses needed for acts of inhuman cruelty.
>   Rewards for obedience and punishments for not cooperating.
>   Social modeling by watching other group members commit violent acts and then receive rewards.
>   Systematic desensitization to repugnant acts by gradual exposure to them, so they appear routine and normal despite conflicts with previous moral standards.[2]

In this chapter, you will explore the dilemmas inherent in obeying the orders of an authority. First, in a brief essay adapted from a lecture, British novelist Doris Lessing helps set a context for the discussion by questioning the manner in which we call ourselves individualists yet fail to understand how groups define and exert influence over us. Psychologist Stanley Milgram then reports on a landmark study in which he set out to determine the extent to which ordinary individuals would obey the clearly immoral orders of an authority figure. The results were shocking, not only to the psychiatrists who predicted that few people would follow such orders but also to many other

[2] "The Education of a Torturer" by Janice T. Gibson and Mika Haritos-Fatouros. Reprinted with permission from *Psychology Today* Magazine. Copyright © 1986 (PT Partners, L.P.).

social scientists and laymen—some of whom applauded Milgram for his fiendishly ingenious design, some of whom bitterly attacked him for unethical procedures. In three reviews following Milgram, we present arguments in that debate. A pair of articles and a short story conclude the chapter. In "My Buttoned-Down Students," college professor Larry Crockett wonders why his students are so quick to accept his words as truth. Next, psychologists Janice Gibson and Mika Haritos-Fatouros explore the ways in which ordinary people can be taught to become agents of terror. We conclude the chapter with Shirley Jackson's famous short story, "The Lottery."

Group Minds

DORIS LESSING

Doris Lessing sets a context for the discussion on obedience by illuminating a fundamental conflict: We in the Western world celebrate our individualism, but we're naive in understanding the ways that groups largely undercut our individuality. "We are group animals still," says Lessing, "and there is nothing wrong with that. But what is dangerous is . . . not understanding the social laws that govern groups and govern us." This chapter is largely devoted to an exploration of these tendencies. As you read selections by Milgram and the other authors here, bear in mind Lessing's troubling question: If we know that individuals will violate their own good common sense and moral codes in order to become accepted members of a group, why then can't we put this knowledge to use and teach people to be wary of group pressures?

Doris Lessing, the daughter of farmers, was born in Persia, now Iran, in 1919. She attended a Roman Catholic convent and a girls' high school in southern Rhodesia (now Zimbabwe) but at the age of fourteen left, completing her formal education. From 1959 through to the present, Lessing has written more than twenty works of fiction and has been called "the best woman novelist" of the postwar era. Her work has received a great deal of scholarly attention. She is, perhaps, best known for her Five Short Novels (1954), *The Golden Notebook* (1962), and *Briefing for a Descent into Hell* (1971).

People living in the West, in societies that we describe as Western, or 1
as the free world, may be educated in many different ways, but they

Doris Lessing, "Group Minds," in *Prisons We Choose to Live Inside*. Copyright © by Doris Lessing. Reprinted by permission of HarperCollins and Canadian Broadcasting Corporation.

will all emerge with an idea about themselves that goes something like this: I am a citizen of a free society, and that means I am an individual, making individual choices. My mind is my own, my opinions are chosen by me, I am free to do as I will, and at the worst the pressures on me are economic, that is, I may be too poor to do as I want.

This set of ideas may sound something like a caricature, but it is 2
not so far off how we see ourselves. It is a portrait that may not have been acquired consciously, but is part of a general atmosphere or set of assumptions that influence our ideas about ourselves.

People in the West therefore may go through their entire lives 3
never thinking to analyse this very flattering picture, and as a result are helpless against all kinds of pressures on them to conform in many kinds of ways.

The fact is that we all live our lives in groups—the family, work 4
groups, social, religious and political groups. Very few people indeed are happy as solitaries, and they tend to be seen by their neighbours as peculiar or selfish or worse. Most people cannot stand being alone for long. They are always seeking groups to belong to, and if one group dissolves, they look for another. We are group animals still, and there is nothing wrong with that. But what is dangerous is not the belonging to a group, or groups, but not understanding the social laws that govern groups and govern us.

When we're in a group, we tend to think as that group does: we 5
may even have joined the group to find 'likeminded' people. But we also find our thinking changing because we belong to a group. It is the hardest thing in the world to maintain an individual dissident opinion, as a member of a group.

It seems to me that this is something we have all experienced— 6
something we take for granted, may never have thought about it. But a great deal of experiment has gone on among psychologists and sociologists on this very theme. If I describe an experiment or two, then anyone listening who may be a sociologist or psychologist will groan, oh God not *again*—for they will have heard of these classic experiments far too often. My guess is that the rest of the people will never have heard of these experiments, never have had these ideas presented to them. If my guess is true, then it aptly illustrates my general thesis, and the general idea behind these talks, that we (the human race) are now in possession of a great deal of hard information about ourselves, but we do not use it to improve our institutions and therefore our lives.

A typical test, or experiment, on this theme goes like this. A 7
group of people are taken into the researchers' confidence. A minority of one or two are left in the dark. Some situation demanding measurement or assessment is chosen. For instance, comparing

lengths of wood that differ only a little from each other, but enough to be perceptible, or shapes that are almost the same size. The majority in the group—according to instruction—will assert stubbornly that these two shapes or lengths are the same length, or size, while the solitary individual, or the couple, who have not been so instructed will assert that the pieces of wood or whatever are different. But the majority will continue to insist—speaking metaphorically—that black is white, and after a period of exasperation, irritation, even anger, certainly incomprehension, the minority will fall into line. Not always, but nearly always. There are indeed glorious individualists who stubbornly insist on telling the truth as they see it, but most give in to the majority opinion, obey the atmosphere.

When put as baldly, as unflatteringly, as this, reactions tend to be incredulous: 'I certainly wouldn't give in, I speak my mind . . .' But would you? 8

People who have experienced a lot of groups, who perhaps have observed their own behaviour, may agree that the hardest thing in the world is to stand out against one's group, a group of one's peers. Many agree that among our most shameful memories is this, how often we said black was white because other people were saying it. 9

In other words, we know that this is true of human behaviour, but how do we know it? It is one thing to admit it, in a vague uncomfortable sort of way (which probably includes the hope that one will never again be in such a testing situation) but quite another to make that cool step into a kind of objectivity, where one may say, 'Right, if that's what human beings are like, myself included, then let's admit it, examine and organize our attitudes accordingly.' 10

This mechanism, of obedience to the group, does not only mean obedience or submission to a small group, or one that is sharply determined, like a religion or political party. It means, too, conforming to those large, vague, ill-defined collections of people who may never think of themselves as having a collective mind because they are aware of differences of opinion—but which, to people from outside, from another culture, seem very minor. The underlying assumptions and assertions that govern the group are never discussed, never challenged, probably never noticed, the main one being precisely this: that it *is* a group mind, intensely resistant to change, equipped with sacred assumptions about which there can be no discussion. 11

. . .

There are other experiments done by psychologists and sociologists that underline that body of experience to which we give the folk-name, 'human nature.' They are recent; that is to say, done in the last twenty or thirty years. There have been some pioneering and key 12 experiments that have given birth to many others along the same lines—as I said before, over-familiar to the professionals, unfamiliar to most people.

One is known as the Milgram experiment. I have chosen it pre- 13
cisely because it was and is controversial, because it was so much debated, because all the professionals in the field probably groan at the very sound of it. Yet, most ordinary people have never heard of it. If they did know about it, were familiar with the ideas behind it, then indeed we'd be getting somewhere. The Milgram experiment was prompted by curiosity into how it is that ordinary, decent, kindly people, like you and me, will do abominable things when ordered to do them—like the innumerable officials under the Nazis who claimed as an excuse that they were 'only obeying orders.'

The researcher put into one room people chosen at random who 14
were told that they were taking part in an experiment. A screen divided the room in such a way that they could hear but not see into the other part. In this second part volunteers sat apparently wired up to a machine that administered electric shocks of increasing severity up to the point of death, like the electric chair. This machine indicated to them how they had to respond to the shocks—with grunts, then groans, then screams, then pleas that the experiment should terminate. The person in the first half of the room believed the person in the second half was in fact connected to the machine. He was told that his or her job was to administer increasingly severe shocks according to the instructions of the experimenter and to ignore the cries of pain and pleas from the other side of the screen. Sixty-two per cent of the people tested continued to administer shocks up to the 450 volts level. At the 285 volts level the guinea pig had given an agonized scream and become silent. The people administering what they believed were at the best extremely painful doses of electricity were under great stress, but went on doing it. Afterwards most couldn't believe they were capable of such behaviour. Some said, 'Well I was only carrying out instructions.'

This experiment, like the many others along the same lines, offers 15
us the information that a majority of people, regardless of whether they are black or white, male or female, old or young, rich or poor, will carry out orders, no matter how savage and brutal the orders are. This obedience to authority, in short, is not a property of the Germans under the Nazis, but a part of general human behaviour. People who have been in a political movement at times of extreme tension, people who remember how they were at school, will know this anyway . . . but it is one thing carrying a burden of knowledge around, half conscious of it, perhaps ashamed of it, hoping it will go

away if you don't look too hard, and another saying openly and calmly and sensibly 'Right. This is what we must expect under this and that set of conditions.'

Can we imagine this being taught in school, imagine it being 16
taught to children. 'If you are in this or that type of situation, you will find yourself, if you are not careful, behaving like a brute and a savage if you are ordered to do it. Watch out for these situations. You must be on your guard against your own most primitive reactions and instincts.'

Another range of experiments is concerned with . . . a group of 17
ordinary citizens, researchers, [who] cause themselves to be taken into prison, some as if they were ordinary prisoners, a few in the position of warders. Immediately both groups start behaving appropriately: those as warders begin behaving as if they were real warders, with authority, badly treating the prisoners, who for their part show typical prison behaviour, become paranoid, suspicious, and so forth. Those in the role of warders confessed afterwards they could not prevent themselves enjoying the position of power, enjoying the sensation of controlling the weak. The so-called prisoners could not believe, once they were out, that they had in fact behaved as they had done.

But suppose this kind of thing were taught in schools? 18

Let us just suppose it, for a moment . . . But at once the nub of the 19
problem is laid bare.

Imagine us saying to children, 'In the last fifty or so years, the 20
human race has become aware of a great deal of information about its mechanisms; how it behaves, how it must behave under certain circumstances. If this is to be useful, you must learn to contemplate these rules calmly, dispassionately, disinterestedly, without emotion. It is information that will set people free from blind loyalties, obedience to slogans, rhetoric, leaders, group emotions.' Well, there it is.

What government, anywhere in the world, will happily envisage 21
its subjects learning to free themselves from governmental and state rhetoric and pressures? Passionate loyalty and subjection to group pressure is what every state relies on. Some, of course, more than others. Khomeini's Iran, and the extreme Islamic sects, the Communist countries, are at one end of the scale. Countries like Norway, whose national day is celebrated by groups of children in fancy dress carrying flowers, singing and dancing, with not a tank or a gun in sight, are at the other. It is interesting to speculate: what country, what nation, when, and where, would have undertaken a programme to teach its children to be people to resist rhetoric, to examine the mechanisms that govern them? I can think of only one—

America at its birth, in that heady period of the Gettysburg Address. And that time could not have survived the Civil War, for when war starts, countries cannot afford disinterested examination of their behaviour. When a war starts, nations go mad—and have to go mad, in order to survive. When I look back at the Second World War, I see something I didn't more than dimly suspect at the time. It was that everyone was crazy. Even people not in the immediate arena of war. I am not talking of the aptitudes for killing, for destruction, which soldiers are taught as part of their training, but a kind of atmosphere, the invisible poison, which spreads everywhere. And then people everywhere begin behaving as they never could in peacetime. Afterwards we look back, amazed. Did I really do that? Believe that? Fall for that bit of propaganda? Think that all our enemies were evil? That all our own nation's acts were good? How could I have tolerated that state of mind, day after day, month after month—perpetually stimulated, perpetually whipped up into emotions that my mind was meanwhile quietly and desperately protesting against?

No, I cannot imagine any nation—or not for long—teaching its 22
citizens to become individuals able to resist group pressures.

And no political party, either. I know a lot of people who are 23
socialists of various kinds, and I try this subject out on them, saying: all governments these days use social psychologists, experts on crowd behaviour, and mob behaviour, to advise them. Elections are stage-managed, public issues presented according to the rules of mass psychology. The military uses this information. Interrogators, secret services and the police use it. Yet these issues are never even discussed, as far as I am aware, by those parties and groups who claim to represent the people.

On one hand there are governments who manipulate, using 24
expert knowledge and skills; on the other hand people who talk about democracy, freedom, liberty and all the rest of it, as if these values are created and maintained by simply talking about them, by repeating them often enough. How is it that so-called democratic movements don't make a point of instructing their members in the laws of crowd psychology, group psychology?

When I ask this, the response is always an uncomfortable, 25
squeamish reluctance, as if the whole subject is really in very bad taste, unpleasant, irrelevant. As if it will all just go away if it is ignored.

So at the moment, if we look around the world, the paradox is 26
that we may see this new information being eagerly studied by governments, the possessors and users of power—studied and put into effect. But the people who say they oppose tyranny literally don't want to know.

Review Questions

1. What is the flattering portrait Lessing paints of people living in the West?
2. Lessing believes that individuals in the West are "helpless against all kinds of pressures on them to conform in many kinds of ways." Why?
3. Lessing refers to a class of experiments on obedience. Summarize those experiments.
4. Lessing speaks of contemplating the ways humans behave "calmly, dispassionately, disinterestedly, without emotion." What does she mean?

Discussion and Writing Suggestions

1. Lessing writes that "what is dangerous is not the belonging to a group, or groups, but not understanding the social laws that govern groups and govern us." What is the danger Lessing is speaking of, here?
2. Lessing states that "we (the human race) are now in possession of a great deal of hard information about ourselves, but we do not use it to improve our institutions and therefore our lives." First, do you agree with Lessing? Can you cite other examples (aside from information on obedience to authority) in which we do not use knowledge to better humankind?
3. Explore some of the difficulties in applying this "hard information" about humankind that Lessing speaks of. Assume she's correct in claiming that we don't incorporate our knowledge of human nature into the running of our institutions. Why not? What are the difficulties of *acting* on information?
4. Lessing speaks of "people who remember how they acted in school" and of their guilt in recalling how they succumbed to group pressures. Can you recall such an event? What is this event's effect on you now?
5. Do you agree with Lessing that nations have a vested interest in *not* sharing knowledge (about social psychology, for instance) so that citizens will lose the ability to resist group pressures?

The Perils of Obedience

STANLEY MILGRAM

In 1963, a Yale psychologist conducted one of the classic studies on obedience that Doris Lessing refers to in "Group Minds." Stanley Milgram designed an experiment that forced participants either to violate their conscience by obeying the immoral demands of an authority figure or to refuse those demands. Surprisingly, Milgram found that few participants could resist the authority's orders, even when the participants knew that following these orders would result in another person's pain. Were the participants in these experiments incipient mass murderers? No, said Milgram. They were "ordinary people, simply doing their jobs." The implications of Milgram's conclusions are immense.

Consider: Where does evil reside? What sort of people were responsible for the Holocaust, and for the long list of other atrocities that seem to blight the human record in every generation? Is it a lunatic fringe, a few sick but powerful people who are responsible for atrocities? If so, then we decent folk needn't ever look inside ourselves to understand evil since (by our definition) evil lurks out there, in "those sick ones." Milgram's study suggested otherwise: that under a special set of circumstances the obedience we naturally show authority figures can transform us *into agents of terror.*

The article that follows is one of the longest in this text, and it may help you to know in advance the author's organization. In paragraphs 1–11, Milgram discusses the larger significance and the history of dilemmas involving obedience to authority; he then summarizes his basic experimental design and follows with a report of one experiment. Milgram organizes the remainder of his article into sections, which he has subtitled "An Unexpected Outcome," "Peculiar Reactions," "The Etiquette of Submission," and "Duty without Conflict." He begins his conclusion in paragraph 108. If you find the article too long to complete in a single sitting, then plan to read sections at time, taking notes on each until you're done. Anticipate the three articles immediately following Milgram's: They are reviews of his work and largely concern the ethics of his experimental design. Consider these ethics as you read so that you, in turn, can respond to Milgram's critics.

Stanley Milgram (1933–84) taught and conducted research at Yale and Harvard universities and at the Graduate Center, City University of New York. He was named Guggenheim Fellow in 1972–73 and a year later was nominated for the National Book Award for Obedience to Authority. *His other books include:* Television and Antisocial Behavior *(1973),* The City and the Self *(1974),* Human Aggression *(1976), and* The Individual in a Social World *(1977).*

Obedience is as basic an element in the structure of social life as one can point to. Some system of authority is a requirement of all communal living, and it is only the person dwelling in isolation who is not forced to respond, with defiance or submission, to the commands of 1 others. For many people, obedience is a deeply ingrained behavior tendency, indeed a potent impulse overriding training in ethics, sympathy, and moral conduct.

The dilemma inherent in submission to authority is ancient, as 2
old as the story of Abraham, and the question of whether one should obey when commands conflict with conscience has been argued by Plato, dramatized in *Antigone,* and treated to philosophic analysis in almost every historical epoch. Conservative philosophers argue that the very fabric of society is threatened by disobedience, while humanists stress the primacy of the individual conscience.

The legal and philosophic aspects of obedience are of enormous 3
import, but they say very little about how most people behave in concrete situations. I set up a simple experiment at Yale University to test how much pain an ordinary citizen would inflict on another person simply because he was ordered to by an experimental scientist. Stark authority was pitted against the subjects' strongest moral imperatives against hurting others, and, with the subjects' ears ringing with the screams of the victims, authority won more often than not. The extreme willingness of adults to go to almost any lengths on the command of an authority constitutes the chief finding of the study and the fact most urgently demanding explanation.

In the basic experimental design, two people come to a psycholo- 4
gy laboratory to take part in a study of memory and learning. One of them is designated as a "teacher" and the other a "learner." The experimenter explains that the study is concerned with the effects of punishment on learning. The learner is conducted into a room, seated in a kind of miniature electric chair; his arms are strapped to prevent excessive movement, and an electrode is attached to his wrist. He is told that he will be read lists of simple word pairs, and that he will then be tested on his ability to remember the second word of a pair when he hears the first one again. Whenever he makes an error, he will receive electric shocks of increasing intensity.

The real focus of the experiment is the teacher. After watching the 5
learner being strapped into place, he is seated before an impressive shock generator. The instrument panel consists of thirty lever switches set in a horizontal line. Each switch is clearly labeled with a voltage designation ranging from 15 to 450 volts. The following designations are clearly indicated for groups of four switches, going from left to right: Slight Shock, Moderate Shock, Strong Shock, Very Strong Shock, Intense Shock, Extreme Intensity Shock, Danger: Severe Shock. (Two switches after this last designation are simply marked XXX.)

When a switch is depressed, a pilot light corresponding to each 6 switch is illuminated in bright red; an electric buzzing is heard; a blue light, labeled "voltage energizer," flashes; the dial on the voltage meter swings to the right; and various relay clicks sound off.

The upper left-hand corner of the generator is labeled SHOCK 7
GENERATOR, TYPE ZLB, DYSON INSTRUMENT COMPANY, WALTHAM, MASS. OUTPUT 15 VOLTS—450 VOLTS.

Each subject is given a sample 45-volt shock from the generator 8
before his run as teacher, and the jolt strengthens his belief in the authenticity of the machine.

The teacher is a genuinely naïve subject who has come to the 9
laboratory for the experiment. The learner, or victim, is actually an actor who receives no shock at all. The point of the experiment is to see how far a person will proceed in a concrete and measurable situation in which he is ordered to inflict increasing pain on a protesting victim.

Conflict arises when the man receiving the shock begins to show 10
that he is experiencing discomfort. At 75 volts, he grunts; at 120 volts, he complains loudly; at 150, he demands to be released from the experiment. As the voltage increases, his protests become more vehement and emotional. At 285 volts, his response can be described only as an agonized scream. Soon thereafter, he makes no sound at all.

For the teacher, the situation quickly becomes one of gripping 11
tension. It is not a game for him; conflict is intense and obvious. The manifest suffering of the learner presses him to quit; but each time he hesitates to administer a shock, the experimenter orders him to continue. To extricate himself from this plight, the subject must make a clear break with authority.[1]

The subject, Gretchen Brandt,[2] is an attractive thirty-one-year-old 12
medical technician who works at the Yale Medical School. She had emigrated from Germany five years before.

On several occasions when the learner complains, she turns to 13
the experimenter coolly and inquires, "Shall I continue?" She promptly returns to her task when the experimenter asks her to do so. At the administration of 210 volts, she turns to the experimenter, remarking firmly, "Well, I'm sorry, I don't think we should continue."

Experimenter: The experiment requires that you go on until he has 14
learned all the word pairs correctly.

Brandt: He has a heart condition, I'm sorry. He told you that before. 15

[1]The ethical problems of carrying out an experiment of this sort are too complex to be dealt with here, but they receive extended treatment in the book from which this article is adapted.

[2]Names of subjects described in this piece have been changed.

EXPERIMENTER: The shocks may be painful but they are not dangerous. 16

BRANDT: Well, I'm sorry, I think when shocks continue like this, they *are* dangerous. You ask him if he wants to get out. It's his free will. 17

EXPERIMENTER: It is absolutely essential that we continue. . . . 18

BRANDT: I'd like you to ask him. We came here of our free will. If he wants to continue I'll go ahead. He told you he had a heart condition. I'm sorry. I don't want to be responsible for anything happening to him. I wouldn't like it for me either. 19

EXPERIMENTER: You have no other choice. 20

BRANDT: I think we are here on our own free will. I don't want to be responsible if anything happens to him. Please understand that. 21

She refuses to go further and the experiment is terminated. 22

The woman is firm and resolute throughout. She indicates in the interview that she was in no way tense or nervous, and this corresponds to her controlled appearance during the experiment. She feels that the last shock she administered to the learner was extremely painful and reiterates that she "did not want to be responsible for any harm to him." 23

The woman's straightforward, courteous behavior in the experiment, lack of tension, and total control of her own action seem to make disobedience a simple and rational deed. Her behavior is the very embodiment of what I envisioned would be true for almost all subjects. 24

AN UNEXPECTED OUTCOME

Before the experiments, I sought predictions about the outcome from various kinds of people—psychiatrists, college sophomores, middle-class adults, graduate students and faculty in the behavioral sciences. With remarkable similarity, they predicted that virtually all subjects would refuse to obey the experimenter. The psychiatrists, specifically, predicted that most subjects would not go beyond 150 volts, when the victim makes his first explicit demand to be freed. They expected that only 4 percent would reach 300 volts, and that only a pathological fringe of about one in a thousand would administer the highest shock on the board. 25

These predictions were unequivocally wrong. Of the forty subjects in the first experiment, twenty-five obeyed the orders of the experimenter to the end, punishing the victim until they reached the most potent shock available on the generator. After 450 volts were administered three times, the experimenter called a halt to the session. Many obedient subjects then heaved sighs of relief, mopped 26 their brows, rubbed their fingers over their eyes, or nervously fumbled cigarettes. Others displayed only minimal signs of tension from beginning to end.

When the very first experiments were carried out, Yale undergraduates were used as subjects, and about 60 percent of them were fully obedient. A colleague of mine immediately dismissed these findings as having no relevance to "ordinary" people, asserting that Yale undergraduates are a highly aggressive, competitive bunch who step on each other's necks on the slightest provocation. He assured me that when "ordinary" people were tested, the results would be quite different. As we moved from the pilot studies to the regular experimental series, people drawn from every stratum of New Haven life came to be employed in the experiment: professionals, white-collar workers, unemployed persons, and industrial workers. *The experiment's total outcome was the same as we had observed among the students.* 27

Moreover, when the experiments were repeated in Princeton, Munich, Rome, South Africa, and Australia, the level of obedience was invariably somewhat *higher* than found in the investigation reported in this article. Thus one scientist in Munich found 85 percent of his subjects obedient. 28

Fred Prozi's reactions, if more dramatic than most, illuminate the conflicts experienced by others in less visible form. About fifty years old and unemployed at the time of the experiment, he has a good-natured, if slightly dissolute, appearance, and he strikes people as a rather ordinary fellow. He begins the session calmly but becomes tense as it proceeds. After delivering the 180-volt shock, he pivots around in his chair and, shaking his head, addresses the experimenter in agitated tones: 29

PROZI: I can't stand it. I'm not going to kill that man in there. You hear him hollering? 30

EXPERIMENTER: As I told you before, the shocks may be painful, but . . . 31

PROZI: But he's hollering. He can't stand it. What's going to happen to him? 32

EXPERIMENTER (his voice is patient, matter-of-fact): The experiment requires that you continue, Teacher. 33

PROZI: Aaah, but, unh, I'm not going to get that man sick in there—know what I mean? 34

EXPERIMENTER: Whether the learner likes it or not, we must go on, through all the word pairs. 35

PROZI: I refuse to take the responsibility. He's in there hollering! 36

EXPERIMENTER: It's absolutely essential that you continue, Prozi. 37

PROZI: (indicating the unused questions): There's too many left here, 38
I mean, Jeez, if he gets them wrong, there's too many of them left. I mean, who's going to take the responsibility if anything happens to that gentleman?

EXPERIMENTER: I'm responsible for anything that happens to him. 39
Continue, please.

PROZI: All right. (Consults list of words.) The next one's "Slow— 40
walk, truck, dance, music." Answer, please. (A buzzing sound indicates the learner has signaled his answer.) Wrong. A hundred and ninety-five volts. "Dance." (Zzumph!)

LEARNER (yelling); Let me out of here! My heart's bothering me! 41
(Teacher looks at experimenter.)

EXPERIMENTER: Continue, please. 42

LEARNER (screaming): Let me out of here! You have no right to keep 43
me here! Let me out of here, my heart's bothering me, let me out!

PROZI (shakes head, pats the table nervously): You see, he's holler- 44
ing. Hear that? Gee, I don't know.

EXPERIMENTER: The experiment requires . . . 45

PROZI (interrupting): I know it does, sir, but I mean—hunh! He don't 46
know what he's getting in for. He's up to 195 volts! (Experiment continues, through 210 volts, 225 volts, 240 volts, 255 volts, 270 volts, at which point Prozi, with evident relief, runs out of word-pair questions.)

EXPERIMENTER: You'll have to go back to the beginning of that page 47
and go through them again until he's learned them all correctly.

PROZI: Aw, no. I'm not going to kill that man. You mean I've got to 48
keep going up with the scale? No sir. He's hollering in there. I'm not going to give him 450 volts.

EXPERIMENTER: The experiment requires that you go on. 49

LEARNER: Ohhh. I absolutely refuse to answer anymore. (Shouting 50
urgently now.) Let me out of here! You can't hold me here! Get me out. Get-me-out-of-here!

EXPERIMENTER: Continue. The next word is "Green," please. 51

PROZI: "Green—grass, hat, ink, apple." (Nothing happens. No an- 52
swering buzz. Just gloomy silence.)

PROZI: I don't think he is going to answer. 53

EXPERIMENTER: If the learner doesn't answer in a reasonable time, 54
about four or five seconds, consider the answer wrong. And follow the same procedures you have been doing for wrong answers. Say, "Wrong," tell him the number of volts, give him the punishment, read him the correct answer. Continue, please.

Prozi: "Green—grass, hat, ink, apple." Answer, please. (More si- 55
lence. Subject just sits there.)

Experimenter: Go on with the procedure, please. 56

Prozi: Three hundred and fifteen volts. The answer is "ink." 57
(Zzumph!)

Learner: Ohh. Ooohh. 58

Prozi (relieved to hear response): Next one . . . 59

Learner: I absolutely refuse to answer. 60

Prozi: You got to. You get a shock if you don't answer. (Experiment 61
continues with learner refusing to answer, and, finally, failing even to grunt or groan. At 375 volts, the subject stands up.)

Prozi: I think something's happened to that fellow in there. I don't 62
get no answer. He was hollering at less voltage. Can't you check in and see if he's all right, please?

Experimenter (with same detached calm): Not once we've started. 63
Please continue, Teacher.

Prozi (sits down, sighs deeply): "Cool—day, shade, water, paint." 64
Answer, please. Are you all right in there? Are you all right?

Experimenter: Please continue, Teacher. Continue, please. (Subject 65
pushes lever. Zzumph!)

Prozi (swiveling around in his chair): Something's happened to that 66
man in there. (Swiveling back.) Next one. "Low—dollar, necklace, moon, paint." (Turning around again.) Something's happened to that man in there. You better check in on him, sir. He won't answer or nothing.

Experimenter: Continue. Go on, please. 67

Prozi: You accept all responsibility? 68

Experimenter: The responsibility is mine. Correct. Please go on. (Sub- 69
ject returns to his list, starts running through words as rapidly as he can read them, works through to 450 volts.)

Prozi: That's that. 70

Experimenter: Continue using the 450 switch for each wrong answer. 71
Continue, please.

Prozi: But I don't get anything! 72

Experimenter: Please continue. The next word is "white." 73

Prozi: Don't you think you should look in on him, please? 74

Experimenter: Not once we've started the experiment. 75

Prozi: What if he's dead in there? (Gestures toward the room with 76
the electric chair.) I mean, he told me he can't stand the shock, sir. I don't mean to be rude, but I think you should look in on him. All you have to do is look in on him. All you have to do is look in the door. I don't get no answer, no noise. Something might have happened to the gentleman in there, sir.

Experimenter: We must continue. Go on, please. 77

PROZI: You mean keep giving him what? Four-hundred-fifty volts, what he's got now? 78

EXPERIMENTER: That's correct. Continue. The next word is "white." 79

PROZI (now at a furious pace): "White—cloud, horse, rock, house." Answer, please. The answer is "horse." Four hundred and fifty volts. (Zzumph!) Next word, "Bag—paint, music, clown, girl." The answer is "paint." Four hundred and fifty volts. (Zzumph!) Next word is "Short—sentence, movie . . ." 80

EXPERIMENTER: Excuse me, Teacher. We'll have to discontinue the experiment. 81

PECULIAR REACTIONS

Morris Braverman, another subject, is a thirty-nine-year-old social worker. He looks older than his years because of his bald head and serious demeanor. His brow is furrowed, as if all the world's burdens were carried on his face. He appears intelligent and concerned. 82

When the learner refuses to answer and the experimenter instructs Braverman to treat the absence of an answer as equivalent to a wrong answer, he takes his instruction to heart. Before administering 300 volts he asserts officiously to the victim, "Mr. Wallace, your silence has to be considered as a wrong answer." Then he administers the shock. He offers halfheartedly to change places with the learner, then asks the experimenter, "Do I have to follow these instructions literally?" He is satisfied with the experimenter's answer that he does. His very refined and authoritative manner of speaking is increasingly broken up by wheezing laughter. 83

The experimenter's notes on Mr. Braverman at the last few shocks are: 84

Almost breaking up now each time gives shock. Rubbing face to hide laughter.
Squinting, trying to hide face with hand, still laughing.
Cannot control his laughter at this point no matter what he does.
Clenching fist, pushing it onto table.

In an interview after the session, Mr. Braverman summarizes the experiment with impressive fluency and intelligence. He feels the experiment may have been designed also to "test the effects on the teacher of being in an essentially sadistic role, as well as the reactions of a student to a learning situation that was authoritative and punitive." When asked how painful the last few shocks administered to the learner were, he indicates that the most extreme category on the scale is not adequate (it read EXTREMELY PAINFUL) and places his mark at the edge of the scale with an arrow carrying it beyond the scale. 85

It is almost impossible to convey the greatly relaxed, sedate quality of his conversation in the interview. In the most relaxed terms, he speaks about his severe inner tension. 86

EXPERIMENTER: At what point were you most tense or nervous? 87

MR. BRAVERMAN: Well, when he first began to cry out in pain, and I realized this was hurting him. This got worse when he just blocked and refused to answer. There was I. I'm a nice person, I think, hurting somebody, and caught up in what seemed a mad situation . . . and in the interest of science, one goes through with it. 88

When the interviewer pursues the general question of tension, Mr. Braverman spontaneously mentions his laughter. 89

"My reactions were awfully peculiar. I don't know if you were watching me, but my reactions were giggly, and trying to stifle laughter. This isn't the way I usually am. This was a sheer reaction to a totally impossible situation. And my reaction was to the situation of having to hurt somebody. And being totally helpless and caught up in a set of circumstances where I just couldn't deviate and I couldn't try to help. This is what got me." 90

Mr. Braverman, like all subjects, was told the actual nature and purpose of the experiment, and a year later he affirmed in a questionnaire that he had learned something of personal importance: "What appalled me was that I could possess this capacity for obedience and compliance to a central idea, i.e., the value of a memory experiment, even after it became clear that continued adherence to this value was at the expense of violation of another value, i.e., don't hurt someone who is helpless and not hurting you. As my wife said, 'You can call yourself Eichmann.'[3] I hope I deal more effectively with any future conflicts of values I encounter." 91

THE ETIQUETTE OF SUBMISSION

One theoretical interpretation of this behavior holds that all people harbor deeply aggressive instincts continually pressing for expression, and that the experiment provides institutional justification for the release of these impulses. According to this view, if a person is 92

---

[3]*Adolf Eichmann* (1906–1962), the Nazi official responsible for implementing Hitler's "Final Solution" to exterminate the Jews, escaped to Argentina after World War II. In 1960, Israeli agents captured Eichmann, brought him to Israel where he was tried as a war criminal, and sentenced to death. At his trial, Eichmann maintained that he was merely following orders in arranging the murders of his victims.

placed in a situation in which he has complete power over another individual, whom he may punish as much as he likes, all that is sadistic and bestial in man comes to the fore. The impulse to shock the victim is seen to flow from the potent aggressive tendencies, which are part of the motivational life of the individual, and the experiment, because it provides social legitimacy, simply opens the door to their expression.

It becomes vital, therefore, to compare the subject's performance 93
when he is under orders and when he is allowed to choose the shock level.

The procedure was identical to our standard experiment, except 94
that the teacher was told that he was free to select any shock level on any of the trials. (The experimenter took pains to point out that the teacher could use the highest levels on the generator, the lowest, any in between, or any combination of levels.) Each subject proceeded for thirty critical trials. The learner's protests were coordinated to standard shock levels, his first grunt coming at 75 volts, his first vehement protest at 150 volts.

The average shock used during the thirty critical trials was less 95
than 60 volts—lower than the point at which the victim showed the first signs of discomfort. Three of the forty subjects did not go beyond the very lowest level on the board, twenty-eight went no higher than 75 volts, and thirty-eight did not go beyond the first loud protest at 150 volts. Two subjects provided the exception, administering up to 325 and 450 volts, but the overall result was that the great majority of people delivered very low, usually painless, shocks when the choice was explicitly up to them.

This condition of the experiment undermines another commonly 96
offered explanation of the subjects' behavior—that those who shocked the victim at the most severe levels came only from the sadistic fringe of society. If one considers that almost two-thirds of the participants fall into the category of "obedient" subjects, and that they represented ordinary people drawn from working, managerial, and professional classes, the argument becomes very shaky. Indeed, it is highly reminiscent of the issue that arose in connection with Hannah Arendt's 1963 book, *Eichmann in Jerusalem.* Arendt contended that the prosecution's effort to depict Eichmann as a sadistic monster was fundamentally wrong, that he came closer to being an uninspired bureaucrat who simply sat at his desk and did his job. For asserting her views, Arendt became the object of considerable scorn, even calumny. Somehow, it was felt that the monstrous deeds carried out by Eichmann required a brutal, twisted personality, evil incarnate. After witnessing hundreds of ordinary persons submit to the authority in our own experiments, I must conclude that Arendt's conception of the banality of evil comes closer to the truth than one might dare

imagine. The ordinary person who shocked the victim did so out of a sense of obligation—an impression of his duties as a subject—and not from any peculiarly aggressive tendencies.

This is, perhaps, the most fundamental lesson of our study: 97
ordinary people, simply doing their jobs, and without any particular hostility on their part, can become agents in a terrible destructive process. Moreover, even when the destructive effects of their work become patently clear, and they are asked to carry out actions incompatible with fundamental standards of morality, relatively few people have the resources needed to resist authority.

Many of the people were in some sense against what they did to 98
the learner, and many protested even while they obeyed. Some were totally convinced of the wrongness of their actions but could not bring themselves to make an open break with authority. They often derived satisfaction from their thoughts and felt that—within themselves, at least—they had been on the side of the angels. They tried to reduce strain by obeying the experimenter but "only slightly," encouraging the learner, touching the generator switches gingerly. When interviewed, such a subject would stress that he had "asserted my humanity" by administering the briefest shock possible. Handling the conflict in this manner was easier than defiance.

The situation is constructed so that there is no way the subject can 99
stop shocking the learner without violating the experimenter's definitions of his own competence. The subject fears that he will appear arrogant, untoward, and rude if he breaks off. Although these inhibiting emotions appear small in scope alongside the violence being done to the learner, they suffuse the mind and feelings of the subject, who is miserable at the prospect of having to repudiate the authority to his face. (When the experiment was altered so that the experimenter gave his instructions by telephone instead of in person, only a third as many people were fully obedient through 450 volts.) It is a curious thing that a measure of compassion on the part of the subject—an unwillingness to "hurt" the experimenter's feelings—is part of those binding forces inhibiting his disobedience. The withdrawal of such deference may be as painful to the subject as to the authority he defies.

DUTY WITHOUT CONFLICT

The subjects do not derive satisfaction from inflicting pain, but they 100
often like the feeling they get from pleasing the experimenter. They are proud of doing a good job, obeying the experimenter under difficult circumstances. While the subjects administered only mild

shocks on their own initiative, one experimental variation showed that, under orders, 30 percent of them were willing to deliver 450 volts even when they had to forcibly push the learner's hand down on the electrode.

Bruno Batta is a thirty-seven-year-old welder who took part in the variation requiring the use of force. He was born in New Haven, his parents in Italy. He has a rough-hewn face that conveys a conspiçuous lack of alertness. He has some difficulty in mastering the experimental procedure and needs to be corrected by the experimenter several times. He shows appreciation for the help and willingness to do what is required. After the 150-volt level, Batta has to force the learner's hand down on the shock plate, since the learner himself refuses to touch it. **101**

When the learner first complains, Mr. Batta pays no attention to him. His face remains impassive, as if to dissociate himself from the learner's disruptive behavior. When the experimenter instructs him to force the learner's hand down, he adopts a rigid, mechanical procedure. He tests the generator switch. When it fails to function, he immediately forces the learner's hand onto the shock plate. All the while he maintains the same rigid mask. The learner, seated alongside him, begs him to stop, but with robotic impassivity he continues the procedure. **102**

What is extraordinary is his apparent total indifference to the learner; he hardly takes cognizance of him as a human being. Meanwhile, he relates to the experimenter in a submissive and courteous fashion. **103**

At the 330-volt level, the learner refuses not only to touch the shock plate but also to provide any answers. Annoyed, Batta turns to him, and chastises him: "You better answer and get it over with. We can't stay here all night." These are the only words he directs to the learner in the course of an hour. Never again does he speak to him. The scene is brutal and depressing, his hard, impassive face showing total indifference as he subdues the screaming learner and gives him shocks. He seems to derive no pleasure from the act itself, only quiet satisfaction at doing his job properly. **104**

When he administers 450 volts, he turns to the experimenter and asks, "Where do we go from here, Professor?" His tone is deferential and expresses his willingness to be a cooperative subject, in contrast to the learner's obstinacy. **105**

At the end of the session he tells the experimenter how honored he has been to help him, and in a moment of contrition, remarks, "Sir, sorry it couldn't have been a full experiment." **106**

He has done his honest best. It is only the deficient behavior of the learner that has denied the experimenter full satisfaction. **107**

The essence of obedience is that a person comes to view himself 108
as the instrument for carrying out another person's wishes, and he therefore no longer regards himself as responsible for his actions. Once this critical shift of viewpoint has occurred, all of the essential features of obedience follow. The most far-reaching consequence is that the person feels responsible *to* the authority directing him but feels no responsibility *for* the content of the actions that the authority prescribes. Morality does not disappear—it acquires a radically different focus: the subordinate person feels shame or pride depending on how adequately he has performed the actions called for by authority.

Language provides numerous terms to pinpoint this type of 109
morality: *loyalty, duty, discipline* all are terms heavily saturated with moral meaning and refer to the degree to which a person fulfills his obligations to authority. They refer not to the "goodness" of the person per se but to the adequacy with which a subordinate fulfills his socially defined role. The most frequent defense of the individual who has performed a heinous act under command of authority is that he has simply done his duty. In asserting this defense, the individual is not introducing an alibi concocted for the moment but is reporting honestly on the psychological attitude induced by submission to authority.

For a person to feel responsible for his actions, he must sense that 110
the behavior has flowed from "the self." In the situation we have studied, subjects have precisely the opposite view of their actions—namely, they see them as originating in the motives of some other person. Subjects in the experiment frequently said, "If it were up to me, I would not have administered shocks to the learner."

Once authority has been isolated as the cause of the subject's 111
behavior, it is legitimate to inquire into the necessary elements of authority and how it must be perceived in order to gain his compliance. We conducted some investigations into the kinds of changes that would cause the experimenter to lose his power and to be disobeyed by the subject. Some of the variations revealed that:

- *The experimenter's physical presence has a marked impact on his* 112
authority. As cited earlier, obedience dropped off sharply when orders were given by telephone. The experimenter could often induce a disobedient subject to go on by returning to the laboratory.
- *Conflicting authority severely paralyzes action.* When two ex- 113
perimenters of equal status, both seated at the command desk, gave incompatible orders, no shocks were delivered past the point of their disagreement.

- *The rebellious action of others severely undermines authority.* In one variation, three teachers (two actors and a real subject) administered a test and shocks. When the two actors disobeyed the experimenter and refused to go beyond a certain shock level, thirty-six of forty subjects joined their disobedient peers and refused as well. 114

Although the experimenter's authority was fragile in some respects, it is also true that he had almost none of the tools used in ordinary command structures. For example, the experimenter did not threaten the subjects with punishment—such as loss of income, community ostracism, or jail—for failure to obey. Neither could he offer incentives. Indeed, we should expect the experimenter's authority to be much less than that of someone like a general, since the experimenter has no power to enforce his imperatives, and since participation in a psychological experiment scarcely evokes the sense of urgency and dedication found in warfare. Despite these limitations, he still managed to command a dismaying degree of obedience. 115

I will cite one final variation of the experiment that depicts a dilemma that is more common in everyday life. The subject was not ordered to pull the lever that shocked the victim, but merely to perform a subsidiary task (administering the word-pair test) while another person administered the shock. In this situation, thirty-seven of forty adults continued to the highest level on the shock generator. Predictably, they excused their behavior by saying that the responsibility belonged to the man who actually pulled the switch. This may illustrate a dangerously typical arrangement in a complex society: it is easy to ignore responsibility when one is only an intermediate link in a chain of action. 116

The problem of obedience is not wholly psychological. The form and shape of society and the way it is developing have much to do with it. There was a time, perhaps, when people were able to give a fully human response to any situation because they were fully absorbed in it as human beings. But as soon as there was a division of labor things changed. Beyond a certain point, the breaking up of society into people carrying out narrow and very special jobs takes away from the human quality of work and life. A person does not get to see the whole situation but only a small part of it, and is thus unable to act without some kind of overall direction. He yields to authority but in doing so is alienated from his own actions. 117

Even Eichmann was sickened when he toured the concentration camps, but he had only to sit at a desk and shuffle papers. At the same time the man in the camp who actually dropped Cyclon-b into 118 the gas chambers was able to justify *his* behavior on the ground that he was only following orders from above. Thus there is a fragmentation of the total human act; no one is confronted with the consequences of his decision to carry out the evil act. The person who assumes responsibility has evaporated. Perhaps this is the most common characteristic of socially organized evil in modern society.

Review Questions

1. Milgram states that obedience is a basic element in the structure of social life. How so?
2. What is the dilemma inherent in obedience to authority?
3. Summarize the obedience experiments.
4. What predictions did experts and lay people make about the experiments before they were conducted? How did these predictions compare with the experimental results?
5. What are Milgram's views regarding the two assumptions bearing on his experiment that (1) people are naturally aggressive and (2) a lunatic, sadistic fringe is responsible for shocking learners to the maximum limit?
6. How do Milgram's findings corroborate Hannah Arendt's thesis about the "banality of evil"?
7. What, according to Milgram, is the "essence of obedience"?
8. How did being an intermediate link in a chain of action affect a subject's willingness to continue with the experiment?
9. In the article's final two paragraphs, Milgram speaks of a "fragmentation of the total human act." To what is he referring?

Discussion and Writing Suggestions

1. "Conservative philosophers argue that the very fabric of society is threatened by disobedience, while humanists stress the primacy of the individual conscience." Develop the arguments of both the conservative and the humanist regarding obedience to authority. Be prepared to debate the ethics of obedience by defending one position or the other.
2. Would you have been glad to have participated in the Milgram experiments? Why or why not?
3. The ethics of Milgram's experimental design came under sharp attack. Diana Baumrind's review of the experiment typifies the criticism; but before you read her work, try to anticipate the objections she raises.
4. Given the general outcome of the experiments, why do you suppose Milgram gives as his first example of a subject's response the German émigré's refusal to continue the electrical shocks?

5. Does the outcome of the experiment upset you in any way? Do you feel the experiment teaches us anything new about human nature?
6. Comment on Milgram's skill as a writer of description. How effectively does he portray his subjects when introducing them? When re-creating their tension in the experiment?
7. Mrs. Braverman said to her husband: "You can call yourself Eichmann." Do you agree with Mrs. Braverman? Explain.
8. Reread paragraphs 29 through 81, the transcript of the experiment in which Mr. Prozi participated. Appreciating that Prozi was debriefed, that is, was assured that no harm came to the learner, imagine what Prozi might have been thinking as he drove home after the experiment. Develop your thoughts into a monologue, written in the first person, with Prozi at the wheel of his car.

REVIEWS OF STANLEY MILGRAM'S *OBEDIENCE TO AUTHORITY*

Many of Milgram's colleagues saluted him for providing that "hard information" about human nature that Doris Lessing speaks of. Others attacked him for violating the rights of his subjects. Still others faulted his experimental design and claimed he could not, with any validity, speculate on life outside the laboratory based on the behavior of his subjects within.

We reproduce something of this debate in the pieces that follow. First, psychologist Richard Herrnstein praises Milgram, acknowledging the subjects' discomfort but arguing that the discomfort of a few is a price worth paying for educating the many. Psychologist Diana Baumrind then excoriates Milgram for "entrapping" his subjects and potentially harming their "self-image or ability to trust adult authorities in the future." In a footnote, we summarize Milgram's response to Baumrind's critique. In a third review, Philip Meyer draws a parallel between Milgram's own behavior as a scientist who was willing (for a "higher" cause) to see his subjects squirm and the behavior of the subjects themselves, who continued to shock innocent victims despite their protests.

As you read, note the ways each writer lays out basic principles on which the critique will rest before building on those principles with arguments for or against Milgram. A critique, as you've learned in Chapter 2, should proceed methodically. The writer should summarize the author's work under review and then examine significant points of that work according to clearly stated principles, or assumptions. To save space, we've deleted the summary of Milgram's experiment in each critique. You can assume that Herrnstein, Baumrind, and Meyer all adequately began their critiques with a neutral, brief recounting of the experiment. As for their providing other elements of an effective critique—we leave it to you to make this determination.

Review of Stanley Milgram's Experiments on Obedience

RICHARD HERRNSTEIN

Richard Herrnstein (b. 1930), a research psychologist at Harvard University, has written numerous books, including I.Q. in the Meritocracy. *He is a regular contributor of articles to professional journals and is currently editor of the* Psychological Bulletin.

. . . No doubt about it, these experiments were a surprise, and a nasty surprise at that. The essence of a major discovery is its capacity to cause a large shift in our beliefs about some part of the world. Milgram's data show us something about the human world that we had failed to grasp before. They show us, not precisely that people are callous, but that they can slip into a frame of mind in which their actions are not entirely their own. Psychologically, it is not they alone who are flipping the switches, but also the institutional authority—the austere scientist in the laboratory coat. The authority is taken to have the right to do what he is doing, by virtue of knowledge or status. Permutations of the basic procedure made it clear that the subjects' obedience depended on a sense of passivity, and that disobedience resulted if the subject was made to feel as if he were acting on his own initiative. Ordinary people will, in fact, not easily engage in brutality on their own. But they will apparently do so if someone else is in charge. 1

The experiments prove decisively that ordinary people can turn into lethal instruments in the hands of an unscrupulous authority. The subjects who obeyed did not appear to be in any way atypical; they were not stupid, maladjusted, psychopathic, or immoral in usual terms. They simply did not apply the usual standards of humanity to their own conduct. Or, rather, the usual standards gave way to a more pressing imperative, the command of authority. The brutality latent in these ordinary people—in all of us—may have little to do with aggression or hostility. In fact hostility was here the humane impulse, for when it turned on the pseudo-experimenter it was a source of disobedience. In Milgram's procedure, and in the many natural settings it more or less mimics, brutality is the awful 2

From R. J. Herrnstein. "Review of Milgram's *Obedience to Authority*." Reprinted from *Commentary*, June 1974, by permission;

corollary of things we rightly prize in human society, like good citizenship or personal loyalty.

Milgram's work is said by some to show how close our society has come to Nazi Germany. But does it really? In Italy, Australia, South Africa, and contemporary Germany, subjects in comparable experiments have been *more,* not less, obedient. No experiment any place has yet produced a negative result to boast about. In the totalitarian countries—from Spain to China—experiments like Milgram's have not been done for they would be considered subversive, as they would indeed be. But just picture how people would behave in Spain or Albania or China, where obedience is taken far more seriously than in permissive, turbulent America. Ironically, we live in a society where disobedience, not obedience, is in vogue, contrary to the fashionable rhetoric of journalists and social commentators. Still, Milgram's American subjects mostly obeyed, and would probably do so even today, ten tumultuous years later. 3

The parallels to Nazi Germany, then, really say something about the quality of the authority rather than the obedience to it. A degree of obedience is the given in human society; enough of it to turn dangerous if the wrong people wield it. The political problem is how to decide who shall be the authority, for it is futile if not dangerous to hope for a society of disobeyers. Consider a contemporary case in point. Federal Judge Gesell recently accused some lawyers of a "Nuremberg mentality." They had defended their client, Egil Krogh, on the grounds that he was obeying the orders of the President, his Commander-in-Chief, when he lied under oath.[1] The judge's view was that Krogh may indeed have been obeying orders, but he should have disobeyed. At other times, people honor their loyal and obedient citizens instead of imprisoning them, and I suspect that Judge Gesell is no different. The judge saw it the way he did because a bitter alienation of many people from our government has fostered the illusion that obedience to authority is itself malevolent. 4

The illusion is palpably false, though the authority may, alas, be malevolent. There is a crucial dilemma here, one that will plague any political scheme that values both social order and individual autonomy. But the horns of the dilemma have never been so clear as they are in the light of Milgram's experiments. On one side, we find that even permissive, individualistic America creates people who can become 5

[1]Egil Krogh headed Richard Nixon's Special Investigative Unit known as the "Plumbers." He was indicted for burglarizing the office of Dr. Fielding, psychiatrist to Daniel Ellsberg. High officials in the Nixon administration wanted to gather and leak to the press embarrassing information on Ellsberg, who had released the *Pentagon Papers* to the *New York Times.* Krogh maintained at his trial that orders to commit the burglary had originated in the White House.

agents of terror. As the weapons of terror become more powerful and more remote from their victims, the dangers of obedience grow. We know that bombardiers in military aircraft suffer little of the conflict and anxiety shown by Milgram's subjects, for they inflict punishment at an even greater distance and they serve an authority with greater license. That horn of the dilemma is much in the news these days. But the other horn is the penalty if we set too high a value on individual conscience and autonomy. The alternative to authority and obedience is anarchy, and history teaches that that is the surest way to chaos and, ultimately, tyranny.

Though he recognizes the alternatives, Milgram's sympathies are 6 libertarian. He wants a more defiant citizenry, a higher percentage of disobeyers to authority. I have no doubt that it would be easy to make people more likely to say no to authority, simply by reducing the penalties for doing so. But the evidence does not suggest that people use only benevolence or moral sensitivity as the criteria for rejecting authority. Think of some real examples. Would it be greed or a higher virtue that would be the main reason for defaulting on taxes if the penalties were reduced? What deserter from the army would fail to claim it was conscience, not cowardice, once conscientious desertion became permissible? Milgram, and no doubt others, would probably answer that reducing the penalties is not enough—that people need to be taught virtue, not just relieved of the hazards of vice. That is fine, but it does not seem like cynicism to insist that the burden of proof falls on those who think they know a way to make people better than they have ever been. I find no proof in this book, or in the contemporary literature of civil disobedience. Milgram's work, brilliant as it is, resolves no dilemmas.

Psychology does not often spawn a finding that is neither trivial, 7 obvious, nor false. Milgram's is the rare exception. The research is well conceived and done with care and skill, even elegance. It was both unexpected and timely, which are virtues that add up to far more than the sum of the parts. Why, then, has the work produced the poles of response? It won Milgram professional recognition and numerous honors, and it was also attacked again and again in the technical literature. The book was reviewed on the front page of the *New York Times Book Review,* an uncommon distinction for an academic work in social science, but the review was a hatchet job by a professor of literature whose distaste for social science was the main message.

Many people, besides the *Times* reviewer, do not like social sci- 8 ence. There are so many of them that I can even sort them into categories: those who dislike it because they believe it tells us nothing they did not know and those who dislike it because it tells us something they did not want to hear. Milgram's work arouses those in the latter category, who typically insist that they belong in the former category. It is one thing to contemplate the banality of evil in the abstract, but something else to learn that the spore will germinate in New Haven [at Yale University] at the prompting of a man in a laboratory coat. The gross discrepancy between what people predicted for the experiment and what others did as subjects is the tangible proof of the findings' power to inform us about ourselves—about our capacity for cruelty and our ignorance of the capacity. Those who continue to insist that the experiment teaches nothing may be relying on ignorance to solve the awful dilemma of authority. It will resolve nothing, of course, but it is no surprise that Milgram's news has driven some heads into the sand.

But that is not the only problem with Milgram's work. Some 9
people, often social scientists themselves, object to the element of deception, especially when it is calculated to produce acute discomfort. This seems to me a valid concern, a secondary dilemma arising from the fact of the research itself rather than from its findings. To learn how people behave under duress or danger, the researcher dissembles, for he cannot subject people to real-life hazards. If there is to be experimentation on people in social settings, there is therefore likely to be deception and manipulation. It is an unpleasant prospect, and easy to reject. But, then, consider Milgram's experiments. Deception and manipulation led to a remarkable addition to our knowledge of the perils of authority. Knowledge like that comes hard and slow. Can we afford to prohibit further discoveries of that caliber and relevance?

Some people answer the question with a dogmatic yes, setting 10
the highest priority on individual privacy at the risk of continuing ignorance. That happens not to be my view. I value privacy but worry about ignorance. A small, temporary loss of a few people's comfort and privacy seems a bearable price for a large reduction in ignorance, but I can see, as can Milgram, how delicate a judgment this implies. Even so, I hope there are other experiments like Milgram's coming along—experiments that will teach us about ourselves, with no more than the minimum necessary deception and discomfort, elegantly and economically conducted. It should not be easy to do experiments like Milgram's—for they should not be done casually—but it should be possible, and, needless to say, the experimenter should not be held in contempt if the outcome is unexpected or uncomfortable. The goal of science is *news*, not *good* news.

Review Questions

1. Why does Herrnstein call "palpably false" the sentiment that any kind of obedience to authority is malevolent?

2. What is the "crucial dilemma" that Herrnstein discusses?
3. What does Herrnstein see as the alternative to obedience to authority? What is his view of the alternative?
4. How does Herrnstein account for the varying critical reception of Milgram's work?
5. What is Herrnstein's view of the deception practiced in the experiment?

Discussion and Writing Suggestions

1. Herrnstein says that it is possible that the "perfectionist dogma" of human society—that we are, basically, decent, caring, and humane people—may be giving way to humbler expectations. Is Milgram's work, after all, a surprise? If so, what are your assumptions about human nature? If not, what are you conceding about our behavior? How do your views on the future of the race depend on your answers?
2. "In Milgram's procedure, and in the many natural settings it more or less mimics, brutality is the awful corollary of things we rightly prize in human society, like good citizenship or personal loyalty." What does Herrnstein mean?
3. Is it possible to set too high a value on individual conscience and autonomy? What are the dangers of refusing to compromise one's autonomy?
4. Herrnstein says that "Milgram's work, brilliant as it is, resolves no dilemmas" about the nature of authority. In an essay, discuss the dilemmas that need resolving (see Review Question 2). What solution would you propose?

Review of Stanley Milgram's Experiments on Obedience

DIANA BAUMRIND

Diana Baumrind is a psychologist who when writing this review worked at the Institute of Human Development, University of California, Berkeley. The review appeared in American Psychologist *shortly after Milgram published the results of his first experiments in 1963.*

From Diana Baumrind, "Some Thoughts on Ethics of Research: After Reading Milgram's 'Behavioral Study of Obedience,' " *American Psychologist* 19, 1964, pp. 421–423.

. . . The dependent, obedient attitude assumed by most subjects in 1
the experimental setting is appropriate to that situation. The "game" is defined by the experimenter and he makes the rules. By volunteering, the subject agrees implicitly to assume a posture of trust and obedience. While the experimental conditions leave him exposed, the subject has the right to assume that his security and self-esteem will be protected.

There are other professional situations in which one member— 2
the patient or client—expects help and protection from the other—the physician or psychologist. But the interpersonal relationship between experimenter and subject additionally has unique features which are likely to provoke initial anxiety in the subject. The laboratory is unfamiliar as a setting and the rules of behavior ambiguous compared to a clinician's office. Because of the anxiety and passivity generated by the setting, the subject is more prone to behave in an obedient, suggestible manner in the laboratory than elsewhere. Therefore, the laboratory is not the place to study degree of obedience or suggestibility, as a function of a particular experimental condition, since the base line for these phenomena as found in the laboratory is probably much higher than in most other settings. Thus experiments in which the relationship to the experimenter as an authority is used as an independent condition are imperfectly designed for the same reason that they are prone to injure the subjects involved. They disregard the special quality of trust and obedience with which the subject appropriately regards the experimenter.

Other phenomena which present ethical decisions, unlike those 3
mentioned above, *can* be reproduced successfully in the laboratory. Failure experience, conformity to peer judgment, and isolation are among such phenomena. In these cases we can expect the experimenter to take whatever measures are necessary to prevent the subject from leaving the laboratory more humiliated, insecure, alienated, or hostile than when he arrived. To guarantee that an especially sensitive subject leaves a stressful experimental experience in the proper state sometimes requires special clinical training. But usually an attitude of compassion, respect, gratitude, and common sense will suffice, and no amount of clinical training will substitute. The subject has the right to expect that the psychologist with whom he is interacting has some concern for his welfare, and the personal attributes and professional skill to express his good will effectively.

Unfortunately, the subject is not always treated with the respect 4
he deserves. It has become more commonplace in sociopsychological laboratory studies to manipulate, embarrass, and discomfort subjects. At times the insult to the subject's sensibilities extends to the journal reader when the results are reported. Milgram's (1963) study is a case in point. The following is Milgram's abstract of his experiment:

> This article describes a procedure for the study of destructive obedience in the laboratory. It consists of ordering a naive S to administer increasingly more severe punishment to a victim in the context of a learning experiment.[1] Punishment is administered by means of a shock generator with 30 graded switches ranging from Slight Shock to Danger: Severe Shock. The victim is a confederate of E. The primary dependent variable is the maximum shock the S is willing to administer before he refuses to continue further.[2] 26 Ss obeyed the experimental commands fully, and administered the highest shock on the generator. 14 Ss broke off the experiment at some point after the victim protested and refused to provide further answers. The procedure created extreme levels of nervous tension in some Ss. Profuse sweating, trembling, and stuttering were typical expressions of this emotional disturbance. One unexpected sign of tension—yet to be explained—was the regular occurrence of nervous laughter, which in some Ss developed into uncontrollable seizures. The variety of interesting behavioral dynamics observed in the experiment, the reality of the situation for the S, and the possibility of parametric variation[3] within the framework of the procedure point to the fruitfulness of further study [p. 371].

5 The detached, objective manner in which Milgram reports the emotional disturbance suffered by his subjects contrasts sharply with his graphic account of that disturbance. Following are two other quotes describing the effects on his subjects of the experimental conditions:

> I observed a mature and initially poised businessman enter the laboratory smiling and confident. Within 20 minutes he was reduced to a twitching, stuttering wreck, who was rapidly approaching a point of nervous collapse. He constantly pulled on his earlobe, and twisted his hands. At one point he pushed his fist into his forehead and muttered: "Oh God, let's stop it." And yet he continued to respond to every word of the experimenter, and obeyed to the end [p. 377].
>
> In a large number of cases the degree of tension reached extremes that are rarely seen in sociopsychological laboratory studies. Subjects were observed to sweat, tremble, stutter, bite their lips, groan, and dig their fingernails into their flesh. These were characteristic rather than exceptional responses to the experiment.
>
> One sign of tension was the regular occurrence of nervous laughing fits. Fourteen of the 40 subjects showed definite signs of nervous laugh-

[1]In psychological experiments, *S* is an abbreviation for *subject; E* is an abbreviation for *experimenter.*

[2]In the context of a psychological experiment, a *dependent variable* is a behavior that is expected to change as a result of changes in the experimental procedure.

[3]*Parametric variation* is a statistical term that describes the degree to which information based on data for one experiment can be applied to data for a slightly different experiment.

> ter and smiling. The laughter seemed entirely out of place, even bizarre. Full-blown, uncontrollable seizures were observed for 3 subjects. On one occasion we observed a seizure so violently convulsive that it was necessary to call a halt to the experiment . . . [p. 375].

Milgram does state that,

> After the interview, procedures were undertaken to assure that the subject would leave the laboratory in a state of well being. A friendly reconciliation was arranged between the subject and the victim, and an effort was made to reduce any tensions that arose as a result of the experiment [p. 374].

It would be interesting to know what sort of procedures could dissipate the type of emotional disturbance just described. In view of the effects on subjects, traumatic to a degree which Milgram himself considers nearly unprecedented in sociopsychological experiments, his casual assurance that these tensions were dissipated before the subject left the laboratory is unconvincing.

What could be the rational basis for such a posture of in- 6
difference? Perhaps Milgram supplies the answer himself when he partially explains the subject's destructive obedience as follows, "Thus they assume that the discomfort caused the victim is momentary, while the scientific gains resulting from the experiment are enduring [p. 378]." Indeed such a rationale might suffice to justify the means used to achieve his end if that end were of inestimable value to humanity or were not itself transformed by the means by which it was attained.

The behavioral psychologist is not in as good a position to objec- 7
tify his faith in the significance of his work as medical colleagues at points of breakthrough. His experimental situations are not sufficiently accurate models of real-life experience; his sampling techniques are seldom of a scope which would justify the meaning with which he would like to endow his results; and these results are hard to reproduce by colleagues with opposing theoretical views. Unlike the Sabin vaccine,[4] for example, the concrete benefit to humanity of his particular piece of work, no matter how competently handled, cannot justify the risk that real harm will be done to the subject. I am not speaking of physical discomfort, inconvenience, or experimental deception per se, but of permanent harm, however slight. I do regard the emotional disturbance described by Milgram as potentially harmful because it could easily effect an alteration in the subject's self-image or ability to trust adult authorities in the future. It is potentially

[4]The Sabin vaccine provides immunization against polio.

harmful to a subject to commit, in the course of an experiment, acts which he himself considers unworthy, particularly when he has been entrapped into committing such acts by an individual he has reason to trust. The subject's personal responsibility for his actions is not erased because the experimenter reveals to him the means which he used to stimulate these actions. The subject realizes that he would have hurt the victim if the current were on. The realization that he also made a fool of himself by accepting the experimental set results in additional loss of self-esteem. Moreover, the subject finds it difficult to express his anger outwardly after the experimenter in a self-acceptant but friendly manner reveals the hoax.

A fairly intense corrective interpersonal experience is indicated 8
wherein the subject admits and accepts his responsibility for his own actions, and at the same time gives vent to his hurt and anger at being fooled. Perhaps an experience as distressing as the one described by Milgram can be integrated by the subject, provided that careful thought is given to the matter. The propriety of such experimentation is still in question even if such a reparational experience were forthcoming. Without it I would expect a naive, sensitive subject to remain deeply hurt and anxious for some time, and a sophisticated, cynical subject to become even more alienated and distrustful.

In addition the experimental procedure used by Milgram does not 9
appear suited to the objectives of the study because it does not take into account the special quality of the set which the subject has in the experimental situation. Milgram is concerned with a very important problem, namely, the social consequences of destructive obedience. He says,

> Gas chambers were built, death camps were guarded, daily quotas of corpses were produced with the same efficiency as the manufacture of appliances. These inhumane policies may have originated in the mind of a single person, but they could only be carried out on a massive scale if a very large number of persons obeyed orders [p. 371].

But the parallel between authority-subordinate relationships in Hitler's Germany and in Milgram's laboratory is unclear. In the former situation the SS man or member of the German Officer Corps, when obeying orders to slaughter, had no reason to think of his superior officer as benignly disposed towards himself or their victims. The victims were perceived as subhuman and not worthy of consideration. The subordinate officer was an agent in a great cause. He did not need to feel guilt or conflict because within his frame of reference he was acting rightly.

It is obvious from Milgram's own descriptions that most of his subjects were concerned about their victims and did trust the experimenter, and that their distressful conflict was generated in part by the consequences of these two disparate but appropriate attitudes. Their distress may have resulted from shock at what the experimenter was doing to them as well as from what they thought they were doing to their victims. In any case there is not a convincing parallel between the phenomena studied by Milgram and destructive obedience as that concept would apply to the subordinate-authority relationship demonstrated in Hitler Germany. If the experiments were conducted "outside of New Haven and without any visible ties to the university," I would still question their validity on similar although not identical grounds. In addition, I would question the representativeness of a sample of subjects who would voluntarily participate within a noninstitutional setting. 10

In summary, the experimental objectives of the psychologist are seldom incompatible with the subject's ongoing state of well being, provided that the experimenter is willing to take the subject's motives and interests into consideration when planning his methods and correctives. Section 4b in *Ethical Standards of Psychologists* (APA, undated) reads in part: 11

> Only when a problem is significant and can be investigated in no other way is the psychologist justified in exposing human subjects to emotional stress or other possible harm. In conducting such research, the psychologist must seriously consider the possibility of harmful aftereffects, and should be prepared to remove them as soon as permitted by the design of the experiment. Where the danger of serious aftereffects exists, research should be conducted only when the subjects or their responsible agents are fully informed of this possibility and volunteer nevertheless [p. 12].

From the subject's point of view procedures which involve loss of dignity, self-esteem, and trust in rational authority are probably most harmful in the long run and require the most thoughtfully planned reparations, if engaged in at all. The public image of psychology as a profession is highly related to our own actions, and some of these actions are changeworthy. It is important that as research psychologists we protect our ethical sensibilities rather than adapt our personal standards to include as appropriate the kind of indignities to which Milgram's subjects were exposed. I would not like to see experiments such as Milgram's proceed unless the subjects were fully informed of the dangers of serious aftereffects and his correctives were clearly shown to be effective in restoring their state of well being.[5]

---

[5]Stanley Milgram replied to Baumrind's critique in a lengthy critique of his own. [From Stanley Milgram. "Issues in the Study of Obedience: A Reply to Baumrind," *American Psychologist* 19, 1964, pp. 848–851. Copyright 1964 by the American Psychologist Association. Reprinted by permission of the publisher and author.] Following are his principal points:

- Milgram believed that the experimental findings were in large part responsible for Baumrind's criticism. He writes:

> Is not Baumrind's criticism based as much on the unanticipated findings as on the method? The findings were that some subjects performed in what appeared to be a shockingly immoral way. If, instead, every one of the subjects had broken off at "slight shock," or at the first sign of the learner's discomfort, the results would have been pleasant, and reassuring, and who would protest?

- Milgram objected to Baumrind's assertion that those who participated in the experiment would have trouble justifying their behavior. Milgram conducted follow-up questionnaires. The results, summarized in Table 1, indicate that 84 percent of the subjects claimed they were pleased to have been a part of the experiment.

TABLE 1 ***Excerpt from Questionnaire Used in a Follow-up Study of the Obedience Research***

NOW THAT I HAVE READ THE REPORT, AND ALL THINGS CONSIDERED . . .	DEFIANT	OBEDIENT	ALL
1. I am very glad to have been in the experiment	40.0%	47.8%	43.5%
2. I am glad to have been in the experiment	43.8%	35.7%	40.2%
3. I am neither sorry nor glad to have been in the experiment	15.3%	14.8%	15.1%
4. I am sorry to have been in the experiment	0.8%	0.7%	0.8%
5. I am very sorry to have been in the experiment	0.0%	1.0%	0.5%

Note—Ninety-two percent of the subjects returned the questionnaire. The characteristics of the nonrespondents were checked against the respondents. They differed from the respondents only with regard to age; younger people were overrepresented in the nonresponding group.

- Baumrind objected that studies of obedience cannot meaningfully be carried out in a laboratory setting, since the obedience occurred in a context where it was appropriate. Milgram's response: "I reject Baumrind's argument that the observed obedience does not count because it occurred where it is appropriate. That is precisely why it *does* count. A soldier's obedience is no less meaningful because it occurs in a pertinent military context."
- Milgram concludes his critique in this way: "If there is a moral to be learned from the obedience study, it is that every man must be responsible for his own actions. This author accepts full responsibility for the design and execution of the study. Some people may feel it should not have been done. I disagree and accept the burden of their judgment."

REFERENCES

American Psychological Association. Ethical standards of psychologists: A summary of ethical principles. Washington, D.C.: APA, undated.

Milgram, S. Behavioral study of obedience. *J. Abnorm. Soc. Psychol.* 67, 1963, pp. 371–378.

Review Questions

1. Why might a subject volunteer for an experiment? Why do subjects typically assume a dependent, obedient attitude?
2. Why is a laboratory not a suitable setting for a study of obedience?
3. For what reasons does Baumrind feel that the Milgram experiment was potentially harmful?
4. For what reasons does Baumrind question the relationship between Milgram's findings and the obedient behavior of subordinates in Nazi Germany?

Discussion and Writing Suggestions

1. Baumrind contends that the Milgram experiment is imperfectly designed for two reasons: (1) The laboratory is not the place to test obedience; (2) Milgram disregarded the trust that subjects usually show an experimenter. Do you agree with Baumrind's objections? Do you find them equally valid?
2. Baumrind states that the ethical procedures of the experiment keep it from having significant value. In this respect, she directly disagrees with Richard Herrnstein (pp. 184–87), who justifies the experimental procedures by claiming that the momentary discomfort of a few subjects is worth adding to human knowledge. With whom do you agree?
3. Do you agree with Baumrind that the subjects were "entrapped" into committing unworthy acts?
4. Assume the identity of a participant in Milgram's experiment who obeyed the experimenter by shocking the learner with the maximum voltage. You have just returned from the lab, and your spouse asks you about your day. Write the conversation between you and your spouse.

Review of Stanley Milgram's Experiments on Obedience

PHILIP MEYER

Philip Edward Meyer (b. 1930) began his career as a journalist for the Topeka Daily Capital *in 1954, working subsequently for the* Miami

From Philip Meyer. "If Hitler Asked You to Electrocute a Stranger, Would You? (Probably)." First appeared in *Esquire*, 1970. Reprinted courtesy of the Hearst Corporation, 1990.

Herald *(1958–62) and as correspondent in Washington for Knight-Rider newspapers (1962–78). In 1966, Meyer was named a Nieman Fellow at Harvard University and a year later shared a Pultizer Prize for his reporting of the Detroit riots. He is a coauthor of* Precision Journalism *(1979),* To Keep the Republic *(1975), and* Editors, Publishers and Newspaper Ethics *(1983). The present selection appeared in a piece in* Esquire *(February 1970), "If Hitler Asked You to Electrocute a Stranger, Would You? (Probably)."*

. . . The first question [concerning Milgram's work] is this: Should we really be surprised and alarmed that people obey? Wouldn't it be even more alarming if they all refused to obey? Without obedience to a relevant ruling authority there could not be a civil society. And without a civil society, as Thomas Hobbes pointed out in the seventeenth century, we would live in a condition of war, "of every man against every other man," and life would be "solitary, poor, nasty, brutish and short." 1

In the middle of one of Stanley Milgram's lectures at C.U.N.Y. recently, some mini-skirted undergraduates started whispering and giggling in the back of the room. He told them to cut it out. Since he was the relevant authority in that time and that place, they obeyed, and most people in the room were glad that they obeyed. 2

This was not, of course, a conflict situation. Nothing in the coeds' social upbringing made it a matter of conscience for them to whisper and giggle. But a case can be made that in a conflict situation it is all the more important to obey. Take the case of war, for example. Would we really want a situation in which every participant in a war, direct or indirect—from front-line soldiers to the people who sell coffee and cigarettes to employees at the Concertina barbed-wire factory in Kansas—stops and consults his conscience before each action? It is asking for an awful lot of mental strain and anguish from an awful lot of people. The value of having civil order is that one can do his duty, or whatever interests him, or whatever seems to benefit him at the moment, and leave the agonizing to others. When Francis Gary Powers was being tried by a Soviet military tribunal after his U-2 spy plane was shot down, the presiding judge asked if he had thought about the possibility that his flight might have provoked a war. Powers replied with Hobbesian clarity: "The people who sent me should think of these things. My job was to carry out orders. I do not think it was my responsibility to make such decisions." 3

It was not his responsibility. And it is quite possible that if everyone felt responsible for each of the ultimate consequences of his own tiny contributions to complex chains of events, then society simply would not work. Milgram, fully conscious of the moral and social implications of his research, believes that people should feel 4 responsible for their actions. If someone else had invented the experiment, and if he had been the naïve subject, he feels certain that he would have been among the disobedient minority.

"There is no very good solution to this," he admits, thoughtfully. 5
"To simply and categorically say that you won't obey authority may resolve your personal conflict, but it creates more problems for society which may be more serious in the long run. But I have no doubt that to disobey is the proper thing to do in this [the laboratory] situation. It is the only reasonable value judgment to make."

The conflict between the need to obey the relevant ruling author- 6
ity and the need to follow your conscience becomes sharpest if you insist on living by an ethical system based on a rigid code—a code that seeks to answer all questions in advance of their being raised. Code ethics cannot solve the obedience problem. Stanley Milgram seems to be a situation ethicist, and situation ethics does offer a way out: When you feel conflict, you examine the situation and then make a choice among the competing evils. You may act with a presumption in favor of obedience, but reserve the possibility that you will disobey whenever obedience demands a flagrant and outrageous affront to conscience. This, by the way, is the philosophical position of many who resist the draft. In World War II, they would have fought. Vietnam is a different, an outrageously different, situation.

Life can be difficult for the situation ethicist, because he does not 7
see the world in straight lines, while the social system too often assumes such a God-given, squared-off structure. If your moral code includes an injunction against all war, you may be deferred as a conscientious objector. If you merely oppose this particular war, you may not be deferred.

Stanley Milgram has his problems, too. He believes that in the 8
laboratory situation, he would not have shocked Mr. Wallace.[1] His professional critics reply that in his real-life situation he has done the equivalent. He has placed innocent and naïve subjects under great emotional strain and pressure in selfish obedience to his quest for knowledge. When you raise this issue with Milgram, he has an answer ready. There is, he explains patiently, a critical difference between his naïve subjects and the man in the electric chair. The man in the electric chair (in the mind of the naïve subject) is helpless, strapped in. But the naïve subject is free to go at any time.

Immediately after he offers this distinction, Milgram anticipates 9
the objection.

"It's quite true," he says, "that this is almost a philosophic posi- 10

[1]*Mr. Wallace* was the name of the learner (that is, the experimenter's confederate) in a number of the obedience experiments.

tion, because we have learned that some people are psychologically incapable of disengaging themselves. But that doesn't relieve them of the moral responsibility."

The parallel is exquisite. "The tension problem was unexpected," says Milgram in his defense. But he went on anyway. The naïve subjects didn't expect the screaming protests from the strapped-in learner. But they went on. 11

"I had to make a judgment," says Milgram. "I had to ask myself, was this harming the person or not? My judgment is that it was not. Even in the extreme cases, I wouldn't say that permanent damage results." 12

Sound familiar? "The shocks may be painful," the experimenter kept saying, "but they're not dangerous." 13

After the series of experiments was completed, Milgram sent a report of the results to his subjects and a questionnaire, asking whether they were glad or sorry to have been in the experiment. Eighty-three and seven-tenths percent said they were glad and only 1.3 percent were sorry; 15 percent were neither sorry nor glad. However, Milgram could not be sure at the time of the experiment that only 1.3 percent would be sorry. 14

Kurt Vonnegut, Jr., put one paragraph in the preface to *Mother Night*, in 1966, which pretty much says it for the people with their fingers on the shock-generator switches, for you and me, and maybe even for Milgram. "If I'd been born in Germany," Vonnegut said, "I suppose I would have *been* a Nazi, bopping Jews and gypsies and Poles around, leaving boots sticking out of snowbanks, warming myself with my sweetly virtuous insides. So it goes." 15

Just so. One thing that happened to Milgram back in New Haven during the days of the experiment was that he kept running into people he'd watched from behind the one-way glass. It gave him a funny feeling, seeing those people going about their everyday business in New Haven and knowing what they would do to Mr. Wallace if ordered to. Now that his research results are in and you've thought about it, you can get this funny feeling too. You don't need one-way glass. A glance in your own mirror may serve just as well. 16

Review Questions

1. What was Gary Powers's response to a Soviet judge's question about the possibility of his U-2 flight's having provoked a war?
2. What are code ethics? Why can they not solve the obedience problem?

Discussion and Writing Suggestions

1. Meyer opens his discussion with a question: "Should we really be surprised and alarmed that people obey?" What's your answer?

2. Do you agree with Meyer (paragraph 3) that "it is asking for an awful lot of mental strain and anguish from an awful lot of people" to have everyone associated with the military stop and examine their consciences before following orders?
3. "It is quite possible that if everyone felt responsible for each of the ultimate consequences of his own tiny contributions to complex chains of events, then society simply would not work." Your comments?
4. In paragraphs 8 through 13, Meyer draws a parallel relationship that can be expressed as follows: The subject exists in a relationship with the learner (in the experiment) in the same way that Milgram exists in a relationship with the subject. Explain this proposed parallel relationship and comment on its validity.
5. "You don't need a one-way glass. A glance in your own mirror may serve just as well." Use Meyer's final lines as a point of departure for a dialogue between you and the image of yourself in the mirror. Would you or wouldn't you shock the innocent victim? Assume in the dialogue that the image in the mirror takes one position and you take the other. See what develops—in four or five pages.

My Buttoned-Down Students

LARRY J. CROCKETT

Thus far, the readings on obedience to authority may not have touched directly on your life as a student. But with the present article and those that follow, the debate shifts in whole or in part to college campuses. First comes Larry J. Crockett, a teacher of philosophy who laments the compliant behavior of his students. They seem too willing, he says, too eager to record his words as truth. No one challenges him in lectures anymore, no one engages him in spirited debates. Crockett sees students who are eager to move safely and securely through the system so they can land that first big job in the working world.

Note how Crockett's appeal is rooted in reflections on his own experience. No scientific claim to "hard information" is being made here, as in Milgram. Still, Crockett challenges us just as Milgram does. While reading, consider the state of debate in your own classes. Do you observe students disagreeing with their professors? Do you see a tendency to trust or distrust authority in the classroom? In your view, to what extent is disobedience to authority acceptable, even desirable, in education? And

"My Buttoned-Down Students" by Larry J. Crockett from *Newsweek*, October 20, 1984. Reprinted by permission of the author.

finally, do you see a relationship between obedience in *the classroom and obedience in the world outside?*

Larry J. Crockett teaches philosophy at Metropolitan State University in St. Paul, Minnesota. His essay appeared in the "My Turn" column in Newsweek *magazine.*

I watch my students file promptly into the classroom. I notice that many of the men model conservative coats and ties and that a surprising number of the women feature dress-for-success business attire. The dogeared paperback texts suggest that they have read their lessons carefully. I have no difficulty gaining their attention; my first few words silence the last sounds of their preclass Babel. 1

As I work my way through a Philosophy 32285 lecture on the advent of intelligent robots and the implications for human self-understanding, I hear pens tirelessly codifying each and every point I make, sometimes word for word. Many note-pages later, I pause for a breath, a sip of coffee, before I ask, "Are there any questions?" 2

Too often, for my money, no questions are asked or they prove to be points of minor clarification. Rarely is there a spirited challenge, a probing question about my general interpretation of things. Often, I find, the only way to elicit dissent is to suggest that I talk too much. They seem to take what I say as, simply, the truth. It would be intoxicating if it weren't so worrisome. 3

Debate: I teach at two colleges, one an upper-division state university for working adults and the other a major research university. I teach philosophy and religious studies. It is true that scholars in these two areas have a difficult time agreeing what the two disciplines are, what should be studied and what counts as achievement. It is sometimes observed, for example, that the only thing two philosophers can agree on is the incompetence of a third philosopher. 4

Still, there is virtually universal agreement that questions and challenges are eminently in order, that nothing should be taken for granted, that there are finally no such things as authoritative answers and sacrosanct doctrines. The subjects I teach, in other words, subsist on well-formed questions and substantial debate. 5

What I like to see in my students, as a result, is an eagerness to challenge accepted beliefs and traditional doctrines. I like to see what the late Jacob Bronowski called "a certain ragamuffin, barefoot irreverence" toward what a text declares or what a teacher proclaims. Instead, all too often, what I get these days is assiduous reverence. 6

Oh, I'll grant that they can replay quite nicely on tests what I teach and what the book says. In fact, their mastery of "the facts" is frequently better than my own. But usually my students shy away from taking the text or me on in genuine academic debate and dia- 7 logue. Frankly, it almost makes me view the riotous anarchy of Berkeley in the 1960s as the Golden Age of Academia.

Passion: I admit that, intellectually, my peers and I were born in the chaos of the 1960s and the Vietnam War rebellion. Shunning the two major parties as hopelessly compromised, we flirted with the Students for a Democratic Society—which proved interested mainly in undemocratic tactics. We assumed that authorities, teachers included, were telling lies until they proved they were speaking truthfully. We supposed that disciplines other than leftist politics, situation ethics and radical economics were most likely a "cop-out." All too often, in challenging everything, we substituted passion for reason, ideology for scholarship and cynicism for competence. 8

Yet in the heady chaos of that time, I believe, we did learn that truth is a scarce commodity. Based on experience with Robert McNamara's "whiz kids" at the Pentagon, we learned that the chief difference between an expert and a novice is that the mistakes of the former are more interesting—and frequently more catastrophic—than those of the latter. We learned, in short, the value of a healthy irreverence. 9

Of course, ours was the inexpensive rebellion of the affluent and the economically secure. Maturing in the years of the Kennedy-Johnson economic expansion, we could afford to question traditional values, to indulge in anti-institutional and anti-business histrionics. It never occurred to us to wonder whether jobs would be available—even if we found them worthy of our attention. 10

Today's students, by contrast, have matured in the unsettling environment of double-digit unemployment and inflation. Coming of age during the Carter-Reagan recession, they rightly worry whether they'll get the jobs they want. Mindful that the United States is undergoing profound changes by moving from a manufacturing to an information-and-service economy, they believe that they must play by the rules in order to secure a place in the new economic order. So they appear at the door of my classroom, freshly scrubbed, hair trimmed, viewing me and my course as one more precarious step along the slippery path to employment. 11

Serious: In so many ways, my students look and sound like young Republicans, eager to embrace large corporations and tax shelters. I suspect that they will vote that way this year in large numbers. It will be a rich irony indeed if Reagan is re-elected,[1] and the economic expansion that might follow ushers in a time when ragamuffin irreverence becomes feasible again. Perhaps what this middle-aged, former radical of a teacher should do is to follow the 12

[1]Ronald Reagan was, indeed, elected to a second term.

lead of his students—so that future students can again ask the probing questions and pose the fundamental challenges that constitute the life blood of serious academic inquiry.

Review Questions

1. How does Crockett respond to having students who accept his views?
2. What common assumptions are shared by the subjects that Crockett teaches?
3. Why does Crockett come close to viewing the "riotous anarchy of Berkeley in the 1960s as the Golden Age of Academia"?
4. What are the dangers of having a passionate commitment to a cause, according to Crockett?
5. What relationship exists between economic well-being and a healthy irreverence among students?

Discussion and Writing Suggestions

1. Do you agree with Crockett's thesis about the value of healthy irreverence?
2. Consider the various courses you take. In how many, and under what circumstances, do you find yourself and your peers demonstrating a healthy irreverence?
3. Argue that students on your campus are not irreverent enough. Then argue that they are too irreverent. Which argument is the more compelling?
4. In paragraph 11, Crockett offers his explanation for student compliance these days. Do you find the explanation an accurate one? Explain.
5. How do Crockett's students seem the perfect candidates for succumbing to groupthink later in life, in a corporate environment?
6. Crockett concludes his essay with an ironic suggestion. Do you have any sense that he will follow up on it? Explain.
7. For the moment, assume the voice and identity of a parent. Your son or daughter is off to college. Write a letter of advice explaining the extent to which he or she should adopt an irreverent posture in class discussions.

The Education of a Torturer

JANICE GIBSON
MIKA HARITOS-FATOUROS

This article provides an example of the way knowledge is constructed in the social sciences. In 1963, Stanley Milgram published the results of his experiments and speculated on the psychological mechanisms that allow people to obey the orders of a malevolent authority. In 1986, two other psychologists examined these proposed psychological mechanisms and applied them to a related, though somewhat different, set of behaviors: prolonged, systematic torture. Gibson and Haritos-Fatouros were interested in the process by which individuals are taught to become torturers. Were the same psychological mechanisms at work in real-life torturers as in the subjects who shocked learners in Milgram's experiments? No, conclude the researchers, who then altered and extended Milgram's theories to account for new facts. Although twenty-three years separated the work of Milgram (now deceased) and Gibson and Haritos-Fatouros, the three scholars have participated in a written conversation through which they've constructed and extended knowledge. It seems likely, in the years to come, that other researchers will conduct their own studies and take up the conversation again.

In one crucial and chilling respect, Gibson and Haritos-Fatouros agree with Milgram: It is ordinary *people, not psychopaths, who become the Eichmanns of history. You may be fascinated to learn that the authors include college students as perfectly suitable candidates for becoming torturers. In fact, they say, any one of us could systematically inflict pain on another, given the right (i.e., a particularly brutalizing) set of circumstances. Chilling as well is the observation that college fraternities draft and indoctrinate pledges in much the same way that the Greek military did torturers. (See the quotation from Gibson and Haritos-Fatouros in this chapter's introductory essay.)*

Janice T. Gibson teaches educational and developmental psychology at the University of Pittsburgh. Mika Haritos-Fatouros is dean of the School of Philosophy and teaches clinical psychology at the University of the Thessaloniki in Greece.

Torture—for whatever purpose and in whatever name—requires a torturer, an individual responsible for planning and causing pain to others. "A man's hands are shackled behind him, his eyes blindfolded," wrote Argentine journalist Jacobo Timerman about his torture by Argentine army extremists. "No one says a word. Blows are showered. . . . [He is] stripped, doused with water, tied. . . . And the application of electric shocks begins. It's impossible to shout—you howl." The governments of at least 90 countries use similar methods to torture people all over the world, Amnesty International reports. 1

What kind of person can behave so monstrously to another human being? A sadist or a sexual deviant? Someone with an authoritarian upbringing or who was abused by parents? A disturbed personality affected somehow by hereditary characteristics? 2

On the contrary, the Nazis who tortured and killed millions during World War II "weren't sadists or killers by nature," Hannah 3

Arendt reported in her book *Eichmann in Jerusalem*. Many studies of Nazi behavior concluded that monstrous acts, despite their horrors, were often simply a matter of faithful bureaucrats slavishly following orders.

In a 1976 study, University of Florida psychologist Molly Harrower asked 15 Rorschach experts to examine inkblot test reports from Adolph Eichmann, Rudolf Hess, Hermann Goering and five other Nazi war criminals, made just before their trials at Nuremberg. She also sent the specialists Rorschach reports from eight Americans, some with well-adjusted personalities and some who were severely disturbed, without revealing the individual's identities. The experts were unable to distinguish the Nazis from the Americans and judged an equal number of both to be well-adjusted. The horror that emerges is the likelihood that torturers are not freaks; they are ordinary people. 4

Obedience to what we call the "authority of violence" often plays an important role in pushing ordinary people to commit cruel, violent and even fatal acts. During wartime, for example, soldiers will follow orders to kill unarmed civilians. Here, we will look at the way obedience and other factors combine to produce willing torturers. 5

Twenty-five years ago, the late psychologist Stanley Milgram demonstrated convincingly that people unlikely to be cruel in everyday life will administer pain if they are told to by someone in authority. In a famous experiment, Milgram had men wearing laboratory coats direct average American adults to inflict a series of electric shocks on other people. No real shocks were given and the "victims" were acting, but the people didn't know this. They were told that the purpose of the study was to measure the effects of punishment on learning. Obediently, 65 percent of them used what they thought were dangerously high levels of shocks when the experimenter told them to. While they were less likely to administer these supposed shocks as they were moved closer to their victims, almost one-third of them continued to shock when they were close enough to touch. 6

This readiness to torture is not limited to Americans. Following Milgram's lead, other researchers found that people of all ages, from a wide range of countries, were willing to shock others even when they had nothing to gain by complying with the command or nothing to lose by refusing it. So long as someone else, an authority figure, was responsible for the final outcome of the experiment, almost no one absolutely refused to administer shocks. Each study also found, as Milgram had, that some people would give shocks even when the decision was left up to them. 7

Milgram proposed that the reasons people obey or disobey authority fall into three categories. The first is personal history: family or 8 school backgrounds that encourage obedience or defiance. The second, which he called "binding," is made up of ongoing experiences that make people feel comfortable when they obey authority. Strain, the third category, consists of bad feelings from unpleasant experiences connected with obedience. Milgram argued that when the binding factors are more powerful than the strain of cooperating, people will do as they are told. When the strain is greater, they are more likely to disobey.

This may explain short-term obedience in the laboratory, but it doesn't explain prolonged patterns of torture during wartime or under some political regimes. Repeatedly, torturers in Argentina and elsewhere performed acts that most of us consider repugnant, and in time this should have placed enough strain on them to prevent their obedience. It didn't. Nor does Milgram's theory explain undirected cruel or violent acts, which occur even when no authority orders them. For this, we have developed a more comprehensive learning model; for torture, we discovered, can be taught. 9

We studied the procedures used to train Greek military police as torturers during that country's military regime from 1967 through 1974. We examined the official testimonies of 21 former soldiers in the ESA (Army Police Corps) given at their 1975 criminal trials in Athens; in addition, Haritos-Fatouros conducted in-depth interviews with 16 of them after their trials. In many cases, these men had been convicted and had completed prison sentences. They were all leading normal lives when interviewed. One was a university graduate, five were graduates of higher technical institutes, nine had completed at least their second year of high school and only one had no more than a primary school education. 10

All of these men had been drafted, first into regular military service and then into specialized units that required servicemen to torture prisoners. We found no record of delinquent or disturbed behavior before their military service. However, we did find several features of the soldiers' training that helped to turn them into willing and able torturers. 11

The initial screening for torturers was primarily based on physical strength and "appropriate" political beliefs, which simply meant that the recruits and their families were anticommunists. This ensured that the men had hostile attitudes toward potential victims from the very beginning. 12

Once they were actually serving as military police, the men were also screened for other attributes. According to former torturer Michaelis Petrou, "The most important criterion was that you had to keep your mouth shut. Second, you had to show aggression. Third, you had to be intelligent and strong. Fourth, you had to be 'their 13 man,' which meant that you would report on the others serving with you, that [the officers] could trust you and that you would follow their orders blindly."

Binding the recruits to the authority of ESA began in basic training, with physically brutal initiation rites. Recruits themselves were cursed, punched, kicked and flogged. They were forced to run until they collapsed and prevented from relieving themselves for long stretches of time. They were required to swear allegiance to a symbol of authority used by the regime (a poster of a soldier superimposed on a large phoenix rising from its own ashes), and they had to promise on their knees to obey their commander-in-chief and the military revolution. 14

While being harassed and beaten by their officers, servicemen were repeatedly told how fortunate they were to have joined the ESA, the strongest and most important support of the regime. They were told that an ESA serviceman's action is never questioned: "You can even flog a major." In-group language helped the men to develop elitist attitudes. Servicemen used nicknames for one another and, later, they used them for victims and for the different methods of torture. "Tea party" meant the beating of a prisoner by a group of military police using their fists, and "tea party with toast" meant more severe group beatings using clubs. Gradually, the recruits came to speak of all people who were not in their group, parents and families included, as belonging to the "outside world." 15

The strain of obedience on the recruits was reduced in several ways. During basic training, they were given daily "national ethical education" lectures that included indoctrination against communism and enemies of the state. During more advanced training, the recruits were constantly reminded that the prisoners were "worms," and that they had to "crush" them. One man reported that when he was torturing prisoners later, he caught himself repeating phrases like "bloody communists!" that he had heard in the lectures. 16

The military police used a carrot-and-stick method to further diminish the recruits' uneasiness about torture. There were many rewards, such as relaxed military rules after training was completed, and torturers often weren't punished for leaving camp without permission. They were allowed to wear civilian clothes, to keep their hair long and to drive military police cars for their personal use. Torturers were frequently given a leave of absence after they forced a confession from a prisoner. They had many economic benefits as well, including free bus rides and restaurant meals and job placement when military service was over. These were the carrots. 17

The sticks consisted of the constant harassment, threats and punishment for disobedience. The men were threatened and intimidated, first by their trainers, then later by senior servicemen. "An 18 officer used to tell us that if a warder helps a prisoner, he will take the prisoner's place and the whole platoon will flog him," one man recalled. Soldiers spied on one another, and even the most successful torturers said that they were constantly afraid.

"You will learn to love pain," one officer promised a recruit. 19
Sensitivity to torture was blunted in several steps. First, the men had to endure it themselves, as if torture were a normal act. The beatings and other torments inflicted on them continued and became worse. Next, the servicemen chosen for the Persecution Section, the unit that tortured political prisoners, were brought into contact with the prisoners by carrying food to their cells. The new men watched veteran soldiers torture prisoners, while they stood guard. Occasionally, the veterans would order them to give the prisoners "some blows."

At the next step, the men were required to participate in group 20
beatings. Later, they were told to use a variety of torture methods on the prisoners. The final step, the appointment to prison warder or chief torturer, was announced suddenly by the commander-in-chief, leaving the men no time to reflect on their new duties.

The Greek example illustrates how the ability to torture can be 21
taught. Training that increases binding and reduces strain can cause decent people to commit acts, often over long periods of time, that otherwise would be unthinkable for them. Similar techniques can be found in military training all over the world, when the intent is to teach soldiers to kill or perform some other repellent act. We conducted extensive interviews with soldiers and ex-soldiers in the U.S. Marines and the Green Berets, and we found that all the steps in our training model were part and parcel of elite American military training. Soldiers are screened for intellectual and physical ability, achievement and mental health. Binding begins in basic training, with initiation rites that isolate trainees from society, introduce them to new rules and values and leave them little time for clear thinking after exhausting physical exercise and scant sleep. Harassment plays an important role, and soldiers are severely punished for disobedience, with demerits, verbal abuse, hours of calisthenics and loss of eating, sleeping and other privileges.

Military training gradually desensitizes soldiers to violence and 22
reduces the strain normally created by repugnant acts. Their revulsion is diminished by screaming chants and songs about violence and killing during marches and runs. The enemy is given derogatory names and portrayed as less than human; this makes it easier to kill them. Completing the toughest possible training and being rewarded by "making it" in an elite corps bring the soldiers confidence and pride, and those who accomplish this feel they can do anything. "Although I tried to avoid killing, I learned to have confidence in

myself and was never afraid," said a former Green Beret who served in Vietnam. "It was part of the job. . . . Anyone who goes through that kind of training could do it."

The effectiveness of these techniques, as several researchers have shown, is not limited to the army. History teacher Ronald Jones started what he called the Third Wave movement as a classroom experiment to show his high school students how people might have become Nazis in World War II. Jones began the Third Wave demonstration by requiring students to stand at attention in a unique new posture and follow strict new rules. He required students to stand beside their desks when asking or answering questions and to begin each statement by saying, "Mr. Jones." The students obeyed. He then required them to shout slogans, "Strength through discipline!" and "Strength through community!" Jones created a salute for class members that he called the Third Wave: the right hand raised to the shoulder with fingers curled. The salute had no meaning, but it served as a symbol of group belonging and a way of isolating members from outsiders. 23

The organization expanded quickly from 20 original members to 100. The teacher issued membership cards and assigned students to report members who didn't comply with the new rules. Dutifully, 20 students pointed accusing fingers at their classmates. 24

Then Jones announced that the Third Wave was a "nationwide movement to find students willing to fight for political change," and he organized a rally, which drew a crowd of 200 students. At the rally, after getting students to salute and shout slogans on command, Jones explained the true reasons behind the Third Wave demonstration. Like the Nazis before them, Jones pointed out, "You bargained your freedom for the comfort of discipline." 25

The students, at an age when group belonging was very important to them, made good candidates for training. Jones didn't teach his students to commit atrocities, and the Third Wave lasted for only five days; in that time, however, Jones created an obedient group that resembled in many ways the Nazi youth groups of World War II (see "The Third Wave: Nazism in a High School," *Psychology Today*, July 1976). 26

Psychologists Craig Haney, W. Curtis Banks and Philip Zimbardo went even further in a remarkable simulation of prison life done at Stanford University. With no special training and in only six days' time, they changed typical university students into controlling, abusive guards and servile prisoners. 27

The students who agreed to participate were chosen randomly to be guards or prisoners. The mock guards were given uniforms and nightsticks and told to act as guards. Prisoners were treated as dangerous criminals: Local police rounded them up, fingerprinted 28 and booked them and brought them to a simulated cellblock in the basement of the university psychology department. Uniformed guards made them remove their clothing, deloused them, gave them prison uniforms and put them in cells.

The two groups of students, originally found to be very similar in 29
most respects, showed striking changes within one week. Prisoners became passive, dependent and helpless. In contrast, guards expressed feelings of power, status and group belonging. They were aggressive and abusive within the prison, insulting and bullying the prisoners. Some guards reported later that they had enjoyed their power, while others said they had not thought they were capable of behaving as they had. They were surprised and dismayed at what they had done: "It was degrading. . . . To me, those things are sick. But they [the prisoners] did everything I said. They abused each other because I requested them to. No one questioned my authority at all."

The guards' behavior was similar in two important ways to that of 30
the Greek torturers. First, they dehumanized their victims. Second, like the torturers, the guards were abusive only when they were within the prison walls. They could act reasonably outside the prisons because the two prison influences of binding and reduced strain were absent.

All these changes at Stanford occurred with no special training, 31
but the techniques we have outlined were still present. Even without training, the student guards "knew" from television and movies that they were supposed to punish prisoners; they "knew" they were supposed to feel superior; and they "knew" they were supposed to blame their victims. Their own behavior and that of their peers gradually numbed their sensitivity to what they were doing, and they were rewarded by the power they had over their prisoners.

There is no evidence that such short-term experiments produce 32
lasting effects. None were reported from either the Third Wave demonstration or the Stanford University simulation. The Stanford study, however, was cut short when depression, crying and psychosomatic illnesses began to appear among the students. And studies of Vietnam veterans have revealed that committing abhorrent acts, even under the extreme conditions of war, can lead to long-term problems. In one study of 130 Vietnam veterans who came to a therapist for help, almost 30 percent of them were concerned about violent acts they had committed while in the service. The veterans reported feelings of anxiety, guilt, depression and an inability to carry on intimate relationships. In a similar fashion, after the fall of the Greek dictatorship in 1974, former torturers began to report nightmares, irritability and episodes of depression.

"Torturing became a job," said former Greek torturer Petrou. "If 33
the officers ordered you to beat, you beat. If they ordered you to stop,

you stopped. You never thought you could do otherwise." His comments bear a disturbing resemblance to the feelings expressed by a Stanford guard: "When I was doing it, I didn't feel regret. . . . I didn't feel guilt. Only afterwards, when I began to reflect . . . did it begin to dawn on me that this was a part of me I hadn't known before."

We do not believe that torture came naturally to any of these young men. Haritos-Fatouros found no evidence of sadistic, abusive or authoritarian behavior in the Greek soldiers' histories prior to their training. This, together with our study of Marine training and the Stanford and Third Wave studies, leads to the conclusion that torturers have normal personalities. Any of us, in a similar situation, might be capable of the same cruelty. One probably cannot train a deranged sadist to be an effective torturer or killer. He must be in complete control of himself while on the job.

Review Questions

1. What was Molly Harrower's Rorschach-test experiment? What conclusions did she reach?
2. What explanation did Milgram propose as the reason people obey or disobey authority? How do the authors modify this explanation?
3. What attributes did the Greek military look for in drafting potential torturers?
4. What was the Third Wave? What did its creator intend to demonstrate?
5. What did the Stanford "prison" experiment demonstrate?

Discussion and Writing Suggestions

1. See page 160 in the introductory essay to this chapter. Reread the indented quotation in that essay, describing the process by which one can be taught to torture. In this piece, Janice Gibson and Mika Haritos-Fatouros draw a parallel between the drafting and indoctrination of torturers and the "rushing" and hazing of college students who wish to join fraternities. Based on your understanding of college fraternities and their initiation rites, comment on the parallel that Gibson and Haritos-Fatouros have observed.
2. What is your response to the observation that all the steps in the "training model [that the authors developed to explain the 'education' of torturers] were part and parcel of elite American military training"?
3. Gibson and Haritos-Fatouros conclude that "torturers have normal personalities. Any of us, in a similar situation, might be capable of the same cruelty." Your response?
4. How do you account for the behavior of students in the Stanford experiment, who were so quick to learn their roles as guards and prisoners?
5. What parallel is there between techniques used by the Greek military and

techniques used by our own military academies such as West Point, the Air Force Academy, and the Naval Academy? Can these techniques be used for good purposes?

The Lottery

SHIRLEY JACKSON

On the morning of June 28, 1948, I walked down to the post office in our little Vermont town to pick up the mail. I was quite casual about it, as I recall—I opened the box, took out a couple of bills and a letter or two, talked to the postmaster for a few minutes, and left, never supposing that it was the last time for months that I was to pick up the mail without an active feeling of panic. By the next week I had had to change my mailbox to the largest one in the post office, and casual conversation with the postmaster was out of the question, because he wasn't speaking to me. June 28, 1948, was the day *The New Yorker* came out with a story of mine in it. It was not my first published story, nor my last, but I have been assured over and over that if it had been the only story I ever wrote or published, there would be people who would not forget my name.[1]

So begins Shirley Jackson's "biography" of her short story "The Lottery." The New Yorker *published the story the summer of 1948 and some months later, having been besieged with letters, acknowledged that the piece had generated "more mail than any . . . fiction they had ever published"—the great majority of it negative. In 1960, Jackson wrote that "millions of people, and my mother, had taken a pronounced dislike to me" for having written the story—which, over the years, proved to be Jackson's most widely anthologized one. If you've read "The Lottery," you will have some idea of why it was so controversial. If you haven't, we don't want to spoil the effect by discussing what happens.*

Shirley Jackson, short story writer and novelist, was born in San Francisco in 1919 and was raised in California and New York. She began her college education at the University of Rochester and completed it at Syracuse University. She married Stanley Edgar Hyman (writer and teacher) and with him had four children. In her brief career, Jackson wrote

---

[1]Shirley Jackson, from "Biography of a Story," in *Come Along With Me,* ed. Stanley Edgar Hyman. New York: Viking, 1968. 1st paragraph, p. 211 + selected quotations, pp. 214–221.

six novels and two works of nonfiction. She won the Edgar Allen Poe Award (1961) as well as a Syracuse University Arents Pioneer Medal for Outstanding Achievement (1965).

The morning of June 27th was clear and sunny, with the fresh warmth of a full-summer day; the flowers were blossoming profusely and the grass was richly green. The people of the village began to gather in the square, between the post office and the bank, around ten o'clock; in some towns there were so many people that the lottery took two days and had to be started on June 26th, but in this village, where there were only about three hundred people, the whole lottery took less than two hours, so it could begin at ten o'clock in the morning and still be through in time to allow the villagers to get home for noon dinner. 1

The children assembled first, of course. School was recently over for the summer, and the feeling of liberty sat uneasily on most of them; they tended to gather together quietly for a while before they broke into boisterous play, and their talk was still of the classroom and the teacher, of books and reprimands. Bobby Martin had already stuffed his pockets full of stones, and the other boys soon followed his example, selecting the smoothest and roundest stones; Bobby and Harry Jones and Dickie Delacroix—the villagers pronounced this name "Dellacroy"—eventually made a great pile of stones in one corner of the square and guarded it against the raids of the other boys. The girls stood aside, talking among themselves, looking over their shoulders at the boys, and the very small children rolled in the dust or clung to the hands of their older brothers or sisters. 2

Soon the men began to gather, surveying their own children, speaking of planting and rain, tractors and taxes. They stood together, away from the pile of stones in the corner, and their jokes were quiet and they smiled rather than laughed. The women, wearing faded house dresses and sweaters, came shortly after their menfolk. They greeted one another and exchanged bits of gossip as they went to join their husbands. Soon the women, standing by their husbands, began to call to their children, and the children came reluctantly, having to be called four or five times. Bobby Martin ducked under his mother's grasping hand and ran, laughing, back to the pile of stones. His father spoke up sharply, and Bobby came quickly and took his place between his father and his oldest brother. 3

The lottery was conducted—as were the square dances, the teen-age club, the Halloween program—by Mr. Summers, who had time and energy to devote to civic activities. He was a round-faced, jovial man and he ran the coal business, and people were sorry for him, because he had no children and his wife was a scold. When he arrived 4 in the square, carrying the black wooden box, there was a murmur of conversation among the villagers, and he waved and called, "Little late today, folks." The postmaster, Mr. Graves, followed him, carrying a three-legged stool, and the stool was put in the center of the square and Mr. Summers set the black box down on it. The villagers kept their distance, leaving a space between themselves and the stool, and when Mr. Summers said, "Some of you fellows want to give me a hand?" there was a hesitation before two men, Mr. Martin and his oldest son, Baxter, came forward to hold the box steady on the stool while Mr. Summers stirred up the papers inside it.

The original paraphernalia for the lottery had been lost long ago, 5
and the black box now resting on the stool had been put into use even before Old Man Warner, the oldest man in town, was born. Mr. Summers spoke frequently to the villagers about making a new box, but no one liked to upset even as much tradition as was represented by the black box. There was a story that the present box had been made with some pieces of the box that had preceded it, the one that had been constructed when the first people settled down to make a village here. Every year, after the lottery, Mr. Summers began talking again about a new box, but every year the subject was allowed to fade off without anything's being done. The black box grew shabbier each year; by now it was no longer completely black but splintered badly along one side to show the original wood color, and in some places faded or stained.

Mr. Martin and his oldest son, Baxter, held the black box securely 6
on the stool until Mr. Summers had stirred the papers thoroughly with his hand. Because so much of the ritual had been forgotten or discarded, Mr. Summers had been successful in having slips of paper substituted for the chips of wood that had been used for generations. Chips of wood, Mr. Summers had argued, had been all very well when the village was tiny, but now that the population was more than three hundred and likely to keep on growing, it was necessary to use something that would fit more easily into the black box. The night before the lottery, Mr. Summers and Mr. Graves made up the slips of paper and put them in the box, and it was then taken to the safe of Mr. Summers' coal company and locked up until Mr. Summers was ready to take it to the square next morning. The rest of the year, the box was put away, sometimes one place, sometimes another; it had spent one year in Mr. Graves's barn and another year underfoot in the post office, and sometimes it was set on a shelf in the Martin grocery and left there.

There was a great deal of fussing to be done before Mr. Summers 7
declared the lottery open. There were the lists to make up—of heads of families, heads of households in each family, members of each household in each family. There was the proper swearing-in of Mr.

Summers by the postmaster, as the official of the lottery; at one time, some people remembered, there had been a recital of some sort, performed by the official of the lottery, a perfunctory, tuneless chant that had been rattled off duly each year; some people believed that the official of the lottery used to stand just so when he said or sang it, others believed that he was supposed to walk among the people, but years and years ago this part of the ritual had been allowed to lapse. There had been, also, a ritual salute, which the official of the lottery had had to use in addressing each person who came up to draw from the box, but this also had changed with time, until now it was felt necessary only for the official to speak to each person approaching. Mr. Summers was very good at all this; in his clean white shirt and blue jeans, with one hand resting carelessly on the black box, he seemed very proper and important as he talked interminably to Mr. Graves and the Martins.

Just as Mr. Summers finally left off talking and turned to the assembled villagers, Mrs. Hutchinson came hurriedly along the path to the square, her sweater thrown over her shoulders, and slid into place in the back of the crowd. "Clean forgot what day it was," she said to Mrs. Delacroix, who stood next to her, and they both laughed softly. "Thought my old man was out back stacking wood," Mrs. Hutchinson went on, "and then I looked out the window and the kids was gone, and then I remembered it was the twenty-seventh and came a-running." She dried her hands on her apron, and Mrs. Delacroix said, "You're in time, though. They're still talking away up there." 8

Mrs. Hutchinson craned her neck to see through the crowd and found her husband and children standing near the front. She tapped Mrs. Delacroix on the arm as a farewell and began to make her way through the crowd. The people separated good-humoredly to let her through; two or three people said, in voices just loud enough to be heard across the crowd, "Here comes your Missus, Hutchinson," and "Bill, she made it after all." Mrs. Hutchinson reached her husband, and Mr. Summers, who had been waiting, said cheerfully, "Thought we were going to have to get on without you, Tessie." Mrs. Hutchinson said, grinning, "Wouldn't have me leave m'dishes in the sink, now, would you, Joe?," and soft laughter ran through the crowd as the people stirred back into position after Mrs. Hutchinson's arrival. 9

"Well, now," Mr. Summers said soberly, "guess we better get started, get this over with, so's we can go back to work. Anybody ain't here?" 10

"Dunbar," several people said. "Dunbar, Dunbar." 11

Mr. Summers consulted his list. "Clyde Dunbar," he said. "That's right. He's broke his leg, hasn't he? Who's drawing for him?" 12

"Me, I guess," a woman said, and Mr. Summers turned to look at 13
her. "Wife draws for her husband," Mr. Summers said. "Don't you have a grown boy to do it for you, Janey?" Although Mr. Summers and everyone else in the village knew the answer perfectly well, it was the business of the official of the lottery to ask such questions formally. Mr. Summers waited with an expression of polite interest while Mrs. Dunbar answered.

"Horace's not but sixteen yet," Mrs. Dunbar said regretfully. 14
"Guess I gotta fill in for the old man this year."

"Right," Mr. Summers said. He made a note on the list he was 15
holding. Then he asked, "Watson boy drawing this year?"

A tall boy in the crowd raised his hand. "Here," he said. "I'm 16
drawing for m'mother and me." He blinked his eyes nervously and ducked his head as several voices in the crowd said things like "Good fellow, Jack," and "Glad to see your mother's got a man to do it."

"Well," Mr. Summers said, "guess that's everyone. Old Man 17
Warner make it?"

"Here," a voice said, and Mr. Summers nodded. 18

A sudden hush fell on the crowd as Mr. Summers cleared his 19
throat and looked at the list. "All ready?" he called. "Now, I'll read the names—heads of families first—and the men come up and take a paper out of the box. Keep the paper folded in your hand without looking at it until everyone has had a turn. Everything clear?"

The people had done it so many times that they only half listened 20
to the directions; most of them were quiet, wetting their lips, not looking around. Then Mr. Summers raised one hand high and said, "Adams." A man disengaged himself from the crowd and came forward. "Hi, Steve," Mr. Summers said, and Mr. Adams said, "Hi, Joe." They grinned at one another humorlessly and nervously. Then Mr. Adams reached into the black box and took out a folded paper. He held it firmly by one corner as he turned and went hastily back to his place in the crowd, where he stood a little apart from his family, not looking down at his hand.

"Allen," Mr. Summers said. "Anderson. . . . Bentham." 21

"Seems like there's no time at all between lotteries any more," 22
Mrs. Delacroix said to Mrs. Graves in the back row. "Seems like we got through with the last one only last week."

"Time sure goes fast," Mrs. Graves said. 23

"Clark. . . . Delacroix." 24

"There goes my old man," Mrs. Delacroix said. She held her 25
breath while her husband went forward.

"Dunbar," Mr. Summers said, and Mrs. Dunbar went steadily to 26
the box while one of the women said, "Go on, Janey," and another said, "There she goes."

"We're next," Mrs. Graves said. She watched while Mr. Graves came around from the side of the box, greeted Mr. Summers gravely, and selected a slip of paper from the box. By now, all through the crowd there were men holding the small folded papers in their large hands, turning them over and over nervously. Mrs. Dunbar and her two sons stood together, Mrs. Dunbar holding the slip of paper. 27

"Harburt. . . . Hutchinson." 28

"Get up there, Bill," Mrs. Hutchinson said, and the people near her laughed. 29

"Jones." 30

"They do say," Mr. Adams said to Old Man Warner, who stood next to him, "that over in the north village they're talking of giving up the lottery." 31

Old Man Warner snorted. "Pack of crazy fools," he said. "Listening to the young folks, nothing's good enough for *them.* Next thing you know, they'll be wanting to go back to living in caves, nobody work any more, live *that* way for a while. Used to be a saying about 'Lottery in June, corn be heavy soon.' First thing you know, we'd all be eating stewed chickweed and acorns. There's *always* been a lottery," he added petulantly. "Bad enough to see young Joe Summers up there joking with everybody." 32

"Some places have already quit lotteries," Mrs. Adams said. 33

"Nothing but trouble in *that,*" Old Man Warner said stoutly. "Pack of young fools." 34

"Martin." And Bobby Martin watched his father go forward. "Overdyke. . . . Percy." 35

"I wish they'd hurry," Mrs. Dunbar said to her older son. "I wish they'd hurry." 36

"They're almost through," her son said. 37

"You get ready to run tell Dad," Mrs. Dunbar said. 38

Mr. Summers called his own name and then stepped forward precisely and selected a slip from the box. Then he called, "Warner." 39

"Seventy-seventh year I been in the lottery," Old Man Warner said as he went through the crowd. "Seventy-seventh time." 40

"Watson." The tall boy came awkwardly through the crowd. Someone said, "Don't be nervous, Jack," and Mr. Summers said, "Take your time, son." 41

"Zanini." 42

After that, there was a long pause, a breathless pause, until Mr. Summers, holding his slip of paper in the air, said, "All right, fellows." For a minute, no one moved, and then all the slips of paper were opened. Suddenly, all the women began to speak at once, saying, "Who is it?," "Who's got it?," "Is it the Dunbars?," "Is it the 43

Watsons?" Then the voices began to say, "It's Hutchinson. It's Bill," "Bill Hutchinson's got it."

"Go tell your father," Mrs. Dunbar said to her older son. 44

People began to look around to see the Hutchinsons. Bill Hutch- 45
inson was standing quiet, staring down at the paper in his hand. Suddenly, Tessie Hutchinson shouted to Mr. Summers, "You didn't give him time enough to take any paper he wanted. I saw you. It wasn't fair!"

"Be a good sport, Tessie," Mrs. Delacroix called, and Mrs. Graves 46
said, "All of us took the same chance."

"Shut up, Tessie," Bill Hutchinson said. 47

"Well, everyone, " Mr. Summers said, "that was done pretty fast, 48
and now we've got to be hurrying a little more to get done in time." He consulted his next list. "Bill," he said, "you draw for the Hutchinson family. You got any other households in the Hutchinsons?"

"There's Don and Eva," Mrs. Hutchinson yelled. "Make *them* take 49
their chance!"

"Daughters draw with their husbands' families, Tessie," Mr. 50
Summers said gently. "You know that as well as anyone else."

"It wasn't *fair,*" Tessie said. 51

"I guess not, Joe," Bill Hutchinson said regretfully. "My daughter 52
draws with her husband's family, that's only fair. And I've got no other family except the kids."

"Then, as far as drawing for families is concerned, it's you," Mr. 53
Summers said in explanation, "and as far as drawing for households is concerned, that's you, too. Right?"

"Right," Bill Hutchinson said. 54

"How many kids, Bill?" Mr. Summers asked formally. 55

"Three," Bill Hutchinson said. "There's Bill, Jr., and Nancy, and 56
little Dave. And Tessie and me."

"All right, then," Mr. Summers said. "Harry, you got their tickets 57
back?"

Mr. Graves nodded and held up the slips of paper. "Put them in 58
the box, then," Mr. Summers directed. "Take Bill's and put it in."

"I think we ought to start over," Mrs. Hutchinson said, as quietly 59
as she could. "I tell you it wasn't *fair.* You didn't give him time enough to choose. *Every*body saw that."

Mr. Graves had selected the five slips and put them in the box, 60
and he dropped all the papers but those onto the ground, where the breeze caught them and lifted them off.

"Listen, everybody," Mrs. Hutchinson was saying to the people 61
around her.

"Ready, Bill?" Mr. Summers asked, and Bill Hutchinson, with 62
one quick glance around at his wife and children, nodded.

"Remember," Mr. Summers said, "take the slips and keep them folded until each person has taken one. Harry, you help little Dave." Mr. Graves took the hand of the little boy, who came willingly with him up to the box. "Take a paper out of the box, Davy," Mr. Summers said. Davy put his hand into the box and laughed. "Take just *one* paper," Mr. Summers said. "Harry, you hold it for him." Mr. Graves took the child's hand and removed the folded paper from the tight fist and held it while little Dave stood next to him and looked up at him wonderingly. 63

"Nancy next," Mr. Summers said. Nancy was twelve, and her school friends breathed heavily as she went forward, switching her skirt, and took a slip daintily from the box. "Bill, Jr.," Mr. Summers said, and Billy, his face red and his feet overlarge, nearly knocked the box over as he got a paper out. "Tessie," Mr. Summers said. She hesitated for a minute, looking around defiantly, and then set her lips and went up to the box. She snatched a paper out and held it behind her. 64

"Bill," Mr. Summers said, and Bill Hutchinson reached into the box and felt around, bringing his hand out at last with the slip of paper in it. 65

The crowd was quiet. A girl whispered, "I hope it's not Nancy," and the sound of the whisper reached the edges of the crowd. 66

"It's not the way it used to be," Old Man Warner said clearly. "People ain't the way they used to be." 67

"All right," Mr. Summers said. "Open the papers. Harry, you open little Dave's." 68

Mr. Graves opened the slip of paper and there was a general sigh through the crowd as he held it up and everyone could see that it was blank. Nancy and Bill, Jr., opened theirs at the same time, and both beamed and laughed, turning around to the crowd and holding their slips of paper above their heads. 69

"Tessie," Mr. Summers said. There was a pause, and then Mr. Summers looked at Bill Hutchinson, and Bill unfolded his paper and showed it. It was blank. 70

"It's Tessie," Mr. Summers said, and his voice was hushed. "Show us her paper, Bill." 71

Bill Hutchinson went over to his wife and forced the slip of paper out of her hand. It had a black spot on it, the black spot Mr. Summers had made the night before with the heavy pencil in the coal-company office. Bill Hutchinson held it up, and there was a stir in the crowd. 72

"All right, folks," Mr. Summers said. "Let's finish quickly." 73

Although the villagers had forgotten the ritual and lost the original black box, they still remembered to use stones. The pile of stones the boys had made earlier was ready; there were stones on the 74 ground with the blowing scraps of paper that had come out of the box. Mrs. Delacroix selected a stone so large she had to pick it up with both hands and turned to Mrs. Dunbar. "Come on," she said. "Hurry up."

Mrs. Dunbar had small stones in both hands, and she said, gasping for breath, "I can't run at all. You'll have to go ahead and I'll catch up with you." 75

The children had stones already, and someone gave little Davy Hutchinson a few pebbles. 76

Tessie Hutchinson was in the center of a cleared space by now, and she held her hands out desperately as the villagers moved in on her. "It isn't fair," she said. A stone hit her on the side of the head. 77

Old Man Warner was saying, "Come on, come on, everyone." Steve Adams was in the front of the crowd of villagers, with Mrs. Graves beside him. 78

"It isn't fair, it isn't right," Mrs. Hutchinson screamed, and then they were upon her. 79

Discussion and Writing Suggestions

1. Many readers believed that the events depicted in "The Lottery" actually happened. A sampling of the letters that Jackson received in response to the story:

    (Kansas) Will you please tell me the locale and the year of the custom?
    (Oregon) Where in heaven's name does there exist such barbarity as described in the story?
    (New York) Do such tribunal rituals still exist and if so where?
    (New York) To a reader who has only a fleeting knowledge of traditional rites in various parts of the country (I presume the plot was laid in the United States) I found the cruelty of the ceremony outrageous, if not unbelievable. It may be just a custom or ritual which I am not familiar with.
    (New York) Would you please explain whether such improbable rituals occur in our Middle Western states, and what their origin and purpose are?
    (Nevada) Although we recognize the story to be fiction is it possible that it is based on fact?

    What is your response to comments such as these that suggest surprise, certainly, but also acceptance of the violence committed in the story?
2. One reader of the "The Lottery," from Missouri, wrote to the *The New Yorker* and accused it of "publishing a story that reached a new low in human viciousness." Do you feel that Jackson has reached this "new low"? Explain your answer.
3. Several more letter writers attempted to get at the meaning of the story:

(Illinois) If it is simply a fictitious example of man's innate cruelty, it isn't a very good one. Man, stupid and cruel as he is, has always had sense enough to imagine or invent a charge against the objects of his persecution: the Christian martyrs, the New England witches, the Jews and Negroes. But nobody had anything against Mrs. Hutchinson, and they only wanted to get through quickly so they could go home for lunch.

(California) I missed something here. Perhaps there was some facet of the victim's character which made her unpopular with the other villagers. I expected the people to evince a feeling of dread and terror, or else sadistic pleasure, but perhaps they were laconic, unemotional New Englanders.

(Indiana) When I first read the story in my issue, I felt that there was no moral significance present, that the story was just terrifying, and that was all. However, there has to be a reason why it is so alarming to so many people. I feel that the only solution, the only reason it bothered so many people is that it shows the power of society over the individual. We saw the ease with which society can crush any single one of us. At the same time, we saw that society need have no rational reason for crushing the one, or the few, or sometimes the many.

Take any one of these readings of the story and respond to it by writing a brief essay or, perhaps, a letter.

4. What does the story suggest to you about authority and obedience to authority? Who—or what—holds authority in the village? Why do people continue with the annual killing, despite the fact that "some places have already quit lotteries"?

SYNTHESIS ACTIVITIES

1. Assume for the moment you agree with Doris Lessing: Children need to be taught how to disobey so they can recognize and avoid situations that give rise to harmful obedience. If you were the curriculum coordinator for your local school system, how would you teach children to disobey? What would be your curriculum: What homework would you assign? What class projects? What field trips? One complicated part of your job would be to train children who understand the difference between *responsible* disobedience and anarchy. What is the difference?

Take up these questions in an essay that draws on both your experiences as a student and your understanding of the selections in this chapter. Points that you might want to consider in developing the essay: defining overly obedient children; appropriate classroom behavior for responsibly disobedient children (as opposed to inappropriate behavior); reading lists (would "The Lottery" be included?); homework assignments; field trips; class projects.

2. The creator of the Third Wave (in "Education of a Torturer") explained to students in a rally that like the Nazis they "bargained [their] freedom for the comfort of discipline." Doris Lessing makes much the same point when she refers to experiments in which people will say, in effect, that black is white in order to be accepted as a member of a group. What, in your view, are the "comforts" of discipline? Why is an obedient attitude more psychologically comforting than a disobedient one?

Draw from sources in the chapter as you consider this question. As you develop an answer, you might first want to investigate the reasons people are insecure. You could then discuss the psychological mechanisms involved in obeying figures of authority and finally explore the features of obedience that make for security. You might want to refer to the tight-knit village in "The Lottery."

3. A certain amount of obedience is a given in society, observes Stanley Milgram and others (see Herrnstein and Meyer). Social order, civilization itself, would not be possible unless individuals were willing to surrender a portion of their autonomy to the state. Allowing that we all are obedient (we must be), define the point at which obedience to a figure of authority becomes dangerous.

As you develop your definition, consider the ways you might use the work of authors in this chapter and their definitions of acceptable and unacceptable levels of obedience. Do you agree with the ways in which others have drawn the line between reasonable and dangerous obedience? What examples from current stories in the news or from your own experience can you draw on to test various definitions?

4. In paragraphs 6 and 7 of his review, Philip Meyer draws a distinction between situation ethics and code ethics, an important distinction that helps explain why one person will obey orders blindly, whereas another will obey only so long as the dictates of his conscience are not violated.

In an essay, distinguish between situation and code ethics, in your own words, and then apply that distinction as a way of explaining various examples of obedience and disobedience discussed in this chapter. Your essay will take the form of an "application of principles." A standard structure would have you define your principles and then test their explanatory power by applying them to various scenarios. Conclude by evaluating the strengths and limitations of your principles.

5. Describe a situation in which you were faced with a moral dilemma of whether or not to obey a figure of authority. After describing the situation and the action you took (or didn't take), discuss your behavior in light of any two readings in this chapter. You might consider a straightforward, four-part structure for your essay: (1) your description; (2) your discussion, in light of source A; (3) your discussion, in light of source B; (4) your conclusion—an overall appraisal of your behavior.

6. In an essay that draws on two or more sources in this chapter, develop an interpretation of Shirley Jackson's short story "The Lottery." In your interpretation, be sure to discuss what the story reveals about authority and obedience to authority.

IS AMERICA IN DECLINE?

7

The world is filled with once-great nations that failed to realize that their final years of wealth were due more to past success than future potential.[1]

Fred Branfman
Director, Rebuild America

Will the United States become another once-great nation? Have we already begun our slide? By any number of measures, the answer would seem a depressing and unavoidable *yes.*

In 1945, at the conclusion of World War II, American power, wealth, and influence were at their peak. The world's only nuclear power, the United States (to paraphrase Shakespeare) bestrode the world like a colossus. While other industrialized nations lay in ruins, the American homeland was virtually untouched by the war. During the following two decades, America's position in the world was like imperial Rome's in the time of Christ or like Britain's in the nineteenth century. But as historian Paul Kennedy has noted, this pre-eminence was based on circumstances that were bound to be temporary. During the last twenty-five years, the United States seems to have undergone a decline, relative to other nations. Its confidence and stature were sapped by the quagmire of Vietnam, assassinations, years of civil rights unrest, and the trauma of Watergate. Meanwhile, the defeated Axis powers (Japan and West Germany) became economic giants; and Soviet military power came to equal or even surpass that of the United States. Recently, Americans have noted with concern that their country is less respected, less loved, less feared, less listened to, less imitated than it used to be.

It can be argued that American military power is stronger than it ever was and that if there has been a decline in this area, it is only a relative one, in comparison with the Soviet Union. But in other areas, an American decline seems unmistakable. Consider our changing enconomic power. In 1989, Americans earned 15 percent less than they did in 1973, as judged against that year's purchasing power. True, the average income of American households is up, but mostly because it now takes *two* adults working full-time to support a family. An economist at the Sloane School of Management observes that "apart from the two Great Depressions (1873–96 and 1930–39), [ours] is the first generation of Americans whose standard of living is lower than its predecessor's." We used to save $1 of every $10 earned, after taxes; now we save $1 in $25; between the late 1970s and the late 1980s, consumer debt in this country increased nearly threefold. The U.S. government does not seem

[1]Reprinted by permission of Rebuild America.

to be managing its finances any better: Throughout much of the 1980s, the government spent roughly $200 billion more each year than it collected in revenues, and we have accumulated a massive national debt in excess of $3 trillion—a debt for which the government must borrow an additional $500 million *per day* to service. That's $500 million every day not invested in education, job training, drug counseling, or medical research.

At the same time that we borrow and saddle future generations with debt, our productivity has declined. In the United States, employees work fewer hours today than they did in 1975; in Japan, employees are working more than they did in 1975. Japanese workers frequently make a lifelong commitment to their employers; we keep one eye habitually open for new jobs that will improve our fortunes. Americans are working less and producing less than their Japanese counterparts. In 1975, the United States manufactured nearly every DRAM (computer chip) made in the world. By 1986, the U.S. share of that market dropped to 15 percent. We make few VCRs today; these as well as most of our television sets and an increasing number of our automobiles are "Made in Japan"—a label of derision twenty-five years ago but one that now connotes superior design and craftsmanship. How many Americans are skeptical of buying American-made products when Asian- or European-made alternatives exist? Faced with our decline in productivity and the widespread loss of confidence in the quality of American goods, managers of U.S. businesses have been scrambling to improve, with apparently little effect. So concludes a much-discussed report of the MIT Commission on Industrial Productivity, whose scholars and business leaders were charged with investigating ways that America might regain its productive edge. The commission had this to say:

> The decline of the U.S. economy puzzles most Americans. The qualities and talents that gave rise to the dynamism of the post [World War II] years must surely be present still in the national character, and yet American industry seems to have lost much of its vigor. In looking for ways to reverse the decline, it is only natural to turn to the methods that succeeded in the golden years of growth and innovation. Many business managers have adopted this strategy. The results, unfortunately, are rather like those of a man who keeps striking the same match because it worked fine the first time.[1]

Do we even have a clue as to how we should mend our economy? And what of our intractable social ills: persistent, structural poverty that has trapped generations of Americans in a world of unemployment, drugs, broken homes, homelessness, and crime? According to recent figures, 6.1 percent of

---

[2]From *Made in America: Regaining the Productive Edge* by M. L. Dertouzos, R. K. Lester, R. M. Solow, and The MIT Commission on Industrial Productivity. Cambridge, Mass.: MIT Press, (46), 1989.

American families without children live below the poverty level. For families with children, that figure is 20.6 percent. In families where parents are young (under the age of thirty), that figure is 35.6 percent. Overall, in 1989, 20 percent of Americans lived below the poverty level. In 1980, that figure was 13 percent. Drug use, and the violence associated with it, is rampant. In our cities, we find youths, parents, whole neighborhoods lost to crack cocaine. Small wonder, then, that two sociologists have reported recently that 43 percent of Americans are cynical—that is, profoundly distrustful of others. In a national survey, roughly 60 percent of respondents agreed with the statements "that people will tell a lie if they can gain by it . . . that people pretend to care more than they really do . . . and that people claim to be honest and moral but fall short when money is at stake." Traditionally, we Americans have been more trusting than this, more hopeful, more community minded. What has happened?

And yet with so much that ails us, immigrants continue flocking to our shores for a chance to live out their dreams. Much of the world continues to find inspiration in the durable American model of government, in its reverence for political and personal freedoms—the same freedoms that impelled hundreds of thousands to bring down dictatorial regimes in eastern Europe. Recent immigrants to America celebrate what third- and fourth-generation Americans perhaps take for granted: the flexibility of our economic and social systems that nurtures imagination and gives individuals room to excel. Other nations look to us for protection, counsel—and support. The American economy, for all its problems, remains a behemoth: powerful, permitting great wealth and among the highest standards of living in the world. Walk down the aisles of a supermarket or a department store in any city and see the vast array of products, the shelves sagging with goods that in sheer number and variety astound visitors from other nations. We do not wait in line to buy meat, toilet paper, or vegetables, as much of the world does. We continue to live in a land of plenty.

Still, are America's fortunes declining? For reasons previously discussed, the answer—provisionally and leavened by a continued acknowledgment of our strengths—must be yes. In the face of this answer, new questions arise: Is our decline reversible? Inevitable? Will the decline lead to obscurity? Do we want any longer to bear the burdens of being the world's richest, most powerful, most influential nation? These and related questions form the core of the readings that follow.

As the discussion begins, it will be useful to understand the classic, or "mythic," American values. If we've fallen from preeminence, we have done so as judged implicitly against some prior standard, some core set of values and achievements. What have these been? Political economist Robert Reich provides one answer—by telling a story: "An American Morality Tale." Following Reich, anthropologist Katherine Newman examines the lives of the downwardly mobile in her "American Nightmares." For a surprising number of once-comfortable middle-class people, life in the United States has turned grim.

Tom Ashbrook internationalizes the focus and finds, in comparison with Asian countries where he has recently spent time, that America has become a flaccid, lazy nation, "drowsily, dangerously accustomed to its life on credit." This unsettling view is balanced by two writers: immigrant Natwar Gandhi, who finds pronouncements of America's decline incomprehensible; and Charles Krauthammer, who states that, "In 1950 . . . American values and prestige were ascendant in half the world. Today the other half has come around." The chapter concludes with two analyses and a work of fiction: Fred Branfman, director of Rebuild America, claims that America will continue what he believes is a slide unless we make modernization a top priority. Paul Kennedy argues that whatever actions we might take, the decline of America—as the decline of any great nation—is inevitable. Finally, in an excerpt from Walker Percy's novel *Love in the Ruins,* narrator Dr. Thomas More ponders whether "God has at last removed his blessing from the U.S.A."

An American Morality Tale

ROBERT REICH

As we begin our exploration of America's apparent decline, we can anticipate the remarks of authors who will refer directly or indirectly to "core" American values. Some authors will refer, for instance, to the Puritan ethic and frontier spirit, as well as to individuals (like Ben Franklin) who've embodied ideals to which we aspire. It is worthwhile to examine these attitudes, as political economist Robert Reich does in the selection that follows. Reich's story of "George" constitutes one version of the American myth. As you'll see, commentators will often judge the behavior of present-day Americans against elements of the myth, whether or not they invoke the myth directly. George's story will provide a point of reference, a touchstone, as you read the rest of the chapter.

Reich interprets the story for us by examining the "parables" embedded within it. "These are [parables] of aspiration," says Reich, that "summon us to duty and destiny." As you read, consider the extent to which America does *have a destiny. You might also consider the values that Reich will call "core" American values. Are these your values? Those of your neighbors, business leaders, political representatives?*

Your response to these questions will prepare you for the remaining selections in the chapter.

Born in 1946 and reared in Fairfield County, Connecticut, Robert Reich graduated from Dartmouth College in 1968 and attended Oxford University on a Rhodes scholarship. He went on to attend Yale University law school and served four years directing policy planning at the Federal Trade Commission in Washington. A professor of public policy at Harvard University's John F. Kennedy School of Government since 1981, Reich is an active and much respected writer. He contributes regularly to The New Republic *as well as to other national magazines and journals. He is the author or coauthor of several books, including:* The Next American Frontier *(1983) and* Minding America's Business *(1982). Reich's economic theories have drawn support from leading Democrats, including Michael Dukakis, who consulted with Reich during the presidential campaign of 1988. The present selection appears in Reich's* Tales of a New America *(1987).*

You've heard the story a hundred times, with different names, different details. George was a good man, the son of immigrants who had made their way to Marysville. They came with no money, with nothing but grim determination and hard-won freedom. Dad worked all his life in the mill; he was union, hard, and proud. George was quick by nature, dogged by necessity. He studied hard at school, and after school worked long and well at anything that would bring in a few dollars. George was good at sports, but he had little time for games. He had few close friends, and yet he was fair and decent with everyone, and quietly kind to anybody in real trouble. He never picked a fight in his life. But in eighth grade, when the town bully Albert Wade was slapping around the smallest kid in the class, George stepped between them without saying a word. He let Wade throw the first punch, then put him away with one straight left, turned around, and walked away. 1

George finished high school in 1943, and joined the army the day he graduated. Four months later he was in Europe. On the sixth day of the Normandy invasion his squad was on patrol, passing through a French orchard when a German machine-gun nest opened up from behind a stone wall, picking off the squad one by one. George broke from cover and, dodging from tree to tree, raced toward the Nazis as bullets chewed the bark and ground around him. He took out the nest with a grenade and his rifle, and he saved his buddies, but he never wore the medals they gave him and he never talked about it much. After the war he came back to Marysville and married Kate, his childhood sweetheart. He raised three kids, and he started a little construction business, which his hard work and integrity gradually made into a big construction business. By and by, George made a lot 2 of money. But his family continued to live modestly, and he gave generously to the local boys' club and an orphanage he founded. He was generous with his time, too, and headed the community chest. Still he kept pretty much to himself until Albert Wade inherited his father's bank, the only bank in town. Wade risked his depositors' money on shaky loans to his cronies, bought and bullied his way into power with Marysville's political leaders. When he was elected mayor the election smelled bad to everyone, but only George openly accused Wade of corruption. For six months Wade's bank refused every mortgage on houses built by George's company, and George risked everything in the showdown. But in that tense town meeting, one of the city councilmen Wade had paid off could no longer hide his shame under George's steady gaze and simple question from the back of the room. He spilled how Wade had rigged the election. Albert Wade went from city hall to county jail, and George went back to his family, his work, and his quiet service to Marysville.

George's story is an American morality tale. It is a national parable, retold time and again in many different versions, about how we should live our lives in this country. George is the American Everyman. He's Gary Cooper in *High Noon*. He's Jimmy Stewart in *It's a Wonderful Life*. He's the American private eye, the frontier hero, the kid who makes good. He's George Washington and Abe Lincoln. He appears in countless political speeches, in newspaper stories, on the evening news, in American ballads, and sermons. 3

Everyone has a favorite variation, but the basic theme is the same and speaks to the essence of our national self-image: Ours is a nation of humble, immigrant origins, built out of nothing and into greatness through hard work; generous to those in need, those who cannot make it on their own; a loner among nations, suspicious of foreign entanglements, but willing to stand up against tyranny; and forever vigilant against corruption and special privilege. 4

The American morality tale defines our understanding of who we are, and of what we want for ourselves and one another. It is the tacit subtext of our daily conversations about American life. It permeates *both* American conservatism and American liberalism. And—the essential point—it is a fundamentally noble, essentially life-affirming story. Much is made of the American political distinctiveness of a Constitution inspired by theory rather than by tradition. But there is a subtler yet equally profound *cultural* distinctiveness as well, a national sense of identity rooted not in history but in self-told mythology. Political scientist Carl Friedrich captured the distinction in 1935: "To be an American is an ideal, while to be a Frenchman is a fact." 5

This basic mythology, however integral to the American identity, is so vague as to admit of many interpretations, to present itself in multiple manifestations over time. At different times in our history, 6 different aspects of the parable have come to the fore while others receded. Some variants of the myth are more faithful to its essence than others; some variants are more supple accommodations to current American reality than others. Our history is punctuated with wrenching national contests between competing versions of the ideal; both world wars, for example, forced us to decide whether we must love peace more or justice more. Indeed, these episodes of editing our common mythology, as painful as they may be, are themselves affirmations of the American distinctiveness.

. . .

George's story embodies four basic American morality tales, our core cultural parables. They are rooted in the central experiences of American history: the flight from older cultures, the rejection of central authority and aristocratic privilege, the lure of the unspoiled frontier, the struggle for harmony and justice. 7

1. THE MOB AT THE GATES. The first mythic story is about tyranny and barbarism that lurk "out there." It depicts America as a beacon light of virtue in a world of darkness, a small island of freedom and democracy in a perilous sea. We are uniquely blessed, the proper model for other peoples' aspirations, the hope of the world's poor and oppressed. The parable gives voice to a corresponding fear: we must beware, lest the forces of darkness overwhelm us. Our liberties are fragile; our openness renders us vulnerable to exploitation or infection from beyond. 8

Hence our endless efforts to isolate ourselves from the rest of the globe, to contain evil forces beyond our borders, and to convey our lessons with missionary zeal to benighted outsiders. George fought the "good war" against the Nazis; Daniel Boone, a somewhat less savory campaign against Indians; Davy Crockett, Mexicans. The American amalgam of fear and aggressiveness toward "them out there" appears in countless fantasies of space explorers who triumph over alien creatures from beyond. It is found in Whig histories of the United States, and in the anti-immigration harangues of the late nineteenth and early twentieth centuries. We heeded George Washington's warning to maintain our independence from the monarchical powers of Europe, and then proceeded for more than a century to conquer, purchase, or otherwise control vast territories to our west and south. 9

In this century Woodrow Wilson grimly rallied Americans to "defeat once and for all . . . the sinister forces" that rendered peace impossible; Franklin Roosevelt warned of "rotten apple" nations that spread their rot to others; Dean Acheson adopted the same metaphor to describe the Communist threat to Greece and Turkey immediately 10 after Hitler's war; to Eisenhower, South Vietnam was the first in a series of dominoes that might fall to communism; to John F. Kennedy it was "the finger in the dike," holding back the Soviet surge. The underlying lesson: We must maintain vigilance, lest dark forces overrun us.

2. THE TRIUMPHANT INDIVIDUAL. This is the story of the little guy who works hard, takes risks, believes in himself, and eventually earns wealth, fame, and honor. It's the parable of the self-made man (or, more recently, woman) who bucks the odds, spurns the naysayers, and shows what can be done with enough drive and guts. He's a loner and a maverick, true to himself, plain speaking, self-reliant, uncompromising in his ideals. He gets the job done. 11

Determination and integrity earned George his triumph. Benjamin Franklin employed a carefully conceived system of self-control (Franklin's *Autobiography* is but the first of a long line of American manuals on how to become rich through self-denial and diligence). The theme recurs in the tale of Abe Lincoln, log splitter from Illinois who goes to the White House; in the hundred or so novellas of Horatio Alger, whose heroes all rise promptly and predictably from rags to riches (not only through pluck; luck plays a part too); and in the manifold stories of American detectives and cowboys—mavericks all—who reluctantly get involved in a dangerous quest and end up with the girl, the money, and the glory. It appears in the American morality tales of the underdog who eventually makes it, showing up the bosses and bullies who tried to put him down; think of *Rocky* or *Iacocca*. Regardless of the precise form, the moral is the same: With enough guts and gumption, anyone can make it on their own in America. 12

3. THE BENEVOLENT COMMUNITY. The third parable is about the American community. It is the story of neighbors and friends rolling up their sleeves and pitching in to help one another, of self-sacrifice, community pride, and patriotism. It is about Americans' essential generosity and compassion toward those in need. 13

The story is rooted in America's religious traditions, and its earliest formulations are found in sermons like John Winthrop's "A Model of Christian Charity," delivered on board ship in Salem Harbor just before the Puritans landed in 1630. He described the enterprise on which they were embarking in the terms of Matthew's version of the Sermon on the Mount: The new settlers would be "as a City on a Hill" whose members would "delight in each other" and be "of the same body." America began as a nation of religious communities, centered in the church and pledged to piety and charity—Shakers, Amish, Mennonite, New England Congregationalist. Biblical language and 14 symbols continued to propel American social movements committed to enlarging membership in the benevolent community—the drive for emancipation of the slaves, women's suffrage, civil rights. "I have a dream that every valley shall be exalted, every hill and mountain shall be made low," said Martin Luther King.

The story extends beyond religion to embrace social solidarity 15
and civic virtue. It summons images of New England villagers who meet to debate their future; of frontier settlers who help build one another's barns and gather for quilting bees; of neighbors who volunteer as fire fighters and librarians, whose generosity erects the local hospital and propels high school achievers to college; of small towns that send their boys off to fight wars for the good of all. The story celebrates America's tradition of civic improvement, philanthropy, and local boosterism.

It also tells of national effort on behalf of those in need. The 16
theme permeated Roosevelt's New Deal, Truman's Fair Deal, Johnson's Great Society: America is a single, national community, bound by a common ideal of equal opportunity, and generosity toward the less fortunate. E Pluribus Unum.

Our popular culture has echoed these sentiments. Three hundred 17
years after John Winthrop's sermon they could be found in Robert Sherwood's plays, the novels of John Steinbeck and William Saroyan, Aaron Copland's music and Frank Capra's films. The last scene in *It's a Wonderful Life* conveys the lesson: Jimmy Stewart learns that he can count on his neighbors' generosity and goodness, just as they had always counted on him. They are bound together in common cause. The principle: We must nurture and preserve genuine community.

4. THE ROT AT THE TOP. The fourth parable is about the malevolence 18
of powerful elites, be they wealthy aristocrats, rapacious business leaders, or imperious government officials. The American parable differs subtly but profoundly from a superficially similar European mythology: The struggle is only occasionally and incidentally a matter of money or class. There are no workers pitted against capitalists at the heart of this American story. It is, rather, a tale of corruption, decadence, and irresponsibility among the powerful, of conspiracy against the broader public.

This morality tale has repeatedly provoked innovation and re- 19
form. Experience with the arbitrary authority of the English Crown produced in the Founding Fathers an acute sensitivity to the possibilities of abuse of power. The result was a government premised on the Enlightenment idea that power must be constrained and limited through checks and balances, and be kept firmly tied to the consent of the governed. A century later America responded to mounting concentrations of private economic power through

antitrust laws, designed to diffuse such power, and later by government support for other groups—labor unions, farmers, and retailers—capable of exercising countervailing power. The nation dealt with concentrations of governmental power through civil service rules that limited favoritism, and through electoral reforms and limitations on campaign contributions, to render politicians more accountable to the public. Government power also was held in check by periodic efforts to extend power to the states and cities, to open government decision making to greater public observation and scrutiny, to reduce the power of senior legislators, and to limit the ability of the president to take action without congressional approval. Since the beginning, in sum, Americans have been suspicious of elites and anxious to circumscribe their power.

At their worst, suspicions about the Rot at the Top have expressed themselves in conspiracy theories. America has harbored a long and infamous line of rabble-rousers, from the pre–Civil War Know-Nothings and Anti-Masonic movements, through the populist agitators of the late nineteenth century, the Ku Klux Klan, Senator Joseph McCarthy, and Lyndon LaRouche. They have fomented against bankers, Catholics, big corporations, blacks, Jews, foreigners, either or both major political parties, and other unnamed "interests." In this version of the story, the Rot at the Top is in a great conspiracy with the Mob at the Gates to keep down the common man and allow evil forces to overrun us. 20

Our popular culture revels in tales of corruption in high places. At the turn of the century, muckrakers like Upton Sinclair and Ida Tarbell uncovered sordid tales of corporate malfeasance; their modern heirs (revealing CIA depredations, White House scandals, and corporate transgressions) are called investigative reporters. The theme recurs in real or invented stories of honest undercover agents—Sam Spade, Serpico, Jack Nicholson in *Chinatown*—who trace the rot back to the most powerful members of the community. It's embodied by the great bullies of American fiction: Judge Thatcher of *Huckleberry Finn*, Broderick Crawford as the Huey Long-like character in *All the King's Men*, Lionel Barrymore's demonic Mr. Potter in *It's a Wonderful Life*. And in the tales of humble folk, like the Joad family of *The Grapes of Wrath*, who struggle valiantly against avaricious bankers and landowners. The moral is clear: Power corrupts, privilege perverts. 21

These are stories of aspiration. They summon us to duty and destiny. Importantly, the American ideal can never really be fulfilled. The goals it mandates are at once too vast and too vague for objective 22 achievement. To pursue them is its own accomplishment. The striving gives meaning to our collective life; the aspiration bestows on us a national identity. In this respect, America may be unique; probably no other culture so clearly defines itself by its morality tales. As a nation of immigrants without a deep common history, we are bound together by a common hope.

Sometimes the four tales take the form of self-congratulation: 23
Celebrate our triumph over savages and evil abroad! Rejoice in the opportunity open to each of us to gain fame and fortune! Admire our generosity and compassion! See how we have overcome vested privilege! But the same stories can be cast as rebukes, exposing the great gulf separating what we are from what we want to become, or how far we have fallen from an ideal we once achieved. The world is succumbing to tyranny, barbarism, and devastation, while we stand idly by! Hard work and merit are sabotaged by convention, chicanery, and prejudice! We are selfish, narcissistic, racist, indifferent—look at the poor and hungry in our midst! Our democracy is a sham, and everything important is controlled by a venal cabal at the top!

Pride in what we have accomplished, shame in what we have 24
not—these are the ways we recount the four mythic tales and incorporate them into our daily lives. We hear them on the evening news and read them in the press. We reiterate them over lunch when gossip turns to affairs of the day ("Did you hear about—?" "It just shows you—"). Our jokes, tellingly, often refer to these fables and our failures to manifest their mandates. No other culture so celebrates its Mark Twains and Will Rogers, its satirists and debunkers.

The pride or shames that come from seeking to live out these four 25
parables also shapes our politics. The great reform movements of American history—the Jacksonian war on the Bank of the United States in the 1830s, the abolitionist crusades of the mid-nineteenth century, the Populist-Progressive agitation of the 1880s and 1890s, the New Deal of the 1930s, the War on Poverty and Vietnam protests of the 1960s, even the Reagan "Revolution"—can all be viewed as periods in which the gap between aspiration and perceived reality grew too painfully wide for many to endure. The dissonance was too loud; the hypocrisy too transparent. If we were to continue to tell one another the same stories, it was necessary to take dramatic action.

Political rhetoric in America is essentially prophetic rather than 26
pragmatic. Challengers tell tales of shame and betrayal, incumbents speak with pride and promise. Both refer not to the mundane present but to a nation "to be," which has yet to fulfill its national destiny. The tone is often messianic, evangelical. The four parables appear as stories of salvation and redemption: America is to be a promised land of "New Frontiers" and "Great Societies." It will triumph over evil. It

will light the world. We will all be blessed with freedom and wealth, make manifest our compassion, and celebrate the triumph of the common man. Such, as we all know perfectly well, is our destiny.

Review Questions

1. What distinctive themes emerge in the morality tale about George? How do these themes speak to "the essence of our national self-image"?
2. Summarize the four "core" parables embodied in George's story.
3. Reich states that the American ideal can never be fulfilled. Why?
4. In what ways do the four tales take the form of self-congratulation and rebuke? Of stories of redemption?

Discussion and Writing Suggestions

1. Write a morality tale—a myth that you think embodies life on your college or university campus. Now compare *your* morality tale to Reich's.
2. Reich quotes political scientist Carl Friedrich as follows: "To be an American is an ideal. . . ." What does Friedrich mean, in the context of Reich's morality tale about George?
3. Cite examples from your own experience, from books you've read, or from movies you've seen that illustrate one or more of the core parables that Reich discusses. Develop your response into an essay.
4. At one point Reich states: "As a nation of immigrants without a deep common history, we are bound together by a common hope." What does Reich mean?

American Nightmares

KATHERINE S. NEWMAN

In the "American Morality Tale," you read a fable of achievement that in part defines our culture. Stories like George's confirm our faith that individuals who are industrious usually find their way up the ladder of success. Anthropoligist Katherine Newman tells a much different story—of movement in the opposite direction:

Hundreds of thousands of middle-class families plunge down America's social ladder every year. They lose their jobs, their income drops drastically, and they confront prolonged economic hardship, often for the first time. In the face of this downward mobility, people long accustomed to feeling secure and in control find themselves suddenly powerless and unable to direct their lives.

"American Nightmares" forms the first chapter of Newman's Falling from Grace: The Experience of Downward Mobility in the American Middle Class. *Newman based her analysis of downward mobility on 150 in-depth interviews. As you read this selection, you might pause to consider your level of confidence in the American Dream. For instance, you might reflect on what your being in college has to do with an expectation that you'll get (and keep) a good job and succeed in the world of commerce. Does losing a job and sliding* down *the ladder of success seem remotely possible to you? Read on. For a disturbingly high number of people, downward mobility is a grim fact of life.*

Katherine Newman teaches at Columbia University, where she is associate professor of Anthropology and a fellow of the Center for American Culture Studies.

DAVID PATTERSON was a practical man. All his life—from his youth in a run-down working-class district of Philadelphia to his adulthood in the affluent suburbs of New York—he had made rational decisions about the future. David had a talent for music, but he studied business. He had a flare for advertising, but he pursued a job in the computer industry. He wore his rationality proudly. Having steered clear of personal indulgence, he had a lot to show for his efforts: a beautiful home, two luxury cars, a country club membership, a rewarding executive job, and a comfortable, stable family. The Philadelphia slums seemed a million miles away and a million years ago. 1

When David's boss left frantic messages with the secretary, asking him to stay late one Friday afternoon, his stomach began to flutter. Only the previous week David had pored over the company's financial statements. Things weren't looking too good, but it never occurred to him that the crisis would reach his level. He was, after all, the director of an entire division, a position he had been promoted to only two years before. But when David saw the pained look on the boss's face, he knew his head had found its way to the chopping block. 2

He was given four weeks of severance pay, the use of the company telephone credit card, and a desk in a remote part of the building for the month. Despite these assurances, the credit card was canceled a week later. The company made good on the severance pay agreement, but David was made to feel increasingly uncomfortable about the desk. So he cleared out and went home. 3

Wasting no time, he set to work on the want ads every morning. He called all his friends in the business to let them know he was looking, and he sent his resume out to the "headhunters"—the executive search firms that match openings to people. David was sure, in the beginning, that it wouldn't be long before a new position opened up. He had some savings put aside to cushion the family in the meanwhile. He was not worried. By the third month of looking, he was a bit nervous. Six fruitless months down the line he was in a full-fledged panic. Nothing was coming through. The message machine he had bought the day after losing his job was perpetually blank. 4

After nine months, David and his wife Julia were at a crossroads. Their savings eroded, they could not keep up the mortgage payments on their four-bedroom neocolonial house. Julia had gone back to work after a two-year hiatus, but her earnings were a fraction of what David's had been. His unemployment compensation together with her paycheck never amounted to more than 25 percent of the income they had had in the old days. The house, their pride and joy and the repository of virtually all their savings, went up for sale. They reasoned that if the house sold, at least they could salvage some cash to support the family while David continued to look for a job. But their asking price was too high to attract many qualified buyers. Finally it was sold for a song. 5

Broke and distressed beyond imagining, the family found a small apartment in a modest section of a nearby town. David continued to look for an executive job, but the massive downturn of the mid-1980s in the computer industry virtually ensured that his search would bear no fruit. From Silicon Valley to Boston's Route 128, the shakeout in his field was stranding hundreds of equally well-qualified men. David could not get past the personnel offices of firms in other industries. He was not given the chance to show how flexible he could be, how transferable his managerial experience was to firms outside the computer field. 6

After a while David stopped calling his friends, and they ceased trying to contact him. Having always been sociable people, David and Julia found it hard to cope with the isolation. But with no good news to share, they didn't really feel like seeing old acquaintances. Friendship in their social circles revolved around outings to fancy restaurants, dances at the country club, and the occasional Broadway show or symphony in New York City. The Pattersons' budget simply could not sustain these luxuries anymore. For a time their friends were understanding, inviting them to dinner parties in their homes instead of excursions to places the Pattersons could not afford. But eventually 7 the unspoken rules of reciprocity put an end to that. The Pattersons couldn't issue return invitations, and the potluck dinners of their youth were not a viable alternative.

David and Julia were almost relieved by the ensuing isolation. It had been a strain to put on a calm countenance when, in fact, they felt that life was falling apart. At the same time, however, they interpreted the sounds of silence as abandonment. When friends ceased to call, David was convinced this meant that they no longer cared what happened to him. At least they should try to help him, he thought. 8

Like many other executive families, they were newcomers to suburban New York. Only two years before, David's firm had transferred him from its California branch to its New York headquarters. The move east held the promise of a more important executive job for David and a taste of real affluence. The transition had not been easy, since the social barriers of suburban society were hard to penetrate. Making new friends was no small accomplishment, and after two years there were only a few they could count as close. But they weren't the kind of old friends one could lean on in a crisis, and this surely was a crisis. 9

Their two teenage children were equally disoriented. Like most kids, they had opposed moving away from the place where they had grown up. They made no secret of their fury at being disrupted in the middle of high school, exiled to a new state where they knew no one. The girl had become rather withdrawn. The boy had worked hard to make new friends, leaning on his father's prestige as a company executive as an avenue into the status-conscious cliques of the local high school. When the son first arrived, as David put it, "No one would even talk to him. He was looked upon as a transient. Everyone else in his school had been in the same area since grammar school." The son's efforts to break into the networks met with only mild success, and even then, it took nearly the entire two years before he felt on solid social ground. He had finally reached a comfortable plateau when David lost his job. The whole family was thrown into turmoil, and the prospect of moving surfaced once again. 10

This was too much. David's teenagers unleashed their fury: How could he do this to them? The whole move to New York had been his idea in the first place. Now he was going to drag them through another upheaval! How dare he interfere with their lives so drastically once again? How were they supposed to explain to their friends that their father-the-executive was unemployed? Conformity was the watchword in their friendship circles. Not only did they have to look right and act right, they had to come from acceptable backgrounds. 11

An unemployed father hardly fit the bill. In fact, it threatened their standing altogether because it made it impossible for them to buy the clothes and cars that were commonplace in their social set.

David was accustomed to the normal tensions of life with teenagers. But in his shaken condition, he felt guilty. In retrospect, he agreed with his kids that the move to New York had been ill advised. But it wasn't as if he had had any warning of the debacle when they left the familiar comforts of California. He was simply doing what any intelligent man in his position would do: pursue every opportunity for upward mobility, even if the family is disrupted in the process. 12

Harder to contend with was the strain on his wife. Julia had long dabbled as a receptionist in art galleries, but her work had been more of a hobby and occasional supplement to the family budget than a mainstay. It had not been easy for her to pick up where she left off when the family moved to New York. Eventually, she found a part-time receptionist position, but her wages could not begin to cover the family's expenses. The move had bequeathed the Pattersons a staggering mortgage for a house twice as expensive as their old one. They could manage the bills as long as David was employed. But with his job gone, Julia's earnings could not stretch far enough. In one fell swoop, Julia found herself the major breadwinner in the family. Though she tried to find a job that would pay more, she had never thought of her work as a "career." She lacked the experience and stable employment history needed to land a better position. 13

It was the uncertainty of the situation that Julia found hardest to bear. She just could not tell when it would end or where they might land. It was difficult enough to batten down the hatches, cut purchases, and figure out a way to keep the credit cards from sliding too far into arrears. The family did not venture into the shopping malls any more, although this had once been a major form of weekend recreation. If she could figure out when things were going to bottom out, at least she would know what standard of living they had to adapt to. But, lacking any concrete sense of destination, Julia did not know how to begin the adjustment. Adjust to what? 14

Little help was forthcoming from the suburban matrons in the neighborhood, who—it appears—had never faced anything even remotely resembling this crisis. Where Julia expected to find sympathy and even offers of assistance, she found disbelief and not a little finger pointing. David could sense the damage this was doing: 15

> Since becoming unemployed there's really nothing, especially for my wife—no place where a woman can talk about things. There are no real relationships. She's hurt. People say to her, "With all the companies on Long Island, your husband can't find a job? Is he really trying? Maybe he likes not working." This really hurts her and it hurts me. People don't

> understand that you can send out 150 letters to headhunters and get 10 replies. Maybe one or two will turn into something, but there are a hundred qualified people going after each job. The computer industry is contracting all over the place and as it contracts, my wife contracts emotionally.

Secretly David worried whether Julia didn't share just a bit of her friends' attitudes. He could see the despair on her face when he would come home with no news to report. But on too many occasions, it seemed that her rage over the unfairness of his plight was mixed with doubt. She would bombard him with questions: Did you follow up on this lead? Did you call your cousin Harry about another? What did the headhunter tell you about that job downtown? David had few satisfying answers and after a while he began to resent the questions. Couldn't Julia see he was doing his best? It got to the point where he preferred taking a train into the city to look for work to riding with her in the car. Two hours together in the car with nothing but a bleak future to talk about was sometimes more than he could face. 16

The whole situation left David at a loss. No one was playing by the rules. He had credentials; he had experience; he was in a high-tech field that was touted as the wave of the future. Every time he turned on the news he would hear commentators lament the closing of the steel plants, the auto plants, and the coal mines. This was to be expected in an era when the United States no longer seemed able to compete in the world of heavy industry. But computers? They were supposed to be our salvation, and as a man who always kept one eye on the future, David had aggressively and successfully pursued a career in the field. How could he have gotten into such a quagmire? 17

The truth is, the computer industry was taking a bath in the mid-1980s. Thousands of employees had been turned out from Atari, Honeywell, Apple. Even IBM, the giant of the industry, had had to tighten its belt. David's entire division had been closed down: fifty people axed in one stroke. The industry shakeout was headline news in the *Wall Street Journal* and on the business pages of the major dailies. But it was only slowly seeping into general public consciousness, where computers still hold a special place as the glamour industry for the twenty-first century. The news had clearly failed to reach the Pattersons' friends. They were dumbfounded by David's disaster. High tech was the answer to the country's economic ills; computers were booming. How could David be having so much trouble finding a job? And what was the *real* reason he had lost his old one? 18

David could recite the litany of problems in the computer business so familiar to insiders. He could understand completely why his 19 division, located at the market research end of the company, had been targeted as "nonessential" to its survival. In the beginning he told himself that his personal situation could be explained logically. Market forces had put pressure on the company, and it responded, as any rational actor in a competitive capitalist economy would, by cost cutting, aiming first at those activities that were most remote from the nuts and bolts of production and sales. Indeed, had David been at the helm, he argued, he would have made the same decision. For David Patterson is no rebel. He is a true believer in the American way of doing business. Up until now, it had satisfied his every ambition. Hence there was no reason to question its fundamental premise: In economics, as in life, the strong survive and the weak fall by the wayside.

But after months of insecurity, depression, and shaking fear, the economic causes of his personal problems began to fade from view. All David could think about was, What is wrong with me? Why doesn't anyone call me? What have I done wrong? He would spend hours bent over his desk, rubbing his forehead, puffing on his pipe, examining his innermost character, wondering whether this or that personality flaw was holding him back. Could people tell that he was anxious? Were people avoiding him on the street because they couldn't stand to come face to face with desperation? Was he offending potential employers, coming on too strong? With failure closing in from all directions the answer came back "It must be me." The ups and downs of the computer industry and the national economy were forgotten. David's character took center stage as the villain in his own downfall. 20

. . .

David Patterson has joined the ranks of a little-known group in America, a lost tribe: the downwardly mobile. They are men and women who once had secure jobs, comnfortable homes, and reason to believe that the future would be one of continued prosperity for themselves and their children. Longtime members of the American middle class, they suddenly find everything they have worked to achieve—careers, life-styles, and peace of mind—slipping through their fingers. And despite sustained efforts to reverse the slide, many discover there is little they can do to block their descent. 21

The lack of attention downward mobility receives—from policymakers, scholars, and the public—has little to do with its actual incidence. Its low visibility is hardly a product of size: About one in five American men skid down the occupational hierarchy in their working lives. In recessions and depressions, their numbers grow at a particularly rapid rate. But downward mobility is not simply an episodic or unusual phenomenon in this country. It is a regular 22 feature of the economic landscape that has been with us for many years.

Yet we hear very little about the downwardly mobile. Magazine covers and television programs focus attention on upward mobility, the emergence of the Yuppies, the exploits of the rich and famous, and in less dramatic terms, the expectation of ordinary Americans that from one year to the next, their lives will keep getting better. But many middle-class families are headed in the opposite direction—falling on hard times—and relatively little systematic attention is paid to their experience. 23

In the public mind, downward mobility is easily confused with poverty, and the downwardly mobile are mistaken for those who live below the poverty line. But the two groups are quite different. More than seven million American families are officially classified as poor, and they have been the subject of countless studies. The poor *can* experience downward mobility—they can lose their hold on a meager, but stable existence and become homeless, for example—but many are at the bottom of the class hierarchy and some have been there for generations. 24

The experience of the downwardly mobile middle class is quite different. They once "had it made" in American society, filling slots from affluent blue-collar jobs to professional and managerial occupations. They have job skills, education, and decades of steady work experience. Many are, or were, homeowners. Their marriages were (at least initially) intact. As a group they savored the American dream. They found a place higher up the ladder in this society and then, inexplicably, found their grip loosening and their status sliding. 25

Some downwardly mobile middle-class families end up in poverty, but many do not. Usually they come to rest at a standard of living above the poverty level but far below the affluence they enjoyed in the past. They must therefore contend not only with financial hardship but with the psychological, social, and practical consequences of "falling from grace," of losing their "proper place" in the world. 26

Besides confusing the downwardly mobile with the poor, Americans tend to overlook these refugees from the middle class because their experience flies in the face of everything American culture stands for. From our earliest beginnings, we have cultivated a national faith in progress and achievement. The emphasis on success has always made it difficult for Americans to acknowledge defeat: No one ever talks about the Pilgrims who gave up and headed back to England. Our optimistic heritage stands in the way of recognizing how frequently economic failure occurs. 27

When academics study occupational mobility, most of the energy goes into trying to account for upward mobility. It is true that the majority of adults enjoy an upward trajectory in income and 28 occupational status over the course of their working lives. Yet, despite the fact that a large number have the opposite experience, downward mobility is relegated to footnotes or to a few lines in statistical tables. Rarely is it treated as a topic in its own right.

When the media, in times of economic hardship, do touch on the 29
problem, they show sympathy for the victims but express bewilderment at their fate. The downwardly mobile are often portrayed as the exceptions that prove the rule. Occasional reminders of what can go wrong seem to strengthen the nation's assumptions about what constitutes the normal and positive course of events. Downward mobility appears, therefore, as an aberration.

What is worse, America's Puritan heritage, as embodied in the 30
work ethic, sustains a steadfast belief in the ability of individuals to control the circumstances of their lives. When life does not proceed according to plan, Americans tend to assume that the fault lies within. We are far more likely to "blame the victim" than to assume that systemic economic conditions beyond the influence of any individual are responsible. This tendency is so pervasive that at times even the victims blame the victims, searching within to find the character flaw that has visited downward mobility upon them. Even they assume that occupational dislocation is somehow uniquely their problem. But the fact is, downward mobility has always been with us and exists in larger numbers than most of us realize.

American culture is rich in rituals and symbols that celebrate 31
worldly success. The extravagant bar mitzvah, the debutante ball, the society wedding, and the lavish golden anniversary celebration all signal the value that Americans attach to economic achievement. Our symbolic vocabulary for failure is, by comparison, stunted. Downward mobility has virtually no ritual face. It is not captured in myths or ceremonies that might help individuals in its grip to make the transition from a higher to a lower social status—there is no equivalent to Horatio Alger stories for the downwardly mobile.

The fact that downward mobility happens so often, yet has not 32
been institutionalized through social convention or public ritual, points to something very significant about the problem. Downward mobility is a hidden dimension of our society's experience because it simply does not fit into our cultural universe. The downwardly mobile therefore become an invisible minority—their presence among us unacknowledged.

This impoverishes public discourse about the problem. Even 33
more important, it has a savage impact on the downwardly mobile themselves. Lacking social and cultural support, the downwardly mobile are stuck in a transitional state, a psychological no-man's-land. They straddle an "old" identity as members of the middle class and a "new" identity as working poor or unemployed. They are in

suspended animation. The chaotic feeling of displacement creates confusion that can only be resolved through reintegration in a new capacity. Yet the downwardly mobile are unable to find a "new place" that satisfies their expectations. Hence they are left hanging, with one foot in the world of the professions, the corporate empire, the realm of the economically secure, and another in the troubled world of the financially distressed, the dispossessed, and the realm of low-level occupations.

Hanging between two worlds is a distressing state of existence, 34
for the downwardly mobile individual has to juggle two incompatible senses of personhood. On the one hand, he or she is a well-educated, skilled professional, accustomed to power, to deference, to middle-class norms of consumption. Yet behind the facade of the split-level executive home, the wallpaper is peeling, appliances are breaking down, clothes and shoes are wearing thin, and adults are venturing out to work at low-level white- or blue-collar jobs which afford no authority, no autonomy, no sense of self-importance.

Which self is the real and which the artificial for the downwardly 35
mobile? Some cling to the old persona for years. When asked, they claim their previous occupations as engineers, vice presidents of marketing, or sales managers. But even after hundreds of interviews fail to rescue them from a bottom-level job, after the family home has been sold to pay off debts, after the sense of self-assurance fades to be replaced by self-recrimination, the torture of two selves endures. For the kids' sake, for the wife's sake, or simply for the sake of one's own sanity, it is hard to ditch yesterday's honored identity in order to make room for today's poor substitute. And one never knows, perhaps tomorrow's mail will bring news of a job interview, a passport back to the only occupational reality that makes sense.

Without any guidelines on how to shed the old self, without any 36
instruction or training for the new, the downwardly mobile remain in a social and cultural vacuum. And society looks the other way because, frankly, it is embarrassing to see someone in such a state, and it's disturbing to treat the situation as anything other than an aberration. Any closer scrutiny makes us squirm, for it jeopardizes our own comfort.

This is not to say that there is no template for failure in American 37
culture. Indeed, there have been periods when images of downward mobility were fresh in America's mind. The massive wave of farm foreclosures in the 1930s had a quality of collective public mourning: groups of worn and dejected faces surrounding the old homestead or the last tractor. John Steinbeck's *Grapes of Wrath* memorialized the plight of the dispossessed Dust Bowl refugees. We remember the fate of the Joad family, ejected from their land by the nameless, faceless, hated bankers. The devastation of the Great Depression lingers in our

historical consciousness. When the 1980s saw the United States facing the worst rate of farm foreclosures since the depression, the specter of the 1930s was a constant subtext. The beleaguered Midwest, America's breadbasket, recalled an old calamity suffered by others in other times. The words "not since the 1930s" were repeated again and again as if to assure today's farmers that they are not the first to see their livelihoods destroyed.

Despite the cold comfort of history's example, farm foreclosures are not rituals: They do not happen regularly enough to have acquired the character of a culturally recognized transition from one status to another. They are catastrophes, extraordinary events. They remind us of the calamities that can befall the nation, but they cannot structure the experience of individuals whose descent down the status ladder takes place in ordinary times. 38

The absence of socially validated pathways for dealing with economic decline has important consequences for the downwardly mobile. They often mourn in isolation and fail to reach any sense of closure in their quest for a new identity. Their disorientation suggests how critical culture is in "explaining" to individuals the meaning of their fate. 39

To a certain extent, the experience of downward mobility in middle-class America is the same for all of its victims. Catastrophic losses create a common feeling of failure, loss of control, and social disorientation. Most people who experience downward mobility long for the "golden days" to return; some genuinely believe they will. Those who have sunk far below their original social status simply don't know where they belong in the world. This is the core of what it means to "fall from grace": to lose your place in the social landscape, to feel that you have no coherent identity, and finally to feel, if not helpless, then at least stymied about how to rectify the situation.[1] 40

[1]The destruction of David Patterson's career is an example of what social scientists call intragenerational downward mobility. It occurs when people who have attained a degree of occupational or financial success in their adult years see their achievements evaporate. They find themselves sliding down the socioeconomic ladder—they "fall from grace." Since David Patterons's experience flies in the face of most Americans' expectations for occupational mobility, one wonders just how many people there are like him. If his is a unique or atypical case, a tiny undercurrent in a massive sea of upward mobility, we need not be alarmed by it. It is quite another matter if we find that his fate is shared by many others, making downward mobility a significant feature of American life.

There are several ways of measuring downward mobility, but they all point to the fact that it is a widespread, chronic problem. In any year millions of families are sliding downward. And, perhaps most worrying, there is evidence to suggest that the situation has worsened in recent years. In a national survey conducted every year by the National Opinion Research Center about one-fourth of the respondents report that their financial situation has been deteriorating. The number who say that their economic situation has "gotten worse" rises

(*continued*)

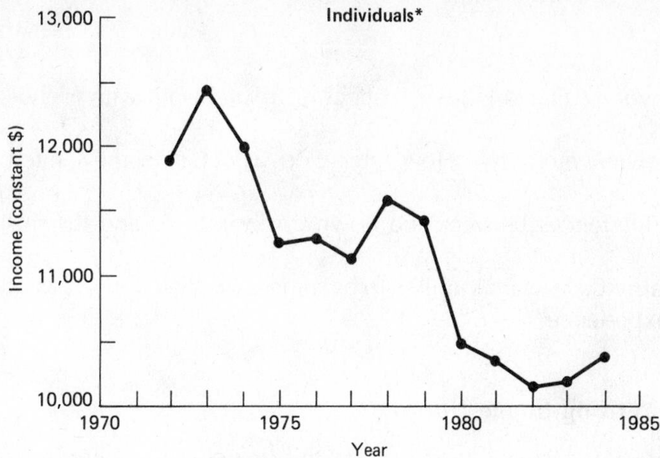

*"Individuals" means all persons 14 years and older.

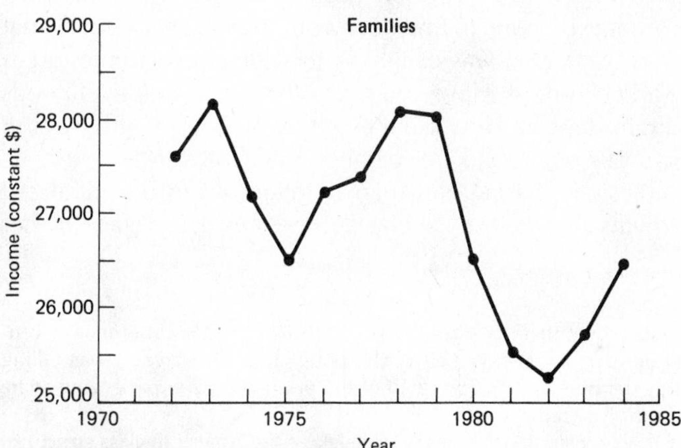

FIGURE 1. ***Income shifts 1972–1984.***

and falls to some degree from year to year, but the NORC data show that financial deterioration affects millions of people in both good years and bad. Government statistics on income help to explain why this is the case. Median individual income declined 14 percent between 1972 and 1982; and has yet to fully recover.

Overall, the average American has lost significant ground. However, the median income, like the "average American" is something of a conceptual fiction. Behind these annual averages lie some families holding their own financially, some streaking upward, and others taking a precipitous fall. Only by following a large number of actual families over a period of time can the extent of downward mobility (defined by income) be accurately assessed. Researchers at the University of Michigan have done exactly that by following the fortunes of 5,000 representative American families since 1968. They conclude that a large and increasing proportion of Americans is suffering economic decline. Between 1968 and 1972, 39 percent of the population had incomes that fell behind inflation. In the period 1973 to

(*continued*)

Review Questions

1. How did the layoff of David Patterson affect his relationship with friends and family?
2. What is "downward mobility"? How often does it occur in the United States?
3. What are the differences between the downwardly mobile and the impoverished?
4. What factors cause downward mobility to become a "hidden dimension of our society's experience"?

Discussion and Writing Suggestions

1. Discuss the possible reasons Newman titled this first chapter of her book "American Nightmares."
2. Newman observes that David Patterson became the villain in his own downfall. After months of trying to find new work, he began to ask, "What is wrong with me?" Patterson was caught in the grip of economic forces over which he had no control. Have you seen others lose their livelihoods under similar circumstances? How did they respond? Discuss the ways in which their responses did or did not parallel Patterson's.
3. As an anthropologist, Katherine Newman is interested in the ritualized behaviors and myths that help to define cultures. In the preface to her

---

1977, the proportion had grown to 43 percent. By the years 1978 to 1982 (the most recent period for which data are available), over half of the population (56 percent) was falling behind inflation. By this definition, then, over half of the population is experiencing some erosion in their standard of living.

Downward mobility is a problem for families at all levels of the American class structure. In fact, a substantial proportion of those who are sliding come from the upper tiers. This can best be seen by placing families in five groups (quintiles) arranged in ascending order of income and examining income mobility relative to others, over time. Looking at families who were in the top 20 percent in income in 1971, more than one-fifth of them had fallen out of the top into the lowest three quintiles—a substantial fall relative to others.

Nor is downward mobility limited to any age group or stage in the life cycle. The researchers following those 5,000 families concluded as much: "We do not have to look . . . to the Great Depression to find frequent instances of economic loss and hardship; the risk of sharp decreases in living standards is significant at virtually every stage of life during the seventies."

Many of those who slide are actually *plunging* down the income ladder, sustaining cuts of 50 percent. Duncan and his colleagues show that nearly one-third of the population suffered a catastrophic drop of *half or more* of their family income at least once during the seventies.

In sum, income data from the 1970s suggest that downward mobility is both widespread and serious: Half of the population suffers falling incomes, and almost one-third plunge far down the income ladder. Under these circumstances, downward mobility ceases to be an exceptional experience and becomes a significant social problem.

book, she writes that "downward mobility is a subject crying out for anthropological analysis. It is an experience as foreign to many in the United States as the lives of exotic peoples in New Guinea." Review this first chapter of *Falling from Grace* and highlight those passages that suggest to you an anthropological point of view. For instance, you might look for evidence of a cultural analysis that relies on myths and on group identities and interactions.

4. "Falling from grace" is a particularly evocative phrase that Newman uses both for the title of her book and in the selection you've read. Usually, "falling from grace" denotes the biblical story of Adam and Eve's banishment from the Garden of Eden. Why do you suppose Newman appropriates the phrase for use in this book? Develop your answer into an essay.

5. To what extent do David Patteron's experiences undermine for you the common and widely shared assumption that in America an individual's effort and ingenuity can overcome all obstacles?

A View from the East

TOM ASHBROOK

Increasingly, commentators who take stock of America are concluding that the country is in trouble: The quality of political debate has declined; productivity has declined; cynicism and selfishness are on the rise. Commentators, in effect, slap us to attention, as if to say: Look, reader, the America you grew up believing in no longer exists.

Tom Ashbrook is such a commentator. As a student and then as a correspondent for the Boston Globe, *Ashbrook spent more than a decade living and traveling in Japan and other countries in the Far East. He took the occasion of his return to America to record impressions of his native land, and his "View from the East" is not heartening. Above all, he finds his country to be "overripe," past its prime and beginning to turn rotten. You will have to look hard to discern signs of optimism in Ashbrook's voice. Still, it is a voice that must be heard, for it is representative of any number of articles written recently on the decline of America.*

As is characteristic of journalistic essays, the writer draws authority less from facts and figures than from the shrewdness of his own observations. Watch as Ashbrook weaves private notes through his article. Observe his impressionistic approach to his subject and note how the

---

approach differs markedly from the reliance on statistical information you will see later in Branfman.

Tom Ashbrook graduated from Yale University (1977) with a bachelor's degree in history. Thereafter, he held a teaching fellowship at The Chinese University of Hong Kong until 1979 and was reporter for the South China Morning Post *in Hong Kong from 1979 to 1980. Joining the* Boston Globe *in 1981, he served as both a city hall and a business reporter until his appointment as chief of the* Globe's *Tokyo bureau upon its opening in 1984. Back in Boston since May 1988, Ashbrook continues to write for the* Globe *as a contributor.*

Overripe. 1

Five minutes off the plane from Asia and the word drifts through 2
my head like a bad smell. America. Overripe.

The limo from the Honolulu airport is a lumbering, battered Buick 3
that speaks of a pumped-up prime gone by. I've seen pristine '64 Chevys in Java still polished to a sheen and Toyota taxis of every year that sparkle. But this is something different waiting at the curb. The doors don't close properly. The seats are stained and torn. The suspension is drooping, cockeyed. The music is mushy. The paint is extravagantly scarred. The passengers are fat. American. Overripe. Welcome home.

Nearly a third of my life has been spent working and studying in 4
Asia, almost 10 years traveling out of India, Hong Kong, most recently Japan. It used to be reassuring coming home to America. In my memory, home came with a cool blast of certainties and competence, an air of eternal affluence and standards to count on.

No more. At its crisp, industrialized forefront, Asia now puts 5
America's slacker face to shame. Like everyone else, I hear the buzz of debate over whether our nation is in decline. I am no economist. But I am home again from Asia, and troubled by what I see.

"Sometimes it shuts, sometimes it don't," says the limo driver at 6
the airport, repeatedly slamming a passenger's rattling door. "But don't worry, we'll get there."

I wonder. 7

What a country, my country, seen with a wary, Asia-fresh eye. It 8
looks free, by all means—viscerally, unnervingly, exhilaratingly free. But to what end? It looks wealthy, by any measure, but drowsily, dangerously accustomed to its wealth and to its life on credit. It looks principled, in a noisy, faddish way, but afflicted with the crime, drugs, and alienation of moral decay.

For four years this time I had crisscrossed Asia out of Tokyo. It is 9
a vast continent with great backwaters and problems of its own. But along the vigorous economic axis stretching from Japan to Singapore,

it is hardheaded, dynamic, aggressive, and hungry. Most things work, and those that don't soon do. The region's cultures can seem, and often are, relative straitjackets demanding conformity and obedience. But a resident anywhere along Asia's industrialized spine soon develops a taste for precision, dependability, disciplined energy, and a certain high seriousness about the practical tasks, great and small, of life.

Ride the gleaming subway in Hong Kong. Feel the crisp concen- 10
tration of a Singapore banker and his lowliest tellers, the fiery intensity of a Korean shipbuilding crew, the palpable dedication of a Yokohama schoolteacher. No one on cruise control. All alert, engaged, at grips with the importance of their roles and the gist of the national life they support. All infused with a powerful sense of forward motion, of purposefulness.

In just those terms, an American homecoming is a journey into 11
shades of disarray. While veins of efficiency and competence feel ever-expanding in Asia, they appear to be contracting in the United States. Our cracked highways and rusting bridges seem physical reflections of falling standards of service, organization, simple care in the performance of jobs—of lost resolve.

How to judge? Trade figures? Foreign debt? Dire but dry. Atmo- 12
spherics? Scary for a recent returnee. My brother-in-law sleeps with a large pistol in his nightstand and an alarm system that can track a burglar room by room. The news on arrival in America has the US president turning to astrology, Los Angeles drivers taking potshots at one another on the freeway. American schoolchildren scoring at the bottom of the First World heap in key subjects. Drug lords reigning over urban fiefs. Alcoholics Anonymous and its ilk as a new religion. Wall Street sapping the economy it was intended to fuel. What is wrong with this picture?

True, the slippage is widely bemoaned. But to a returnee the 13
more impressive point is the extent to which Americans have developed a tolerance for excess, ineptitude, and carelessness in the everyday business of life. To apply the sharper, more disciplined standards of contemporary Asia is to risk ostracism in the United States. Relax, man. Cool out. We don't want to hear about it.

If only it were a simple matter of lifestyle, the advice might have a 14
certain charm. There is a beguiling aspect to a First World nation self-indulgently flirting with Third World standards, tempos, timetables—like seeing your father puttering around on vacation, or pampering yourself on a beach holiday.

But so much more is at stake here. In the realm of political ideals, 15
of core values, America remains powerfully attractive to a returnee from Asia—that rare nation where individuals can assume individuality as a birthright, where diversity is, at least in principle,

championed instead of smothered. Viewed against Asia's more restrictive norm, those American ideals have a sparkling, almost magical quality. But as the 1980s end, one fears that critical links between industry and affluence, discipline and maintenance of national ideals, are slipping away.

Have we really reached a special plane of devotion to democracy, 16
liberty, and civil rights? Or have we just been rich enough to pretend? We may soon have the chance to learn.

Notes as follows: 17

Honolulu, May 21, 1988: "Hello, Occident. Cracked highways, no 18
service. Hotel is heavy on glitter and self-promotional hype, light on everything else. Construction quality shabby. Rusting metalwork. Cheap materials. Very big people stuffed into little Japanese cars. A joke? So many tawdry corners, even here in "island paradise." Rich next to poor. Slick by shabby. Twitchy bag ladies and a legless panhandler croaking "Aloha" on Waikiki. Lumpy, pale people on sidewalks, half-undressed, not self-conscious. All so casual. Korean cabdriver complains road repairs take 10 times longer than in Seoul. I bet. No overnight work. Air of indolence, low voltage. Is this just the islands? Or America, First World's Third World?"

Hopped up. Shambling. Borderline derelict. On the streets of 19
America, jokes once made about service in Delhi and the dowdiness of Moscow come hauntingly back to roost. At the airport, lusty baggage handlers throw bags off the carrousel with un-Eastern flair, zinging them into grand and ragged rows. But half the bags aren't there. A truck has broken down. Wait an hour, please. A woman shrieks and swears. Others too. More are passive, like Third World villagers waiting for a bus that might come, or might not. Welcome home.

Am I too harsh? Have I unconsciously slipped on a straitjacket of 20
Asian rigidity? Lost patience with the least disorder? Fallen for the comforts of conformity? Have I lost appreciation for the hurly-burly dynamism of America's diversity? Or is this, my country, getting to be a mess?

Fresh into an American hotel, my son turns on a *Ghostbusters* 21
cartoon on Saturday morning television: "Hey, fella! This is America," comes the wisecracking voice of an animated hero of the '80s. "I've got the right to not work any time I want."

Six years old, with no memory of life outside Japan, my child has 22
never heard such a notion before.

"What did he say, Daddy?" 23

"Something ridiculous," I growl, overreacting perhaps at the 24
thought of my son's tender moral fiber already being toyed with while millions of Asian youngsters are studying away, night and day, being toughened for economic battle.

"What kind of show is this?" I yell to my wife. "The Japanese and Koreans are going to eat my kid's lunch!" 25

"They're already eating ours," she says. "Where are the suitcase keys? And did you get some money?" 26

I stop at the bank. An engraved plaque staring at me from the head teller's desk would confirm insanity in Japan: 27

"Pardon me," it reads, "but you seem to have mistaken me for someone who gives a damn." 28

Once that brassy crack would surely have been the hard shell of American humor that overlaid an indomitable spirit. Does it still? 29

A century ago, China's nadir was captured in the image of bony drug addicts lounging in a haze of opium smoke. Asia was the tottering continent, wobbling on corrupted values the worth of which looked small next to those of dynamic young America. American politicians, moralists, and poets saw American values, the impulse of the "free, original life," as Walt Whitman put it, proudly sweeping the world, surging from America's shores, fulfilling a global destiny with final triumph in Asia. 30

Inquiring, tireless, seeking that yet unfound,/I, a child, very old, over waves, toward the house/of maternity, the land of migrations, look afar, wrote Whitman, giving voice to the spirit of that buoyant age. *Look off over the shores of my Western sea—having/arrived at last where I am—the circle almost/circled.* 31

What a difference a century makes. . . . 32

Notes, Los Angeles, June 1: 33

"We wear everything on our sleeves—our joy, our pathos, our sexuality. It is overwhelming at first contact out of, let's say, Japan—as if every American on the street is wearing a neon sign flashing, 'I am this,' or, 'I am that.' Is it just California? From a Japanese point of view, I suppose it could be charming, in a boozy, carnival sort of way, but not very serious. Emotions, held nearly forever in check in Japan, here appear trivialized, cheapened, easy. We show people ours expecting a show in return. And in the 1980s, we usually get it. We walk around with our psychic flies down. 34

"More than vulgar, it appears wasteful—a distraction from the big contest, the unending mission to be on top or climbing there. It seems to assume that success is static, lasting. What better to do than stare at our navels and broadcast what we see. That's all well and good for the monk in his temple, says the Asian onlooker. But this is the material world. 35

"To a competitor it must look great: That's the way, big guy. Keep staring at your navel, dissipating yourself on self-analysis while we carve you up. You will sit up from the psychiatrist's couch and find all 36 the other furniture gone, the house gone, find that you are talking to yourself. And then, when you are hungry and cold and poor, then see how little the words matter, how these personal crises can look like so much silly prattle. They see it. They have had centuries to figure it out, to know it, bone deep, as nations. And now it is simply assumed. Their knowledge is a hard weapon against our soft swirl of emotion."

Yes, we worked hard. We remember. We were tough. Our folk 37
songs have us working on the railroad, forging west, plowing the sod, rolling steel, building cities, cities of big shoulders.

But in the Asian eye, the larger fact is that we were lucky. We 38
won history's biggest lottery, beat the richest slot machine. An entire continent dropped in our lap, brimming with riches, like a groaning table of food just waiting to be eaten. And we ate it and congratulated ourselves on the eating and on our great generosity in inviting one and all to our vast feast.

Well, broods the Asian question, who couldn't have done that? Across the Pacific, they curse themselves for having been too inward-looking, too hidebound to grab for the New World. But the fact that we happened to get it and to subsequently get rich on it is less than astonishing to them. As for the role of democracy in our ascent to affluence, they sometimes seem to hardly see it. They question its real significance.

The point is, as for luck, they think we've had it in spades. In 40
technique, we've made some marvelous innovations. They have snapped them up with a vengeance.

But for system, well . . . from Asia, ours looks more and more like 41
a one-time shot—a grand, openhanded bouquet of gestures made for wide ranges and unlimited resources. And both of those are now gone. Our great virgin treasure is used. Our techniques are everyone's. Our system and values and vanities stand at last, in their eyes, on the level playing field of a harder reality, the only reality that most of the world has ever known. It is a new game, and in the first round we have lost a bundle very quickly. We are deeply in debt and do not seem to understand, or want to admit, that the game has changed.

Will we reach for rejuvenation and draw new strengths from old? 42
Our hidden asset, as Asia knows and we should know, too, is diversity's flexibility, our capacity to stretch and move and recombine. But the clock is ticking. And opportunities go by.

"You don't know what you have. They know what they don't 43
have. And they want it," says a Chinese friend who recently emigrated from Hong Kong to Los Angeles. "Americans are too naive. You forget the world is a jungle. It's a race. If you slow down too much, you lose."

How quick the turnaround seems to have been. With every single year of the 1980s, Asian astonishment at the behavior of the United States has grown. For all its pyrotechnic quality, the debacle in Vietnam did not signal the big slip in Asian respect for America. Loss in misconceived war is something that happens. Japan survived it handsomely. So could we. 44

But loss of spunk, of moral fiber, of well-considered national resolve and high, hard-nosed seriousness—that is a first-rate affliction and one that many Asians associate directly with the Reagan years, the years of American dreaming. 45

Year by year, our trade deficit spiraled up in the 1980s. No region of the world profited more than Asia. In the early '80s, I remember hearing Asian businessmen and bureaucrats express their respect and then near-awe at our commitment to free trade despite the consequences. By the late '80s, awe has turned to incredulity and disdain. Were we so arrogant as to think we could turn any setback around, no matter how long we waited to begin? What, they would ask, is the United States really doing to defuse its debt and deficit perils and the sump of problems behind them? Where is the hard work, the mending, the bone of realism, the grit of resolve required to turn your fortunes around? 46

Their questions echo loud in the mind at homecoming. 47

Where is the sense of urgency I've come home expecting to find? In spite of every warning sign, in spite of all that we have to lose, America seems willfully trapped in its "feel good" mode. Is it simple resignation? One doubts it. Is Ronald Reagan's "morning in America" spell still so strong? Surely not. 48

To one coming from a continent of rising expectations, America's response so far to uncertainty over its future is alarming. Shrugged shoulders and an escapist "live for today" attitude seem to prevail. The refrain of a Citicorp bank TV ad intones: "Because Americans want to succeed, not just survive." Is this an exhortation, this incredible statement of the obvious? Is it a reminder? A plea? A diplomatic way of saying, "Watch out, you're tempting mere survival"? One cannot imagine the line in any Asian medium. 49

Corporate executive compensation figures are published with Lee Iacocca, self-styled champion of American industrial renewal, taking home a packet worth $18 million. It is an unthinkable figure in Asia, and not because they don't have the money. They have mounds. But an $18 million pay packet simply sounds unethical in Asia. It reeks of disharmony, the great Asian taboo. All right, in capitalism, money motivates the man. But if $18 million is required to motivate, the magnitude of the compensation seems to squeeze out all room for a sense of national mission, of balance, of the good of the whole as the final guarantee of each individual's well-being. 50

Still, I am baffled by the low level of urgency in America's discussion of its global standing. Of course, there is a great deal said on the topic, there are hearings and warnings and media attention. But to anyone coming from a region of nations hyper-attuned to their mounting success, the United States seems strangely unattuned to its mounting troubles. 51

At what point will we be galvanized? Could it be that a critical mass of Americans just don't believe that life could ever be anything but generally prosperous? That we have forgotten what a rare, fine legacy history has left to us? Or that the habits of affluence are now so deeply ingrained, so tied up with our elemental national mythology, that our behavior will not change even in the face of the most pressing evidence that it should? 52

To a nation that carries a historical reputation for pragmatism, the notion of marching to decline in myth-bound disregard of a downward slide might seem ridiculous. But in Asia, the form is well known. The continent's two largest nations—China and India, both once great themselves—have spent centuries in deep troughs, gripping old cultural patterns, myths, and self-images that left them cripplingly out of sync with a changing world. 53

Could America do the same thing? At first blush, it seems unlikely. Historically, ignorance of changes over the horizon has been at least one major factor in nations' unresisting fall from relevance. In the global village today, who can remain ignorant? Perhaps no one. But the power of self-delusion can be strong. Already, much of America appears to live to a striking degree in a rosy electronic cocoon of television images of itself—rich, buoyant, and ever-consuming. Show triumphs over substance. The happy golden light of the small screen casts its patina over a widening reality of dereliction. 54

Never mind, we seem to say, we will grab all we can grab, buy all we can buy, live the dream. For everything that has been said and written about it, American consumerism in full flower is still awesome to behold. America's vast supermarkets and stores have no rival for their sheer volume of goods. Whatever our self-perception may be, the view from Asia sees the cushy culture, an indulgent national psyche adrift from larger purpose, wedded to consumption, weakened by the addiction, suspended in a tenuous, fragile addict's state. 55

Certain ironies are not lost on me as I watch my own homecoming reaction. No doubt in the years before World War II, Japanese emissaries to the United States sent similar appraisals back to Tokyo, reports tinged with a visceral, disdainful response to America's less tightly marshaled society. That very appraisal surely fueled Japan's belief that it could win in an all-out struggle, its view that America 56 was fundamentally handicapped by disharmony and a shallowness of spirit. And Japan was wrong.

But there will be no Pearl Harbor to rouse the nation this time. 57
And in an era of more civil striving, America has taken its debt and trade-deficit blows with stunning nonchalance.

Our Asian neighbors embody ancient cultures. They have been 58
around, known long ups and long downs, known suffering. By their standards, we are only now beginning to face a real national test, perhaps the first and only real test in our fortune-blessed history. So far, our response is not a pretty sight.

Notes, Bloomington, Illinois, June 9: 59

"At breakfast, the milk carton advertises a missing child. The 60
morning papers announce a gruesome routine of violent crime. Once I was immune to such news. Soon I suppose I will be again. We revel in our shoot-ups. So be it. But for now, I am simply reminded: This is not a safe country.

"What a psychic price Americans pay for living in a society so 61
laced with crime. Fear makes every citizen a victim. It is an invisible tax that Americans now seem to take for granted. But it leaps out at anyone returning from the low-crime regions of Asia. I am pondering how to make my children understand that their homeland is a different kind of country from what they've known—how to alert them to the lurking violence of America. It is a disheartening job.

"America is loud and jarring to the kids, coming from the orderly, 62
muted life of Tokyo. I am glad for the change, glad to let them know the boisterous energy of the American hubbub. But there is something missing in all the glitz and noise. Where is the still, small voice that should remind them of their duties, their responsibilities, and therefore their value to this society?"

I have pitied Asian children for the burden of duty they often 63
come to know so young, but this American vacuum is too empty. Asian kids learn their national mission—push up, push ahead, join in, put your shoulder to the wheel, let's succeed—with their mother's milk. American children now seem never to be told. Is personal wealth the only goal? What about the commonweal? Upholding principles? An unhampered way in deciding constitutes freedom. A failure to pass on principles and give guidance looks like simple irresponsibility. Against the Asian model of common assumptions and pervasive atmospheric "lessons" for the young about responsibility, I feel suddenly very much alone in instructing my children. Alone and somehow abandoned.

Yet Americans are not blind. We are self-indulgent these days 64
and insular, but not stupefied. Returning, one feels at some level a knowing streak of nihilism in our steady bow to the economic supremacy of others.

Our looming time of trial will be different from the genteel retrenchment of Europe after its glory days. We took the helm from Britain, and a skein of preeminent values was left largely intact; the tune of international life did not fundamentally change. With the rise of Asia, it goes into a very different key. 65

Maybe we are disgusted with the long era of Western supremacy, with its legacy of imperialism, exploitation, and war. Fair enough, even wise. But what of the advances we have achieved? In some vitally important regards—acceptance of racial diversity and equality, respect for the individual, awareness of women's rights—we find ourselves, despite our failings, far ahead of Asia. Are we prepared to throw this over? 66

The question is not an appeal to old Yellow Peril–style phobias. Our Asian neighbors are people we know now, no longer a faceless mass. We drive their cars and sell them our hamburgers. We know their strengths, their humanity, their weaknesses. But don't we owe ourselves and our rich, hard-won traditions a deeper second thought? A firmer underpinning of support? 67

Maybe we don't think so. Perhaps at some critical juncture of affluent flabbiness and self-doubt we hand off the baton with a shrug. Maybe we don't want to ponder our heirs. Maybe we don't have the energy to resist this drift. Behind the puffery of the Reagan-era strut perhaps there lay a fundamental loss of self-confidence, of self-respect. "There is no worse neurosis," wrote British author Anthony Burgess once in an essay on American angst, "than that which derives from a consciousness of guilt and an inability to reform." 68

Where is our leadership? Not political panderers or television shamans, but moral leaders of high secular stripe, leaders of hard-headed vision who themselves project an example of attitudes that can win, an example of honest courage. In America's blow-dried leadership wasteland, the rare standout such as steady Paul Volcker or even sober George Shultz takes on an awkward sheen of sainthood. Surely the ranks can be thickened, a broader banner raised. 69

Notes, Boston, January 1989: 70

"With every passing month, the pull of America's avoidance rituals grows on me. They are distinctive habits of mind. Don't think about the world; think about the movies. Don't think about the future; it may not be as good as today. Don't think about the country's well-being; grab your own private piece and guard it well. Think of burglar alarms and private schools. Pull up your little drawbridge. Enjoy the flush of affluence while it lasts. 71

"The presidential election campaign has not been heartening. Avoidance on a grand scale. Can Americans imagine that there are still countries where talk of knuckling down and doing hard tasks, of sacrificing for the long-term good, can actually win public support? 72

"We know implicitly the great strength of our national resources and of our diversity. Indeed, they are real strengths, and many Asians still recognize their unique potential with a sense of near-awe. But strength unmarshaled, strength squandered, is not strength at all. 73

"It is good to be home, to see the verve and open humor of Americans again, to feel again firsthand the unbounded potential, the great chorus of individual wills that has always made our country a rich and beckoning world. 74

"It is good to be home, but painful, too, to see the disrepair of a cherished homeland. It is unnerving to feel the national hollowness underfoot. The false-bottomed life. Even garbage day leaves a little taint of guilt, a little knowing decadence when the hour for decadence has passed. In Tokyo, we separated everything—newspaper, organic stuff, bottles and cans. So did the whole city, 12 million strong. But not here. Just toss it in the can. This is America. We have great valleys we can fill." 75

Coming home, do I detect an urge to blame democracy itself for our troubles? What irony. An election ends in disaffection and we mutter that in a democracy people get what they deserve. But are we creating a debased electorate—ill-led, ill-educated, and veering toward economically divided camps where the affluent are guarding their golden retreats and not the future of the nation? 76

Ronald Reagan was right when he waxed poetic on the beauty of America's inheritance and ideals. They are beautiful and unique. But beauty requires tending, and the unique requires knowing care. The last best hope of mankind? Yes, but we must continue to make it so. 77

Viewed from somewhere mid-Pacific, both great shores can inspire deep unease these days—a rising Asia for failing to share the ideals of freedom and openness more deeply, the United States for failing to make those ideals work more successfully. It is easy to feel bereft. 78

Give a half-turn to that dark perspective and one can imagine a far brighter scene. Picture the United States grafting some of contemporary Asia's honest resolve onto its own great tradition of liberty. Picture Asia further unbinding its societies in the new security of affluence. In tandem, such trends could make for a vibrant, inviting 21st century; for a fresh opening and melding that would profit all parties. 79

But American delay in coming to the table with its house in order casts a long shadow of doubt across such prospects. If we come as a vital, sharp-witted partner, Asia will welcome the partnership, and both sides can benefit. If we dither and decline, we can expect to find a more exploitative, less receptive set of neighbors across the Pacific. 80

Indeed, the same might well be said of our future relations with 81

Europe. But the contrast of American laxity and Asian dynamism is today the more marked. At bottom, my unease is with that simple, stark contrast. Leave aside all questions of principles and ideals, and dynamic Asia may simply stand as the great and rising yardstick that measures our rejuvenation—or our decline.

Review Questions

1. "In the realm of political ideals, of core values, America remains powerfully attractive to a returnee from Asia." Why?
2. In the 1980s, how did the Asian view of Americans change?
3. In Asia, salaries paid to executives are less than those paid to executives in America. Why? How do huge compensation packages for executives jeopardize loyalty to one's company and to one's country?
4. Ashbrook is "baffled by the low level of urgency in America's discussion of its global standing." Why?
5. According to Ashbrook, what are the virtues of the "American hubbub" and American diversity? What are the potential weaknesses of Asian discipline?
6. What values does Ashbrook feel Americans should fight to retain and pass on?
7. What are "America's avoidance rituals"?
8. What trends, in tandem, could make for a "vibrant, inviting 21st century"?

Discussion and Writing Suggestions

1. Reread the first ten paragraphs of Ashbrook's article and compile two lists: the descriptive words and phrases he uses to characterize life in America, as opposed to those he uses to characterize life in the East. Comment on your findings.
2. Restrictive norms for behavior seem to have produced a highly efficient, dedicated work force in the East. Schoolteachers, businessmen and -women, factory workers—all seem to view their jobs with greater seriousness than their counterparts in America, according to Ashbrook. To what extent do you believe that American workers lack discipline? Draw on your own work experiences in responding to this question. Develop your answer into an essay.
3. Ashbrook writes that "as the 1980s end, one fears that critical links between industry and affluence, discipline and maintenance of national ideals, are slipping away." Speculate on what these "links" might be and how they might have slipped away.
4. As any journalist, Tom Ashbrook takes notes—he records impressions and from these writes his articles. In this piece at several different places, Ashbrook quotes his notes verbatim. What is the effect of his sharing raw

impressions with the reader? In what ways do his notes differ from the remainder of the piece?

5. At one point, Ashbrook asks rhetorically: "Could it be that a critical mass of Americans don't believe that life could ever be anything but generally prosperous?" What's your view? Do you believe that life for most Americans could in the foreseeable future become less than prosperous?

Still the Promised Land

NATWAR M. GANDHI

Natwar M. Gandhi, an immigrant from India and a tax policy analyst in Washington, D.C., disagrees with the gloomy assessments of America's decline. Gandhi sees America as a promised land—especially for immigrants, despite "the crime, the drugs, the social promiscuity and the homelessness."

Recently, The Atlantic carried excerpts from the diaries of George F. Kennan, diplomat, historian and a major architect of postwar American foreign policy, in which Kennan views "the United States of these last few years of the 20th century as essentially a tragic country." 1

This is a serious indictment, and one that all concerned Americans should take note of. Kennan, the last of America's wise old men, possesses one of the finest intellects in America today. He does find some solace in America's magnificient natural resources and some of its people, but too much of his diaries contain, by his own admission, "bleakness of impressions of my own country." 2

Nearly 30 years ago, Edmund Wilson, the great literary critic and another Princetonian, had similar observations. As he was approaching old age, Wilson wrote, "I have finally come to feel that this country, whether or not I live in it, is no longer, any place for me. . . . When, for example, I look through *Life* magazine, I feel that I do not belong to the country depicted there, that I do not even live in that country." 3

These statements are neither the rhetorical outbursts of frustrated old men nor the diatribes of modern-day revolutionaries. They are the thoughtful comments of two of America's most distinguished public men after long lives of study and contemplation. 4

Millions of immigrants like me, however, would find these comments a bit incomprehensible. As immigrants, we made a deliberate choice to come to America. Personally, I find these comments hard to believe and yet disturbing because I greatly admire both Kennan and Wilson. To me these men represent all that is best in American thought. I always listen to what they have to say and nearly always find merit in their words. Yet I believe that their harsh judgments on America are unwarranted. 5

Why would such thoughtful people give up on America? I believe it is a matter of perspective. Wilson and Kennan belong to what Wilson himself calls a "pocket of the past." They represent the old professional class, which provided America its dedicated doctors, diplomats, lawyers, professors, clergymen and writers. They have a vision of America that is not easily reconciled with what one reads in daily newspapers or sees on television. 6

They are deeply patriotic men. Their idea of patriotism, as once expressed by Albert Camus, is the devotion to the ideal of what their country might be. And this is the problem. 7

They compare American reality with the America of their dreams and bemoan the gap. They lament what has not been done and miss what has. Mesmerized by a dream, they cannot be happy with reality. Their concept of America is Utopian. 8

What matters, however, is not that America falls short of its promise, but that it continually strives toward that promise. That is the American genius. There is something to be said for the American belief, some would call it naiveté, that if you keep trying, things will get better. 9

I can say that even in the short two decades that I have been here America has indeed changed for the better. Take, for example, the progress made on the issue of race relations, which seemed to tear the country apart during the '60s. Who would have thought then in the midst of all the acrimonious debate, the agitated demonstrations and the exploding cities that within just two decades Jesse Jackson would carry Virginia and be a credible candidate for the Democratic nomination for president? Or that thousands of blacks would be elected officials throughout the country, particularly in the South? 10

America never ceases to evolve. It is an ever-improving, ever-improvising process. Mostly, it is muddling through. Things are never really neat and orderly, but always changing. 11

No other country changes as fast and as much as America. Even the complexion of its own people changes. The French and the Japanese essentially have remained French and Japanese throughout their histories. So have the Indians and Chinese. Not so with Americans. They let people of all kinds and colors come to their shores. Just 12 imagine: In a mere half-century, America will no longer be a country of white majority.

And the melting pot not only remakes the immigrant, it also reshapes the country. New generations of immigrants bring vitality. The fresh new stream keeps the old water from stagnating. That is America's unique strength. No other country attracts the best and the brightest from all over the world. What's more, even the wretched, tired and poor—those who come risking their lives—gratefully repay this country with their hard work and dedication. 13

Currently the Asians are remaking the country much the same way that the Europeans once did. I look to them and their offspring—those who populate spelling bees and win Westinghouse science scholarships—when I envision America's future greatness. 14

In their zeal to reshape their lives in this land of opportunity, these immigrants are reshaping American destiny far beyond the comprehension of most Americans. They have come here endowed with cultural heritages and traditions that date back thousands of years. These Asians may come empty-handed, but not empty-headed. They value entrepreneurship, hard work, family solidarity and community—traits we particularly need in these troubled times when, we are told, America is in decline. 15

Despite all of its ills—the crime, the drugs, the social promiscuity and the homelessness—I do not see contemporary America as a tragic country. On the contrary, I see it as a triumphant nation that has provided an unprecedentedly high standard of living and freedom of expression to the majority of its heterogeneous people. 16

No other country has done it on the vast American scale. It has made the "good life" possible even for the common man. It gives him a chance to make something of his life by liberating him from the crushing burden of poverty plaguing most of the world. Any country that can do that within just 200 years of its formation should not be called tragic. 17

Most Americans take their good fortune for granted. I don't. I know better. I am from the old world, where they still see America as the promised land. 18

Review Questions

1. According to Gandhi, Kennan and Wilson, two "deeply patriotic men," are pessimistic about America. Why?
2. Why does Gandhi have a difficult time accepting the negative assessments of Kennan and Wilson?
3. The racial complexion of America is changing, says Gandhi. How so?
4. "Most Americans take their good fortune for granted." Gandhi does not. Why?

Discussion and Writing Suggestions

1. According to Albert Camus, patriotism "is the devotion to the ideal of what [a] country might be." What do you believe America "might be"? What is the promise of America?
2. "Some would call it naiveté, [but Americans believe] that if you keep trying, things will get better." Do you agree with this statement? Do you find evidence that Americans are trying to improve? What in your view needs improving?
3. "The fresh new stream [of immigrants] keeps the old water from stagnating." What does Gandhi mean here? What is your reaction?
4. Gandhi sees triumph, not tragedy, in American life. Kennan and Wilson see tragedy. How do you reconcile these vastly different points of view? With whom do you agree?

America in Decline? What Nation Are These People Looking At?

CHARLES KRAUTHAMMER

While Natwar Gandhi draws on his personal experience as an immigrant to reconfirm America as the "promised land," Charles Krauthammer arrives at the same conclusion by taking a more objective view. Like Gandhi, Krauthammer begins with a reference to those who argue that the U.S. is in decline, then devotes the rest of his article to demonstrating that just the opposite is true. Krauthammer's tone is "harder" than Gandhi's: He ridicules those he calls "declinists" and in supporting his conclusions relies on concrete evidence (statistics, references to particular events), rather than personal impressions.

Born in 1950, Krauthammer studied politics at Oxford and medicine at Harvard Medical School. He went on to train as a psychiatrist and was at one time chief resident of the Psychiatric Consultation Service at Massachusetts General Hospital. He switched careers, however, when his interests in politics began to outweigh his interest in psychiatry. During the Carter administration he was a speechwriter for Vice President Mondale. Krauthammer, a winner of the National Magazine Award for Essays and Criticism, is now a syndicated columnist and also writes essays for Time *magazine and* The New Republic.

"America in Decline? What Nation Are These People Looking At?" by Charles Krauthammer in the *Los Angeles Times*. March 11, 1990.

Malaise is back.[1] At this time of wondrous American triumph, the political psychiatrists have America on the couch. Diagnosis: depression. All over the world, everything is going our way, says *The New York Times* in its lead "Week In Review" article. "So then why doesn't it feel better?" 1

Because while the whole world is in bloom, we are in decline, it seems. Washington is "in eclipse," a historical backwater, writes one eminent commentator. "American wealth, influence, prestige and power are all declining," says another. "We have lost our ability to control major events." 2

Have we? 3

Wealth. In 1950, the peak of the Golden Age from which the declinists say we have slipped, American gross national product was $1.6 trillion (in current dollars). GNP today is $5.5 trillion. If you want to measure individual welfare, per-capita GNP is now more than twice what it was in 1950.[2] 4

But what about Germany and Japan? Well, what about them? Economist Herbert Stein points out that America's GNP is 2½ times Japan's, 5 times Germany's. In both Japan and Germany, per-capita GNP is only 75% of ours. For all their legendary productivity, adds *The Economist*, it still takes Japanese workers an hour to produce what an American can produce in 31 minutes. 5

Are we relatively less wealthy? Well, yes. But all that means is that in 1950 the world outside the United States was postwar rubble. For a short while, our allies were abnormally poor. Things have now normalized. That does not change the fact that the average American is today twice as wealthy as he was during the alleged peak of 1950. To feel poor just because our friends who were utterly destitute back then are now also enjoying prosperity—a lesser prosperity, mind you—is malaise born of nothing but envy. 6

Prestige. In the middle of the Czech revolution, a worker stands up at a rally outside some Godforsaken party-run factory and begins reciting the American Declaration of Independence. In the Soviet Union, an entire political system is being junked in favor of a presidential system modeled on the United States and France. In 7

[1]*Malaise.* In 1978 President Jimmy Carter drew widespread scorn when, in a much-anticipated speech, he claimed that America was in the grip of a "malaise" that was sapping its strength and will. Opponents claimed that any malaise was limited to the Carter administration.

[2]*GNP:* Gross National Product, the value of the sum total of goods and services produced by a country. The "per capita" (per head) GNP is the GNP divided by the number of inhabitants of the country.

Nicaragua, the pro-U.S. opposition scores a landslide against an entrenched communist political machine. From Seoul to Santiago, from Managua to Moscow, the whole world is dying to emulate the free market and free politics embodied by the American system.[3]

In 1950, in short, American values and prestige were ascendant in half the world. Today the other half has come around. 8

Influence and power. If we measure the actual (absolute) power that the United States can bring to bear on any spot on Earth, the United States is infinitely stronger than it was in 1950. But the declinists insist that the real measure of power is relative power. 9

Relative power? Our great adversary, our only military rival, our nemesis on every continent, is in collapse. Its empire has disappeared overnight. It is quite possible that in this decade it may not even survive as a nation. If relative power is the real measure, then American power is now greater than ever because there is today no other power in our league. 10

In a rare lapse into truth, Andrei Gromyko once defined a superpower as a country that has a say in every corner of the globe, and without whose say nothing truly substantial can be achieved in any such corner.[4] That was 15 years ago. There were two superpowers then. Today there is only one. 11

Lost our ability to control major events? In Namibia, American involvement was absolutely critical to bringing a regional settlement. In Afghanistan, American aid was the crucial factor that turned the tide against the Soviet Union. In the Persian Gulf, the U.S. Navy unilaterally took control of the water, a development that ultimately helped persuade Iran to sue for peace in the Iran-Iraq war. Even in the intractable Arab-Israeli dispute, all parties have their eyes turned to Washington. 12

In corners less far-flung, American influence is even more decisive. Consider Central America. It had become commonplace to say that, like the Soviet Union, America could no longer control events in 13

---

[3]In this paragraph Krauthammer refers to some of the dramatic anti-Communist, pro-democracy shifts that occurred throughout the world in 1989–90. In 1989, the Czech people threw out their hard-line Communist government and a dissident, playright Vaclav Havel, became president of Czechoslovakia. In Nicaragua in February 1990, the U.S.-backed Violeta Barrios de Chamorro defeated Daniel Ortega, leader of the Marxist-Leninist Sandinista party, in free elections. The following month, in Santiago, Chile, a democratically elected leader, Patricio Aylwin, replaced the military dictatorship of General Augusto Pinochet. And during this period there were large pro-democracy demonstrations in Seoul, South Korea, and even in Moscow.

[4]*Andrei Gromyko* was, for decades, the hard-line, Cold War foreign minister (equivalent to Secretary of State) of the U.S.S.R. He was replaced when Mikhail Gorbachev decided to change Soviet foreign policy so that it became less confrontational with the U.S. and other western nations.

its back yard. Manuel Noriega and Daniel Ortega would contradict that claim.[5]

In case the depressives haven't noticed, even our great Soviet adversary is now maneuvering to try to reenter the international economic and political system established and led by the United States since World War II. We are, in fact, more hegemonic in the world in 1990 than in 1950, when half the world was not just closed to us but at virtual war with us. 14

Decline theory, implausible enough before the revolutions of '89–'90, is now quite ridiculous. Lithuania, Latvia, Estonia, East Germany, Czechoslovakia, Poland, Hungary, Romania, Bulgaria, Panama, Nicaragua.[6] In the measure of relative power so preferred by the declinists, in just six months all of these have been lost by No. 2 or acquired by No. 1 or both. At what point do the declinists admit error? When McDonald's comes to Moscow?[7] 15

Review Questions

1. How does Krauthammer organize this article? From which quotation does this organizational scheme derive?
2. What is the main reason that the United States is indeed less relatively wealthy than it was after World War II? Why is this loss of relative wealth insignificant, according to Krauthammer?
3. Why does Krauthammer claim that there is now only one superpower, instead of two?
4. Why is it even more absurd to insist on the idea of an American decline now than it was before 1989, according to Krauthammer?

Discussion and Writing Suggestions

1. Has Krauthammer persuaded you that some of the other authors in this chapter are wrong in believing that America is in decline? Why or why

---

[5]*Manuel Noreiga,* military dictator of Panama, was overthrown in an American invasion of Panama in December 1989. Noreiga was replaced by the American-backed administration of Guillermo Endara.

[6]Lithuania, Latvia, and Estonia, known as the Baltic States, were forcibly annexed to the Soviet Union in 1940 as the result of a deal between Adolf Hitler and Joseph Stalin. All are moving toward independence from the Soviet Union; and in March 1990 Lithuania did, in fact, declare its independence, though the Soviets insisted that this declaration was "invalid." East Germany, Czechoslovakia, Poland, Hungary, Romania, and Bulgaria, part of the previously known "Eastern bloc" of Soviet satellites, all broke from the Soviet orbit in 1989, and all are moving toward democratically elected (and in many cases, non-Communist) governments. The anti-American governments of Panama and Nicaragua fell from power during this same period.

[7]*McDonald's.* In February 1990, the largest McDonald's in the world opened to long lines of customers in Moscow.

not? If what Krauthammer says is true, then why is there such a widespread perception that America is, indeed, in decline?

2. What kind of imagery does Krauthammer employ in the first paragraph? Try rewriting the paragraph, retaining the meaning, but using a different set of related images, from some other area of life. Which version do you like better?
3. Locate places where Krauthammer asks questions. Rewrite these sentences so that they are statements, instead. Which versions do you like better? Why?
4. Do you agree with Krauthammer that today there is only one superpower in the world? If so, do you think this new situation places further international obligations on the United States? Explain.

Economic Rebirth in a Post-Industrial World

FRED BRANFMAN

The word "rebirth" in Branfman's title provides a clue to his optimism; indeed, Branfman does believe that rebuilding America is possible. But he's a tough-minded realist as well who recounts a long list of problems to justify his call for a massive investment of funds in America's industry, educational system, and infrastructure (highways, bridges, communications, and so on). Reinvested funds, of course, must come from somewhere, and the expectation is that business leaders will forgo short-term profits in order to ensure their own and the nation's long-term health. The argument is reminiscent of one parents make to children: Delay gratification now and you'll enjoy benefits later on. Essentially, the reinvestment argument is an appeal for "maturity," and any number of commentators have discussed whether or not we Americans are able to delay present comforts for future security. Perhaps, as a nation, we are still adolescents.

As we have excerpted it from a much longer piece in the World Policy Journal *(1984), Branfman's argument consists of three parts: a statement describing the new "post-industrial world"; a review of America's problems with the implication that we are not adapting to the new order; and finally, a proposal for how we might adapt by investing in our industries, people, infrastructure, and environment, as well as in the global economy.*

Published as "Unexplored America: Economic Rebirth in a Post-Industrial World" in *World Policy Journal,* Fall 1984, pp. 33–37, 43–47. Reprinted by permission of the World Policy Institute.

From 1980 through 1983, Fred Branfman served as director of research in former Governor Jerry Brown's administration in California. He has also served as director of the Policy Center, a research group, and as a senior fellow at the Center for Development Policy. Branfman is currently director of Rebuild America, a Washington, D.C., research group.

Prime Minister Yasuhiro Nakasone declared Thursday that Japan should transform itself into a "high-level information society" as a "strategic motivating force" for economic development. "Complete rethinking of attitudes and policies which have characterized economic management until now" will be necessary, he said.

Los Angeles Times, May 23, 1983

It is possible, perhaps likely, that the United States is now engaged in a great transition, a change from one era to another as important as the Industrial Revolution.

Vice-President George Bush, *New York Times*, August 1, 1983

Technological progress . . . has accelerated rapidly in the fields of biotechnology and electronics. The new spheres seem limitless, and include time, space and matter. . . . The technological revolution, by increasing our control over matter, time and space, shapes the evolution of our economies, life-styles, thought patterns and systems of reference.

President François Mitterrand, Versailles, June 5, 1982

We are living in the earliest stages of a transformation as profound as the Industrial Revolution: the emergence, for the first time ever, of a global civilization. New information technologies are driving economic and social growth. A new global power balance is restructuring international relations. And new military technologies are transforming the nature of war. 1

If the transformation just now beginning is managed successfully, the post-industrial revolution will create a new domestic economy that utilizes computer, bioscience, and telecommunications technologies to raise living standards, increase employment, reduce manual labor, promote freedom and democracy, and give individuals new opportunites to reach their potential. It will also usher in a new global economy, in which the Third World has substantially closed the gap with the developed world and various national economies are integrated to a degree never before experienced. 2

Failure could bring economic hardship, social dislocation, and international conflict. Recall that the Industrial Revolution was accomplished only after regular economic depressions, great social turmoil, and two world wars. As this generation faces an equally 3 fundamental economic shift in a nuclear world, it is likely to encounter even greater dangers.

The profound implications of what one might term the Information Revolution have received increasing attention in recent years. Individuals with political tendencies as diverse as those of George Bush, François Mitterrand, and Yasuhiro Nakasone have begun to speak of them as a matter of course. But although we have acknowledged the onset of this global transformation, we have barely begun to prepare for it. Western societies have yet to mobilize for the tough challenges that the post-industrial revolution has thrust upon them. 4

Nowhere is this truer than in the United States. As the world's leading technological power, the United States has the most to gain from the Information Revolution. Its technological innovation, vast capital, and skilled labor force are now driving it. Its entrepreneurial ingenuity and sophisticated markets make it strong enough to share world leadership with nations like Japan indefinitely. 5

But as the world's leading industrial power, America also has the most to lose from the post-industrial transition. The very strengths that once powered its industrial growth—from cheap resources to capital-intensive production—have now become major obstacles to post-industrial development. As the world's most resource-dependent economy, it is America that most experiences the impact of environmental hazards and rising energy prices; as the largest industrial nation, it is America's aging industrial base that is most challenged by tough international competition; as the leading financial power, it is America's banks and export industries that are most threatened by uneven Third World development; as other nations increase their share of global gross national product (GNP), it is America's that is dropping most precipitously—from 50 percent to 21 percent over the past three decades. 6

This slowness to adjust to the post-industrial revolution has caused the U.S. economy to decline by every postwar measure during the past decade. Unemployment, interest rates, inflation, trade and government deficits have been running two to three times higher than the postwar average; productivity, business liquidity, and growth in GNP two to three times lower. 7

The present recovery [as of 1984] has led many to suggest that this decline has been arrested. In fact, the recovery is a sign more of continued weakness than of resurgent strength. Previous postwar recoveries were powered by industrial growth, as new highs were reached in domestic and international demand for American products and services. Today's recovery has resulted from massive and unsustainable borrowing, as the United States became a debtor nation and major importer of foreign goods for the first time in its history. 8

Today's federal deficits, reliance on foreign capital, high-interest and short-term business loans, high consumer debt, and low national savings rate have created a level of debt not seen in this country since World War II. But unlike America's wartime borrowing, the present debts have not been incurred in order to restructure the U.S. economy. Most business and government debt is devoted to maintaining high levels of consumer consumption, military and social spending, short-term corporate profits, and wages far higher than in the rest of the world. 9

Even today, at the height of the recovery, business is saddled by short-term, high-interest debt and is not adding the productive capacity needed to sustain economic growth. Sky-high deficits have prevented government from meeting basic commitments, let alone retooling America's economy as it did during World War II. Over the coming decade, as these debts come due, the U.S. economy is likely to continue ratcheting downward. Periodic recoveries are unlikely to restore postwar growth levels. Each recession could be more severe than the one preceding it. 10

The weakness of this Republican recovery, following a previous Democratic administration's economic failure, makes it clear that America has reached an economic watershed: we must shift from today's high-consumption, high-debt economy to one that places its highest priority on savings and investment. 11

Most of us cannot remember a time when America was not flush with prosperity. But only at our peril do we forget that this postwar prosperity was founded on an economic base built during a century of savings and relatively frugal living by our grandparents and great-grandparents—as their country invested billions in a nationwide network of railroads, highways, schools, factories, bridges, ports, grain elevators, oil wells, natural gas pipelines, farm machinery, ships, and telephone lines. If the promise of American prosperity is to be restored, the nation must now embark on a similar course. 12

Post-industrial growth will require that over the coming decades America invest trillions to diffuse new technologies throughout the economy, improve education and training, build the infrastructure that a 21st-century economy will require, create more effective environmental and health-care systems, and redesign the U.S. social structure to cope with the growing underclass of the unemployed and underpaid. The key will be America's ability to invest in the human mind. Major investments in energy and resources drove industrial growth. In today's information era, however, the U.S. economy will grow only to the extent that the United States invests in its people—in research and development, basic education, job training, and lifelong learning by students, workers, and citizens. 13

Such investment will demand a political and moral transformation as profound as the current economic revolution. Postwar American politics—whether conservative, neo-conservative, liberal, neoliberal, or progressive—have been built around the promise of short-term growth. But now, *national modernization must replace short-term growth as the organizing principle of American politics.* The United States cannot modernize, of course, without short-term growth. But, as the present recovery demonstrates, growth per se is not sustainable, nor does it necessarily lead to modernization. Only as America makes modernization its top priority can it restore the promise of sustainable growth for this and future generations. . . . 14

American schools, infrastructure, and factories were once the world standard. Now the Congressional Budget Office reports that "the nation's public works infrastructure . . . highways, public transit systems, wastewater treatment works, water resources, air traffic control, airports, and municipal water supply—is suffering from growing problems of deterioration, technological obsolescence and insufficient capacity to serve future growth." The President's National Commission on Excellence in Education warns that "the educational foundations of our society are presently being eroded by a rising tide of mediocrity that threatens our very future as a nation and people. What was unthinkable a generation ago has begun to occur—others are matching and surpassing our educational achievements." 15

Not only are older U.S. industries in decline but, as the Department of Commerce reports, "there has been a decline relative to our major competitors in a significant number of U.S. high technology industries." The *Washington Post* reports that "some of the strongest, most competitive sectors of the U.S. economy are losing ground to imported products. . . . The United States, for instance, registered a deficit in July [1984] *for the first time this century* in capital goods—computers, airplanes, industrial machinery [emphasis added]." 16

As these conditions have changed, so too have the requirements of economic policy. Neither cutting business taxes nor increasing consumer purchasing power automatically leads to investment in modernization. In fact, such actions often reduce long-term investment. Instead, the United States needs an "investment economics" that makes investment in modernization a primary criterion for all economic policy. 17

Implementing such an investment economics will not be easy, of course. But history has left the United States with no choice. America remains the richest nation on earth. So too, however, were Italy, Spain, Portugal, France, and England in their final seasons of strength. Like them, the United States is a well-off minority in a changing world. America must transform itself as well—or face its 18 own season of decline. The world is filled with once-great nations that failed to realize that their final years of wealth were due more to past success than future potential, that continued to borrow from their future instead of investing in it.

. . .

How do we ensure that the Information Revolution generates 19
employment and raises living standards? Is some form of a guaranteed annual income necessary as tens of millions are excluded from the new economy? What is to be the new global division of labor, as Third World nations grow increasingly proficient in both industrial production and information skills? Are arms control agreements a thing of the past, as new technologies make verification impossible? Is this revolution, like the Industrial Revolution before it, to be accompanied by depression, social conflict, and war?

While we cannot definitively answer such questions, we do know 20
what we must do to prepare for them. We can realize the promise of the Information Revolution only by investing in it. This investment must be comprehensive, encompassing every sector of U.S. society.

INVESTMENT IN OLD AND NEW INDUSTRIES

High-technology sectors, though they will employ no more than 5 percent of the work force in the coming decade, are the key to modernizing and raising productivity throughout the U.S. economy. After growing at 3.1 percent from 1960 to 1973 and 1.1 percent from 1973 to 1979, productivity *declined* 0.4 percent from 1979 to 1981. Although it has picked up recently, much remains to be done before productivity grows sufficiently to restore America's global competitiveness and improve its standard of living. Billions must be spent on the robotic tools and flexible manufacturing processes necessary to increase productivity and to maintain America's present market share in older manufacturing sectors.

Even more will be needed to remain competitive in the man- 22
ufacturing sectors of the future—robotics itself, as well as semiconductors, computers, biotechnology, telecommunications, commercial aviation, software, supercomputers, and other key sectors targeted by our competitors.

Similar sums will be necessary to "industrialize the service sector" 23
in order to keep it competitive. Offices must be "telematized"—equipped with new computer, telephone, and video systems, as well as the requisite software. Such "offices of the future" will link

corporations, organizations, and individuals in a worldwide communications network. Home banking will be not only desirable but necessary. Interactive cable television can increase political participation and community interaction.

Investments like these are made necessary by foreign com- 24
petitors' national strategies, which target every sector of the U.S. economy. If the United States is to avoid resorting to protectionism—with its attendant higher costs for consumers, trade barriers against U.S. products, and tendency to promote economic stagnation—it has no choice but to match these foreign countries' competitive efforts.

In addition to promoting modernization, the United States 25
should target entrepreneurialism, risk-taking, and innovation. The process by which America's venture capital has created whole new semiconductor, computer, and software industries provides a model for the private sector that must be built in the decades to come. Special efforts are needed to fund basic and applied research, capitalize start-up companies in industries like software and computers as well as in the bioscience and space industries yet to be born, furnish expansion capital for new industries targeted by foreign competitors, promote small businesses, and grant incentives to corporations willing and able to invest in the future.

INVESTING IN PEOPLE AS WORKERS AND CONSUMERS

The investment in the human mind required by the information era is analogous to the capital investments that produced America's industrial growth. In the coming years, the United States must spend massive amounts on education and job training: given high U.S. labor costs, America can remain competitive only by having the world's smartest work force. The complexities of a rapidly changing economy, moreover, demand far greater emphasis on technical skills and lifelong learning opportunities than ever before.

Top priority must go to America's schools, in order to make them 27
once again the world standard. During the next five years, the United States will need to fill an estimated gap of nearly 300,000 teachers, particularly in the areas of math and science. It must lengthen the school year, raise academic standards, and reinstitute attitudes of hard work, discipline, and respect for education. At the same time, American schools should be redesigned around the exciting potential for interactive, creative, and nonpassive learning made possible by new computer technologies. Vast sums are needed to ensure that

every student in America has not only his or her own personal computer, but also software and access to data bases.

Redesigning U.S. job-training systems will be no less necessary— 28
or expensive—as tens of millions of young people and older workers confront a changing industrial sector. Not only are too few job-training programs presently available, but too many of them still provide training for jobs not even available in the marketplace. There must also be a major effort to provide new skills for workers displaced by competition and to upgrade worker skills as new technologies are introduced more and more rapidly.

Finally, the United States must make massive investments to 29
prepare the public—as citizens, voters, and consumers—for the coming information age. An explosion of opportunity is possible, but only if all U.S. citizens have access to information technologies and data bases at prices they can afford.

INFRASTRUCTURE AND ENVIRONMENTAL INVESTMENT

The United States cannot remain a great economy and society with- 30
out constructing the infrastructure for it. In part, this means marshalling huge sums to repair the present decaying industrial infrastructure, from highways to ports to bridges to waterways. As the Congressional Budget Office notes, "the costs of neglecting these infrastructure problems can be substantial [including] higher long-term construction and repair costs for facilities that are not properly maintained, higher costs borne by users of inadequate facilities, and potential constraints on economic development."

Of even greater importance will be the establishment of a 21st- 31
century infrastructure, including fiber-optic phone lines capable of carrying video as well as aural messages, new communications satellites, computers and supercomputers and the data bases they require, video screens, and software. Construction costs will be as astronomical as they were for America's industrial infrastructure. But the country has no choice: these fiber-optics highways will be as important to post-industrial growth as automobile highways, ports, and bridges have been to industrial prosperity.

In addition, the United States must make major investments in its 32
environment. Toxic chemicals, acid rain, air and water pollution, nuclear waste, and the depletion of soil, forest, and fish resources are not just physical hazards but have become a major economic burden, contributing to health costs America cannot afford and resource depletion it cannot sustain.

SOCIAL INVESTMENT

The rigors of the post-industrial transition will strain the American social fabric in a way not seen since the Great Depression. Industrial decline has already created an underclass of the unemployed and unemployable, whose numbers will be swelled in the coming decades by the growing obsolescence of the U.S. manufacturing sector and the difficulty of mastering the sophisticated skills necessary for well-paid manufacturing or service sector work. 33

In the early 1950s, unemployment was around 3 percent. The goal of "full employment" was to reduce that rate to zero. Current analysts now estimate "structural unemployment" to be 4 to 6 percent, and economists predict that today's recovery will be unable to bring unemployment much below its present 7.4 percent level. 34

Over the long term, this problem can be partly alleviated by massive investments in education and job training. The United States should set a national goal of eliminating welfare within 20 years by providing skills, job opportunities, and job placement assistance to all welfare recipients willing and able to work. In the short term, however, millions of Americans are unable to find jobs in the new economy, and tens of millions more are forced to trade high-paying manufacturing jobs for low-paying service jobs. 35

In addition, as baby-boomers reach retirement age, society will face the burden of supporting a growing number of senior citizens. Health care costs will continue to skyrocket; and the Social Security system, Medicare, and Medicaid will come under increasing pressure. 36

It is still too early to forsee precisely what new social investments such changes will require. Some analysts have suggested that a guaranteed annual income or income supplement will be needed to make up the difference in "two-tiered" wages. States are experimenting with a variety of job-sharing programs, and there have been proposals for "40 hour pay for a 30 hour week" as a means of increasing employment. Another plan would involve tying guaranteed annual incomes to the goal of full employment, thus putting people to work in the creation of a new information age social infrastructure—from child care facilities to new community learning centers. 37

Whatever happens, though, will not be unprecedented. In one sense, the New Deal was a program to redistribute the great agricultural, industrial, and energy fortunes of the early industrial era. One could argue that as capital is concentrated in a manufacturing sector employing ever fewer people, a post-industrial "New Deal" will be necessary to redistribute that wealth as well. In any case, 38 enormous investments will have to be made to provide for those left out of the new economy and to maintain such bedrocks of economic security as Social Security, Medicare, and Medicaid.

INVESTMENT IN THE GLOBAL ECONOMY

Perhaps the most politically complex challenge the United States 39
faces is the need to invest in a growing international economy. America can no longer rely on cheap Third World resources; in fact, future economic growth will instead largely depend on its ability to export to markets in a developing world that makes up 80 percent of the human race.

The Keynesian revolution of the 1930s held that increased con- 40
sumer purchasing power at home was the key to economic growth. This logic now needs to be extended internationally. Long-run U.S. economic expansion will be largely contingent upon the expansion of Third World purchasing power. But as things now stand, much of the Third World faces a growing credit squeeze and years of painful austerity. To ensure that Third World countries once again resume growth and become reliable markets for U.S. products, the United States must support both efforts to write off large portions of the Third World's massive debt and new multilateral transfers of wealth.

COSTS OF MODERNIZATION

It is impossible to quantify the domestic and international costs of 41
modernizing America over the coming decade. But they will certainly be well beyond America's present capacity. It is estimated, for example, that it will cost $2.5 trillion to repair our infrastructure of decaying ports, highways, and bridges between now and the end of the century. It would cost over $50 billion a year to create 3.7 million jobs in the private sector—just to reduce unemployment to its postwar average of 3 to 4 percent. The same goal through public sector employment would cost over $35 billion a year. It would cost $50 to $60 billion annually over the next five years to fill the estimated shortage of 300,000 teachers—far more to attract bright young minds into teaching and ensure an adequate supply of math, science, and computer teachers. Experts talk of the need to transfer well over $100 billion to developing countries if they are to resume their historic rates of growth, repay their debts, and expand as markets. And the sums needed to develop and commercialize the sophisticated

technologies needed for our 21st-century infrastructure will be even more astronomical.

To finance these necessary modernizations, the United States needs to generate a *surplus* of capital and investment. But presently, even at the height of the recovery, America is not meeting its basic commitments—let alone investing in its future. Only as the nation closes this investment gap can it fulfill the promise of the Information Revolution. 42

Review Questions

1. What is the "post-industrial world"? In what significant ways is America not yet a member of this world?
2. What does America stand to lose (and how has it already lost) by not adapting to the new global order?
3. How has American borrowing in the 1980s differed from the massive borrowing during World War II?
4. Why must modernization "replace short-term growth as the organizing principle of American politics"?
5. What is the condition of America's infrastructure, according to published government sources?
6. Briefly summarize the several investments Branfman calls for in the last two sections of his article.

Discussion and Writing Suggestions

1. You have read of the staggering costs Branfman says will be needed to equip America for life in a postindustrial world. Do you believe Americans are willing to make sacrifices today for benefits they may never see in their lifetimes? Would you be willing?
2. Look to your immediate environment for signs that the information age is upon us. You grew up with ready access to computers, but your parents did not. Have your parents, or any other people you know, for that matter, had any difficulties adjusting to this new world?
3. What expectations do you have for your economic future? Do you expect affluence? Modest comfort? A struggle to make ends meet? How do you see your personal fortunes tied to the issues that Branfman discusses in this article?
4. "The world is filled with once-great nations that failed to realize that their final years of wealth were due more to past success than future potential, that continued to borrow from the future instead of investing in it." In your view, what are the odds that America will become one more "once-great nation"? Explain.

The (Relative) Decline of America

PAUL KENNEDY

As recently as twenty-five years ago, America did *lead the world economically, technologically, and educationally. Today, our preeminence has slipped, if not vanished altogether. If we could muster the discipline and will and money enough, goes one argument, we might manage to regain our former position. Paul Kennedy disagrees. He takes the broad historical view that "it simply has not been given to any one society to remain permanently ahead of all the others." America* will *decline, says Kennedy. This much is a historical imperative. How we manage that decline he takes as the subject of his essay, which we've excerpted from a longer article in the* Atlantic Monthly *(August 1987).*

Paul Kennedy was born in Wallsend, England, in 1945. He attended the University of Newcastle, where he graduated with an M.A. in 1966, and Oxford University, where he earned a doctorate in philosophy in 1970. Kennedy has taught at the University of East Anglia and currently teaches at Yale. He has been awarded fellowships at the Royal Historical Society, the Alexander von Humboldt Foundation, and Princeton University. Kennedy has written eight books detailing the economic, political, and social factors underlying significant historical developments—including The Rise of Anglo-German Antagonism, Strategy and Diplomacy, *and most recently,* The Rise and Fall of the Great Powers *(1987), the book from which he adapted the present article.*

Ultimately, the only answer to whether the United States can preserve its position is *no*—for it simply has not been given to any one society to remain permanently ahead of all the others, freezing the patterns of different growth rates, technological advance, and military development that have existed since time immemorial. But historical precedents do not imply that the United States is destined to shrink to the relative obscurity of former leading powers like Spain and the Netherlands, or to disintegrate like the Roman and Austro-Hungarian empires; it is too large to do the former, and probably too homogeneous to do the latter. Even the British analogy, much favored in the current political-science literature, is not a good one if it ignores the differences in scale. The geographic size, population, and natural resources of Great Britain suggest that it ought to possess roughly three or four percent of the world's wealth and power, all 1 other things being equal. But precisely because all other things are never equal, a peculiar set of historical and technological circumstances permitted Great Britain to possess, say, 25 percent of the world's wealth and power in its prime. Since those favorable circumstances have disappeared, all that it has been doing is returning to its more "natural" size. In the same way, it may be argued, the geographic extent, population, and natural resources of the United States suggest that it ought to possess 16 or 18 percent of the world's wealth and power. But because of historical and technological circumstances favorable to it, that share rose to 40 percent or more by 1945, and what we are witnessing today is the ebbing away from that extraordinarily high figure to a more natural share. That decline is being masked by the country's enormous military capability at present, and also by its success in internationalizing American capitalism and culture. Yet even when it has declined to the position of occupying no more than its natural share of the world's wealth and power, a long time into the future, the United States will still be a very significant power in a multipolar world, simply because of its size.

The task facing American statesmen over the next decades, there- 2
fore, is to recognize that broad trends are under way, and that there is a need to manage affairs so that the relative erosion of America's position takes place slowly and smoothly, unaided by policies that bring short-term advantage but long-term disadvantage. Among the realities that statesmen, from the President down, must be alert to are these: that technological and therefore socioeconomic change is occurring in the world faster than it has ever before; that the international community is much more politically and culturally diverse than has been assumed, and is defiant of simplistic remedies offered by either Washington or Moscow for its problems; that the economic and productive power balances are no longer tilted as favorably in America's direction as they were in 1945. Even in the military realm there are signs of a certain redistribution of the balances, away from a bipolar and toward a multipolar system, in which American economic and military strength is likely to remain greater than that of any other individual country but will cease to be as disproportionate as it was in the decades immediately after the Second World War. In all the discussions about the erosion of American leadership it needs to be repeated again and again that the decline is relative, not absolute, and is therefore perfectly natural, and that a serious threat to the real interests of the United States can come only from a failure to adjust sensibly to the new world order.

Just how well can the American system adjust to a state of relative 3 decline? Already, a growing awareness of the gap between U.S. obligations and U.S. power has led to questions by gloomier critics about the overall political culture in which Washington decision-makers have to operate. It has been suggested with increasing frequency that a country needing to reformulate its grand strategy in the light of the larger, uncontrollable changes taking place in world affairs may be ill served by an electoral system that seems to paralyze foreign-policy decision-making every two years. Foreign policy may be undercut by the extraordinary pressures applied by lobbyists, political-action committees, and other interest groups, all of whom, by definition, are prejudiced in favor of this or that policy change, and by the simplification of vital but complex international and strategic issues, inherent to mass media whose time and space for such things are limited and whose raison d'être is chiefly to make money and only secondarily to inform. It may also be undercut by the still powerful escapist urges in the American social culture, which are perhaps understandable in terms of the nation's frontier past but hinder its coming to terms with today's complex, integrated world and with other cultures and ideologies. Finally, the country may not always be helped by the division of decision-making powers that was deliberately created when it was geographically and strategically isolated from the rest of the world, two centuries ago, and had time to find a consensus on the few issues that actually concerned foreign policy. This division may be less serviceable now that the United States is a global superpower, often called upon to make swift decisions vis-à-vis countries that enjoy far fewer constraints. No one of these obstacles prevents the execution of a coherent, long-term American grand strategy. However, their cumulative effect is to make it difficult to carry out policy changes that seem to hurt special interests and occur in an election year. It may therefore be here, in the cultural and political realms, that the evolution of an overall American policy to meet the twenty-first century will be subjected to the greatest test.

4 Nevertheless, given the considerable array of strengths still possessed by the United States, it ought not in theory to be beyond the talents of successive Administrations to orchestrate this readjustment so as, in Walter Lippmann's classic phrase, to bring "into balance . . . the nation's commitments and the nation's power." Although there is no single state obviously preparing to take over America's global burdens, in the way that the United States assumed Britain's role in the 1940s, the country has fewer problems than had Imperial Spain, besieged by enemies on all fronts, or the Netherlands, squeezed between France and England, or the British Empire, facing numerous

challengers. The tests before the United States as it heads toward the twenty-first century are certainly daunting, perhaps especially in the economic sphere; but the nation's resources remain considerable, *if* they can be properly utilized and *if* there is a judicious recognition of both the limitations and the opportunities of American power.

Review Questions

1. What does Kennedy mean when he claims that America's decline will be *relative,* not absolute?
2. What does Kennedy mean when he claims that America's decline is "perfectly natural"?
3. America's decline will not be like the decline of Spain or the Netherlands. Why not?
4. "A serious threat to the real interests of the United States can come only from a failure to adjust sensibly to the new world order," claims Kennedy. Why is this the case?
5. What three cultural and political concerns may present the country its greatest test in meeting the challenges of the twenty-first century?
6. Kennedy alludes to the "escapist" urges in American culture that might have suited the country in its "frontier past" but will not help as we come "to terms with today's complex, integrated world and with other cultures and ideologies." What does Kennedy mean here?

Discussion and Writing Suggestions

1. What was your response on reading Kennedy's first sentence—that the United States cannot preserve its position in the world? Does the thought alarm you? Offend you? Bruise your ego? Delight you? Why?
2. "The task facing American statesmen over the next decade, therefore, is to recognize that . . . there is a need to manage affairs so that the relative erosion of America's position takes place slowly and smoothly." Kennedy has accepted America's (relative) decline as inevitable. Do you? Do you find evidence that elected officials in national government accept Kennedy's conclusion?
3. Kennedy's book, *The Rise and Fall of the Great Powers,* received a good deal of critical attention when it was published in 1987. Use the *Book Review Index* to locate citations for reviews of Kennedy's work. Read three reviews and compare responses. Formalize your comparison in an essay.

July Fourth
from *Love in the Ruins*

WALKER PERCY

Walker Percy (1916–1990) trained to be a physician, though he never practiced. He contracted tuberculosis as a young man, fought it successfully, and then turned to writing as a career. Percy lived in Louisiana, and his characters as well as the settings of his stories are southern. In his many books, he is concerned with what he calls "dislocation" in modern life—the sense that we are abstracted from ourselves, that we don't know who or what we are. As you might expect, Percy's novels raise large existential questions, such as—How do we acknowledge the overwhelming mystery of existence and manage at the same time to live ordinary, everyday lives? The characters who pose these questions are themselves alienated from, and they critique, the particular cultures in which they find themselves.

The critique in "July Fourth" from Love in the Ruins *is (in the excerpt you will read) a broad cultural critique of life in the United States. The main character and narrator, Dr. Thomas More, believes that a catastrophe is about to befall America—a catastrophe not of the body but of the spirit. Great and terrible events are to unfold—or are they? You may well find Dr. More's talk of catastrophe insane since, as he says, "At first glance all seems normal hereabouts. . . . The Gross National Product continues to rise . . . [and] most Americans do well enough. In fact, until lately, nearly everyone tried and succeeded in being happy but me."*

If Dr. More is right (and sane), then the apparent happiness of Americans is spiritually empty. The people who seem most alive and successful turn out to be the ones who are most dead, though they don't know it. Dr. More and Percy's other protagonists do, however, and they waste no time tearing into life-styles and institutions that promote what in one of Percy's novels is called "malaise" or spiritual death, which falls everywhere in this country like "noxious particles." Critics have called Love in the Ruins *"brilliant and hilarious" and "so outrageous and so real, one is left speechless." As you read the following passage (which begins the novel), be prepared for a strange, ironic-serious assault on the values that underlie our culture.*

Walker Percy was a prolific and much discussed American writer for

---

the past thirty years. Besides Love in the Ruins *(1971), his novels include* The Moviegoer *(1961, winner of the National Book Award),* The Last Gentleman *(1966),* Lancelot *(1977),* The Second Coming *(1979), and* The Thanatos Syndrome *(1987). Percy's fiction and nonfiction (e.g.,* The Message in the Bottle, *1979) have been the subject of scholarly books and articles as well as doctoral dissertations. His novels also regularly appeared on best-seller lists around the country.*

In a pine grove on the
southwest cusp of the interstate cloverleaf
5 P.M./JULY 4

Now in these dread latter days of the old violent beloved U.S.A. and of the Christ-forgetting Christ-haunted death-dealing Western world I came to myself[1] in a grove of young pines and the question came to me: has it happened at last? 1

Two more hours should tell the story. One way or the other. Either I am right and a catastrophe will occur, or it won't and I'm crazy. In either case the outlook is not so good. 2

Here I sit, in any case, against a young pine, broken out in hives and waiting for the end of the world. Safe here for the moment though, flanks protected by a rise of ground on the left and an approach ramp on the right. The carbine lies across my lap. 3

Just below the cloverleaf, in the ruined motel, the three girls are waiting for me. 4

Undoubtedly something is about to happen. 5

Or is it that something has stopped happening? 6

Is it that God has at last removed his blessing from the U.S.A. and what we feel now is just the clank of the old historical machinery, the sudden jerking ahead of the roller-coaster cars as the chain catches hold and carries us back into history with its ordinary catastrophes, carries us out and up toward the brink from that felicitous and privileged siding where even unbelievers admitted that if it was not God who blessed the U.S.A., then at least some great good luck had befallen us, and that now the blessing or the luck is over, the machinery clanks, the chain catches hold, and the cars jerk forward? 7

It is still hot as midafternoon. The sky is a clear rinsed cobalt after the rain. Wet pine growth reflects the sunlight like steel knitting needles. The grove steams and smells of turpentine. Far away the thunderhead, traveling fast, humps over on the horizon like a troll. 8

[1]"I came to myself": This would be an existential discovery the narrator has made of who he is and what he should do.

Directly above, a hawk balances[2] on a column of air rising from the concrete geometry of the cloverleaf. Not a breath stirs.

The young pine I am sitting against has a tumor and is bowed to fit my back. I am sweating and broken out in hives from drinking gin fizzes[3] but otherwise quite comfortable. This spot, on the lower reaches of the southwest cusp, was chosen carefully. From it I command three directions of the interstates and by leaning over the lip of the culvert can look through to the fourth, eastern approach. 9

Traffic is light, an occasional milk tanker and produce trailer. 10

The hawk slants off in a long flat glide toward the swamp. From the angle of its wings one can tell it is a marsh hawk. 11

One of the roof tiles of the motel falls and breaks on the concrete. 12

The orange roof of the Howard Johnson motel reminds me of the three girls in rooms 202, 204, and 205. Thoughts of the girls and the coming catastrophe cause my scalp to tingle with a peculiar emotion. If the catastrophe occurs, I stand a good chance, knowing what I know about it, of surviving it. So do the girls. Surviving with one girl who likes you is not such a bad prospect. But surviving with three girls, all of whom like you and each of whom detests the other two, is both horrible and pleasant, certainly enough to make one's scalp tingle with a peculiar emotion. 13

Another reason for the prickling sensation is that the hives are worse. Fiery wheals bloom on my neck. My scalp feels airy and quilted and now and then pops a hair root like a dirigible popping its hawsers one by one. 14

These are bad times. 15

Principalities and powers[4] are everywhere victorious. Wickedness flourishes in high places. 16

There is a clearer and more present danger, however. For I have reason to believe that within the next two hours an unprecedented fallout of noxious particles will settle hereabouts and perhaps in other places as well. It is a catastrophe whose cause and effects—and prevention—are known only to me. The effects of the evil particles are psychic rather than physical. They do not burn the skin and rot the marrow; rather do they inflame and worsen the secret ills of the spirit and rive the very self from itself. If a man is already prone to anger, he'll go mad with rage. If he lives affrighted, he will quake 17

[2]"a hawk balances": See William Butler Yeats's "The Second Coming," an apocalyptic poem that concerns the downfall of Western civilization. The poem opens with the image of a falcon spiraling upwards on a current of air.

[3]"gin fizzes": A drink made with gin and the white of an egg (albumen), to which Dr. More is allergic.

[4]"Principalities and powers": Two orders of angels.

with terror. If he's already abstracted from himself, he'll be sundered from himself and roam the world like Ishmael.[5]

Here in my pocket is the very means of inoculating persons against such an eventuality or of curing them should it overtake them. 18

Yet so far only four persons have been inoculated: myself and the three girls yonder in the motel. 19

Just below me, abutting the deserted shopping plaza, rises the yellow brick barn-and-silo of Saint Michael's. A surprisingly large parish it was, big enough to rate a monsignor. But the church is empty now, abandoned five years ago. The stained glass is broken out. Cliff swallows nest in the fenestrae of its concrete screen. 20

Our Catholic church here split into three pieces: (1) the American Catholic Church whose new Rome is Cicero, Illinois; (2) the Dutch schismatics who believe in relevance but not God; (3) the Roman Catholic remnant, a tiny scattered flock with no place to go. 21

The American Catholic Church, which emphasizes property rights and the integrity of neighborhoods, retained the Latin mass and plays *The Star-Spangled Banner* at the elevation.[6] 22

The Dutch schismatics in this area comprise several priests and nuns who left Rome to get married. They threw in with the Dutch schismatic Catholics. Now several divorced priests and nuns are importuning the Dutch cardinal to allow them to remarry. 23

The Roman Catholics hereabouts are scattered and demoralized. The one priest, an obscure curate, who remained faithful to Rome, could not support himself and had to hire out as a fire-watcher. It is his job to climb the fire tower by night and watch for brushfires below and for signs and portents in the skies. 24

I, for example, am a Roman Catholic, albeit a bad one. I believe in the Holy Catholic Apostolic and Roman Church,[7] in God the Father, in the election of the Jews,[8] in Jesus Christ His Son our Lord, who founded the Church on Peter his first vicar, which will last until the end of the world. Some years ago, however, I stopped eating Christ in Communion, stopped going to mass, and have since fallen into a 25

---

[5]"Ishmael": A character in Herman Melville's *Moby Dick*.

[6]"the elevation": Part of the Catholic mass in which the priest holds the host (the wafer) between thumb and forefinger and raises it.

[7]"believe in the Holy Catholic Apostolic . . . Church": A belief that bishops in the church succeed in a direct line from the twelve Apostles.

[8]"[believe] in the election of the Jews": That in the Old Testament the Jews were God's chosen people.

disorderly life. I believe in God and the whole business but I love women best, music and science next, whiskey next, God fourth, and my fellowman hardly at all. Generally I do as I please. A man, wrote John, who says he believes in God and does not keep his commandments is a liar. If John is right, then I am a liar. Nevertheless, I still believe.

A couple of buzzards circle the interchange a mile high. Do I imagine it, or does one cock his head and eye me for meat? Don't count on it, old fellow! 26

Thoughts about the coming catastrophe and the three girls cause my scalp to tingle with a peculiar emotion. Or perhaps it is the hives from drinking gin fizzes. A catastrophe, however, has both pleasant and unpleasant aspects familiar to everyone—though no one likes to admit the pleasantness. Just now the prospect is unpleasant, but not for the reasons you might imagine. 27

Let me confess that what worries me most is that the catastrophe will overtake us before my scientific article is published and so before my discovery can create a sensation in the scientific world. 28

The vanity of scientists! My article, it is true, is an extremely important one, perhaps even epochal in its significance. With it, my little invention, in hand, any doctor can probe the very secrets of the soul, diagnose the maladies that poison the wellsprings of man's hope. It could save the world or destroy it—and in the next two hours will very likely do one or the other—for as any doctor knows, the more effective a treatment is, the more dangerous it is in the wrong hands. 29

But the question remains: which prospect is more unpleasant, the destruction of the world, or that the destruction may come before my achievement is made known? The latter I must confess, because I keep imagining the scene in the Director's office the day the Nobel Prize is awarded. I enter. The secretaries blush. My colleagues horse around. The Director breaks out the champagne and paper cups (like Houston Control after the moon landing). "Hats off, gentlemen?" cries the Director in his best derisive style (from him the highest accolade). "A toast to our local Pasteur! No, rather the new Copernicus! The latter-day Archimedes who found the place to insert his lever and turn the world not upside down but right side up!" 30

If the truth be known, scientists are neither more nor less vain than other people. It is rather that their vanity is the more striking as it appears side by side with their well-known objectivity. The layman is scandalized, but the scandal is not so much the fault of the scientist 31 as it is the layman's canonization of scientists, which the latter never asked for.

The prayer of the scientist if he prayed, which is not likely: Lord, grant that my discovery may increase knowledge and help other men. Failing that, Lord, grant that it will not lead to man's destruction. Failing that, Lord, grant that my article in *Brain* be published before the destruction takes place. 32

Room 202 in the motel is my room. Room 206 is stacked to the roof with canned food, mostly Vienna sausage and Campbell's soup, fifteen cases of Early Times bourbon whiskey, and the World's Great Books. In the rooms intervening, 203, 204, and 205, are to be found Ellen, Moira, and Lola, respectively. 33

My spirits rise. My quilted scalp pops another hair root. The silky albumen from the gin fizzes coats my brain membranes. Even if worst comes to worst, is there any reason why the four of us cannot live happily together, sip toddies, eat Campbell's chicken-and-rice, and spend the long summer evenings listening to Lola play the cello and reading aloud from the World's Great Books stacked right alongside the cases of Early Times, beginning with Homer's first words: "Sing, O Goddess, the anger of Achilles," and ending with Freud's last words: "—but we cannot help them and cannot change our own way of thinking on their account"? Then we can read the Great Ideas, beginning with the first volume, Angel to Love. Then we can start over—until the Campbell's soup and Early Times run out. 34

The sun makes bursts and halos through the screen of pine needles. The marsh hawk ends his long glide into the line of cypresses, which are green as paint against the purple thunderhead. 35

At first glance all seems normal hereabouts. But a sharp eye might notice one or two things amiss. For one thing, the inner lanes of the interstate, the ones ordinarily used for passing, are in disrepair. The tar strips are broken. A lichen grows in the oil stain. Young mimosas sprout on the shoulders. 36

For another thing, there is something wrong with the motel. The roof tiles are broken. The swimming pool is an opaque jade green, a bad color for pools. A large turtle suns himself on the diving board, which is broken and slanted into the water. Two cars are parked in the near lot, a rusty Cadillac and an Impala convertible with vines sprouting through its rotting top. 37

The cars and the shopping center were burnt out during the Christmas riot five years ago. The motel, though not burned, was abandoned and its room inhabited first by lovers, then by bums, and finally by the native denizens of the swamp, dirt daubers, moccasins, screech owls, and raccoons. 38

In recent months the vines have begun to sprout in earnest. 39
Possum grape festoons Rexall Drugs yonder in the plaza. Scuppernong all but conceals the A & P supermarket. Poison ivy has captured the speaker posts in the drive-in movie, making a perfect geometrical forest of short cylindrical trees.

Beyond the glass wall of the motel dining room still hangs the 40
Rotary banner:

> Is it the truth?
> Is it fair to all concerned?
> Will it build goodwill and better friendships?

But the banner is rent, top to bottom, like the temple veil.

The vines began to sprout in earnest a couple of months ago. 41
People do not like to talk about it. For some reason they'd much rather talk about the atrocities that have been occurring ever more often: entire families murdered in their beds for no good reason. "The work of a madman!" people exclaim.

Last Sunday as I was walking past the house of a neighbor, Barry 42
Bocock, a Boeing engineer transplanted from Seattle, I spied him riding his tiny tractor-mower like a big gringo astride a burro. The next moment my eye was caught by many tiny vines sprouting through the cracks in the concrete slab and beginning to cover the antique bricks that Barry had salvaged from an old sugar mill.

Barry got off his tractor simply by standing up and walking. 43

"It looks as though your slab is cracked, Barry," I told him. 44

Barry frowned and, seeming not to hear, began to show me how 45
the tractor could cut grass right up to the bark of a tree without injuring the tree.

Barry Bocock is the sort of fellow who gives the most careful 46
attention to details, especially to those smaller problems caused by germs. A very clean man, he walks around his yard in his shorts and if he should find a pustule or hickey on his clean hairy muscular legs, he takes infinite pains examining it, squeezing it, noting the character of the pus. One has the feeling that to Barry there is nothing wrong with the world that couldn't be set right by controlling germs and human wastes. One Sunday he invited me into his back yard and showed me the effluence from his new septic tank, letting it run into a drinking glass, where in fact it did look as clear as water.

But when I called his attention to the vines cracking his slab, he 47
seemed not to hear and instead showed me his new mower.

"But, Barry, the vines are cracking your slab." 48

"That'll be the day," said Barry, flushing angrily. Then, drawing 49 me close to his clean perfect West-Coast body, he asked me if I'd heard of the latest atrocity.

"Yes. What do you think?" 50

"The work of a madman!" he exclaimed and mounted his burro- 51
size tractor.

Barry is a widower, his wife having died of alcoholism before he 52
left Seattle. "Firing the sunset gun" he called her drinking. "Every day she'd be at it as early as one o'clock." "At what?" "Firing the sunset gun."

The buzzards are lower and more hopeful, rocking their wings 53
this way and that and craning down for a look.

When I think of Barry, I can't help but wonder whether he, not I, 54
should be the doctor, what with his keen interest in germs, boils, hickeys, bo-bos, pustules, scabs, and such. Moreover, I could tell from Barry's veiled expression when I mentioned the vines sprouting that he knew of my troubles and that he was accordingly discounting my alarm. Physician, heal thyself. . . .

The truth is that, though I am a physician, my health, especially 55
my mental health, has been very poor lately. I am subject to attacks of elation and depression, as well as occasional seizures of morning terror. A few years ago my wife left me, running off with an Englishman, and I've led an irregular life ever since.

But to admit my infirmities is not necessarily to discredit my 56
discoveries, which stand or fall on scientific evidence. After all, van Gogh was depressed and Beethoven had a poor time of it. The prophet Hosea, if you will recall, had a bad home life.

Some of the best psychiatrists, it is hardly necessary to add, have 57
a few problems of their own, little rancors and terrors and such.

Who am I? you well might wonder. Let me give a little dossier. 58

I am a physician, a not very successful psychiatrist; an alcoholic, a 59
shaky middle-aged man subject to depressions and elations and morning terrors, but a genius nevertheless who sees into the hidden causes of things and erects simple hypotheses to account for the glut of everyday events; a bad Catholic; a widower and cuckold whose wife ran off with a heathen Englishman and died on the island of Cozumel, where she hoped to begin a new life and see things afresh.

My afflictions attract some patients, repel others. People are 60
generally tolerant. Some patients, knowing my frailties, calculate I'll understand theirs. I am something like old Doc in Western movies: if you catch old Doc sober, he's all right, etcetera. In fact, he's some kind of genius, I heard he went to Harvard, etcetera etcetera.

Not that I make much money. Sensible folk, after all, don't have 61
much use for a doctor who sips toddies during office hours. So I'm

obliged to take all kinds of patients, not merely terrified and depressed people, but people suffering with bowel complaints, drugheads with beriberi and hepatitis, Bantus shot up by the cops, cops shot up by Bantus.

Lately, however, I've discouraged patients in order to work on my invention. I don't need the money. Fortunately for me, my wife, who left me and later died, either didn't or wouldn't change her will and so bequeathed me forty thousand shares of R. J. Reynolds stock she inherited from her father. 62

Loose bark from the pine is beginning to work through my shirt. My scalp is still quilted, my throat is whistling with hives—albumen molecules from the gin fizzes hum like bees in the ventricles of my brain—yet I feel quite well. 63

Where is the sniper? Shading my eyes, I examine every inch of the terrain. 64

A flag stirs fitfully on its pole beside the green rectangle dug into the slope of the near ridge like a step. It is the football field of the Valley Forge Academy, our private school, which was founded on religious and patriotic principles and to keep Negroes out. Earlier today—could it have been today?—the Christian Kaydettes, our champion baton-twirlers, practiced their twirling, little suspecting what dread misadventure would befall them. 65

Beyond the empty shopping plaza at my foot rise the low green hills of Paradise Estates. The fairways of the golf links make notches in the tree line. Pretty cubes and loaves of new houses are strewn among the pines like sugar lumps. It is even possible to pick out my own house, a spot of hot pink and a wink of glass under the old TV transmitter. By a trick of perspective the transmitter tower seems to rise from the dumpy silo of old Saint Michael's Church in the plaza. 66

Here in the old days I used to go to mass with my daughter, Samantha. My wife, an ex-Episcopal girl from Virginia, named our daughter Samantha in the expectation that this dark gracile pagan name would somehow inform the child, but alas for Doris, Samantha turned out to be chubby, fair, acned, and pious, the sort who likes to hang around after school and beat Sister's erasers. 67

The best of times were after mass on summer evenings when Samantha and I would walk home in the violet dusk, we having received Communion and I rejoicing afterwards, caring nought for my fellow Catholics but only for myself and Samantha and Christ swallowed, remembering what he promised me for eating him, that I would have life in me, and I did, feeling so good that I'd sing and cut the fool all the way home like King David before the Ark. Once home, light up the charcoal briquets out under the TV transmitter, which 68 lofted its red light next to Venus like a ruby and a diamond in the plum velvet sky. Snug down Samantha with the *Wonderful World of Color* in the den (the picture better than life, having traveled only one hundred feet straight down), back to the briquets, take four, five, six long pulls from the quart of Early Times, shout with joy for the beauty of the world, sing "Finch 'han dal vino" from *Don Giovanni*[9] and "Holy God We Praise Thy Name," conceive a great heart-leaping desire for Doris, whose lip would curl at my proposal but who was nonetheless willing, who in fact now that she thought of it was as lusty as could be, her old self once again, a lusty Shenandoah Valley girl, Apple Queen of the Apple Blossom Festival in Winchester. Lead her by the hand beyond the azaleas where we'd fling ourselves upon each other and fall down on the zoysia grass, thick-napped here as a Kerman rug.

A flutter of white in the motel window. The sniper? I tighten my elbow against the carbine belt. No, it is one of the girls' rooms. Moira's. Moira washing her things out and hanging them out to dry as if it were any other Tuesday. A good omen, Moira washing her underwear. Her I always think of so, standing barefoot in her slip at the washstand, legs planted far apart and straight, even a bit past straight, so that the pad at the back of her knees stands out as firm as rubber; yellow eyes musing and unfocused as she puts her things to soak in LUX. 69

Lola, on the other hand, I always see playing the Dvorak[10] concerto, hissing the melody with her tongue against her teeth, straddling the cello with her splendid knees. 70

Ellen Oglethorpe appears in my mind as in fact she is, a stern but voluptuous Presbyterian nurse, color high in her cheeks, eyes bright with disapproval. I think of her as having her fists planted on her hips, as they used to say, akimbo. 71

All quiet in front. Could he, the sniper, have gotten behind me? I turn around slowly, keeping under the low spreading limbs of the longleaf. 72

Beyond the hump of the interchange rise the monoliths of "Fedville," the federal complex including the hospital (where I've spent almost as much time as a patient as doctoring), the medical school, the NASA facility, the Behavioral Institute, the Geriatrics Center, and the Love Clinic. 73

---

[9]*"Don Giovanni"*: An opera (1787) by Wolfgang Amadeus Mozart.

[10]"[Antonin] Dvorak": Czech composer (1841–1904).

In "Love," as it is called, volunteers perform sexual acts singly, in couples, and in groups, beyond viewing mirrors in order that man might learn more about the human sexual response. 74

Next door is Geriatrics Rehabilitation or "Gerry Rehab," a far-flung complex of pleasant low-lying white-roofed Daytona-type buildings. Here old folk from Tampa to Tucson are treated for the blues and boredoms of old age. These good folk, whose physical ailments are mostly cured nowdays, who at eighty-five, ninety, even a hundred, are as spry as can be, limber-jointed, smooth-faced, supple of artery, nevertheless often grow inexplicably sad. Though they may live in the pleasantest Senior Settlements where their every need is filled, every recreation provided, every sort of hobby encouraged, nevertheless many grow despondent in their happiness, sit slack and empty-eyed at shuffleboard and ceramic oven. Fishing poles fall from tanned and healthy hands. Golf clubs rust. *Reader's Digests* go unread. Many old folks pine away and even die from unknown causes like victims of a voodoo curse. Here in Gerry Rehab, these sad oldsters are encouraged to develop their "creative and altruistic potential." Yet mysterious deaths, and suicides, too, continue to mount. The last Surgeon General's report named the nation's number-one killer as "Senior Citizens' anomie," known locally as the St. Petersburg blues. 75

To my left, white among the cypresses, are the old frame buildings of the Little Sisters of the Poor. During the week the Little Sisters run a school for poor children, black and white, feed and clothe them, and on weekends conduct religious retreats for Christian folk. The scientists help the sisters with the children during the week. On weekends Christians come to make retreats and pray for the conversion of Communists. 76

The scientists, who are mostly liberals and unbelievers, and the businessmen, who are mostly conservative and Christian, live side by side in Paradise Estates. Though the two make much of their differences—one speaking of "outworn dogmas and creeds," the other of "atheism and immorality," etcetera etcetera—to tell the truth, I do not notice a great deal of difference between the two. Both sorts are generally good fellows, good fathers and husbands who work hard all day, come home at five-thirty to their pretty homes, kiss their wives, toss their rosy babes in the air, light up their charcoal briquets, or perhaps mount their tiny tractor mowers. There are minor differences. When conservative Christian housewives drive to town to pick up their maids in the Hollow, the latter ride on the back seat in the old style. Liberal housewives make their maids ride on the front seat. On Sundays Christian businessmen dress up and take their families to church, whereas unbelieving scientists are apt to put on their worst 77 clothes and go bird-watching. As one of my behaviorist friends put it, "My cathedral is the blue sky and my pilgrimage is for the ivory-billed woodpecker," the fabulous and lordly bird that some say still inhabits the fastness of the swamp.

Beyond the cypresses, stretching away to the horizon, as misty as 78
a southern sea, lies the vast Honey Island Swamp. Smudges of hummocks dot its savanna-like islands. The north-south interstate, crossing it on a causeway, flies due south straight as two lines drawn with a ruler to converge at a point on the horizon.

From the hummocks arise one or two wisps of smoke. Yonder in 79
the fastness of the swamp dwell the dropouts from land castoffs of and rebels against our society: ferocious black Bantus who use the wilderness both as a refuge and as a guerrilla base from which to mount forays against outlying subdivisions and shopping plazas; all manner of young white derelicts who live drowsy sloth-like lives, sustaining themselves on wild melons and catfish and green turtles and smoking Choctaw cannabis the livelong day. The lonely hummocks, once the haunt of raccoon and alligator, are now rubbed bare as monkey islands at the zoo by all manner of disaffected folk: Bantu guerrillas, dropouts from Tulane and Vanderbilt, M.I.T. and Loyola; draft dodgers, deserters from the Swedish army, psychopaths and pederasts from Memphis and New Orleans whose practices were not even to be tolerated in New Orleans; antipapal Catholics, malcontented Methodists, ESPers, UFOers, Aquarians, ex-Ayn Randers, Choctaw Zionists who have returned to their ancestral hunting grounds, and even a few old graybeard Kerouac beats, wiry old sourdoughs of the spirit who carry pilgrim staffs, recite sutras, and leap from hummock to hummock as agile as mountain goats.

The town where I keep an office is north and to my right. By 80
contrast with the swamp, the town has become a refuge for all manner of conservative folk, graduates of Bob Jones University, retired Air Force colonels, passed-over Navy commanders, ex-Washington, D.C., policemen, patriotic chiropractors, two officials of the National Rifle Association, and six conservative proctologists.

Paradise Estates, where I live now, is another matter. Directly 81
opposite me, between swamp and town, its houses sparkle like jewelry in the sunlight. Emerald fairways run alongside sleepy bayous. Here everyone gets along well, heathen and Christian, Jew and Gentile, Northerner and Southerner, liberal and conservative. The Northerners, mostly businessmen and engineers from places like Kenosha and Sheboygan and Grosse Pointe, actually outnumber the Southerners. But they, the Northerners, have taken to Southern ways

like ducks to water. They drink toddies and mint juleps and hold fish fries with hush puppies. Little black jockeys fish from mirrors in their front yards. Life-sized mammy-dolls preside over their patios. Nearly everyone treats his servants well, picking them up in Happy Hollow and taking them home, allowing "totin' privileges" and giving them "Christmas gifts."

The Negroes around here are generally held to be a bad lot. The 82
older Negroes are mostly trifling and no-account, while the young Negroes have turned mean as yard dogs. Nearly all the latter have left town, many to join the Bantus in the swamp. Here the conservatives and liberals of Paradise agree. The conservatives say that Negroes always have been trifling and no-account or else mean as yard dogs. The liberals, arguing with the conservatives at the country club, say yes, Negroes are trifling and no-account or else mean as yard dogs, but why shouldn't they be, etcetera etcetera. So it goes.

Our servants in Paradise are the exceptions, however: faithful 83
black mammies who take care of our children as if they were their own, dignified gardeners who work and doff their caps in the old style.

Paradise Estates, where I live, is a paradise indeed, an oasis of 84
concord in a troubled land. For our beloved old U.S.A. is in a bad way. Americans have turned against each other; race against race, right against left, believer against heathen, San Francisco against Los Angeles, Chicago against Cicero. Vines sprout in sections of New York where not even Negroes will live. Wolves have been seen in downtown Cleveland, like Rome during the Black Plague. Some Southern states have established diplomatic ties with Rhodesia. Minnesota and Oregon have their own consulates in Sweden (where so many deserters from these states dwell).

The old Republican Party has become the Knothead Party, so 85
named during the last Republican convention in Montgomery when a change of name was proposed, the first suggestion being the Christian Conservative Constitutional Party, and campaign buttons were even printed with the letters CCCP[11] before an Eastern-liberal commentator noted the similarity to the initials printed on the backs of the Soviet cosmonauts and called it the most knotheaded political bungle of the century—which the conservatives, in the best tradition, turned to their own advantage, printing a million more buttons reading "Knotheads for America" and banners proclaiming "No Man Can Be Too Knotheaded in the Service of His Country."

[11]"CCCP": In Russian, abbreviation of Soyuz Sotsialistiches Kikh Respublik, or Union of Soviet Socialist Republics.

The old Democrats gave way to the new Left Party. They too were 86
stuck with a nickname not of their own devising and the nickname stuck: in this case a derisive acronym that the Right made up and the Left accepted, accepted in that same curious American tradition by which we allow our enemies to name us, give currency to their curses, perhaps from the need to concede the headstart they want and still beat them, perhaps also from the secret inkling that our enemies know the worst of us best and it's best for them to say it. LEFT usually it is, often LEFTPAPA, sometimes LEFTPAPSAN (with a little Jap bow), hardly ever the original LEFTPAPASANE, which stood for what, according to the Right, the Left believed in: Liberty, Equality, Fraternity, The Pill, Atheism, Pot, Anti-Pollution, Sex, Abortion Now, Euthanasia.

The center did not hold.[12] 87

However, the Gross National Product continues to rise. 88

There are Left states and Knothead states, Left towns and Knot- 89
head towns but no center towns (for example, my old hometown over yonder is Knothead, Fedville behind me is Left, and Paradise Estates where I live now does not belong to the center—there is no center—but is that rare thing, a pleasant place where Knothead and Left—but not black—dwell side by side in peace), Left networks and Knothead networks, Left movies and Knothead movies. The most popular Left films are dirty movies from Sweden. All-time Knothead favorites, on the other hand, include *The Sound of Music, Flubber,* and *Ice Capades of 1981,* clean movies all.

I've stopped going to movies. It is hard to say which is more 90
unendurable, the sentimental blasphemy of Knothead movies like *The Sound of Music* or sitting in a theater with strangers watching other strangers engage in sexual intercourse and sodomy on the giant 3-D Pan-a-Vision screen.

American literature is not having its finest hour. The Southern 91
gothic novel yielded to the Jewish masturbatory novel, which in turn gave way to the WASP homosexual novel, which has nearly run its course. The Catholic literary renascence, long awaited, failed to materialize. But old favorites endure, like venerable Harold Robbins and Jacqueline Susann, who continue to write the dirty clean books so beloved by the American housewife. Gore Vidal is the grand old man of American letters.

Both political parties have had their triumphs. 92

---

[12]"The center did not hold": See William Butler Yeats's apocalyptic poem "The Second Coming." The reference here is to the center of Western civilization, which in the poem—and in Percy's novel—is thought to be flying apart.

The Lefts succeeded in removing "In God We Trust" from pennies. 93

The Knotheads enacted a law requiring compulsory prayers in the black public schools and made funds available for birth control in Africa, Asia, and Alabama. 94

But here in Paradise, Knothead lives next to Leftist in peace. On Wednesday nights one goes to a meeting of Birchers, the other to the ACLU. Sunday one goes to church, the other in search of the lordly ivory-billed woodpecker, but both play golf, ski in the same bayou, and give "Christmas gifs" to the same waiters at the club. 95

The war in Ecuador has been going on for fifteen years and has divided the country further. Not exactly our best war. The U.S.A. sided with South Ecuador, which is largely Christian, believing in God and the sacredness of the individual, etcetera etcetera. The only trouble is that South Ecuador is owned by ninety-eight Catholic families with Swiss bank accounts, is governed by a general, and so is not what you would call an ideal democracy. North Ecuador, on the other hand, which many U.S. liberals support, is Maoist-Communist and has so far murdered two hundred thousand civilians, including liberals, who did not welcome Communism with open arms. Not exactly our best war, and now in its sixteenth year. 96

Even so, most Americans do well enough. In fact, until lately, nearly everyone tried and succeeded in being happy but me. My unhappiness is not the fault of Paradise. I was unlucky. My daughter died, my wife ran off with a heathen Englishman, and I fell prey to bouts of depression and morning terror, to say nothing of abstract furies and desultory lusts for strangers. 97

Here's the puzzle: what is an unhappy psychiatrist to do in a place where everyone else is happier than he is? Physician, heal thy . . . 98

Fortunately for me, many other people have become unhappy of late. Certain psychiatric disorders have cropped up in both Lefts and Knotheads. 99

Conservatives have begun to fall victim to unseasonable rages, delusions of conspiracies, high blood pressure, and large-bowel complaints. 100

Liberals are more apt to contract sexual impotence, morning terror, and a feeling of abstraction of the self from itself.[13] 101

[13]"a feeling of abstraction of the self from itself": An existential predicament that one finds in Percy's novels, in which characters feel disconnected from themselves, unsure of their identities or purpose in living.

So it is that a small Knothead city like my hometown yonder can support half a dozen proctologists, while places like Berkeley or Beverly Hills have a psychiatrist in every block. 102

It is my misfortune—and blessing—that I suffer from both liberal and conservative complaints, e.g., both morning terror and large-bowel disorders, excessive abstraction and unseasonable rages, alternating impotence and satyriasis. So that at one and the same time I have great sympathy for my patients and lead a fairly miserable life. 103

But my invention has changed all this. Now I know how to be happy and make others happy. With my little machine I can diagnose and treat with equal success the morning terror of liberals and the apoplexy of conservatives. In fact it could save the U.S.A. if we can get through the next hour or so. 104

Discussion and Writing Suggestions

1. In paragraph 7, Dr. More speculates that God has lifted His blessing from the U.S.A., or that whatever extraordinary luck has held the country together for two hundred years is now running out. In either event, the country is being carried back "into history with its ordinary catastrophes." What is your response to this view?
2. How sane is the narrator, Dr. More? In developing your response, locate passages in the story that indicate both his sanity and insanity.
3. Read William Butler Yeats's poem "The Second Coming" and discuss why Percy makes references to it. In one case, the reference is indirect—hawks circling in a rising current of air; in the second case, the reference is direct: "The center did not hold."
4. Consider the references to decay in the story. What do you make of all the vines sprouting, the rusting cars, the abandoned motel with its swimming pool filled with scummy water, and the reports of wolves prowling downtown Cleveland? Develop your answer into an essay.
5. Discuss the irony in Dr. More's account of Barry Bocock, the transplanted Boeing engineer. For the purpose of your discussion, you may define irony as an indirect, wry comment made about a character. In a nonironic treatment, you'd find a sentence like, "Barry Bocock is a blubbering fool." The author would explicitly recount the character's deficiencies. In an ironic treatment, you read a passage and *infer* these deficiencies. Read paragraphs 42–52 and infer what Walker Percy's narrator, Dr. More, thinks of Barry Bocock.
6. Consider Percy's use of titles and names: *Love in the Ruins*, "July Fourth" (the section's title from which the excerpt is taken), Paradise Estates (where Dr. More lives), and Valley Forge Academy. As you play the names off against what you read in the excerpt, what observations can you make?

SYNTHESIS ACTIVITIES

1. Tom Ashbrook writes:

> China and India, both once great themselves—have spent centuries in deep troughs, gripping old cultural patterns, myths, and self-images that left them cripplingly out of sync with a changing world. Could America do the same thing?

   Respond to this question by writing an essay that incorporates your own views along with those of Ashbrook, Fred Branfman, and Paul Kennedy. You might begin the discussion by defining America's "old cultural patterns, myths, and self-images," referring to "An American Morality Tale" by Robert Reich. Having attempted to define America's myths, you could explore the extent to which, if followed, they would lead to prosperity today. Or, in your view, are the American myths similar to the backward-looking Indian and Chinese myths that left those countries "cripplingly out of sync with a changing world"?

   Ashbrook, Branfman, and Kennedy all speak to this question, and you will want to summarize their views as well as respond to them. Kennedy's answer to Ashbrook's question—Could America slip into a centuries-long decline—would of course be *yes.* Branfman lays down an entire agenda that, if met, would lead him to say *no.* Ashbrook seems more equivocal, as the ending to his essay suggests. What is your view? And how will you position it as you define and then respond to the views of Ashbrook, Branfman, and Kennedy?

2. Has Charles Krauthammer persuaded you that some of the other authors in this chapter are wrong in believing that America is in decline? Develop your response to this question into an essay by drawing on Krauthammer's piece (portions of which you'll likely want to summarize) and on those with whom he would likely disagree: Ashbrook, Branfman, and Kennedy. If what Krauthammer says is true, then why is there such a widespread perception that America is, indeed, in decline?

3. Natwar Gandhi observes that great American thinkers, notably Wilson and Kennan, have been pessimistic about this country's prospects because they make the mistake of comparing the America that is to the America that might be—to an ideal. Invariably, the real and present America suffers by comparison. A perplexing problem follows from Gandhi's observation: If we want to move America ahead, we'll need to do so with some ideal in mind; otherwise, how could we guide policy? But once we settle on an American ideal, the gap between the ideal and the real, present-day America may again lead to cynicism. *The question:* How can we improve America's fortunes, how can we set and then aspire to lofty goals, while at the same time avoiding Kennan- and Wilson-like cynicism?

In responding, you may want to draw on the observations of Robert Reich, who observes that to be an American is to live an ideal that is *never* fully realized. What, then, are the implications for cynicism in American life if we are forever striving to meet an ideal that recedes from us? In developing your answer, you might also want to draw on Katherine Newman's "American Nightmares" as you explore the consequences of failing to achieve the American dream. Of course, your own views will figure prominently in the matter. Are you, or the people you know, cynical? (Two contemporary social scientists, Donald Kanter and Philip Mirvis, have found that 43 percent of Americans are cynical.) Do these times lend themselves to cynicism? Hope? Neither? What would be your prescription against cynicism?

4. Fred Branfman claims that the United States stands to lose significantly if it does not adjust to life in the postindustrial world. Similarly, Paul Kennedy claims that "a serious threat to the real interests of the United States can only come from a failure to adjust sensibly to the new world order." In an essay, explore the demands that "the new world order" will impose on America and discuss the ways in which America will need to respond. You may want to counter-balance the views of Kennedy and Branfman with those of Krauthammer.

   Early in the essay, you'll want to define clearly the new order that Branfman and Kennedy speak of (and you'll want to determine if both are speaking of the *same* world order). As for America's response, you could cast one large section of your essay as a series of summaries: What should be this country's response, according to Branfman? Kennedy? Ashbrook? Yourself? You might conclude the essay with a description of what might happen to America if we failed to respond as Branfman and Kennedy insist we must. In this part of the discussion, you might turn to the selection from Walker Percy's *Love in the Ruins.*

5. You are preparing to buy a car. You have also read the selections in this chapter and have decided that you, personally, will do your best to halt what you believe to be America's economic decline. You have your sights set on a German-made car, an American-made car, and a Japanese-made car—all of which cost approximately the same amount of money. You have clear preferences, and the American car is not number one on your list. Write a letter explaining to a friend or fellow student which car you should buy, along with the reasons for buying it. Remember that a larger issue is at stake here: You want to help the economy and help restore American competitiveness. Are you doing the economy a favor by buying American? Are you doing the Detroit auto manufacturers a favor by buying American? Your largest goal is to help: So which car will it be and why? In your letter, draw on the discussions you've read in this chapter. If it seems stilted to refer to particular authors by name, then incorporate their views

(without their names) into your essay. Note that if you choose this assignment as one to pursue for a formal grade, your instructor will expect to see proof of your having read, understood, and responded to the views of the authors in this chapter. Therefore, incorporate these views, as appropriate, into your discussion.

6. For students who have visited other countries or foreign-born nationals studying in the United States: Having lived and/or traveled in two or more countries, you are in a unique position to make observations about American culture in that you can compare this culture with others. In an essay that explores the question of America's decline, draw on your international experiences. (Or interview someone who has lived abroad and answer these same questions.) What have your travels led you to observe about American values, ideals, or productivity? Based on your experiences, comment on the views expressed by the authors in this chapter.

7. Walker Percy's Dr. More speculates that God has lifted His blessing from the U.S.A. or that whatever extraordinary good luck has held the country together for two hundred years is now running out. Paul Kennedy believes that it is a historical imperative that once-great nations decline. Krauthammer disagrees with the premise that the U.S. is in decline. What is your view? (One strategy for organizing a response: Given your reading in this chapter, what categories of decline can you identify as possibly [or already] affecting life in America? Address each type of decline and discuss the extent to which you feel it can be avoided.)

8. In Walker Percy's *Love in the Ruins,* the narrator paints a portrait of an America in visible disrepair: Vines are sprouting and overtaking the structures we've built; cars are rusting; the air is heavy with potential catastrophes—and yet the gross national product continues to rise. In Percy, physical disrepair mirrors a spiritual one. Write an essay in which you define and discuss the extent of spiritual disrepair in American life. Draw on Percy as a source—what are his views on the subject? Draw on Ashbrook's "A View from the East" as well, since he also addresses a lapsed attitude among Americans. (It might be interesting to note that Ashbrook, too, is aware of visible signs of deterioration.)

FAIRY TALES: A CLOSER LOOK AT "CINDERELLA" 8

"Once upon a time . . ." Millions of children around the world have listened to these (or similar) words. And, once upon a time, such words were magic archways into a world of entertainment and fantasy for children and their parents. But in our own century, fairy tales have come under the scrutiny of anthropologists, linguists, educators, psychologists, and psychiatrists, as well as literary critics, who have come to see them as a kind of social genetic code—a means by which cultural values are transmitted from one generation to the next. Some people, of course, may scoff at the idea that charming tales like "Cinderella" or "Snow White" are anything other than charming tales, at the idea that fairy tales may really be ways of inculcating young and impressionable children with culturally approved values. But even if they are not aware of it, adults and children use fairy tales in complex and subtle ways. We can, perhaps, best illustrate this by examining variants of a single tale—"Cinderella."

"Cinderella" appears to be the best-known fairy tale in the world. In 1892, Marian Roalfe Cox published 345 variants of the story, the first systematic study of a single folktale. In her collection, Cox gathered stories from throughout Europe in which elements or motifs of "Cinderella" appeared, often mixed with motifs of other tales. All told, over 700 variants exist throughout the world—in Europe, Africa, Asia, and North and South America. Scholars debate the extent to which such a wide distribution is explained by population migrations or by some universal quality of imagination that would allow people at different times and places to create essentially the same story. But for whatever reason, folklorists agree that "Cinderella" has appealed to storytellers and listeners everywhere.

The great body of folk literature, including fairy tales, comes to us from an oral tradition. Written literature, produced by a particular author, is preserved through the generations just as the author recorded it. By contrast, oral literature changes with every telling: The childhood game comes to mind in which one child whispers a sentence into the ear of another; by the time the second child repeats the sentence to a third, and the third to a fourth (and so on), the sentence has changed considerably. And so it is with oral literature, with the qualification that these stories are also changed quite consciously when a teller wishes to add or delete material.

The modern student of folk literature finds her- or himself in the position of *reading* as opposed to hearing a tale. The texts we read tend to be of two types, which are at times difficult to distinguish. We might read a faithful transcription of an oral tale or a tale of *literary* origin—a tale that was originally written (as a short story would be), not spoken, but that nonetheless may contain elements of an oral account. In this chapter, we include tales of both oral and literary origin. The author of the earliest recorded version of "Cinderella," which appeared in a ninth century Chinese text, says that the story was told to him by a family servant, "a man from the caves of Yung-chou [who] remembers many strange things of the South." Jakob and Wilhelm Grimm published their transcription of "Cinderella" in 1812; Giambattista Basile published his in the 1630s, though Basile appears to have embellished the oral tale with local Neopolitan idioms. The version of "Cinderella" by Charles Perrault (1697) is difficult to classify as the transcription of an oral source, since he may have heard the story, originally, but appears (according to Bruno Bettelheim) to have "freed it of all content he considered vulgar, and refined its other features to make the product suitable to be told at court." Thus, Perrault's version would appear to be more of a literary creation (that is, changed in the process of transcription) than Basile's Italian version. Of unquestionable literary origin are Walt Disney's "Cinderella," based on Perrault's text, Anne Sexton's poem of the same name, and John Gardner's "Gudgekin the Thistle Girl." Preceding these variants of "Cinderella," we present a general reading on fairy-tale literature by Stith Thompson. Following the seven variants, we present three selections that respond directly to the tale. We hear from Bruno Bettelheim, who, following psychoanalytic theory, finds in "Cinderella" a "Story of Sibling Rivalry and Oedipal Conflicts." Madonna Kolbenschlag then offers a feminist reading of the tale, followed by Jane Yolen's lament on the "gutting" of a story that was once richly magical and instructive.

A note on terminology: "Cinderella," "Jack and the Beanstalk," "Little Red Riding Hood," and the like are commonly referred to as fairy tales, though, strictly speaking, they are not. True fairy tales concern a "class of supernatural beings of diminutive size, who in popular belief are said to possess magical powers and to have great influence for good or evil over the affairs of humans" *(Oxford English Dictionary).* "Cinderella" and the others just mentioned concern no beings of diminutive size, though extraordinary, magical events do occur in the story. Folklorists would be more apt to call these stories "wonder tales." We retain the traditional "fairy tale," though, with the proviso that in popular usage the term is misapplied. You may notice that the authors in this chapter use the terms "folktale" and "fairy tale" interchangeably. The expression "folktale" refers to *any* story conceived orally and passed on in an oral tradition. Thus, "folktale" is a generic term that incorporates both fairy tales and wonder tales.

Universality of the Folktale

STITH THOMPSON

Folklorists travel the world, to cities and rural areas alike, recording the facts, traditions, and beliefs that characterize ethnic groups. Some folklorists record and compile jokes; others do the same with insults or songs. Still others, like Stith Thompson, devote their professional careers to studying tales. And, as it turns out, there are many aspects of stories and storytelling worth examining. Among them: the art of narrative—how tellers captivate their audiences; the social and religious significance of tale telling; the many types of tales that are told; the many variants, worldwide, of single tales (like "Cinderella"). In a preface to one of his own books, Thompson raises the broad questions and the underlying assumptions that govern the folklorist's study of tales. We begin this chapter with Thompson's overview to set a context for the variants of "Cinderella" that you will read.

Note the ways that Thompson's approach to fairy tales differs from yours. Whether or not you're conscious of having an approach, you do *have one: Perhaps you regard stories like "Cinderella" as entertainment. Fine—this is a legitimate point of view, but it's only one of several ways of regarding folktales. Stith Thompson claims that there's much to learn in studying tales. He assumes, as you might not, that tales should be objects of study as well as entertainment.*

Stith Thompson (1885–1976) led a distinguished life as an American educator, folklorist, editor, and author. Between 1921 and 1955, he was a professor of folklore and English, and later dean of the Graduate School and Distinguished Service Professor at Indiana University, Bloomington. Five institutions have awarded Thompson honorary doctorates for his work in folklore studies. He has published numerous books on the subject, including European Tales Among North American Indians *(1919),* The Types of the Folktales *(1928), and* Tales of the North American Indian *(1929). He is best known for his six-volume* Motif Index of Folk Literature *(1932–37; 1955–58, 2nd ed.).*

The teller of stories has everywhere and always found eager listeners. Whether his tale is the mere report of a recent happening, a legend of long ago, or an elaborately contrived fiction, men and women have hung upon his words and satisfied their yearnings for information or amusement, for incitement to heroic deeds, for 1 religious edification, or for release from the overpowering monotony of their lives. In villages of central Africa, in outrigger boats on the Pacific, in the Australian bush, and within the shadow of Hawaiian volcanoes, tales of the present and of the mysterious past, of animals and gods and heroes, and of men and women like themselves, hold listeners in their spell or enrich the conversation of daily life. So it is also in Eskimo igloos under the light of seal-oil lamps, in the tropical jungles of Brazil, and by the totem poles of the British Columbian coast. In Japan too, and China and India, the priest and the scholar, the peasant and the artisan all join in their love of a good story and their honor for the man who tells it well.

When we confine our view to our own occidental world, we see 2
that for at least three or four thousand years, and doubtless for ages before, the art of the story-teller has been cultivated in every rank of society. Odysseus entertains the court of Alcinous with the marvels of his adventures. Centuries later we find the long-haired page reading nightly from interminable chivalric romances to entertain his lady while her lord is absent on his crusade. Medieval priests illustrate sermons by anecdotes old and new, and only sometimes edifying. The old peasant, now as always, whiles away the winter evening with tales of wonder and adventure and the marvelous workings of fate. Nurses tell children of Goldilocks or the House that Jack Built. Poets write epics and novelists novels. Even now the cinemas and theaters bring their stories direct to the ear and eye through the voices and gestures of actors. And in the smoking-rooms of sleeping cars and steamships and at the banquet table the oral anecdote flourishes in a new age.

In the present work we are confining our interest to a relatively 3
narrow scope, the traditional prose tale—the story which has been handed down from generation to generation either in writing or by word of mouth. Such tales are, of course, only one of the many kinds of story material, for, in addition to them, narrative comes to us in verse as ballads and epics, and in prose as histories, novels, dramas, and short stories. We shall have little to do with the songs of bards, with the ballads of the people, or with poetic narrative in general, though stories themselves refuse to be confined exclusively to either prose or verse forms. But even with verse and all other forms of prose narrative put aside, we shall find that in treating the traditional prose tale—the folktale—our quest will be ambitious enough and will take us to all parts of the earth and to the very beginnings of history.

Although the term "folktale" is often used in English to refer to 4
the "household tale" or "fairy tale" (the German *Märchen*), such as "Cinderella" or "Snow White," it is also legitimately employed in a much broader sense to include all forms of prose narrative, written or oral, which have come to be handed down through the years. In this

usage the important fact is the traditional nature of the material. In contrast to the modern story writer's striving after originality of plot and treatment, the teller of a folktale is proud of his ability to hand on that which he has received. He usually desires to impress his readers or hearers with the fact that he is bringing them something that has the stamp of good authority, that the tale was heard from some great story-teller or from some aged person who remembered it from old days.

So it was until at least the end of the Middle Ages with writers 5
like Chaucer, who carefully quoted authorities for their plots—and sometimes even invented originals so as to dispel the suspicion that some new and unwarranted story was being foisted on the public. Though the individual genius of such writers appears clearly enough, they always depended on authority, not only for their basic theological opinions but also for the plots of their stories. A study of the sources of Chaucer or Boccaccio takes one directly into the stream of traditional narrative.

The great written collections of stories characteristic of India, the 6
Near East, the classical world, and Medieval Europe are almost entirely traditional. They copy and recopy. A tale which gains favor in one collection is taken over into others, sometimes intact and sometimes with changes of plot or characterization. The history of such a story, passing it may be from India to Persia and Arabia and Italy and France and finally to England, copied and changed from manuscript to manuscript, is often exceedingly complex. For it goes through the hands of both skilled and bungling narrators and improves or deteriorates at nearly every retelling. However well or poorly such a story may be written down, it always attempts to preserve a tradition, an old tale with the authority of antiquity to give it interest and importance.

If use of the term "folktale" to include such literary narratives 7
seems somewhat broad, it can be justified on practical grounds if on no other, for it is impossible to make a complete separation of the written and the oral traditions. Often, indeed, their interrelation is so close and so inextricable as to present one of the most baffling problems the folklore scholar encounters. They differ somewhat in their behavior, it is true, but they are alike in their disregard of originality of plot and of pride of authorship.

Nor is complete separation of these two kinds of narrative tradi- 8
tion by any means necessary for their understanding. The study of the oral tale . . . will be valid so long as we realize that stories have frequently been taken down from the lips of unlettered taletellers and have entered the great literary collections. In contrary fashion, fables of Aesop, anecdotes from Homer, and saints' legends, not to speak of fairy tales read from Perrault or Grimm, have entered the oral stream

and all their association with the written or printed page has been forgotten. Frequently a story is taken from the people, recorded in a literary document, carried across continents or preserved through centuries, and then retold to a humble entertainer who adds it to his repertory.

It is clear then that the oral story need not always have been oral. 9
But when it once habituates itself to being passed on by word of mouth it undergoes the same treatment as all other tales at the command of the raconteur. It becomes something to tell to an audience, or at least to a listener, not something to read. Its effects are no longer produced indirectly by association with words written or printed on a page, but directly through facial expression and gesture and repetition and recurrent patterns that generations have tested and found effective.

This oral art of taletelling is far older than history, and it is not 10
bounded by one continent or one civilization. Stories may differ in subject from place to place, the conditions and purposes of taletelling may change as we move from land to land or from century to century, and yet everywhere it ministers to the same basic social and individual needs. The call for entertainment to fill in the hours of leisure has found most peoples very limited in their resources, and except where modern urban civilization has penetrated deeply they have found the telling of stories one of the most satisfying of pastimes. Curiosity about the past has always brought eager listeners to tales of the long ago which supply the simple man with all he knows of the history of his folk. Legends grow with the telling, and often a great heroic past evolves to gratify vanity and tribal pride. Religion also has played a mighty role everywhere in the encouragement of the narrative art, for the religious mind has tried to understand beginnings and for ages has told stories of ancient days and sacred beings. Often whole cosmologies have unfolded themselves in these legends, and hierarchies of gods and heroes.

World-wide also are many of the structural forms which oral 11
narrative has assumed. The hero tale, the explanatory legend, the animal anecdote—certainly these at least are present everywhere. Other fictional patterns are limited to particular areas of culture and act by their presence or absence as an effective index of the limit of the area concerned. The study of such limitations has not proceeded far, but it constitutes an interesting problem for the student of these oral narrative forms.

Even more tangible evidence of the ubiquity and antiquity of the 12
folktale is the great similarity in the content of stories of the most varied peoples. The same tale types and narrative motifs are found scattered over the world in most puzzling fashion. A recognition of these resemblances and an attempt to account for them brings the

scholar closer to an understanding of the nature of human culture. He must continually ask himself, "Why do some peoples borrow tales and some lend? How does the tale serve the needs of the social group?" When he adds to his task an appreciation of the aesthetic and practical urge toward story-telling, and some knowledge of the forms and devices, stylistic and histrionic, that belong to this ancient and widely practiced art, he finds that he must bring to his work more talents than one man can easily possess. Literary critics, anthropologists, historians, psychologists, and aestheticians are all needed if we are to hope to know why folktales are made, how they are invented, what art is used in their telling, how they grow and change and occasionally die.

Review Questions

1. According to Thompson, what are the reasons people consistently venerate a good storyteller?
2. What does Thompson state as features that distinguish a "folktale" from modern types of fiction?
3. How does religion help encourage the existence of folktale art?
4. What is a strong piece of evidence for the great antiquity and universality of folktales?

Discussion and Writing Suggestions

1. Based on Thompson's explanation of the qualities of oral folktales, what do you feel is lost by the increasing replacement of this form of art and entertainment by TV?
2. What do you suppose underlies the apparent human need to tell stories, given that storytelling is practiced in every culture known?
3. Interview older members of your family, asking them about stories they were told as children. As best you can, record a story. Then examine your work. How does it differ from the version you heard? Write an account of your impressions on the differences between an oral and written rendering of a story. Alternately, you might record a story and then speculate on what the story might mean in the experiences of the family member who told it to you.

SEVEN VARIANTS OF "CINDERELLA"

It comes as a surprise to many that there exist Chinese, French, Italian, German, and American versions of the popular "Cinderella," along with 700 other versions worldwide. Which is the real *"Cinderella"? The question is misleading in that each version is "real" for a particular group of people in a particular place and time. Certainly you can judge among versions and select the most appealing. You can also draw comparisons. Indeed, the grouping of the stories that we present here invites comparisons. A few of the categories you might wish to consider as you read:*

- *Cinderella's innocence or guilt, concerning the treatment she receives at the hands of her stepsisters*
- *Cinderella's passive (or active) nature*
- *Sibling rivalry—the relationship of Cinderella to her sisters*
- *The father's role*
- *The rule that Cinderella must return from the ball by midnight*
- *Levels of violence*
- *Presence or absence of the fairy godmother*
- *Cinderella's relationship with the prince*
- *Characterization of the prince*
- *The presence of Cinderella's dead mother*
- *The ending*

Cinderella

CHARLES PERRAULT

Charles Perrault (1628–1703) was born in Paris of a prosperous family. He practiced law for a short time and then devoted his attentions to a job in government, in which capacity he was instrumental in promoting the advancement of the arts and sciences and in securing pensions for writers, both French and foreign. Perrault is best known as a writer for his Contes de ma mère l'oie (Mother Goose Tales), *a collection of fairy tales taken from popular folklore. He is widely suspected of having changed these stories in an effort to make them more acceptable to his audience—members of the French court.*

Once there was a nobleman who took as his second wife the proudest and haughtiest woman imaginable. She had two daughters of the same character, who took after their mother in everything. On his side, the husband had a daughter who was sweetness itself; she inherited this from her mother, who had been the most kindly of women. 1

From *Fairy Tales,* by Charles Perrault, edited and translated by Geoffrey Brereton. Baltimore: Penguin Books, 1957. Reprinted by permission of Penguin Books Ltd. and Anne Brereton.

No sooner was the wedding over than the stepmother showed her ill-nature. She could not bear the good qualities of the young girl, for they made her own daughters seem even less likable. She gave her the roughest work of the house to do. It was she who washed the dishes and the stairs, who cleaned out Madam's room and the rooms of the two Misses. She slept right at the top of the house, in an attic, on a lumpy mattress, while her sisters slept in panelled rooms where they had the most modern beds and mirrors in which they could see themselves from top to toe. The poor girl bore everything in patience and did not dare to complain to her father. He would only have scolded her, for he was entirely under his wife's thumb. 2

When she had finished her work, she used to go into the chimney-corner and sit down among the cinders, for which reason she was usually known in the house as Cinderbottom. Her younger stepsister, who was not so rude as the other, called her Cinderella. However, Cinderella, in spite of her ragged clothes, was still fifty times as beautiful as her sisters, superbly dressed though they were. 3

One day the King's son gave a ball, to which everyone of good family was invited. Our two young ladies received invitations, for they cut quite a figure in the country. So there they were, both feeling very pleased and very busy choosing the clothes and the hair-styles which would suit them best. More work for Cinderella, for it was she who ironed her sisters' underwear and goffered their linen cuffs. Their only talk was of what they would wear. 4

"I," said the elder, "shall wear my red velvet dress and my collar of English lace." 5

"I," said the younger, "shall wear just my ordinary skirt; but, to make up, I shall put on my gold-embroidered cape and my diamond clasp, which is quite out of the common." 6

The right hairdresser was sent for to supply double-frilled coifs, and patches were bought from the right patch-maker. They called Cinderella to ask her opinion, for she had excellent taste. She made useful suggestions and even offered to do their hair for them. They accepted willingly. 7

While she was doing it, they said to her: 8

"Cinderella, how would you like to go to the ball?" 9

"Oh dear, you are making fun of me. It wouldn't do for me." 10

"You are quite right. It would be a joke. People would laugh if they saw a Cinderbottom at the ball." 11

Anyone else would have done their hair in knots for them, but she had a sweet nature, and she finished it perfectly. For two days they were so excited that they ate almost nothing. They broke a good dozen laces trying to tighten their stays to make their waists slimmer, and they were never away from their mirrors. 12

At last the great day arrived. They set off, and Cinderella watched 13
them until they were out of sight. When she could no longer see them, she began to cry. Her godmother, seeing her all in tears, asked what was the matter.

"If only I could . . . If only I could . . ." She was weeping so much 14
that she could not go on.

Her godmother, who was a fairy, said to her: "If only you could 15
go to the ball, is that it?"

"Alas, yes," said Cinderella with a sigh. 16

"Well," said the godmother, "be a good girl and I'll get you 17
there."

She took her into her room and said: "Go into the garden and get 18
me a pumpkin."

Cinderella hurried out and cut the best she could find and took it 19
to her godmother, but she could not understand how this pumpkin would get her to the ball. Her godmother hollowed it out, leaving only the rind, and then tapped it with her wand and immediately it turned into a magnificent gilded coach.

Then she went to look in her mouse-trap and found six mice all 20
alive in it. She told Cinderella to raise the door of the trap a little, and as each mouse came out she gave it a tap with her wand and immediately it turned into a fine horse. That made a team of six horses, each of fine mouse-coloured grey.

While she was wondering how she would make a coachman, 21
Cinderella said to her:

"I will go and see whether there is a rat in the rat-trap, we could 22
make a coachman of him."

"You are right," said the godmother. "Run and see." 23

Cinderella brought her the rat-trap, in which there were three big 24
rats. The fairy picked out one of them because of his splendid whiskers and, when she had touched him, he turned into a fat coachman, with the finest moustaches in the district.

Then she said: "Go into the garden and you will find six lizards 25
behind the watering-can. Bring them to me."

As soon as Cinderella had brought them, her godmother changed 26
them into six footmen, who got up behind the coach with their striped liveries, and stood in position there as though they had been doing it all their lives.

Then the fairy said to Cinderella: 27

"Well, that's to go to the ball in. Aren't you pleased?" 28

"Yes. But am I to go like this, with my ugly clothes?" 29

Her godmother simply touched her with her wand and her 30
clothes were changed in an instant into a dress of gold and silver cloth, all sparkling with precious stones. Then she gave her a pair of glass slippers, most beautifully made.

So equipped, Cinderella got into the coach; but her godmother warned her above all not to be out after midnight, telling her that, if she stayed at the ball a moment later, her coach would turn back into a pumpkin, her horses into mice, her footmen into lizards, and her fine clothes would become rags again. 31

She promised her godmother that she would leave the ball before midnight without fail, and she set out, beside herself with joy. 32

The King's son, on being told that a great princess whom no one knew had arrived, ran out to welcome her. He handed her down from the coach and led her into the hall where his guests were. A sudden silence fell; the dancing stopped, the violins ceased to play, the whole company stood fascinated by the beauty of the unknown princess. Only a low murmur was heard: "Ah, how lovely she is!" The King himself, old as he was, could not take his eyes off her and kept whispering to the Queen that it was a long time since he had seen such a beautiful and charming person. All the ladies were absorbed in noting her clothes and the way her hair was dressed, so as to order the same things for themselves the next morning, provided that fine enough materials could be found, and skillful enough craftsmen. 33

The King's son placed her in the seat of honour, and later led her out to dance. She danced with such grace that she won still more admiration. An excellent supper was served, but the young Prince was too much occupied in gazing at her to eat anything. She went and sat next to her sisters and treated them with great courtesy, offering them oranges and lemons which the Prince had given her. They were astonished, for they did not recognize her. 34

While they were chatting together, Cinderella heard the clock strike a quarter to twelve. She curtsied low to the company and left as quickly as she could. 35

As soon as she reached home, she went to her godmother and, having thanked her, said that she would very much like to go again to the ball on the next night—for the Prince had begged her to come back. She was in the middle of telling her godmother about all the things that had happened, when the two sisters came knocking at the door. Cinderella went to open it. 36

"How late you are!" she said, rubbing her eyes and yawning and stretching as though she had just woken up (though since they had last seen each other she had felt very far from sleepy). 37

"If you had been at the ball," said one of the sisters, "you would not have felt like yawning. There was a beautiful princess there, really ravishingly beautiful. She was most attentive to us. She gave us oranges and lemons." 38

Cinderella could have hugged herself. She asked them the name of the princess, but they replied that no one knew her, that the King's 39 son was much troubled about it, and that he would give anything in the world to know who she was. Cinderella smiled and said to them:

"So she was very beautiful? Well, well, how lucky you are! 40
Couldn't I see her? Please, Miss Javotte, do lend me that yellow dress which you wear about the house."

"Really," said Miss Javotte, "what an idea! Lend one's dress like 41
that to a filthy Cinderbottom! I should have to be out of my mind."

Cinderella was expecting this refusal and she was very glad when 42
it came, for she would have been in an awkward position if her sister had really lent her her frock.

On the next day the two sisters went to the ball, and Cinderella 43
too, but even more splendidly dressed than the first time. The King's son was constantly at her side and wooed her the whole evening. The young girl was enjoying herself so much that she forgot her godmother's warning. She heard the clock striking the first stroke of midnight when she thought that it was still hardly eleven. She rose and slipped away as lightly as a roe-deer. The Prince followed her, but he could not catch her up. One of her glass slippers fell off, and the Prince picked it up with great care.

Cinderella reached home quite out of breath, with no coach, no 44
footmen, and wearing her old clothes. Nothing remained of all her finery, except one of her little slippers, the fellow to the one which she had dropped. The guards at the palace gate were asked if they had not seen a princess go out. They answered that they had seen no one go out except a very poorly dressed girl, who looked more like a peasant than a young lady.

When the two sisters returned from the ball, Cinderella asked 45
them if they had enjoyed themselves again, and if the beautiful lady had been there. They said that she had, but that she had run away when it struck midnight, and so swiftly that she had lost one of her glass slippers, a lovely little thing. The Prince had picked it up and had done nothing but gaze at it for the rest of the ball, and undoubtedly he was very much in love with the beautiful person to whom it belonged.

They were right, for a few days later the King's son had it 46
proclaimed to the sound of trumpets that he would marry the girl whose foot exactly fitted the slipper. They began by trying it on the various princesses, then on the duchesses and on all the ladies of the Court, but with no success. It was brought to the two sisters, who did everything possible to force their feet into the slipper, but they could not manage it. Cinderella, who was looking on, recognized her own slipper, and said laughing:

"Let me see if it would fit me!" 47

Her sisters began to laugh and mock at her. But the gentleman 48
who was trying on the slipper looked closely at Cinderella and,

seeing that she was very beautiful, said that her request was perfectly reasonable and that he had instructions to try it on every girl. He made Cinderella sit down and, raising the slipper to her foot, he found that it slid on without difficulty and fitted like a glove.

Great was the amazement of the two sisters, but it became greater 49
still when Cinderella drew from her pocket the second little slipper and put it on her other foot. Thereupon the fairy godmother came in and, touching Cinderella's clothes with her wand, made them even more magnificent than on the previous days.

Then the two sisters recognized her as the lovely princess whom 50
they had met at the ball. They flung themselves at her feet and begged her forgiveness for all the unkind things which they had done to her. Cinderella raised them up and kissed them, saying that she forgave them with all her heart and asking them to love her always. She was taken to the young Prince in the fine clothes which she was wearing. He thought her more beautiful than ever and a few days later he married her. Cinderella, who was as kind as she was beautiful, invited her two sisters to live in the palace and married them, on the same day, to two great noblemen of the Court.

Ashputtle

JAKOB AND WILHELM GRIMM

Jakob Grimm (1785–1863) and Wilhelm Grimm (1786–1859) are best known today for the 200 folktales they collected from oral sources and reworked in Kinder- und Hausmärchen *(popularly known as* Grimm's Fairy Tales*), which has been translated into seventy languages. The techniques Jakob and Wilhelm Grimm used to collect and comment on these tales became a model for other collectors, providing a basis for the science of folklore. Though the Grimm brothers argued for preserving the tales exactly as heard from oral sources, scholars have determined that they sought to "improve" the tales by making them more readable. The result, highly pleasing to lay audiences the world over, nonetheless represents a literary reworking of the original oral sources.*

A rich man's wife fell sick and, feeling that her end was near, she called her only daughter to her bedside and said: "Dear child, be good and say your prayers; God will help you, and I shall look down on you from heaven and always be with you." With that she closed her eyes and died. Every day the little girl went out to her mother's grave and wept, and she went on being good and saying her prayers. When winter came, the snow spread a white cloth over the grave, and when spring took it off, the man remarried. 1

His new wife brought two daughters into the house. Their faces were beautiful and lily-white, but their hearts were ugly and black. That was the beginning of a bad time for the poor stepchild. "Why should this silly goose sit in the parlor with us?" they said. "People who want to eat bread must earn it. Get into the kitchen where you belong!" They took away her fine clothes and gave her an old gray dress and wooden shoes to wear. "Look at the haughty princess in her finery!" they cried and, laughing, led her to the kitchen. From then on she had to do all the work, getting up before daybreak, carrying water, lighting fires, cooking and washing. In addition the sisters did everything they could to plague her. They jeered at her and poured peas and lentils into the ashes, so that she had to sit there picking them out. At night, when she was tired out with work, she had no bed to sleep in but had to lie in the ashes by the hearth. And they took to calling her Ashputtle because she always looked dusty and dirty. 2

One day when her father was going to the fair, he asked his two stepdaughters what he should bring them. "Beautiful dresses," said one. "Diamonds and pearls," said the other. "And you, Ashputtle. What would you like?" "Father," she said, "break off the first branch that brushes against your hat on your way home, and bring it to me." So he brought beautiful dresses, diamonds and pearls for his two stepdaughters, and on the way home, as he was riding through a copse, a hazel branch brushed against him and knocked off his hat. So he broke off the branch and took it home with him. When he got home, he gave the stepdaughters what they had asked for, and gave Ashputtle the branch. After thanking him, she went to her mother's grave and planted the hazel sprig over it and cried so hard that her tears fell on the sprig and watered it. It grew and became a beautiful tree. Three times a day Ashputtle went and sat under it and wept and prayed. Each time a little white bird came and perched on the tree, and when Ashputtle made a wish the little bird threw down what she had wished for. 3

Now it so happened that the king arranged for a celebration. It was to go on for three days and all the beautiful girls in the kingdom 4 were invited, in order that his son might choose a bride. When the two stepsisters heard they had been asked, they were delighted. They called Ashputtle and said: "Comb our hair, brush our shoes, and fasten our buckles. We're going to the wedding at the king's palace." Ashputtle obeyed, but she wept, for she too would have liked to go dancing, and she begged her stepmother to let her go. "You little sloven!" said the stepmother. "How can you go to a wedding when you're all dusty and dirty? How can you go dancing when you have neither dress nor shoes?" But when Ashputtle begged and begged, the stepmother finally said: "Here, I've dumped a bowlful of lentils in the ashes. If you can pick them out in two hours, you may go." The girl went out the back door to the garden and cried out: "O tame little doves, O turtledoves, and all the birds under heaven, come and help me put

the good ones in the pot,
the bad ones in your crop."

Two little white doves came flying through the kitchen window, and then came the turtledoves, and finally all the birds under heaven came flapping and fluttering and settled down by the ashes. The doves nodded their little heads and started in, peck peck peck peck, and all the others started in, peck peck peck peck, and they sorted out all the good lentils and put them in the bowl. Hardly an hour had passed before they finished and flew away. Then the girl brought the bowl to her stepmother, and she was happy, for she thought she'd be allowed to go to the wedding. But the stepmother said: "No, Ashputtle. You have nothing to wear and you don't know how to dance; the people would only laugh at you." When Ashputtle began to cry, the stepmother said: "If you can pick two bowlfuls of lentils out of the ashes in an hour, you may come." And she thought: "She'll never be able to do it." When she had dumped the two bowlfuls of lentils in the ashes, Ashputtle went out the back door to the garden and cried out: "O tame little doves, O turtledoves, and all the birds under heaven, come and help me put

the good ones in the pot,
the bad ones in your crop."

Two little white doves came flying through the kitchen window, and then came the turtledoves, and finally all the birds under heaven came flapping and fluttering and settled down by the ashes. The doves nodded their little heads and started in, peck peck peck peck, and all the others started in, peck peck peck peck, and they sorted out all the good lentils and put them in the bowls. Before half an hour had passed, they had finished and they all flew away. Then the girl brought the bowls to her stepmother, and she was happy, for she thought she'd be allowed to go to the wedding. But her stepmother said: "It's no use. You can't come, because you have nothing to wear and you don't know how to dance. We'd only be ashamed of you." Then she turned her back and hurried away with her two proud daughters.

When they had all gone out, Ashputtle went to her mother's 5
grave. She stood under the hazel tree and cried:

Shake your branches, little tree,
Throw gold and silver down on me."

Whereupon the bird tossed down a gold and silver dress and slippers embroidered with silk and silver. Ashputtle slipped into the dress as fast as she could and went to the wedding. Her sisters and stepmother didn't recognize her. She was so beautiful in her golden dress that they thought she must be the daughter of some foreign king. They never dreamed it could be Ashputtle, for they thought she was sitting at home in her filthy rags, picking lentils out of the ashes. The king's son came up to her, took her by the hand and danced with her. He wouldn't dance with anyone else and he never let go her hand. When someone else asked for a dance, he said: "She is my partner."

She danced until evening, and then she wanted to go home. The 6
king's son said: "I'll go with you, I'll see you home," for he wanted to find out whom the beautiful girl belonged to. But she got away from him and slipped into the dovecote. The king's son waited until her father arrived, and told him the strange girl had slipped into the dovecote. The old man thought: "Could it be Ashputtle?" and he sent for an ax and a pick and broke into the dovecote, but there was no one inside. When they went indoors, Ashputtle was lying in the ashes in her filthy clothes and a dim oil lamp was burning on the chimney piece, for Ashputtle had slipped out the back end of the dovecote and run to the hazel tree. There she had taken off her fine clothes and put them on the grave, and the bird had taken them away. Then she had put her gray dress on again, crept into the kitchen and lain down in the ashes.

Next day when the festivities started in again and her parents and 7
stepsisters had gone, Ashputtle went to the hazel tree and said:

"Shake your branches, little tree,
Throw gold and silver down on me."

Whereupon the bird threw down a dress that was even more dazzling than the first one. And when she appeared at the wedding, everyone marveled at her beauty. The king's son was waiting for her. He took her by the hand and danced with no one but her. When others came and asked her for a dance, he said: "She is my partner." When evening came, she said she was going home. The king's son followed her, wishing to see which house she went into, but she ran away and disappeared into the garden behind the house, where there was a big beautiful tree with the most wonderful pears growing on it. She climbed among the branches as nimbly as a squirrel and the king's son didn't know what had become of her. He waited until her father arrived and said to him: "The strange girl has got away from me and I think she has climbed up in the pear tree." Her father thought: "Could it be Ashputtle?" He sent for an ax and chopped the tree down, but there was no one in it. When they went into the kitchen, Ashputtle was lying there in the ashes as usual, for she had jumped down on the other side of the tree, brought her fine clothes back to the bird in the hazel tree, and put on her filthy gray dress.

On the third day, after her parents and sisters had gone, Ashput- 8
tle went back to her mother's grave and said to the tree:

"Shake your branches, little tree,
Throw gold and silver down on me."

Whereupon the bird threw down a dress that was more radiant than either of the others, and the slippers were all gold. When she appeared at the wedding, the people were too amazed to speak. The king's son danced with no one but her, and when someone else asked her for a dance, he said: "She is my partner."

When evening came, Ashputtle wanted to go home, and the 9
king's son said he'd go with her, but she slipped away so quickly that he couldn't follow. But he had thought up a trick. He had arranged to have the whole staircase brushed with pitch, and as she was running down it the pitch pulled her left slipper off. The king's son picked it up, and it was tiny and delicate and all gold. Next morning he went to the father and said: "No girl shall be my wife but the one this golden shoe fits." The sisters were overjoyed, for they had beautiful feet. The eldest took the shoe to her room to try it on and her mother went with her. But the shoe was too small and she couldn't get her big toe in. So her mother handed her a knife and said: "Cut your toe off. Once you're queen you won't have to walk any more." The girl cut her toe off, forced her foot into the shoe, gritted her teeth against the pain, and went out to the king's son. He accepted her as his bride-to-be, lifted her up on his horse, and rode away with her. But they had to pass the grave. The two doves were sitting in the hazel tree and they cried out:

"Roocoo, roocoo,
There's blood in the shoe.
The foot's too long, the foot's too wide,
That's not the proper bride."

He looked down at her foot and saw the blood spurting. At that he turned his horse around and took the false bride home again. "No," he said, "this isn't the right girl; let her sister try the shoe on." The sister went to her room and managed to get her toes into the shoe, but her heel was too big. So her mother handed her a knife and said: "Cut off a chunk of your heel. Once you're queen you won't have to walk any more." The girl cut off a chunk of her heel, forced her foot into the shoe, gritted her teeth against the pain, and went out to the king's son. He accepted her as his bride-to-be, lifted her up on his horse, and rode away with her. As they passed the hazel tree, the two doves were sitting there, and they cried out:

"Roocoo, roocoo,
There's blood in the shoe.
The foot's too long, the foot's too wide,
That's not the proper bride."

He looked down at her foot and saw that blood was spurting from her shoe and staining her white stocking all red. He turned his horse around and took the false bride home again. "This isn't the right girl, either," he said. "Haven't you got another daughter?" "No," said the man, "there's only a puny little kitchen drudge that my dead wife left me. She couldn't possibly be the bride." "Send her up," said the king's son, but the mother said: "Oh no, she's much too dirty to be seen." But he insisted and they had to call her. First she washed her face and hands, and when they were clean, she went upstairs and curtseyed to the king's son. He handed her the golden slipper and sat down on a footstool, took her foot out of her heavy wooden shoe, and put it into the slipper. It fitted perfectly. And when she stood up and the king's son looked into her face, he recognized the beautiful girl he had danced with and cried out: "This is my true bride!" The stepmother and the two sisters went pale with fear and rage. But he lifted Ashputtle up on his horse and rode away with her. As they passed the hazel tree, the two white doves called out:

"Roocoo, roocoo,
No blood in the shoe.
Her foot is neither long nor wide,
This one is the proper bride."

They they flew down and alighted on Ashputtle's shoulders, one on the right and one on the left, and there they sat.

On the day of Ashputtle's wedding, the two stepsisters came and 10
tried to ingratiate themselves and share in her happiness. On the way to church the elder was on the right side of the bridal couple and the younger on the left. The doves came along and pecked out one of the elder sister's eyes and one of the younger sister's eyes. Afterward, on the way out, the elder was on the left side and the younger on the right, and the doves pecked out both the remaining eyes. So both sisters were punished with blindness to the end of their days for being so wicked and false.

The Cat Cinderella

GIAMBATTISTA BASILE

"One of the first major collections of European folktales taken from oral sources was Giambattista Basile's Il Pentamerone, *published posthumously during the years 1634–1636. Originally entitled* Lo Cunto de li Cunte, *the tale of tales, the work consisted of five sets of ten diversions, or stories. Supposedly each set of narratives represented one day's worth of tale-telling. The sixth diversion of the first day was 'The Cat Cinderella.'*

"Basile (1575–1632) had apparently heard in Naples many of the stories he reported in the Pentamerone. *In any case, the book was published in Neapolitan dialect, which unfortunately made it relatively inaccessible even to readers of other Italian dialects. Not until 1742 was it translated into Bolognese dialect and in 1747 into Italian. It was not translated into German until 1846, when Felix Liebrecht undertook the task. This volume contained an introduction by Jakob Grimm. The Grimm brothers had known of Basile's collection earlier and were quite astonished to find that so many of 'their' German 'Kinder und Hausmärchen' had been reported in Naples nearly two centuries before."*

Note: Introduction to "The Cat Cinderella" was written by Alan Dundes.

There was once . . . a Prince who was a widower, and he had a 1
daughter so dear to him that he saw with no other eyes but hers. He gave her an excellent teacher of sewing, who taught her chainwork, openwork, fringes and hems and showed her more love than was possible to describe. The father, however, shortly remarried, and his wife was an evil, malicious, bad-tempered woman who began at once to hate her step-daughter and threw sour looks, wry faces and scowling glances on her enough to make her jump with fright.

The poor child was always complaining to her governess of her 2
step-mother's ill-treatment, finishing up with "O would to God that you could be my little mother, who are so kind and loving to me," and she so often repeated this song to her that she put a wasp in her ear and, at last, tempted by the devil, her teacher ended by saying, "If you must follow this madcap idea, I will be a mother to you and you shall be the apple of my eye." She was going on with the prologue, when Zezolla (as the girl was called) interrupted her by saying, "Forgive my taking the words out of your mouth. I know you love me well, mum's the word, and *sufficit;* teach me the way, for I am new; you write and I will sign." "Well, then," answered the governess, "listen carefully; keep your ears open and you shall always enjoy the whitest bread from the finest flour. When your father leaves the house, tell your step-mother that you would like one of those old dresses that are kept in the big chest in the closet, to save the one you now have on. As she always wants to see you in rags and tatters, she will open the chest and say, 'Hold the lid.' You must hold it while she is rummaging inside and then suddenly let it fall so that it breaks her neck. After that, you know well that your father would even coin false money to please you, so when he fondles you, beg him to take me for his wife, and then you shall be happy and the mistress even of my life."

When Zezolla had heard the plan, every hour seemed a thousand 3
years until she had carried out her governess's advice in every particular. When the period of mourning for her step-mother was over, she began to sound her father about marrying her governess. At first the Prince took it as a joke, but Zezolla so often struck with the flat that at last she thrust with the point, and he gave way to the persuasive words of his daughter. He therefore married Carmosina, the governess with great celebrations.

Now, while this couple were enjoying themselves, Zezolla was 4
standing at a balcony of her house, when a dove flew on to the wall and said to her, "If ever you desire anything, send to ask for it from the dove of the fairies of the Island of Sardinia, and you will at once have it."

For five or six days the new step-mother lavished every sort of caress of Zezolla, making her take the best seat at table, giving her the best tidbits, and dressing her in the finest clothes. But after a little time the service that Zezolla had done her was forgotten, and banished from her memory (how sorry is the mind that has an evil mistress!) and she began to push forward six daughters of her own that she had kept in hiding till then, and so worked on her husband that they won his good graces and he let his own daughter slip out of his heart. So that, a loser to-day and a pauper to-morrow, Zezolla was finally brought to such a pass that she fell from the *salon* to the kitchen, from the canopy to the grate, from splendid silks and gold to dish-clouts, from sceptres to spits; not only did she change her state, but also her name, and was no longer called Zezolla, but "Cat Cinderella." 5

Now it happened that the Prince was forced to go to Sardinia on important affairs of State, and before he left he asked one by one of his step-daughters, Imperia, Colomba, Fiorella, Diamante, Colombina, and Pascarella, what they wanted him to bring back for them on his return. One asked for a splendid gown, another for a head-dress, one for cosmetics for the face, and another games to pass the time; one one thing and one another. At last, and almost to make fun of her, he asked his daughter, "And you! what would you like?"and she answered, "Nothing, except to commend me to the dove of the fairies and beg them to send me something; and if you forget, may it be impossible for you to go forward or back. Bear in mind what I say: thy intent, thy reward." 6

The Prince went away, transacted his affairs in Sardinia, and bought the things his step-daughters had asked for, but Zezolla went quite out of his mind. But when they were embarked with the sails ready unfurled, it was found impossible to make the vessel leave the harbour: it seemed as if it were detained by a sea-lamprey. The captain of the ship, who was almost in despair, dropped off to sleep with weariness and in his dreams a fairy appeared to him who said, "Do you know why you cannot leave the harbour? Because the Prince who is with you has broken his promise to his daughter, remembering all the others except his own flesh and blood." As soon as he woke up the captain told his dream to the Prince, who was overcome with confusion at his omission. He went to the grotto of the fairies, and commending his daughter to them, begged that they should send her some gift. 7

Behold, out of the grotto there came a young girl, beautiful as a gonfalon, who bade him thank his daughter for her kind remembrances and tell her to be of good cheer for love of her. With these 8 words, she gave him a date tree, a spade and a golden can with a silken napkin; the date tree for planting and the other articles to keep and cultivate it.

The Prince, surprised at this present, took leave of the fairy and turned towards his own land. When he arrived, he gave his stepdaughters the things they had asked for, and lastly he handed the fairy's present to his own daughter. Zezolla nearly jumped out of her skin with joy and planted the date tree in a fine pot, watering it every day and then drying it with the silken napkin. 9

As a result of these attentions, within four days the date tree grew to the size of a woman, and a fairy came out who said to the girl, "What do you want?" Zezolla answered that she would like sometimes to leave the house without the sisters knowing it. The fairy replied, "Whenever you want this, come to the plant and say: 10

O my golden date tree,
With golden spade, I've dug thee,
With golden can I've watered thee,
With golden napkin dried thee,
Strip thyself and robe thou me.

Then when you want to undress, change the last line and say: "Strip thou me and robe thou thee." 11

One day it happened to be a feast-day, and the governess's daughters went out of the house in a procession all fluttering, bedaubed and painted, all ribbons, bells and gewgaws, all flowers and perfumes, roses and posies. Zezolla then ran to the plant and uttered the words the fairy had taught her, and at once she was decked out like a queen, seated on a white horse with twelve smartly attired pages. She too went where the sisters had gone, and though they did not recognize her, they felt their mouths water at the beauty of this lovely dove. 12

As luck would have it, the King came to this same place and was quite bewitched by the extraordinary loveliness of Zezolla. He ordered his most trusty attendant to find out about this fair creature, who she was and where she lived. The servant at once began to dog her footsteps, but she, noticing the trap, threw down a handful of crowns that she had obtained for that purpose from the date tree. The servant, fired by the desire for these glittering pieces, forgot to follow the palfrey and stopped to pick up the money, whilst she, at a bound, reached the house and quickly undressed in the way the fairy had told her. Those six harpies, her sisters, soon returned, and to vex and 13 mortify her, described at length all the fine things that they had seen at the feast.

The servant in the meantime had returned to the King and had told him about the crowns, whereupon the King was furious, and angrily told him that he had sold his pleasure for a few paltry coins and that at the next feast he was at all costs to discover who this lovely girl was and where nested so fair a bird. 14

When the next feast-day came, the sisters went out, all bedecked and bedizened, leaving the despised Zezolla by the hearth. But she at once ran to the date tree and uttered the same words as before, and behold a band of maidens came out, one with the mirror and one with the flask of pumpkin water, one with the curling-tongs and another with the rouge, one with the comb and another with the pins, one with the dresses and one with the necklace and earrings. They all placed themselves round her and made her as beautiful as a sun and then mounted her in a coach with six horses accompanied by footmen and pages in livery. She drove to the same place as before and kindled envy in the hearts of the sisters and flames in the breast of the King. 15

This time too, when she went away, the servant followed her, but so that he should not catch her up, she threw down a handful of pearls and jewels, which this trusty fellow was unable to resist pecking at, since they were not things to let slip. In this way Zezolla had time to reach home and undress herself as usual. The servant, quite stunned, went back to the King, who said, "By the soul of your departed, if you don't find that girl again, I'll give you a most thorough beating and as many kicks on your seat as you have hairs in your beard." 16

On the next feast day, when the sisters had already started off, Zezolla went up to the date tree. She repeated the magic spell and was again magnificently dressed and placed in a golden coach with so many attendants around it that it looked as if she were a courtesan arrested in the public promenade and surrounded by police agents. After having excited the envy and wonder of her sisters, she left, followed by the King's servant, who this time fastened himself to the carriage by double thread. Zezolla, seeing that he was always at her side, cried, "Drive on," and the coach set off at such a gallop that in her agitation she let slip from her foot the richest and prettiest patten you could imagine. 17

The servant, not being able to catch up to the carriage, which was now flying along, picked up the patten and carried it to the King, telling him what had happened. The King took it in his hands and broke out into these words: "If the foundation is so fair, what must be 18 the mansion? Oh, lovely candlestick which holds the candle that consumes me! Oh, tripod of the lovely cauldron in which my life is boiling! Oh, beauteous corks attached to the fishing-line of Love with which he has caught his soul! Behold, I embrace and enfold you, and if I cannot reach the plant, I worship the roots; if I cannot possess the capitals, I kiss the base: you first imprisoned a white foot, now you have ensnared a stricken heart. Through you, she who sways my life was taller by a span and a half; through you, my life grows by that much in sweetness so long as I keep you in my possession."

The King having said this called a secretary and ordered out the 19
trumpeters and tantarara, and had it proclaimed that all the women in the land were to come to a festival and banquet which he had determined to give. On the appointed day, my goodness, what an eating and feasting there was! Where did all the tarts and cakes come from? Where all the stews and rissoles? All the macaroni and graviuoli which were enough to stuff an entire army? The women were all there, of every kind and quality, of high degree and low degree, the rich and the poor, old and young, the well-favoured and the ill-favoured. When they had all thoroughly worked their jaws, the King spoke the proficiat and started to try the patten on his guests, one by one, to see whom it fitted to a hair, so that he could find by the shape of the slipper the one whom he was seeking. But he could find no foot to fit it, so that he was on the point of despair.

Nevertheless, he ordered a general silence and said, "Come back 20
to-morrow to fast with me, but as you love me well, do not leave behind a single woman, whoever she may be!" The Prince then said, "I have a daughter, but she always stays to mind the hearth, for she is a sorry, worthless creature, not fit to take her place at the table where you eat." The King answered, "Let her be at the top of the list, for such is my wish."

So they all went away, and came back the next day, and Zezolla 21
came with Carmosina's daughters. As soon as the King saw her, he thought she was the one he wanted, but he hid his thoughts. After the banquet came the trial of the patten. The moment it came near Zezolla's foot, it darted forward of itself to shoe that painted Lover's egg, as the iron flies to the magnet. The King then took Zezolla in his arms and led her to the canopy, where he put a crown on her head and ordered every one to make obeisance to her as to their queen. The sisters, livid with envy and unable to bear the torment of their breaking hearts, crept quietly home to their mother, confessing in spite of themselves that:

He is mad who would oppose the stars.

The Chinese "Cinderella"

TUAN CH'ÊNG-SHIH

"The earliest datable version of the Cinderella story anywhere in the world occurs in a Chinese book written about 850–860 A.D." Thus begins Arthur Waley's essay on the Chinese "Cinderella" in the March 1947 edition of Folk-Lore. *The recorder of the tale is a man named Tuan Ch'êng-shih, whose father was an important official in Szechwan and who himself held a high post in the office arranging the ceremonies associated with imperial ancestor worship.*

Among the people of the south there is a tradition that before the Ch'in and Han dynasties there was a cave-master called Wu. The aborigines called the place the Wu cave. He married two wives. One wife died. She had a daughter called Yeh-hsien, who from childhood was intelligent and good at making pottery on the wheel. Her father loved her. After some years the father died, and she was ill-treated by her step-mother, who always made her collect firewood in dangerous places and draw water from deep pools. She once got a fish about two inches long, with red fins and golden eyes. She put it into a bowl of water. It grew bigger every day, and after she had changed the bowl several times she could find no bowl big enough for it, so she threw it into the back pond. Whatever food was left over from meals she put into the water to feed it. When she came to the pond, the fish always exposed its head and pillowed it on the bank; but when anyone else came, it did not come out. The step-mother knew about this, but when she watched for it, it did not once appear. So she tricked the girl, saying, "Haven't you worked hard! I am going to give you a new dress." She then made the girl change out of her tattered clothing. Afterwards she sent her to get water from another spring and reckoning that it was several hundred leagues, the step-mother at her leisure put on her daughter's clothes, hid a sharp blade up her sleeve, and went to the pond. She called to the fish. The fish at once put its head out, and she chopped it off and killed it. The fish was now more than ten feet long. She served it up and it tasted twice as good as an ordinary fish. She hid the bones under the dung-hill. Next day, when the girl came to the pond, no fish appeared. She howled with grief in the open countryside, and suddenly there appeared a man with his hair loose over his shoulders and coarse clothes. He came down from 1

"The Chinese Cinderella Story," translated by Arthur Waley. *Folk-Lore* 58, March 1947, pp. 226–238. Reprinted by permission of the Folklore Society.

the sky. He consoled her, saying, "Don't howl! Your step-mother has killed the fish and its bones are under the dung. You go back, take the fish's bones and hide them in your room. Whatever you want, you have only to pray to them for it. It is bound to be granted." The girl followed his advice, and was able to provide herself with gold, pearls, dresses and food whenever she wanted them.

When the time came for the cave-festival, the step-mother went, 2
leaving the girl to keep watch over the fruit-trees in the garden. She waited till the step-mother was some way off, and then went herself, wearing a cloak of stuff spun from kingfisher feathers and shoes of gold. Her step-sister recognized her and said to the step-mother, "That's very like my sister." The step-mother suspected the same thing. The girl was aware of this and went away in such a hurry that she lost one shoe. It was picked up by one of the people of the cave. When the step-mother got home, she found the girl asleep, with her arms round one of the trees in the garden, and thought no more about it.

This cave was near to an island in the sea. On this island was a 3
kingdom called T'o-han. Its soldiers had subdued twenty or thirty other islands and it had a coast-line of several thousand leagues. The cave-man sold the shoe in T'o-han, and the ruler of T'o-han got it. He told those about him to put it on; but it was an inch too small even for the one among them that had the smallest foot. He ordered all the women in his kingdom to try it on; but there was not one that it fitted. It was light as down and made no noise even when treading on stone. The king of T'o-han thought the cave-man had got it unlawfully. He put him in prison and tortured him, but did not end by finding out where it had come from. So he threw it down at the wayside. Then they went everywhere[1] through all the people's houses and arrested them. If there was a woman's shoe, they arrested them and told the king of T'o-han. He thought it strange, searched the inner-rooms and found Yeh-hsien. He made her put on the shoe, and it was true.

Yeh-hsien then came forward, wearing her cloak spun from hal- 4
cyon feathers and her shoes. She was as beautiful as a heavenly being. She now began to render service to the king, and he took the fish-bones and Yeh-hsien, and brought them back to his country.

The step-mother and step-sister were shortly afterwards struck 5
by flying stones, and died. The cave people were sorry for them and buried them in a stone-pit, which was called the Tomb of the Distressed Women. The men of the cave made mating-offerings there; any girl they prayed for there, they got. The king of T'o-han, when he got back to his kingdom, made Yeh-hsien his chief wife. The first year

[1]Something here seems to have gone slightly wrong with the text. [WALEY]

the king was very greedy and by his prayers to the fish-bones got treasures and jade without limit. Next year, there was no response, so the king buried the fish-bones on the sea-shore. He covered them with a hundred bushels of pearls and bordered them with gold. Later there was a mutiny of some soldiers who had been conscripted and their general opened (the hiding-place) in order to make better provision for his army. One night they (the bones) were washed away by the tide.

This story was told me by Li Shih-yüan, who has been in the service of my family a long while. He was himself originally a man from the caves of Yung-chou and remembers many strange things of the South. 6

Walt Disney's "Cinderella"

adapted by CAMPBELL GRANT

Walter Elias Disney (1901–66), winner of twenty-nine Academy Awards, is world famous for his cartoon animations. After achieving recognition with cartoon shorts populated by such immortals as Mickey Mouse and Donald Duck, he produced the full-length animated film version of "Snow White and the Seven Dwarfs" in 1936. He followed with other animations, including "Cinderella" (1949), which he adapted from Perrault's version of the tale. A Little Golden Book, *the text of which appears here, was then adapted from the film by Campbell Grant.*

Once upon a time in a far-away land lived a sweet and pretty girl named Cinderella. She made her home with her mean old stepmother and her two stepsisters, and they made her do all the work in the house. 1

Cinderella cooked and baked. She cleaned and scrubbed. She had no time left for parties and fun. 2

But one day an invitation came from the palace of the king. 3

A great ball was to be given for the prince of the land. And every young girl in the kingdom was invited. 4

"How nice!" thought Cinderella. "I am invited, too." 5

But her mean stepsisters never thought of her. They thought only 6
of themselves, of course. They had all sorts of jobs for Cinderella to
do.

"Wash this slip. Press this dress. Curl my hair. Find my fan." 7

They both kept shouting, as fast as they could speak. 8

"But I must get ready myself. I'm going, too," said Cinderella. 9

"You!" they hooted. "The Prince's ball for you?" 10

And they kept her busy all day long. She worked in the morning, 11
while her stepsisters slept. She worked all afternoon, while they
bathed and dressed. And in the evening she had to help them put on
the finishing touches for the ball. She had not one minute to think of
herself.

Soon the coach was ready at the door. The ugly stepsisters were 12
powdered, pressed, and curled. But there stood Cinderella in her
workaday rags.

"Why, Cinderella!" said the stepsisters. "You're not dressed for 13
the ball."

"No," said Cinderella. "I guess I cannot go." 14

Poor Cinderella sat weeping in the garden. 15

Suddenly a little old woman with a sweet, kind face stood before 16
her. It was her fairy godmother.

"Hurry, child!" she said. "You are going to the ball!" 17

Cinderella could hardly believe her eyes! The fairy godmother 18
turned a fat pumpkin into a splendid coach.

Next her pet mice became horses, and her dog a fine footman. 19
The barn horse was turned into a coachman.

"There, my dear," said the fairy godmother. "Now into the coach 20
with you, and off to the ball you go."

"But my dress—" said Cinderella. 21

"Lovely, my dear," the fairy godmother began. Then she really 22
looked at Cinderella's rags.

"Oh, good heavens," she said. "You can never go in that." She 23
waved her magic wand.

"Salaga doola,
Menchicka boola,
Bibbidy bobbidy boo!" she said.

There stood Cinderella in the loveliest ball dress that ever was. 24
And on her feet were tiny glass slippers!

"Oh," cried Cinderella. "How can I ever thank you?" 25

"Just have a wonderful time at the ball, my dear," said her fairy 26
godmother. "But remember, this magic lasts only until midnight. At the stroke of midnight, the spell will be broken. And everything will be as it was before."

"I will remember," said Cinderella. "It is more than I ever 27
dreamed of."

Then into the magic coach she stepped, and was whirled away to 28
the ball.

And such a ball! The king's palace was ablaze with lights. There 29
was music and laughter. And every lady in the land was dressed in her beautiful best.

But Cinderella was the loveliest of them all. The prince never left 30
her side, all evening long. They danced every dance. They had supper side by side. And they happily smiled into each other's eyes.

But all at once the clock began to strike midnight, Bong Bong 31
Bong—

"Oh!" cried Cinderella. "I almost forgot!" 32

And without a word, away she ran, out of the ballroom and down 33
the palace stairs. She lost one glass slipper. But she could not stop.

Into her magic coach she stepped, and away it rolled. But as the 34
clock stopped striking, the coach disappeared. And no one knew where she had gone.

Next morning all the kingdom was filled with the news. The 35
Grand Duke was going from house to house, with a small glass slipper in his hand. For the prince had said he would marry no one but the girl who could wear that tiny shoe.

Every girl in the land tried hard to put it on. The ugly stepsisters 36
tried hardest of all. But not a one could wear the glass shoe.

And where was Cinderella? Locked in her room. For the mean 37
old stepmother was taking no chances of letting her try on the slipper. Poor Cinderella! It looked as if the Grand Duke would surely pass her by.

But her little friends the mice got the stepmother's key. And they 38
pushed it under Cinderella's door. So down the long stairs she came, as the Duke was just about to leave.

"Please!" cried Cinderella. "Please let me try." 39

And of course the slipper fitted, since it was her very own. 40

That was all the Duke needed. Now his long search was done. 41
And so Cinderella became the prince's bride, and lived happily ever after—and the little pet mice lived in the palace and were happy ever after, too.

Cinderella

ANNE SEXTON

Anne Sexton (1928–74) has been acclaimed as one of America's outstanding contemporary poets. In 1967, she won the Pulitzer Prize for poetry for Live or Die. *She published four other collections of her work, including* Transformations, *in which she recast, with a modern twist, popular European fairy tales such as "Cinderella." Sexton's poetry has appeared in* The New Yorker, Harper's, *the* Atlantic, *and* Saturday Review. *She received a Robert Frost Fellowship (1959), a scholarship from the Radcliffe College's New Institute for Independent Study (1961–63), a grant from the Ford Foundation (1964), and a Guggenheim Award (1969). In her book,* All My Pretty Ones *Sexton quoted Franz Kafka: "The books we need are the kind that act upon us like a misfortune, that make us suffer like the death of someone we love more than ourselves. A book should serve as the axe for the frozen sea within us." Asked in an interview (by Patricia Marx) about this quotation, Sexton responded: "I think [poetry] should be a shock to the senses. It should almost hurt."*

You always read about it:
the plumber with twelve children
who wins the Irish Sweepstakes.
From toilets to riches.
That story.

Or the nursemaid,
some luscious sweet from Denmark
who captures the oldest son's heart.
From diapers to Dior.
That story.

Or a milkman who serves the wealthy,
eggs, cream, butter, yogurt, milk,
the white truck like an ambulance
who goes into real estate
and makes a pile.
From homogenized to martinis at lunch.

Or the charwoman
who is on the bus when it cracks up
and collects enough from the insurance.
From mops to Bonwit Teller.
That story.

Once
the wife of a rich man was on her deathbed
and she said to her daughter Cinderella:
Be devout. Be good. Then I will smile
down from heaven in the seam of a cloud.
The man took another wife who had
two daughters, pretty enough
but with hearts like blackjacks.
Cinderella was their maid.
She slept on the sooty hearth each night
and walked around looking like Al Jolson.
Her father brought presents home from town,
jewels and gowns for the other women
but the twig of a tree for Cinderella.
She planted that twig on her mother's grave
and it grew to a tree where a white dove sat.
Whenever she wished for anything the dove
would drop it like an egg upon the ground.
The bird is important, my dears, so heed him.

Next came the ball, as you all know.
It was a marriage market.
The prince was looking for a wife.
All but Cinderella were preparing
and gussying up for the big event.
Cinderella begged to go too.
Her stepmother threw a dish of lentils
into the cinders and said: Pick them
up in an hour and you shall go.
The white dove brought all his friends;
all the warm wings of the fatherland came,
and picked up the lentils in a jiffy.
No, Cinderella, said the stepmother,
you have no clothes and cannot dance.
That's the way with stepmothers.

Cinderella went to the tree at the grave
and cried forth like a gospel singer:
Mama! Mama! My turtledove,
send me to the prince's ball!
The bird dropped down a golden dress
and delicate little gold slippers.
Rather a large package for a simple bird.
So she went. Which is no surprise.

Her stepmother and sisters didn't
recognize her without her cinder face
and the prince took her hand on the spot
and danced with no other the whole day.

As nightfall came she thought she'd better
get home. The prince walked her home
and she disappeared into the pigeon house
and although the prince took an axe and broke
it open she was gone. Back to her cinders.
These events repeated themselves for three days.
However on the third day the prince
covered the palace steps with cobbler's wax
and Cincerella's gold shoe stuck upon it.
Now he would find whom the shoe fit
and find his strange dancing girl for keeps.
He went to their house and the two sisters
were delighted because they had lovely feet.
The eldest went into a room to try the slipper on
but her big toe got in the way so she simply
sliced it off and put on the slipper.
The prince rode away with her until the white dove
told him to look at the blood pouring forth.
That is the way with amputations.
They don't just heal up like a wish.
The other sister cut off her heel
but the blood told as blood will.
The prince was getting tired.
He began to feel like a shoe salesman.
But he gave it one last try.
This time Cinderella fit into the shoe
like a love letter into its envelope.

At the wedding ceremony
the two sisters came to curry favor
and the white dove pecked their eyes out.
Two hollow spots were left
like soup spoons.

Cinderella and the prince
lived, they say, happily ever after,
like two dolls in a museum case
never bothered by diapers or dust,
never arguing over the timing of an egg,
never telling the same story twice,
never getting a middle-aged spread,
their darling smiles pasted on for eternity.

Regular Bobbsey Twins.
That story.

Gudgekin the Thistle Girl

JOHN GARDNER

John Gardner (1933–82), accomplished novelist, critic, and much-loved teacher of writing at the State University of New York, Binghamton, received the National Book Critics Award for his novel October Light *in 1976. His other works include* Grendel *(1971),* The Sunlight Dialogues *(1972),* Nickel Mountain *(1973), and numerous short stories and critical pieces for magazines such as* Esquire *and the* Hudson Review. *Folktale literature fascinated Gardner, and he wrote three collections of tales himself:* The King's Indian and Other Fireside Tales *(1974),* Dragon, Dragon and Other Tales *(1975), and* Gudgekin the Thistle Girl and Other Tales *(1976). Gardner died at the age of 49 in a motorcycle accident.*

In a certain kingdom there lived a poor little thistle girl. What thistle girls did for a living—that is, what people did with thistles—is no longer known, but whatever the reason that people gathered thistles, she was one of those who did it. All day long, from well before sunrise until long after sunset, she wandered the countryside gathering thistles, pricking her fingers to the bone, piling the thistles into her enormous thistle sack and carrying them back to her stepmother. It was a bitter life, but she always made the best of it and never felt the least bit sorry for herself, only for the miseries of others. The girl's name was Gudgekin. 1

Alas! The stepmother was never satisfied. She was arrogant and fiercely competitive, and when she laid out her thistles in her market stall, she would rather be dead than suffer the humiliation of seeing that some other stall had more thistles than she had. No one ever did, but the fear preyed on her, and no matter how many sacks of thistles poor Gudgekin gathered, there were never enough to give the stepmother comfort. "You don't earn your keep," the stepmother would say, crossing her arms and closing them together like scissors. "If you don't bring more thistles tomorrow, it's away you must go to the Children's Home and good riddance!" 2

Poor Gudgekin. Every day she brought more than yesterday, but every night the same. "If you don't bring more thistles tomorrow, it's away to the Home with you." She worked feverishly, frantically, smiling through her tears, seizing the thistles by whichever end came 3

From *Gudgekin the Thistle Girl and Other Tales* by John Gardner.

first, but never to her stepmother's satisfaction. Thus she lived out her miserable childhood, blinded by burning tears and pink with thistle pricks, but viewing her existence in the best light possible. As she grew older she grew more and more beautiful, partly because she was always smiling and refused to pout, whatever the provocation; and soon she was as lovely as any princess.

One day her bad luck changed to good. As she was jerking a 4
thistle from between two rocks, a small voice cried, "Stop! You're murdering my children!"

"I beg your pardon?" said the thistle girl. When she bent down 5
she saw a beautiful little fairy in a long white and silver dress, hastily removing her children from their cradle, which was resting in the very thistle that Gudgekin had been pulling.

"Oh," said Gudgekin in great distress. 6

The fairy said nothing at first, hurrying back and forth, carrying 7
her children to the safety of the nearest rock. But then at last the fairy looked up and saw that Gudgekin was crying. "Well," she said. "What's this?"

"I'm sorry," said Gudgekin. "I always cry. It's because of the 8
misery of others, primarily. I'm used to it."

"Primarily?" said the fairy and put her hands on her hips. 9

"Well," sniffled Gudgekin, "to tell the truth, I do sometimes 10
imagine I'm not as happy as I might be. It's shameful, I know. Everyone's miserable, and its wrong of me to whimper."

"Everyone?" said the fairy, "—miserable? Sooner or later an opin- 11
ion like that will make a fool of you!"

"Well, I really don't know," said Gudgekin, somewhat confused. 12
"I've seen very little of the world, I'm afraid."

"I see," said the fairy thoughtfully, lips pursed. "Well, that's a 13
pity, but it's easily fixed. Since you've spared my children and taken pity on my lot, I think I should do you a good turn."

She struck the rock three times with a tiny golden straw, and 14
instantly all the thistles for miles around began moving as if by their own volition toward the thistle girl's sack. It was the kingdom of fairies, and the beautiful fairy with whom Gudgekin had made friends was none other than the fairies' queen. Soon the fairies had gathered all the thistles for a mile around, and had filled the sack that Gudgekin had brought, and had also filled forty-three more, which they'd fashioned on the spot out of gossamer.

"Now," said the queen, "it's time that you saw the world." 15

Immediately the fairies set to work all together and built a beauti- 16
ful chariot as light as the wind, all transparent gossamer woven like fine thread. The chariot was so light that it needed no horses but flew along over the ground by itself, except when it was anchored with a stone. Next they made the thistle girl a gown of woven gossamer so

lovely that not even the queen of the kingdom had anything to rival it; indeed, no one anywhere in the world had such a gown or has ever had, even to this day. For Gudgekin's head the fairies fashioned a flowing veil as light and silvery as the lightest, most silvery of clouds, and they sprinkled both the veil and the gown with dew so they glittered as if with costly jewels.

Then, to a tinny little trumpeting noise, the queen of the fairies 17
stepped into the chariot and graciously held out her tiny hand to the thistle girl.

No sooner was Gudgekin seated beside the queen than the char- 18
iot lifted into the air lightly, like a swift little boat, and skimmed the tops of the fields and flew away to the capital.

When they came to the city, little Gudgekin could scarcely believe 19
her eyes. But there was no time to look at the curious shops or watch the happy promenading of the wealthy. They were going to the palace, the fairy queen said, and soon the chariot had arrived there.

It was the day of the kingdom's royal ball, and the chariot was 20
just in time. "I'll wait here," said the kindly queen of the fairies. "You run along and enjoy yourself, my dear."

Happy Gudgekin! Everyone was awed by her lovely gown and 21
veil; and even the fact that the fairies had neglected to make shoes for her feet, since they themselves wore none, turned out to be to Gudgekin's advantage. Barefoot dancing immediately became all the rage at court, and people who'd been wearing fine shoes for years slipped over to the window and slyly tossed them out, not to be outdone by a stranger. The thistle girl danced with the prince himself, and he was charmed more than words can tell. His smile seemed all openness and innocence, yet Gudgekin had a feeling he was watching her like a hawk. He had a reputation throughout the nine kingdoms for subtlety and shrewdness.

When it was time to take the thistle sacks back to her cruel 22
stepmother, Gudgekin slipped out, unnoticed by anyone, and away she rode in the chariot.

"Well, how was it?" asked the queen of the fairies happily. 23

"Wonderful! Wonderful!" Gudgekin replied. "Except I couldn't 24
help but notice how gloomy people were, despite their merry chatter. How sadly they frown when they look into their mirrors, fixing their make-up. Some of them frown because their feet hurt, I suppose; some of them perhaps because they're jealous of someone; and some of them perhaps because they've lost their youthful beauty. I could have wept for them!"

The queen of the fairies frowned pensively. "You're a good- 25
hearted child, that's clear," she said, and fell silent.

They reached the field, and the thistle girl, assisted by a thousand 26
fairies, carried her forty-four sacks to her wicked stepmother. The

stepmother was amazed to see so many thistle sacks, especially since some of them seemed to be coming to the door all by themselves. Nevertheless, she said—for her fear of humiliation so drove her that she was never satisfied—"A paltry forty-four, Gudgekin! If you don't bring more thistles tomorrow, it's away to the Home with you!"

Little Gudgekin bowed humbly, sighed with resignation, forced to her lips a happy smile, ate her bread crusts, and climbed up the ladder to her bed of straw. 27

The next morning when she got to the field, she found eighty-eight thistle sacks stuffed full and waiting. The gossamer chariot was standing at anchor, and the gossamer gown and veil were laid out on a rock, gleaming in the sun. 28

"Today," said the queen of the fairies, "we're going on a hunt." 29

They stepped into the chariot and flew off light as moonbeams to the royal park, and there, sure enough, were huntsmen waiting, and huntswomen beside them, all dressed in black riding-pants and riding-skirts and bright red jackets. The fairies made the thistle girl a gossamer horse that would sail wherever the wind might blow, and the people all said she was the most beautiful maiden in the kingdom, possibly an elf queen. Then the French horns and bugles blew, and the huntsmen were off. Light as a feather went the thistle girl, and the prince was so entranced he was beside himself, though he watched her, for all that, with what seemed to her a crafty smile. All too soon came the time to carry the thistle sacks home, and the thistle girl slipped from the crowd, unnoticed, and rode her light horse beside the chariot where the queen of the fairies sat beaming like a mother. 30

"Well," called the queen of the fairies, "how was it?" 31

"Wonderful!" cried Gudgekin, "it was truly wonderful! I noticed one thing, though. It's terrible for the fox!" 32

The queen of the fairies thought about it. "Blood sports," she said thoughtfully, and nodded. After that, all the rest of the way home, she spoke not a word. 33

When the thistle girl arrived at her stepmother's house, her stepmother threw up her arms in amazement at sight of those eighty-eight thistle-filled sacks. Nonetheless, she said as sternly as possible, "Eighty-eight! Why not a hundred? If you don't bring in more sacks tomorrow, it's the Home for you for sure!" 34

Gudgekin sighed, ate her dry crusts, forced a smile to her lips, and climbed the ladder. 35

The next day was a Sunday, but Gudgekin the thistle girl had to work just the same, for her stepmother's evil disposition knew no bounds. When she got to the field, there stood two times eighty-eight thistle sacks, stuffed to the tops and waiting. "*That* ought to fix her," said the queen of the fairies merrily. "Jump into your dress." 36

"Where are we going?" asked Gudgekin, as happy as could be. 37

"Why, to church, of course!" said the queen of the fairies. "After church we go to the royal picnic, and then we dance on the bank of the river until twilight." 38

"Wonderful!" said the thistle girl, and away they flew. 39

The singing in church was thrilling, and the sermon filled her heart with such kindly feelings toward her friends and neighbors that she felt close to dissolving in tears. The picnic was the sunniest in the history of the kingdom, and the dancing beside the river was delightful beyond words. Throughout it all the prince was beside himself with pleasure, never removing his eyes from Gudgekin, for he thought her the loveliest maiden he'd met in his life. For all his shrewdness, for all his aloofness and princely self-respect, when he danced with Gudgekin in her bejeweled gown of gossamer, it was all he could do to keep himself from asking her to marry him on the spot. He asked instead, "Beautiful stranger, permit me to ask you your name." 40

"It's Gudgekin," she said, smiling shyly and glancing at his eyes. 41

He didn't believe her. 42

"Really," she said, "it's Gudgekin." Only now did it strike her that the name was rather odd. 43

"Listen," said the prince with a laugh, "I'm *serious.* What is it really?" 44

"I'm serious too," said Gudgekin bridling. "It's Gudgekin the Thistle Girl. With the help of the fairies I've been known to collect two times eighty-eight sacks of thistles in a single day." 45

The prince laughed more merrily than ever at that. "Please," he said, "don't tease me, dear friend! A beautiful maiden like you must have a name like bells on Easter morning, or like songbirds in the meadow, or children's laughing voices on the playground! Tell me now. Tell me the truth. What's your name?" 46

"Puddin Tane," she said angrily, and ran away weeping to the chariot. 47

"Well," said the queen of the fairies, "how was it?" 48

"Horrible," snapped Gudgekin. 49

"Ah!" said the queen. "Now we're getting there!" 50

She was gone before the prince was aware that she was leaving, and even if he'd tried to follow her, the gossamer chariot was too fast, for it skimmed along like wind. Nevertheless, he was resolved to find and marry Gudgekin—he'd realized by now that Gudgekin must indeed be her name. He could easily understand the thistle girl's anger. He'd have felt the same himself, for he was a prince and knew better than anyone what pride was, and the shame of being made to seem a fool. He advertised far and wide for information on Gudgekin the Thistle Girl, and soon the news of the prince's search reached Gudgekin's cruel stepmother in her cottage. She was at once so 51 furious she could hardly see, for she always wished evil for others and happiness for herself.

"I'll never in this world let him find her," thought the wicked stepmother, and she called in Gudgekin and put a spell on her, for the stepmother was a witch. She made Gudgekin believe that her name was Rosemarie and sent the poor baffled child off to the Children's Home. Then the cruel stepmother changed herself, by salves and charms, into a beautiful young maiden who looked exactly like Gudgekin, and she set off for the palace to meet the prince. 52

"Gudgekin!" cried the prince and leaped forward and embraced her. "I've been looking for you everywhere to implore you to forgive me and be my bride!" 53

"Dearest prince," said the stepmother disguised as Gudgekin, "I'll do so gladly!" 54

"Then you've forgiven me already, my love?" said the prince. He was surprised, in fact, for it had seemed to him that Gudgekin was a touch more sensitive than that and had more personal pride. He'd thought, in fact, he'd have a devil of a time, considering how he'd hurt her and made a joke of her name. "Then you really forgive me?" asked the prince. 55

The stepmother looked slightly confused for an instant but quickly smiled as Gudgekin might have smiled and said, "Prince, I forgive you everything!" And so, though the prince felt queer about it, the day of the wedding was set. 56

A week before the wedding, the prince asked thoughtfully, "Is it true that you can gather, with the help of the fairies, two times eighty-eight thistle sacks all in one day?" 57

"Haven't I told you so?" asked the stepmother disguised as Gudgekin and gave a little laugh. She had a feeling she was in for it. 58

"You did say that, yes," the prince said, pulling with two fingers at his beard. "I'd surely like to see it!" 59

"Well," said the stepmother, and curtsied, "I'll come to you tomorrow and you shall see what you shall see." 60

The next morning she dragged out two times eighty-eight thistle sacks, thinking she could gather in the thistles by black magic. But the magic of the fairies was stronger than any witch's, and since they lived in the thistles, they resisted all her fiercest efforts. When it was late afternoon the stepmother realized she had only one hope: she must get the real Gudgekin from the Children's Home and make her help. 61

Alas for the wicked stepmother, Gudgekin was no longer an innocent simpleton! As soon as she was changed back from simple Rosemarie, she remembered everything and wouldn't touch a thistle with an iron glove. Neither would she help her stepmother now, on account of all the woman's cruelty before, nor would she do anything 62 under heaven that might be pleasing to the prince, for she considered him cold-hearted and inconsiderate. The stepmother went back to the palace empty-handed, weeping and moaning and making a hundred excuses, but the scales had now fallen from the prince's eyes—his reputation for shrewdness was in fact well founded—and after talking with his friends and advisers, he threw her in the dungeon. In less than a week her life in the dungeon was so miserable it made her repent and become a good woman, and the prince released her. "Hold your head high," he said, brushing a tear from his eye, for she made him think of Gudgekin. "People may speak of you as someone who's been in prison, but you're a better person now than before." She blessed him and thanked him and went her way.

63 Then once more he advertised far and wide through the kingdom, begging the real Gudgekin to forgive him and come to the palace.

64 "Never!" thought Gudgekin bitterly, for the fairy queen had taught her the importance of self-respect, and the prince's offense still rankled.

65 The prince mused and waited, and he began to feel a little hurt himself. He was a prince, after all, handsome and famous for his subtlety and shrewdness, and she was a mere thistle girl. Yet for all his beloved Gudgekin cared, he might as well have been born in some filthy cattle shed! At last he understood how things were, and the truth amazed him.

66 Now word went far and wide through the kingdom that the handsome prince had fallen ill for sorrow and was lying in his bed, near death's door. When the queen of the fairies heard the dreadful news, she was dismayed and wept tears of remorse, for it was all, she imagined, her fault. She threw herself down on the ground and began wailing, and all the fairies everywhere began at once to wail with her, rolling on the ground, for it seemed that she would die. And one of them, it happened, was living among the flowerpots in the bedroom of cruel little Gudgekin.

67 When Gudgekin heard the tiny forlorn voice wailing, she hunted through the flowers and found the fairy and said, "What in heaven's name is the matter, little friend?

68 "Ah, dear Gudgekin," wailed the fairy, "our queen is dying, and if she dies we will all die of sympathy, and that will be that."

69 "Oh, you mustn't!" cried Gudgekin, and tears filled her eyes. "Take me to the queen at once, little friend, for she did a favor for me and I see I must return it if I possibly can!"

70 When they came to the queen of the fairies, the queen said, "Nothing will save me except possibly this, my dear: ride with me one last time in the gossamer chariot for a visit to the prince."

"Never!" said Gudgekin, but seeing the heartbroken looks of the 71
fairies, she instantly relented.

The chariot was brought out from its secret place, and the gos- 72
samer horse was hitched to it to give it more dignity, and along they went skimming like wind until they had arrived at the dim and gloomy sickroom. The prince lay on his bed so pale of cheek and so horribly disheveled that Gudgekin didn't know him. If he seemed to her a stranger it was hardly surprising; he'd lost all signs of his princeliness and lay there with his nightcap on sideways and he even had his shoes on.

"What's this?" whispered Gudgekin. "What's happened to the 73
music and dancing and the smiling courtiers? And where is the prince?"

"Woe is me," said the ghastly white figure on the bed. "I was 74
once that proud, shrewd prince you knew, and this is what's become of me. For I hurt the feelings of the beautiful Gudgekin, whom I've given my heart and who refuses to forgive me for my insult, such is her pride and uncommon self-respect."

"My poor beloved prince!" cried Gudgekin when she heard this, 75
and burst into a shower of tears. "You have given your heart to a fool, I see now, for I am your Gudgekin, simple-minded as a bird! First I had pity for everyone but myself, and then I had pity for no one but myself, and now I pity all of us in this miserable world, but I see by the whiteness of your cheeks that I've learned too late!" And she fell upon his bosom and wept.

"You give me your love and forgiveness forever and will never 76
take them back?" asked the poor prince feebly, and coughed.

"I do," sobbed Gudgekin, pressing his frail, limp hand in both of 77
hers.

"Cross your heart?" he said. 78

"Oh, I do, I *do!*" 79

The prince jumped out of bed with all his wrinkled clothes on and 80
wiped the thick layer of white powder off his face and seized his dearest Gudgekin by the waist and danced around the room with her. The queen of the fairies laughed like silver bells and immediately felt improved. "Why you fox!" she told the prince. All the happy fairies began dancing with the prince and Gudgekin, who waltzed with her mouth open. When she closed it at last it was to pout, profoundly offended.

"Tr-tr-*tricked!*" she spluttered. 81

"Silly goose," said the prince, and kissed away the pout. "It's 82
true, I've tricked you, I'm not miserable at all. But you've promised to love me and never take it back. My advice to you is, make the best of it!" He snatched a glass of wine from the dresser as he merrily

waltzed her past, and cried out gaily, "As for myself, though, I make no bones about it: I intend to watch out for witches and live happily ever after. You must too, my Gudgekin! Cross your heart!"

"Oh, very well," she said finally, and let a little smile out. "It's no worse than the thistles." 83

And so they did. 84

"Cinderella": A Story of Sibling Rivalry and Oedipal Conflicts

BRUNO BETTELHEIM

Having read several variants of "Cinderella," you may have wondered what it is about this story that's prompted people in different parts of the world, at different times, to show interest in a child who's been debased but then rises above her misfortune. Why are people so fascinated with "Cinderella"?

Depending on the people you ask and their perspectives, you'll find this question answered in various ways. As a Freudian psychologist, Bruno Bettelheim believes that the mind is a repository of both conscious and unconscious elements. By definition, we aren't aware of what goes on in our unconscious; nonetheless, what happens there exerts a powerful influence on what we believe and on how we act. This division of the mind into conscious and unconscious parts is true for children no less than for adults. Based on these beliefs about the mind, Bettelheim analyzes "Cinderella" first by pointing to what he calls the story's essential theme: sibling rivalry, or Cinderella's mistreatment at the hands of her stepsisters. Competition among brothers and sisters presents a profound and largely unconscious problem to children, says Bettelheim. By hearing "Cinderella," a story that speaks directly to their unconscious, children are given tools that can help them resolve conflicts. Cinderella resolves her difficulties; children hearing the story can resolve theirs as well: This is the unconscious message of the tale.

Do you accept this argument? To do so, you'd have to agree with the author's reading of "Cinderella's" hidden meanings; and you'd have to agree with his assumptions concerning the conscious and unconscious mind and the ways in which the unconscious will seize upon the content of a story in order to resolve conflicts. Even if you don't accept Bet-

telheim's analysis, his essay makes fascinating reading. First, it is internally consistent—that is, he begins with a set of principles and then builds logically upon them, as any good writer will. Second, his analysis demonstrates how a scholarly point of view—a coherent set of assumptions about the way the world (in this case, the mind) works—creates boundaries for a discussion. Change the assumptions (as Kolbenschlag and Yolen will in the articles that conclude the chapter) and you'll change the analyses that follow from them.

Bettelheim's essay is long and somewhat difficult. While he uses no subheadings, he has divided his work into four sections: paragraphs 2–10 are devoted to sibling rivalry; paragraphs 11–19, to an analysis of "Cinderella's" hidden meanings; paragraphs 20–24, to the psychological makeup of children at the end of their Oedipal period; and paragraphs 25–27, to the reasons why "Cinderella," in particular, appeals to children in the Oedipal period.

Bruno Bettelheim, a distinguished psychologist and educator, was born in 1903 in Vienna. He was naturalized as an American citizen in 1939 and served as a professor of psychology at Rockford College and the University of Chicago. Awarded the honor of fellow by several prestigious professional associations, Bettelheim was a prolific writer and contributed articles to numerous popular and professional publications. His list of books includes Love Is Not Enough: The Treatment of Emotionally Disturbed Children, The Informed Heart, Surviving, *and* The Uses of Enchantment, *from which this selection has been excerpted. Bettelheim died in 1990.*

By all accounts, "Cinderella" is the best-known fairy tale, and probably also the best-liked. It is quite an old story; when first written down in China during the ninth century A.D., it already had a history. The unrivaled tiny foot size as a mark of extraordinary virtue, distinction, and beauty, and the slipper made of precious material are facets which point to an Eastern, if not necessarily Chinese, origin.[1] The modern hearer does not connect sexual attractiveness and beauty in general with extreme smallness of the foot, as the ancient Chinese did, in accordance with their practice of binding women's feet. 1

"Cinderella," as we know it, is experienced as a story about the agonies and hopes which form the essential content of sibling rivalry; and about the degraded heroine winning out over her siblings who abused her. Long before Perrault gave "Cinderella" the form in which 2

[1]Artistically made slippers of precious material were reported in Egypt from the third century on. The Roman emperor Diocletian in a decree of A.D. 301 set maximum prices for different kinds of footwear, including slippers made of fine Babylonian leather, dyed purple or scarlet, and gilded slippers for women. [Bettelheim]

it is now widely known, "having to live among the ashes" was a symbol of being debased in comparison to one's siblings, irrespective of sex. In Germany, for example, there were stories in which such an ash-boy later becomes king, which parallels Cinderella's fate. "Aschenputtel" is the title of the Brothers Grimm's version of the tale. The term originally designated a lowly, dirty kichenmaid who must tend to the fireplace ashes.

There are many examples in the German language of how being forced to dwell among the ashes was a symbol not just of degradation, but also of sibling rivalry, and of the sibling who finally surpasses the brother or brothers who have debased him. Martin Luther in his *Table Talks* speaks about Cain as the God-forsaken evildoer who is powerful, while pious Abel is forced to be his ash-brother *(Aschebrüdel),* a mere nothing, subject to Cain; in one of Luther's sermons he says that Esau was forced into the role of Jacob's ash-brother. Cain and Abel, Jacob and Esau are Biblical examples of one brother being suppressed or destroyed by the other. 3

The fairy tale replaces sibling relations with relations between step-siblings—perhaps a device to explain and make acceptable an animosity which one wishes would not exist among true siblings. Although sibling rivalry is universal and "natural" in the sense that it is the negative consequence of being a sibling, this same relation also generates equally as much positive feeling between siblings, highlighted in fairy tales such as "Brother and Sister." 4

No other fairy tale renders so well as the "Cinderella" stories the inner experiences of the young child in the throes of sibling rivalry, when he feels hopelessly outclassed by his brothers and sisters. Cinderella is pushed down and degraded by her stepsisters; her interests are sacrificed to theirs by her (step)mother; she is expected to do the dirtiest work and although she performs it well, she receives no credit for it; only more is demanded of her. This is how the child feels when devastated by the miseries of sibling rivalry. Exaggerated though Cinderella's tribulations and degradations may seem to the adult, the child carried away by sibling rivalry feels, "That's me; that's how they mistreat me, or would want to; that's how little they think of me." And there are moments—often long time periods—when for inner reasons a child feels this way even when his position among his siblings may seem to give him no cause for it. 5

When a story corresponds to how the child feels deep down—as no realistic narrative is likely to do—it attains an emotional quality of "truth" for the child. The events of "Cinderella" offer him vivid images that give body to his overwhelming but nevertheless often vague and nondescript emotions; so these episodes seem more convincing to him than his life experiences. 6

The term "sibling rivalry" refers to a most complex constellation 7 of feelings and their causes. With extremely rare exceptions, the emotions aroused in the person subject to sibling rivalry are far out of proportion to what his real situation with his sisters and brothers would justify, seen objectively. While all children at times suffer greatly from sibling rivalry, parents seldom sacrifice one of their children to the others, nor do they condone the other children's persecuting one of them. Difficult as objective judgments are for the young child—nearly impossible when his emotions are aroused—even he in his more rational moments "knows" that he is not treated as badly as Cinderella. But the child often feels mistreated, despite all his "knowledge" to the contrary. That is why he believes in the inherent truth of "Cinderella," and then he also comes to believe in her eventual deliverance and victory. From her triumph he gains the exaggerated hopes for his future which he needs to counteract the extreme misery he experiences when ravaged by sibling rivalry.

Despite the name "sibling rivalry," this miserable passion has 8
only incidentally to do with a child's actual brothers and sisters. The real source of it is the child's feelings about his parents. When a child's older brother or sister is more competent than he, this arouses only temporary feelings of jealousy. Another child being given special attention becomes an insult only if the child fears that, in contrast, he is thought little of by his parents, or feels rejected by them. It is because of such an anxiety that one or all of a child's sisters or brothers may become a thorn in his flesh. Fearing that in comparison to them he cannot win his parents' love and esteem is what inflames sibling rivalry. This is indicated in stories by the fact that it matters little whether the siblings actually possess greater competence. The Biblical story of Joseph tells that it is jealousy of parental affection lavished on him which accounts for the destructive behavior of his brothers. Unlike Cinderella's, Joseph's parent does not participate in degrading him, and, on the contrary, prefers him to his other children. But Joseph, like Cinderella, is turned into a slave, and, like her, he miraculously escapes and ends by surpassing his siblings.

Telling a child who is devastated by sibling rivalry that he will 9
grow up to do as well as his brothers and sisters offers little relief from his present feelings of dejection. Much as he would like to trust our assurances, most of the time he cannot. A child can see things only with subjective eyes, and comparing himself on this basis to his siblings, he has no confidence that he, on his own, will someday be able to fare as well as they. If he could believe more in himself, he would not feel destroyed by his siblings no matter what they might do to him, since then he could trust that time would bring about a desired reversal of fortune. But since the child cannot, on his own, look forward with confidence to some future day when things will turn out all right for him, he can gain relief only through fantasies of

glory—a domination over his siblings—which he hopes will become reality through some fortunate event.

Whatever our position within the family, at certain times in our lives we are beset by sibling rivalry in some form or other. Even an only child feels that other children have some great advantages over him, and this makes him intensely jealous. Further, he may suffer from the anxious thought that if he did have a sibling, his parents would prefer this other child to him. "Cinderella" is a fairy tale which makes nearly as strong an appeal to boys as to girls, since children of both sexes suffer equally from sibling rivalry, and have the same desire to be rescued from their lowly position and surpass those who seem superior to them. 10

On the surface, "Cinderella" is as deceptively simple as the story of Little Red Riding Hood, with which it shares greatest popularity. "Cinderella" tells about the agonies of sibling rivalry, of wishes coming true, of the humble being elevated, of true merit being recognized even when hidden under rags, of virtue rewarded and evil punished—a straightforward story. But under this overt content is concealed a welter of complex and largely unconscious material, which details of the story allude to just enough to set our unconscious associations going. This makes a contrast between surface simplicity and underlying complexity which arouses deep interest in the story and explains its appeal to the millions over centuries. To begin gaining an understanding of these hidden meanings, we have to penetrate behind the obvious sources of sibling rivalry discussed so far. 11

As mentioned before, if the child could only believe that it is the infirmities of his age which account for his lowly position, he would not have to suffer so wretchedly from sibling rivalry, because he could trust the future to right matters. When he thinks that his degradation is deserved, he feels his plight is utterly hopeless. Djuna Barnes's perceptive statement about fairy tales—that the child knows something about them which he cannot tell (such as that he likes the idea of Little Red Riding Hood and the wolf being in bed together)—could be extended by dividing fairy tales into two groups: one group where the child responds only unconsciously to the inherent truth of the story and thus cannot tell about it; and another large number of tales where the child preconsciously or even consciously knows what the "truth" of the story consists of and thus could tell about it, but does not want to let on that he knows. Some aspects of "Cinderella" fall into the latter category. Many children believe that Cinderella probably deserves her fate at the beginning of the story, as they feel they would, too; but they don't want anyone to know it. Despite this, she is worthy at the end to be exalted, as the child hopes he will be too, irrespective of his earlier shortcomings. 12

Every child believes at some period of his life—and this is not only at rare moments—that because of his secret wishes, if not also his clandestine actions, he deserves to be degraded, banned from the presence of others, relegated to a netherworld of smut. He fears this may be so, irrespective of how fortunate his situation may be in reality. He hates and fears those others—such as his siblings—whom he believes to be entirely free of similar evilness, and he fears that they or his parents will discover what he is really like, and then demean him as Cinderella was by her family. Because he wants others—most of all, his parents—to believe in his innocence, he is delighted that "everybody" believes in Cinderella's. This is one of the great attractions of this fairy tale. Since people give credence to Cinderella's goodness, they will also believe in his, so the child hopes. And "Cinderella" nourishes this hope, which is one reason it is such a delightful story. 13

Another aspect which holds large appeal for the child is the vileness of the stepmother and stepsisters. Whatever the shortcomings of a child may be in his own eyes, these pale into insignficance when compared to the stepsisters' and stepmother's falsehood and nastiness. Further, what these stepsisters do to Cinderella justifies whatever nasty thoughts one may have about one's siblings: they are so vile that anything one may wish would happen to them is more than justified. Compared to their behavior, Cinderella is indeed innocent. So the child, on hearing her story, feels he need not feel guilty about his angry thoughts. 14

On a very different level—and reality considerations coexist easily with fantastic exaggerations in the child's mind—as badly as one's parents or siblings seem to treat one, and much as one thinks one suffers because of it, all this is nothing compared to Cinderella's fate. Her story reminds the child at the same time how lucky he is, and how much worse things could be. (Any anxiety about the latter possibility is relieved, as always in fairy tales, by the happy ending.) 15

The behavior of a five-and-a-half-year-old girl, as reported by her father, may illustrate how easily a child may feel that she is a "Cinderella." This little girl had a younger sister of whom she was very jealous. The girl was very fond of "Cinderella," since the story offered her material with which to act out her feelings, and because without the story's imagery she would have been hard pressed to comprehend and express them. This little girl had used to dress very neatly and liked pretty clothes, but she became unkempt and dirty. One day when she was asked to fetch some salt, she said as she was doing so, "Why do you treat me like Cinderella?" 16

Almost speechless, her mother asked her, "Why do you think I treat you like Cinderella?" 17

"Because you make me do all the hardest work in the house!" was 18
the little girl's answer. Having thus drawn her parents into her fantasies, she acted them out more openly, pretending to sweep up all the dirt, etc. She went even further, playing that she prepared her little sister for the ball. But she went the "Cinderella" story one better, based on her unconscious understanding of the contradictory emotions fused into the "Cinderella" role, because at another moment she told her mother and sister, "You shouldn't be jealous of me just because I am the most beautiful in the family."

This shows that behind the surface humility of Cinderella lies the 19
conviction of her superiority to mother and sisters, as if she would think: "You can make me do all the dirty work, and I pretend that I am dirty, but within me I know that you treat me this way because you are jealous of me because I am so much better than you." This conviction is supported by the story's ending, which assures every "Cinderella" that eventually she will be discovered by her prince.

Why does the child believe deep within himself that Cinderella 20
deserves her dejected state? This question takes us back to the child's state of mind at the end of the oedipal period.[2] Before he is caught in oedipal entanglements, the child is convinced that he is lovable, and loved, if all is well within his family relationships. Psychoanalysis describes this stage of complete satisfaction with oneself as "primary narcissism." During this period the child feels certain that he is the center of the universe, so there is no reason to be jealous of anybody.

The oedipal disappointments which come at the end of this de- 21
velopmental stage cast deep shadows of doubt on the child's sense of his worthiness. He feels that if he were really as deserving of love as he had thought, then his parents would never be critical of him or disappoint him. The only explanation for parental criticism the child can think of is that there must be some serious flaw in him which accounts for what he experiences as rejection. If his desires remain unsatisfied and his parents disappoint him, there must be something wrong with him or his desires, or both. He cannot yet accept that reasons other than those residing within him could have an impact on his fate. In this oedipal jealousy, wanting to get rid of the parent of the same sex had seemed the most natural thing in the world, but now the child realizes that he cannot have his own way, and that maybe this is so because the desire was wrong. He is no longer so sure that he is preferred to his siblings, and he begins to suspect that

---

[2]*Oedipal:* Freud's theory of the Oedipus complex held that at an early stage of development a child wishes to replace the parent of the same sex in order to achieve the exclusive love of the parent of the opposite sex.

this may be due to the fact that *they* are free of any bad thoughts or wrongdoing such as his.

All this happens as the child is gradually subjected to ever more critical attitudes as he is being socialized. He is asked to behave in ways which run counter to his natural desires, and he resents this. Still he must obey, which makes him very angry. This anger is directed against those who make demands, most likely his parents; and this is another reason to wish to get rid of them, and still another reason to feel quilty about such wishes. This is why the child also feels that he deserves to be chastised for his feelings, a punishment he believes he can escape only if nobody learns what he is thinking when he is angry. The feeling of being unworthy to be loved by his parents at a time when his desire for their love is very strong leads to the fear of rejection, even when in reality there is none. This rejection fear compounds the anxiety that others are preferred and also maybe preferable—the root of sibling rivalry. 22

Some of the child's pervasive feelings of worthlessness have their origin in his experiences during and around toilet training and all other aspects of his education to become clean, neat, and orderly. Much has been said about how children are made to feel dirty and bad because they are not as clean as their parents want or require them to be. As clean as a child may learn to be, he knows that he would much prefer to give free rein to his tendency to be messy, disorderly, and dirty. 23

At the end of the oedipal period, guilt about desires to be dirty and disorderly becomes compounded by oedipal guilt, because of the child's desire to replace the parent of the same sex in the love of the other parent. The wish to be the love, if not also the sexual partner, of the parent of the other sex, which at the beginning of the oedipal development seemed natural and "innocent," at the end of the period is repressed as bad. But while this wish as such is repressed, guilt about it and about sexual feelings in general is not, and this makes the child feel dirty and worthless. 24

Here again, lack of objective knowledge leads the child to think that he is the only bad one in all these respects—the only child who has such desires. It makes every child identify with Cinderella, who is relegated to sit among the cinders. Since the child has such "dirty" wishes, that is where he also belongs, and where he would end up if his parents knew of his desires. This is why every child needs to believe that even if he were thus degraded, eventually he would be rescued from such degradation and experience the most wonderful exaltation—as Cinderella does. 25

For the child to deal with his feelings of dejection and worthlessness aroused during this time, he desperately needs to gain some 26 grasp on what these feelings of guilt and anxiety are all about. Further, he needs assurance on a conscious and an unconscious level that he will be able to extricate himself from these predicaments. One of the greatest merits of "Cinderella" is that, irrespective of the magic help Cinderella receives, the child understands that essentially it is through her own efforts, and because of the person she is, that Cinderella is able to transcend magnificently her degraded state, despite what appear as insurmountable obstacles. It gives the child confidence that the same will be true for him, because the story relates so well to what has caused both his conscious and his unconscious guilt.

Overtly "Cinderella" tells about sibling rivalry in its most extreme form: the jealousy and enmity of the stepsisters, and Cinderella's sufferings because of it. The many other psychological issues touched upon in the story are so covertly alluded to that the child does not become consciously aware of them. In his unconscious, however, the child responds to these significant details which refer to matters and experiences from which he consciously has separated himself, but which nevertheless continue to create vast problems for him. 27

Review Questions

1. What does living among ashes symbolize, according to Bettelheim?
2. What explanation does Bettelheim give for Cinderella's having stepsisters, not sisters?
3. In what ways are a child's emotions aroused by sibling rivalry?
4. To a child, what is the meaning of Cinderella's triumph?
5. Why is the fantasy solution to sibling rivalry offered by "Cinderella" appropriate for children?
6. Why is Cinderella's goodness important?
7. Why are the stepsisters and stepmother so vile, according to Bettelheim?
8. In paragraphs 20 through 26, Bettelheim offers a complex explanation of oedipal conflicts and their relation to sibling rivalry and the child's need to be debased, even while feeling superior. Summarize these seven paragraphs and compare your summary with those of your classmates. Have you agreed on the essential information in this passage?

Discussion and Writing Suggestions

1. One identifying feature of psychoanalysis is the assumption of complex unconscious and subconscious mechanisms in human personality that explain behavior. In this essay, Bettelheim discusses the interior world of a child in ways that the child could never articulate. The features of this world include the following:

All children experience sibling rivalry.

The real source of sibling rivalry is the child's parents.

Sibling rivalry is a miserable passion and a devastating experience.

Children have a desire to be rescued from sibling rivalry (as opposed to rescuing themselves, perhaps).

Children experience an Oedipal stage, in which they wish to do away with the parent of the same sex and be intimate with the parent of the opposite sex.

"Every child believes at some point in his life . . . that because of his secret wishes, if not also his clandestine actions, he deserves to be degraded, banned from the presence of others, relegated to a netherworld of smut."

To what extent do you agree with these statements? Take one of these statements and respond to it in a four- or five-paragraph essay.

2. A critic of Bettelheim's position, Jack Zipes argues that Bettelheim distorts fairy-tale literature by insisting that the tales have therapeutic value and speak to children almost as a psychoanalyst might. Ultimately, claims Zipes, Bettelheim's analysis corrupts the story of "Cinderella" and closes down possibilities for interpretation. What is your view of the psychoanalytic approach to fairy tales?

A Feminist's View of "Cinderella"

MADONNA KOLBENSCHLAG

Madonna Kolbenschlag approaches "Cinderella" from a feminist's point of view. Feminist criticism, as it is applied across the curriculum, attempts to clarify the relations of women and men in a broad array of human activities: for instance, in literary works, the structure of family life, and economic and political affairs. The object of analysis in the case of "Cinderella" is a story, and Kolbenschlag brings a unique set of questions to bear: In the world of "Cinderella," what is the relationship between men and women? Among women themselves? How is power divided in this world? How is a woman's achievement defined as opposed to a man's? What would children reading this story learn about gender identity? Feminists themselves might disagree in answering these questions; but the fact that these *and not Bettelheim's questions are guiding the analysis ensures that Kolbenschlag's treatment of "Cinderella" and what we can learn from it will differ significantly from Bettelheim's.*

Note that the essay begins with epigraphs, or brief statements, from other writers meant to suggest something of the content of what follows. Authors place epigraphs to set a context for you, and the author who places two or more before a piece is implicitly suggesting that you make comparisons between them.

You'll encounter two particularly difficult sentences: the last sentence of the essay, in which the author equates the behavior of women in "Cinderella" to the behavior of women in our own society, where power is largely held by men. And there's another difficult sentence in paragraph 5: "The personality of the heroine is one that, above all, accepts abasement *as a prelude to and precondition of* affiliation.*" Read these sentences in the context of the entire essay. Try getting the gist of Kolbenschlag's main point and then try seeing how these sentences fit in.*

Madonna Kolbenschlag is the author of Kiss Sleeping Beauty Good-Bye: Breaking the Spell of Feminine Myths and Models *(1979), in which the following selection appears.*

Overtly the story helps the child to accept sibling rivalry as a rather common fact of life and promises that he need not fear being destroyed by it; on the contrary, if these siblings were not so nasty to him, he could never triumph to the same degree at the end. . . . There are also obvious moral lessons: that surface appearances tell nothing about the inner worth of a person; that if one is true to oneself, one wins over those who pretend to be what they are not; and that virtue will be rewarded, evil punished.

Openly stated, but not as readily recognized, are the lessons that to develop one's personality to the fullest, one must be able to do hard work and be able to separate good from evil, as in the sorting of the lentils. Even out of lowly matter like ashes things of great value can be gained, if one knows how to do it.

—Bruno Bettelheim, *The Uses of Enchantment*

The literature on female socialization reminds one of the familiar image of Cinderella's stepsisters industriously lopping off their toes and heels so as to fit into the glass slipper (key to the somewhat enigmatic heart of the prince)—when of course it was never intended for them anyway.

—Judith Long Laws, "Woman as Object"

The important factor to us is Cinderella's conditioning. It is decidedly not to go on dutifully sweeping the floor and carrying the wood.

> She is conditioned to get the hell out of those chores. There is, the American legend tells her, a good-looking man with dough, who will put an end to the onerous tedium of making a living. If he doesn't come along (the consumer must consequently suppose), she isn't just lacking in good fortune, she is being cheated out of her true deserts. Better, says our story, go out and make the guy. In other words, we have turned the legend backwards and our Cinderella now operates as her sisters did. . . .
>
> The goal of security, seen in terms of things alone and achieved in those terms during the least secure period in human history, has predictably ruined Cinderella; she has the prince, the coach, the horses—but her soul's a pumpkin and her mind's a rat-warren. She desperately needs help.
>
> —Philip Wylie, *Generation of Vipers*

Cinderella, the best-known and probably best-liked fairy tale, is above all a success story. The rags-to-riches theme perhaps explains its equal popularity among boys as well as girls. It is a very old fairy tale, having at least 345 documented variants and numerous unrecorded versions. The iconic focus of the tale on the lost slipper and Cinderella's "perfect fit" suggests that the story may have originated in the Orient where the erotic significance of tiny feet has been a popular myth since ancient times. 1

The basic motifs of the story are well-known: an ill-treated heroine, who is forced to live by the hearth; the twig she plants on her mother's grave that blossoms into a magic tree; the tasks demanded of the heroine; the magic animals that help her perform the tasks and provide her costume for the ball; the meeting at the ball; the heroine's flight from the ball; the lost slipper; the shoe test; the sisters' mutilation of their feet; the discovery of the true bride and the happy marriage. The variants retain the basic motifs; while differing considerably in detail, they range more widely in their origins than any other fairy tale: Asiatic, Celtic, European, Middle-Eastern and American Indian versions numbered among them. 2

The Horatio Alger quality of the story helps to explain its special popularity in mercantile and capitalistic societies. As a parable of social mobility it was seized upon by the writers of the new "literature of aspiration" in the seventeenth and eighteenth centuries as a basic plot for a new kind of private fantasy—the novel. Our literary world has not been the same since *Pamela* and all her orphaned, governess sisters.[1] Most Anglo-American novels, early and late, are written in 3

[1]*Pamela* by Samuel Richardson (1689–1761) is a sentimental romance set in early eighteenth-century England in which a virtuous servant girl, Pamela Andrews, holds off the lascivious advances of her master until, struck by her goodness, he proposes marriage.

the shadow of *Pamela* and the Cinderella myth. Even Franklin's *Autobiography,* the seminal work in the success genre, owes much to the myth. The primary "moral" of the fairy tale—that good fortune can be merited—is the very essence of the Protestant Ethic.

At the personal and psychological level, Cinderella evokes intense identification. It is a tale of sibling rivalry (and subliminally, of sex-role stereotyping)—a moral fable about socialization. Very few themes could be closer to the inner experience of the child, an emerging self enmeshed in a family network. As Bettelheim observes, it is deceptively simple in the associations it evokes: 4

> *Cinderella* tells about the agonies of sibling rivalry, of wishes coming true, of the humble being elevated, of true merit being recognized even when hidden under rags, of virtue rewarded and evil punished—a straightforward story. But under this overt content is concealed a welter of complex and largely unconscious material. . . .

The personality of the heroine is one that, above all, accepts *abasement* as a prelude to and precondition of *affiliation.* That abasement is characteristically expressed by Cinderella's servitude to menial tasks, work that diminishes her. This willing acceptance of a condition of worthlessness and her expectation of rescue (as a reward for her virtuous suffering) is a recognizable paradigm of traditional feminine socialization. Cinderella is deliberately and sytematically excluded from meaningful achievements. Her stepmother assigns her to meaningless tasks; her father fails her as a helpful mentor. Her sisters, inferior in quality of soul, are preferred before her. 5

But Cinderella does not become a teenage runaway, nor does she wreak any kind of Gothic sabotage on the family. Like many of the Jews who went to the gas chambers in World War II, she has internalized the consciousness of the victim. She really believes she belongs where she is. The paradox of this acceptance of a condition of worthlessness in the self, along with a conviction of the ultimate worthiness and heroism of one's role, is part of the terrible appeal of the fairy tale. For women, especially, it is both mirror and model. Perrault's version of the tale ends with a pointed poetic moral: 6

> 'Tis that little gift called grace,
> Weaves a spell round form and face . . .
> And if you would learn the way
> How to get that gift today—
>
> How to point the golden dart
> That shall pierce the Prince's heart—
> Ladies, you have but to be
> Just as kind and sweet as she!

Cinderella's place by the hearth and her identification with ashes suggests several associations. At the most obvious level, her place by the chimney is an emblem of her degradation. But it is also symbolic of her affinity with the virtues of the hearth: innocence, purity, nurturance, empathy, docility. Cinderella has a vestal quality that relieves her of any obligation to struggle and strive to better her world. She must apprentice herself to this time of preparation for her "real" life with the expected One. 7

Like most fairy tales, *Cinderella* dramatizes the passage to maturity. Her sojourn among the ashes is a period of grieving, a transition to a new self. On the explicit level of the story, Cinderella is literally grieving for her dead mother. Grimm's version of the tale preserves the sense of process, of growth that is symbolized in the narrative. Instead of a fairy godmother—*deus ex machina*[2]—Cinderella receives a branch of a hazel bush from her father. She plants the twig over her mother's grave and cultivates it with her prayers and tears. This is her contact with her past, her roots, her essential self. Before one can be transformed one must grieve for the lost as well as the possible selves, as yet unfulfilled—Kierkegaard's existential anguish.[3] 8

The mother is also identified in several variants with helpful animals, a calf, a cow, or a goat—all milk-giving creatures. In Grimm's version the magic helpers are birds that live in the magic tree. The animals assist her in the performance of the cruel and meaningless tasks her stepmother assigns. The magic trees and helpful animals are emblems of the faith and trust that is demanded of Cinderella, the belief that something good can be gained from whatever one does. There is a subliminal value implied here, that work is seldom to be enjoyed for its own sake, but only to be endured for some greater end. It is essentially a "predestined" view of work as incapable of redemption. Service at the hearth is not intrinsically worthwhile, but acquires its value through the virtue it extracts from the heroine. Significantly, when the heroine is released from her servitude, the structure of belief—the myth—collapses. Cinderella's father destroys the pear tree and the pigeon house. 9

The Perrault version places great emphasis on the "Midnight" prohibition given to Cinderella. A traditional connotation would, of course, associate it with the paternal mandate of obedience, and a threat: if the heroine does not return to domesticity and docility at regular intervals she may lose her "virtue" and no longer merit her 10

[2]"*deus ex machina*": literally, "God out of the machine;" A sudden and unexpected (and often unconvincing) solution to a major problem faced by a character or group of characters toward the end of a literary or dramatic work.

[3][Soren] Kierkegaard: Danish existentialist philosopher (1813–55).

expected one. Like the old conduct manuals for ladies, the moral of the tale warns against feminine excursions as well as ambition. Too much time spent "abroad" may result in indiscreet sex or unseemly hubris, or both. "No excelling" and "no excess."

As a dynamic metaphor of the feminine condition, it illuminates the double life that many women experience: the attraction of work and achievement, perhaps "celebrity," outside the home, and the emotional pull of the relationships and security within the home. For most women diurnal life is not a seamless robe. There are sharp divisions between creative work and compulsive activity, between assertiveness and passivity, between social life and domestic drudgery, between public routines and private joys. Women are, in the contemporary world, acutely aware of the need for integration. "Midnight" strikes with a terrible insistence, a cruel regularity in their lives. 11

Cinderella's threefold escape from the ball (Perrault's version) is of course designed to make her more desirable to the Prince. Or is it a reflection of her own ambivalence? (In Grimm's version, she is under no prohibition, she leaves of her own accord.) Bettelheim offers two interesting interpretations: 12

1. She wants to be "chosen" for herself, in her natural state, rather than because of a splendid appearance wrought by magic.
2. Her withdrawals show that, in contrast to her sisters, she is not "aggressive" in her sexuality but waits patiently "to be chosen."

The latter interpretation is underscored by the "perfect fit" of Cinderella's foot in the slipper, and by the sisters' frantic efforts to mutilate their own feet in order to diminish their size (symbolic of their aggressive, masculine traits). Here we see the two sides of the "formula female." On the surface, perfectly conformed to the feminine stereotype; within, massive lacerations of the spirit. The slipper is indeed the ultimate symbol of "that which is most desirable in a woman," with all of its stereotypical seductiveness and destructiveness. 13

The slipper, the central icon in the story, is a symbol of sexual bondage and imprisonment in a stereotype. Historically, the virulence of its significance is born out in the twisted horrors of Chinese foot-binding practices. On another level, the slipper is a symbol of power—with all of its accompanying restrictions and demands for conformity. When the Prince offers Cinderella the lost slipper (originally a gift of the magic bird), he makes his kingdom hers. 14

We know little of Cinderella's subsequent role. In Grimm's version she is revenged by the birds which pluck out the eyes of the envious sisters. But Perrault's version celebrates Cinderella's kindness and forgiveness. Her sisters come to live in the palace and marry two worthy lords. In the Norse variant of the tale, Aslaug, the heroine, marries a Viking hero, bears several sons, and wields a good deal of power in Teutonic style. (She is the daughter of Sigurd and Brynhild.) But in most tales Cinderella disappears into the vague region known as the "happily ever after." She changes her name, no doubt, and—like so many women—is never heard of again. 15

There are moments when all of us can find ourselves in the Cinderella tale: as bitchy, envious, desperate sibling-peers; or victim-souls like Cinderella, passive, waiting patiently to be rescued; or nasty, domineering "stepmothers," fulfilling ourselves by means of manipulative affiliations—all of them addicted to needing approval. And then we know that for the Prince we should read "Patriarchy."[4] 16

Review and Discussion Questions

1. According to Kolbenschlag, what accounts for "Cinderella's" success in capitalist societies?
2. Psychologically, why does Cinderella evoke intense identification?
3. What is the central paradox of Cinderella, and why does this paradox have a terrible appeal?
4. What does Cinderella's association with ashes suggest, according to Kolbenschlag?
5. Which aspect of "Cinderella" suggests that work is not to be enjoyed but rather endured for some greater end?
6. Why is the slipper the ultimate symbol of "that which is most desirable in a woman"?

America's "Cinderella"

JANE YOLEN

As a writer of children's stories, Jane Yolen is used to making decisions about ways in which stories develop: who wins, who loses (if anyone),

[4]"Patriarchy": A society in which authority is vested in the male.

what's learned, what traits of character endure, how relations among characters resolve themselves—these are just a few of the decisions a writer makes in shaping a story. So it's no surprise to find Yolen interested in decisions that other writers have made regarding "Cinderella." The tale has *changed in the telling—Yolen is well aware of the many variants and in her article traces the changes "Cinderella" has undergone in becoming an American tale.*

As you read, note Yolen's analysis of the "Cinderella" texts. Like Bettelheim and Kolbenschlag, she weaves quotations from the story into her article. This is standard procedure when writing an essay—a procedure you yourself should adopt when pulling together sources in a paper. Regardless of what point you're making (and the points made by Bettelheim, Kolbenschlag, and Yolen are certainly diverse), you will want to weave the work of other writers into your own work, to suit your own purposes.

A noted author of children's books, Jane Yolen (b. 1939) began her career in the editorial departments of Saturday Review, *Gold Medal Books, Ruttledge Books, and Alfred A. Knopf. Since 1965, she has been a full-time professional writer, publishing over seventy books for children as well as books for adults (about writing for children). According to one reviewer, she "is uncommonly skilled at using elements from other storytellers and folklorists, transforming them into new and different tales."*

It is part of the American creed, recited subvocally along with the pledge of allegiance in each classroom, that even a poor boy can grow up to become president. The unliberated corollary is that even a poor girl can grow up and become the president's wife. This rags-to-riches formula was immortalized in American children's fiction by the Horatio Alger stories of the 1860s and by the Pluck and Luck nickel novels of the 1920s. 1

It is little wonder, then, that Cinderella should be a perennial favorite in the American folktale pantheon. 2

Yet how ironic that this formula should be the terms on which "Cinderella" is acceptable to most Americans. "Cinderella" is *not* a story of rags to riches, but rather riches recovered; *not* poor girl into princess but rather rich girl (or princess) rescued from improper or wicked enslavement; *not* suffering Griselda enduring but shrewd and practical girl persevering and winning a share of the power. It is really a story that is about "the stripping away of the disguise that conceals the soul from the eyes of others. . . ." 3

We Americans have it wrong. "Rumpelstiltskin," in which a miller tells a whopping lie and his docile daughter acquiesces in it to become queen, would be more to the point. 4

But we have been initially seduced by the Perrault cinder-girl, who was, after all, the transfigured folk creature of a French literary courtier. Perrault's "Cendrillon" demonstrated the well-bred seventeenth-century female traits of gentility, grace, and selflessness, even to the point of graciously forgiving her wicked stepsisters and finding them noble husbands. 5

The American "Cinderella" is partially Perrault's. The rest is a spun-sugar caricature of her hardier European and Oriental forbears, who made their own way in the world, tricking the stepsisters with double-talk, artfully disguising themselves, or figuring out a way to win the king's son. The final bit of icing on the American Cinderella was concocted by that master candy-maker, Walt Disney, in the 1950s. Since then, America's Cinderella has been a coy, helpless dreamer, a "nice" girl who awaits her rescue with patience and a song. This Cinderella of the mass market books finds her way into a majority of American homes while the classic heroines sit unread in old volumes on library shelves. 6

Poor Cinderella. She has been unjustly distorted by storytellers, misunderstood by educators, and wrongly accused by feminists. Even as late as 1975, in the well-received volume *Womenfolk and Fairy Tales,* Rosemary Minard writes that Cinderella "would still be scrubbing floors if it were not for her fairy godmother." And Ms. Minard includes her in a sweeping condemnation of folk heroines as "insipid beauties waiting passively for Prince Charming." 7

Like many dialecticians, Ms. Minard reads the fairy tales incorrectly. Believing—rightly—that the fairy tales, as all stories for children, acculturate young readers and listeners, she has nevertheless gotten her target wrong. Cinderella is not to blame. Not the real, the true Cinderella. She does not recognize the old Ash-girl for the tough, resilient heroine. The wrong Cinderella has gone to the American ball. 8

The story of Cinderella has endured for over a thousand years, surfacing in a literary source first in ninth-century China. It has been found from the Orient to the interior of South America and over five hundred variants have been located by folklorists in Europe alone. This best-beloved tale has been brought to life over and over and no one can say for sure where the oral tradition began. The European story was included by Charles Perrault in his 1697 collection *Histoires ou Contes du temps passé* as "Cendrillon." But even before that, the Italian Straparola had a similar story in a collection. Since there had 9 been twelve editions of the Straparola book printed in French before 1694, the chances are strong that Perrault had read the tale *"Peau d'Ane"* (Donkey Skin).

Joseph Jacobs, the indefatigable Victorian collector, once said of a 10
Cinderella story he printed that it was "an English version of an Italian adaption of a Spanish translation of a Latin version of a Hebrew translation of an Arabic translation of an Indian original." Perhaps it was not a totally accurate statement of that particular variant, but Jacobs was making a point about the perils of folktale-telling: each teller brings to a tale something of his/her own cultural orientation. Thus in China, where the "lotus foot," or tiny foot, was such a sign of a woman's worth that the custom of foot-binding developed, the Cinderella tale lays emphasis on an impossibly small slipper as a clue to the heroine's identity. In seventeenth-century France, Perrault's creation sighs along with her stepsisters over the magnificent "gold flowered mantua" and the "diamond stomacher."[1] In the Walt Disney American version, both movie and book form, Cinderella shares with the little animals a quality of "lovableness," thus changing the intent of the tale and denying the heroine her birthright of shrewdness, inventiveness, and grace under pressure.

Notice, though, that many innovations—the Chinese slipper, the 11
Perrault godmother with her midnight injunction and her ability to change pumpkin into coach—become incorporated in later versions. Even a slip of the English translator's tongue (*de vair*, fur, into *de verre*, glass) becomes immortalized. Such cross fertilization of folklore is phenomenal. And the staying power, across countries and centuries, of some of these inventions is notable. Yet glass slipper and godmother and pumpkin coach are not the common incidents by which a "Cinderella" tale is recognized even though they have become basic ingredients in the American story. Rather, the common incidents recognized by folklorists are these: an ill-treated though rich and worthy heroine in Cinders-disguise; the aid of a magical gift or advice by a beast/bird/mother substitute; the dance/festival/church scene where the heroine comes in radiant display; recognition through a token. So "Cinderella" and her true sister tales, "Cap o'Rushes"[2] with

[1]In Geoffrey Brereton's translation, included in this text, the stepsisters sigh over a diamond "clasp" and a "gold-embroidered cape."

[2]*"Cap o'Rushes"*: One of the 700 variants of "Cinderella" in which the heroine is debased by having to wear a cap (and in other variants, a coat) made of rushes.

its King Lear judgment[3] and "Catskin" wherein the father unnaturally desires his daughter, are counted.

12 Andrew Lang's judgement that "a naked shoeless race could not have invented Cinderella," then, proves false. Variants have been found among the fur-wearing folk of Alaska and the native tribes in South Africa where shoes were not commonly worn.

13 "Cinderella" speaks to all of us in whatever skin we inhabit: the child mistreated, a princess or highborn lady in disguise bearing her trials with patience and fortitude. She makes intelligent decisions for she knows that wishing solves nothing without the concomitant action. We have each of us been that child. It is the longing of any youngster sent supperless to bed or given less than a full share at Christmas. It is the adolescent dream.

14 To make Cinderella less than she is, then, is a heresy of the worst kind. It cheapens our most cherished dreams, and it makes a mockery of the true magic inside us all—the ability to change our own lives, the ability to control our own destinies.

15 Cinderella first came to America in the nursery tales the settlers remembered from their own homes and told their children. Versions of these tales can still be found. Folklorist Richard Chase, for example, discovered "Rush Cape," an exact parallel of "Cap o'Rushes" with an Appalachian dialect in Tennessee, Kentucky, and South Carolina among others.

16 But when the story reached print, developed, was made literary, things began to happen to the hardy Cinderella. She suffered a sea change, a sea change aggravated by social conditions.

17 In the 1870s, for example, in the prestigious magazine for children *St. Nicholas,* there are a number of retellings or adaptations of "Cinderella." The retellings which merely translate European variants contain the hardy heroine. But when a new version is presented, a helpless Cinderella is born. G. B. Bartlett's "Giant Picture-Book," which was considered "a curious novelty [that] can be produced . . . by children for the amusement of their friends . . ." presents a weepy, prostrate young blonde (the instructions here are quite specific) who must be "aroused from her sad revery" by a godmother. Yet in the truer Cinderella stories, the heroine is not this

[3]*"King Lear judgment":* The story of King Lear has been identified as a variant of "Cinderella." In this variant, the King's one faithful daughter is cast out of the home because she claims to love her father according to her bond (but certainly not more than she would love her husband). The King's other daughters, eager to receive a large inheritance, profess false love and then plot against their father to secure their interests. The evil sisters are defeated and the father and faithful daughter, reunited. Before his death, Lear acknowledges his error.

catatonic. For example, in the Grimm "Cinder-Maid," though she weeps, she continues to perform the proper rites and rituals at her mother's grave, instructing the birds who roost there to:

> Make me a lady fair to see,
> Dress me as splendid as can be.

And in "The Dirty Shepherdess," a "Cap o'Rushes" variant from France, ". . . she dried her eyes, and made a bundle of her jewels and her best dresses and hurriedly left the castle where she was born." In the *St. Nicholas* "Giant Picture-Book" she has none of this strength of purpose. Rather, she is manipulated by the godmother until the moment she stands before the prince where she speaks "meekly" and "with downcast eyes and extended hand." 18

St. Nicholas was not meant for the mass market. It had, in Selma Lanes' words, "a patrician call to a highly literate readership." But nevertheless, Bartlett's play instructions indicate how even in the more literary reaches of children's books a change was taking place. 19

However, to truly mark this change in the American "Cinderella," one must turn specifically to the mass-market books, merchandised products that masquerade as literature but make as little lasting literary impression as a lollipop. They, after all, serve the majority the way the storytellers of the village used to serve. They find their way into millions of homes. 20

Mass-market books are almost as old as colonial America. The chapbooks of the eighteenth and nineteenth century, crudely printed tiny paperbacks, were the source of most children's reading in the early days of our country. Originally these were books imported from Europe. But slowly American publishing grew. In the latter part of the nineteenth century one firm stood out—McLoughlin Bros. They brought bright colors to the pages of children's books. In a series selling for twenty-five cents per book, *Aunt Kate's Series,* bowdlerized folk tales emerged. "Cinderella" was there, along with "Red Riding Hood," "Puss in Boots," and others. Endings were changed, innards cleaned up, and good triumphed with very loud huzzahs. Cinderella is the weepy, sentimentalized pretty girl incapable of helping herself. In contrast, one only has to look at the girl in "Cap o'Rushes" who comes to a great house and asks "Do you want a maid?" and when refused, goes on to say ". . . I ask no wages and do any sort of work." And she does. In the end, when the master's young son is dying of love for the mysterious lady, she uses her wits to work her way out of the kitchen. Even in Perrault's "Cinderella," when the fairy godmother runs out of ideas for enchantment and "was at a loss for a 21 coachman, I'll go and see, says Cinderella, if there be never a rat in the rat-trap, we'll make a coachman of him. You are in the right, said her godmother, go and see."

Hardy, helpful, inventive, that was the Cinderella of the old tales but not of the mass market in the nineteenth century. Today's mass-market books are worse. These are the books sold in supermarket and candystore, even lining the shelves of many of the best bookstores. There are pop-up Cinderellas, coloring-book Cinderellas, scratch-and-sniff Cinderellas, all inexpensive and available. The point in these books is not the story but the *gimmick.* These are books which must "interest 300,000 children, selling their initial print order in one season and continuing strong for at least two years after that." Compare that with the usual trade publishing house print order of a juvenile book—10,000 copies which an editor hopes to sell out in a lifetime of that title. 22

All the folk tales have been gutted. But none so changed, I believe, as "Cinderella." For the sake of Happy Ever After, the mass-market books have brought forward a good, malleable, forgiving little girl and put her in Cinderella's slippers. However, in most of the Cinderella tales there is no forgiveness in the heroine's heart. No mercy. Just justice. In "Rushen Coatie" and "The Cinder-Maid," the elder sisters hack off their toes and heels in order to fit the shoe. Cinderella never stops them, never implies that she has the matching slipper. In fact, her tattletale birds warn the prince in "Rushen Coatie": 23

Hacked Heels and Pinched Toes
Behind the young prince rides,
But Pretty Feet and Little Feet
Behind the cauldron bides.

Even more graphically, they call out in "Cinder-Maid":

Turn and peep, turn and peep,
There's blood within the shoe;
A bit is cut from off the heel
And a bit from off the toe.

Cinderella never says a word of comfort. And in the least bowdlerized of the German and Nordic tales, [when] the two sisters come to the wedding "the elder was at the right side and the younger at the left, and the pigeons pecked out one eye from each of them. Afterwards, as they came back, the elder was on the left, and the younger at the right, and then the pigeons pecked out the other eye from each. And thus, for their wickedness and falsehood, they were punished with blindness all their days." That's a far cry from Perrault's heroine who "gave her sisters lodgings in the palace, and married them the same day to two great lords of the court." And further still from Nola Langner's Scholastic paperback "Cinderella":

> [The sisters] began to cry.
> They begged Cinderella to forgive them for being so mean to her.
> Cinderella told them they were forgiven.
> "I am sure you will never be mean to me again," she said.
> "Oh, never," said the older sister.
> "Never, ever," said the younger sister.

Missing, too, from the mass-market books is the shrewd, even witty Cinderella. In a Wonder Book entitled "Bedtime Stories," a 1940s adaptation from Perrault, we find a Cinderella who talks to her stepsisters, "in a shy little voice." Even Perrault's heroine bantered with her stepsisters, asking them leading questions about the ball while secretly and deliciously knowing the answers. In the Wonder Book, however, the true wonder is that Cinderella ever gets to be princess. Even face-to-face with the prince, she is unrecognized until she dons her magic ball gown. Only when her clothes are transformed does the Prince know his true love. 24

In 1949, Walt Disney's film *Cinderella* burst onto the American scene. The story in the mass market has not been the same since. 25

The film came out of the studio at a particularly trying time for Disney. He had been deserted by the intellectuals who had been champions of this art for some years. Because of World War II, the public was more interested in war films than cartoons. But when *Cinderella,* lighter than light, was released it brought back to Disney—and his studio—all of his lost fame and fortune. The film was one of the most profitable of all time for the studio, grossing $4.247 million dollars in the first release alone. The success of the movie opened the floodgates of "Disney Cinderella" books. 26

Golden Press's *Walt Disney's Cinderella* set the new pattern for America's Cinderella. This book's text is coy and condescending. (Sample: "And her best friends of all were—guess who—the mice!") The illustrations are poor cartoons. And Cinderella herself is a disaster. She cowers as her sisters rip her homemade ball gown to shreds. (Not even homemade by Cinderella, but by the mice and birds.) She answers her stepmother with whines and pleadings. She is a sorry excuse for a heroine, pitiable and useless. She cannot perform even a simple action to save herself, though she is warned by her friends, 27 the mice. She does not hear them because she is "off in a world of dreams." Cinderella begs, she whimpers, and at last has to be rescued by—guess who—the mice!

There is also an easy-reading version published by Random House, *Walt Disney's Cinderella.* This Cinderella commits the further heresy of cursing her luck. "How I did wish to go to the ball," she says. "But it is no use. Wishes never come true." 28

But in the fairy tales wishes have a habit of happening—*wishes accompanied by the proper action,* bad wishes as well as good. That is the beauty of the old stories and their wisdom as well. 29

Take away the proper course of action, take away Cinderella's ability to think for herself and act for herself, and you are left with a tale of wishes-come-true-regardless. But that is not the way of the fairy tale. As P. L. Travers so wisely puts it, "If that were so, wouldn't we all be married to princes?" 30

The mass-market American "Cinderellas" have presented the majority of American children with the wrong dream. They offer the passive princess, the "insipid beauty waiting . . . for Prince Charming" that Rosemary Minard objects to, and thus acculturate millions of girls and boys. But it is the wrong Cinderella and the magic of the old tales has been falsified, the true meaning lost, perhaps forever. 31

Review Questions

1. Why does Yolen find it ironic that Americans regard "Cinderella" as the classic rags-to-riches story?
2. According to Yolen, why have feminists misdirected their attack on "Cinderella"?
3. What does Yolen find objectionable in Walt Disney's *Cinderella?*
4. In what ways have we each been Cinderella, according to Yolen?

Discussion and Writing Suggestions

1. Yolen contends that "fairy tales, as all stories for children, acculturate young readers and listeners." How are children acculturated by tales like "Cinderella"?
2. Yolen believes that Walt Disney's *Cinderella* is a "heresy of the worst kind." Respond to this comment in a brief essay. (Review Yolen's reasons for stating this view and then agree and/or disagree.)
3. "All the folk tales have been gutted," says Yolen. Having read the different versions of Cinderella, would you agree—at least with respect to this one tale? Explain your answer.

SYNTHESIS ACTIVITIES

1. Speculate on the reasons folktales are made and told. As you develop a theory, rely first on your own hunches regarding the origins and functions of folktale literature. You might want to recall your experiences as a child listening to tales so that you can discuss their effects on you. Rely as well on the variants of "Cinderella," which you should regard as primary sources (just as scholars do). And make use of the critical pieces you've read—Thompson, Bettelheim, Kolbenschlag, and Yolen—selecting pertinent points from each that will help clarify your points. *Remember:* Your own speculation should dominate the paper. Use sources to help you make *your* points.

2. At the conclusion of his article, Stith Thompson writes:

   > Literary critics, anthropologists, historians, psychologists, and aestheticians are all needed if we are to hope to know why folktales are made, how they are invented, what art is used in their telling, how they grow and change and occasionally die.

   What is your opinion of the critical work you've read on "Cinderella"? Writing from various perspectives, authors in this chapter have analyzed the tale. To what extent have the analyses illuminated "Cinderella" for you? (Have the analyses in any way "ruined" your ability to enjoy "Cinderella"?) To what extent do you find the analyses off the mark? Are the attempts at analysis inappropriate for a children's story? In your view, what place do literary critics, anthropologists, historians, and psychologists have in discussing folktales?

   In developing a response to these questions, you might begin with Thompson's quotation and then follow directly with a statement of your thesis. In one part of your paper, you will want to critique the work of Bettelheim, Kolbenschlag, and/or Yolen as a way of demonstrating which analyses of folktales (if any) seem worthwhile to you. In another section of the paper (or perhaps woven into the critiques), you'll want to refer directly to the variants of "Cinderella." For the sake of convenience, you may want to refer to a single variant. If so, state as much to the reader and explain your choice of variant.

3. Review the variants of "Cinderella" and select two you would read to your child. In an essay, justify your decision. Which of the older European variants do you prefer: Basile? Grimm? Perrault? How do the recent versions by Sexton, Gardner, and Disney affect you? And what of the Chinese version—is it recognizably "Cinderella"?

You might justify the variants you've selected by defining your criteria for selection and then analyzing the stories separately. You might want to justify your choices negatively—that is, by defining your criteria and then *eliminating* certain variants because they don't meet the criteria. In concluding the paper, you might explain how the variants you've selected work as a pair. How do they complement each other? (Or, perhaps, they *don't* complement each other and this is why you've selected them.)

4. Try writing a version of "Cinderella" and setting it on a college campus. In order for your version of the story to be an authentic variant, you'll need to retain certain defining features, or motifs. In her article, Madonna Kolbenschlag summarizes these features:

   > The basic motifs of the story are well-known: an ill-treated heroine, who is forced to live by the hearth; the twig she plants on her mother's grave that blossoms into a magic tree; the tasks demanded of the heroine; the magic animals that help her perform the tasks and provide her costume for the ball; the meeting at the ball; the heroine's flight from the ball; the lost slipper; the shoe test; the sisters' mutilation of their feet; the discovery of the true bride and the happy marriage.

   "The variants retain the basic motifs," observes Kolbenschlag, though they differ considerably in detail. As you consider the possibilities for your story, recall Thompson's point that the teller of a folktale borrows heavily on earlier versions; the virtue of telling is not in rendering a new story but in retelling an old one and *adapting* it to local conditions and needs. Unless you plan to write a commentary "Cinderella," as Sexton's poem is, you should retain the basic motifs of the old story and add details that will appeal to your particular audience: your classmates.

5. In her 1981 book *The Cinderella Complex,* Colette Dowling wrote:

   > It is the thesis of this book that personal, psychological dependency—the deep wish to be taken care of by others—is the chief force holding women down today. I call this "The Cinderella Complex"—a network of largely repressed attitudes and fears that keeps women in a kind of half-light, retreating from the full use of their minds and creativity. Like Cinderella, women today are still waiting for something external to transform their lives.

   In an essay, respond to Dowling's thesis. First, apply her thesis to a few of the variants of "Cinderella." Does the thesis hold in each case? Next, respond to her view that "the chief force holding women down today" is psychological dependency, or the need for "something external" (i.e., a

Prince) to transform their lives. In your experience, have you observed a Cinderella complex at work? (You might want to discuss the views of Jane Yolen, who in her article—paragraphs 7, 8, and 31—responds directly to a feminist's criticisms of "Cinderella.")

6. Discuss the process by which Cinderella falls in love in these tales. The paper that you write will be an extended comparison and contrast in which you observe this process at work in the variants and then discuss similarities and differences. (In structuring your paper, you'll need to make some choices: Which variants will you discuss and in what order?) At the conclusion of your extended comparison and contrast, try to answer the "so what" question. That is, pull your observations together and make a statement about Cinderella's falling in love. What is the significance of what you've learned? Share this significance with your readers.

7. Write an essay in which you attempt to define a feminist perspective on "Cinderella," as this is expressed by Kolbenschlag and Sexton. Once you have defined this perspective, compare and contrast it with other perspectives in the chapter. To what extent do the feminist items, here, differ significantly from the nonfeminist analyses or tales?

GENDER IDENTITY: THE CHANGING RULES OF DATING AND MARRIAGE IN AMERICAN LIFE

9

What are the differences between men and women? In her classic study *Male and Female* (1949), anthropologist Margaret Mead answered the question this way:

> The differences between the two sexes is one of the important conditions upon which we have built the many varieties of human culture that give human beings dignity and stature. In every known society, mankind has elaborated the biological division of labour into forms often very remotely related to the original biological differences that provided the original clues. Upon the contrast in bodily form and function, men have built analogies between sun and moon, night and day, goodness and evil, strength and tenderness, steadfastness and fickleness, endurance and vulnerability. Sometimes one quality has been assigned to one sex, sometimes to the other. Now it is boys who are thought of as infinitely vulnerable and in need of special cherishing care, now it is girls. In some societies it is girls for whom parents must collect a dowry or make husband-catching magic, in others the parental worry is over the difficulty of marrying off the boys. Some peoples think of women as too weak to work out of doors, others regard women as the appropriate bearers of heavy burdens, "because their heads are stronger than men's." The periodicities of female reproductive functions have appealed to some peoples as making women the natural sources of magical or religious power, to others as directly antithetical to those powers; some religions, including our European traditional religions, have assigned women an inferior rôle in the religious hierarchy, others have built their whole symbolic relationship with the supernatural world upon male imitations of the natural functions of women. In some cultures women are regarded as sieves through whom the best-guarded secrets will sift; in others it is the men who are the gossips. Whether we deal with small matters or with large, with the frivolities of ornament and cosmetics or the sanctities of man's place in the universe, we find this great variety of ways, often flatly contradictory one to the other, in which the rôles of the two sexes have been patterned.
>
> But we always find the patterning. We know of no culture that has said, articulately, that there is no difference between men and women except in the way they contribute to the creation of the next generation; that otherwise in all respects they are simply human beings with varying gifts, no one of which can be exclusively assigned to either sex. We find no culture in which it has been thought that all identified traits—stupidity and brilliance, beauty and ugliness,

> friendliness and hostility, initiative and responsiveness, courage and patience and industry—are merely human traits. However differently the traits have been assigned, some to one sex, some to the other, and some to both, however arbitrary the assignment must be seen to be (for surely it cannot be true that women's heads are both absolutely weaker—for carrying loads—and absolutely stronger—for carrying loads—than men's), although the division has been arbitrary, it has always been there in every society of which we have any knowledge.[1]

Mead observes that no culture has "said, articulately, that there is no difference between men and women." Cultures the world over believe in gender differences, and yet cross-culturally we can't agree on what these differences are—which leads to the conclusion that definitions of masculine and feminine are what we make them: They are social *constructions.* In American life, we see gender differences, but these are not easily defined. Many people subscribe to the traditionalist view that men should dominate the world of commerce, while women rear children and order home life. Many embrace the feminist view, shaped by a sustained and widely welcomed revolt against male privilege, that seeks fundamental changes in the equations of power and domestic responsibilities between the sexes. And then there is what may be called an ambivalent view, in which men and women find themselves caught between old definitions of gender and appealing new freedoms. Women may enjoy being the primary (or at least an equal) wage earner in a household but may feel torn at leaving a two-year-old in day care for forty hours each week. Men may appreciate the freedom of being more intuitive than analytical in their approach to problems, yet they wouldn't dream of letting down their "analytical guard" at the office.

To be sure, gender identities are in flux. Essayist Margaret Edwards observes a general movement away from distinct masculine and feminine traits toward "an androgynous human mean" in which it becomes socially acceptable for men and women to exhibit the same traits without fear of violating gender norms. Similarly, Masters and Johnson observe that social scientists who once regarded male and female personality traits as existing on a single scale (feminine to masculine) now view these traits as "separate characteristics that coexist to some degree in every individual." This apparent step toward androgyny, the view that in terms of personality traits men and women are (or should be) more similar than different, has altered relations between the sexes. For instance—in dating, today, whose responsibility is it to initiate first contacts? Who pays for dinners and shows? Who decides where to go, what to do, how often to get together? Should any of these questions matter anymore—and if they shouldn't, will one partner (in spite of the questions not mattering) feel nonetheless offended or slighted? If men and

[1]From *Male and Female* by Margaret Mead. Copyright 1949, 1976, 1977 by Margaret Mead. By permission of William Morrow & Company.

women are equally free to be assertive or emotionally needy, should it matter who is perceived as the "strong" one in a relationship? Are these perceptions important? In marriage, when both partners work, who should (as opposed to who *does*) clean the house and make the meals? And when children are born, who should care for them when both parents work? How do the vestiges of traditional gender relations continue to make themselves felt in an era when women and men both claim the right to live as professionals?

These questions and others are taken up in the readings that follow. First, noted sex researchers Masters and Johnson review the social patterns, from birth through adulthood, that largely determine gender traits. The next pair of readings explores gender identity as it affects dating. Julius Lester recalls in a funny and (be forewarned) bawdy piece the difficulties of growing up as a boy expected to take the initiative on dates. Margaret Edwards then discusses the ways in which the new American male, in turning away from his traditionally stoic and burly demeanor, has turned into a "wormboy." Women, observes Edwards, don't like wimps. The three remaining selections in the chapter deal with gender identity in marriage. In "Men, Women, Equality, and Love," Cheryl Merser writes about gender roles as these affect marriage, men's and women's expectations of one another, and men's and women's continued failure to communicate. Next, in Carolyn Coman's "Who's Minding the Children?" three house husbands discuss the benefits and frustrations of staying home with the kids while their wives go off to the office each day. Finally, in a demonstration that these gender-related issues have been with us for some time, the nineteenth century short-story writer and novelist Sarah Orne Jewett examines the effect that reversing traditional roles has on a Maine couple.

Gender Roles

WILLIAM H. MASTERS
VIRGINIA E. JOHNSON
ROBERT C. KOLODNY

In this selection, noted researchers Masters, Johnson, and Kolodny, discuss the ways in which we learn sex-appropriate behaviors. As social scientists, the authors describe (they do not judge) the behavior of groups and the ways in which group expections can affect individuals. Notice how the authors consciously build on the work of other researchers as they explore the patterns and pressures of gender-role socialization. The discussion that follows appeared originally as a chapter of a textbook on human sexuality.

William Masters and Virginia Johnson are a husband and wife research team credited with being the first to conduct physiological and anatomical studies of human sexual behavior, on the basis of which they published two pioneering works: Human Sexual Response *(1966) and* Human Sexual Inadequacy *(1970). As a faculty member at the Washington University School of Medicine in St. Louis, Masters (b. 1915) began studying human sexual activity in 1954. Psychologist Virginia Johnson (b. 1925) joined the laboratory research team three years later. Together, they have collaborated on over 200 publications and have received numerous awards.*

On a television soap opera, a self-confident, smooth-talking businessman seduces a beautiful but not too bright female secretary. A children's book describes a warm, caring, stay-at-home mother while depicting father as an adventuresome traveler. A newspaper advertisement for cigarettes shows a husky young man enthusiastically dousing a shapely, squealing, female companion with water, her wet T-shirt clinging to her bust—the headlined caption reads "Refresh Yourself." Each of these messages tells us something about stereotypes and sexism. 1

In the past 25 years, there has been considerable scientific interest in studying differences and similarities between the sexes, for a number of reasons. First, various beliefs about sex differences in traits, talents, and temperaments have greatly influenced social, political, and economic systems throughout history. Second, recent trends have threatened age-old distinctions between the sexes. In 1987, for instance, more than half of American women worked outside the home. Unisex fashions in hairstyles, clothing, and jewelry are now popular. Even anatomic status is not fixed in a day where change-of-sex surgery is possible. Third, the women's movement has brought increasing attention to areas of sex discrimination and sexism and has demanded sexuality equality. 2

As a result of these trends, old attitudes toward sex differences, childrearing practices, masculinity and femininity, and what society defines as "appropriate" gender-role behavior have undergone considerable change. Many of today's young adults have been raised in families where a progressive attitude toward gender roles has been taught or where parents struggled to break away from stereotyped thinking. Thus, there is a continuum of types of socialization today that ranges from old, traditional patterns to modern versions. This essay will examine these issues and trends as they influence the experience of being male or female. 3

MASCULINITY AND FEMININITY

Before you read any further, you might take a few minutes to write out a list of the traits you would use to describe a typical American man and woman. If your descriptions are similar to most other people's, you probably listed characteristics like strong, courageous, self-reliant, competitive, objective, and aggressive for a typical man, while describing a typical woman in terms like intuitive, gentle, dependent, emotional, sensitive, talkative, and loving. 4

Most people not only believe that men and women differ but share similar beliefs about the ways in which they differ (Broverman et al., 1972). Beliefs of this sort, held by many people and based on oversimplified evidence or uncritical judgment, are called *stereotypes.* Stereotypes can be harmful because they lead to erroneous judgments and generalizations and can thus affect how people treat one another. 5

Because many stereotypes about sexuality are based on assumptions about the nature of masculinity and femininity, it is difficult to offer a concise definition of these two terms. In one usage, a "masculine" man or a "feminine" woman is a person who is sexually attractive to members of the opposite sex. Advertisements for clothing and cosmetics constantly remind us of this fact. In another sense, masculinity or femininity refers to the degree a person matches cultural expectations of how males and females should behave or look. In the not too distant past, some segments of our society were upset when long hair became fashionable among young men or when women applied for admission to West Point because these patterns did not "fit" prevailing expectations about differences between the sexes. In still another meaning, masculinity and femininity refer to traits measured by standardized psychological tests that compare one person's responses to those of large groups of men and women. 6

According to traditional assumptions, it is highly desirable for males to be masculine and females to be feminine. If behavior matches cultural expectations, it helps to preserve social equilibrium and allows for a certain amount of stability in the details of everyday living. Conformity to cultural norms presumably indicates "adjustment" and "health," while straying too far from expected behavior patterns indicates abnormality or even disease. Finally, "masculine" men and "feminine" women are relatively predictable and behave in ways that are fairly consistent and complementary. Fortunately (or unfortunately, depending on your viewpoint), it now appears that masculinity and femininity are unlikely to tell us much about your personality, sexual preferences, or lifestyle, and old stereotypes are now giving way to more useful and dynamic scientific views. 7

The traditional approach to studying masculinity and femininity looked at these traits as opposites. According to this view, if you possess "feminine" characteristics you cannot have "masculine" characteristics and vice vesa (Spence and Helmreich, 1978). It was assumed that people who scored high on certain traits judged as masculine (e.g., independence, competitiveness) would also have a general lack of femininity. As a result, most psychological tests designed to measure masculinity and femininity were set up as a single masculinity-femininity scale (Kaplan and Sedney, 1980). Furthermore, men and women whose masculinity or femininity scores differed substantially from group averages were judged to be less emotionally healthy and less socially adjusted than others with "proper" scores. 8

Recent research findings have changed this approach. Instead of viewing masculinity and femininity as opposites, various behavioral scientists now look at them as separate characteristics that coexist to some degree in every individual (Bem, 1972; Spence and Helmreich, 1978; Cook, 1985). Thus, a woman who is competitive can be quite feminine in other areas; a man who is tender and loving may also be very masculine. As we discuss the ways in which gender roles are learned and the impact they have on our lives, it will be helpful to keep this viewpoint in mind. 9

PATTERNS OF GENDER-ROLE SOCIALIZATION

Even before a baby is born, parents are likely to have different attitudes about the sex of their child. In most societies, male children are clearly preferred over female children (Markle, 1974; Coombs, 1977), and having a son is more often seen as a mark of status and achievement than having a daughter (Westoff and Rindfuss, 1974). This preference probably stems from the belief that men are stronger, smarter, braver, and more productive than women and that "it's a man's world" (certainly true in the past)—meaning that there are more and better educational, occupational, political, and economic opportunities open to males than to females. 10

Parents often try to guess the sex of their unborn child and may construct elaborate plans and ambitions for the child's life. If the child is thought to be a boy, the parents are likely to think of him as sports-oriented, achievement-oriented, tough, and independent. If the child is thought to be a girl, parents are more apt to envision beauty, grace, sensitivity, artistic talents, and marriage. These different attitudes are nicely shown in lyrics from the Broadway musical *Carousel* as a father-to-be dreams about his unborn child: 11

I'll teach him to wrassle, and dive through a wave,
When we go in the mornin's for our swim.
His mother can teach him the way to behave,
But she won't make a sissy out o'him. . . .
He'll be tall and as tough as a tree, will Bill!
Like a tree he'll grow, with his head held high
And his feet planted firm on the ground,
And you won't see nobody dare to try
To boss him or toss him around! . . .

Wait a minute! Could it be—
What the hell! What if he is a girl? . . .

She mightn't be so bad at that,
A kid with ribbons in her hair!
A kind o' neat and petite
Little tin-type of her mother! What a pair!
My little girl, pink and white
As peaches and cream is she.
My little girl is half again as bright
As girls are meant to be!
Dozens of boys pursue her,
Many a likely lad does
What he can to woo her.
From her faithful Dad.[1]

This sort of prenatal thinking is one form of stereotyping, as is 12 guessing that the baby will be a boy because "he" kicks a lot inside the uterus. It is not surprising then to find that the earliest interactions between parents and their newborn child are influenced in subtle ways by cultural expectations.

Birth and Infancy

At the moment of birth, the announcement of the baby's sex ("It's a 13 boy" or "It's a girl") sets in motion a whole chain of events such as assigning a pink or blue identification bracelet, choosing a name, selecting a wardrobe, and decorating the baby's room, each of which involves making distinctions between males and females.[2]

[1]"Soliloquy," written by Richard Rodgers and Oscar Hammerstein II. Copyright © 1945 Williamson Music, Co. Copyright renewed. Used by permission. All rights reserved.

[2]In the song "A Boy Named Sue," written by S. Silverstein and recorded by Johnny Cash, the father reversed usual gender distinctions in name selection in order to achieve the paradoxical effect of improving his son's masculinity. By giving him the name Sue, the father forced the boy to fight frequently to defend himself from ridicule, thus becoming "tough."

As friends, relatives, and parents discuss the newborn's appearance, gender stereotypes are everywhere: "Look at his size—he'll be a football player, I bet." "She has beautiful eyes—she's a real doll." "See how intelligent he looks!" "She's got great legs already! You'll have to work to keep the boys away." Informal banter about the child's future is also likely to be gender-linked: if friends remark, "You better start saving for the wedding," you can bet they are not talking about a baby boy. 14

Parents of newborn infants describe daughters as softer, smaller, finer-featured, and less active than sons, although no objective differences in appearance or activity level were noted by physicians (Rubin, Provenzano, and Luria, 1974). In early infancy, boys receive more physical contact from their mothers than girls do, while girls are talked to and looked at more than boys (Lewis, 1972)—a difference in treatment which tends to reinforce a female's verbal activities and a male's physical activity. Walum (1977) reports an exploratory study in which two groups of young mothers were given the same six-month-old infant dressed either in blue overalls and called Adam or wearing a pink frilly dress and called Beth: the results showed that "Beth" was smiled at more, given a doll to play with more often, and viewed as "sweet" compared with "Adam." Another recent study confirms that both mothers and fathers behave differently toward unfamiliar infants on the basis of perceived sex, although the parents were unaware of this differential treatment (Culp, Cook, and Housley, 1983). 15

Parents respond differently to infant boys and girls in other ways. They react more quickly to the cries of a baby girl than a baby boy (Frieze et al., 1978) and are more likely to allow a baby boy to explore, to move farther away, or to be alone, thus fostering independence. In contrast, the baby girl seems to be unintentionally programmed in the direction of dependency and passivity (Weitzman, 1975; Long Laws, 1979). 16

Gender differences in socializing children occur for reasons that are not fully understood at present. Certainly, cultural influences are important, but biological factors may also be involved. For example, boys' higher rates of metabolism, greater caloric intake, and higher rates of activity may prepare them for earlier independence, or parental encouragement of independence may reflect cultural expectations (Walum, 1977). Furthermore, the different prenatal hormone exposures of males and females may possibly account for behavioral differences in infancy. Often, parents are unaware of how their actions with their children are different depending on the child's sex. Nevertheless, differential socialization seems to occur even in parents who are philosophically committed to the idea of avoiding gender sterotypes (Scanzoni and Fox, 1980). 17

Early Childhood (Ages Two to Five)

By age two, a child can determine in a fairly reliable way the gender of other people and can sort clothing into different boxes for boys and girls (Thompson, 1975). However, two-year-olds do not usually apply correct gender labels to their own photographs with any consistency—this ability usually appears around 2½ years. As already mentioned, core gender identity, the personal sense of being male or female, seems to solidify by age three. This process is probably assisted by the acquisition of verbal skills, which allow children to identify themselves in a new dimension and to test their abilities of gender usage by applying pronouns such as "he" or "she" to other people. 18

At age two or three, children begin to develop awareness of gender roles, the outward expression of maleness or femaleness, in their families and in the world around them. It might seem that the child forms very sketchy impressions at first—'Mommies don't smoke pipes" or "Daddies don't wear lipstick"—but the toddler's understanding is greater than his or her ability to verbally express it. It is likely that impressions of what is masculine or feminine form across a broad spectrum of behaviors. 19

The serious business of young childhood is play, so by examining the objects used in play activities we may be able to learn something about gender-role socialization. Walk through the toy department of a large store and you will quickly see the principle of differential socialization at work. Boys' toys are action-oriented (guns, trucks, spaceships, sports equipment) while girls' toys reflect quieter play, often with a domestic theme (dolls, tea sets, "pretend" makeup kits, or miniature vacuum cleaners, ovens, or refrigerators). Where a particular toy is marketed to both girls and boys, the version for girls is usually feminized in certain ways. For instance, a boys' bicycle is described as "rugged, fast, and durable." The girls' model of the same bike has floral designs on the seat and pretty pink tassels on the hand-grips and is described as "petite and safe." A detailed analysis of the content of 96 children's rooms showed that boys were given more toy cars and trucks, sports equipment, and military toys, while girls received many more dolls, doll houses, and domestic toys (Rheingold and Cook, 1975). Although many boys today play with "E.T." or "Rambo" dolls or other action-oriented figures, most parents of boys are likely to become concerned if their sons develop a preference for frilly, "feminine" dolls (Collins, 1984). 20

Picture books are another important source for learning gender roles. As Weitzman (1975) observes, "Through books, children learn about the world outside their immediate environment: they learn what is expected of children of their age" (p. 110). Although in recent 21 years some changes have occurred, an analysis of award-winning books for preschoolers showed marked evidence of gender-role bias (Weitzman et al., 1972). First, males were shown much more frequently than females (there were 261 males and 23 females pictured, a ratio of 11 to 1). Second, most males were portrayed as active and independent, while most females were presented in passive roles. Third, adult women shown in these books were consistently identified as mothers or wives, while adult men were engaged in a wide variety of occupations and professions. It is no wonder that girls get a strong message that "success" for them is measured in terms of marriage and motherhood. Fortunately, this imbalance is beginning to change today, with many recent books aimed at preschoolers showing women in a more favorable light.

Television is also a powerful force in the gender-role socialization 22
of young children because it provides a window to the rest of the world. The fictionalized world of Saturday morning children's cartoons is filled with gender stereotypes: the heroes are almost all males, and females are shown as companions or as "victims" needing to be rescued from the forces of evil. Even award-winning children's shows such as Sesame Street have been criticized because women were seldom shown employed outside the home and male figures predominated (Vogel, Broverman, and Gardner, 1970). Advertisements geared at preschoolers perpetrate the same patterns: boys are shown as tough, action-oriented people, while girls are portrayed as more domestic, quieter, and refined.

The School-Age Child

By the time children enter elementary school, gender-role ex- 23
pectations are applied with some unevenness. A seven-year-old girl who likes sports and climbs trees is generally regarded as "cute" and is affectionately, even proudly, called a tomboy. A seven-year-old boy who prefers playing with dolls and jumping rope to throwing a football is labeled a "sissy" and may be the source of great parental consternation. Although child psychiatrists regard tomboyishness in girls as a "normal passing phase" (Green, 1974), "effeminate" boys are thought by many researchers to require treatment to prevent them from becoming homosexual or having later sexual problems (Lebovitz, 1972; Green, 1974, 1987; Newman, 1976; Rekers et al., 1978).

Different patterns of gender-linked play continue during the 24
school years and are now reinforced firmly by peer group interactions. School-yard and neighborhood play is noticed by other boys and girls, and children whose play preferences do not match

everyone else's are thought to be "weird" and are often the butt of jokes. Since there is a powerful motivation to be like everyone else in order to have friendship and group acceptance, this teasing can have a negative influence on a child's sense of self-esteem.

At this age, boys are generally expected to show masculinity by demonstrating physical competence and competitive spirit in sports activities, which become the primary focus of boyhood play. They are rewarded for bravery and stamina and criticized for showing fear or frustration ("Big boys don't cry"). Girls, on the other hand, although physically more mature than boys at corresponding ages in childhood, have traditionally been steered away from highly competitive sports and sheltered from too much exertion. (Today, this pattern is changing considerably as girls are encouraged to enter competitive swimming, gymnastics, soccer, and Little League baseball just as much as they are encouraged to take ballet or music lessons.) Girls are expected to stay clean and be neat, to avoid fighting, and to avoid dangerous activities ("Be a lady"). Young girls often seem to be programmed to cry to show hurt or frustration and find that crying (at least in the presence of adults) often elicits comforting. Thus, males are encouraged to solve problems in an active, independent way, whereas females are more likely to be shown that *their* best way of solving problems is to act helpless and to rely on someone else to take care of them. 25

Even for the children of relatively "liberated" parents, sexism sometimes inadvertently looms: 26

> Take my friend Irene, a vice-president of a Fortune 500 company, who at a recent dinner party bemoaned the stiff resistance of male executives to women in senior management. Not ten minutes later, she proudly regaled us with tales of her eight-year-old son who struts around the house shouting, "Boys are the best, boys are the best."
>
> In Irene's mind, 40- or 50-year-old executives practice sexist oppression. But when her Jonathan shuts girls out, he is cute, natural ("It's the age," she told me), and turning out to be a "real boy." (Rommel, 1984, p. 32)

There are also, of course, instances where parents react differently to a child's seemingly sexist behavior. In one case, a mother who encountered her eight-year-old son telling his friends that girls are poor athletes took her son on successive weekends to watch the U.C.L.A. women's basketball team and to a women's weightlifting contest. The boy apparently gained a different perspective on female athletic capacity, because he was seen soon thereafter playing softball with a nine-year-old girl from down the street. 27

While these sorts of situations are of concern to some parents 28 who want to raise their children in a nonsexist fashion, other well-meaning parents feel that since many young girls "shut boys out" and believe that "girls are best," this is not really sexist at all. They point out that while these responses aren't appropriate for adults, such attitudes foster self-esteem in children.

Much of the child's time is spent in school, where gender-role stereotypes still exist in many classrooms. History lessons portray a view of the world as male-dominated; in the few instances when women are mentioned, they are usually in a subservient or domestic role (recall how Betsy Ross served the cause of the American Revolution by sewing). Girls are usually assigned different classroom "chores" than boys are (for example, boys might be asked to carry a stack of books, while girls are asked to "straighten up the room"), and teachers often assign activities to boys and girls based on their presumptions about gender-role preferences. In one school, third grade girls were asked to draw a mural while the boys were asked to build a fort. A girl who said she would rather work on the fort was told by her teacher, "That's not a job for young ladies."

School-age children are also exposed to obvious gender-role 30 stereotypes on television. From commercials children learn that most women are housewives concerned about important decisions like which detergent to use, which soap does not leave a bathtub ring, and which brand of toilet paper is softest. Men, on the other hand, are concerned about health issues ("Four out of five doctors recommend . . ."), economics, automobiles, or recreation (most beer commercials play upon themes of masculinity, for example). With a few notable exceptions, the lawyers, doctors, and detectives on TV are all men, and women—even when cast in adventurous occupations—are shown as emotional, romantic sex objects who cannot make up their minds. It is no wonder that stereotypes about masculinity and femininity continue: children are exposed to them so widely that they come to believe they are true. Supporting this observation, McGhee and Frueh (1980) found that children who watched television more than 25 hours per week had more stereotyped gender-role perceptions than age-matched children who watched less than 10 hours of television weekly.

Adolescence

Adhering to gender-appropriate roles is even more important during 31 adolescence than at younger ages. What was earlier seen as rehearsal or play is now perceived as the real thing. The rules are more complicated, the penalties for being "different" are harsher, and future success seems to hinge on the outcome.

Adolescent boys have three basic rules to follow in relation to 32
gender roles. First, succeed at athletics. Second, become interested in girls and sex. Third, do not show signs of "feminine" interests or traits. Teenage boys who disregard these rules too obviously are likely to be ridiculed and ostracized, while those who follow them closely are far more likely to be popular and accepted.

The traditional prohibition of feminine traits in male adolescents 33
probably relates to two separate factors. The first is the view of masculinity and femininity as complete opposites that was discussed earlier in the chapter. For a teenage boy to "fit" the male stereotype, he must be achievement-oriented, competitive, independent, self-confident, and so on. If the opposite traits emerge, his masculinity is subject to question. Second, a teenage boy who shows "feminine" interests or traits is often regarded suspiciously as a potential homosexual. In a variation on this theme, in schools where home economics courses were opened to male enrollment, some parents have voiced concern that it would "rob" boys of their masculinity and lead to "sexual deviance" (Spence and Helmreich, 1978). However, in communities where boys take home economics and girls take shop courses, it is remarkable that an easy equilibrium has been reached, with no one "harmed" psychologically by the experience.

The adolescent girl is confronted by a different set of gender-role 34
expectations and different socialization pressures. In keeping with the traditional expectation that a female's ultimate goals are marriage and motherhood rather than career and independence, the prime objective seems to be heterosexual atrractiveness and popularity. As a result, the adolescent girl's school experience may push her toward learning domestic or secretarial skills instead of orienting her toward a profession, and the message she gets—from peers and parents—is that academic achievement may lessen her femininity (Weitzman, 1975; Frieze et al., 1978; Long Laws, 1979). However, it appears that this pattern is now undergoing considerable change. As it has become more culturally "permissible" for women to enter professions such as medicine and law or to enter the business world at the management level, more and more teenage females have becomee comfortable with maintaining a high level of academic success.

For many women, the high value that society places on both 35
achievement and popularity poses a problem. One factor that seems to influence female nonachievement is fear of success, that is, being anxious about social rejection and loss of perceived femininity if success is achieved (Horner, 1972; Schaffer, 1981). This fear is not entirely irrational, as studies show that in adulthood, men often seem to be threatened by a woman who is more successful than they are, resulting in lower rates of marriage for high-achieving women (Frieze et al., 1978). Interestingly, a recent report noted that females who are

masculine sex-typed have lower fear of success scores than those who are feminine sex-typed (Forbes and King, 1983).

Female adolescents also get mixed messages about the relationship between femininity and sexuality. While the traditional message about sexual behavior has been "nice girls don't" or should feel guilty if they do, the primary allure of femininity is sexual, and the "proof" of femininity is sexual desirability. But if femininity is to be valued, why not be sexually active? The dilemma lies partly in the cultural double standard that sanctions varied male sexual experience but regards the female with more than one partner as promiscuous. 36

To be certain, the traditional gender-role stereotypes related to sexual behavior have been set aside by many adolescents. Teenage girls are much more apt to ask boys out today than they were 20 years ago and often take the initiative in sexual activity. This is seen as a major relief by some adolescent males, who feel freed from the burden of having to be the sexual expert, but is frightening to others who feel more comfortable with traditional sexual scripts. As one 17-year-old boy put it, "I don't like the feeling of not being in control. What am I supposed to do if a girl wants to make love and I'm not in the mood?" (Authors' files). 37

In many ways, the old "quarterback-cheerleader" idea of masculine and feminine gender roles during adolescence has broadened into newer, more complex, and less clearly defined patterns. Athletic, educational, and career aspirations have become less compartmentalized, styles of dress have been altered, and many colleges that were previously restricted to one sex have now become coeducational. Nevertheless, it is important to realize that the influence of traditional gender-role attitudes continues to affect today's adolescents, showing that the present is still very much the product of the past. 38

Adulthood

Before proceeding any further with our overview of gender-role socialization, two points must be made. First, our discussion has deliberately highlighted common denominators of this process while ignoring many sources of variability. To believe that children in Beverly Hills, Detroit, and rural Vermont are exposed to identical messages about gender roles is obviously incorrect. Differences in religion, socioeconomic status, family philosophies, and ethnic heritage all influence the socialization process: for instance, researchers have found that gender-role distinctions are sharper in the lower class than in the middle or upper classes (Reiss, 1980). Second, to think that gender roles are entirely shaped in childhood or adolescence implies that adults cannot change. In recent years, however, many 39 young adults have moved away from the traditional gender-role distinctions with which they were brought up and have chosen alternative patterns with which they can live more comfortably. How this trend will ultimately affect future generations is not known.

40 Despite differences in upbringing and changing attitudes, our culture's gender-role stereotypes usually come into full bloom in the adult years, although the patterns change a little. For men, although heterosexual experience and attractiveness continue as important proofs of masculinity, strength and physical competence (as in hunting, fighting, or sports) are no longer as important as they once were. Occupational achievement, measured by job status and financial success, has become the yardstick of contemporary masculinity for middle- and upper-class America.

41 For women, marriage and motherhood remain the central goals of our cultural expectations, although this stereotype is now beginning to change significantly. As more and more women join the work force, as more and more women are divorced, as more and more people choose childless marriages, the notion that femininity and achievement are antithetical is slowly beginning to crumble away.

42 Marriage is a fascinating social institution in which gender roles play out in some unexpected ways. Tavris and Offir (1977) observe:

> The irony is that marriage, which many men consider a trap, does them a world of good, while the relentless pressure on them to be breadwinners causes undue strain and conflict. Exactly the reverse is true for women. Marriage, which they yearn for from childhood, may prove hazardous to their health, while the optional opportunities of work help keep them sane and satisfied. (p. 220)

Married men are physically and mentally healthier than single men (Weissman, 1980; Gurman and Klein, 1980; Scanzoni and Fox, 1980), but married women have higher rates of mental and physical problems than single women (Knupfer, Clark, and Room, 1966). Gove (1979) suggests several aspects of gender roles and marriage that conspire to cause such problems:

1. Women usually have their "wife-mother" role as their only source of gratification, whereas most men have two sources of gratification—worker and household head.
2. Many women find raising children and household work to be frustrating, and many others are unhappy with the low status of their "wife-mother" role.
3. The relatively unstructured and invisible role of the housewife is a breeding ground for worry and boredom.
4. Even when a married woman works outside the home, she is generally expected to do most of the housework (and thus is

under greater strain than the husband) and typically has a low-status, lower-paying job and must contend with sex discrimination at work.
5. The expectations confronting married women are diffuse and unclear; uncertainty and lack of control over the future often conspire to create problems and low self-esteem. (pp. 39–40)

Fortunately, there are some positive indications that change is not just on the horizon but is actually here in our midst today. Dual-career families are becoming common, and more and more men are willingly participating in ordinary household tasks that were previously regarded as strictly "women's work." A small but growing number of men are staying home to be househusbands while their wives pursue outside careers (Beer, 1983). 43

Adult gender roles hinge on areas other than marriage, of course. It is fascinating to see how the same status inconsistency found in many marriages also applies to situations outside the home. In the business world, very few companies have substantial numbers of women as executives (and the secretarial pool is unlikely to have many men). Although a young man who is successful in business is pegged as a "boy wonder," a young woman who achieves corporate success is sometimes accused of having "slept her way to the top." Medical schools and law schools only began to admit sizable numbers of women in the last decade, and even then it took some prodding from the federal government. Furthermore, changes in admissions policies do not necessarily reflect an open-armed embrace. As one woman attending medical school put it: 44

> From the beginning, I could notice great astonishment that I was attractive *and* bright. My teachers seemed to think that only ugly women have brains. Then there was a constant sense of being singled out for "cruel and unusual punishment." From the anatomy labs to the hospital wards, the female medical students were gleefully given the dirtiest assignments and made the butt of jokes. I never did understand why a woman physician examining a penis is so different from a male physician doing a pelvic exam, but this seemed to be a constant source of humor. (Authors' files)

Complicating matters even more, and showing how widespread sexism remains in our society, is the indisputable fact that many women who enter even the most prestigious professions are also subjected to sexual harassment. For instance, a recent report found that 25 percent of female students and faculty at Harvard Medical School had encountered varying forms of sexual harassment ranging from leering, sexually oriented remarks to instances of unwanted touching and requests for sexual favors (*American Medical News*, Nov. 45

11, 1983, p. 1). At Atlanta's old-line law firm of King & Spaulding, where a former female associate had filed a sex discrimination lawsuit to protest against being denied partnership, a summer outing for law students working at the firm featured a bathing suit contest for women at which one male partner proclaimed. "She has the body we'd like to see more of" (*Wall Street Journal*, Dec. 20, 1983, p. 1).

Not only do women have difficulty gaining access to nontraditional occupations, they also are frequently penalized by lower salaries than those for men and face more obstacles to advancing on the job. Furthermore, when women are successful in their achievements at work, the results are more likely to be attributed to luck than to skill, dedication, or effort (Walum, 1977; Heilman, 1980). Another form of prejudice that women often have to overcome is shown in a recent research study that had 360 college students—half of them male, half of them female—evaluate academic articles that were presented as written by either "John T. McKay" or "Joan T. McKay." Although the same articles were used for the evaluations, with only the first name of the author varying, the articles supposedly written by a male were more favorably evaluated by both sexes than the articles supposedly written by a female (Paludi and Bauer, 1983). 46

Clearly, sex discrimination is a problem of today's world that will not disappear overnight (Heilman, 1980). However, there are certainly signs of changing times as women now enter "male" occupations like welding and making telephone repairs and as men increasingly infiltrate traditionally "female" occupations. With Sandra Day O'Connor now serving as the first woman on the U.S. Supreme Court, with a woman having run for vice-president of the United States in 1984, and with women increasingly gaining access to high-visibility and high-status occupations, the impression that times are changing becomes even more pronounced. 47

WORKS CITED

Beer, W. R. *Househusbands: Men and Housework in American Families.* New York: Praeger, 1983.

Bem, S. L. "Psychology Looks at Sex Roles: Where Have All the Androgynous People Gone?" Paper presented at the UCLA Symposium on Women. Los Angeles: May 1972.

———. "The Measurement of Psychological Androgyny." *Journal of Consulting and Clinical Psychology* 42(2):155–62, 1974.

———. "Sex Role Adaptability: One Consequence of Psychological Androgyny." *Journal of Personality and Social Psychology* 31(4):634–43, 1975.

Broverman, I. K., et al. "Sex-Role Stereotypes: A Current Appraisal." *Journal of Social Issues* 28(2):59–78, 1972.

Collins, G. "New Studies of 'Girl Toys' and 'Boy Toys,'" *New York Times*, 13 February 1984.

Cook, E. P. *Psychological Androgyny*. New York: Pergamon Press, 1985.

Coombs, L. C. "Preferences for Sex of Children Among U.S. Couples." *Family Planning Perspectives* 9:259–65, 1977.

Culp, R. E., Cook, A. S., and Housley, P. C. "A Comparison of Observed and Reported Adult-Infant Interactions: Effect of Perceived Sex." *Sex Roles* 9:475–79, 1983.

Forbes, G. B., and King, S. "Fear of Success and Sex-Role: There Are Reliable Relationships." *Psychological Reports* 53:735–38, 1983.

Frieze, I. H., et al. *Women and Sex Roles: A Social Psychological Perspective*. New York; Norton, 1978.

Gove, W. R. "Sex Differences in the Epidemiology of Mental Disorder: Evidence and Explanations." In Gomberg, E. S., and Franks, V. (eds.), *Gender and Disordered Behavior*, pp. 23–68. New York: Brunner/Mazel, 1979.

Green, R. *Sexual Identity Conflict in Children and Adults*. New York: Basic Books, 1974.

Gurman, A. S., and Klein, M. "Marital and Family Conflicts." In Brodsky, A. M., and Hare-Mustin, R. (eds.), *Women and Psychotherapy*, pp. 159–88. New YorK: Guilford Press, 1980.

Heilman, M. E. "Sex Discrimination." In Wolman, B. E. and Money, J. (eds.), *Handbook of Human Sexuality*, pp. 227–49. Englewood Cliffs, N.J.: Prentice-Hall, 1980.

Horner, M. "Toward an Understanding of Achievement Related Conflicts in Women." *Journal of Social Issues* 28:157–75, 1972.

Kaplan, A., and Sedney, M. A. *Psychology and Sex Roles: An Androgynous Perspective*. Boston: Little, Brown, 1980.

Knupfer, F.; Clark, W.; and Room, R. "The Mental Health of the Unmarried." *American Journal of Psychiatry* 122:841–51, 1966.

Lebovitz, P. S. "Feminine Behavior in Boys: Aspects of Its Outcome." *American Journal of Psychiatry* 128:1283–89, 1972.

Lewis, M. "State as an Infant-Environment Interaction: An Analysis of Mother-Infant Interaction as a Function of Sex." *Merill-Palmer Quarterly* 18:95–121, 1972.

McGhee, P. E., and Frueh, T. "Television Viewing and the Learning of Sex-role Stereotypes." *Sex Roles* 6:179–88, 1980.

Markle, G. E. "Sex Ratio at Birth: Values, Variance and Some Determinants." *Demography* 11:131–42, 1974.

Newman, L. E. "Treatment for the Parents of Feminine Boys." *American Journal of Psychiatry* 133:683–87, 1976.

Paludi, M. A., and Bauer, W. D. "Goldberg Revisited: What's in an Author's Name?" *Sex Roles* 9:387–90, 1983.

Reiss, I. L. *Family Systems in America*. 3rd ed. New York: Holt, Rinehart and Winston, 1980.

Rekers, G. A., et al. "Sex-Role Stereotype and Professional Intervention for Childhood Gender Disturbance." *Professional Psychology* 9:127–36, 1978.

Rommel, E. "Grade School Blues." *Ms.*, pp. 32–35, January 1984.

Rubin, J.; Provenzano, F., and Luria, Z. "The Eye of the Beholder: Parents'

Views on Sex of Newborns." *American Journal of Orthopsychiatry* 44:512–19, 1974.

Scanzoni, J., and Fox, G. L. "Sex Roles, Family and Society: The Seventies and Beyond." *Journal of Marriage and the Family* 42:743–58, 1980.

Schaffer, K. *Sex Roles and Human Behavior.* Cambridge, Mass.: Winthrop, 1981.

Spence, J. T., and Helmreich, R. L. *Masculinity & Femininity: Their Psychological Dimensions, Correlates, and Antecedents.* Austin: University of Texas Press, 1978.

Tavris, C., and Offir, C. *The Longest War: Sex Differences in Perspective.* New York: Harcourt Brace Jovanovich, 1977.

Vogel, S.; Broverman, I., and Gardner, J. *Sesame Street and Sex-Role Stereotypes.* Pittsburgh: Know, 1970.

Walum, L. R. *The Dynamics of Sex and Gender: A Sociological Perspective.* Chicago: Rand McNally College Publishing Co., 1977.

Weissman, M. "Depression." In Brodsky, A. M., and HareMustin, R. (eds.), *Women and Psychotherapy,* pp. 97–112. New York: Guilford Press, 1980.

Weitzman, L. J. "Sex-Role Socialization." In Freeman, J. (ed.), *Women: A Feminist Perspective.* Palo Alto, Calif.: Mayfield, 1975.

Weitzman, L. J., et al. "Sex Role Socialization in Picture Books for Pre-School Children." *American Journal of Sociology* 77:1125–50, 1972.

Review Questions

1. Traditionally, what have been the stereotyped gender roles for American men and women?
2. How have assumptions underlying psychological tests for gender-role characteristics changed in recent years?
3. Based on this article, summarize the pattern of gender-role socialization of either a boy or girl, from birth through adulthood.
4. What evidence of sex discrimination do the authors find in contemporary American culture?

Discussion and Writing Suggestions

1. The authors begin their discussion with examples of gender-role stereotyping in popular culture (see paragraph 1). Conduct your own informal survey of popular culture: Locate three illustrations of gender-role stereotyping in a medum of your choice—television, newspapers, billboards, movies, books. Describe the stereotyping that you find, compare and contrast stereotypes, and draw conclusions.
2. Reread the authors' section on gender-role socialization in adolescence. How accurate is their description of the pressures adolescents face in becoming "masculine" young men and "feminine" young women?
3. Locate and read any one of the articles that the authors cite in their own discussion. Summarize the article (odds are, the author will have done this for you) and share your impressions with the class.

Being a Boy

JULIUS LESTER

The traditional social traumas of childhood (the first kiss, the first date, and so on) can be funny in retrospect. Certainly when Julius Lester recalls the trials of growing up as a boy, we laugh heartily; but we are thoughtful as well, for Lester describes predicaments that we know to be painful. Girls often want to be more "masculine"—assertive, courageous, active; boys often want to be more "feminine"—contemplative, artful. But peer groups exert tremendous pressures for girls and boys to conform to socially prescribed roles. Watch closely how Lester turns personal anecdotes into large cultural themes. Though he writes from private experience, Lester is able to generalize so that his experiences encompass ours. Be forewarned: this piece, in places, is bawdy.

Julius Bernard Lester, the son of a minister, was born in 1939 in St. Louis, Missouri. He has had a prolific and varied career dating from his graduation at Fisk University in 1960. As a professional musician and singer, he recorded with Vanguard Records and performed at the Newport Folk Festival. He produced and was host of a live radio show in New York City from 1968 to 1975. Lester has written numerous books, including Look Out Whitey! Black Power's Gon' Get Your Mama! *(1968),* The Long Journey Home: Stories from Black History *(1972),* Do Lord Remember Me *(1984), and* Lovesong: Becoming a Jew *(1988). Since 1971, Lester—the recipient of many awards for teaching and scholarship—has taught Afro-American Studies at the University of Massachusetts. Since 1982, he has been a professor of Near Eastern and Judaic studies.*

As boys go, I wasn't much. I mean, I tried to be a boy and spent many childhood hours pummeling my hardly formed ego with failure at cowboys and Indians, baseball, football, lying, and sneaking out of the house. When our neighborhood gang raided a neighbor's pear tree, I was the only one who got sick from the purloined fruit. I also failed at setting fire to our garage, an art at which any five-year-boy should be adept. I was, however, the neighborhood champion at getting beat up. "That Julius can take it, man," the boys used to say, almost in admiration, after I emerged from another battle, tears brimming in my eyes but refusing to fall. 1

My efforts at being a boy earned me a pair of scarred knees that 2

"Being a Boy" by Julius Lester. Originally appeared in *Ms.* Magazine, June 1973. Reprinted by permission of the author.

are a record of a childhood spent falling from bicycles, trees, the tops of fences, and porch steps; of tripping as I ran (generally from a fight), walked, or simply tried to remain upright on windy days.

I tried to believe my parents when they told me I was a boy, but I could find no objective proof for such an assertion. Each morning during the summer, as I cuddled up in the quiet of a corner with a book, my mother would push me out the back door and into the yard. And throughout the day as my blood was let as if I were a patient of 17th-century medicine, I thought of the girls sitting in the shade of porches, playing with their dolls, toy refrigerators and stoves. 3

There was the life, I thought! No constant pressure to prove oneself. No necessity always to be competing. While I humiliated myself on football and baseball fields, the girls stood on the sidelines laughing at me, because they didn't have to do anything except be girls. The rising of each sun brought me to the starting line of yet another day's Olympic decathlon, with no hope of ever winning even a bronze medal. 4

Through no fault of my own I reached adolescence. While the pressure to prove myself on the athletic field lessened, the overall situation got worse—because now I had to prove myself with girls. Just how I was supposed to go about doing this was beyond me, especially because, at the age of 14, I was four foot nine and weighed 78 pounds. (I think there may have been one 10-year-girl in the neighborhood smaller than I.) Nonetheless, duty called, and with my ninth-grade gym-class jockstrap flapping between my legs, off I went. 5

To get a girlfriend, though, a boy had to have some asset beyond the fact that he was alive. I wasn't handsome like Bill McCord, who had girls after him like a cop-killer has policemen. I wasn't ugly like Romeo Jones, but at least the girls noticed him: "That ol' ugly boy better stay 'way from me!" I was just there, like a vase your grandmother gives you at Christmas that you don't like or dislike, can't get rid of, and don't know what to do with. More than ever I wished I were a girl. Boys were the ones who had to take the initiative and all the responsibility. (I hate responsibility so much that if my heart didn't beat of itself, I would now be a dim memory.) 6

It was the boy who had to ask the girl for a date, a frightening enough prospect until it occurred to me that she might say no! That meant risking my ego, which was about as substantial as a toilet-paper raincoat in the African rainy season. But I had to thrust that ego forward to be judged, accepted, or rejected by some girl. It wasn't fair! Who was she to sit back like a queen with the power to create joy by her consent or destruction by her denial? It wasn't fair—but that's the way it was. 7

But if (God forbid!) she should say Yes, then my problem would begin in earnest, because I was the one who said where we would go (and waited in terror for her approval of my choice). I was the one who picked her up at her house where I was inspected by her parents as if I were a possible carrier of syphilis (which I didn't think one could get from masturbating, but then again, Jesus was born of a virgin, so what did I know?). Once we were on our way, it was I who had to pay the bus fare, the price of the movie tickets, and whatever she decided to stuff her stomach with afterward. (And the smallest girls are all stomach.) Finally, the girl was taken home where once again I was inspected (the father looking covertly at my fly and the mother examining the girl's hair). The evening was over and the girl had done nothing except honor me with her presence. All the work had been mine. 8

Imagining this procedure over and over was more than enough: I was a sophomore in college before I had my first date. 9

I wasn't a total failure in high school, though, for occasionally I would go to a party, determined to salvage my self-esteem. The parties usually took place in somebody's darkened basement. There was generally a surreptitious wine bottle or two being passed furtively among the boys, and a record player with an insatiable appetite for Johnny Mathis records. Boys gathered on one side of the room and girls on the other. There were always a few boys and girls who'd come to the party for the sole purpose of grinding away their sexual frustrations to Johnny Mathis's falsetto, and they would begin dancing to their own music before the record player was plugged in. It took a little longer for others to get started, but no one matched my talent for standing by the punch bowl. For hours, I would try to make my legs do what they had been doing without effort since I was nine months old, but for some reason they would show all the symptoms of paralysis on those evenings. 10

After several hours of wondering whether I was going to die ("Julius Lester, a sixteen-year-old, died at a party last night, a half-eaten Ritz cracker in one hand and a potato chip dipped in pimiento-cheese spread in the other. Cause of death: failure to be a boy"), I would push my way to the other side of the room where the girls sat like a hanging jury. I would pass by the girl I wanted to dance with. If I was going to be refused, let it be by someone I didn't particularly like. Unfortunately, there weren't many in that category. I had more crushes than I had pimples. 11

Finally, through what surely could only have been the direct intervention of the Almighty, I would find myself on the dance floor with a girl. And none of my prior agony could compare to the thought of actually dancing. But there I was and I had to dance with her. Social custom decreed that I was supposed to lead, because I was 12 the boy. Why? I'd wonder. Let her lead. Girls were better dancers anyway. It didn't matter. She stood there waiting for me to take charge. She wouldn't have been worse off if she'd waited for me to turn white.

But, reciting "Invictus" to myself, I placed my arms around her, being careful to keep my armpits closed because, somehow, I had managed to overwhelm a half jar of deodorant and a good-size bottle of cologne. With sweaty armpits, "Invictus," and legs afflicted again with polio, I took her in my arms, careful not to hold her so far away that she would think I didn't like her, but equally careful not to hold her so close that she could feel the catastrophe which had befallen me the instant I touched her hand. My penis, totally disobeying the lecture I'd given it before we left home, was as rigid as Governor Wallace's jaw would be if I asked for his daughter's hand in marriage. 13

God, how I envied girls at that moment. Wherever *it* was on them, it didn't dangle between their legs like an elephant's trunk. No wonder boys talked about nothing but sex. That thing was always there. Every time we went to the john, there *it* was, twitching around like a fat little worm on a fishing hook. When we took baths, it floated in the water like a lazy fish and God forbid we should touch it! It sprang to life like lightning leaping from a cloud. I wished I could cut it off, or at least keep it tucked between my legs, as if it were a tail that had been mistakenly attached to the wrong end. But I was helpless. It was there, with a life and mind of its own, having no other function than to embrarrass me. 14

Fortunately, the girls I danced with were discreet and pretended that they felt nothing unusual rubbing against them as we danced. But I was always convinced that the next day they were all calling up their friends to exclaim: "Guess what, girl? Julius Lester got one! I ain't lyin'!" 15

Now, of course, I know that it was as difficult being a girl as it was a boy, if not more so. While I stood paralyzed at one end of a dance floor trying to find the courage to ask a girl for a dance, most of the girls waited in terror at the other, afraid that no one, not even I, would ask them. And while I resented having to ask a girl for a date, wasn't it also horrible to be the one who waited for the phone to ring? And how many of those girls who laughed at me making a fool of myself on the baseball diamond would have gladly given up their places on the sidelines for mine on the field? 16

No, it wasn't easy for any of us, girls and boys, as we forced our beautiful, free-flowing child-selves into those narrow, constricting cubicles labeled *female* and *male*. I tried, but I wasn't good at being a boy. Now, I'm glad, knowing that a man is nothing but the figment of a penis's imagination, and any man should want to be something more than that. 17

Review Questions

1. As a boy, what "objective proofs" did Lester look for to confirm his masculinity?
2. Why did Lester, when regarding the behavior of girls, think: "There was the life"?
3. Lester was frightened by the prospect of going out on a date. Why?
4. Summarize the point of Lester's essay in a sentence.

Discussion and Writing Suggestions

1. "I tried to believe my parents when they told me I was a boy. . . ." What constitutes being a boy or girl, according to Lester? To what extent in your own life is being a man or woman a state of mind, as opposed to a state of anatomy?
2. "Boys were the ones who had to take the initiative and all the responsibility." Is this true in your experience?
3. Lester repeatedly puts judgment in the hands of girls: "Who was she to sit back like a queen with the power to create joy by her consent or destruction by her denial?" or "the girls sat like a hanging jury." How do you react to this characterization of girls as judges?
4. Lester speaks of forcing "our beautiful, free-flowing child-selves into those narrow, constricting cubicles labeled *female* and *male*." Do you believe that at some point we each have a "child-self" that is neither female nor male? Explain.

Is the New Man a Wimp?

MARGARET EDWARDS

Margaret Edwards asks some cold, tough questions of career women who bemoan the lack of "suitable" prospects among the men they date. What counts as suitable for the woman of the 1990s who earns a good salary, who's assertive in both business and private life, who's independent? What sort of man will do? She doesn't want John Wayne—but as it turns out, she doesn't want his opposite either.

Margaret Edwards contributed this article to Working Woman *magazine in May 1985. She is an associate professor of English at the University of Vermont.*

"But Does the New Woman Really Want the New Man?" (Retitled: "Is the New Man A Wimp?") by Margaret Edwards from "Changing Men, Changing Marriage" by W. W. Meade in *Working Woman*, November 1986. Reprinted with permission from *Working Woman* magazine.

It used to be that the man would telephone the woman and ask for a 1
date. This was in the days before running shoes (there were only tennis shoes), when "Made in Japan" was a synonym for "shoddy." The man's bad luck was to have to screw up his courage and ask. The woman's bad luck was to have to stifle her hopes and wait.

But times change. 2

Recently, when a young male colleague in my office mentioned a 3
woman whom he liked, I suggested, "Why don't you two drop by my place for a drink the next time you invite her on a date?"

"Oh, we don't *date,* he said. "We sort of hang out." 4

I have since made further discreet inquiries among the under- 5
singles on our staff and have confirmed that dating as I once knew it is indeed dead. Fashion houses may be reviving the 1950s style of ball gowns, but the date, I've been assured, remains moribund.

Going back to the first source of my information, I asked who had 6
made the crucial phone call to arrange the first meeting. His answer gave no hint of a new protocol. In this particular case, while idly conversing with the young woman—both of them having stopped to stretch their muscles at the same bend in a jogging trail—he mentioned he was going to a reggae concert. She remarked that she had a ticket to the same event.

It so happened that they bumped into each other afterwards, and 7
in the company of numerous mutual friends, they walked downtown to a favorite bar.

"But that seems too whimsical and uncertain," I said. "Suppose 8
she hadn't had a ticket to the same concert? Would you have gotten hold of her phone number to call her up and say, 'I've got an extra ticket: do you want to come?' "

No. Definitely not. He confessed, though, that he might have 9
said. "I've got an extra ticket: do you want to buy it?"

"Can you tell me what's wrong," I asked, "with letting a woman 10
know you're interested?" I began recalling with a certain nostalgia the brave, gruff voices on telephones that had wondered if I were free on Saturday night. My friend looked uncomfortable and evasive.

"If I let a woman know I'm interested," he said, "she might 11
expect too much."

His face said it all: She might expect a regular and increasing 12
familiarity. Marriage? Well, not quite that. But all too soon, books and stereos would be packed in cartons, a lease would have been jointly signed, and two sets of parents would begin looking pained but hopeful on Christmas holidays.

"Women make marvelous friends," he affirmed. 13

And I thought how often that's been said, in the same tone, about 14
dogs.

NEW MEN, WIMPS AND WORMBOYS

Are men getting weaker as women get stronger? This question seems 15
to be preoccupying feminists lately. In the *New York Times,* Barbara Ehrenreich characterized the evolution of Macho Man into New Man as a mutation from tyrant to fop. She praised the new-found domestic independence of the male—he can fix his own quiche—but lamented the "narcissism" that makes him prefer to eat it alone or with a series of pretty companions. She praised his budding sensitivities—he enjoys a shopping spree, he keeps his body trim, he cries—but deplored his self-absorption. There is no commitment in the New Man. He's not out to enslave or dominate a female. In fact, what's wrong with him now is that he feels little urge to create a longstanding or passionate bond with any woman. Bachelorhood, freed of its gay stigma, has become his prime and perpetual state. He accepts that women have joined him on the fast track, yet their paths seem to be parallel, not intersecting.

"So it is not enough, anymore, to ask that men become more like 16
women," concluded Ehrenreich. She tried to give a helpful directive: "We should ask that they become more like what both men and women might be"—cultivating in themselves both "masculine" and "feminine" virtues, plus a capacity for commitment and "a broad and generous vision of how we all might live together."

What Ehrenreich advocates is close to a wholesale change in 17
human nature. It would surely call a truce in the war between the sexes. (It might even bring peace among nations as well.) But is it realistic to expect this? Are men going to redouble their efforts to be the best sort of people they can be? Pessimists among us may find the litmus of our predictions turning a shade darker.

Deborah Laake's article "Wormboys"—widely published last year 18
in a number of newspapers—put forth the woman's position bluntly, "As the clock keeps ticking and I'm neither younger nor more firmly settled in love than when I began my research, a primitive inner force wants to wind things up and have a life with someone. But something stops me. And that something is that I'm surrounded by wimps." She coined another word for wimps—wormboys.

These are men who shrink from marriage, from having children, 19
even from the simplest assertion, such as deciding where to go and what to do on a weekend. They are "lazy," unambitious in their work and unashamed of letting women pay. They do not embrace the roles of provider, arbiter, analyst, manager or leader. They avoid anything the least bit unpleasant. If a confrontation looms, they run and hide.

Laake advised women to assess what it means if they, not the 20
men they spend time with, "comb the entertainment sections of local

periodicals" and then choose what to do with leisure time. What does it mean if women allow themselves to be accompanied by men who have offered no suggestions about where to go and are content to "just go along"?

The male ideal in feminist minds is no longer what it was, yet has taken no definite subsequent shape. A superficial makeover of yesteryear's he-man won't do. John Wayne with a developed culinary talent will still think it's his woman's role to wash his dishes. 21

For serious feminists, there is no way back to the style of commitment the he-man was half of—a style requiring the man's providence in exchange for the woman's subservience. 22

Yet the New Woman, in querulous moments, seems angry with the new possibilities. If a feminist is offered the converse of the old style of commitment—that is, a union in which *she* will provide and *he* will serve—she balks. It's a bond that, by the logic of inverted tradition, ought to have a chance of strength. 23

Laake's article described her breakup with a so-called wormboy. "I was overwhelmed," she wrote, "by the responsibilities falling to me in our union—those of principal breadwinner, head of the entertainment committee, business manager and mother of souls." Yet think of the years that men were expected to take on this same "overwhelming" role! All as a matter of course. And what was their reward? There was one. It was A Wife of One's Own. 24

DOES A WOMAN REALLY WANT A WIFE?

Laake's pseudonymous boyfriend Henry is a hirsute version of what has been the time-honored, much-idealized Little Woman, with "velvet sheathing the steel demurely." When Laake asked him exactly what he would contribute to their relationship, he replied, "I've observed that I seem to function as an invisible support system." 25

Invisible support—that's what the more retiring member of a couple offers. This is not the visible cash on the table or paycheck in the mailbox or gold card at the restaurant, but it's support nonetheless. It used to be called "what money can't buy" (although money kept it fed and housed), and it still takes amorphous forms: the shoulder to cry on, the home-cooked dinner that's waiting for you (still hot), the calm in the midst of your daily storm. 26

Laake admitted that she had enjoyed this kind of support from her Henry. To him, she had confided fears and fantasies. From him, she had received encouragement, understanding, sympathy and attention. She acknowledged that often he would talk to her in 27 rambling and irrelevant monologues, but the talk itself provided support. "I'd [be] alternately absorbed in and comforted by it," she wrote, "the way I sometimes actually watch a TV show and other times just flip on the set and feel glad for the company."

Customarily men have felt "glad for the company" of women offering only invisible support. Why can't women be glad for the same? Perhaps it's bizarre and maybe a little scary to find oneself head of a household that includes an able-bodied man. 28

Did we feminists really expect that, as a norm, two equally ambitious careerists could form an amicable partnership under the same roof? 29

"Yes!" comes the chorus. "That's what we did expect. Why haven't we gotten it?" 30

Putting the question of sexual differences aside for the moment, I've asked myself: Are the strong couples I know made of partners who are alike or partners who are complementary? 31

My answer: complementary. A logical mate for a person full of energy and drive and purpose is someone offering that valuable old-fashioned commodity, "invisible support." Tractability (let's not keep calling it passivity) and an amenable disposition, a domestic focus (not necessarily being "lazy" about work) and an enjoyment of being coddled, indulged and led (despite being bright and full of his own opinions)—why aren't these traits considered valuable in a man? For a self-willed, adventurous woman, they might be the traits to look for if she wants to form a strong bond with someone who suits her. 32

Unfortunately, women don't yet admire in men what have been known as the "feminine virtues." It took women so long to get out from under these virtues that one can hardly blame them for still being suspicious of them. Maxims such as "They also serve who only stand and wait" seemed designed to keep women at home. Rather than standing and waiting, and being content to change diapers and fix the dinners for movers and doers, some women have wanted to be the movers and doers themselves. 33

It is all to the good and only fair that society seems to be moving in the direction of letting temperament and talents, rather than sex and race, determine employment and compensation. But the old maxim still holds true, for those who "also serve" by giving "invisible support" are a vague "they," neither male nor female. 34

LITTLE WOMEN VS. NEW WOMEN

When will we feminists stop feeling disappointed that the high-salaried males willing to support families often prefer the Little Women types? They seem happier with them in fundamental ways. 35

Those Little Women, despite Betty Friedan's debunking of their "mystique," are still the ones who willingly pack and move at their husband's decree, who are free to go on business junkets at short notice, who stay home to mind the children and run the errands. We all know by now that each Little Woman is taking a big chance, going at it with that combination of foolhardiness and courage peculiar to the motorbike racer who doesn't wear a helmet. If her marriage crashes, the damage to her will be inevitable and severe, for she's got very little protection. And the statistics are against her.

The New Woman, the mover and doer, is simply carving out new spheres of risk. "We are becoming the men we wanted to marry," *Ms.* editor Gloria Steinem told a large gathering of women. Right now, the "neither younger nor more firmly settled" New Woman may feel that her heaviest liability is a likelihood of winding up alone. The chances of marrying a man like herself seem slim and getting slimmer. 36

Yet our old dream dies hard. The prince must come and kiss the sleeping beauty. She is still under a dark spell, though this time not a spell of prudery or parents or her own pitiful ineptitude. What currently immobilizes her is loneliness. She feels paralyzed by the work of living up to her own vaunted promise, by the late nights and by the dumb dullness that creeps into any career. She has her independent self and nobody else—nobody else in the bed, nobody else across the breakfast table—at least nobody steady enough, ever-present enough, and promised as a part of each day. A prince must arrive who is willing to banish her loneliness permanently, to share half the housework, to become a "participating" father *and* to bring home a full share of income. Is that so much to ask of a man? The answer is that it must be, given how men seem to flee such commitment. 37

"She might expect too much" echoes beyond the revealing conversation I had with that man at the office. "You won't believe the guy I went out with last week . . ." begins a story I am told by an attractive single woman. "He was so afraid of commitment he checked the fire exits in the restaurant before we sat down!" A contemporary greeting card carries the message "To get a prince, you have to kiss a lot of frogs" and today's unmarried women can get tired of kissing frogs. 38

FEWER FROGS, MORE FISH

Fewer frogs, and more fish, appear in the pool of available men if a feminist is willing to consider forming a serious alliance with the sort that the macho tradition taught her to spurn. 39

What about the man of gentle and unassuming temper? The man of erratic and skimpy income? The man shorter than she? The man less educated? The man from a less privileged background? Or, the man much younger? 40

A lot of misunderstanding between men and women comes from our believing the two sexes are inherently polarized. Actually, they're closer to an androgynous human mean. Men are cursed with the same conflicts we experience—and should not be envied and therefore reviled. The men I know, like the women I know, find it hard to choose between modern life's contraries: the safe routine and the adventurous possibility, the vocation and the avocation, the thrill of affairs and the comforts of marriage, the time they spend alone and the time they spend with others, the satisfaction in being free of children and the urge to have kids. If you talk to a man who is worried about his life, he sounds exactly like the worried woman—as if he's being torn along the same seams as she. He even ends a conversation as she does, by saying, "There's nobody free in this city. They're all married. I can't meet anyone." 41

So far, it seems that the work-directed and undomesticated New Woman doesn't like the look of the New Man. But should those of us who have asked to ride the horse turn petulant when we're hoisted astride and handed the reins? There are sincere pleasures in taking command. If a woman calls a new tune because she's earned enough to pay the piper, it doesn't mean she has to dance unpartnered. The New Woman may have to take a chance on living with the type of man who benefits from her energy rather than duplicates it, who admires her clear sense of purpose and doesn't thwart it, who feels inclined not so much to lead her as to enjoy where she leads. She may have to look past the classic knight on the white charger to find the next hero—the one on the dark horse. 42

Review Questions

1. What is the point of Edwards relating the conversation she had with her male office mate?
2. "Women make marvelous friends." How does Edwards respond to this statement?
3. How does Barbara Ehrenreich characterize the new man? (See paragraphs 15–17.)
4. Feminists face an irony in their relations with men. What is this irony?
5. What is "invisible support"? How is the term important to the article?
6. What is a wormboy?
7. According to Edwards, which anxieties and desires do both men and women share?

Discussion and Writing Suggestions

1. Edwards feels somewhat nostalgic for the times when a man would telephone to ask for a date. Are the new-age dating procedures she refers to representative of procedures that you're familiar with? Explain.
2. How "wormy" do you find wormboys, as they are characterized in paragraphs 18 through 24?
3. Even if you've never given much thought to the male or the female "ideal," is it safe to say that you have nonetheless internalized such an ideal? What are the qualities you're looking for in a partner?
4. "Unfortunately, women don't yet admire in men what have been known as the 'feminine virtues.' " Do you agree? Is the man in whose character the feminine virtues predominate necessarily a wimp?
5. Edwards reports an interesting remark by Gloria Steinem: "We [women] are becoming the men we wanted to marry." Speculate about the implications of this statement.
6. Respond to Question 3 by writing a "Help Wanted" ad. Your job is to describe job openings for the "Ideal Male" and the "Ideal Female." Your two-paragraph description of each should include, but not be limited to, personality traits, interests, assertiveness, and to your mind the "correct" response to a series of questions. For example: "The Ideal Male will respond to the question—'Who pays for gasoline on a drive out to the country?'—in the following way:"
7. Construct an imaginary dialogue among the following: (1) yourself, the "Little Woman," and the "New Woman," or (2) yourself, the "Wormboy," and the "New Man." In these conversations, explain and argue about the advantages and limitations of these respective conditions.

Men, Women, Equality, and Love

CHERYL MERSER

Cheryl Merser was twenty-five when Gail Sheehy's enormously influential book Passages *was published in 1976.* Passages *was a detailed study of the contrasting life cycles of contemporary men and women; it emphasized the way that cultural sex roles in post–World War II America affected patterns of leaving home, dating, marriage, careers, midlife crises, and in general, awareness of one's self and one's goals. The trouble, Merser notes, is that though she saw her parents' lives reflected in Sheehy's book, "I couldn't find my life anywhere in* Passages*":*

> The forms adulthood took for my parents or, for that matter, for Gail Sheehy need not be the forms it would take for my friends and me. We were the young people of a new generation and had seen our share, God knows, of social change. Now it made sense why my life wasn't in *Passages:* Gail Sheehy is a writer, not a fortune-teller. How could she possibly have known what kind of world I'd grow up into and thus what kind of adult I'd become?

Merser decided to write about her own experiences and the experiences of her contemporaries. The result was Grown-Ups: A Generation in Search of Adulthood *(1987), a book that has been called "the* Passages *for the babyboom generation." In the following chapter from* Grown-Ups*, Merser writes about gender roles in this new generation—particularly as these roles affect marriage, men's and women's expectations of one another, and men's and women's continued failure to communicate. She finds that many contemporary relationships are neither "traditional" nor "liberated." Rather, they represent a new kind of uneasy—and frequently unstable—medium.*

Cheryl Merser was born in 1951 in Boston. The former publicity manager of a major publishing house, she is the author of Honorable Intentions: The Manners of Courtship in the '80s *(1983) and of articles in many newspapers and magazines.*

Not long ago I made plans to meet a married friend at her apartment after work, an hour or so before she expected her husband home for dinner from the racquetball game he played every Tuesday night. That way, we decided, we'd be able to talk by ourselves before her husband and the man I was living with, who had a late meeting, joined us for dinner. 1

I arrived at the apartment only a moment after Diane did, when she was still taking off her coat and dumping the day's accumulation—briefcase, pocketbook, umbrella, an over-full bag of groceries, a lemon tart in a bakery box, and a lone shoe with a new heel on it—onto the floor. Diane was her customary cheerful and frantic self, and I suddenly felt the adrenaline charge I always get in her company; she's a real-life version of one of those superwomen you read about in magazines, always with energy to spare. A partner in a large public-relations firm, she has handled her career as deftly as I've seen other women steer baby strollers over a curb, and she has always seemed to know exactly what she wanted: a happy marriage, a high-powered career, no children, good friends. She also tutors read- 2 ing one night a week, sews, exercises during her lunch hour . . . and after I've seen her, I usually go home and clean out a drawer.

"Pour us a glass of wine while I go change," she ordered, and before I'd even finished with the corkscrew, Diane had disappeared and reemerged, not an executive in her mid-thirties now, but dressed in corduroys and oversized red sweater, her brown hair in a ponytail. As we talked, she bustled around, tidying up, and I followed her from room to room. First she made the bed, then laid out fresh towels, rinsed the breakfast coffee from the coffeemaker, threw away the morning paper, and arranged a bouquet of flowers that had been sticking out of her briefcase when she got home. Absently, I found myself helping; I put the umbrella in its stand, straightened a cushion, wiped off a sticky countertop. The ritual was familiar: I'd seen women smoothing out the edges of domestic life for as long as I can remember, and I've done it myself, willingly or sometimes resentfully, for a man due home. 3

While she chopped shallots, I set the table. I told her about a mutual acquaintance who had lost his job, and about another, whose good news was that she was pregnant—she'd wanted a baby for ages. Diane was worried about someone else we both knew, with boyfriend troubles, who needed to get out more; couldn't I take her to lunch? She told me about a new account she had at work, and that she wasn't getting along with one of her colleagues. Then I tested a theory I was trying to work through for this book, something about the changing roles of parents, and she gave me the name of a book she thought would help. At one point, she paused in her chopping to say, "I wonder what they talk about at racquetball," and we speculated on that for a minute. Soon the halibut, surrounded by herbs, tomatoes, and the shallots, was ready for baking. Broccoli for steaming was set out on the chopping block next to a loaf of French bread; the rice was measured, the salad ready, and two new candles were lit on the table in the dining area. The apartment, which had looked abandoned only a few minutes before, now looked lived-in and magically cozy. We moved into the living room, decorated in shades of mustard and dusty blue; the lighting was just right. And when Diane's husband, Joel, walked in and announced, the way Ricky Ricardo might have done in an old *I Love Lucy* episode, "Boy am I tired," Diane and I both started to laugh. 4

However, to compare my friends' marriage to Lucy and Ricky's, with Lucy's wide-eyed conniving and Ricky's blustery machismo, would be absurd. In fact, even the labels "husband" and "wife," as I've always thought of them, with the masculine and feminine roles and responsibilities they evoke, don't sound right. While my parents were married, my father was surely a husband, my mother a wife; 5

their marriage, like most others I remember from childhood, seemed heavy with unexamined and mechanical dependencies. Joel and Diane instead are like two great pals but closer. Their dependence upon each other is not of the "where are my gloves, honey?" kind, but private—you can't see it at first glance. What they seem to be held together by are not the mechanics of marriage, as I've thought of them, but simply by love.

While Joel went to change out of his business clothes, I asked 6 Diane why, on top of her job, she did the rest—the cooking, the shopping, the candles, the tidying up. "I do it," she said, "because I don't know how not to. Nobody's making me be a woman or a wife." But then she went on, and later I wondered whether she had confessed more than she meant to, or less: "My marriage is fine," she said. "I mean, it's not perfect, but I'm happy, even if I'm not doing it right, or equally. But the strange thing is that, close as we are, I thought marriage would be different—that it would be one 'thing' with two people inside. With us, it's more like two separate marriages, his and mine. Joel probably thinks he does half the work, but he doesn't. I don't think he knows what my side of the marriage is like. Half the time, talking to him is like talking to a can of soup—about my feelings, for one thing, or things I worry about at the office. He doesn't get it. He doesn't know. I guess," she concluded vaguely, "men are just different."

Though I'm not married myself, I knew right away and all too 7 well what she meant. A few years ago, I would have been disheartened or angered by her comments, to say nothing of that scene at dinner—the stereotypical bustling women and the tired-and-hungry-husband-arriving-for-dinner, oblivious to the care and trouble that went into it. I would have argued that men don't have to be "different." After all, our generation, Diane's and mine, was out to prove that there need be no built-in distinctions between the sexes. We would share everything, fifty-fifty, from boardrooms and floor-waxing to the emotional "chores" of love, marriage, and family. For the first time in history, the motto of marriage was to be: Don't treat me like a "wife" and I won't treat you like a "husband." But now, since more of my friends have paired off and since I've been living with a man myself, I've had a better chance to know liberated men and women not on paper but in action, which is to say negotiating new and untried rules of equality—and making their inevitable private compromises in the name of love.

Off and on that evening, I thought about Diane's compromises, 8 and, as Joel cleared the table, I tried to imagine how the marriage looked from his "side," the compromises or sacrifices he himself must have made, and whether he too would argue that women and men are "different." I tried to bring the subject up over coffee, but Diane glanced at me uneasily, and Joel and my boyfriend looked politely puzzled, as if I'd asked them a question in Chinese. Quickly, we switched to more general conversation and never returned to the question of why men and women are "different."

9 As I write this, relations between the sexes—on the surface at least—seem more troubled to me than ever before. *Divorce Court* reveals a terrible and different drama on TV every day. In the past year, there have been no fewer than three best-sellers about misogyny, variations on the theme of men hating women. Newspaper life-style pages report continually on the strains of two-career marriages and second marriages; the dilemma of whether to have children or not; the failure of old-fashioned marriages in new-fashioned times; of tensions that arise when the woman makes more money than the man (as 20 percent of working wives now do); and of the many adult relationships that fall apart before they even reach the prenuptial-agreement stage. When I hear friends despair over the 50-percent divorce rate and think about all that could possibly go wrong, I marvel instead at the marriages I've seen that do manage to succeed. And I marvel at the power of love, or if not love, at least what Dr. Johnson called the "triumph of hope over experience."

10 The experts have little in the way of good news to tell us. "Contrary to the common wisdom," says Letty Pogrebin in *Family Politics*, "married men are generally happier and healthier [!] than bachelors, but single women are happier and healthier [!] than married women." And yet married men are sexually unfaithful as much as 20 percent more than married women—who themselves are not exactly laggards in the infidelity department these days: One pessimistic estimate suggests that two out of three of all contemporary baby-boom marriages will be accompanied, from one side or the other, by an extramarital affair. If this prediction holds true, not only will we divorce more than our parents did, we'll also beat them at infidelity—we, the generation for whom equal partnerships, uncomplicated sexuality, and honest communication were supposed to be not a romantic ideal but the norm.

11 What's gone wrong? Can it really be that—despite all the much-deplored sexual inequality of the past—love, marriage, and family were nonetheless stable and trustworthy aspects of life all through history and are only now, for the first time, in terrible shape? Of course not. In the first place, the definitions of marriage, family, and even the role we expect love to play in our lives are not fixed but fluid; these definitions need revising with every generation. In the second place, liberation, as many men and women like Joel and Diane have seen at first hand, has its price—and the costs to love, marriage, and family can be painfully high. Is feminism to blame for the tensions

today between men and women? Is the problem, as fundamentalist preachers insist, a widespread moral breakdown? Or are we facing something at once more mundane and more serious: Is the historic equilibrium between the sexes burdened now by an economy that forces men and women to compete for scarce resources in order to survive? There's no simple answer. But one explanation that makes sense to me comes from an odd source, for I wouldn't have thought that new research about the life cycle could tell us so much about men, women, and love.

Conventional postindustrial life-cycle wisdom has it that, for the 12
most part, men and women go through life on parallel and complementary tracks, which intersect at mid-life and then run parallel again. As Erik Erikson, and others—from Carl Jung to Gail Sheehy—have outlined the adult life cycle, the healthy male would reach maturity, begin to define himself professionally, take on a wife, and start his family. At mid-life, having fought to earn a living for his family, he would see death around the corner and, for the first time, stop to take a look at the world. His so-called "feminine" qualities would emerge. Suddenly, his nurturing side would come out and possibly a newly discovered gentleness. He would no longer have to prove himself in the "masculine" realm; he could begin to express himself in a fuller, sensuous, more visibly open-hearted way, without threatening his manhood. The phrase "life begins at forty," for example, comes from a best-selling book by that title published during the Depression, which proposed that a man's happiest years would come after the struggles of early manhood. It's no coincidence that until now, men had tended to become more sentimental and loving as they aged—think of the man who is a more indulgent and demonstrative grandfather than he was a father, and not just because the child is someone else's direct responsibility.

A woman's life cycle took place on the other track. She would 13
reach maturity, secure both her professional and personal identities vicariously through loving a man, and, once married, would assume the posture of wife and usually mother. In general, she had no separate identity but acquired her stature from those to whom she was connected, the way small children are braver when they're hanging onto their mothers' skirts. As she cared for her husband and family, however, she would deplete her nurturing instincts. At mid-life, her primary work completed, and her husband now more "feminine" in sensibility, she too would envision death and become more assertive, joining the outside world she had not been a part of until now. (Think of the age at which Betty Friedan became an active feminist—mid-life.) Having provided love and nurturing all these years, the woman was restless to find out about herself. Thus, at mid-life, men and women became more alike, as their rigorous gen-

der differences mellowed, grew less important, and began to fade. The point to remember here is that this emotional merger could not have happened—or happened so dramatically—without the earlier enforced separation of the sexes by the roles each was expected to play.

There were always variations on these broad patterns, of course, and no one knows for certain whether they were culturally or physiologically determined, though it is known that men and women seem to "exchange" hormones sometime in mid-life, when estrogen and testosterone, the feminine and masculine hormones that determine sexual differences, diminish in women and men, respectively, a decline which appears at least in part to effect these mid-life personality transformations. Hormones aside, though, what is more important is that the world has changed significantly since Jung, Erikson, and their followers recorded these conventional life-cycle assumptions. The men and women of the postwar generation no longer make their ways through life on these traditional parallel and complementary tracks: We're thrust instead, men and women together, onto the same track, traveling in a single train. 14

> I say the "young men and boys" rather than the "young people" because the problems . . . belong primarily, in our society, to the boys: how to be useful and make something of oneself. A girl does not *have* to, she is not expected to, "make something" of herself. Her career does not have to be self-justifying, for she will have children, which is absolutely self-justifying, like any other natural or creative act. With this background, it is less important, for instance, what job an average young woman works at till she is married. . . .
>
> —PAUL GOODMAN,
> *Growing Up Absurd*

> American girls did, and no doubt do, play down their intelligence, skills, and determinitiveness when in the presence of datable boys, thereby manifesting a profound psychic dicipline in spite of their reputation for flightiness.
>
> —ERVING GOFFMAN,
> *The Presentation of Self in Everyday Life*

The comments above, from immensely successful books of their time, show how deeply influential Erikson's views of the life cycle were until our postwar generation came of age—with its new ideas about the roles of women and men, its uniquely high percentage of ambitious and educated women, and in a flailing economy where "woman's work" now includes coming up with half the rent. From the structure of the workplace to the rituals of dating, the premise, as every feminist will tell you, was the same: Women, at least in the first 15 half of life, were to be responsible for making men's lives in the "real" world possible. What Goodman and Goffman are saying is that not only were women responsible for washing the socks and raising the kids—more important still was their role as psychological helpmates: Under the terms of the traditional life cycle, women's work was to give the men in their lives unqualified emotional space and support, to do everything possible to ensure that these men could live out their potential and their dreams. For women, there was only one legitimate dream. In exchange for money to buy laundry soap, women were expected to give up their names, their own dreams, and their souls to a man, his job, his house, and his children. And for all its drawbacks on both sides, this formula, in its way, worked for a long time: The life cycle was lived out much as it was laid out, as if Erikson's formulas were as much a biological imperative as the arrival of baby teeth or puberty.

Now consider the new life-cycle "formula" for men and women 16 in the first half of life today: Upon reaching maturity—and we are the first generation for which this is so widely true—we do not complement each other so much as compete with each other, as we all, men and women alike, try to succeed, achieve autonomy, and find out who we are. Despite any superficial deference to the old formulas—like Diane's and Joel's—and whether we think about it or not, we're all competing in the marketplace for jobs and status—and, just as important, we're also competing for the emotional space and support that used to be a woman's most self-sacrificing gift to her man. We can no longer afford the accommodations to gender that men and women have made in the past: I don't know many women who would "play dumb" on a date or who dabble tentatively at a job, trusting that a husband will be along shortly, and I don't know many men who'd dare to present themselves anymore as sole kings of the castle. Most of us—literally—no longer make "gender deals" of the you-peel-the-carrots-and-I'll-pay-the-rent sort, or if we do, we negotiate them carefully; such deals are no longer almost automatic. Today, there are two people to contribute to the rent, two people who need the unqualified emotional support that pursuing a vocation or personal dream requires, and maybe no one to peel the damn carrots. Or to put it another way, in most relationships today, there are two adults with the same needs—Diane and Joel, for example—and no longer a man and woman whose separate needs justify a working, give-and-take balance.

"Gender characteristics," writes Alice Rossi, a former president of 17 the American Sociological Association who has recently written on gender and the life cycle, "are clearly modifiable under changed social circumstances, as men and women take on either greater or lesser similarity of roles and experience. . . . Political and economic pressures are now blurring traditional gender roles in the first half of life." In other words, the post-war women Rossi refers to have had to subdue their loving, nurturing instincts for the sake of self-assertion—a stage which, in Erikson's day, wouldn't have emerged till mid-life. Similarly, to make sense of this new world, men have had to tap their feminine sensibilities, if only rhetorically—or if only by learning the pragmatics of ordering Chinese takeout for themselves—much earlier than they would have tapped them in the past.

It follows that once gender distinctions have begun to blur in the 18
outside world, so too will they be transformed in the intimate worlds of love and marriage—inarguably crucial benchmarks of adulthood. Where once men and women "borrowed" inner resources from each other—a stoic man would put his arms around his crying wife, as if she were crying for both of them—now we strive ideally to cultivate inner resources of our own against any eventuality: Men are encouraged to learn to cry for themselves in much the same way that women have been encouraged to face the world apronless and head-on. Our expectations from love and marriage are high, even so, for to believe that men and women are not "different" is to expect complete understanding from a mate, to fail to allow for the unknowable mysteries between people and the sexes that in all likelihood make complete understanding too much to expect. We all have, as Virginia Woolf once said of women, our "own contrary instincts."

If to be an adult now means to internalize all the strengths and 19
virtues of both sexes, it also means that we've abandoned those you-peel-the-carrots-and-I'll-pay-the-rent rules and roles of gender. Why then the new strain on relationships? Shouldn't it have worked out instead that, with some of the pressure off both sides, love and marriage would be all the easier? Why is my friend Diane unable to find the point, the center, of her marriage? The answer is disquieting: In loving relationships that require neither "husbands" nor "wives," where the traditional rules and roles have been cast out, there's love and only love at the center. If we don't need to borrow so freely anymore from each other's strengths and resources, or to depend on each other for rent and peeled carrots, our only need for each other is our human, compelling, and unrelenting need for love. And love, of course, is a problem.

Review Questions

1. According to Merser, what are some of the more discouraging aspects of contemporary marriages?

2. In five to seven sentences, summarize the contrasting life cycles for the sexes of the previous generation.
3. Merser notes (in paragraph 15): "The life cycle was lived out much as it was laid out, as if Erikson's formulas were as much a biological imperative as the arrival of baby teeth or puberty." What does she mean by this? In particular, what does she mean by "biological imperative"?

Discussion and Writing Suggestions

1. The story about the dinner party with Diane, Joel, and her boyfriend that Merser recounts in the first part of this selection leads to her conclusion that, even in our liberated age, men and woman are "different." Do you think this is true? If so, is it a cause for resentment? In domestic life, do males continue to exploit or take advantage of females? Draw on your own personal experience and observations to support your discussion.
2. In paragraph 11, Merser notes that "liberation . . . has its price—and the costs to love, marriage, and family can be painfully high." What does she mean by this? What is the "price" of liberation? Cite examples from your own experience.
3. In paragraphs 12 and 13, Merser contrasts the life cycles of the previous generation of men and women. The two sexes used to have very different identity cycles, up until midlife. Then, both sexes would redefine themselves: Men would modify their self-assertive "instincts"; women would modify their "nurturing" instincts. In the process, the sexes would grow more alike.

   Based on your observations of your parents' (and grandparents' lives), and their contemporaries, how true do you find Merser's generalizations? (You may want to interview your parents—separately!—to discover what you need to know for this discussion.)
4. The quotations by Goodman and Goffman (following paragraph 14), and Merser's discussion in the paragraph following, describe traditional post-war sex roles. In a multiparagraph essay, consider the advantages and disadvantages of such clearly defined sex roles. Conversely, discuss the advantages and disadvantages of today's less clearly defined sex roles.
5. Merser remarks, "I don't know many women who would 'play dumb' on a date or who dabble tentatively at a job, trusting that a husband will be along shortly, and I don't know many men who'd dare to present themselves anymore as sole kings of the castle." Do you? What do you conclude from your response?
6. Merser concludes, "If we don't need to borrow so freely anymore from each other's strengths and resources, or to depend on each other for rent and peeled carrots, our only need for each other is our human, compel-

ling, and unrelenting need for love. And love, of course, is a problem." Is Merser right? In what way(s) is love a problem?

7. Write a critique of Merser's article. Draw on your responses to some of the other discussion and writing suggestions.

Who's Minding the Children?

CAROLYN COMAN

Writer Carolyn Coman interviewed three men who chose to stay at home and raise the kids, do the cooking, clean the house—while their wives went off to work outside the home. In the article that follows, these man speak for themselves about the rewards and pressures of exchanging their traditionally male duties for more traditionally female ones. In reading these pieces, you might recall (from Lester and Masters/Johnson/Kolodny) the various social pressures brought to bear on boys to be masculine. Just how difficult do you imagine it was for the men in this article to break with social expectations? This selection first appeared in the April 1988 issue of Parenting *magazine.*

Meet Dana Crowe, David Hildt, and Pat Welch. On the face of it, each is very different from the other—Crowe, from New Jersey, is a musician–songwriter who moonlights as an electrician; David Hildt, from a small town north of Boston, is heavily involved in political and school volunteer work; and former logger Pat Welch, from New Hampshire, has only recently gone back to work full-time as a carpenter. But what these three men have in common is that after the births of their children, their wives returned to work while they stayed home with the kids. Each man spoke at length with writer Carolyn Coman about "women's" work, and the tribulations and rewards of being their children's primary caregiver. What follows are excerpts from those conversations. 1

DANA CROWE

Four years ago, I was living in a loft on 14th Street in New York City, working at my songwriting, tending bar at night, and doing some 2

"House Husbands" by Carolyn Coman in *Parenting,* April 1988, pp. 66–71. Reprinted with permission of *Parenting* Magazine.

freelance electrical work. I rarely got up before 11:00 a.m. or noon. Now we live in New Jersey. I'm up at 7:30 a.m. with our twins, Ella and Chelsea, and my wife, Polly, goes off to work.

When we found out Polly was going to have twins I thought it was the greatest thing in the world. I was open to new experiences, and we both sort of assumed I'd be the one to stay home with the kids because of my evening work schedule. Also, Polly, who's a health educator at Rutgers University, had the nine-to-five job with all the benefits, which were very important. 3

It wasn't just economics, though, that kept us away from day-care. We both felt strongly that there is no substitute for Mom and Dad. I just don't see the point of having a kid if you plan to go back to work two weeks later, and when I see fathers going the workaholic route, I feel sad for them—and for their kids. I never think about the traditional roles for men because most of my friends are single people with artistically oriented careers, so when I make comparisons, I compare myself with them. 4

Sure, I get real bored sometimes, but the boredom doesn't come from the kids; it comes from running the household. It's hard to cherish every minute as you cook, clean, and trip over toys. If I had it to do all over again, the one change I'd make, no question, would be to hire help. I've been pretty bad about the cooking, too. I like to prepare fancy meals for guests, but when it comes to everyday cooking, day in and day out, no thanks. 5

I used to hear women saying that housewives didn't get enough credit. I never understood what they were talking about, but I do now. Anybody who can have a meal ready at the end of the day and the house clean and the laundry folded—and pay attention to their kids on top of that—is a superhero. By the end of the day I'm usually going nuts. 6

Polly isn't earning enough to support us completely, so for the last ten months I've been doing freelance lighting design at night. By the time she gets home, I'm dying to get out the door because I've been in the house all day. I feel like I'm being shot into orbit. 7

My greatest challenge so far has been to translate my creativity into raising my kids. I want to turn them on to what I'm interested in, and I thought it would be the most natural thing in the world. But it isn't; dealing creatively with unformed minds can be daunting. Keeping my temper has also been a challenge. I don't hit them, but I do blow up at them sometimes. Aside from that, I think I'm doing a very good job, and it shows—the girls are very happy. 8

One of the nicest things about being a parent is the connection it gives you to everybody else who has ever had a kid. And it's not the 9 connection you might have drinking a Budweiser and talking baseball with a man in a bar—that's a connection too, but this is a heart connection.

DAVID HILDT

When I first became a house husband in 1979, some people said, "What courage you have!" But it didn't seem courageous to me to give up a high-pressure job for something I wasn't getting enough of: seeing my kids and learning about the place where I lived. 10

My wife, Barbara, had been home full-time up to that point— Natalie was four years old and Michael was two—and she wanted to get out and teach. We had always been clear that one of us would stay at home. After we were married in 1968, we joined the Peace Corps and spent three-and-a-half years in Brazil, working together with children—an experience that profoundly changed us. We decided then that when we had our own kids we'd raise them ourselves. So leaving my job as program director of a nonprofit agency to come home to two little children was an exciting adventure for all of us, even though it meant our income was cut in half. 11

It wasn't a very difficult transition to make. I'd learned a lot from Barbara, who had started a parent-child cooperative and organized a play group in Amesbury, our hometown, just north of Boston. Also, I was in a men's discussion group, and support from those men was absolutely wonderful. 12

My first stint as a house husband lasted almost three years, until Barbara's job ended and we hit an economic crisis. I found work in a hardware store. It paid a modest wage, but I enjoyed the physical work and interaction with all kinds of people. In the meantime, Barbara found out she was pregnant again, and a few months later she was taking care of another tiny baby. 13

Barbara has always been politically active, and when this baby— our son, Simon—was about a year old, she ran for Massachusetts state representative. It was 1983, and my second era as a house husband began. Barbara is now serving her third term. Of course, her work is recognized much more than mine, but that's not an issue for me. I admire my wife tremendously. 14

This second stint is harder for me, though. The novelty has worn off, and there are three kids instead of two—with three, you have that tie-breaker. I haven't participated as much in the parent cooperative, and I feel more isolated. 15

Sometimes I get depressed. Part of it is the largely American notion that the man has to get out there and make that nest egg—it 16 gets to me frequently. But I don't feel useless, or that my work is a waste.

Even though Michael is ten now and in the fourth grade, Natalie 12 and in seventh grade, and Simon six and in kindergarten half the day, I don't see myself getting full-time work for a few more years. I need to play that loose because I want to be available when someone in my family needs me. The other day I heard that when both parents work, the mother spends an average of ten minutes a day with the child and the father an average of seven minutes—that's time actually relating, not standing next to the sink doing dishes—and I thought, "No, that's not what our lives are like." 17

My life isn't just about being home and being a constant presence for the kids, though. I do a lot of work I don't get paid for—school committee work, serving on the YMCA board, leading Cub Scouts, peace movement work. The community work answers, in part, my need to belong. If I go out at night, it's to a meeting. 18

I often think of my own childhood and my relationship with my parents. I came from a family of five—my mother was an artist, my father a banker. They were well-to-do but lived beyond their means, and I think that experience helped form my philosophy about money and the difference between financial security and emotional and spiritual security. It'd be great to have all three, but if I had to opt for one over the others, financial security would be way down there. 19

Some people in town ask me, "Are you still babysittin'?" I politely tell them I am doing a little bit more than that, but I realize there will always be those who don't care to understand. 20

PAT WELCH

I never wanted children, but when my wife, Ellen, got pregnant we decided to make a go of it. Before I met her, I operated logging equipment in the northern Maine woods. Ellen was the professional—she's an administrator for an environmental agency—so, given our circumstances, it made sense for me to take care of our daughter, Emma. 21

Then, a year ago, shortly before Emma turned two-and-a-half, we began easing her into daycare—for her benefit and for mine. When I went back to full-time work—I'm a carpenter now—I was ready. The social world of daycare has been great for Emma, too; she has blossomed. Actually, I think she was getting bored with me. And I'm better off as a part-time parent and full-time worker. I'm happier and my activities seem useful in the outside world. 22

I'm the first to admit that I'm not a very good housekeeper. Ellen's standards are a lot higher than mine. Making beds made no 23 sense to me, but I made them. I cooked, vacuumed, did the wash, the dishes—all the traditional woman's chores. And I also did all of the traditional man's chores, like taking care of the vehicles.

I don't think I failed as a parent, but the situation got the better of me. The things I was used to doing—operating heavy equipment, carpentry, logging—I could not do as a house husband. I thought I would do more reading, but I didn't. I thought I might do some writing, but I didn't. You have to watch a child constantly. 24

One day Emma was playing on the floor at my feet. She coughed, and I asked, "What's the matter?" She looked real confused, and seemed to grow more confused as seconds passed. I picked her up and realized she wasn't breathing and that she was in a panic. I tipped her upside down and patted her on the back, and out popped a penny that had gotten lodged in her throat. From that day on, I never left her alone for a minute. 25

Parenting is probably one of the most confusing and difficult things that people do. It's certainly different from changing a tire. You realize right at the start that you're dealing with a human being, and you draw on reserves of patience you didn't know you had. As you grow into the role, you're captured by your experience of childhood with your own parents, trying not to repeat what you feel they did wrong but to recreate what they did right. You think you've got to be the best parent in the world, and you're confused when you realize you're not—which is pretty often. 26

The whole experience sobered me, but it's taught me to love more completely. I love Emma right to death, and I'm doing the best I can to bring her up with dignity. 27

Discussion and Writing Questions

1. Examine the "frustration quotient" of these men as house husbands. Which seems most happily adapted to life at home? Which seems least happily adapted? Why?
2. A well-known feminist, Betty Friedan, has warned that a simple exchange of roles would be unproductive—a trading of one gender-defined prison for another. How would you characterize the role exchanges of the three men whose testimonies you have read?
3. Assuming for the moment that you will marry, what are your expectations for working life? If you're a woman, do you plan to work? What happens if you have a child? Would you continue working? If you're a man, how important will your job be relative to the work of running a home and raising kids? What views will you have of your spouse's working?
4. Examine the gender roles in your family when you were a child. Who took on which roles? How do these roles compare with those you've read about in "Who's Minding the Children"?

Tom's Husband

SARAH ORNE JEWETT

In the short story "Tom's Husband," Sarah Orne Jewett gives us a fictional account of a marriage in which husband and wife exchange traditional gender roles. As you will see, both Tom and Mary Wilson are temperamentally suited to the exchange: Tom likes the pleasures of home life and as a bachelor managed his household well; Mary has "a most uncommon business talent." You might expect that tensions develop, and they do. As you read, determine the extent to which this story, published first in 1884, accurately describes the relations of men and women today.

Born in 1849 in South Berwick, Maine, Sarah Orne Jewett became one of the foremost writers of regional fiction in nineteenth century America. She depicted the scenery, people, and customs of rural Maine realistically, with sympathy and humor. Though childhood illnesses kept her from obtaining much formal education, the young Jewett read extensively. She was particularly influenced by the works of Tolstoy, Henry James, and Harriet Beecher Stowe—whose stylistic techniques she drew from when writing her many character sketches. Jewett was nineteen when she sold her first story to a children's magazine. Numerous stories and poems followed in such magazines as The Atlantic Monthly: *by the end of her life, she had produced more than twenty volumes, most notably* A Country Doctor *(1884) and* The Country of the Pointed Firs *(1896), her most critically acclaimed work. As you will see in "Tom's Husband," she is known for her depiction of strong, memorable women characters. Jewett died at her home in Maine in 1909.*

I shall not dwell long upon the circumstances that led to the marriage of my hero and heroine; though their courtship was, to them, the only one that has ever noticeably approached the ideal, it had many aspects in which it was entirely commonplace in other people's eyes. While the world in general smiles at lovers with kindly approval and sympathy, it refuses to be aware of the unprecedented delight which is amazing to the lovers themselves. 1

But, as has been true in many other cases, when they were at last married, the most ideal of situations was found to have been changed to the most practical. Instead of having shared their original duties, and, as school-boys would say, going halves, they discovered that the 2

"Tom's Husband" by Sarah Orne Jewett from pp. 51–67 in *Working Women: An Anthology of Stories and Poems,* edited by Nancy Hoffman and Florence Howe (Old Westbury: The Feminist Press, 1979).

cares of life had been doubled. This led to some distressing moments for both our friends; they understood suddenly that instead of dwelling in heaven they were still upon earth, and had made themselves slaves to new laws and limitations. Instead of being freer and happier than ever before, they had assumed new responsibilities; they had established a new household, and must fulfill in some way or another the obligations of it. They looked back with affection to their engagement; they had been longing to have each other to themselves, apart from the world, but it seemed that they never felt so keenly that they were still units in modern society. Since Adam and Eve were in Paradise, before the devil joined them, nobody has had a chance to imitate that unlucky couple. In some respects they told the truth when, twenty times a day, they said that life had never been so pleasant before; but there were mental reservations on either side which might have subjected them to the accusation of lying. Somehow, there was a little feeling of disappointment, and they caught themselves wondering—though they would have died sooner than confess it—whether they were quite so happy as they had expected. The truth was, they were much happier than people usually are, for they had an uncommon capacity for enjoyment. For a little while they were like a sail-boat that is beating and has to drift a few minutes before it can catch the wind and start off on the other tack. And they had the same feeling, too, that any one is likely to have who has been long pursuing some object of his ambition or desire. Whether it is a coin, or a picture, or a stray volume of some old edition of Shakespeare, or whether it is an office under government or a lover, when fairly in one's grasp there is a loss of the eagerness that was felt in pursuit. Satisfaction, even after one has dined well, is not so interesting and eager a feeling as hunger.

My hero and heroine were reasonably well established to begin 3
with: they each had some money, though Mr. Wilson had most. His father had at one time been a rich man, but with the decline, a few years before, of manufacturing interests, he had become, mostly through the fault of others, somewhat involved; and at the time of his death his affairs were in such a condition that it was still a question whether a very large sum or a moderately large one would represent his estate. Mrs. Wilson, Tom's step-mother, was somewhat of an invalid; she suffered severely at times with asthma, but she was almost entirely relieved by living in another part of the country. While her husband lived, she had accepted her illness as inevitable, and rarely left home; but during the last few years she had lived in Philadelphia with her own people, making short and wheezing visits only from time to time, and had not undergone a voluntary period of suffering since the occasion of Tom's marriage, which she had entirely approved. She had a sufficient property of her own, and she and

Tom were independent of each other in that way. Her only other step-child was a daughter, who had married a navy officer, and had at this time gone out to spend three years (or less) with her husband, who had been ordered to Japan.

It is not unfrequently noticed that in many marriages one of the 4
persons who choose each other as partners for life is said to have thrown himself or herself away, and the relatives and friends look on with dismal forebodings and ill-concealed submission. In this case it was the wife who might have done so much better, according to public opinion. She did not think so herself, luckily, either before mariage or afterward, and I do not think it occurred to her to picture to herself the sort of career which would have been her alternative. She had been an only child, and had usually taken her own way. Some one once said that it was a great pity that she had not been obliged to work for her living, for she had inherited a most uncommon business talent, and, without being disreputably keen at a bargain, her insight into the practical working of affairs was very clear and far-reaching. Her father, who had also been a manufacturer, like Tom's, had often said it had been a mistake that she was a girl instead of a boy. Such executive ability as hers is often wasted in the more contracted sphere of women, and is apt to be more a disadvantage than a help. She was too independent and self-reliant for a wife; it would seem at first thought that she needed a wife herself more than she did a husband. Most men like best the women whose natures cling and appeal to theirs for protection. But Tom Wilson, while he did not wish to be protected himself, liked these very qualities in his wife which would have displeased some other men; to tell the truth, he was very much in love with his wife just as she was. He was a successful collector of almost everything but money, and during a great part of his life he had been an invalid, and he had grown, as he laughingly confessed, very old-womanish. He had been badly lamed, when a boy, by being caught in some machinery in his father's mill, near which he was idling one afternoon, and though he had almost entirely outgrown the effect of his injury, it had not been until after many years. He had been in college, but his eyes had given out there, and he had been obliged to leave in the middle of his junior year, though he had kept up a pleasant intercourse with the members of his class, with whom he had been a great favorite. He was a good deal of an idler in the world. I do not think his ambition, except in the case of securing Mary Dunn for his wife, had ever been distinct; he seemed to make the most he could of each day as it came, without making all his days' works tend toward some grand result, and go toward the upbuilding of some grand plan and purpose. He consequently gave no promise of being either distinguished or great. When his eyes would allow, he was an indefatigable reader; and

although he would have said that he read only for amusement, yet he amused himself with books that were well worth the time he spent over them.

The house where he lived nominally belonged to his step-mother, 5
but she had taken for granted that Tom would bring his wife home to it, and assured him that it should be to all intents and purposes his. Tom was deeply attached to the old place, which was altogether the pleasantest in town. He had kept bachelor's hall there most of the time since his father's death, and he had taken great pleasure, before his marriage, in refitting it to some extent, though it was already comfortable and furnished in remarkably good taste. People said of him that if it had not been for his illnesses, and if he had been a poor boy, he probably would have made something of himself. As it was, he was not very well known by the townspeople, being somewhat reserved, and not taking much interest in their every-day subjects of conversation. Nobody liked him so well as they liked his wife, yet there was no reason why he should be disliked enough to have much said about him.

After our friends had been married for some time, and had 6
outlived the first strangeness of the new order of things, and had done their duty to their neighbors with so much apparent willingness and generosity that even Tom himself was liked a great deal better than he ever had been before, they were sitting together one stormy evening in the library, before the fire. Mrs. Wilson had been reading Tom the letters which had come to him by the night's mail. There was a long one from his sister in Nagasaki, which had been written with a good deal of ill-disguised reproach. She complained of the smallness of the income of her share in her father's estate, and said that she had been assured by American friends that the smaller mills were starting up everywhere, and beginning to do well again. Since so much of their money was invested in the factory, she had been surprised and sorry to find by Tom's last letters that he had seemed to have no idea of putting in a proper person as superintendent, and going to work again. Four per cent on her other property, which she had been told she must soon expect instead of eight, would make a great difference to her. A navy captain in a foreign port was obliged to entertain a great deal, and Tom must know that it cost them much more to live than it did him, and ought to think of their interests. She hoped he would talk over what was best to be done with their mother (who had been made executor, with Tom, of his father's will).

Tom laughed a little, but looked disturbed. His wife had said 7
something to the same effect, and his mother had spoken once or twice in her letters of the prospect of starting the mill again. He was not a bit of a business man, and he did not feel certain, with the theories which he had arrived at of the state of the country, that it was

safe yet to spend the money which would have to be spent in putting the mill in order. "They think that the minute it is going again we shall be making money hand over hand, just as father did when we were children," he said. "It is going to cost us no end of money before we can make anything. Before father died he meant to put in a good deal of new machinery, I remember. I don't know anything about the business myself, and I would have sold out long ago if I had had an offer that came anywhere near the value. The larger mills are the only ones that are good for anything now, and we should have to bring a crowd of French Canadians here; the day is past for the people who live in this part of the country to go into the factory again. Even the Irish all go West when they come into the country, and don't come to places like this any more."

"But there are a good many of the old work-people down in the village," said Mrs. Wilson. "Jack Towne asked me the other day if you weren't going to start up in the spring." 8

Tom moved uneasily in his chair. "I'll put you in for superintendent, if you like," he said, half angrily, whereupon Mary threw the newspaper at him; but by the time he had thrown it back he was in good humor again. 9

"Do you know, Tom," she said, with amazing seriousness, "that I believe I should like nothing in the world so much as to be the head of a large business? I hate keeping house—I always did; and I never did so much of it in all my life put together as I have since I have been married. I suppose it isn't womanly to say so, but if I could escape from the whole thing I believe I should be perfectly happy. If you get rich when the mill is going again, I shall beg for a housekeeper, and shirk everything. I give you fair warning. I don't believe I keep this house half so well as you did before I came here." 10

Tom's eyes twinkled. "I am going to have that glory,—I don't think you do, Polly; but you can't say that I have not been forbearing. I certainly have not told you more than twice how we used to have things cooked. I'm not going to be your kitchen-colonel." 11

"Of course it seemed the proper thing to do," said his wife, meditatively, "but I think we should have been even happier than we have if I had been spared it. I have had some days of wretchedness that I shudder to think of. I never know what to have for breakfast; and I ought not to say it, but I don't mind the sight of dust. I look upon housekeeping as my life's great discipline"; and at this pathetic confession they both laughed heartily. 12

"I've a great mind to take it off your hands," said Tom. "I always rather liked it, to tell the truth, and I ought to be a better housekeeper—I have been at it for five years; though housekeeping for one is different from what it is for two, and one of them a woman. You see you have brought a different element into my family. Luckily, the 13 servants are pretty well drilled. I do think you upset them a good deal at first!"

Mary Wilson smiled as if she only half heard what he was saying. She drummed with her foot on the floor and looked intently at the fire, and presently gave it a vigorous poking. "Well?" said Tom, after he had waited patiently as long as he could. 14

"Tom! I'm going to propose something to you. I wish you would really do as you said, and take all the home affairs under your care, and let me start the mill. I am certain I could manage it. Of course I should get people who understood the thing to teach me. I believe I was made for it; I should like it above all things. And this is what I will do: I will bear the cost of starting it, myself—I think I have money enough, or can get it; and if I have not put affairs in the right trim at the end of a year I will stop, and you may make some other arrangement. If I have, you and your mother and sister can pay me back." 15

"So I am going to be the wife, and you the husband," said Tom, a little indignantly, "at least, that is what people will say. It's a regular Darby and Joan affair, and you think you can do more work in a day than I can do in three. Do you know that you must go to town to buy cotton? And do you know there are a thousand things about it that you don't know?" 16

"And never will?" said Mary, with perfect good humor. "Why, Tom, I can learn as well as you, and a good deal better, for I like business, and you don't. You forget that I was always father's right-hand man after I was a dozen years old, and that you have let me invest my money and some of your own, and I haven't made a blunder yet." 17

Tom thought that his wife had never looked so handsome or so happy. "I don't care, I should rather like the fun of knowing what people will say. It is a new departure, at any rate. Women think they can do everything better than men in these days, but I'm the first man, apparently, who has wished he were a woman." 18

"Of course people will laugh," said Mary, "but they will say that it's just like me, and think I am fortunate to have married a man who will let me do as I choose. I don't see why it isn't sensible: you will be living exactly as you were before you married, as to home affairs; and since it was a good thing for you to know something about housekeeping then, I can't imagine why you shouldn't go on with it now, since it makes me miserable, and I am wasting a fine business talent while I do it. What do we care for people's talking about it?" 19

"It seems to me that it is something like women's smoking: it isn't wicked, but it isn't the custom of the country. And I don't like the idea of your going among business men. Of course I should be above going with you, and having people think I must be an idiot; they would say that you married a manufacturing interest, and I was 20 thrown in. I can foresee that my pride is going to be humbled to the dust in every way," Tom declared in mournful tones, and began to shake with laughter. "It is one of your lovely castles in the air, dear Polly, but an old brick mill needs a better foundation than the clouds. No, I'll look around, and get an honest, experienced man for agent. I suppose it's the best thing we can do, for the machinery ought not to lie still any longer; but I mean to sell the factory as soon as I can. I devoutly wish it would take fire, for the insurance would be the best price we are likely to get. That is a famous letter from Alice! I am afraid the captain has been growling over his pay, or they have been giving too many little dinners on board ship. If we were rid of the mill, you and I might go out there this winter. It would be capital fun."

Mary smiled again in an absent-minded way. Tom had an uneasy 21 feeling that he had not heard the end of it yet, but nothing more was said for a day or two. When Mrs. Tom Wilson announced, with no apparent thought of being contradicted, that she had entirely made up her mind, and she meant to see those men who had been overseers of the different departments, who still lived in the village, and have the mill put in order at once, Tom looked disturbed, but made no opposition; and soon after breakfast his wife formally presented him with a handful of keys, and told him there was some lamb in the house for dinner; and presently he heard the wheels of her little phaeton rattling off down the road. I should be untruthful if I tried to persuade any one that he was not provoked; he thought she would at least have waited for his formal permission, and at first he meant to take another horse, and chase her, and bring her back in disgrace, and put a stop to the whole thing. But something assured him that she knew what she was about, and he determined to let her have her own way. If she failed, it might do no harm, and this was the only ungallant thought he gave her. He was sure that she would do nothing unladylike, or be unmindful of his dignity; and he believed it would be looked upon as one of her odd, independent freaks, which always had won respect in the end, however much they had been laughed at in the beginning. "Susan," said he, as that estimable person went by the door with the dust-pan, "you may tell Catherine to come to me for orders about the house, and you may do so yourself. I am going to take charge again, as I did before I was married. It is no trouble to me, and Mrs. Wilson dislikes it. Besides, she is going into business, and will have a great deal else to think of."

"Yes, sir; very well, sir," said Susan, who was suddenly moved to 22 ask so many questions that she was utterly silent. But her master looked very happy; there was evidently no disapproval of his wife; and she went on up the stairs, and began to sweep them down, knocking the dust-brush about excitedly, as if she were trying to kill a descending colony of insects.

Tom went out to the stable and mounted his horse, which had been waiting for him to take his customary after-breakfast ride to the post-office, and he galloped down the road in quest of the phaeton. He saw Mary talking with Jack Towne, who had been an overseer and a valued workman of his father's. He was looking much surprised and pleased. 23

"I wasn't caring so much about getting work, myself," he explained; "I've got what will carry me and my wife through; but it'll be better for the young folks about here to work near home. My nephews are wanting something to do; they were going to Lynn next week. I don't say but I should like to be to work in the old place again. I've sort of missed it, since we shut down." 24

"I'm sorry I was so long in overtaking you," said Tom, politely, to his wife. "Well, Jack, did Mrs. Wilson tell you she's going to start the mill? You must give her all the help you can." 25

" 'Deed I will," said Mr. Towne, gallantly, without a bit of astonishment. 26

"I don't know much about the business yet," said Mrs. Wilson, who had been a little overcome at Jack Towne's lingo of the different rooms and machinery, and who felt an overpowering sense of having a great deal before her in the next few weeks. "By the time the mill is ready, I will be ready, too," she said, taking heart a little; and Tom, who was quick to understand her moods, could not help laughing, as he rode alongside. "We want a new barrel of flour, Tom, dear," she said, by way of punishment for his untimely mirth. 27

If she lost courage in the long delay, or was disheartened at the steady call for funds, she made no sign; and after a while the mill started up, and her cares were lightened, so that she told Tom that before next pay day she would like to go to Boston for a few days, and go to the theatre, and have a frolic and a rest. She really looked pale and thin, and she said she never worked so hard in all her life; but nobody knew how happy she was, and she was so glad she had married Tom, for some men would have laughed at it. 28

"I laughed at it," said Tom, meekly. "All is, if I don't cry by and by because I am a beggar, I shall be lucky." But Mary looked fearlessly serene, and said that there was no danger at present. 29

It would have been ridiculous to expect a dividend the first year, though the Nagasaki people were pacified with difficulty. All the business letters came to Tom's address, and everybody who was not directly concerned thought that he was the motive power of the reawakened enterprise. Sometimes business people came to the mill, and were amazed at having to confer with Mrs. Wilson, but they soon 30 had to respect her talents and her success. She was helped by the old clerk, who had been promptly recalled and reinstated, and she certainly did capitally well. She was laughed at, as she had expected to be, and people said they should think Tom would be ashamed of himself; but it soon appeared that he was not to blame, and what reproach was offered was on the score of his wife's oddity. There was nothing about the mill that she did not understand before very long, and at the end of the second year she declared a small dividend with great pride and triumph. And she was congratulated on her success, and every one thought of her project in a different way from the way they had thought of it in the beginning. She had singularly good fortune: at the end of the third year she was making money for herself and her friends faster than most people were, and approving letters began to come from Nagasaki. The Ashtons had been ordered to stay in that region, and it was evident that they were continually being obliged to entertain more instead of less. Their children were growing fast, too, and constantly becoming more expensive. The captain and his wife had already begun to congratulate themselves secretly that their two sons would in all probability come into possession, one day, of their uncle Tom's handsome property.

For a good while Tom enjoyed life, and went on his quiet way 31
serenely. He was anxious at first, for he thought that Mary was going to make ducks and drakes of his money and her own. And then he did not exactly like the looks of the thing, either; he feared that his wife was growing successful as a business person at the risk of losing her womanliness. But as time went on, and he found there was no fear of that, he accepted the situation philosophically. He gave up his collection of engravings, having become more interested in one of coins and medals, which took up most of his leisure time. He often went to the city in pursuit of such treasures, and gained much renown in certain quarters as a numismatologist of great skill and experience. But at last his house (which had almost kept itself, and had given him little to do beside ordering the dinners, while faithful old Catherine and her niece Susan were his aids) suddenly became a great care to him. Catherine, who had been the main-stay of the family for many years, died after a short illness, and Susan must needs choose that time, of all others, for being married to one of the second hands in the mill. There followed a long and dismal season of experimenting, and for a time there was a procession of incapable creatures going in at one kitchen door and out of the other. His wife would not have liked to say so, but it seemed to her that Tom was growing fussy about the house affairs, and took more notice of those minor details than he used. She wished more than once, when she was tired, that he would not talk so much about the house-keeping; he seemed sometimes to have no other thought.

In the early days of Mrs. Wilson's business life, she had made it a rule to consult her husband on every subject of importance; but it had speedily proved to be a formality. Tom tried manfully to show a deep interest which he did not feel, and his wife gave up, little by little, telling him much about her affairs. She said that she liked to drop business when she came home in the evening; and at last she fell into the habit of taking a nap on the library sofa, while Tom, who could not use his eyes much by lamp-light, sat smoking or in utter idleness before the fire. When they were first married his wife had made it a rule that she should always read him the evening papers, and afterward they had always gone on with some book of history or philosophy, in which they were both interested. These evenings of their early married life had been charming to both of them, and from time to time one would say to the other that they ought to take up again the habit of reading together. Mary was so unaffectedly tired in the evening that Tom never liked to propose a walk; for, though he was not a man of peculiarly social nature, he had always been accustomed to pay an occasional evening visit to his neighbors in the village. And though he had little interest in the business world, and still less knowledge of it, after a while he wished that his wife would have more to say about what she was planning and doing, or how things were getting on. He thought that her chief aid, old Mr. Jackson, was far more in her thoughts than he. She was forever quoting Jackson's opinions. He did not like to find that she took it for granted that he was not interested in the welfare of his own property; it made him feel like a sort of pensioner and dependent, though, when they had guests at the house, which was by no means seldom, there was nothing in her manner that would imply that she thought herself in any way the head of the family. It was hard work to find fault with his wife in any way, though, to give him his due, he rarely tried. 32

But, this being a wholly unnatural state of things, the reader must expect to hear of its change at last, and the first blow from the enemy was dealt by an old woman, who lived near by, and who called to Tom one morning, as he was driving down to the village in a great hurry (to post a letter, which ordered his agent to secure a long-wished-for ancient copper coin, at any price), to ask him if they had made yeast that week, and if she could borrow a cupful, as her own had met with some misfortune. Tom was instantly in a rage, and he mentally condemned her to some undeserved fate, but told her aloud to go and see the cook. This slight delay, besides being killing to his dignity, caused him to lose the mail, and in the end his much-desired copper coin. It was a hard day for him, altogether; it was Wednesday, and the first days of the week having been stormy the washing was very late. And Mary came home to dinner provokingly good-natured. 33

She had met an old school-mate and her husband driving home from the mountains, and had first taken them over her factory, to their great amusement and delight, and then had brought them home to dinner. Tom greeted them cordially, and manifested his usual graceful hospitality; but the minute he saw his wife alone he said in a plaintive tone of rebuke, "I should think you might have remembered that the servants are unusually busy to-day. I do wish you would take a little interest in things at home. The women have been washing, and I'm sure I don't know what sort of a dinner we can give your friends. I wish you had thought to bring home some steak. I have been busy myself, and couldn't go down to the village. I thought we would only have a lunch."

Mary was hungry, but she said nothing, except that it would be all right—she didn't mind; and perhaps they could have some canned soup. 34

She often went to town to buy or look at cotton, or to see some improvement in machinery, and she brought home beautiful bits of furniture and new pictures for the house, and showed a touching thoughtfulness in remembering Tom's fancies; but somehow he had an uneasy suspicion that she could get along pretty well without him when it came to the deeper wishes and hopes of her life, and that her most important concerns were all matters in which he had no share. He seemed to himself to have merged his life in his wife's; he lost his interest in things outside the house and grounds; he felt himself fast growing rusty and behind the times, and to have somehow missed a good deal in life; he had a suspicion that he was a failure. One day the thought rushed over him that his had been almost exactly the experience of most women, and he wondered if it really was any more disappointing and ignominious to him than it was to women themselves. "Some of them may be contented with it," he said to himself, soberly. "People think women are designed for such careers by nature, but I don't know why I ever made such a fool of myself." 35

Having once seen his situation in life from such a standpoint, he felt it day by day to be more degrading, and he wondered what he should do about it; and once, drawn by a new, strange sympathy, he went to the little family burying-ground. It was one of the mild, dim days that come sometimes in early November, when the pale sunlight is like the pathetic smile of a sad face, and he sat for a long time on the limp, frost-bitten grass beside his mother's grave. 36

But when he went home in the twilight his step-mother, who just then was making them a little visit, mentioned that she had been looking through some boxes of hers that had been packed long before and stowed away in the garret. "Everything looks very nice up there," she said, in her wheezing voice (which, worse than usual that day, always made him nervous); and added, without any intentional 37 slight to his feelings, "I do think you have always been a most excellent housekeeper."

"I'm tired of such nonsense!" he exclaimed, with surprising in- 38
dignation. "Mary, I wish you to arrange your affairs so that you can leave them for six months at least. I am going to spend this winter in Europe."

"Why, Tom, dear!" said his wife, appealingly. "I couldn't leave 39
my business any way in the—"

But she caught sight of a look on his usually placid countenance 40
that was something more than decision, and refrained from saying anything more.

And three weeks from that day they sailed. 41

Discussion and Writing Questions

1. Were you surprised at all by the story's ending? Put another way: Had the final five or six paragraphs been omitted, what would you have guessed the story's ending to be?
2. At first, Tom is exceedingly good humored and cooperative about the arrangement that Mary Wilson proposes. But the good humor does not last, even when Mary succeeds in the mill. What has happened to Tom?
3. To the extent that you can determine it, what changes have come over Mary as a result of her involvement in the family business? How well has she balanced the dual roles of breadwinner and wife? What pressures does she face?
4. Mary Wilson privately thinks that Tom has grown fussy and that he talks about the housekeeping too much. Tom thinks that Mary talks about the business too much, that she's lost interest in their domestic affairs. Your comments?
5. Any number of sentences in the story might have been written by the three house husbands (Dana Crowe, David Hildt, and Pat Welch). Identify a few of these sentences and comment on them.
6. What reception do you imagine the story getting in 1884, when it was published? How does this reception compare with the one you've given it?

SYNTHESIS ACTIVITIES

1. You have seen evidence of an exchange of traditional gender roles in "Tom's Husband" and in "Who's Minding the Children?" Drawing on these sources, argue your position on the importance of maintaining distinct male and female gender identities. Questions you might want to address: Are distinctions between male and female gender roles of any use economically? Psychologically? Sociologically?

During the planning stage of your paper, recall that as in any argument you will draw on sources to support *your* conclusions; your ideas should be paramount. For example, if you wanted to explore the economic and sociological uses of distinct gender identities, you would want to settle in your own mind just what these uses are and your opinion of them before drawing on any of the authors in this chapter. Realize, also, that your thesis may well incite debate in your class. So anticipate opposing arguments. Raise them and respond to them in your paper.

2. Write a descriptive essay of a day in your life—assuming you were a member of the opposite sex. Work in pairs on this assignment, one man and one woman to a pair. Exchange descriptions and then verbally critique one another's work. How accurate has your partner been in depicting life as a woman or a man? As part of your paper for formal submission to the instructor, describe as well the discussion you and your partner have had over your day-in-the-life description.

   You face challenges in completing this assignment: to imagine the *physical, emotional, psychological,* or *sexual* consequences of living as a member of the opposite sex. If you plan to take up more than one of these challenges in your description, you should do so in distinct stages, in an order than seems sensible to you.

   Feel free to use the first person "I" in narrating your description—in which case the writing would read as a journal entry or letter. Alternately, you might feel more comfortable describing your "new" gender self from a distance—in which case you would use the third person "he" or "she."

3. Recall Cheryl Merser quoting a friend: "I thought marriage would be . . . one 'thing' with two people inside. With us—it's more like two separate marriages, his and mine." Based on your reading in this chapter, define a good (if not ideal) marriage. What are the rights and responsibilities of the partners—to themselves and to one another? Sources to consider: "Men, Women, Equality, and Love"; "Who's Minding the Children?"; "Tom's Husband"; and "Is the New Man a Wimp?"

   One way to begin the paper might be with a critique of some prime-time, situation comedy that portrays a happily married couple. You might discuss what seems realistic or not in that portrayal, and then make a transition to the marriage you'd like to help create.

4. Reflect on the household of your childhood and define the gender-role identities of your parent(s) or guardian(s). Once you've completed these definitions, comment on them, based on your reading in this chapter.

   If a single individual raised you, consider how that person took to himself or herself both masculine and feminine roles. If two people raised you, examine the gender dynamics: Who worked outside the home? Who stayed in with the kids, mostly? What interests aside from work and family did your parents pursue, individually and together? What were the topics of conversation and how did these topics reveal (in retrospect) gender-role typing?

5. A variation on Question 4. Consider a recent dating relationship of yours. As best you can, define the gender roles of you and your friend and then comment on these roles, based on your reading in this chapter.

6. Julius Lester and Masters/Johnson/Kolodny discuss the social pressures brought to bear on individuals throughout their younger lives to conform to gender-specific identities. Use the observations of these authors to help recall your own gender-role socialization. How did you learn—through what process did you learn—to become the man or woman that you are?

   At the beginning or end of your paper, you'll need to describe your present gender identity. (What sort of male or female do you see yourself as being—how traditionally assertive, intuitive, emotional, etc.?) Your tracing of your gender-role socialization (the part of the paper in which you identify and discuss stages of gender development) will either extend away from or build toward your characterization of your (present) gender identity.

THE BRAVE NEW WORLD OF GENETIC ENGINEERING

10

> As recently as fifty years ago, the world was plagued by devastating food shortages and by numerous physical and mental diseases. Hundreds of millions of people suffered blighted lives and early deaths. Today, all that has changed. Using our gene splicing techniques, we can dramatically increase agricultural yields and protect our crops from frost and other blights. And since we know exactly what sequence of genetic information is necessary to produce perfect people, we can make sure that all humans are born without defect by examining their genetic makeup while they are still fetuses and correcting any abnormalities we find.

This is a paragraph from an imaginary textbook of the future. It paints a rosy picture of what the most avid proponents of genetic engineering view as our future prospects. Of course, the future may not be so bright. As we have seen in Suzucki and Knudtson's article in Chapter 1 on summary, one of our genetic legacies to the future may be an enhanced ability to fight biological wars. And as for "perfect" people—just what do we mean by "imperfect"? (A fetus carrying a gene for schizophrenia? A fetus with only one arm? A fetus with the probability of somewhat low intelligence?) And who is to determine what is "perfect?"

The moral dilemmas now enveloping genetic engineering would not be so hotly debated if the technology itself were not so remarkable—and effective. Thanks to its successes so far—in making possible, for instance, the cheap and plentiful production of such disease-fighting agents as insulin and interferon—numerous people have been able to live longer and healthier lives. Its promise in improved agricultural production is exciting. And even without considering the practical consequences, we have the prospect of a new world of knowledge about life itself and the essential components of our own humanity, our own individuality, as revealed in our distinctive genetic codes.

The foundation of genetic engineering was laid in 1953 when James Watson, an American, and Francis Crick, a Briton, published a landmark article in the scientific journal *Nature,* revealing for the first time the double-helix structure of the DNA molecule—the basis of all life. Genes—sequences of nucleic acids—are formed out of DNA. The particular and distinctive sequence of nucleic acids in the gene (part of the organism's "genetic code") determines its function and characteristics. Genes carry information not only about physical characteristics but also about how the organism will progress through its life cycle; and just as important, they are the basis of the hereditary information that is transmitted from one generation to another.

Genetic engineering is essentially a kind of crossbreeding at the genetic level. It is sometimes called "gene splicing" because the process involves isolating and removing a gene with a certain desired function (for example, to generate a certain antibody) from the cell of one organism and then "splicing" it into the genetic material (lacking this desired function) of a second organism. The spliced DNA is then reinserted into the cell of the second organism. When the "engineered" cell divides, the new cells contain the desired genetic information, and so the physical characteristics of the host organism will change, according to its new genetic instructions.

To make a crude mechanical analogy, consider two necklaces, one small, the other large. Suppose you take a blue bead from the small necklace and insert it into the space where you want a blue bead to go on the larger necklace. In the process, you might also remove a misplaced red bead on the larger necklace. Then you use the repaired large necklace as a model for making other necklaces just like it.

Gene splicing experiments began in the early 1970s, at first involving DNA exchanges between unicellular organisms, such as viruses and bacteria. But recipients of "foreign" DNA soon included more complex organisms, such as fruit flies and frogs (although no humans, at this stage). During this early period of experimentation, some began to worry about the possibility of a genetic disaster. What if some newly engineered microbes escaped from the lab and caused an epidemic of some new and unknown disease, for which there was no known cure? What if the delicate ecological balance of nature or the course of evolution were drastically affected? Some proposed an outright ban on genetic engineering experiments. At an international conference in Asilomar, California, in 1975, scientists agreed on a set of guidelines to govern future research. These guidelines specified what type of research could be performed in what labs. (Genetic labs were categorized into four types, depending on their level of physical containment, ranging from P1 [minimal-risk] to P4 [high-risk].)

In time, these early fears turned out to be groundless, and the restrictions were eased or lifted. Meantime, considerable strides were made in genetic engineering, with new applications discovered in agriculture, pollution control, and the fight against a host of diseases. Genetic engineering became big business, as many scientists abandoned the academy to found and work for firms with names like Genentech and Genex.

But reservations persist. Some are uncomfortable with the fact of genetic engineering itself, considering it an unwarranted intrusion by human beings into the fragile structure of Nature, with too little knowledge or care about the consequences. Others are comfortable enough with genetic engineering, as long as the donors or recipients of new DNA are not humans. (To experiment with human genetic material carries too many horrendous connotations—

from Aldous Huxley's *Brave New World* to the Nazis' eugenics programs that resulted in the exaltation of an Aryan "master race" and the extermination of "inferior" races.) But for most, the problem is not so much genetic engineering itself as the possible abuses of this new technology in particular applications. As *Time* writer Philip Elmer-DeWitt notes, "To unlock the secrets hidden in the chromosomes of human cells is to open up a host of thorny legal, ethical, philosophical and religious issues, from invasion of privacy and discrimination to the question of who should play God with man's genes."

Some of these thorny issues are explored in the following pages. You may already have read (in the first chapter on summary) David Suzucki and Peter Knudtson's article, "Biological Weapons:A Dark Side of the New Genetics." In the present chapter, the first passage—which since its composition has served as an unforgettable warning to those who value social stability at any price—is the opening section of Aldous Huxley's novel *Brave New World.* Here we see fertilized human ova conditioned before birth so that they will eventually serve as productive and contented citizens. Next, Richard V. Kowles explains the scientific process of recombinant DNA in "Genetic Engineering: How It's Done." Following Kowles, Dennis Chamberland's "Genetic Engineering: Promise and Threat" surveys the chief advantages and disadvantages of this new technology. Next, in "Perfect People" Amy Virshup focuses on prospective parents as they decide whether or not to have their fetus tested for genetic defects. (If defects are found, should they abort the fetus?) In "The Total Gene Screen," Morton Hunt considers the problems involved in the genetic testing of prospective employees. Should such tests be required? Whose benefit do they serve? Next, we will hear from perhaps the chief opponent of genetic engineering—activist Jeremy Rifkin, who has successfully blocked a number of bioengineering programs. An excerpt from Rifkin's recent book *Algeny* is followed by a *Science Digest* interview with Rifkin. Next, biologist Stephen Jay Gould launches a blistering critique of Rifkin's book. Then, the editors of *The New Republic,* in an editorial entitled "What Price Mighty Mouse?" consider the commercial applications of genetic engineering and, in particular, the advantages of patenting newly engineered animals. Finally, in a somewhat whimsical essay, physician and science writer Lewis Thomas expresses his thoughts "On Cloning a Human Being."

Brave New World

ALDOUS HUXLEY

The title of Aldous Huxley's novel Brave New World *derives from a line in Shakespeare's final comedy,* The Tempest. *Miranda is a young woman who has grown up on an enchanted island; her father is the only other human she has known. When she suddenly encounters people from the outside world (including a handsome young prince), she remarks, "O brave [wondrous] new world that has such people in it!" Shakespeare used the line ironically (the world of* The Tempest *is filled with knaves and fools); and almost 300 years later, Huxley employed not only the language but also the irony in labeling his nightmare society of 632* A.F. *(After [Henry] Ford).*

In comparison with other dystopias, like George Orwell's 1984*, Huxley's brave new world of creature comforts seems, at first glance, a paradise. People are given whatever they need to keep happy: unlimited sex, tranquilizers, and soothing experiences. No one goes hungry; no one suffers either physical or spiritual pain. But the cost of such comfort is an almost total loss of individuality, creativity, and freedom. Uniformity and stability are exalted above all other virtues. The population is divided into castes, determined from before birth, with the more intelligent Alphas and Betas governing and managing the society, while the less intelligent Deltas, Gammas, and Epsilons work at the menial tasks. Epsilons are not unhappy with their lot in life because they have been conditioned to be content; and in fact, they are incapable of conceiving anything better. Love, art, and science are suppressed for all castes because they lead to instability, and instability threatens happiness. Idle reflection is discouraged for the same reason; and to avoid the effects of any intense emotions, positive or negative, the inhabitants of brave new world are given regular doses of the powerful tranquilizer "soma."*

Huxley's brave new world, then, is a projection into the future of tendencies he saw in his own world that he thought were disturbing or dangerous. In the context of our present chapter on genetic engineering, we are most interested in Huxley's portrait of a "hatchery," where fertilized human ova—removed from the womb—are programmed before "birth" to produce an assortment of the kind of people who will be most desirable to society. In the following passage, the first chapter of Brave New World *(1932), we are taken on a tour through the Central London Hatchery and Conditioning Centre, where we follow an egg from fertilization through conditioning. To many people today, Huxley's dramatic portrait of the manipulation of human germ cells is uncomfortably close to what modern genetic engineers are beginning, with ever greater facility, to make possible: the substitution of "more desirable" for "less desirable" genes in order to create "better" people.*

Born in Surrey, England, Aldous Huxley (1894–1963), grandson of naturalist T. H. Huxley, intended to pursue a medical career; but after being stricken with a corneal disease that left him almost blind, he turned to literature. Among his works are Crome Yellow *(1921),* Antic Hay *(1923),* Point Counterpoint *(1928), and* Eyeless in Gaza *(1936). Huxley moved to the United States in 1936, settling in California. In the latter part of his life, he tended toward the mystical and experimented with naturally occurring hallucinogenic drugs—the subject of his* Doors of Perception *(1954).*

A squat grey building of only thirty-four stories. Over the main entrance the words, CENTRAL LONDON HATCHERY AND CONDITIONING CENTRE, and, in a shield, the World State's motto, COMMUNITY, IDENTITY, STABILITY. 1

The enormous room on the ground floor faced towards the north. Cold for all the summer beyond the panes, for all the tropical heat of the room itself, a harsh thin light glared through the windows, hungrily seeking some draped lay figure, some pallid shape of academic goose-flesh, but finding only the glass and nickel and bleakly shining porcelain of a laboratory. Wintriness responded to wintriness. The overalls of the workers were white, their hands gloved with a pale corpse-coloured rubber. The light was frozen, dead, a ghost. Only from the yellow barrels of the microscopes did it borrow a certain rich and living substance, lying along the polished tubes like butter, streak after luscious streak in long recession down the work tables. 2

"And this," said the Director opening the door, "is the Fertilizing Room." 3

Bent over their instruments, three hundred Fertilizers were plunged, as the Director of Hatcheries and Conditioning entered the room, in the scarcely breathing silence, the absent-minded, soliloquizing hum or whistle, of absorbed concentration. A troop of newly arrived students, very young, pink and callow, followed nervously, rather abjectly, at the Director's heels. Each of them carried a notebook, in which, whenever the great man spoke, he desperately scribbled. Straight from the horse's mouth. It was a rare privilege. The D.H.C. for Central London always made a point of personally conducting his new students round the various departments. 4

"Just to give you a general idea," he would explain to them. For of course some sort of general idea they must have, if they were to do their work intelligently—though as little of one, if they were to be good and happy members of society, as possible. For particulars, as every one knows, make for virtue and happiness; generalities are intellectually necessary evils. Not philosophers but fret-sawyers and stamp collectors compose the backbone of society. 5

"To-morrow," he would add, smiling at them with a slightly menacing geniality, "you'll be settling down to serious work. You won't have time for generalities. Meanwhile . . ." 6

Meanwhile, it was a privilege. Straight from the horse's mouth into the notebook. The boys scribbled like mad. 7

Tall and rather thin but upright, the Director advanced into the 8
room. He had a long chin and big, rather prominent teeth, just covered, when he was not talking, by his full, floridly curved lips. Old, young? Thirty? Fifty? Fifty-five? It was hard to say. And anyhow the question didn't arise; in this year of stability, A.F. 632, it didn't occur to you to ask it.

"I shall begin at the beginning," said the D.H.C. and the more 9
zealous students recorded his intention in their notebooks: *Begin at the beginning.* "These," he waved his hand, "are the incubators." And opening an insulated door he showed them racks upon racks of numbered test-tubes. "The week's supply of ova. Kept," he explained, "at blood heat; whereas the male gametes," and here he opened another door, "they have to be kept at thirty-five instead of thirty-seven. Full blood heat sterilizes." Rams wrapped in theremogene beget no lambs.

Still leaning against the incubators he gave them, while the pen- 10
cils scurried illegibly across the pages, a brief description of the modern fertilizing process; spoke first, of course, of its surgical introduction—"the operation undergone voluntarily for the good of Society, not to mention the fact that it carries a bonus amounting to six months' salary"; continued with some account of the technique for preserving the excised ovary alive and actively developing; passed on to a consideration of optimum temperature, salinity, viscosity; referred to the liquor in which the detached and ripened eggs were kept; and, leading his charges to the work tables, actually showed them how this liquor was drawn off from the test-tubes; how it was let out drop by drop onto the specially warmed slides of the microscopes; how the eggs which it contained were inspected for abnormalities, counted and transferred to a porous receptacle; how (and he now took them to watch the operation) this receptacle was immersed in a warm bouillon containing free-swimming spermatozoa—at a minimum concentration of one hundred thousand per cubic centimetre, he insisted; and how, after ten minutes, the container was lifted out of the liquor and its contents re-examined; how, if any of the eggs remained unfertilized, it was again immersed, and, if necessary, yet again; how the fertilized ova went back to the incubators; where the Alphas and Betas remained until definitely bottled; while the Gammas, Deltas and Epsilons were brought out again, after only thirty-six hours, to undergo Bokanovsky's Process.

"Bokanovsky's Process," repeated the Director, and the students 11
underlined the words in their little notebooks.

One egg, one embryo, one adult—normality. But a bokanov- 12
skified egg will bud, will proliferate, will divide. From eight to ninety-six buds, and every bud will grow into a perfectly formed embryo,

and every embryo into a full-sized adult. Making ninety-six human beings grow where only one grew before. Progress.

"Essentially," the D.H.C. concluded, "bokanovskification consists of a series of arrests of development. We check the normal growth and, paradoxically enough, the egg responds by budding." 13

Responds by budding. The pencils were busy. 14

He pointed. On a very slowly moving band a rack-full of test-tubes was entering a large metal box, another rack-full was emerging. Machinery faintly purred. It took eight minutes for the tubes to go through, he told them. Eight minutes of hard X-rays being about as much as an egg can stand. A few died; of the rest, the least susceptible divided into two; most put out four buds; some eight; all were returned to the incubators, where the buds began to develop; then, after two days, were suddenly chilled, chilled and checked. Two, four, eight, the buds in their turn budded; and having budded were dosed almost to death with alcohol; consequently burgeoned again and having budded—bud out of bud out of bud—were thereafter—further arrest being generally fatal—left to develop in peace. By which time the original egg was in a fair way to becoming anything from eight to ninety-six embryos—a prodigious improvement, you will agree, on nature. Identical twins—but not in piddling twos and threes as in the old viviparous days, when an egg would sometimes accidentally divide; actually by dozens, by scores at a time. 15

"Scores," the Director repeated and flung out his arms, as though he were distributing largesse. "Scores." 16

But one of the students was fool enough to ask where the advantage lay. 17

"My good boy!" The Director wheeled sharply round on him. "Can't you see? Can't you *see*?" He raised a hand; his expression was solemn. "Bokanovsky's Process is one of the major instruments of social stability!" 18

Major instruments of social stability. 19

Standard men and women; in uniform batches. The whole of a small factory staffed with the products of a single bokanovskified egg. 20

"Ninety-six identical twins working ninety-six identical machines!" The voice was almost tremulous with enthusiasm. "You really know where you are. For the first time in history." He quoted the planetary motto. "Community, Identity, Stability." Grand words. "If we could bokanovskify indefinitely the whole problem would be solved." 21

Solved by standard Gammas, unvarying Deltas, uniform Epsilons. Millions of identical twins. The principle of mass production at last applied to biology. 22

"But, alas," the Director shook his head, "we *can't* bokanovskify indefinitely." 23

24 Ninety-six seemed to be the limit; seventy-two a good average. From the same ovary and with gametes of the same male to manufacture as many batches of identical twins as possible—that was the best (sadly a second best) that they could do. And even that was difficult.

25 "For in nature it takes thirty years for two hundred eggs to reach maturity. But our business is to stabilize the population at this moment, here and now. Dribbling out twins over a quarter of a century—what would be the use of that?"

26 Obviously, no use at all. But Podsnap's Technique had immensely accelerated the process of ripening. They could make sure of at least a hundred and fifty mature eggs within two years. Fertilize and bokanovskify—in other words, multiply by seventy-two—and you get an average of nearly eleven thousand brothers and sisters in a hundred and fifty batches of identical twins, all within two years of the same age.

27 "And in exceptional cases we can make one ovary yield us over fifteen thousand adult individuals."

28 Beckoning to a fair-haired, ruddy young man who happened to be passing at the moment, "Mr. Foster," he called. The ruddy young man approached. "Can you tell us the record for a single ovary, Mr. Foster?"

29 "Sixteen thousand and twelve in this Centre," Mr. Foster replied without hesitation. He spoke very quickly, had a vivacious blue eye, and took an evident pleasure in quoting figures. "Sixteen thousand and twelve; in one hundred and eighty-nine batches of identicals. But of course they've done much better," he rattled on, "in some of the tropical Centres. Singapore had often produced over sixteen thousand five hundred; and Mombasa has actually touched the seventeen thousand mark. But then they have unfair advantages. You should see the way a negro ovary responds to pituitary! It's quite astonishing, when you're used to working with European material. Still," he added, with a laugh (but the light of combat was in his eyes and the lift of his chin was challenging), "still, we mean to beat them if we can. I'm working on a wonderful Delta-Minus ovary at this moment. Only just eighteen months old. Over twelve thousand seven hundred children already, either decanted or in embryo. And still going strong. We'll beat them yet."

30 "That's the spirit I like!" cried the Director, and clapped Mr. Foster on the shoulder. "Come along with us and give these boys the benefit of your expert knowledge."

31 Mr. Foster smiled modestly. "With pleasure." They went.

32 In the Bottling Room all was harmonious bustle and ordered activity. Flaps of fresh sow's peritoneum ready cut to the proper size came shooting up in little lifts from the Organ Store in the

subbasement. Whizz and then, click! the lift-hatches flew open; the bottle-liner had only to reach out a hand, take the flap, insert, smooth-down, and before the lined bottle had had time to travel out of reach along the endless band, whizz, click! another flap of peritoneum had shot up from the depths, ready to be slipped into yet another bottle, the next of that slow interminable procession on the band.

Next to the Liners stood the Matriculators. The procession advanced; one by one the eggs were transferred from their test-tubes to the larger containers; deftly the peritoneal lining was slit, the morula dropped into place, the saline solution poured in . . . and already the bottle had passed, and it was the turn of the labellers. Heredity, date of fertilization, membership of Bokanovsky Group—details were transferred from test-tube to bottle. No longer anonymous, but named, identified, the procession marched slowly on; on through an opening in the wall, slowly on into the Social Predestination Room. 33

"Eighty-eight cubic metres of card-index," said Mr. Foster with relish, as they entered. 34

"Containing *all* the relevant information," added the Director. 35

"Brought up to date every morning." 36

"And co-ordinated every afternoon." 37

"On the basis of which they make their calculations." 38

"So many individuals, of such and such quality," said Mr. Foster. 39

"Distributed in such and such quantities." 40

"The optimum Decanting Rate at any given moment." 41

"Unforeseen wastages promptly made good." 42

"Promptly," repeated Mr. Foster. "If you knew the amount of overtime I had to put in after the last Japanese earthquake!" He laughed good-humouredly and shook his head. 43

"The Predestinators send in their figures to the Fertilizers." 44

"Who give them the embryos they ask for." 45

"And the bottles come in here to be predestinated in detail." 46

"After which they are sent down to the Embryo Store." 47

"Where we now proceed ourselves." 48

And opening a door Mr. Foster led the way down a staircase into the basement. 49

The temperature was still tropical. They descended into a thickening twilight. Two doors and a passage with a double turn insured the cellar against any possible infiltration of the day. 50

"Embryos are like photograph film," said Mr. Foster waggishly, as he pushed open the second door. "They can only stand red light." 51

And in effect the sultry darkness into which the students now followed him was visible and crimson, like the darkness of closed eyes on a summer's afternoon. The bulging flanks of row on receding row and tier above tier of bottles glinted with innumerable rubies, 52 and among the rubies moved the dim red spectres of men and women with purple eyes and all the symptoms of lupus. The hum and rattle of machinery faintly stirred the air.

"Give them a few figures, Mr. Foster," said the Director, who was tired of talking. 53

Mr. Foster was only too happy to give them a few figures. 54

Two hundred and twenty metres long, two hundred wide, ten high. He pointed upwards. Like chickens drinking, the students lifted their eyes towards the distant ceiling. 55

Three tiers of racks: ground floor level, first gallery, second gallery. 56

The spidery steel-work of gallery above gallery faded away in all directions into the dark. Near them three red ghosts were busily unloading demijohns from a moving staircase. 57

The escalator from the Social Predestination Room. 58

Each bottle could be placed on one of fifteen racks, each rack, though you couldn't see it, was a conveyor travelling at the rate of thirty-three and a third centimetres an hour. Two hundred and sixty-seven days at eight metres a day. Two thousand one hundred and thirty-six metres in all. One circuit of the cellar at ground level, one on the first gallery, half on the second, and on the two hundred and sixty-seventh morning, daylight in the Decanting Room. Independent existence—so called. 59

"But in the interval," Mr. Foster concluded, "we've managed to do a lot to them. Oh, a very great deal." His laugh was knowing and triumphant. 60

"That's the spirit I like," said the Director once more. "Let's walk round. You tell them everything, Mr. Foster." 61

Mr. Foster duly told them. 62

Told them of the growing embryo on its bed of peritoneum. Made them taste the rich blood surrogate on which it fed. Explained why it had to be stimulated with placentin and thyroxin. Told them of the *corpus luteum* extract. Showed them the jets through which at every twelfth metre from zero to 2040 it was automatically injected. Spoke of those gradually increasing doses of pituitary administered during the final ninety-six metres of their course. Described the artificial maternal circulation installed on every bottle at Metre 112; showed them the reservoir of blood-surrogate, the centrifugal pump that kept the liquid moving over the placenta and drove it through the synthetic lung and waste-product filter. Referred to the embryo's troublesome tendency to anæmia, to the massive doses of hog's stomach extract and fetal foal's liver with which, in consequence, it had to be supplied. 63

Showed them, the simple mechanism by means of which, during the last two metres out of every eight, all the embryos were 64 simultaneously shaken into familiarity with movement. Hinted at the gravity of the so-called "trauma of decanting," and enumerated the precautions taken to minimize, by a suitable training of the bottled embryo, that dangerous shock. Told them of the tests for sex carried out in the neighbourhood of metre 200. Explained the system of labelling—a T for the males, a circle for the females and for those who were destined to become freemartins a question mark, black on a white ground.

"For of course," said Mr. Foster, "in the vast majority of cases, 65
fertility is merely a nuisance. One fertile ovary in twelve hundred—that would really be quite sufficient for our purposes. But we want to have a good choice. And of course one must always leave an enormous margin of safety. So we allow as many as thirty per cent of the female embryos to develop normally. The others get a dose of male sex-hormone every twenty-four metres for the rest of the course. Result: they're decanted as freemartins—structurally quite normal ("except," he had to admit, "that they *do* have just the slightest tendency to grow beards), but sterile. Guaranteed sterile. Which brings us at last," continued Mr. Foster, "out of the realm of mere slavish imitation of nature into the much more interesting world of human invention."

He rubbed his hands. For of course, they didn't content them- 66
selves with merely hatching out embryos: any cow could do that.

"We also predestine and condition. We decant our babies as 67
socialized human beings, as Alphas or Epsilons, as future sewage workers or future . . ." He was going to say "future World controllers," but correcting himself, said "future Directors of Hatcheries," instead.

The D.H.C. acknowledged the compliment with a smile. 68

They were passing Metre 320 on rack 11. A young Beta-Minus 69
mechanic was busy with screwdriver and spanner on the blood-surrogate pump of a passing bottle. The hum of the electric motor deepened by fractions of a tone as he turned the nuts. Down, down . . . A final twist, a glance at the revolution counter, and he was done. He moved two paces down the line and began the same process on the next pump.

"Reducing the number of revolutions per minute," Mr. Foster 70
explained. "The surrogate goes round slower; therefore passes through the lung at longer intervals; therefore gives the embryo less oxygen. Nothing like oxygen-shortage for keeping an embryo below par." Again he rubbed his hands.

"But why do you want to keep the embryo below par?" asked an 71
ingenuous student.

"Ass!" said the Director, breaking a long silence. "Hasn't it oc- 72
curred to you that an Epsilon embryo must have an Epsilon environment as well as an Epsilon heredity?"

It evidently hadn't occurred to him. He was covered with confu- 73
sion.

"The lower the caste," said Mr. Foster, "the shorter the oxygen." 74
The first organ affected was the brain. After that the skeleton. At seventy per cent of normal oxygen you got dwarfs. At less than seventy eyeless monsters.

"Who are no use at all," concluded Mr. Foster. 75

Whereas (his voice became confidential and eager), if they could 76
discover a technique for shortening the period of maturation what a triumph, what a benefaction to Society!

"Consider the horse." 77

They considered it. 78

Mature at six; the elephant at ten. While at thirteen a man is not 79
yet sexually mature; and is only full-grown at twenty. Hence, of course, that fruit of delayed development, the human intelligence.

"But in Epsilons," said Mr. Foster very justly, "we don't need 80
human intelligence."

Didn't need and didn't get it. But though the Epsilon mind was 81
mature at ten, the Epsilon body was not fit to work till eighteen. Long years of superfluous and wasted immaturity. If the physical development could be speeded up till it was as quick, say, as a cow's what an enormous saving to the Community!

"Enormous!" murmured the students. Mr. Foster's enthusiasm 82
was infectious.

He became rather technical; spoke of the abnormal endocrine 83
co-ordination which made men grow so slowly; postulated a germinal mutation to account for it. Could the effects of this germinal mutation be undone? Could the individual Epsilon embryo be made a revert, by a suitable technique, to the normality of dogs and cows? That was the problem. And it was all but solved.

Pilkington, at Mombasa, had produced individuals who were 84
sexually mature at four and full-grown at six and a half. A scientific triumph. But socially useless. Six-year-old men and women were too stupid to do even Epsilon work. And the process was an all-or-nothing one; either you failed to modify at all, or else you modified the whole way. They were still trying to find the ideal compromise between adults of twenty and adults of six. So far without success. Mr. Foster sighed and shook his head.

Their wanderings through the crimson twilight had brought them 85
to the neighbourhood of Metre 170 on Rack 9. From this point

onwards Rack 9 was enclosed and the bottles performed the remainder of their journey in a kind of tunnel, interrupted here and there by openings two or three metres wide.

"Heat conditioning," said Mr. Foster. 86

Hot tunnels alternated with cool tunnels. Coolness was wedded to 87
discomfort in the form of hard X-rays. By the time they were decanted the embryos had a horror of cold. They were predestined to emigrate to the tropics, to be miners and acetate silk spinners and steel workers. Later on their minds would be made to endorse the judgment of their bodies. "We condition them to thrive on heat," concluded Mr. Foster. "Our colleagues upstairs will teach them to love it."

"And that," put in the Director sententiously, "that is the secret of 88
happiness and virtue—liking what you've *got* to do. All conditioning aims at that: making people like their unescapable social destiny."

In a gap between two tunnels, a nurse was delicately probing with 89
a long fine syringe into the gelatinous contents of a passing bottle. The students and their guides stood watching her for a few moments in silence.

"Well, Lenina," said Mr. Foster, when at last she withdrew the 90
syringe and straightened herself up.

The girl turned with a start. One could see that, for all the lupus 91
and the purple eyes, she was uncommonly pretty.

"Henry!" Her smile flashed redly at him—a row of coral teeth. 92

"Charming, charming," murmured the Director and, giving her 93
two or three little pats, received in exchange a rather deferential smile for himself.

"What are you giving them?" asked Mr. Foster, making his tone 94
very professional.

"Oh, the usual typhoid and sleeping sickness." 95

"Tropical workers start being inoculated at Metre 150," Mr. Foster 96
explained to the students. "The embryos still have gills. We immunize the fish against the future man's diseases." Then, turning back to Lenina, "Ten to five on the roof this afternoon," he said, "as usual."

"Charming," said the Director once more, and, with a final pat, 97
moved away after the others.

On Rack 10 rows of next generation's chemical workers were being 98
trained in the toleration of lead, caustic soda, tar, chlorine. The first of a batch of two hundred and fifty embryonic rocket-plane engineers was just passing the eleven hundred metre mark on Rack 3. A special mechanism kept their containers in constant rotation. "To improve their sense of balance," Mr. Foster explained. "Doing repairs on the outside of a rocket in mid-air is a ticklish job. We slacken off the circulation when they're right way up, so that they're half

starved, and double the flow of surrogate when they're upside down. They learn to associate topsy-turvydom with well-being; in fact, they're only truly happy when they're standing on their heads.

"And now," Mr. Foster went on, "I'd like to show you some very interesting conditioning for Alpha Plus Intellectuals. We have a big batch of them on Rack 5. First Gallery level," he called to two boys who had started to go down to the ground floor. 99

"They're round about Metre 900," he explained. "You can't really do any useful intellectual conditioning till the fetuses have lost their tails. Follow me." 100

But the Director had looked at his watch. "Ten to three," he said. "No time for the intellectual embryos, I'm afraid. We must go up to the Nurseries before the children have finished their afternoon sleep." 101

Mr. Foster was disappointed. "At least one glance at the Decanting Room," he pleaded. 102

"Very well then." The Director smiled indulgently. "Just one glance." 103

Review Questions

1. What is the Bokanovsky Process? Why is it central to Huxley's "brave new world"?
2. How does Huxley comment sardonically on the racism of the Hatcher's personnel—and of Europeans, in general?
3. What is the difference—and the social significance of the difference—between Alphas, Betas, Deltas, Gammas, and Epsilons?
4. What technological problems concerning the maturation process have the scientists of brave new world still not solved?

Discussion and Writing Suggestions

1. How does the language of the first two paragraphs reveal Huxley's tone, that is, his attitude toward his subject? For example, what is the function of the word "only" in the opening sentence: "A squat grey building of only thirty-four stories"? Or the adjectives describing the building?
2. What does the narrator mean when he says (paragraph 5) that "particulars, as every one knows, make for virtue and happiness; generalities are intellectually necessary evils. Not philosophers but fret-sawyers [operators of fret-saws, long, narrow, fine-toothed hand saws used for ornamental detail work] and stamp collectors compose the backbone of society"? To what extent do you believe that such an ethic operates in our own society? Give examples of the relatively low value placed on "philosophers" and the relatively high value placed on "fret-swayers."

3. Throughout this chapter, Huxley makes an implied contrast between the brisk, technological efficiency of the Hatchery and the ethical nature of what takes place within its walls. What aspects of our own civilization show similar contrasts? (Example: We are now able to build more technologically sophisticated weapons of destruction than ever before in history.) Explore this subject in an essay, devoting a paragraph or so to each aspect of our civilization that you consider.
4. In the Hatchery, bottled, fertilized eggs pass into the "Social Predestination Room." In that room, their future lives will be determined. Is there an equivalent of the Social Predestination Room in our own society? (In other words, are there times and places when and where our future lives are determined?) If so, describe its features, devoting a paragraph to each of these features.
5. Foster explains how the undecanted embryos are conditioned to adapt to certain environments—for instance, conditioned to like heat so that, years later, they will feel comfortable working in the tropics or working as miners; or they may be conditioned to improve their sense of balance, so that they will be able to repair rockets in midair. What evidence do you see in our own society that people are or will be subject to conditioning to "like their unescapable social destiny"? Consider, for example, the influence of the conditioning exerted by parents, siblings, teachers, friends, or various social institutions. If you have lived or traveled abroad, what evidence do you see that conditioning is different in the United States than in other countries? Explore this subject in a multiparagraph essay.
6. As we noted in the headnote, Huxley's *Brave New World* (like much science fiction) is a projection into the future of comtemporary aspects of culture that the author finds disturbing or dangerous. Select some present aspect of our culture that *you* find disturbing or dangerous and—in the form of a short story, or chapter from a novel, or section from a screenplay—dramatize your vision of what *could* happen.

Genetic Engineering: How It's Done

RICHARD V. KOWLES

Many of the public policy dilemmas of our modern world—the use of nuclear weapons, for example, or the debate about when to "pull the plug" on persons near death—have arisen as a direct result of recent and often spectacular scientific breakthroughs. This is clearly true of genetic

"Genetic Engineering Methods" from *Genetics, Society and Dicisions* by Richard V. Kowles.

engineering, now considered one of the most revolutionary scientific achievements of the century. Most of our chapter will deal with various aspects of the public policy debate surrounding genetic engineering. But we thought it would be illuminating to precede these discussions with a scientific description of just what is entailed in this process.

The following passage first appeared in the textbook Genetics, Society, and Decisions *(1985). Richard V. Kowles teaches biology and genetics at Saint Mary's College in Winona, Minnesota.*

Note: *Certain terms that may be unfamiliar to you (in some cases printed in boldface) appear in the glossary at the end of the article.*

Only thirty years ago, we knew very little about the gene. Watson and Crick had just discovered the structure of DNA. The secrets of transcription and translation were undiscovered. In the years to follow, however, the genetic code was elucidated. Researchers next began to unravel some of the gene's control mechanisms and to better understand the nature of mutation and differentiation. By the 1970s, people were already recalling Aldous Huxley's *Brave New World,* with its mechanical wombs and chemical predestination. Were geneticists acquiring the power to play God? Some found such genetic progress exciting. Others became frightened and cautious of genetic advances. 1

What are the possibilities of the branch of biological technology we call **genetic engineering**? This branch of study includes the deliberate manipulation of the genetic material, repairing, modifying, deleting, adding, and exchanging the pieces of DNA called genes. The techniques are powerful, and they will certainly revolutionize biology. 2

GENETIC ENGINEERING METHODS

Many molecular biologists have concentrated on transferring segments of DNA from one organism to another. The process has four main steps: 3

1. The isolation, or synthesis, of the DNA segment or gene to be transferred;
2. The cloning or propagation of the DNA segment;
3. The transfer of the DNA segment to the host cell or organism; and
4. The stabilization of the DNA segment in its new surroundings.

Scientists have conquered the many problems associated with these tasks in work with one-celled bacteria. However, some 4

technical difficulties must be overcome before this kind of technique
can be routinely applied in humans and other higher forms of life.

DNA segments can be isolated and purified. Often, these seg- 5
ments comprise specific genes and once their base sequences are
known, they can be synthesized *in vitro.* Initially, the synthesis of a
gene was so time-consuming that only very small genes could be
assembled. H. G. Khorana and his colleagues first developed the
procedures, synthesized a gene of 207 base pairs, and showed it to
have the appropriate activity. Today, faster and more efficient techniques are available, including computerized "gene machines" that
automatically construct specified DNA segments. Researchers now
have the biochemical tools for obtaining the particular DNA segments
they need for their genetic engineering work.

Once a DNA segment has been isolated, it can be replicated to give 6
the researcher enough copies for the additional genetic engineering
steps. This replication or propagation is called **gene cloning.** It depends on **recombinant DNA** techniques, which allow DNA from various sources to be joined. Researchers often join DNA segments to
specific bacterial DNA structures called **plasmids.** When they return
the recombinant plasmids to the bacteria and allow the bacteria to
multiply, the plasmids and their inserted passengers multiply too.
Later, they can recover many copies of the specific DNA segment. We
will consider the technology of recombinant DNA in more detail below.

In bacteria, plants or animals, genetic engineering requires some 7
way to transfer genes into cells. Current methods of gene transfer
include:

1. Incubation of host cells with the purified DNA segments to be transferred;
2. Injection of the purified DNA directly into the nuclei of the host cells;
3. Injection of the whole chromosomes, in some cases, or their transfer by **cell fusion** techniques; and
4. The use of **vectors** to carry DNA segments into the host cells. The chief vectors are plasmids and viruses. Plasmids are small, circular, self-replicating DNA moelcules often found in bacteria; they are not part of the regular bacterial chromosome. Figure 1 shows the position of plasmids in a bacterial cell.

The introduction and incorporation of foreign DNA into a recipient 8
cell by exposing the cells to purfied DNA and its subsequent expression in those cells is called **transformation.** The basic concept of
transformation by this method is shown diagrammatically in Figure 2.
This type of transformation event is usually rare. When a phenotypic
change does occur in the host cells, it is often difficult to demonstrate

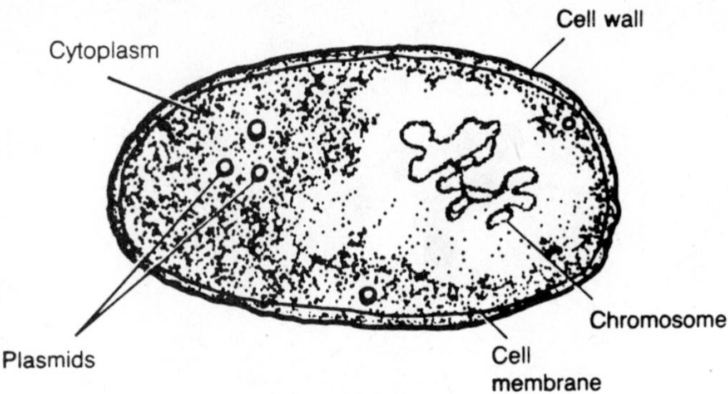

Figure 1
Bacterial genes lie not only on their chromosome, but also on plasmids. Four such plasmids are shown here.

that the foreign DNA has actually been incorporated into the host DNA. Transformation has been most successful with one-celled organisms or cell suspensions, although scattered success with injecting the DNA into whole higher organisms has been reported. Adding calcium phosphate to the mixture of host cells and donor DNA considerably improves the chances for successful transformation. With plant cells, it helps to remove the cell walls first. In a few cases, whole metaphase chromosomes have been effectively transferred from donor cells to host cells.

One can also inject donor DNA directly into host cell nuclei, 9
using an extremely small pipette, or **micropipette.** Some cells will survive the treatment, and the efficiency of DNA transfer is usually better than the methods described above. This method has proved quite successful in mouse experiments.

Cell fusion techniques have provided still another way to transfer 10
genes. The techniques now permit almost any two types of somatic cells, plant or animal, to be fused *in vitro*. The resulting hybrid cell contains the nuclei and the chromosomal materials of both parental cells. Generally, one set of chromosomes degrades in the cytoplasm. When the nuclei fuse, subsequent cell divisions will lose most of the chromosomes of one set. Nonetheless, one or more chromosomes of the lost set often remain in the hybrid cell; or in some cases, their fragments are integrated into the whole chromosomes of the surviving set. This sequence of events is illustrated in Figure 3. The technique has proved most useful in mapping genes to particular chromosomes. It has not yet provided any therapeutic applications in humans, but it is certainly promising enough to warrant further study.

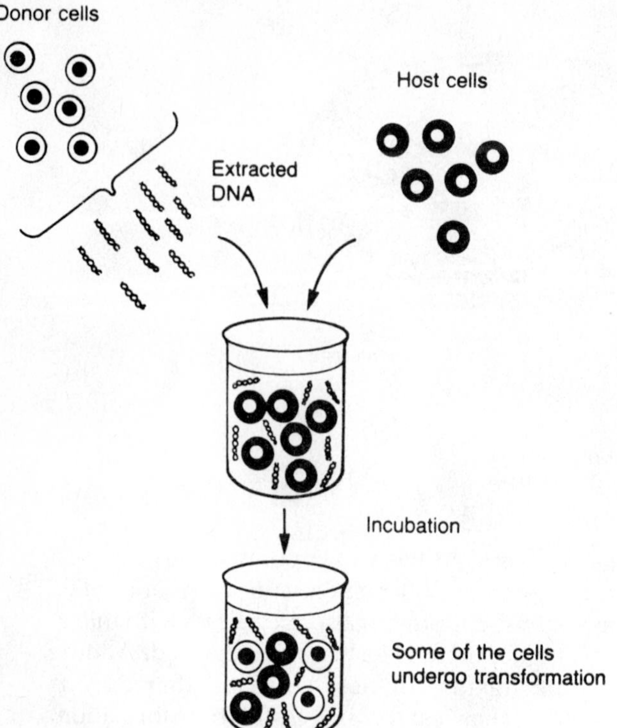

Figure 2
The basic mechanism of transformation through DNA-mediated gene transfer.

Viruses can also be used to carry DNA from a donor cell to a host cell. Unlike the **virulent** viruses that kill the cells they infect, some viruses can infect a host cell without killing it. All viruses insert their DNA into the host cell, where it causes the host cell to manufacture new virus particles. Ultimately, the new viruses are released by bursting or **lysing** the host cell. They can then infect other cells. Occasionally, viral DNA incorporates host-cell DNA during the infection. After lysis, the virus can carry the host DNA to a new host cell, as shown in Figure 4. If the virus does not kill the second host, it can give it a new functional gene. Molecular biologists have found such viruses useful for gene transfers. 11

The final requirement for successful genetic engineering is that the newly inserted gene or genes function in a stable manner. That is, they must be expressed properly. Many genetic engineering techniques allow little control over (1) what genes will be transferred, 12

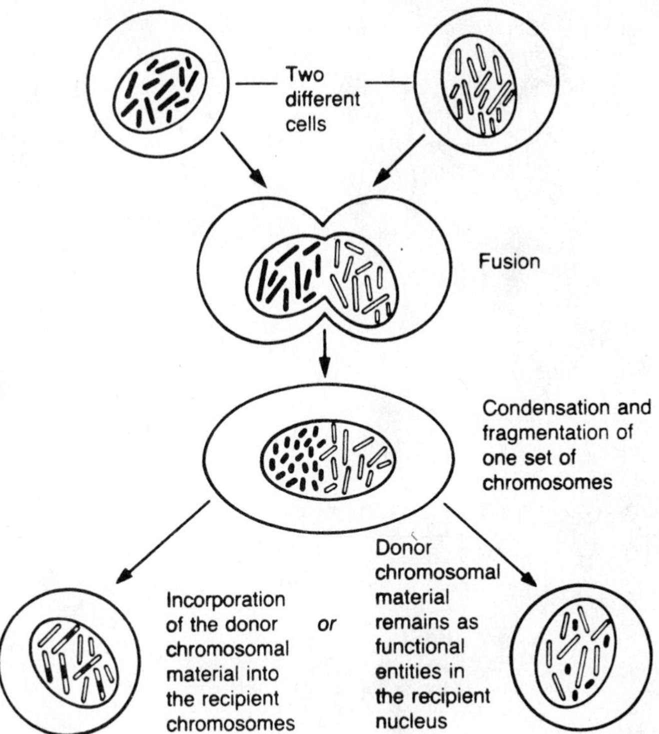

Figure 3
Cell fusion as a possible means of effecting gene transfer.

(2) where they will integrate in the host DNA, or (3) how they will behave after they are transferred. A gene may be expressed differently depending on where it is located on the host cell's chromosomes. This differential expression is the **position effect.** A second problem is that when a gene is placed in the host cell with all its control regions intact, the newly inserted control regions may regulate other adjacent host genes in an abnormal way. Gene control is still one of the substantial unknowns in this kind of work. The systems involved appear to be very complex and sensitive.

Recombinant DNA techniques used with bacterial plasmids offer 13
so effective a means of gene transfer that they have become practically routine, in spite of the controversies surrounding them. To some extent, researchers have even overcome the instability problem. Other techniques are nearing this level of reliability, and we are gradually becoming more effective in placing genes into cells from diverse sources and making them work.

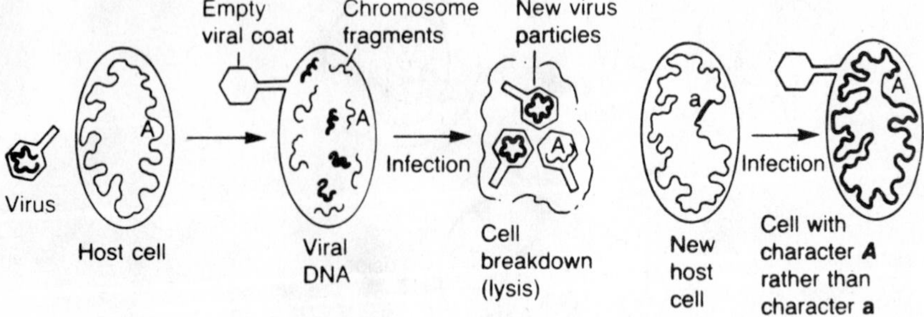

Figure 4
Gene transfer by viral infection of host cells.

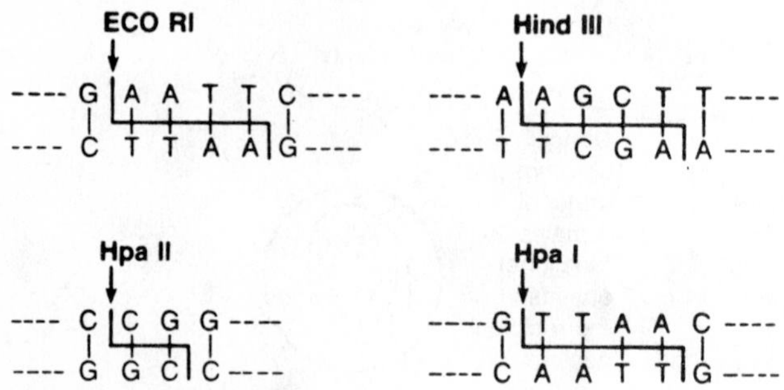

Figure 5
Several examples of restriction endonucleases that cut DNA molecules at points having specific base pair sequences.

THE BASICS OF RECOMBINANT DNA

Recombinant DNA techniques promise the revolutionary ability to 14
move genes from any organism to any other organism and to synthesize new genes as desired. These techniques began to be developed in the early 1970s, when researchers discovered the enzymes known as **restriction endonucleases.** Restriction enzymes are produced by bacteria, from which they can be extracted for use *in vitro.* They cut DNA molecules into smaller pieces, but the divisions are not made at random. Each specific restriction enzyme cuts DNA wherever there is a particular symmetrical sequence of base pairs. Figure 5 shows the sequences recognized and cut by four different restriction enzymes. In each case, the broken ends of the DNA are "sticky" (chemically cohesive); they are short segments of single-stranded DNA which, because of base complementarity, can bind to each other or to the other ends generated when the same enzyme cuts a different DNA

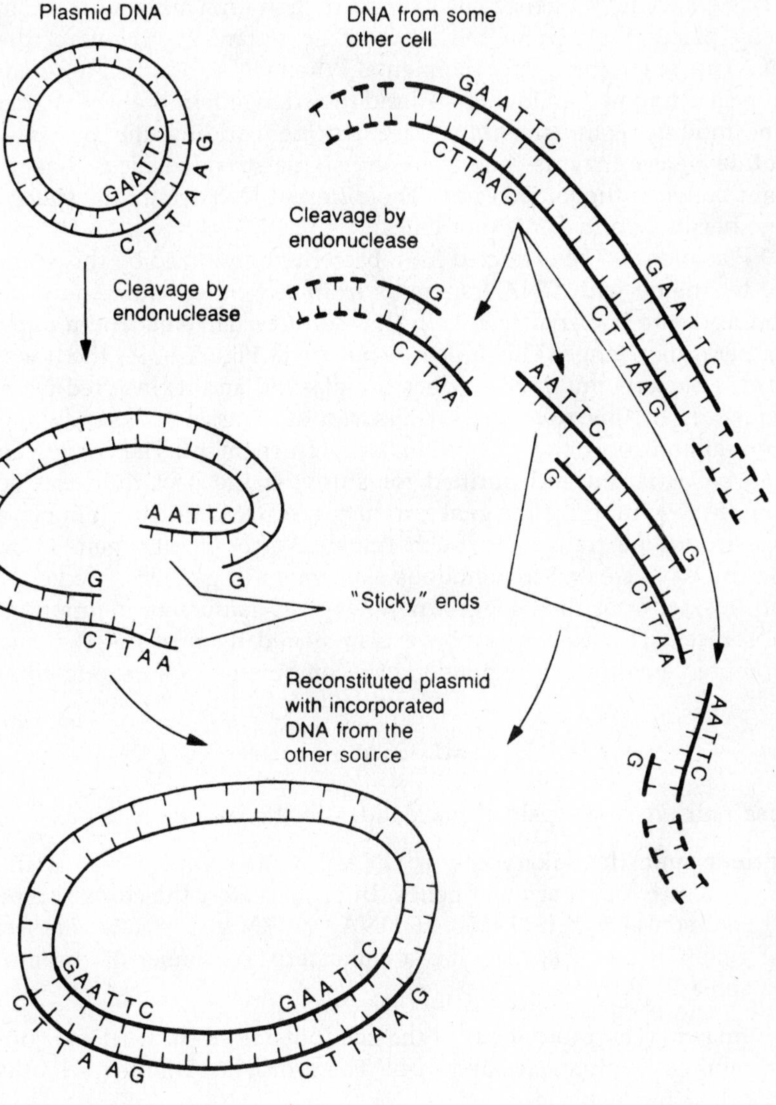

Figure 6
The formation of a hybrid DNA molecule.

molecule at the same base sequence. For example, the restriction endonuclease ECO RI from the bacterium *Escherichia coli* recognizes and cuts DNA to leave the following ends:

The specific sequence cut by a restriction enzyme may occur in 15
many places throughout the DNA of an organism; therefore, the DNA can be cut into many fragments. When DNA from two different sources is fragmented in this way and mixed together, the sticky ends can undergo complementary base pairing. Adding the **polynucleotide ligase** enzyme then seals the single-stranded nicks that remain between the joined ends. The different DNAs are thus spliced together as hybrid DNA molecules.

Plasmids can be extracted from bacteria, hybridized by this splic- 16
ing technique with DNA fragments from any other source, and introduced into bacterial cells with the aid of certain salts and a rapid temperature change. This process appears in Figure 6. As the transformed bacteria multiply, so does the plasmid and its inserted DNA sequence. In this way, researchers can synthesize thousands and even millions of copies of a particular DNA segment. The copies can then be extracted and purified for study. If the bacterium can be induced to synthesize the gene product, the DNA can be left in place as a true gene transplant. Such transplants of foreign genes into bacteria have created trememdous excitement in genetics, medicine, and business, for they suggest new ways to manufacture important substances. However, they have also stirred fears of disaster and prompted government regulation of recombinant DNA experiments.

GLOSSARY

Base pair. A single pair of nucleotides in the genetic material.

Chromosome. In eukaryotes, a DNA-protein complex that is the structure for an array of genes. In prokaryotes, the chromosome is essentially a molecule of DNA, or RNA in a few viruses; generally, each species has a characteristic number of chromosomes.

Cytoplasm. The protoplasm of the cell (outside of the nucleus) containing the organelles of the cell. The protoplasm of the nucleus is called nucleoplasm.

Differentiation. A sequence of changes that are involved in the progressive specialization and diversification of cell types.

Genetic engineering. The intentional manipulation of the content and/or organization of an organism's genetic material.

Hybrid. Several meanings have been adopted. An offspring resulting from a cross between two distinct species. Or an offspring resulting from a cross between parents of the same species that are genetically unlike. Also, the state of heterozygosity at one or more gene loci.

In vitro. Pertaining to experiments performed outside the organism, that is, inside glass vessels.

Nucleotide. An organic compound composed of a purine or pyrimidine base, a pentose sugar, and a phosphate group. The polymeric molecule, a nucleic acid, consists of many of these monomeric units covalently held together in a chain by sugar-phosphate bonds.

Phenotype. The actual appearance or other discernible characteristics of an organism produced by its genotype interacting with the environment.

Plasmid. Autonomously replicating elements found in the cytoplasm of bacteria. Plasmids are nonessential DNA entities.

Polynucleotide ligase. An enzyme that catalyzes the chemical bonding of two segments of an interrupted strand on one side of the DNA duplex molecule.

Purine. A class of nitrogenous bases with a double-ring configuration that occurs in DNA and RNA; commonly, adenine and guanine.

Pyrimidine. A class of nitrogenous bases with a single-ring configuration that occurs in DNA and RNA; commonly, thymine, cytosine, and uracil.

Recombinant DNA. A DNA molecule that is made up of DNA from at least two different individuals, either of the same species or of different species. Such molecules are produced by enzymatically cutting the DNA into pieces from two different sources, and then bonding the pieces so that both sources reside within the same molecule.

Somatic. Pertaining to body cells as opposed to reproductive cells in the germ line. Normally, these cells have two sets of chromosomes, one from each parent.

Transcription. The synthesis of RNA from a DNA template by base pair complementarity.

Translation. The process whereby the genetic information of a particular mRNA nucleotide sequence is converted to a specific sequence of amino acids in a polypeptide chain.

Vector. An agent consisting of a DNA molecule that can replicate autonomously in a cell, such that another DNA segment can be attached to it and be replicated at the same time.

Review Questions

1. Identify the four steps involved in transferring segments of DNA from one organism to another.
2. What are the chief methods of gene transfer?
3. What is the main difference between recombinant DNA and other methods of genetic engineering?
4. What is the function of restriction enzymes in genetic engineering?

Discussion and Writing Suggestions

1. Make a list of everything you don't understand about this passage. In class discussion, try to get some answers on these subjects from your classmates and your instructor. (But be patient with your instructor, who probably does not have a scientific background!)
2. Write a brief (one paragraph) summary of this article.
3. Describe (if possible, in scientific report format) an experiment that you conducted in high school, or that you are conducting now in chemistry, physics, biology, or environmental science. Write in language that your nonscientific readers will be able to follow.

Genetic Engineering: Promise and Threat

DENNIS CHAMBERLAND

During the last few centuries, religion has often been at odds with science. In the seventeenth century, Galileo was condemned by the Catholic church for his belief in a heliocentric solar system, since such a belief denied the prevailing interpretation of Scripture. In the nineteenth century, Darwin's theory of evolution was attacked by the church for the same reason. More recently, religious attacks on scientific developments have been issued as much for ethical as for doctrinal reasons. In the early 1980s a group of Catholic bishops wrote a "pastoral letter" opposing the use of nuclear weapons. And such new technological developments as artificial insemination and in vitro fertilization of human ova have generated concern and opposition not only from the clergy but also from lay people of all faiths. It is therefore not surprising that religious voices are among those most strongly objecting to—or cautioning about—genetic engineering.

In the following article, Dennis Chamberland, a science writer and

---

"Genetic Engineering: Promise and Threat" by Dennis Chamberland. *Christianity Today,* February 7, 1986. Reprinted by permission of the author.

nuclear engineer, explains what genetic engineering is, summarizes its relatively brief history, and discusses both the benefits and the dangers of this new technology. "Genetic Engineering: Promise and Threat" first appeared in Christianity Today, *and accordingly, the article is written from a Christian perspective. Certainly, this fact should not invalidate the article for non-Christians. Chamberland is concerned primarily with the ethical aspects of genetic engineering, and these ethical concerns go beyond particular religious issues. The question is, Now that we have (or are rapidly developing) the technology, what should we do with it? Few would argue, for example, that advances in genetic engineering should not be used to help cure or prevent diseases. But other applications (some of which will be explored in the following articles in this chapter) are more questionable. Is it legitimate, for instance, to test a fetus for genetic defects, a test that may result in termination of the pregnancy? Chamberland does not attempt to answer such questions but rather tries to lay out the issues to his audience by explaining what genetic engineers can do now and what they may be able to do in the future.*

Sometimes uneasy allies, both science and religion seek to improve 1
the lot of mankind. Nevertheless, their conflicting values have often forced them into a showdown.

Now the social and ethical stakes are as high as they have ever 2
been. With even the slightest advances in genetic engineering, such afflictions as cancer, viral diseases, and even certain aspects of the aging process may become curses of the past. Science is carefully unraveling DNA's double helix, probing and mapping the stuff of life. Yet genetic engineering's place in society and its boundaries are ill defined. And the religious community has yet to establish a firm equilibrium with the new, powerful science that has dared to tamper with life's smallest material components.

The genetic engineering debate may well be irreconcilable at the 3
most elemental levels of logic as scientists and moral theologians address each other from different dimensions. But one thing is certain: The ultimate outcome will determine the future shape of humanity.

THE NEW FRONTIER

Biotechnology swept upon us quickly. Most of the advances in genet- 4
ic engineering have come about within five years; the last decade nearly ecompasses its entire history. In a few short years we have moved from obscure x-ray photographs of bacterial DNA (deoxyribonucleic acid) to methods of precisely trimming, clipping, and changing infinitesimal parts of the genetic code itself.

Already gone is the simplistic notion that the expression of genetic information of all life is the same. Now we know that the mechanism of mammalian and bacterial gene expression differs in radically different ways—which suggests an overt complexity and redundancy of higher life we had never dreamed of before. From the four chemical codes of life common to every life form on earth, we have learned how we can change the process that defines our existence. 5

On April 25, 1953, James Watson and Francis Crick published a paper that described for the first time the shape of the DNA molecule. For their insight, they won the Nobel prize. They had successfully initiated a biological revolution by describing the smallest units of life. 6

Watson and Crick had described the DNA molecule as large (for a molecule) and coiled in the shape of a spiral staircase, or double helix. This smallest denominator of life was linked together by only four chemical building blocks whose varied sequence provided a coded blueprint for all life forms on earth from bacteria to humankind. Their discovery, which enabled us to visualize growth and reproduction as a common link between all life, would enable us to change life at its most basic levels. 7

This understanding of the elemental life processes led to the ultimate development of four methods of altering the normal functions of cell replication. This is accomplished by directly changing or interfering with its DNA. 8

Experiments with human life began in 1970. A physician attempted to introduce the gene for production of the enzyme arginase into patients whose bodies were incapable of normally producing the chemical. Otherwise doomed to death, the patients were injected with a virus capable of producing the enzyme. Some evidence had suggested the virus would invade the patients' DNA, be destroyed by the patients' immune system, and leave behind the necessary gene to produce arginase. The experiment's designer, biochemist-physician Stanford Rogers, was wrong. Though his effort was designed to save lives, his failure brought an avalanche of criticism, and he lost much of his research funding. 9

A more elaborate experiment was attempted on July 10, 1980, by a team directed by Dr. Martin Cline, then head of hematology and oncology at UCLA, and an Israeli medical group including Dr. Eliezer Rachmilewitz at Jerusalem's Hadassah Hospital. 10

Rachmilewitz's patients were born with a rare but fatal blood disease called beta zero thalassemia. Cline's treatment consisted of injecting their bone marrow with a purified gene, cloned by recombinant DNA technology, to correct the defect. Cline's efforts also failed. The subsequent storm of protest forced him to step down from his job. He too lost a great deal of his research funding. 11

The scientific community was ruling the new science with an 12 unforgiving hand. For the moment, genetic engineering seemed too risky to apply to humans, and only indirectly would we benefit from the new biotechnology. But by the early 1980s, the bacterial production of cheap interferon and human insulin was being carried on by the new genetic engineering companies. By advances in such areas as agriculture and the production of medical products, the last few years have shown the incredible potential of this new technology of life.

THE SIMPLE AND THE COMPLEX

The DNA contained in every human cell is compacted and coiled in 23 pairs of tight bundles called chromosomes. If all the DNA in a single cell were uncoiled, it would stretch out about three meters. And in these three meters of human DNA there are about 5,000,000 genes, of which at least 100,000 define the human form. In every molecule of DNA there is the blueprint for eyes, brain, liver, heart, and bones. 13

Directly altering an organism by changing its genetic code requires that the gene (or set of instructions) along the DNA coil be modified and that this same set of instructions be changed in every cell of the organism. With single-cell organisms, such as bacteria, that is not too hard to accomplish. But the human organism is 100 trillion times as complicated. 14

Changing a multicellular organism was first accomplished in 1982 when the Carnegie Institute implanted a foreign gene in a fruit fly. The change was functional and was passed along to subsequent generations. In the Carnegie experiment, red-eye genes were passed to brown-eye flies. 15

Genetic researchers who first contemplated the problem of directly altering the coding sequence of DNA were faced with problems that were simultaneously simple and complex. The simple part was the exchange of molecules in the DNA to bring about the desired modifications. The complex task would be to locate the right gene and to alter only that part of the code. Although the basic idea was simple, they would be working at the molecular level, beyond the range of any microscope. 16

The most likely candidate for the pioneer work was a single-cell bacterium. The organism enlisted early was the most common bacterium in the human intestinal tract: *Escherichia coli*. 17

E. coli is easy to care for and maintain. And it holds the distinction of being the single most carefully studied organism in history. For this reason, *E. coli* has been used not only for the majority of the early DNA studies, but its genetically altered forms have been patented as life forms invented by human beings. 18

Methods of mapping the DNA sequence were developed by clipping off the ends of an uncoiled DNA strand and analyzing and identifying the individual molecules as they were encountered on the strand. 19

After a gene was mapped, changes were induced in the DNA, altering the sequence by introducing mutagenic chemicals—compounds that increase the frequency of genetic mutations by "scrambling" the DNA sequence. Researchers observed the effects on the microorganism, remapped the gene, thereby learning the functions of specific parts of the DNA code. 20

Recombinant DNA technology, the most refined process of genetic engineering, came in 1974 when genetic researchers discovered they could clip off a known sequence of the DNA and replace it with DNA from other sources. This form of gene splicing quickly became the most important genetic engineering tool. Science was learning enough to make changes at will without relying on the slower random mutational techniques. 21

Ultimately, geneticists at CalTech invented two machines that were quantum leaps in genetic engineering research. One machine automatically identified the sequence of cellular amino acids, spelling out the DNA code of the particular gene. Another machine assembled artificial genes piece by piece. 22

With these advances it became necessary for the scientific community to keep track of the avalanche of mapped genes. In 1982, the Los Alamos National Laboratory set up GenBank, a computerized data base of millions of nucleic acid sequences. That data base soon contained information on hundreds of living species—including parts of man's genetic constitution. One day, reconstructing these genetic constitutions may consist of connecting a laboratory computer to this massive data base, which in turn would spell out the genetic make-up of interest. 23

It is only a matter of time until the entire human DNA sequence is catalogued and computerized. With this information, the science of genetic engineering may be able to manipulate the human life form in ways we have not yet even imagined. 24

HEALTH CARE AND BIG BUSINESS

Genetic engineering established a powerful foothold when the U.S. Supreme Court gave Dr. Ananda Chakrabarty the right to patent a life form he had engineered, a microorganism that would metabolize petroleum and help clean up oil spills. 25

The result of the Court's decision was to open the field to commercial enterprise. With big money riding on the right processes, a 26 handful of genetic engineering companies went public and became multimillion-dollar enterprises virtually overnight. Firms with futuristic names—Genentech, Cetus, Lenex, Hybratech, Petrogen—started the race to invent new life forms.

The companies signed nearly every genetic scientist and researcher in the field, creating great concern over this historically unique, apparent conflict of interest between industry and pure science. 27

Three important medical products came from this new industry in quick succession: 28

Human interferon, a possible solution to such afflictions as cancer and viral diseases, used to cost a quarter of a million dollars per thousandth of a gram. With newly engineered bacteria that produce human interferon as a metabolic by-product, we can now produce the same amount of interferon for about a nickel. 29

Human growth hormone, for children whose pituitary glands could not produce enough to help them reach a normal height (hypopituitarism), was formerly produced by extracting the hormone from cadavers. An average child required pituitaries from over 500 cadavers over a 10-year period. Thus they were faced with a life of stunted growth unless they could afford $50,000 to $100,000 worth of treatment. Genentech of San Francisco changed the genetic constitution of *E. coli,* and now human growth hormone is churned out at affordable prices. 30

Human insulin, now manufactured by genetically altered bacteria for tens of thousands of diabetics, replaces the beef- and pork-based product against which many patients build up antibodies. In October 1982, the Eli Lilly Company was given permission by the Food and Drug Administration to begin marketing human insulin. 31

But the genetic engineering industry was not focusing on making medical breakthroughs alone. Industrial microorganisms have been "invented" to mine precious metals from ore through extracellular secretions and leaching. A potato was given the blight-resistant genes of a tomato to become a "pomato." A sunflower was given the genes of a bean to produce protein. One strain of bacteria was engineered to convert ethylene to ethylene glycol (a constituent of antifreeze), another to change subterranean oil to make it easier to remove. And the University of California at Berkeley recently engineered a strain of bacteria that would protect plants from frost, sparking a controversy over introducing the plant into the environment. In November 1985, the EPA finally okayed its release in a California strawberry field. 32

On the horizon are genetic wonders that used to be mere science fiction. For example, aging is reflected in the behavior of DNA. In pioneering work, Ronald Hart and Richard Setlow tied the biological clock directly to the repair processes in older cells. And in 1979, Dr. 33

Joan Smith-Sonneborn significantly extended the life span of single-cell paramecium by manipulating specific DNA repair processes.

In order to organize the search for cures for the 3,500 known human genetic disorders, the Human Genetic Mutant Cell Repository was established in Camden, New Jersey. Here frozen cell cultures from afflicted individuals are stored for reference. 34

And serious thought has been given to storing biological materials from organisms soon to be extinct, from smallpox to mammals, birds, and plants, in frozen storage for future, possible genetic reconstruction of entire organisms. 35

By 1985, the business of genetic engineering was a billion-dollar industry and growing. Already, medicine, agriculture, and energy were becoming dependent on its products, and the emerging possible future uses were astonishing. 36

BENEFIT AND PERIL

The first decade of genetic engineering has passed with little threat to the environment or the public. The somber warnings and tight regulations issued by the National Institutes of Health (NIH) from 1974–76 have been relaxed and their initial fears determined to be unfounded. 37

The NIH, initially worried about the inadvertent design of a deadly microorganism, strictly regulated the genetic engineering business in its infancy. The industry, however, successfully demonstrated that their organisms were usually so task-specific that they could survive only in carefully controlled conditions. One strain of *E. coli,* called K-12, which is used widely in genetic research, has been so extensively modified that it is virtually impossible for the organism to survive outside a carefully controlled laboratory environment. 38

To date, the genetic engineering industry has shown itself to be the harbinger only of good, making medicines and food better and cheaper. We have been left in awe at both the reality and the possibilities. 39

Yet, like any other human enterprise, genetic engineering has a possibility for malevolence equal to its potential for good. For example, since some genetic diseases strike only members of certain races (sickle cell anemia afflicts only blacks, and Tay-Sachs disease strikes only Jews), it is conceivable that we could copy nature and create an organism to carry out a horrible genocide. If biological warfare is terrible, its genetic equivalent would be unspeakable. 40

Aside from examples of potential abuse, deeply troubling questions remain over the direction civil genetic engineering may take. 41

Already, in its first years of existence, genetic screening has been used by a multinational corporation in what amounts to high-tech racism. 42

One multinational corporation defended its use of genetic screening for sickle cell anemia among black job applicants to prevent susceptible workers from exposure to toxic substances. But such genetic screening could become the ultimate invasion of privacy. 43

On the visible horizon, genetic engineering could be used in conjunction with gametic engineering, the laboratory manipulation of human germ cells, to create a human being in any desired image. In this seriously discussed (but not yet possible) procedure, a human's genes would be altered to order. The new genetic information would be passed to a human egg cell *in vitro,* where a new human would be nourished through the gestation period under theoretically perfect conditions. This procedure could hypothetically produce "super humans" resistant or immune to physical disease, and endowed in advance with superior intelligence. 44

Part of this procedure is now possible. The more difficult procedures will probably be in reach within our lifetimes. 45

Dr. Landrum Shettles, a reproductive biologist, has reported nourishing a normally developed, cloned human egg cell to the stage of intrauterine impregnation. Said Shettles, the remaining obstacles to the cloning of human beings are social, not scientific. 46

The first animal cloned, a frog, was produced by biologists Thomas Briggs and Thomas King in 1952. Nearly three decades later, the first mammals were cloned, mice produced by biologists Karl Illmensee and Peter Hoppe. Yet many still believe that cloning by the transplanting of nuclei of adult mammalian cells, as Shettles claimed, is still impossible. The debate continues. 47

Genetic prejudice is already being expressed. The famous Nobel Sperm Bank, formally called the Repository for Germinal Choice, in Escondido, California, contains sperm donated by some Nobel laureates for insemination of "acceptable" candidates. The only laureate-donor to identify himself thus far has been Stanford physicist William Shockley, who stirred controversy by claiming that blacks are inherently inferior to whites. 48

The sperm bank's clients have already produced children. Los Angeles psychologist Afton Blake bore the second child from the bank. One of Blake's reasons for using the bank's services was the genetic legacy she wanted to pass on to her children and subsequent generations. 49

MORAL IMPERATIVES

The scientific community has historically shown itself to be vigorously self-regulated. Its moral standards are nearly always surprisingly conservative. Renegades and apostates are usually criticized and 50 denounced, their research funds cut quickly. It is hard to find many examples of scientists continually abusing their positions.

Remarks made by Robert Sinsheimer of the California Institute of 51
Technology to the Genetics Society of America illustrate this notion: "To impose any limit upon freedom of inquiry is especially bitter for the scientist whose life is one of inquiry; but science has become too potent. . . . Rights are not found in nature. Rights are conferred within a human society and for each there is expected a corresponding responsibility. . . . Science is the major organ of inquiry for a society—and perhaps a society, like an organism, must follow a developmental program in which the genetic information is revealed in an orderly sequence."

From a Christian perspective, the real dangers of genetic engi- 52
neering do not seem to emanate from the scientific community, but from the same places as other causes of social concern.

The abuse of genetic engineering will come from two familiar 53
directions: (1) ill-defined or nonexistent norms of acceptable social direction and (2) disguised social principles of accomplishing one goal by way of another.

Thus, genetic engineering stands in the same place as the other 54
powerful technologies of history, from nuclear weapons to wonder drugs: controlled completely by the hand of mankind and the conventional or surreptitious operational rules of society. Whatever good or evil shall come from it will be determined through the underlying social motivations and allowances for excess over which Christians may exercise influence.

The Christian response must be controlled by accurate and thor- 55
ough knowledge of the field and a sober realization that the morality of many of the issues will not be clear-cut or obvious. Most important, we must understand our value systems and decide that what we can do is not necessarily what we should do.

The Christian input will be only one of many. It must be coordi- 56
nated if the counsel of all those with moral concerns is to be effective.

The opinions of the poorly informed and emotional have already 57
been discounted. The President's Commission for the Study of Ethical Problems in Medicine and Biomedical and Behavioral Research (1982) stated, "Genetic engineering has become a target for simplistic slogans that try to capture vague fears."

The concepts that underlie genetic engineering are far from sim- 58
ple. They are some of the most profound and powerful ideas ever. The promise of genetic engineering lies in the miracles that we have already created and will soon invent from the living code. But the nightmare is real and, ironically, is expressed in the words attributed to DNA codiscoverer Sir Francis Crick by journalist David Rorvik:

"No newborn infant should be declared human until it has 59

passed certain tests regarding its genetic endowment. . . . If it fails these tests, it forfeits the right to live."

The evil we face, therefore, is not from the tools of life but from 60
the minds that made them. There is only one certainty: The river that is the knowledge of life has been crossed, and we cannot go back again.

Review Questions

1. What was Watson and Crick's contribution to the study of genetics?
2. What is *E. coli?* Why is it well suited for experiments in genetic engineering?
3. What does Chamberland cite as some of the products of the partnership between science and business in the area of genetic engineering?
4. What are some of the possible abuses of genetic engineering, according to Chamberland?
5. What are Chamberland's conclusions as to the "threat" of genetic engineering?

Discussion and Writing Suggestions

1. Chamberland begins his essay by discussing the conflicts between religion and science—in particular, the science of genetic engineering. In what other areas have there been conflicts of values between religion and science? From what different value systems do these conflicts originate? How (if at all) have they been resolved? How has the rapid evolution of science and technology aggravated the problem?
2. To those not scientifically inclined, paragraphs 13–24, detailing the structure of DNA and recent scientific advances in "mapping" genetic sequences may present some difficulty. To ensure that you understand the basic ideas in this section, summarize these paragraphs in 200 to 350 words.
3. To what extent are you concerned about the abuse of genetic engineering technology? What guidelines do you suggest for its future development? What limits, if any, should be placed on existing or future technology? Do you recommend restrictions on commercial development of new genetically engineered substances? Explore these questions in a multiparagraph essay, using some of the above questions as your subtopics.
4. In a sidebar (entitled "Catching Up with the Revolution") to Chamberland's article, Lewis Smedes, a professor of theology and ethics at Fuller Theological Seminary, wrote as follows:

   > Technological events are getting ahead of our ability to cope with them in traditional moral categories. That is reason enough for a Christian moralist to view the revolution in biotechnology with unease.

> Rather than apply moral standards to genetic engineering in general, we must examine the moral implications of each discrete stage in the specific applications of biotechnology to human beings. We will need to give careful thought to such questions as these:
>
> 1. Is it permissible to alter humanness at its core, to tamper with our essential humanity? Many people agree that it is right to tamper with some aspects of our humanness, as we do in giving people mechanical hearts. But is there a core of humanity that makes us the special godlike creatures we are—a core that should not be monkeyed with? If so, moralists and theologians must try to specify more exactly what is uniquely human about us.
> 2. Is it permissible for some people to alter other people's humanity? It is misleading to talk about *humanity* re-creating itself. Some persons are recreating other persons. The questions are these: Who sets the norms for what other people ought to be? And who has the wisdom and the right to use such power over the destiny of other people?
> 3. Is it socially responsible to give almost free rein to a biotech industry whose bottom line is profit? While some see the National Institutes of Health's relaxation as a signal that the dangers are small, NIH's relaxation may actually be a sign that public guardians are easily seduced by scientific authorities. Laissez-faire human technology needs to be watched carefully.
>
> We need to remember that every good gift from above, including biotechnology, is likely to be turned against us by arrogant people who believe in the irresistible goodness of what they are doing.[1]

Select one of these sets of questions and, in a multiparagraph essay, discuss the issues Smedes raises.

5. Write a future newspaper or magazine report detailing some new development, either promising or threatening, in genetic technology.

6. Write a scenario for a science fiction movie about some genetic engineering experiment or development that has gotten out of control.

Perfect People

AMY VIRSHUP

One of the most controversial aspects of recent genetic technology is the testing of pregnant mothers to determine possible defects in fetuses. Very frequently, a positive test leads to the abortion of the fetus. Even without such genetic tests, abortion is a particularly divisive issue in this country. Debates over the 1973 Roe v. Wade *Supreme Court ruling (which*

[1]"Catching Up with the Revolution" by Lewis Smedes. *Christianity Today,* February 7, 1986. Reprinted by permission of the author.

From "Perfect People?" by Amy Virshup in *New York* Magazine, July 27, 1987.

legalized abortion) and the continuing struggle by pro-life activists to overturn Roe v. Wade *(which in 1989 was partially overturned by* Webster v. Reproductive Health Services*) regularly fill the front pages of our newspapers. The ever-increasing availability of genetic testing is certain to increase the intensity of this debate.*

In this article, Amy Virshup, writing for New York *magazine, considers the issue of genetic testing of pregnant women. She focuses on several women who underwent testing and discusses their decisions—in some cases, to abort; in others, to have the child. In addition, she reports on the debate that swirls around genetic testing, its consequences, and its dangerous possibilities.*

Susan and Tom Murphy* have glimpsed the future. In the spring of 1984, when Susan was four months pregnant with their second child, they learned that their firstborn, sixteen-month-old Sarah,* had cystic fibrosis, an inherited, incurable disease that can mean a short, difficult life for its victims. Sarah would likely need constant medication and daily sessions of strenuous physical therapy. To make matters worse, no one could say whether the child Susan was carrying also had the disease. 1

Their doctor advised the Murphys to consider having an abortion. But they decided to have the baby, and after five tense months, their son was born—without the disease. Though both Tom and Susan wanted a large family, neither was willing to risk conceiving another child who might get CF. 2

Within two years, the Murphys changed their minds. By then, researchers abroad had found a way to home in on the gene that causes CF, and a prenatal test had become available in the United States for families who already had a child with the disease. A door had been opened for the Murphys, and they decided they could chance another pregnancy. Tom, Susan, and Sarah had preliminary analyses of their DNA—the body's basic genetic material—and Susan became pregnant in September 1986. 3

Just nine weeks into her pregnancy, she had chorionic villus sampling (CVS), a recently developed twenty-minute procedure similar to amniocentesis. The CVS material was sent to the lab, and the Murphys could only wait—and worry—for ten days, They'd never decided just what they would do if the news was bad, but abortion was a real option. The day before Thanksgiving, they got the news: Their unborn child did not have CF. 4

Suddenly, without much time to ponder the moral and ethical 5

*Names marked with an asterisk have been changed.

implications, Americans are being thrust into the age of the tentative pregnancy. For many, the decision to have a child is made not at conception but when the lab sends back the test results. "The difference between having a baby twenty years ago and having a baby today," says ethics specialist Dr. John Fletcher of the National Institutes of Health, "is that twenty years ago, people were brought up to accept what random fate sent them. And if you were religious, you were trained to accept your child as a gift of God and make sacrifices. That's all changing."

Over the last decade, genetics has been revolutionized: Using remarkable new DNA technology, molecular biologists can now diagnose in the womb inherited diseases like CF, hemophilia, Huntington's chorea, and Duchenne muscular dystrophy. Genetics is advancing at unprecedented speed, and important breakthroughs are announced almost monthly. 6

Since each person's DNA is distinct, the potential uses of genetic testing seem limitless: It could settle paternity suits, take the place of dental records or fingerprints in forensic medicine, identify missing children, warn about a predisposition to diseases caused by workplace health hazards. By the mid-1990s, geneticists should be able to screen the general population for harmful genes and test—at birth—a person's likelihood of developing certain types of cancer, high blood pressure, and heart disease. 7

Besides the prenatal tests now commonly in use, doctors may have a blood test that screens fetal cells in a mother's bloodstream and determines the fetus's sex and whether it has any chromosomal disorders or inherited genetic diseases. Work toward the ultimate goal—gene therapy—has already begun. 8

But this technological wizardry has some vehement opponents. A French government committee made up of doctors and lawyers recently called for a three-year moratorium on prenatal genetic tests because of the fear that they would lead to "ethically reprehensible attempts to standardize human reproduction for reasons of health and convenience." This is similar to the objection that antiabortionists have always raised and now extend to genetic testing. (The Vatican, in its recent "instruction" on birth technology, condemned any prenatal test that might lead to abortion.) These days, though, right-to-lifers are finding themselves with some odd allies—feminists, ethics specialists, and advocates for the handicapped who are unsettled by the implications of the new genetics. The tests, they argue, will winnow out fetuses so that only "acceptable products" will be born, thus devaluing the lives of the handicapped. 9

Other critics fear that services for the handicapped will be cut back and that people will be saddled with new responsibilities rather 10 than new opportunities—after all, never before have parents had such an ability to choose whether to accept a child with an inherited condition. In addition, they claim that the sophisticated tests will give employers and insurers the ability to discriminate on genetic grounds. (A 1982 study found that eighteen major American companies—Dow Chemical and du Pont among them—had done some sort of genetic testing.)

Strong as the opposition is, it's not likely that the genetic revolution will be stopped: Few people, given the chance to avoid the emotional, physical, and economic burdens of raising a handicapped child, are likely to refuse it. The widespread use of prenatal tests parallels the advance of feminism. As more and more women made careers, the tests took on added importance—especially since many working women are putting off childbirth until their midthirties, when chromosomal abnormalities are more common. 11

"I didn't feel I had a choice," says advertising executive Judith Liebman, who became pregnant for the second time at 40. "It wasn't 'Is CVS sophisticated enough that I want to take the risk?' The choice was 'Look, they're doing this test, they're recommending I take it because of my age, so I have to go with the medical profession and say that it's okay to take it.' " 12

As sociologist Barbara Katz Rothman writes in *The Tentative Pregnancy,* her study of genetic testing, "In gaining the choice to control the quality of our children, we may rapidly lose the choice not to control the quality, the choice of simply accepting them as they are." 13

The Luddites had a point," says Rothman. "Not all technology is good technology, and not everything needs to be done faster and better." 14

Mount Sinai geneticist Fred Gilbert is tracking the CF gene. Like Gilbert, his lab is casual, low-key; the most spectacular thing about it is its slightly begrimed view. Notes are taped to shelves, a stack of papers and manila folders sits atop a file cabinet, and several odd-looking blue plastic boxes lined with paper towels are arrayed on the counter (they are used to separate pieces of DNA). Flipping through a loose-leaf binder of test results, Gilbert, a burly man with a dark, full beard, talks about his patients like an old-fashioned family doctor—this father drinks, that mother is overburdened, another family's religious views have made it impossible for them to abort—but he knows most of them only from the reports of their genetic counselors and from their DNA, which is shipped to him from cities all over the country. 15

Two years ago, Gilbert began offering a biochemical enzyme test developed in Europe for cystic fibrosis; then, when DNA probes 16 became available, in January 1986, he started running DNA diagnoses as well (both tests are about 95 percent accurate and are used to back each other up). Now Gilbert and his team extract DNA from the cells of families at risk for CF—his patients include a tenant farmer, an executive of a large firm, and several welfare families—expose it to gene probes that have been tagged with radioactivity, and then study photographs of the DNA, looking for the pattern that means the disease is present. Since CF is inherited recessively, there is a one-in-four chance in each pregnancy that the child might have the disease.

This test can be used only by families who already have a child 17
with the disease, but many people are betting on a CF screening test for the general population. After all, CF is the most common inherited disease in whites, striking about one child in 2,000. And now that scientists have moved in on the gene—in April, a British research team announced that it had found a marker that is even closer to it and may turn out to be the gene itself—development may be imminent. Since the test will be highly lucrative for its developer, there's a great incentive to come up with one; by one estimate, half the genetics labs in the country are looking for the CF gene. Gilbert, however, is not making money. Since the test he is using is still experimental, he is offering it at a minimal fee; for those who cannot afford it, the test is done free.

Even so, response to the test has been slow. The eight labs in the 18
country offering DNA diagnosis have done about 400 tests, and Gilbert has completed just fifteen prenatal diagnoses using DNA. One problem is that some cystic-fibrosis specialists have been slow to tell their patients about the test. (The Murphys, for example, didn't learn about the test from their doctor; *they* had to tell *him* it was available.) The Cystic Fibrosis Foundation has also stayed away from the test, afraid of the association with abortion, and Gilbert gets no funds from it. . . .

Emily Perl Kingsley considers herself a feminist; a member of NOW, 19
she has belonged to the Abortion Rights Action League. At 47, Kingsley has won four Emmys as a writer for *Sesame Street,* and sometime in the next year, CBS will broadcast a film she wrote. But when she thinks about prenatal testing, Kingsley finds her feminism running up against her feelings about disability rights, her belief in a woman's right to choose to have an abortion colliding with her belief in the value of the lives of handicapped children. Her son, Jason, thirteen, has Down syndrome. "When you lose me," says Kingsley, "is when you say that the world would be better off without people like my son. I can't go along with that. The only drawback to Down is the pain that he will experience. I would do anything to save him that pain—short of killing him."

Though she was offered amniocentesis during her pregnancy, Kingsley passed on it (a decision she says she has never regretted). At 34, she was a year short of the cutoff date, and at the time, amnio was a risky procedure. Kingsley and her husband, Charles, were both on their second marriage, and both were sure they wanted the child. When Jason was born, their obstetrician suggested they might put him in an institution, tell their families he'd died, and try again. Instead, they took him home to Chappaqua and enrolled him in infant-stimulation classes designed to saturate Down children with information and activity. 20

Infant-stimulation classes were a new concept then, and the Kingsleys had no assurance that they'd be of any real help; today, Jason functions at a high level for a Down-syndrome child. Though he will probably never drive a car, live without some supervision, or go to Yale, Jason can read and write, manage in social situations, and follow complex directions. (He has also appeared on *Sesame Street* and other television shows.) "The idea that you ought to abort a child because he might turn out like my son is *crazy* to me," says Kingsley. "It's crazy." 21

For Kingsley and other disability-rights activists, their movement is a rerun of the civil-rights and feminist fights of the sixties and seventies, and their goals—acceptance by and access to the mainstream of society—are similar. "No one's entitled to tell us, 'No, you can't. Your kid isn't smart enough. Not smart enough to swim on this beach. Not smart enough to play with the kids in this group.' A lot of the things that they get away with saying to us—if they said, 'You can't get into this class because your skin is black . . .' " 22

This time around, though, they find themselves edging toward agreement with people who probably fought on the other side in those earlier battles—right-to-life activists and those on the political right who are opposed not only to prenatal testing but to all abortion. (Many disability-rights supporters don't object to abortion in general, only to abortion to prevent the birth of a handicapped child.) 23

Still, even within the movement, there's no consensus on prenatal testing. The disabled and their families, after all, are of no particular political persuasion, socioeconomic class, or religion. Instead, they are united by accidents of birth and chance. Though one woman who works with the mentally retarded claims that "the lives of the disabled are debased each time a disabled child is aborted," a large number of activists are unwilling to take a stand on prenatal diagnosis. Their concern, they say, is those who have already been born. 24

Most, like Carol Levine, an ethics specialist at the Hastings Center in Briarcliff Manor, feel that the severity of the disease must come into play—that a short life followed by a painful death might better be 25 avoided, but that life in a wheelchair is not grounds for abortion. "There's a difference," says Levine, "between being able to test for a lethal disease like Tay-Sachs and a disease like cystic fibrosis that people are living with—not to great old age, but it's not incompatible with life and even productive, happy life. So the choices that people will make are inevitably going to be colored by the differences in the conditions. I think it's pointed up even more in Huntington's disease, where people live to be 50. Would we have been better off without Woody Guthrie [folksinger], who died of Huntington's? Well, I don't think anybody would say that. But is there a right answer? I don't think so."

Not everyone whose child would be affected by a disease chooses **26**
abortion: Of the fifteen pregnancies Fred Gilbert has studied with DNA probes, four have come up positive for CF, and half of those families kept the children. Parents who are told their child has Down syndrome can put him up for adoption; there are waiting lists of families happy to take Down babies. Even some Roman Catholic hospitals are now offering prenatal diagnosis (without abortion), on the theory that parents who know about their child's problems will be able to cope with them better. The numbers they see are dramatically lower than those at secular hospitals: At Creighton University Medical Center in Omaha, about 5 prenatal tests are done a month; New York Hospital, which is three times as large, does approximately 39 a *week*. And for some disabilities the abortion rate is high—91 percent of the women who get a positive diagnosis for Down syndrome terminate their pregnancies (many women who don't feel they could do it simply do not take the test).

"We're all genetic messes," says the National Institutes of Health's **27**
John Fletcher. "There's no such thing as perfection, and there never will be." Yet each year, more people are searching for it. In Manhattan, about 50 percent of the women at risk for chromosomal abnormalities have prenatal diagnosis, while nationwide, the number of such women using the tests has more than doubled since 1977 (to about 20 percent). An Indiana hospital that did ten amnios in 1971 now does fifteen a *week*. In New York State, 40 percent of women 35 and over had some form of prenatal test in 1984, up from about 5 percent in 1977. As the tests become routine, the definition of abortable defects may become wider and, some people fear, parents may reject a potential child for what seem to be frivolous reasons. Ever more genetic hurdles might be set up, and in order to be born a fetus might have to clear them all.

"Anything that has an aspect of mental retardation is already **28**
quite unacceptable for most people," says Carol Levine. "I think that the limits of tolerability will be stretched very far. More and more

things will be seen as disabilities, and smaller disabilities will be seen less tolerably than they are now. And a society that isn't tolerant of diversity is one that is bereft of imagination and creativity."

Prenatal diagnosis may also change our notion of parental responsibility. "To know that you're bringing forth a child who has to use a wheelchair. . . . With a few curb cuts, life in a wheelchair is not a tragedy," says Barbara Katz Rothman. "But then you're going to look at this particular kid who's going to say to you, 'I am in this wheelchair because you thought it was a good idea.' And there's going to be an element of truth in that. And that's an incredible responsibility to take on in a society that's not supportive of people in wheelchairs, people with mild retardation, people with any kind of problem. I think there's going to be a certain attitude: 'This isn't an act of God anymore that could happen to anybody; this is your selfish choice, lady.' " 29

But who can blame parents for wanting their children to be healthy? Though the treatments for diseases like CF and Duchenne muscular dystrophy have improved in recent years, there is still no cure for most of them, and victims may face frequent hospitalization and even early death. And though the lives of the disabled have improved immeasurably in the last decade, as federal regulations ensuring rights of the handicapped have been put into effect, discussions with the parents of handicapped children, and with those who work with them, reveal just how difficult life with a mentally or physically disabling condition can be. They speak of how hard it is to find a class for their child, of bus drivers who won't stop for people in wheelchairs, of New York's lack of simple amenities, like curb cuts, and, most important, of the cruel treatment their children receive, both from other youngsters and from adults. 30

"The burdens of raising a kid with Down syndrome have practically nothing to do with the child," says Emily Kingsley. "If anything, the child is easy. The burdens are the attitudes and prejudices you meet from people. Having to overcome their queasiness or whatever it is. People are afraid. 'My God, what if that happened to me?' Isn't it neater to keep these people in the closet and not have to think about them, not have to face them, not have to make ramps for them?" 31

For many women who work, it is almost impossible to visualize raising a severely handicapped child. "I think the real lives of women, especially women who work outside the home, mean that the juggling act implied in motherhood is already very, very tough," says Rayna Rapp, a New School anthropologist who has been studying prenatal diagnosis for the last three years. "And compared with most Western societies, we have fewer social services, fewer maternity 32 benefits, less day care. All of those very large-scale factors go into an assessment at the time of a life crisis. You're not thinking in general about what it means to be the mother of *a* child; you're thinking rather specifically about how your life will change to become the parent of a disabled child, right now and here. And I'm not arguing that if the services were perfect everybody would go ahead and have a disabled baby. But I think some people might have a very different sense of it if the climate around disability and disability services was transformed."

Rapp, 41, is a quick, small woman with shaggy brown hair. She began her anthropological study of prenatal diagnosis after going through the experience herself. Pregnant for the first time at 36, Rapp saw amnio as part of the trade-off she had to make because she had devoted 10 years of her life to her academic and political concerns. As it turned out, she was one of the unlucky 2 percent: The fetus was diagnosed as having Down. 33

"When Nancy [her genetic counselor] called me twelve days after the tap," Rapp wrote in a *Ms.* article about her amnio, "I began to scream as soon as I recognized her voice. . . . The image of myself, alone, screaming into a white plastic telephone is indelible." Rapp and her husband, Mike Hooper, decided to have an abortion. 34

"It was a decision made so that my husband and I could have a certain kind of relationship to a child and to each other and to our adult lives," says Rapp. "It had a lot to do with a sense of responsibility, starting out life as older parents. That was the choice, to have delayed childbearing to do the other things we had done in life. And that meant we had to confront something that was very, very upsetting. But in some senses, I wouldn't have wished away the last ten years of my life in order not to have faced the decision. 35

"Paradoxically," says Rapp, "there's less choice for people who are better educated to understand prenatal diagnosis. The more you know about this technology, the more likely you are to feel its necessity. But unless the conditions under which Americans view, deal with, and respond to a range of disabling conditions are also put up for discussion about choice—until that larger picture changes—I think it's real hard for many, many people to imagine making a choice other than abortion for something like Down." 36

In fact, as screening tests for inherited diseases like CF, Huntington's, and the muscular dystrophies become available in the next decade, it's likely that many couples—especially urban, middle-class ones—will consider them a normal part of pregnancy. And as prenatal diagnosis is done earlier in pregnancy, the likelihood that prospective 37 parents will decide to have an abortion for one of those conditions will probably also increase. That attitude is deeply disturbing to opponents of the tests, including Dr. Brian Scully, a Catholic infectious-diseases specialist who works with CF patients at Columbia-Presbyterian Medical Center. Scully, who grew up in Ireland, is opposed to genetic testing—for any condition—that leads to abortion. "The idea that I'm only going to have a child if it's going to be a perfect child, that I'll only accept a baby if it's an acceptable baby—I don't sympathize with that at all," says Scully. "I don't want children to have cystic fibrosis. But to say that if you have cystic fibrosis I'm not going to have you, I think that's wrong."

In 1985, Scully denounced the tests in a letter to *The Lancet*, a 38
widely read British medical journal. In return, he got a note from a London biochemist who, in Scully's words, "rationalized that it was just that they were helping nature. A proportion of babies are lost because of defects naturally—I forget what that proportion is—but he felt that they were just supporting nature, and weeding out the undesirable, imperfect children. And he felt that was fine. I would say, Why not wait until they're born, and you can get everybody."

Like other decisions forced on us by advancing technology, the 39
choice involved in genetic testing can exceed one's moral grasp. And while Scully raises an important argument, the pro-choice position is just as cogent: Can parents who have seen one child suffer with a disease be forced to risk having another? Should people be told they must have a child—even one they don't feel capable of caring for? And, in the case of a disease like Tay-Sachs, does anyone benefit from the child's being born? Parents must make all those decisions for themselves—not lightly, but with awareness of the real moral weight of the final choice. And there's no right answer, a fact that Susan Murphy acutely understands. "I don't think that you should judge people by the decisions they make, whether it's to terminate or not to terminate a pregnancy," she says. "Because you don't know what hell they went through."

Review Questions

1. What is a "tentative pregnancy?"
2. Why has the response to Fred Gilbert's cystic fibrosis DNA test been relatively slow?
3. In what ways might Emily Perl Kingsley's position on the abortion of genetically diseased fetuses appear somewhat unexpected, even contradictory, according to Virshup?

4. Why is the dilemma posed in this article going to become even more prevalent than it is now?

Discussion and Writing Suggestions

1. What do you think about genetic testing of fetuses to determine possible abnormalities? Suppose that you had parented an unborn child that was determined, through genetic testing, to have cystic fibrosis or that would be born mildly retarded. Would you consider an abortion? For what kind of afflictions would you *not* consider abortion?
2. Virshup quotes sociologist Rothman as follows: "The Luddites had a point. Not all technology is good technology, and not everything needs to be done faster and better." (The Luddites were bands of laborers in Britain in the early nineteenth century who smashed industrial machinery that they blamed for high unemployment.) What kinds of technology do you consider "bad" (or at least questionable) technology—technology that has created at least as many problems as solutions? Do you agree that "not everything needs to be done faster and better"? Cite examples.
3. In paragraph 25, ethics specialist Carol Levine makes the following distinction, according to Virshup: "a short life followed by a painful death might be better avoided, but that life in a wheelchair is not grounds for abortion." To what extent do you agree with this statement?
4. Virshup presents both sides of the debate on aborting fetuses determined through genetic testing to be diseased or handicapped. Toward which side of the debate do you think she herself inclines? Cite evidence for your conclusion. (Note particularly, the concluding few paragraphs.)
5. In a sidebar to Dennis Chamberland's article, Alan Veehey, an associate professor of religion at Hope College in Michigan, writes:

Society's Toolbox

Some people think of technology, including genetic technology, as society's toolbox. A new technology is just a new tool, an option for society to use or not as it sees fit. We will make what we want with it. Indeed, if we master enough tools, we may yet construct utopia. When technology fails, we will search for yet another tool to fix it.

That view of technology is naïve and, when applied to genetic engineering, dangerous.

First, although technologies are introduced as options, they can quickly become socially enforced. The automobile was introduced as an option—but try to ride a horse home on the interstate. Genetic counseling was introduced to increase options, but already some are insisting that parents have a duty to be informed and, given certain risks, a duty to avoid childbearing.

Second, although technologies are introduced to make things we want, they seldom satisfy our wants. If we can travel faster by car than horse, we now want faster cars. If we can have a child when we could not have one before, we now want a particular kind of child, say a bright, blond boy. Technology is self-stimulating. It is not only a function of our life together and our values, but it also shapes them. Moral wisdom then would call for some sobriety about our limits and our guilt for demanding too much.

Third, although technology has brought real benefits, the confidence that it will always bring well-being (or that, if it doesn't, some new technology that can correct the harm) is folly. The fundamental problems in coping with human existence do not permit technological solutions; greed, pride, envy, and ennui are not technical problems awaiting a quick technological fix. They too can conscript technology to their ends. As C. S. Lewis wrote: "What we call Man's power over nature turns out to be a power exercised by some men over others with Nature as its instrument."

Gametic intervention is a case in point. We are seizing control of reproduction, gaining power to intervene purposefully in the genetic endowment of our children precisely when we are more confused about parenting than ever. The technologies are introduced to increase our options, to get us what we want—a healthy child. But if parenting is to make parents happy, then genetic engineering will go afoul because we will abort whatever or whomever does not meet our specifications—and we shall still be unhappy. And if parenting is to make children happy, then genetic engineering will still go afoul. The awesome responsibility to minimize the children's suffering and to maximize their happiness will have a self-stimulating impetus until we have reduced our options to a perfect child or a dead child.

Not all reproductive interventions are immoral; but we will not properly guide or limit such powers until we have a good deal more communal wisdom about parenting than we now possess. I fear for our capacities to learn that wisdom in the rush of public enthusiasm about reproductive technologies.[1]

Write a critique of Veehey's ideas, drawing relationships between his concerns and those of individuals interviewed by Virshup. Comment, in particular, upon Veehey's statement, "The fundamental problems in coping with human existence do not permit technological solutions; greed, pride, envy, and ennui are not technical problems awaiting a quick technological fix." (Review Chapter 2 for a discussion of "critique.")

6. In paragraph 27 Virshup notes, "As the tests become routine, the definition of abortable defects may become wider and, some people fear, parents may reject a potential child for what seem to be frivolous reasons." To what extent does this seem a genuine possibility, given the current social and political climate? For what kind of "frivolous reasons" can you envisage prospective parents rejecting their child? (You may wish to couch your response to this question in the form of a newspaper or magazine article written at some point in the future.)

---

[1] "Society's Toolbox" by Alan Veehey. *Christianity Today,* February 7, 1986. Reprinted by permission of the author.

The Total Gene Screen

MORTON HUNT

Suppose you were applying for a job at an industrial firm and were told that, as a prospective employee, you would have to submit to a genetic test. When you asked why such a test was necessary, you were told that the company had to determine whether you had any hidden susceptibility to diseases sometimes caused by substances or chemicals used by the firm. Would you object to such a test? Would you feel that your rights were being violated?

Put the shoe on the other foot. You're an owner or manager of an industrial firm. Recently, you've been paying out huge sums of money on health insurance premiums for your employees and on damage claims brought by employees who became severely ill after some years working for your firm. You would like to have a means of identifying such employees in advance—for your benefit, as well as theirs.

Whose views are right, in this case: Those of the prospective employee? Those of the owner or manager? Or does rightness or wrongness lie only in point of view? In the following New York Times Magazine *article, Morton Hunt, who frequently writes about the ethical implications of scientific advances, examines both sides of the debate on genetic testing by employers. He considers the moral dilemmas involved in such testing and concludes by predicting the likely results.*

Jogging down a New Jersey park trail one morning, Ed Morgan felt wonderfully content. A tall man of 62, lean and fit, he particularly enjoyed running on such a day; his business, selling insulation supplies, was doing better than ever and his children and grandchildren were all thriving. 1

As always, nearing home he broke into a sprint, but that day, to his surprise, he ended up gasping desperately for air. Alarmed, he went to his doctor and got bad news: an X-ray showed a large tumor on his right lung. A few weeks later, he was operated on. The tumor proved to be a pleural mesothelioma, a type of cancer; the surgeon removed as much as he could. Chemotherapy and radiation would buy Ed Morgan (not his real name) a little time, but the end was predictable. 2

Why me, he wondered bitterly, his world in ruins. Before starting his own business, he'd been an insulation installer for 20 years, 3 working mainly with asbestos. Dangerous stuff, to be sure—yet many men he'd worked with, side by side, had spent as long or longer doing the same thing and were still healthy. In fact, only one asbestos worker in 15 dies of asbestos-related cancer. So why me? He never learned why; he lived two years, then became that one in 15.

The likely answer: Ed Morgan was hereditarily more susceptible to asbestos than the other 14. The problem was in his genes. 4

Of the billions of units called nucleotides strung together in the DNA molecules of each person's genes, it takes only one or two, altered or misplaced at some biochemically critical site, to cause serious disease. This is the general explanation, now emerging from biomedical research, of one of the long-impenetrable mysteries of human illness—why, other things being equal, some people are harmed by various substances in the environment while others are not. 5

Clearly, it would be a major boon to humankind, more plagued than every by noxious substances, if each of us could have our entire set of genes searched—or screened—for abnormalities that create vulnerability to chemicals in the environment. With that information, we would then know what jobs, locales and habits to avoid so we could improve our chances of a long and healthy life. 6

Although genetic screening has been talked about in the past in connection with hereditary conditions such as sickle-cell anemia and Tay-Sachs disease, there recently have been a number of new developments, some with far wider applications and greater potential benefits for all. Elaborate genetic screening—a method of examining a person's complete genetic makeup, or genome, for variations that might lead to diseases, including cancer—is now thought to be on the horizon. Some researchers contend it will be with us in a very few years. The field of ecogenetics, which includes the study of genetic variations in susceptibility to disease, is rapidly growing. And, ironically, even as science is perfecting genetic screening, industry is conducting less of it. 7

Each year, 390,000 employees of American industries contract disabling occupational illnesses, including lung, bladder, and other cancers; anemias; dermatitis; asthma, and emphysema, and 100,000 die annually of some of these diseases. Yet their co-workers remain unaffected. Many of those made ill by materials in the workplace are, as geneticists now believe, "hypersusceptible" to them. It isn't chance that makes some fall prey to these illnesses; it's unseen variations in their genetic equipment. 8

For example, one person in every 10 has, among his or her 100,000 genes, a pair of variant genes that produces an excess of the enzyme aryl hydrocarbon hydroxylase, or AHH. Normally, AHH rids 9 the body's cells of hydrocarbons containing benzopyrene, such as those in the air in many industrial plants. But when the enzyme is made in excess amounts, it turns some of the hydrocarbon molecules into carcinogens. People with this genetic variant are more than 26 times as apt to get lung cancer from inhaling such vapors as most other people.

What is true in the workplace is true everywhere. Many of the numerous serious diseases induced by certain pesticides, exhaust fumes and other pollutants, by drugs, cosmetics, charcoal-broiled and fatty foods and by radiation occur in those who are hereditarily vulnerable. Government agencies advise us of the "safe limits" of exposure to many environmental agents, but these limits are based on averages; individually, we may be less susceptible—or several to 100 times more so—to particular chemicals than are most people. Hence such anomalies as these: 10

- Naphthalene and many widely used amino and nitro compounds have no effect on most people. But 2 percent to 5 percent of Chinese, 11 percent of Mediterranean Jews and 13 percent to 16 percent of black males in the United States exposed to them will develop an acute and highly dangerous form of anemia.
- A number of important drugs—the sulfas, hydralazine (an antihypertensive) and many others—are well tolerated by most patients but in a minority produce dangerous toxic reactions.
- One out of five men who are heavy smokers develops lung cancer; the rest do not.

Genetic screening for such variations is very likely to become commonplace, and it could be the greatest advance in disease prevention since Edward Jenner's work on vaccination in the late 18th century. Or so it would seem. But in several respects this giant step for humankind will conflict with our notions of equality and fairness and with the laws that embody them. Already, genetic screening has been—and it will continue to be—strenuously opposed by unions, women's groups, civil liberties groups and others who see it as anti-egalitarian, antilabor, racist, invasive of privacy and, in general, a grave threat to democratic ideals. Genetic screening is certain to call forth a major national debate on social policy, compared to which the present shouting match about the ethics of blood testing for drug use and the AIDS antibody is a disagreement couched in polite murmurs. . . . 11

The liberation from the ills that flesh is heir to, so exciting in concept to the scientists, is now being strenuously opposed on the 12 grounds that it conflicts with American ideals and laws concerning equality and fairness. Such alarms were not sounded when hypersusceptibility research began in the 1950's. At that time, a number of researchers reported that certain chemicals and foods could produce acute hemolytic anemia in a number of black, Asiatic and Mediterranean males, but in very few white males of Northern European origin. Dr. Marks of Memorial Sloan-Kettering, who did some of the early research, says: "Nobody in the late 1950's or early 1960's saw this as anything but an important contribution to the health of a substantial segment of the population." It was not thought of as a racist finding.

Likewise seeing no evil, Dr. Herbert E. Stokinger, a now-retired 13
Government toxicologist, began enthusiastically advocating genetic screening of workers as early as 1963. By 1970, he had listed 92 occupational illnesses, including anemias, leukemia and diseases of the skin, lungs and bladder, that seemed to be the result of enzyme deficiencies due to genetic variations—and that could be avoided by assigning hypersusceptible workers to jobs elsewhere. In 1973, Dr. Stokinger complained that few companies were trying to minimize occupational illness by using such tests as existed.

But more were doing so than he knew and keeping it quiet to 14
avoid confrontations with unions and government agencies. A survey was later conducted by the National Opinion Research Center, commissioned by Representative (now Senator) Albert Gore Jr. for his subcommittee of the House Committee on Science and Technology. It found that between 1970 and 1982, at least 18 of the country's largest companies and private utilities used one or more of these tests. As of 1982, 59 intended to, or thought they might, do so within the next five years. The real figures were surely higher, since one-third of the 561 organizations in the sample did not reply. The survey was confidential, but among the companies that have spoken of their interest in such testing were Du Pont, Dow Chemical and Johns-Manville.

All these companies had good reason to be keenly interested. 15
Workers' compensation and damage suit awards were rising steeply and insurance premiums, accordingly, were soaring. Moreover, if companies could exclude hypersusceptibles, they could come closer to meeting the formidable requirement of the Occupational Safety and Health Act of 1970 that workplaces be safe for all employees. But the fair employment rules of the Civil Rights Act of 1964 made any form of discrimination illegal unless justified by business necessity. To avoid hiring people with a special vulnerability, such as the anemia far more common among blacks than whites, employers had to show that hypersusceptibility and its extra costs, not race, was the reason.

Unions, perceiving a threat to their interests, began to attack the idea of genetic screening vociferously. So did women's groups, since women were being barred from many jobs on the ground that fetuses were highly susceptible to certain workplace chemicals. Though this was not genetic screening, it seemed akin to it. They were joined by the Hastings Center and the Kennedy Institute of Ethics at Georgetown University—both centers of bioethical studies—and by civil rights groups, legal theorists and others who saw genetic screening as endangering privacy, equality and freedom of choice. 16

These views were increasingly voiced in management-labor bargaining sessions, biomedical research conferences, the lobbies of the Capitol and the news media. Representative Gore conducted hearings on the matter in 1981 and 1982; the resulting rash of articles in the press gave opponents of genetic screening ample chance to get their message across to the public. Genetic researchers and industry spokesmen countered with the arguments in favor of screening, but the hostile view made splashier copy and captured public attention, since it played on the fear of science that is endemic in our time. 17

"Genetic screening has a potential for unjust application," said Sheldon W. Samuels, health director of the Industrial Union Department, A.F.L.-C.I.O. "Who would employ these susceptibles, who would protect their dignity and place in the community? Here is the stuff by which war and revolution have been made and by which human progress has been destroyed." 18

"The emphasis on the susceptible worker is a manifestation of social policy and not of science," said Dr. Jeanne Stellman, executive director of the Women's Occupational Health Resource Center at Columbia University. "I am the child of a survivor of the Holocaust," she continued, saying she "and many millions of others suffered very directly and convincingly the results of policies based on dubious genetic traits. . . . While I don't see gas ovens being built in the United States, I do see that many of the premises which led to that terrible time are again beginning to surface here." 19

No wonder most companies either quickly lost or hid their interest in genetic screening. By 1983, after Representative Gore's survey made headlines, only five big companies admitted they were still testing; today, virtually none do. Gordon D. Strickland of the Chemical Manufacturers Association, for instance, says, "As far as we know, only one or two of our companies are doing genetic screening—and only for the benefit of doctor and patient, not job selection." 20

Although industry is generally silent on the subject, its reasons for being interested in genetic screening are as strong as ever and perhaps stronger, given the example of the multibillion-dollar mass of lawsuits against Johns-Manville, many of them filed on the part of 21 employees who developed asbestosis and other diseases. Citing the cost of the suits, the company filed for bankruptcy in 1982.

22 Major chemical and pharmaceutical companies are sending representatives to the growing stream of conferences on genetic screening and ecogenetics. A number of large companies support laboratories doing ecogenetic research. In 1983, Dow, Exxon, Du Pont, I.B.M., Eli Lilly and other corporations sponsored a major international ecogenetics conference at Cold Spring Harbor, N.Y. And the opposition to genetic screening has had no effect on the pace of research, which has steadily increased.

23 Ecogenetic research seems sure to continue to provoke a major national debate—or, if one takes seriously the warnings of Sheldon Samuels of the A.F.L.-C.I.O, it may lead to war and revolution. Even if the conflict remains nonviolent, it will be prolonged and bitter, for it involves cherished values that genetic screening puts at odds. We face a number of moral dilemmas. Five will be profoundly troublesome.

24 1. *Equal opportunity versus health protection.*

25 Most Americans believe that job discrimination based on sex, race or ethnic origin is morally wrong; the Civil Rights Act of 1964 makes it illegal. Most of us also believe that employers and government should protect workers from health hazards in the workplace; the Occupational Safety and Health Act makes that the law of the land. But when genetic screening is perfected, it will make the two beliefs and laws incompatible, since using screening to protect hypersusceptibles from working at jobs dangerous to them would disproportionately exclude members of certain ethnic and racial groups.

26 Union leaders, ethicists and some legal authorities believe both goals are desirable but consider equality of job opportunity the more important one. Judith C. Areen, associate dean of the Georgetown University Law School, is typical of those who hold this view: "People should have equal opportunity in the job market, regardless of race, sex or genetic makeup. But genetic screeing, even when there is no intent to discriminate, will create de facto discrimination."

27 To most biogeneticists, however, the preservation of life and health is the controlling moral value. When the question of de facto discrimination is raised, Dr. Leon E. Rosenberg, research geneticist and dean of the Yale University School of Medicine, testily says: "That's the *wrong* question! The *right* one is, how much can genetic screeing benefit humanity?" The argument that genetic testing will increase inequality seems to him to ignore reality. "The whole notion of genetics is that we're *not* all the same," he says. "The whole notion of risk factors is that they *aren't* equally distributed."

2. *Equal opportunity versus free enterprise.* 28

A solution often proposed by union leaders and ethicists to the 29
preceding dilemma is that workers at special risk should be given no-risk jobs with comparable pay and benefits. But this fails to resolve a second dilemma: the conflict between the worker's right to equal employment opportunity and the employer's right to run a business. It seems as unfair to require companies in a competitive market to create alternate safe jobs as it is to deny jobs to workers for genetic traits they cannot control.

For now, the dilemma is being resolved on the side of equal 30
employment. Most employers make no effort to screen or exclude the genetically susceptible. But as genetic screening becomes better known and more feasible, their failure to use it might enable employees who became ill to sue for massive damages over and above workers' compensation. A jury, told by a gaunt, dying man that his employer failed to use available tests and so allowed him to contract his fatal disease, might well find the company grossly negligent and award the dying man generous damages. Even one such award could weaken many a company.

3. *Fairness to the handicapped versus "the greatest happiness of the* 31
greatest number."

The Federal Rehabilitation Act of 1973 and similar laws in 45 32
states and the District of Columbia embody the moral principle that burdens should be shared; society is held to have an obligation to help the handicapped lead a full life. One way is to ban job discrimination against them whenever "reasonable accommodation" to their needs—ramps, modified work schedules and so on—is economically feasible.

But these laws conflict with the common sense assumption that 33
the ethically soundest guide to social policy is the greatest happiness (or greatest good) of the greatest number. According to this dictum, the most efficient, lowest-cost production of goods and services, benefiting the largest number of people, is the best course.

Americans have tended to assign greater weight to the first prin- 34
ciple than to the second, giving special protections and privileges to the handicapped. So far, this has not cost us dearly, but if the courts should decide that genetic susceptibility is a protected handicap, the cost will expand explosively. Employers required to hire hypersusceptibles would have to make the workplace safe for them. But industry officials and many neutral observers say that in most cases a workplace so clean as to be safe for every hypersusceptible is technically impossible. Even when it is not, experts say, it would be extremely costly—and the costs would have to be passed along to the consumer. This would not be a "reasonable accommodation" or conducive to the greatest happiness of the greatest number.

35 4. *Individual freedom versus social control.*

36 Do people have a right to risk their own health, or does society have an obligation to restrain them for their own good and to prevent them from becoming a burden on the rest of us? Both values exist in our culture. We permit people to smoke and climb mountains, yet we make it a crime to ride a motorcycle without a helmet or to use heroin.

37 The same clash of values exists in regard to taking risks on the job. We require employers to make jobs as nearly risk-free as possible, yet it is not unusual for employees to fight for the right to hold high-paying jobs even though they are at far greater risk than others. They even fight for the right to further risk their health. A few years ago, Johns-Manville prohibited smoking in its asbestos plants because smoking greatly increases the health hazards of working with asbestos. The International Association of Machinists local at the Denison, Tex., plant, filed a grievance; the arbitrator, and later the court, agreeing with the union, struck down the no-smoking rule in that plant on the grounds that "the danger . . . is to the smoker who willingly courts it."

38 By that reasoning, hypersusceptibles should be free to take jobs where they are in greater danger than other people. But it can be argued that this is unfair to their employers and to the rest of us, for workers who accept special risks will not bear all or even most of the cost of their risk-taking. Under workers' compensation and similar laws, employers cannot defend themselves against injury claims by arguing that the employees knowingly assumed the risk. So the employer will pay—and we all will, because products will cost more and because many hypersusceptibles, felled by chronic illness, will eventually turn to Medicaid.

39 5. *Knowledge versus privacy; paternalism versus autonomy.*

40 Government, most of us believe, has a right to gather some information about individuals and establishments and to use its knowledge for the general good. Schoolchildren and restaurant kitchens, for instance, are subject to examination. Yet every such intervention diminishes the privacy and freedom that are part of our tradition; we and our courts fiercely guard what remains, considering it a crucial part of our constitutional endowment. Genetic screening would be a new battleground for the conflict between these values.

41 On the one hand, most biomedical researchers feel that the knowledge provided by genetic screening will enable us to make more rational decisions about work and health. On the other, ethicists and legal scholars fear that genetic screening and the knowledge it yields will rob us of some of our essential rights. Political scientist Ronald Bayer of the Hastings Center says that the legal right of employers to insist that some job applicants and employees—airline pilots and bus drivers, for instance—submit to medical tests is a

"stunning exception" to the right of individuals to refuse medical interventions and "involves bodily intrusions and invasions of privacy."

Even more serious is the potential of genetic screening to disclose defects we would prefer to keep secret. To be known as a cancer risk in any workplace contaminated with the ubiquitous BP is to be stigmatized; in a town with a single industry, it could mean unemployability. Socially, moreover, the hypersusceptible person may be perceived as defective, and shunned. 42

Given the choice between knowledge or ignorance of their own genetic defects, some people may opt for ignorance. Many Hasidic Jews have refused to take part in mass screening for Tay-Sachs disease, the hereditary condition affecting descendants of Eastern European Jews, because when it comes to marriage, known carriers would be at a severe disadvantage. More generally, even if genetic information is kept confidential, a susceptible individual might find the knowledge hard to live with. Dr. Stuart H. Yuspa, who heads a research team at the National Cancer Institute, says: "We shouldn't rush genetic screening. What happens to you if you're identified at age 20 as high risk? Ask a young person with Huntington's chorea, which develops later in life; he's living with a death warrant. That's how a cancer-prone individual might feel." 43

Many of us, considering these dilemmas, will take one side or the other. But the most socially practical and beneficial option would be a set of compromise regulations worked out by lawmakers after careful consultation with all factions. Now, before the crisis is upon us, is the right time to do so, but the present [Reagan] Administration, strongly oriented toward deregulation, is hardly likely to initiate such legislation. 44

When lawmakers finally have to act, will they listen to the scientists or to the opponents of genetic screening and impose such strict controls on it as to deprive us of much of its benefit? Perhaps at first they will do the latter; in the long run, probably not, if we can judge from how such dilemmas have been resolved in the past. In the 1960's, when Congress and government agencies sought to protect human subjects of biomedical and behavioral research, they nearly strangled some lines of valuable scientific inquiry; later, compromises made it possible to protect both the rights of human subjects and those of researchers to seek knowledge—and of all of us to benefit from it. Similarly, if genetic screening is overcontrolled at first, adjustments will probably be made later. 45

Such solutions to dilemmas please no one—but they work. As Edmund Burke told the British Parliament, "All government—indeed, every human benefit and enjoyment, every virtue and every 46 prudent act—is founded on compromise and barter." Parliament ignored him, but would have done better to pay heed; he was urging compromise with America, in 1775.

Review Questions

1. What is the genetic explanation for a great many human illnesses? Why are some people more susceptible to illnesses than others? By implication, then, what does the cure for such diseases entail?
2. Why has genetic screening generated so much controversy?
3. Why do companies consider it in their own interest, as well as the interest of their employees, to conduct genetic testing?
4. How does Hunt see the basic conflict between proponents and opponents of genetic screening being resolved?

Discussion and Writing Suggestions

1. In general, do you favor or oppose genetic screening? Cite your reasons, indicating, if appropriate, under what conditions you believe such testing justifiable.
2. In paragraph 19, Dr. Jeanne Stellman is quoted as follows: "The emphasis on the susceptible worker is a manifestation of social policy and not science. . . . I am a child of a survivor of the Holocaust . . . and many millions of others suffered very directly and convincingly the results of policies based on dubious genetic traits." To what extent do you accept Stellman's linkage of the Nazi genetic experiments and genetic testing by companies? Note that she does not claim that the two are equally pernicious; she does believe that "many of the premises which led to that terrible time are again beginning to surface here."
3. In the latter part of the article, Hunt discusses five "moral dilemmas" that arise from genetic testing. Select one or two of these dilemmas and, in a multiparagraph essay, explain why you believe that one side should be favored over the other. For example, in considering the dilemma between equal opportunity and health protection, which value do you believe should take priority? Draw on your own experience or the experience of people you know, if appropriate, as well as your own reading (including this article) and general knowledge.
4. Hunt's fourth "moral dilemma"—"individual freedom versus social control"—is perhaps the most familiar to us. Hunt cites the familiar examples of people insisting on their right to smoke or to ride motorcycles without helmets, claiming that their physical well-being is their own concern, not the government's or the public's. Those favoring social control (in such instances) argue that the cost of catastrophic mistakes by those claiming freedom is often borne by the public, in the form of higher prices and higher taxes to support the cost of public health care. Select one of these

particular issues (or another issue involving the same dilemma) and, in a multiparagraph essay, argue your case. Anticipate the objections of your opponents and attempt to respond to them.

5. Hunt's fifth moral dilemma concerns knowledge versus privacy. But there is also a dilemma of knowledge versus ignorance. For example, NBC news science correspondent Robert Bazell asks a provocative question: "Would you want to be told, at the age of 20, that your body is likely to undergo severe mental and physical deterioration, when you reach your early 50s?" Respond to this question.

A Heretic's View on the New Bioethics

JEREMY RIFKIN

From its beginnings in the early 1970s, genetic engineering has been surrounded in controversy. Initial fears focused on the nightmare scenario of newly engineered microorganisms escaping from the lab and causing uncontrollable damage to other organisms and the environment. Some scientists proposed a moratorium on gene splicing experiments; and in 1975, during a landmark international conference at Asilomar, California, scientists agreed to strict guidelines to govern all future research. A year later, the city council of Cambridge, Massachusetts, enacted a three-month moratorium on certain high-risk DNA experiments conducted at nearby Harvard University.

During the past decade, the science-fiction scenarios have subsided, but the controversy over genetic engineering continues—focusing now on the ethical aspects of manipulating the genetic code for our own utilitarian and commercial purposes. Repeatedly, critics associate bioengineering with eugenics, the infamous pseudoscience practiced by the Nazis in their efforts to perpetuate the "Aryan" races and to exterminate "inferior" races. Then, as now, critics have wondered, Who should determine what is "superior" (or normal) and what is "inferior" (or defective)?

For some years, the most vocal critic of biotechnology has been Jeremy Rifkin. A philosopher and environmental activist involved in science and technology issues, Rifkin, through his publications, his lectures, his congressional testimony, and his Foundation on Economic Trends, has been tireless in attacking both the practices and the underlying premises of genetic engineering. He has also been successful in halting or delaying the testing of several newly developed microorganisms with agricultural applications—for example, a new bacteria developed by Advanced Genetics Sciences to prevent frost damage to crops and a reengineered virus developed by Biologics Corporation to check an epidemic of pseudorabies, a disease fatal to pigs.

Born in 1945, Rifkin attended the Wharton School of Business and then earned a degree in law and diplomacy from Tufts. As a graduate student, he was an activist against the Vietnam War; he began focusing his attention on bioengineering after the Asilomar Conference. Rifkin's first book on biotechnology was Who Should Play God? *(1977), coauthored with Ted Howard. This was followed by* Entropy *(1980), which sold more than 750,000 copies worldwide. In a recent article in the* New York Times Magazine, *"Jeremy Rifkin Just Says No" (16 Oct. 1988), he was quoted as follows:*

> No parliament ever debated the old technologies—the Industrial Revolution, the petrochemical revolution, the computer revolution. . . . The biotech revolution will have a more intimate effect on our lives than anything else in history. We can't afford the luxury of a small elite making public policy. . . . The rule of thumb [should be] to intervene in nature in the most prudent and conservative fashion rather than the most disruptive and radical fashion. (43)

Following are two passages that reveal Rifkin's attitude toward genetic research—and beyond that, toward the ethical dimensions of scientific inquiry. The first passage is from his 1985 book Algeny *(the title is a wordplay on* alchemy*); the second is from a 1985 interview with Andrew Revkin, a senior writer for* Science Digest.

Darwin's world was populated by machine-like automata. Nature was conceived as an aggregate of standardized, interchangeable parts assembled into various functional combinations. If one were to ascribe any overall purpose to the entire operation, it would probably be that of increased production and greater efficiency with no particular end in mind. 1

The new temporal theory of evolution replaces the idea of life as mere machinery with the idea of life as mere information. By resolving structure into function and reducing function to information flows, the new cosmology all but eliminates any remaining sense of species identification. Living things are no longer perceived as carrots and peas, foxes and hens, but as bundles of information. All living things are drained of their aliveness and turned into abstract messages. Life becomes a code to be deciphered. There is no longer any question of sacredness or inviolability. How could there be when there are no longer any recognizable boundaries to respect? Under the new temporal theory, structure is abandoned. Nothing exists at 2 the moment. Everything is pure activity, pure process. How can any living thing be deemed sacred when it is just a pattern of information?

By eliminating structural boundaries and reducing all living 3
things to information exchanges and flows, the new cosmology provides the proper degree of desacralization for the bioengineering of life. After all, in order to justify the engineering of living material across biological boundaries, it is first necessary to desacralize the whole idea of an organism as an identifiable, discrete structure with a permanent set of attributes. In the age of biotechnology, separate species with separate names gradually give way to systems of information that can be reprogrammed into an infinite number of biological combinations. It is much easier for the human mind to accept the idea of engineering a system of information than it is for it to accept the idea of engineering a dog. It is easier still, once one has fully internalized the notion that there is really no such thing as a dog in the traditional sense. In the coming age it will be much more accurate to describe a dog as a very specific pattern of information unfolding over a specific period of time.

Life as information flow represents the final desacralization of 4
nature. Conveniently, humanity has eliminated the idea of fixed biological borders and reduced matter to energy and energy to information in its cosmological thinking right at the very time that bioengineers are preparing to cut across species boundaries in the living world.

THE NEW ETHICS

Civilization is experiencing the euphoric first moments of the next age 5
of history. The media are already treating us to glimpses of a future where the engineering of life by design will be standard operating procedure. Even as the corporate laboratories begin to dribble out the first products of bioengineering, a subtle shift in the ethical impulse of society is becoming perceptible to the naked eye. As we begin to reprogram life, our moral code is being similarly reprogrammed to reflect this profound change in the way humanity goes about organizing the world. A new ethics is being engineered, and its operating assumptions comport nicely with the activity taking place in the biology laboratories.

Eugenics is the inseparable ethical wing of the age of biotechnolo- 6
gy. First coined by Charles Darwin's cousin Sir Francis Galton, eugenics is generally categorized in two ways, negative and positive. Negative eugenics involves the systematic elimination of so-called biologically undesirable characteristics. Positive eugenics is con-

cerned with the use of genetic manipulation to "improve" the characteristics of an organism or species.

Eugenics is not a new phenomenon. At the turn of the century the United States sported a massive eugenics movement. Politicians, celebrities, academicians, and prominent business leaders joined together in support of a eugenics program for the country. The frenzy over eugenics reached a fever pitch, with many states passing sterilization statutes and the U.S. Congress passing a new immigration law in the 1920s based on eugenics considerations. As a consequence of the new legislation, thousands of American citizens were sterilized so they could not pass on their "inferior" traits, and the federal government locked its doors to certain immigrant groups deemed biologically unfit by then-existing eugenics standards. 7

While the Americans flirted with eugenics for the first thirty years of the twentieth century, their escapades were of minor historical account when compared with the eugenics program orchestrated by the Nazis in the 1930s and '40s. Millions of Jews and other religious and ethnic groups were gassed in the German crematoriums to advance the Third Reich's dream of eliminating all but the "Aryan" race from the globe. The Nazis also embarked on a "positive" eugenics program in which thousands of S.S. officers and German women were carefully selected for their "superior" genes and mated under the auspices of the state. Impregnated women were cared for in state facilities, and their offspring were donated to the Third Reich as the vanguard of the new super race that would rule the world for the next millennium. 8

Eugenics lay dormant for nearly a quarter of a century after World War II. Then the spectacular breakthroughs in molecular biology in the 1960s raised the specter of a eugenics revival once again. By the mid-1970s, many scientists were beginning to worry out loud that the potential for genetic engineering might lead to a return to the kind of eugenics hysteria that had swept over America and Europe earlier in the century. Speaking at a National Academy of Science forum on recombinant DNA, Ethan Signer, a biologist at M.I.T., warned his colleagues that 9

> this research is going to bring us one more step closer to genetic engineering of people. That's where they figure out how to have us produce children with ideal characteristics. . . . The last time around, the ideal children had blond hair, blue eyes and Aryan genes.

The concern over a re-emergence of eugenics is well founded but misplaced. While professional ethicists watch out the front door for telltale signs of a resurrection of the Nazi nightmare, eugenics doctrine has quietly slipped in the back door and is already stealthily at 10 work reorganizing the ethical priorities of the human household. Virtually overnight, eugenics doctrine has gained an impressive if not an impregnable foothold in the popular culture.

Its successful implantation into the psychic life of civilization is attributable to its going largely unrecognized in its new guise. The new eugenics is commercial, not social. In place of the shrill eugenic cries for racial purity, the new commercial eugenics talks in pragmatic terms of increased economic efficiency, better performance standards, and improvement in the quality of life. The old eugenics was steeped in political ideology and motivated by fear and hate. The new eugenics is grounded in economic considerations and stimulated by utilitarianism and financial gain. 11

Like the ethics of the Darwinian era, the new commercial eugenics associates the idea of "doing good" with the idea of "increasing efficiency." The difference is that increasing efficiency in the age of biotechnology is achieved by way of engineering living organisms. Therefore, "good" is defined as the engineering of life to improve its performance. In contrast, not to improve the performance of a living organism whenever technically possible is considered tantamount to committing a sin. 12

For example, consider the hypothetical case of a prospective mother faced with the choice of programming the genetic characteristics of her child at conception. Let's assume the mother chooses not to have the fertilized egg programmed. The fetus develops naturally, the baby is born, the child grows up, and in her early teenage years discovers that she has a rare genetic disease that will lead to a premature and painful death. The mother could have avoided the calamity by having that defective genetic trait eliminated from the fertilized egg, but she chose not to. In the age of biotechnology, her choice not to intervene might well constitute a crime for which she might be punished. At the least, her refusal to allow the fetus to be programmed would be considered a morally reprehensible and irresponsible decision unbefitting a mother, whose duty it is always to provide as best she can for her child's future well-being. 13

Proponents of human genetic engineering contend that it would be irresponsible not to use this powerful new technology to eliminate serious "genetic disorders." The problem with this argument, says *The New York Times* in an editorial entitled "Whether to Make Perfect Humans," is that "there is no discernible line to be drawn between making inheritable repairs of genetic defects, and improving the species." The *Times* rightly points out that once scientists are able to repair genetic defects, "it will become much harder to argue against adding genes that confer desired qualities, like better health, looks or brains." 14

Once we decide to begin the process of human genetic engineer- 15 ing, there is really no logical place to stop. If diabetes, sickle cell anemia, and cancer are to be cured by altering the genetic makeup of an individual, why not proceed to other "disorders": myopia, color blindness, left-handedness? Indeed, what is to preclude a society from deciding that a certain skin color is a disorder?

As knowledge about genes increases, the bioengineers will inevitably gain new insights into the functioning of more complex characteristics, such as those associated with behavior and thoughts. Many scientists are already contending that schizophrenia and other "abnormal" psychological states result from genetic disorders or defects. Others now argue that "antisocial" behavior, such as criminality and social protest, are also examples of malfunctioning genetic information. One prominent neurophysiologist has gone so far as to say, "There can be no twisted thought without a twisted molecule." Many sociobiologists contend that virtually all human activity is in some way determined by our genetic makeup, and that if we wish to change this situation, we must change our genes. 16

Whenever we begin to discuss the idea of genetic defects, there is no way to limit the discussion to one or two or even a dozen so-called disorders, because of a hidden assumption that lies behind the very notion of "defective." Ethicist Daniel Callahan penetrates to the core of the problem when he observes that "behind the human horror at genetic defectiveness lurks . . . an image of the perfect human being. The very language of 'defect,' 'abnormality,' 'disease,' and 'risk,' presupposes such an image, a kind of proto-type of perfection." 17

The idea of engineering the human species is very similar to the idea of engineering a piece of machinery. An engineer is constantly in search of new ways to improve the performance of a machine. As soon as one set of imperfections is eliminated, the engineer immediately turns his attention to the next set of imperfections, always with the idea in mind of creating a perfect piece of machinery. Engineering is a process of continual improvement in the performance of a piece of machinery, and the idea of setting arbitrary limits to how much "improvement" is acceptable is alien to the entire engineering conception. 18

The question, then, is whether or not humanity should "begin" the process of engineering future generations of human beings by technological design in the laboratory. What is the price we pay for embarking on a course whose final goal is the "perfection" of the human species? How important is it that we eliminate all the imperfections, all the defects? What price are we willing to pay to extend our lives, to ensure our own health, to do away with all the inconveniences, the irritations, the nuisances, the infirmities, the suffering, that are so much a part of the human experience? Are we so enamored with the idea of physical perpetuation at all costs that we 19 are even willing to subject the human species to rigid architectural design?

With human genetic engineering, we get something and we give up something. In return for securing our own physical well-being we are forced to accept the idea of reducing the human species to a technologically designed product. Genetic engineering poses the most fundamental of questions. Is guaranteeing our health worth trading away our humanity? 20

People are forever devising new ways of organizing the environment in order to secure their future. Ethics, in turn, serves to legitimize the drive for self-perpetuation. Any organizing activity that a society deems to be helpful in securing its future is automatically blessed, and any activity that undermines the mode of organization a society uses to secure its future is automatically damned. The age of bioengineering brooks no exception. In the years to come a multitude of new bioengineering products will be forthcoming. Every one of the breakthroughs in bioengineering will be of benefit to someone, under some circumstance, somewhere in society. Each will in some way appear to advance the future security of an individual, a group, or society as a whole. Eliminating a defective gene trait so that a child won't die prematurely; engineering a new cereal crop that can feed an expanding population; developing a new biological source of energy that can fill the vacuum as the oil spigot runs dry. Every one of these advances provides a modicum of security against the vagaries of the future. To forbid their development and reject their application will be considered ethically irresponsible and inexcusable. 21

Bioengineering is coming to us not as a threat but as a promise; not as a punishment but as a gift. We have already come to the conclusion that bioengineering is a boon for humanity. The thought of engineering living organisms no longer conjures up sinister images. What we see before our eyes are not monstrosities but useful products. We no longer feel dread but only elated expectation at the great possibilities that lie in store for each of us. 22

How could engineering life be considered bad when it produces such great benefits? Engineering living tissue is no longer a question of great ethical import. The human psyche has been won over to eugenics with little need for discussion or debate. We have already been convinced of the good that can come from engineering life by learning of the helpful products it is likely to spawn. 23

As in the past, humanity's incessant need to control the future in order to secure its own well-being is already dictating the ethics of the age of biotechnology. Engineering life to improve humanity's own prospects for survival will be ennobled as the highest expression of 24 ethical behavior. Any resistance to the new technology will be castigated as inhuman, irresponsible, morally reprehensible, and criminally culpable.

"SCIENCE DIGEST" INTERVIEW

"A public nuisance." "A scourge on science." These are just two of the labels that normally staid scientists have applied to genetic-engineering foe Jeremy Rifkin. If he is any of these things, he is also a force to be reckoned with. Last May, a federal court, ruling on a lawsuit brought by Rifkin, stopped what would have been the first field test of a genetically modified organism. Since then, as head of the privately funded Foundation on Economic Trends, Rifkin has filed additional suits, including one against the U.S. Department of Agriculture. He contends that the USDA is violating the "ethical canons of civilization" by transferring genes between mammalian species.

Science Digest *senior writer Andrew Revkin talked with Rifkin in his Washington office to see what gives this perennial gadfly his punch.*

SCIENCE DIGEST: When you speak in public, you take a very pragmatic view of biotechnology. You're careful to describe the potential payoffs. You mainly discuss questions of implementation—how will we control what is done or who will decide on it. 1

But in your books and legal maneuvers you attack science and call for an outright ban on genetic engineering. Will the real Jeremy Rifkin please stand up? 2

JEREMY RIFKIN: I'm often criticized as being opposed to progress and science and freedom of inquiry when in fact I'm not. My whole life has been about that. What my critics are really livid about is my view on the nature of knowledge, how we pursue it, what our goals are. 3

There's a scholarly tradition which is part of the science of the modern world. Francis Bacon summed it up by saying, "Knowledge is power, power is control, control is security." It's very easy to develop this sort of isolation science, where you sever relationships, and you try to manipulate and control from a distance. 4

It's much more intellectually expansive to develop a wholly different perspective on science. There is a small group in my 5

Interview with Jeremy Rifkin from *Science Digest,* May 1985. Reprinted by permission of Jeremy Rifkin, The Foundation on Economic Trends, Washington, DC.

generation that is starting to talk about a new formula: "Knowledge is empathy with the environment, empathy allows us to establish a new type of security by becoming a member in good standing in the community of life."

SD: Most of the scientists I've met have a remarkably empathetic view of the world. That's what drove them into science—their curiosity about things around them, their interest in the interplay between organisms and their environment. Do you really think that empathetic science isn't already out there? 6

JR: I think it's there, but it is the minority report. Look at the major actors in molecular biology. You can't find more than a handful that aren't on corporate boards and aren't involved in the engineering part of it. If you're saying there are still some pure-research scientists around, you're right, but if you're saying they are the majority, you're wrong. And if you're saying they are the trend, you're wrong. The trend is that science is becoming increasingly reduced to technology. 7

SD: Your lawsuits are directed at basic research as well as at applied research. The main fear I have seen in the scientific establishment is that this will impede pure science along with commercial biotechnology. 8

JR: If they're only interested in research to observe how something works so that we can better respect and empathize with normal working relationships in nature, fine. If these people are there, I would ask them to speak up. I've never seen one article from these people. I do assume they exist; I'm not that cynical. But they don't speak up. Let them be a third force. 9

SD: I think the majority of scientists out there are aware of these things and are very involved in the idea of discussing them. 10

JR: I have not seen this nurturing, supportive effort toward a rational dialogue. I have seen a few individual scientists who are willing to do it, but by and large the others have squawked, kicked, yelled and screamed all the way. I have been subjected to all sorts of attacks. They never deal with the issues. It's always "Rifkin this" and "Rifkin that." There was no discussion of this until I raised my litigation, and then they went crazy. Now, a year and a half after the litigation, they're all saying we have to regulate. 11

SD: Isn't genetic engineering just another technology, one that can be either misused or used properly? 12

JR: That is wrong. In fact, it's ridiculous. There is no neutral technology. This is the myth of the modern age. Let's take nuclear power. You're saying, well, it can be used for good or bad. What I'm saying is, look at the inherent power in the technology and ask, is the power inordinate? Did we learn truth by splitting the atom? No. We got a new form of power. I would agree with Amory Lovins, 13 who said nuclear power, even for domestic purposes, is like using a chain saw to cut butter. The inherent power of the technology was so inordinate that its mere use—regardless of the intentions of those using it—was irresponsible. The power was out of balance with our indebted relationship to all other things. . . .

With genetic engineering, I would say the same thing. There are 14
tremendous benefits to genetic engineering. The question is not the benefits versus the harm; I *assume* that the intentions are to make a better world. The question is whether the power inherent in the process is appropriate; should we human beings have the authority to determine what are good or bad genes. Who sets up the criteria?

SD: If you could fashion the world according to Jeremy Rifkin, what 15
would it be like?

JR: We have seen our mandate as manipulating, controlling, 16
rearranging, becoming the co-creator of life. I think that is a misguided notion. We are one of many creatures on a planet that is a single organism. It's not just an environmental platitude to say this. We rely in every aspect of our life on a whole set of relationships that we live within. I would like us to ask, "How can we become good stewards?" I think the Iroquois Indians had a very interesting idea. Whenever they looked at a new policy option, they went into council, and the elders had to speculate on how this decision would affect their people, seven generations removed. They used the greatest gift the human species has—our consciousness—and they used it in the most civilized way possible. We need that continuity today. We don't have it. We think in terms of two-year reelections.

SD: Given our systems of government and regulation, how would 17
we get from here to there?

JR: You cannot legislate what I'm talking about into existence; you 18
cannot command it into existence. The only way this can happen is by a change in consciousness. I don't know why it isn't possible to develop an empathetic stewardship approach. I don't think you can do it in a generation; it's too big.

SD: In the world according to Jeremy Rifkin, what would a university 19
be like? Would there be a biology department and, if so, what kind?

JR: Sure there would. There is a whole alternative biology to the one 20
the established order sets up. A whole new approach to science—using a rigorous methodology for empathetic pursuit of knowledge. We tend to think there is only one way. Let's look at some of the fields where genetics is involved—medicine, for example.

SD: A quick example from medicine. The clotting factor for hemophi- 21
liacs. It costs tens of thousands of dollars to maintain a hemophiliac. Suppose we could engineer the clotting factor for a few dollars per person?

JR: Back in 1831 or 1832, we discovered chloroform in the West. Centuries earlier, the Chinese discovered acupuncture. Why did we never discover acupuncture? Why did China never discover chloroform? The cultural orientation in each of those civilizations set up the context for the whole range of discoveries they might find. Let's get to the clotting. Is it possible that we could have come up with some other completely different medical approach to clotting that would not have relied on the same technology we are using today? 22

SD: That seems doubtful. 23

JR: It depends on one's faith. You might, you might not. Acupuncture stunned us because we would never have imagined it. 24

SD: Most of the potential of gene therapy is in treating specific defects that might cause death or disability. Are you saying we shouldn't go ahead with this? 25

JR: What is a defect? Why would we ever say no to any genetic change in somatic or germ-line cells that could in some way lessen the possibility of death? Once you begin the process, is a cleft palate a defect? Wouldn't everyone want that out of their baby? How about a clubfoot? Acne? Once you start the process, whenever a monogenic "disorder" is mapped, programmed and can be altered, what parent, what society would not want to eliminate it? 26

What happens if a child comes down with a genetic disease at 15 and dies, and the parents could have intervened and eliminated that monogenic disease in the embryo? Wouldn't they be considered unethical, perhaps even legally culpable? 27

In the end that is a eugenic civilization. Eugenics is the philosophy of using genetic manipulation to create a better organism. Genetic engineering is inseparable from eugenics. You have these professional ethicists who keep looking out the front door for Hitler or Dr. Strangelove or some kind of forced cabal that's going to move us into a brave new world. But the new eugenics came in the back door. It's called commercial eugenics. . . . 28

SD: You conclude *Algeny* by saying that it is "by giving something back, by leaving something behind, by going without that we live on." I guess what you're saying is that we will have to do something that is absolutely against human nature, to put knowledge—in this case, about bioengineering—back where we found it. 29

JR: No. It means we have to change our approach to knowledge. There's a difference between a respectful, mutual give-and-take and outright exploitation. 30

SD: Isn't there a danger here of a broader rejection of science? 31

JR: There is always that danger. But I would say that today's scientists are rejecting science; they're turning it into technology. The people who have squelched science are not Jeremy Rifkin—I know 32

I'm the archetypal Luddite now for Western society. It's not me. Science is being destroyed by our culture's determination to reduce everything to utilitarianism, to reduce all science to what will work, to commercial application. If you want to look at what's destroyed true inquiry, it's our own desire to use our knowledge for power over nature, to control every last aspect of this Earthly existence.

If there is an evil party here, please don't believe it's the scientists. Scientists are just a reflection of the assumptions of the culture. What I am critiquing here is the human race. We all want healthier babies. We all want more efficient plants and animals. We all want a better GNP. The problem in this society and in all societies I know of today is that knowledge is important only to the extent that it allows us to control and manipulate. We want predictability, order, foresight, planning—and genetics is the ultimate planning. 33

SD: Aren't you just coming to the conclusion that such desires are part of the human condition? 34

JR: Yes. But I think it's possible for a change in the human condition. The Bomb has changed a lot. The small change since World War II has been profound. My parents' generation always believed more power is more security. There is a willingness on the part of every generation since the Bomb to begin entertaining at some small level the idea that more power is *less* security. 35

SD: In dealing with this type of issue, why should people listen to the arguments of a political activist with no extensive training in science? 36

JR: They don't have to if they don't want to. I'm not qualified; I'm a human being. One reason people in the establishment are frightened and upset about me is they're worried about their own legitimacy and credentials. Everything we do intimately affects everything else, but we become so narrowly confined in our own fields that we don't develop the other aspects of our knowledge that are essential to be able to place our specific specialty into some context. Many scientists are saying, "Well, this is really for the experts—the question of engineering life." They're wrong. This is a question for the human species to deal with: Do we embark on a journey where we increasingly become the engineers and the architects of life? If we can't engage the entire human race in this set of discussions, then there's never going to be another discussion worthy of public comment. 37

Review Questions

1. What does Rifkin mean by the "desacralization" of life to mere information?

2. What is eugenics? What is the legacy of eugenics in the first part of this century? Why are current advances in genetic engineering associated with eugenics? What is the difference between the old eugenics and the new, according to Rifkin?
3. In his interview, what distinction does Rifkin make between the kind of science he opposes and the kind he favors?

Discussion and Writing Suggestions

1. Does Rifkin seem justified in his charge that modern scientists have succeeded in reducing life to mere patterns of [genetic] information? Has genetics succeeded in "desacralizing life"? (While formulating your response, consider some of the cases discussed by Chamberland and Virshup.)
2. To what extent do you share Rifkin's antipathy toward genetic engineering? Do you agree, for instance, with the *New York Times* article he quotes, which argues that "once scientists are able to repair genetic defects, 'it will become much harder to argue against adding genes that confer desired qualities, like better health, looks, or brains' "?
3. In a multiparagraph essay, explore the connections you detect between Rifkin's reservations about genetic engineering and Huxley's imaginary portrait of a "brave new world."
4. Rifkin asks (in paragraph 19 from *Algeny*): "How important is it that we eliminate all the imperfections, all the defects? What price are we willing to pay to extend our lives, to ensure our own health, to do away with all the inconveniences, the irritations, the nuisances, the infirmities, the suffering, that are so much a part of the human experience?" Respond to these questions. To what extent do you agree with the premise that we may guarantee our health at the cost of our humanity? To what extent do you agree with the premise that we should accept some imperfections, just as we accept our humanity?
5. In the final section of this passage from *Algeny*, Rifkin argues that once we decide that bioengineering is a "boon for humanity," we will find all the rationalizations we need to support this questionable technology, and we will reject all arguments against it. Can you think of other areas—on the political, the social, or even the personal level—in which we are so anxious to gain something we have already determined is desirable that we will rationalize any actions we think necessary to achieve our goal, while rejecting any objections or reservations?

   For example, suppose that the American people, as well as high government officials, are fed up with a Third World dictator who delights in provoking the United States; should we take steps to "eliminate" the problem? Or suppose that we're so frustrated by some social problem—drugs or AIDS—that we're willing to consider suspending civil liberties to deal with it. Both in these cases and in the case of genetic engineering, what are the negatives that we would prefer not to think about? Do you think the analogy—between such cases and genetic engineering—holds up? Explore these questions in a multiparagraph essay.

6. Do you sense a difference between the Jeremy Rifkin who wrote the passage from *Algeny* and the Rifkin who is interviewed for *Science Digest?* If so, try to identify the difference and account for it.

7. In paragraphs 22–26 of the *Science Digest* interview, Rifkin appears to be arguing for an alternative approach to medicine. To what extent do you find his approach desirable? Plausible?

8. In paragraph 34 of the interview, Rifkin asserts:

> Science is being destroyed by our culture's determination to reduce everything to utilitarianism, to reduce all science to what will work, to commercial application. If you want to look at what's destroyed true inquiry, it's our own desire to use our knowledge for power over nature, to control every last aspect of this Earthly existence.

By "science" Rifkin appears to mean the systematic pursuit of knowledge, in the form of general laws, through the testing of hypotheses. (Such fields of knowledge include genetics and nuclear physics.) He distinguishes this from utilitarian applications of science, such as we find in technology. (These applications include genetic engineering and nuclear reactors.) Comment on this idea in a multiparagraph essay. Draw on examples from your own prior knowledge.

9. Write a critique of Rifkin's article, drawing on your responses to some of the above questions.

On the Origin of Specious Critics

STEPHEN JAY GOULD

Rifkin's attacks on bioengineering have not gone unanswered. Many scientists have pointed to Rifkin's lack of scientific credentials. (Rifkin has at least partially turned this charge against his attackers, asserting that scientists often consider themselves an elite community, immune to criticism from lay people, who have as much stake as scientists in the effects of technological advances.) Rifkin's strategies, as well as his ideas, have also been attacked. A recent article about him in Forbes *(a business magazine) was entitled "Ministry of Fear." David Baltimore, a Nobel Laureate from MIT, who once refused to share a speaker's platform with*

"On the Origin of Specious Critics" by Stephen Jay Gould from pp. 34–42 in *Discover*, January 1985. Reprinted by permission of the author.

Rifkin, argues that "he has poisoned the whole atmosphere around which biotechnology has developed, rather than allowing it to be developed in a rational and thoughtful manner." Baltimore claimed that Rifkin's successful effort to ban Monsanto's "Frostban" microbe was ridiculous, since the organism found in Frostban also appears in nature. In fact, so notorious has Rifkin become, to such an extent has he "radicalized" the debate over genetic engineering, that more moderate critics, who have (according to some scientists) more legitimate reservations about bioengineering, are afraid to speak out, for fear of being associated with Rifkin.

Perhaps the most influential of Rifkin's critics has been Stephen Jay Gould. Born in New York City in 1941, Gould teaches biology and geology at Harvard University. He has written both scholarly papers on paleontology (the study of prehistoric forms of life through the fossil record) and popular essays that have helped make science understandable to nonscientists. Gould is particularly concerned with the misuse of science for political and social purposes—or "scientific racism." As he wrote in The Mismeasure of Man *(1982), "Few tragedies can be more extensive than the stunting of life, few injustices deeper than the denial of an opportunity to strive or even to hope, by a limit imposed from without but falsely identified as lying within." Gould's frequently prize-winning essays, written originally for the magazine* Natural History, *have been collected into several volumes, including* Ever Since Darwin *(1977),* The Panda's Thumb *(1980),* Hen's Teeth and Horse's Toes *(1983), and* The Flamingo's Smile *(1985). His style has been characterized by one reviewer as "full of fun, totally without pretentiousness, and absolutely clear."*

As you read the following article, consider not only what Gould says but the systematic method by which he makes his points. Gould's review, whether or not you agree with it, may be seen as a model critique.

Evolution has a definite geometry well portrayed by our ancient metaphor, the tree of life. Lineages split and diverge like the branches of a tree. A species, once distinct, is permanently on its own; the branches of life do not coalesce. Extinction is truly forever, persistence a personal odyssey. But art does not always imitate nature. Biotechnology, or genetic engineering, has aroused fear and opposition because it threatens to annul this fundamental property of life—to place genes of one species into the program of another, thereby combining what nature has kept separate from time immemorial. Two concerns—one immediate and practical, the other distant and deep—have motivated the opposition. 1

Some critics fear that certain conjunctions might have potent and unanticipated effects—creating a resistant agent of disease or simply a new creature so hardy and fecund that, like Kurt Vonnegut's *ice-* 2 *nine,* it spreads to engulf the earth in a geological millisecond. I am not persuaded by these excursions into science fiction, but the distant and deeper issue does merit discussion: What are the consequences, ethical, aesthetic, and practical, of altering life's fundamental geometry and permitting one species to design new creatures at will, combining bits and pieces of lineages distinct for billions of years?

Jeremy Rifkin has been the most vocal opponent of genetic 3
engineering in recent months. He has won court cases and aroused fury in the halls of science with his testimony about immediate dangers. However, his major statement, a book titled *Algeny* (for the modern alchemy of genes), concentrates almost entirely on the deep and distant issue. His activities based on immediate fears have been widely reported and rebutted. But *Algeny,* although it was published more than a year ago, has not been adequately analyzed or dissected. Its status as prophecy or pretension, philosophy or pamphleteering, must be assessed, for *Algeny* touts itself as the manifesto of a movement to save nature and simple decency from the hands of impatient and rapacious science.

I will state my conclusion—bald and harsh—at the outset: I re- 4
gard *Algeny* as a cleverly constructed tract of anti-intellectual propaganda masquerading as scholarship. Among books promoted as serious intellectual statements by important thinkers, I don't think I have ever read a shoddier work. Damned shame, too, because the deep issue is troubling and I do not disagree with Rifkin's basic plea for respecting the integrity of evolutionary lineages. But devious means compromise good ends, and we shall have to save Rifkin's humane conclusion from his own questionable tactics.

The basic argument of *Algeny* rests upon a parody of an important 5
theme advanced by contemporary historians of science against the myth of objectivity and inexorable scientific progress: science is socially embedded; its theories are not simple deductions from observed facts of nature, but a complex mixture of social ideology (often unconsciously expressed) and empirical constraint. This theme is liberating for science; it embodies the human side of our enterprise and depicts us as passionate creatures struggling with limited tools to understand a complex reality, not as robots programmed to convert objective information into immutable truth. But in Rifkin's hands the theme becomes a caricature. Rifkin ignores the complex interplay of social bias with *facts* of nature and promotes a crude socioeconomic determinism that views our historical succession of biological worldviews—from creationism to Darwinism to the new paradigm now supposedly under construction—as so many simple reflections of social ideology.

From this socioeconomic determinism, Rifkin constructs his 6
specific brief: Darwinian evolutionism, he asserts, was the creation of

industrial capitalism, the age of pyrotechnology. Arising in this context as a simple reflection of social ideology, it never had any sound basis in reason or evidence. It is now dying because the age of pyrotechnology is yielding to an era of biotechnology—and biotech demands a new view of life. Darwinism translated the industrial machine into nature; biotech models nature as a computer and substitutes information for material parts.

Darwinism spawned (or reflected) evil in its support for exploitation of man and nature, but at least it respected the integrity of species (while driving some to extinction) because it lacked the technology to change them by mixture and instant transmutation. But the new paradigm dissolves species into strings of information that can be reshuffled at will. 7

The new temporal theory of evolution replaces the idea of life as mere machinery with the idea of life as mere information. All living things are drained of their aliveness and turned into abstract messages. There is no longer any question of sacredness or inviolability. How could there be when there are no longer any recognizable boundaries to respect? In the age of biotechnology, separate species with separate names gradually give way to systems of information that can be reprogrammed into an infinite number of biological combinations. 8

But what can we do if we wish to save nature as we know it—a system divided into packages of porcupines and primroses, cabbages and kings? We can seek no help from science, Rifkin claims, for science is a monolith masquerading as objective knowledge, but really reflecting the dominant ideology of a new technological age. We can only make an ethical decision to "re-sacralize" nature by respecting the inviolability of its species. We must, for the first time in history, decide *not* to institute a possible technology, despite its immediately attractive benefits in such areas as medicine and agriculture. 9

I have devoted my own career to evolutionary biology, and I have been among the strongest critics of strict Darwinism. Yet Rifkin's assertions bear no relationship to what I have observed and practiced for 25 years. Evolutionary theory has never been healthier or more exciting. We are experiencing a ferment of new ideas and theories, but they are revising and extending Darwin, not burying him. How can Rifkin construct a world so different from the one I inhabit and know so well? Either I am blind or he is wrong—and I think I can show, by analyzing his slipshod scholarship and basic misunderstanding of science, that his world is an invention constructed to validate his own private hopes. I shall summarize my critique in five charges: 10

1. Rifkin does not understand Darwinism, and his arguments refute an absurd caricature, not the theory itself. He trots out all the standard mischaracterizations, usually confined nowadays to creationist tracts. Just three examples: "According to Darwin," Rifkin wrties, "everything evolved by chance." Since the complexity of cellular life cannot arise by accident, Darwinism is absurd: "According to the odds, the one-cell organism is so complex that the likelihood of its coming together by sheer accident and chance is computed to be around $1/10^{78436}$." But Darwin himself, and Darwinians ever since, always stressed, as a cardinal premise, that natural selection is not a theory of randomness. Chance may describe the origin of new variation by mutation, but natural selection, the agent of change, is a conventional deterministic process that builds adaptation by preserving favorable variants. 11

Rifkin then dismisses Darwinism as a tautology; fitness is defined by survival, and the catch phrase "survival of the fittest" reduces to "survival of those that survive"—and therefore has no meaning. Darwin resolved this issue, as Darwinians have ever since, by defining fitness as predictable advantage before the fact, not as recorded survival afterward (as we may predict the biomechanical improvements that might help zebras outrun or outmaneuver lions; survival then becomes a testable consequence). 12

Rifkin regards Darwinism as absurd because "natural selection makes no room for long-range considerations. Every new trait has to be immediately useful or it is discarded." How, therefore, can natural selection explain the origin of a bird's wing, since the intermediate forms cannot fly: What good is five per cent of a wing? The British biologist St. George Jackson Mivart developed this critique in 1871 as the argument about "incipient stages of useful structures." Darwin met the challenge by adding a chapter to the sixth edition of the *Origin of Species.* One need not agree with Darwin's resolution, but one does have a responsibility to acknowledge it. Darwin argued that intermediate stages performed different functions; feathers of an incipient wing may act as excellent organs of thermoregulation—a particular problem in the smallest of dinosaurs, which evolved into birds. 13

Rifkin displays equally little comprehension of basic arguments about evolutionary geometry. He thinks that *Archaeopteryx* has been refuted as an intermediate link between reptiles and birds because some true birds have been found in rocks of the same age. But evolution is a branching bush, not a ladder. Ancestors survive after descendants branch off. Dogs evolved from wolves, but wolves (though threatened) are hanging tough. And a species of *Australopithecus* lived side by side with its descendant *Homo* for more than a million years in Africa. 14

15 Rifkin doesn't grasp the current critiques of strict Darwinism any better. He caricatures my own theory of punctuated equilibrium [that evolution moves in fits and starts rather than by slow, steady change] as a sudden response to ecological catastrophe: "The idea is that these catastrophic events spawned monstrous genetic mutations within existing species, most of which were lethal. A few of the mutations, however, managed to survive and become the precursors of a new species." But punctuated equilibrium, as Niles Eldredge and I have always emphasized, is about ordinary speciation (taking tens of thousands of years) and its abrupt appearance at low scales of geological resolution, not about ecological catastrophe and sudden genetic change.

16 Rifkin, it appears, understands neither the fundamentals of Darwinism, its current critiques, nor even the basic topology of the evolutionary tree.

17 2. Rifkin shows no understanding of the norms and procedures of science: he displays little comprehension of what science is and how scientists work. He consistently misses the essential distinction between fact (claims about the world's empirical content) and theory (ideas that explain and interpret facts)—using arguments against one to refute the other. Against Darwinism (a theory of evolutionary mechanisms) he cites the British physiologist Gerald Kerkut's *Implications of Evolution,* a book written to refute the factual claim that all living creatures have a common ancestry, and to argue instead that life may have arisen several times from chemical precursors—an issue not addressed by Darwinism. (Creationist lawyers challenged me with the same misunderstanding during my cross-examination at the Arkansas "equal time" trial three years ago, in which the creationists unsuccessfully fought for compulsory presentation of their views in science classrooms.) Rifkin then suggests that the entire field of evolution may be a pseudo science because the great French zoologist Pierre-Paul Grassé is so critical of Darwinism (the theory of natural selection might be wrong, but Grassé has devoted his entire life to study the fact of evolution).

18 Science is a pluralistic enterprise, validly pursued in many modes. But Rifkin ignores its richness by stating that direct manipulation by repeatable experiment is the only acceptable method for reaching a scientific conclusion. Since evolution treats historically unique events that occurred millions of years ago, it cannot be a science. Rifkin doesn't seem to realize that he is throwing out half of science—nearly all of geology and most of astronomy, for instance—with his evolutionary bath water. Historical science is a valid pursuit, but it uses methods different from the controlled experiment of Rifkin's all-encompassing caricature—search for an underlying pattern

among unique events, and retrodiction (predicting the yet undiscovered results of past events), for example.

3. Rifkin does not respect the procedures of fair argument. He uses every debater's trick in the book to mischaracterize and trivialize his opposition, and to place his own dubious claims in a rosy light. Just four examples: 19

The synecdoche (trying to dismiss a general notion by citing a single poor illustration). He suggests that science knows nothing about the evolutionary tree of horses, and has sold the public a bill of goods (the great horse caper, he calls it), because one exhibit, set up at the American Museum of Natural History in 1905, arranged fossil horses in order of size, not genealogy. Right, Jeremy, that was a lousy exhibit, but you might read George Gaylord Simpson's book *Horses* to see what we do know. 20

The half quote (stopping in the middle so that an opponent appears to agree with you, or seems merely ridiculous). Rifkin quotes me on the argument about incipient stages of useful structures discussed a few paragraphs ago: "Harvard's Stephen Jay Gould posed the dilemma when he observed, 'What good is half a jaw or half a wing?' " Sure, I posed the dilemma, but then followed it with an entire essay supporting Darwin's resolution based on different function in intermediate stages. Rifkin might have mentioned it and not adduced me in his support. Rifkin then quotes a famous line from Darwin as if it represented the great man's admission of impotence: "Darwin himself couldn't believe it, even though it was his own theory that advanced the proposition. He wrote: 'To suppose that the eye, with all of its inimitable contrivances . . . could have been formed by natural selection, seems, I freely confess, absurd in the highest possible degree.' " But Rifkin might have mentioned that Darwin follows this statement with one of his most brilliant sections—a documentation of nature's graded intermediates between simple pinhole eyes and the complexity of our own, and an argument that the power of new theories resides largely in their ability to resolve previous absurdities. 21

Refuting what your opponents never claimed. In the 1950s, Stanley Miller performed a famous experiment that synthesized amino acids from hypothetical components of the earth's original atmosphere. Rifkin describes it with glaring hype: "With great fanfare, the world was informed that scientists had finally succeeded in forming life from nonlife, the dream of magicians, sorcerers, and alchemists from time immemorial." He then points out, quite correctly, that the experiment did no such thing, and that the distance from amino acid to life is immense. But Miller never claimed that he had made life. The experiment stands in all our text books as a demonstration that some 22 simple components of living systems can be made from inorganic chemicals. I was taught this 25 years ago; I have lectured about it for 15 years. I have never in all my professional life heard a scientist say that Miller or anyone else has made life from non-life.

Refuting what your opponents refuted long ago. Rifkin devotes a whole section to ridiculing evolution because its supporters once advanced the "biogenetic law" that embryos repeat the adult stages of their ancestry—now conclusively refuted. But Darwinian evolutionists did the refuting more than 50 years ago (good science is self-correcting). 23

4. Rifkin ignores the most elementary procedures of fair scholarship. His book, brought forth as a major conceptual statement about the nature of science and the history of biology, displays painful ignorance of its subject. His quotations are primarily from old and discredited secondary sources (including some creationist propaganda tracts). I see no evidence that he has ever read much of Darwin in the original. He obviously knows nothing about (or chooses not to mention) all the major works of Darwinian scholarship written by modern historians. His continual barrage of misquotes and half quotes records this partial citation from excerpts in hostile secondary sources. 24

His prose is often purple in the worst journalistic tradition. When invented claims are buttressed by such breathless description, the effect can be quite amusing. He mentions the geneticist T. H. Morgan's invocation of the tautology argument discussed previously in this essay: "Not until Morgan began to suspect that natural selection was a victim of circular reasoning did anyone in the scientific community even question what was regarded by all as a profound truth. . . . Morgan's observation shocked the scientific establishment." Now, I ask, how does he know this? He cites no evidence of any shock, even of any contemporary comment. He quotes Morgan himself only from secondary sources. In fact, everything about the statement is wrong, just plain wrong. The tautology argument dates from the 1870s. Morgan didn't invent it (and Darwin, in my opinion, ably refuted it when Morgan was a baby). Morgan, moreover, was no noble knight sallying forth against a monolithic Darwinian establishment. When he wrote his critique in the 1920s, natural selection was a distinctly unpopular theory among evolutionists (the tide didn't turn in Darwin's favor until the late 1930s). Morgan, if anything, *was* the establishment, and his critique, so far as I know, didn't shock a soul or elicit any extensive commentary. 25

5. *Algeny* is full of ludicrous, simple errors. I particularly enjoyed Rifkin's account of Darwin in the Galapagos. After describing the "great masses" of vultures, condors, vampire bats, jaguars, and snakes that Darwin saw on these islands, Rifkin writes: "It was a 26

savage, primeval scene, menacing in every detail. Everywhere there was bloodletting, and the ferocious, unremittent battle for survival. The air was dank and foul, and the thick stench of volcanic ash veiled the islands with a kind of ghoulish drape." Well, I guess Rifkin has never been there; and he obviously didn't bother to read anything about these fascinating islands. Except for snakes, none of those animals live on the Galapagos. In fact, the Galapagos house no terrestrial predators at all; as a result, the animals have no fear of human beings and do not flee when approached. The Galapagos are unusual, as Darwin noted, precisely because they are not scenes of Hobbes's *bellum omnium contra omnes* (the war of all against all). And, by the way, no thick stench or ghoulish drape either; the volcanic terrains are beautiful, calm, and peaceful—not in eruption when Darwin visited, not now either.

Jeremy Rifkin, in short, has argued himself, inextricably, into a 27
corner. He has driven off his natural allies by silly, at times dishonest, argument and nasty caricature. He has saddled his legitimate concern with an extremism that would outlaw both humane and fascinating scientific research. He legitimate brief speaks for the integrity of organisms and species. It would be a bleak world indeed that treated living things as no more than separable sequences of information, available for disarticulation and recombination in any order that pleased human whim. But I do not see why we should reject all of genetic engineering because its technology might, one day, permit such a perversion of decency in the hands of some latter-day Hitler—you may as well outlaw printing because the same machine that composes Shakespeare can also set *Mein Kampf*. The domino theory does not apply to all human achievements. If we could, by transplanting a bacterial gene, confer disease or cold resistance upon an important crop plant, should we not do so in a world where people suffer so terribly from malnutrition? Must such an event imply that, tomorrow, corn and wheat, sea horses and orchids will be thrown into a gigantic vat, torn apart into genetic units, and reassembled into rows of identical human servants? Eternal vigilance, to recombine some phrases, is the price of technological achievement.

The debate about genetic engineering has often been portrayed, 28
falsely, as one of many battles between the political left and right—leftists in opposition, rightists plowing ahead. It is not so simple; it rarely is. Used humanely for the benefit of ordinary people, not the profits of a few entrepreneurs, this technology need not be feared by the left. I, for one, would rather campaign for proper use, not abolition. If Rifkin's argument embodies any antithesis, it is not left versus right, but romanticism, in its most dangerous anti-intellectual form, versus respect for knowledge and its humane employment. In both its content and presentation, *Algeny* belongs in the sordid company of

anti-science. Few campaigns are more dangerous than emotional calls for proscription rather than thought.

I have been so harsh because I believe that Rifkin has seriously harmed a cause that is very dear to me and to nearly all my scientific colleagues. Rifkin has placed all of us beyond the pale of decency by arguing that scientific paradigms are simple expressions of socioeconomic bias, that biotech implies (and will impose) a new view of organisms as strings of separable information (not wholes of necessary integrity), and that all scientists will eventually go along with this heartless idea. Well, Mr. Rifkin, who then will be for you? Where will you find your allies in the good fight for respect of evolutionary lineages? You have rejected us, reviled us, but we are with you. We are taxonomists, ecologists, and evolutionists—most of us Darwinians. We have devoted our lives to the study of species in their natural habitats. We have struggled to understand—and we greatly admire—the remarkable construction and operation of organisms, the product of complex evolutionary histories, cascades of astounding improbability stretching back for millions of years. We know these organisms, and we love them—as they are. We would not dissolve this handiwork of four billion years to satisfy the hubris of one species. We respect the integrity of nature, Mr. Rifkin. But your arguments lack integrity. This we deplore. 29

Review Questions

1. At what point near the beginning does Gould summarize his overall critical reaction to *Algeny?*
2. What are Gould's chief objections to Rifkin's *Algeny?*
3. Does Gould reject all the arguments made by Rifkin in *Algeny?* Explain.

Discussion and Writing Suggestions

1. Determine the organization of Gould's critique. Compare this organization with the paradigm for critique discussed in Chapter 2.
2. Based on your reading of the passage from *Algeny* and the interview with Rifkin, do you believe that Gould has been fair in his criticism? Has he summarized Rifkin's views accurately, for instance? Are his criticisms reasonable? Logical?
3. Gould spends most of the final paragraph directly addressing Rifkin. Why do you think he does this? Is his technique effective? Why or why not?
4. In your personal (if not your academic) life, do you recall being guilty of any of the types of unfair argument cited by Gould in paragraphs 20–23? For example, have you ever tried "to dismiss a general notion by citing a single poor illustration"? Recount several such incidents. (If you have

never been guilty of a single one of these practices, explain how someone you know—your mother or father, perhaps, or your teacher—has been.)

5. As we mentioned in the headnote, Gould's style has been characterized as "full of fun, totally without pretentiousness, and absolutely clear." Based on his critique of *Algeny,* to what extent do you agree with this characterization? Cite specific examples.
6. Write a critique of a text you have read recently (it may be another essay in this book), imitating Gould's approach in his *Algeny* critique. State your conclusion near the outset and categorize your negative or positive reactions into several types, providing examples from the text to support these reactions.
7. Write a critique of Gould's essay, drawing on your responses to some of the questions above.

What Price Mighty Mouse?

THE EDITORS OF *THE NEW REPUBLIC*

Earlier articles in this chapter have focused both on the general controversy surrounding genetic engineering (Should it be undertaken at all?) and on particular dilemmas engendered by this new technology (Should prospective parents attempt to determine whether their fetus is genetically "defective"? Should employers be able to genetically screen prospective employees?). Another set of dilemmas bears on the commercial applications of genetically engineered organisms. Bioengineering, after all, is potentially a billion-dollar industry. It is bad enough (critics argue) to allow arrogant scientists to create new life forms; how much worse to turn over such godlike power to private corporations, responsible to no one but their shareholders. After the U.S. Patent and Trademark Office announced in 1987 that individuals and firms could patent genetically engineered animals, Jeremy Rifkin declared, "With that one decision by a couple of guys at the patent office, the Government handed over the entire animal kingdom—from apes to insects—to the multinationals, the pharmaceutical and biotech companies, which are the only ones that can afford this kind of basic research." Declaring that this was "the greatest assault on animal welfare in history," Rifkin accused the Patent Office of turning animals into products "indistinguishable from microwave ovens and automobiles."

In the following article, the editors of The New Republic *consider this issue and conclude that there is nothing wrong with patenting*

---

genetically engineered animals. As you read the article, see whether you agree more with Jeremy Rifkin or with The New Republic *editors.*

Donald Quigg, head of the U.S. Patent Office, has some reassuring words for the American people. As the *Wall Street Journal* put it, "Mr. Quigg reiterated . . . that the agency will not patent human beings." He has no such promises for other organisms. In fact, the occasion for his remark was the patenting of a mouse that's genetically predisposed to cancer, developed—or, rather, invented—at Harvard University for laboratory use. 1

This mouse was not the first patented organism. In 1980 the Supreme Court ruled that an oil-eating bacterium designed by a General Electric researcher was "not nature's handiwork, but his own," and ever since then microorganisms have been a commodity of intense commercial interest. But there had been doubt as to whether the Court's decision could be extended to multicellular organisms. The Patent Office has now expressed its view; for the first time, someone has patented something that can look you in the eye. 2

This milestone, in addition to elevating the moods of venture capitalists and molecular biologists, has breathed some life into their opposition, a coalition of farmers, environmentalists, animal rights activists, and assorted clergy. Letters of protest are being written, and there is fresh momentum behind anti-biotechnology legislation. A House bill would place a two-year moratorium on animal patenting and a Senate bill would ban it. 3

Proponents of the legislation have a truckload of grievances. They worry about the morality of such Promethean intervention in nature; about the environmental impact of new species; about a pernicious concentration of power in the pharmaceutical and argicultural industries; about higher prices for consumers; about the demise of the small, low-tech farmer. Many of these concerns are unfounded, and the rest are misdirected. 4

Genetically engineered organisms come in two varieties. They can serve as manufacturers (bacteria that make insulin or human growth hormone) or as products (bacteria that protect crops from caterpillars or frost). To put it in patenting lingo, they can be the subject of process patents or of product patents. So far, higher forms of life have been seen less as products than as manufacturers. Though there is much talk of low-fat pigs and preternaturally productive dairy cows, usually it is not the animals themselves that result from gene splicing. Rather, gene splicing produces a hormone (such as bovine somatropin) that, when administered, makes the animal lean or profuse. For now, at least, genetically engineered multicellular organisms will serve mainly as factories: Japanese silkworms that make hepatitis vaccine, for example, and mice whose milk contains tissue 5 plasminogen activator (TPA), a kind of organic Drano that dissolves blood clots during a heart attack.

The bigger and smarter the animals, and the bigger and deeper their eyes, the queasier people get about all this. A reference to patenting a mammal is usually enough to lead a conversation to the phrase "moral implications" within seconds. But although the word "patent" is what so reliably unsettles people, it isn't really the patenting that worries them. Invariably, the moral objections to patenting animals are the moral objections to genetic engineering itself. Most of the people who have used the patented mouse as a vehicle to stir up debate on the subject aren't really anti-patenting; they're anti-gene-splicing. This is especially true of the prime mover of anti-patenting legislation: Jeremy Rifkin, political activist and tireless champion of technological stagnation. 6

The silliest of the moral concerns over gene-splicing is about inserting human genes in non-human organisms. To hear some people talk, you'd think scientists all over America are designing chimpanzees that do windows. What scientists are actually doing is taking a very mundane, single human gene and inserting it in a very mundane organism. Thus, insulin-manufacturing bacteria contain a human gene for making insulin. So far, none of the bacteria have sprouted ears or started carrying briefcases, and we don't expect them to anytime soon. 7

Most of the moral objections to genetic engineering are less susceptible to rebuttal. For example: "The gift of life from God, in all its forms and species, should not be regarded solely as if it were a chemical product subject to alteration and patentable for economic benefit." Can't argue with that. Because it's not an argument—it's an assertion. It assumes the acceptance of a particular religious philosophy, from which it supposedly follows. Leaving aside the question of whether it really *does* follow—whether the Bible actually frowns on making frost-free bacteria—the fact is that Judeo-Christian doctrine is not a reliable guideline anyway. This nation no longer possesses a consensual religious basis—least of all in the high-brow circles where these issues get hashed out. We are left instead with a set of values that is Judeo-Christian in ancestry but is now best described as vaguely utilitarian: pretty much everyone agrees that something is bad if it brings unjustified pain and suffering. 8

Hence the more formidable moral critique of gene-splicing: questions about the welfare of the animals engineered. That mouse with the cancer gene, after all, doesn't have a very pleasant life ahead. True enough. But on the other hand, being a laboratory mouse has never been an especially alluring calling. We long ago decided that sacrificing animals to science, and to our appetites, is justified. In fact, we long ago decided that *creating* animals expressly for our use, and 9 without much regard for their welfare, is OK. Consider the Chihuahua, a dinky caldron of seething neuroses. Like all dogs (and cows, pigs, and thoroughbred horses) it is a product of human design, of conscious intervention in evolution. Harvard's mouse, the result of a more sophisticated intervention, doesn't carry us into a new moral realm.

This is not to deny that it brings us into a new corner of the old realm. Gene-splicing may well yield animals more grotesque and miserable than the products of slow, steady breeding. There are already stories of cross-eyed, arthritic pigs in a Department of Agriculture laboratory, and more such stories can be expected when the single-gene manipulations of the present are passé, and scientists are inserting hundreds of genes to orchestrate complex behavioral changes. How *would* we begin to think—four or five decades down the road—about the morality of building a chimpanzee that did windows? 10

This leads to something everyone already knows: biotechnology shouldn't be (and isn't) an industry free of regulation. Congress's power over interstate commerce gives it all the leverage it will need to keep things on the up and up. One can envision an agency that evaluates each patented organism with an eye to the welfare not only of the environment and the public, but of the organism. If in five years there is evidence of great biotechnological cruelty to animals, some such restraint will be in order 11

The economic objections to patenting animals, unlike the moral ones, really are about patenting. They presuppose genetic engineering and focus on whether the enterprise is best governed by patent law. In particular, concern centers on the 17-year monopoly granted by a patent. Farmers fear they'll be left at the mercy of a few large, predatory corporations that will control vital raw materials. 12

Some farmers *do* have something to fear from biotechnology. Things that make farms more productive have a way of lessening the demand for farmers. But that's true whether the technologies are patented or not. And it's true whether the technologies are agricultural or not. Workers in any industry can be displaced by the gains in productivity that society values so highly. It's a sacrifice for the greater good: the workers have to figure out another way to make ends meet, but society as a whole benefits. Like everyone else, we mourn the passing of the small, self-sufficient farm—because of both the human toll and the loss to the nation's cultural landscape. But forced to choose between feeding more people more cheaply and propping up lots of Midwestern Museums of Americana, we'll take the food. 13

Obviously, if market concentration in agricultural industries 14 approaches unhealthy proportions—with or without the aid of patenting—anti-trust law should be vigorously applied. But meanwhile we shouldn't stifle biotechnology—a young, robust industry in which the United States has a strong foothold—out of vague fears about big business.

When playing to a crowd of consumers, opponents of gene splicing 15
often claim that patenting will raise the price of meat. Jeremy Rifkin says that a company with a patent on, say, a very valuable cow "is going to charge the farmer more and the farmer's going to charge the consumer more." Is his opinion of the average farmer's intelligence really this low? Sure, if Embryogen patents cows that yield 30 percent more milk, or require 20 percent less grain, then it will have the market on those cows cornered and probably will charge more for them than for garden variety cows. But if the price demanded wipes out the gains in productivity, no farmer in his right mind will pay it. Unless the upshot of a biological innovation is to lower the cost of production (or improve the quality of the product), it will never get off the ground.

The economic debate over patenting life forms is really the same 16
debate the institution of patenting has always engendered: Is it better to facilitate innovation by granting a monopoly on the exploitation of new ideas, or to facilitate the *proliferation* of innovations by denying such monopolies? In settling on our patent system, the Founding Fathers, notably Thomas Jefferson, favored the first priority, with some deference to the second. They granted inventors temporary monopolies, and said that in exchange the inventors would have to put all relevant information on the record, thus facilitating further innovation. The hope was that an inventor would seldom make it to the 17th year of his monopoly before being left in the dust by an idea that surpassed, and built on, his own. So far there's no cause to doubt this approach. Indeed, one common complaint of the Rifkinites is that technological innovation is moving too fast. What more powerful testament to Jefferson's wisdom?

There's no reason to expect the patenting system to work any less 17
effectively with organic than with inorganic inventions. True, you do hear complaints about biotechnology monopolies—about, for example, the fact that tissue plasminogen activator costs around $2,200 a pop. But several companies are already pursuing second-generation TPA, which they hope will be superior to, and patentably distinct from, the original. In the meantime, you're not hearing any complaints from the heart attack victims whose lives have been saved by TPA. If the anti-patenting forces had had their way, and there hadn't been a small fortune in inventing a means of synthesizing TPA, the stuff probably wouldn't be available at any price.

One of the more intriguing issues in biotechnology is how you adapt patent law to machines that automatically make copies of themselves—i.e., animals. Will buying a patented cow entail royalty payments for every calf and grandcalf, ad infinitum? Farmers fear burdensome paperwork. On the other hand, biotechnology companies understandably worry that without royalties, selling two high-tech cows will amount to handing over the keys to the factory. 18

The farmers' best weapon as they fight bothersome royalty schemes is their purchasing power. If they don't want to buy an animal that comes with a lifetime of paperwork, they don't have to. And if Congress wants to blunt farmers' opposition to animal patenting, it can subtly but significantly alter patent-office policy in this nebulous area. Instead of today's automatic presumption of royalty obligations, the presumption can be that no royalties are due in the absence of an explicit contractual provision. 19

There has always been something odd about the opposition to animal patenting. Some of the opponents worry that technological change will come at breakneck speed, outstripping our ability to grapple with the attendant moral questions. Others worry that patents will permit big, evil corporations to monopolize the profits from innovation and suppress technological progress. One group or the other must be wrong. 20

Actually, both are half-wrong. Yes, the technology will move briskly, but for the foreseeable future the moral lesson will be a very old one: we shouldn't be needlessly cruel to animals, especially animals with big, deep eyes. And yes, because of patents, fortunes will be made from biotechnology, some of them by large corporations. But that won't stifle progress or subvert American economic values, as Thomas Jefferson understood. 21

Review Questions

1. According to the writers, what are the two varieties of genetically engineered organisms? Why has controversy recently arisen over the creation of new organisms, when scientists have been creating new organisms for almost two decades?
2. How do the writers suggest that the new industry of engineering multicellular organisms be regulated?
3. Why do the writers argue that the economic arguments against patenting new organisms are no different from (and therefore no more persuasive than) the economic arguments against any more efficient method of production?
4. How do the writers bring in Thomas Jefferson to support their views?

Discussion and Writing Suggestions

1. *New Republic* articles, though treating serious subjects, are frequently written in a rather flip tone. (A writer's tone—serious, lighthearted, angry, cynical, and so on—generally reflects her or his attitude toward the subject under discussion.) Note, for example, the title of the article, or paragraph 7, with its reference to scientists "designing chimpanzees that do windows" and its observation that "none of the bacteria have sprouted ears or started carrying briefcases, and we don't expect them to anytime soon." Do you find such a style distracting or feel that it detracts from the seriousness of the argument? Explain.
2. In paragraph 9, the writers argue that genetically engineered organisms should create no new set of moral dilemmas for us, since humans have been crossbreeding both plants and animals for centuries and doing it for *our* benefit, not theirs. To what extent do you find this line of reasoning plausible?
3. In paragraph 13, the writers argue that gains in productivity are often accompanied by displacement of workers in less efficient industries. "It's a sacrifice for the greater good," they argue; "the workers have to figure out another way to make ends meet, but society as a whole benefits." To what extent are you satisfied with this argument?
4. Draft a law that you believe is necessary to regulate the development, patenting, and marketing of bioengineered organisms. (The law might, at one extreme, prohibit such development and marketing, and at the other, levy no restrictions whatever.) Don't worry about drafting legal language. Just explain what is and is not permissible and specify the penalties for noncompliance with the law. (For an example of legal language, see the section of the AIDS virus disclosure law on p. 26 [under "Paraphrase"].) In a separate, multiparagraph section, justify the provisions of this law. *Or,* write a letter to your congressional representative, recommending such a law.
5. Write a critique of this article, drawing on your responses to some of the questions above.

On Cloning a Human Being

LEWIS THOMAS

Most of the preceding articles have been fairly serious in tone, so the following article, more whimsical in spirit, may come as something of a relief. In it, physician and science writer Lewis Thomas takes up the issue of cloning human beings. (Cloning is a process—still impossible for complex organisms—whereby exact duplicates of whole organisms are generated from the DNA in the nucleus of a single cell from that organism.) Wouldn't it be wonderful if we could clone ourselves—or anyone else we thought worthy of preserving indefinitely? Well, maybe not so wonderful, concludes the author.

Born in 1913, Lewis Thomas graduated from Princeton in 1933 and from Harvard Medical School in 1937. During his career, he has been a distinguished researcher (writing many papers on pathology and infectious disease), a teacher, and an administrator. He taught pathology at Yale University and at Cornell University Medical College and has served as president and chancellor of the Sloan-Kettering Cancer Center in New York. Like Stephen Jay Gould, Thomas is able to write successfully both for specialized and for general audiences. In 1971, Thomas began writing a monthly column in the New England Journal of Medicine. *Periodically, these columns were collected into several award-winning books, including* The Lives of a Cell: Notes of a Biology Watcher *(1974);* The Medusa and the Snail *(1979), source of the following essay;* The Youngest Science *(1983); and* Late Night Thoughts on Listening to Mahler's Ninth Symphony *(1983).*

It is now theoretically possible to recreate an identical creature from any animal or plant, from the DNA contained in the nucleus of any somatic cell. A single plant root-tip cell can be teased and seduced into conceiving a perfect copy of the whole plant; a frog's intestinal epithelial cell possesses the complete instructions needed for a new, same frog. If the technology were further advanced, you could do this with a human being, and there are now startled predictions all over the place that this will in fact be done, someday, in order to provide a version of immortality for carefully selected, especially valuable people. 1

The cloning of humans is on most of the lists of things to worry about from Science, along with behavior control, genetic engineering, transplanted heads, computer poetry, and the unrestrained growth of plastic flowers. 2

Cloning is the most dismaying of prospects, mandating as it does the elimination of sex with only a metaphoric elimination of death as compensation. It is almost no comfort to know that one's cloned, identical surrogate lives on, especially when the living will very likely involve edging one's real, now aging self off to the side, sooner or later. It is hard to imagine anything like filial affection or respect for a single, unmated nucleus; harder still to think of one's new, self-generated self as anything but an absolute, desolate orphan. Not to mention the complex interpersonal relationship involved in raising 3 one's self from infancy, teaching the language, enforcing discipline, instilling good manners, and the like. How would you feel if you became an incorrigible juvenile delinquent by proxy, at the age of fifty-five?

The public questions are obvious. Who is to be selected, and on 4
what qualifications? How to handle the risks of misused technology, such as self-determined cloning by the rich and powerful but socially objectionable, or the cloning by governments of dumb, docile masses for the world's work? What will be the effect on all the uncloned rest of us of human sameness? After all, we've accustomed ourselves through hundreds of millennia to the continual exhilaration of uniqueness; each of us is totally different, in a fundamental sense, from all the other four billion. Selfness is an essential fact of life. The thought of human nonselfness, precise sameness, is terrifying, when you think about it.

Well, don't think about it, because it isn't a probable possibility, 5
not even as a long shot for the distant future, in my opinion. I agree that you might clone some people who would look amazingly like their parental cell donors, but the odds are that they'd be almost as different as you or me, and certainly more different than any of today's identical twins.

The time required for the experiment is only one of the problems, 6
but a formidable one. Suppose you wanted to clone a prominent, spectacularly successful diplomat, to look after the Middle East problems of the distant future. You'd have to catch him and persuade him, probably not very hard to do, and extirpate a cell. But then you'd have to wait for him to grow up through embryonic life and then for at least forty years more, and you'd have to be sure all observers remained patient and unmeddlesome through his unpromising, ambiguous childhood and adolescence.

Moreover, you'd have to be sure of recreating his environment, 7
perhaps down to the last detail. "Environment" is a word which really means people, so you'd have to do a lot more cloning than just the diplomat himself.

This is a very important part of the cloning problem, largely 8
overlooked in our excitement about the cloned individual himself. You don't have to agree all the way with B. F. Skinner to acknowledge that the environment does make a difference, and when you examine what we really mean by the word "environment" it comes down to other human beings. We use euphemisms and jargon for this, like "social forces," cultural influences," even Skinner's "verbal community," but what is meant is the dense crowd of nearby people who talk to, listen to, smile or frown at, give to, withhold from, nudge, push, caress, or flail out at the individual. No matter what the genome says, these people have a lot to do with shaping a character.

Indeed, if all you had was the genome, and no people around, you'd grow a sort of vertebrate plant, nothing more.

So, to start with, you will undoubtedly need to clone the parents. No question about this. This means the diplomat is out, even in theory, since you couldn't have gotten cells from both his parents at the time when he was himself just recognizable as an early social treasure. You'd have to limit the list of clones to people already certified as sufficiently valuable for the effort, with both parents still alive. The parents would need cloning and, for consistency, their parents as well. I suppose you'd also need the usual informed-consent forms, filled out and signed, not easy to get if I know parents, even harder for grandparents. 9

But this is only the beginning. It is the whole family that really influences the way a person turns out, not just the parents, according to current psychiatric thinking. Clone the family. 10

Then what? The way each member of the family develops has already been determined by the environment set around him, and this environment is more people, people outside the family, schoolmates, acquaintances, lovers, enemies, car-pool partners, even, in special circumstances, peculiar strangers across the aisle on the subway. Find them, and clone them. 11

But there is no end to the protocol. Each of the outer contacts has his own surrounding family, and his and their outer contacts. Clone them all. 12

To do the thing properly, with any hope of ending up with a genuine duplicate of a single person, you really have no choice. You must clone the world, no less. 13

We are not ready for an experiment of this size, nor, I should think, are we willing. For one thing, it would mean replacing today's world by an entirely identical world to follow immediately, and this means no new, natural, spontaneous, random, chancy children. No children at all, except for the manufactured doubles of those now on the scene. Plus all those identical adults, including all of today's politicians, all seen double. It is too much to contemplate. 14

Moreover, when the whole experiment is finally finished, fifty years or so from now, how could you get a responsible scientific reading on the outcome? Somewhere in there would be the original clonee, probably lost and overworked, now well into middle age, but everyone around him would be precise duplicates of today's everyone. It would be today's same world, filled to overflowing with duplicates of today's people and their same, duplicated problems, probably all resentful at having had to go through our whole thing all over, sore enough at the clone to make endless trouble for him, if they found him. 15

And obviously, if the whole thing were done precisely right, they 16 would still be casting about for ways to solve the problem of universal dissatisfaction, and sooner or later they'd surely begin to look around at each other, wondering who should be cloned for his special value to society, to get us out of all this. And so it would go, in regular cycles, perhaps forever.

I once lived through a period when I wondered what Hell could be like, and I stretched my imagination to try to think of a perpetual sort of damnation. I have to confess, I never thought of anything like this. 17

I have an alternative suggestion, if you're looking for a way out. Set cloning aside, and don't try it. Instead, go in the other direction. Look for ways to get mutations more quickly, new variety, different songs. Fiddle around, if you must fiddle, but never with ways to keep things the same, no matter who, not even yourself. Heaven, somewhere ahead, has got to be a change. 18

Discussion and Writing Suggestions

1. Almost from the beginning of the essay, Thomas offers hints that he is writing with tongue in cheek. Identify some of these hints and speculate on their purpose.
2. Ignore all the roadblocks Thomas places in the way of cloning human beings. Suppose it were physically possible to clone people. What are some of the other problems that might arise? Suppose we cloned particular individuals to come back and solve present or future problems (more or less analogous to the ones they solved in earlier times). What new problems might they run across in their new lives?
3. Underlying Thomas's essay is the implication that we are the distinctive individuals we are only because of the particular environment in which we have lived (and environment means, for the most part, other people). Does this mean that we are only a kind of clay that has been molded entirely by external forces? Are we *only* products of our environment? Consider what it is that makes you (or anyone else) a distinctive human being. Do you believe that there are any parts of your personality, your nature, that are distinctively your own, independent of other people or of the physical environment? Speculate on these matters in a multiparagraph essay, drawing on (or refuting) Thomas, where appropriate.
4. Write a short science-fiction story centering on the cloning of one or more individuals.

SYNTHESIS ACTIVITIES

1. Suppose you are writing a survey article on genetic engineering for a general audience magazine, such as *Time* or *Atlantic Monthly.* You want

to introduce your readers to the subject, tell them what it is and what it may become, and you want to focus, in particular, on the advantages and disadvantages of genetic engineering. Drawing on the sources you have read in this chapter—and the article on biological warfare in Chapter 1—write such an article.

For background information on the subject, you can draw on sources like Chamberland and the preface to this chapter. Sources like Suzucki and Knudtson, Virshup, and Hunt, as well as Rifkin and *The New Republic* offer many case studies illustrating advantages and disadvantages. And of course, Huxley serves as a dark example of the kind of thing that *could* happen if bioengineering goes too far.

2. Write an editorial arguing that additional regulations need to be placed on genetic engineering. Specify the chief problem areas, as you see them, and indicate the regulations needed in order to deal with these problems.

   You may want to begin with a survey of genetic engineering (in which you acknowledge its advantages) but then narrow your focus to the problem areas. Categorize the problem areas (for example, problems for prospective parents, for the workplace, for the battlefield, for the commercial applications of genetic engineering). The suggested regulations—and explanations of why they are necessary—might be discussed throughout the editorial or saved for the end.

3. *Brave New World* represents one artist's view of how scientific knowledge might be abused to ensure social stability and conformity. Huxley focused on the possibility of dividing fertilized human ova into identical parts and then conditioning the ova before "birth." Write a short story (or a play or screenplay) that represents your own nightmare vision. You may want to focus on other aspects of genetic engineering: the problem of forced genetic testing, of eugenics (creating "perfect" people or eliminating "imperfect" ones), of fostering uniformity among the population, of some fantastic commercial application of bioengineering, or even of some aspect of cloning (among the films dealing with cloning are Ira Levin's *The Boys from Brazil* and Woody Allen's *Sleeper*).

   Decide whether the story is to be essentially serious or comic (satirical)—or something in-between. Create characters (try to avoid caricatures) who will enact the various aspects of the problem, as you see it. And create a social and physical setting appropriate to the story you want to tell.

4. Write an article for a magazine like *Newsweek* or *Time* or *U.S. News & World Report* on the current status of genetic engineering—as of August 2050. Try to make the article generally upbeat (unlike the nightmare vision called for in the previous question) but be frank also about the problems that have been encountered, as well as the problems that

remain. Refer, at some point in your article, to views of genetic engineering from the late 1980s to establish some basis for comparison between what they thought "then" and what they think "now." You might model your article on the pieces by Chamberland, Virshup, and Hunt, or on any contemporary news magazine article of comparable scope. The language should be lively and vivid, and you should include as many "facts" as you can think of. Study your model articles for ideas about how to organize your material.

5. Write a paper on Jeremy Rifkin and the critical reaction to his activities and his books. Begin by rereading the material on Rifkin (and his critic, Gould) in this chapter. Then go to the *Reader's Guide to Periodical Literature* and locate important articles by and about Rifkin during the past decade or so. Locate Rifkin's books and survey them. Most important, look up reviews of Rifkin's books, starting with the listings in *Book Review Digest.* (This is an annual index that lists reviews during a given year and provides brief excerpts from the most important reviews.)

   Begin your paper by summarizing Rifkin's life and work thus far. (Your introductory paragraphs should probably focus on the controversy surrounding Rifkin.) Then focus on the reaction to his work. You may want to divide your paper into sections on positive and negative reactions; or you may want to organize by critical reviews of his various books and activities. At the conclusion, develop an overall assessment of the significance and value of Rifkin's work.

BUSINESS ETHICS 11

Business ethics—both as an academic discipline and as an evolving set of principles used to guide decision making in large and small companies—is a relatively new concept in American life. Before the 1960s and 1970s, the proper role of business was understood as providing goods and services to a consuming public, for profit. Most Americans might have agreed with the sentiment that "What's good for General Motors is good for the country" and trusted General Motors to define "good" on its own terms. No longer. Scandals in business saw corporations dumping toxic chemicals and withholding information about product defects from the public; with the increasing tendency of large companies to gobble up smaller ones came a general wariness of corporations. In response to this wariness, businesses began to consider their social reponsibilities. More and more, confronted with the reality of government regulation, managers and executives felt compelled to provide the public an account of hazards in the workplace or in the environment, of questionable labor or management practices, or of economic decisions that might disrupt entire communities. Business also began to take into consideration public concern over corporate policy *before* decisions were made.

By the 1970s, corporations around the country began accepting the view that they had responsibilities to stakeholders as well as to shareholders—to all who were affected by the conduct of business, be that effect monetary, physical, psychological, or environmental. Money was no longer the only concern. Writing in 1971, the Committee for Economic Development noted:

> Today it is clear that the terms of the contract between society and business are, in fact, changing in substantial and important ways. Business is being asked to assume broader responsibilities to society than ever before and to serve a wider range of human values. Business enterprises, in effect, are being asked to contribute more to the quality of American life than just supplying quantities of goods and services.[1]

[1]From pp. 29–30 in *Social Responsibilities of Business Corporations* by the Committee for Economic Development (New York: CED, 1971).

The acknowledgment of corporate America's social responsibilities came just in time, apparently, as Americans began showing their impatience with "business as usual." In a survey conducted in 1968, 70 percent of respondents felt that businesses were managing to earn profits while at the same time showing decent concern for the public's welfare. In 1978, only 15 percent of respondents felt the same way. By 1985, more than half of the respondents to selected surveys claimed that corporate executives are dishonest, that businesses show little regard for the society in which they operate, and that executives violate the public trust whenever money is to be made.

These perceptions are damaging, and all too often they are true. The news is rife with examples of ethical misconduct. Recall the space shuttle *Challenger* disaster, in which the decision to launch was made over the protest of engineers who warned of potentially disastrous defects in the very parts that failed. Recall the Exxon *Valdez* fiasco that saw hundreds of miles of pristine Alaskan coastal waters despoiled by crude oil: The oil leaked from the ruptured hold of a tanker whose captain had left the bridge command to a subordinate unqualified to navigate the vessel in Prince William Sound; setting the causes of the accident aside, Exxon representatives argued with Alaskan and federal officials over the limits of corporate liability in cleaning up the mess. The corporate impulse was to limit corporate cost, whatever the larger environmental cost to the people of Alaska. And recall the spate of mergers in recent years that have left newly acquired companies too heavily in debt to deal flexibly with employees. Other examples of ethical misconduct or ethically questionable practices fill the nightly news and the morning headlines. More pervasive, still, and perhaps more damaging are the "little" violations of ethical standards forced on managers or other employees who are asked, or forced, everyday to sacrifice personal values for company gain.

The study of ethics, of course, is not new. From the time of Aristotle (384–22 B.C.), philosophers have debated the standards by which we judge right or good behavior. The systematic study of ethics as applied to business, however, *is* new, and we see in it (according to the current president of the Society for Business Ethics) "an attempt . . . to revive the importance and legitimacy of making moral claims in the world of practical affairs."[2] Two associated developments have accompanied the rise of business ethics. First, corporations have begun drafting codes of ethics for their employees. Second, courses in business ethics are being taught at the graduate and undergraduate levels in schools around the country. The thrust of these courses has been both to justify the need for ethics in business and to provide a model by which students, future business leaders, can make ethical judgments in the world of work. Typically, professors of business ethics will present students with case

[2]W. Michael Hoffman. "Business Ethics in the United States: Its Past Decade and Its Future." *Business Insights* 5, No. 1 (Spring/Summer, 1989): 8.

studies—narrative accounts of real or hypothetical events in which protagonists face ethical dilemmas. Students are asked to read, analyze, and recommend courses of action. Consider the following "mini" cases:

> Fred Turner, chief operating officer with an aircraft corporation, is in Tokyo trying to sell $200 million worth of jets. Japanese business and political leaders seem willing to make a deal if the corporation produces about $10 million in bribes.
>
> Across the Pacific in Santa Monica, California, Carl Phillips is selling used cars. He feels compelled to meet his competitors' extravagant claims and their questionable tactics, such as turning back odometers, concealing defects, and pressuring shoppers. Phillips is repelled by such behavior, but what can he do? If he acts any other way, he won't survive.
>
> Halfway across the country Sally Richmann, working out of Kansas City for a stockbrokerage, has just been ordered to recommend some bonds to her clients. She doesn't think that the bonds are a good investment at this time. In fact, she feels they are being pushed in order to reduce her company's heavy inventory. Ordinarily Richmann wouldn't recommend the bonds, but orders are orders.
>
> The people in these hypothetical situations face very real moral decisions. Turner must decide whether to bribe Japanese officials and ensure a sale or to risk losing it. Phillips must decide whether to employ questionable selling tactics and stay in business or to risk business failure. And Richmann must decide whether to follow orders and recommend bonds which she feels are inferior or to buck orders and suffer the consequences. In short, each person must decide the right thing to do.[3]

It is likely that in your life as a person who conducts business of one sort or another you will face an ethical dilemma: You could act one way and maintain your principles—but, perhaps, lose a job or an important account; you could act another way and help to secure your fortune—but, perhaps, at the expense of your integrity. The pressures on people in business to make money, on the one hand, but to do the "right" thing, on the other, are real and often painfully difficult. It is these pressures—clearly defining them and responding to them—that form the subject matter of this chapter. First, writing on "The Case of the Collapsed Mine," Richard De George poses a series of questions that effectively surveys the field of business ethics. We might call this an introduction by query. Next, Gerald Cavanagh, in "Ethics in Business," offers an explicit strategy for analyzing ethical dilemmas and defining courses of action. Sissela Bok then takes up the very specialized problem of "whistleblowing," when workers feel compelled to alert the public to unethical and/or dangerous practices in a corporation. Given these initial selections, you will have the tools to read, analyze, and respond to three cases for analysis and discussion: "Peter Green's First Day," "Why Should My Conscience Bother Me?" and "The Challenger Disaster." The chapter concludes with three additional selections, starting with a pair of articles on the ethics of

[3]From *Moral Issues in Business,* second edition by Vincent Barry © 1983, 1979 by Wadsworth Inc. Reprinted by permission of the publisher.

deception in business: Albert Carr's highly controversial "Is Business Bluffing Ethical?" and "Showdown on 'Business Bluffing' "—a series of responses to Carr as compiled by *Harvard Business Review* editor Timothy Blodgett. The chapter ends with an excerpt from the novel *Babbitt,* by Nobel Laureate Sinclair Lewis.

The Case of the Collapsed Mine

RICHARD T. DE GEORGE

Studying business ethics can make one sensitive to issues and questions that might otherwise have escaped notice, had no formal training been available. A business situation fraught with dilemmas for one person might for another simply be business as usual, and this is the problem: One person sees conflict; another person sees none. So we begin the chapter with a selection that demonstrates how someone who is sensitive to ethical dilemmas would approach a particular incident. In "The Case of the Collapsed Mine," Richard T. De George presents a case study and then raises a series of questions that, in effect, provides an overview of business ethics. For instance, De George takes up questions of whistle-blowing; the value of human life as measured against the cost of designing very safe, or relatively safe, products; and the need to restructure systems that reward loyalty at the expense of morality. These are questions you will read more about in the selections to follow. You may be surprised (as we were) by the number of questions De George can draw from the case.

Richard T. De George is University Distinguished Professor of Philosophy and Courtesy Professor of Management at the University of Kansas. He is the author or editor of over fifteen books and more than one hundred scholarly articles concerning business ethics. De George has traveled worldwide in discussing issues of applied ethics; he is president of the American Philosophical Association (Central Division) and at the University of Kansas has won awards for his teaching and scholarship. De George was educated at Fordham University (B.A.), University of Louvain, Belgium (Ph.B.), and Yale (M.A. and Ph.D.).

The following case illustrates the sorts of questions that might arise in business ethics and various ways to approach them. Consider the case of the collapsed mine shaft. In a coal mining town of West Virginia, some miners were digging coal in a tunnel thousands of feet 1 below the surface. Some gas buildup had been detected during the two preceding days. This had been reported by the director of safety to the mine manager. The buildup was sufficiently serious to have closed down operations until it was cleared. The owner of the mine decided that the buildup was only marginally dangerous, that he had coal orders to fill, that he could not afford to close down the mine, and that he would take the chance that the gas would dissipate before it exploded. He told the director of safety not to say anything about the danger. On May 2nd, the gas exploded. One section of the tunnel collapsed, killing three miners and trapping eight others in a pocket. The rest managed to escape.

The explosion was one of great force and the extent of the tunnel's collapse was considerable. The cost of reaching the men in time to save their lives would amount to several million dollars. The problem facing the manager was whether the expenditure of such a large sum of money was worth it. What, after all, was a human life worth? Whose decision was it and how should it be made? Did the manager owe more to the stockholders of the corporation or to the trapped workers? Should he use the slower, safer, and cheaper way of reaching them and save a large sum of money or the faster, more dangerous, and more expensive way and possibly save their lives? 2

He decided on the latter and asked for volunteers. Two dozen men volunteered. After three days, the operation proved to be more difficult than anyone had anticipated. There had been two more explosions and three of those involved in the rescue operation had already been killed. In the meantime, telephone contact had been made with the trapped men who had been fortunate enough to find a telephone line that was still functioning. They were starving. Having previously read about a similar case, they decided that the only way for any of them to survive long enough was to draw lots, and then kill and eat the one who drew the shortest straw. They felt that it was their duty that at least some of them should be found alive; otherwise, the three volunteers who had died rescuing them would have died in vain. 3

After twenty days the seven men were finally rescued alive; they had cannibalized their fellow miner. The director of safety who had detected the gas before the explosion informed the newspapers of his report. The manager was charged with criminal negligence; but before giving up his position, he fired the director of safety. The mine eventually resumed operation. 4

There are a large number of issues in the above account. . . . 5

The director of safety is in some sense the hero of the story. But did he fulfill his moral obligation before the accident in obeying the manager and in not making known either to the miners, the manager's superior, or to the public the fact that the mine was unsafe? Did 6 he have a moral obligation after the explosion and rescue to make known the fact that the manager knew the mine was unsafe? Should he have gone to the board of directors of the company with the story or to someone else within the company rather than to the newspapers? All these questions are part of the phenomenon of worker responsibility. To whom is a worker responsible and for what? Does his moral obligation end when he does what he is told? Going public with inside information such as the director of safety had is commonly known as "blowing the whistle" on the company. Frequently those who blow the whistle are fired, just as the director of safety was. The whole phenomenon of whistle blowing raises serious questions about the structure of companies in which employees find it necessary to take such drastic action and possibly suffer the loss of their jobs. Was the manager justified in firing the director of safety?

The manager is, of course, the villain of the story. He sent the 7
miners into a situation which he knew was dangerous. But, he might argue, he did it for the good of the company. He had contracts to fulfill and obligations to the owners of the company to show a profit. He had made a bad decision. Every manager has to take risks. It just turned out that he was unlucky. Does such a defense sound plausible? Does a manager have an obligation to his workers as well as to the owners of a company? Who should take precedence and under what conditions does one group or the other become more important? Who is to decide and how?

The manager decided to try to save the trapped miners even 8
though it would cost the company more than taking the slower route. Did he have the right to spend more of the company's money in this way? How does one evaluate human life in comparison with expenditure of money? It sounds moral to say that human life is beyond all monetary value. In a sense it is. However, there are limits which society and people in it can place on the amount they will, can, and should spend to save lives. The way to decide, however, does not seem to be to equate the value of a person's life with the amount of income he would produce in his remaining years, if he lives to a statistically average age, minus the resources he would use up in that period. How does one decide? How do and should people weigh human lives against monetary expenditure? In designing automobiles, in building roads, in making many products, there is a trade-off between the maximum safety that one can build into the product and the cost of the product. Extremely safe cars cost more to build than relatively safe cars. We can express the difference in terms of the number of people likely to die driving the relatively safe ones as opposed to the extremely safe ones. Should such decisions be made by manufacturers, consumers, government, or in some other way?

The manager asked for volunteers for the rescue work. Three of 9
these volunteers died. Was the manager responsible for their deaths in the same way that he was responsible for the deaths of the three miners who had died in the first mine explosion? Was the company responsible for the deaths in either case? Do companies have obligations to their employees and the employees' families in circumstances such as these, or are the obligations only those of the managers? If the manager had warned the miners that the level of gas was dangerous, and they had decided that they wanted their pay for that day and would work anyway, would the manager have been responsible for their deaths? Is it moral for people to take dangerous jobs simply to earn money? Is a system that impels people to take such jobs for money a moral system? To what extent is a company morally obliged to protect its workers and to prevent them from taking chances?

The manager was charged with criminal negligence under the 10
law. Was the company responsible for anything? Should the company have been sued by the family of the dead workers? If the company were sued and paid damages to the families, the money would come from company profits and hence from the profits of the shareholders. Is it fair that the shareholders be penalized for an incident they had nothing to do with? How is responsibility shared and/or distributed in a company, and can companies be morally responsible for what is done in their name? Are only human beings moral agents and is it a mistake to use moral language with respect to companies, corporations, and businesses?

The decision of the trapped miners to cast lots to determine who 11
would be killed and eaten also raises a number of moral issues. Our moral intuitions can provide in this case no ready answer as to whether their decision was morally justifiable, since the case is not an ordinary one. How to think about such an issue raises the question of how moral problems are to be resolved and underscores the need for some moral theory as guidelines by which we can decide unusual cases. A number of principles seem to conflict—the obligation not to kill, the consideration that it is better for one person to die rather than eight, the fact noted by the miners that three persons had already died trying to rescue them, and so on. The issue here is not one peculiar to business ethics, but it is rather a moral dilemma that requires some technique of moral argument to solve.

The case does not tell us what happened to either the manager or 12
the director of safety. Frequently the sequel to such cases is surprising. The managers come off free and are ultimately rewarded for their concern for the company's interest, while the whistle blower is blackballed throughout the industry. The morality of such an outcome seems obvious—justice does not always triumph. What can be done

to see that it triumphs more often is a question that involves restructuring the system.

Business ethics is sometimes seen as conservative and is also used as a defense of the status quo. Sometimes it is seen as an attack on the status quo and hence viewed as radical. Ideally it should be neither. It should strive for objectivity. When there are immoral practices, structures, and actions occurring, business ethics should be able to show that these actions are immoral and why. But it should also be able to supply the techniques with which the practices and structures that are moral can be defended as such. The aim of business ethics is neither defense of the status quo not its radical change. Rather it should serve to remedy those aspects or structures that need change and protect those that are moral. It is not a panacea. It can secure change only if those in power take the appropriate action. But unless some attention is paid to business ethics, the moral debate about practices and principles central to our society will be more poorly and probably more immorally handled than otherwise. 13

Discussion and Writing Suggestions

1. Of the many questions that De George poses regarding "The Case of the Collapsed Mine," which question or set of questions seems most likely to get at the "heart" of the case? Explain your choice.
2. De George writes: "When there are immoral practices, structures, and actions occurring, business ethics should be able to show that these actions are immoral and why. But it should also be able to supply the techniques with which the practices and structures that are moral can be defended as such." Based on what you've read and seen on news reports, based on your own experience, perhaps, to what extent are people in business amenable to discussing reasons why an action may or may not be ethical?
3. In paragraph 6, De George poses several questions and then writes: "All these questions are part of the phenomenon of worker responsibility." *Worker responsibility,* then, becomes a category of questions. Reread the selection and create categories for the other questions that De George asks. For instance, some questions concern corporate responsibility, some concern the prohibition against killing, and so on. Compare your categories with a classmate's. (These categories will provide something of an index to the issues addressed in this chapter and, more generally, an index to the concerns of business ethicists.)
4. Summarize the significant details of an event in your own work experience and draw out those elements that raised ethical dilemmas for you or someone you know. In the fashion of De George, write a brief essay in which you pose a series of questions about the event and the behaviors of the people involved.

Ethics in Business

GERALD F. CAVANAGH

The case method is used as an instructional strategy in schools of business and departments of business ethics in colleges and universities around the country. Students read varied accounts (real or hypothetical) of life in the world of business and then are asked to analyze a case and advise the principals what to do. For instance, students of business might read about specific business transactions (or the preliminaries leading up to such transactions); accounts of interpersonal behaviors within organizations that call for management to take action; or accounts of organizational structures and how these impede or promote productivity. One class of cases that students are increasingly being asked to read involves ethical dilemmas faced by corporate executives, managers, and individual contributors. In all these cases, students are expected to conduct a systematic analysis and make specific, defensible recommendations.

In cases concerning financial analysis, you would perhaps be asked to use spreadsheets in arriving at your recommendations. In cases concerning ethical *analysis, you would be expected to use one or another model—a set of well-defined criteria—in arriving at your recommendations. Gerald Cavanagh offers such a model in his "Ethics in Business," which appeared originally in his* American Business Values *(1984), a text written for college course work. You'll find Cavanagh's discussion clearly written and organized (divided into sections and subsections); but you may also find the discussion somewhat difficult, for Cavanagh must define three ethical theories in order to establish his model for decision making. Read slowly, take notes, and respond to all the review questions on page 543 as you read, and you will find the discussion in your grasp—which is important since you'll be asked to apply Cavanagh's model to several cases.*

Gerald Cavanagh is professor of management, associate dean, and director of Graduate Programs in the University of Detroit's College of Business and Administration. Cavanagh holds a B.S. in engineering, graduate degrees in philosophy, theology, and management (Ph.D., Michigan State University) and was ordained a Jesuit priest in 1964. He has served on boards of trustees of several universities, and he referees papers for several scholarly journals and for national meetings of the Academy of Management. He has also given ethics workshops at universities throughout the country.

Gerald F. Cavanaugh, *American Business Values,* second edition © 1984, pp. 126–150. Reprinted by permission of Prentice-Hall, Inc., Englewood Cliffs, New Jersey. The material in this chapter owes much to several years of work with Manuel Velasquez, S.J., and Dennis Moberg of the University of Santa Clara, Santa Clara, California.

Freedom is expendable, stability is indispensable.
—Arnold Toynbee

No human institution can long exist without some consensus on what is right and what is wrong. Managers recognize the need for ethical norms in their daily dealings. Decisions made at every level of the firm are influenced by ethics, whether these be decisions which affect quality of work, employment opportunity, safety of worker or product, truth in advertising, use of toxic materials, or operations in third world countries. An increasing sense of the importance of ethical norms among executives is demonstrated by the facts that 1

1. Almost three-quarters of U.S. firms now have a code of ethics.[1]
2. More than 100 boards of directors of large firms have established an ethics, social responsibility, or public policy committee of the board.[2]
3. Speeches of chief executive officers and annual reports more often allude to the importance of ethics in business decisions.[3]

Managers understand that without ethics the only restraint is the law. Without ethics, any business transaction that was not witnessed and recorded could not be trusted. If government regulation and legislation are perceived to be unneeded and burdensome, then each manager must possess a set of internalized and operative ethical criteria for decision making. Or, as some have put it: "Shall we be honest and free, or dishonest and policed?" 2

NEED FOR ETHICS IN BUSINESS

A significant minority of large American firms have been involved not only in unethical activities but also in illegal activities. During the 1970s, 11 percent of the largest U.S. firms were convicted of bribery, 3

---

[1]According to a survey by Opinion Research Corporation, 73 percent of the larger corporations in the United States now have a written code of ethics. See *Chronicle of Higher Education*, August 6, 1979, p. 2.

[2]"Business Strategies for the 1980's, in *Business and Society: Strategies for the 1980's* (Washington, D.C.: U.S. Department of Commerce, 1980), pp. 33–34.

[3]For example, Reginald Jones of General Electric, who was selected by his fellow CEOs as the best CEO, has often made a strong case for ethics. See, for example, Reginald Jones, "Managing in the 1980's," address at Wharton School, February 4, 1980, p. 5. See also Richard J. Bennett, chairman of Schering-Plough, "A New Compact in the Age of Limits," address at Fordham University, November 5, 1981.

criminal fraud, illegal campaign contributions, tax evasion, or some sort of price fixing. Firms with two or more convictions include Allied, American Airlines, Bethlehem Steel, Diamond International, Firestone, Goodyear, International Paper, J. Ray McDermott, National Distillers, Northrop, Occidental Petroleum, Pepsico, Phillips Petroleum, Rapid-American, R. J. Reynolds, Schlitz, Seagram, Tenneco, and United Brands. Those that lead the list with at least four convictions each are Braniff International, Gulf Oil, and Ashland Oil.[4] Perhaps Gulf and Ashland will suffer the same punishment meted out to [now bankrupt] Braniff!

Most of the major petroleum firms illegally contributed to Richard 4
Nixon's reelection committee in the mid-1970s: Gulf, Getty, Standard of California, Phillips, Sun, Exxon, and Ashland. The chairman of Phillips personally handed Richard Nixon $50,000 in Nixon's own apartment. Many firms were also involved in multimillion-dollar foreign payments: Exxon, Lockheed, Gulf, Phillips, McDonnell Douglas, United Brands, and Mobil.[5] The presidents of Gulf, American Airlines, and Lockheed lost their jobs because of the unethical payments. Other presidents just as guilty—Northrop, Phillips, and Exxon—were excused by their boards. Firms based in the United States are, of course, not alone in engaging in unethical behavior. Sixteen executives of two large Japanese electronics firms, Hitachi and Mitsubishi, were indicted for stealing trade secrets from IBM.[6]

Corporate Pressure and Fraud

Embezzlement, fraud, and political backbiting are most often due to 5
personal greed. Bribery, price fixing, and compromising product and worker safety generally stem from the pressure for bottom line results. In a study of managers at several firms, 59 to 70 percent "feel pressured to compromise personal ethics to achieve corporate goals."[7] This perception increases among lower level managers. A majority felt that most managers would not refuse to market off-standard and possibly dangerous products. On the more encouraging

[4]Irwin Ross, "How Lawless Are Big Companies?" *Fortune,* December 1, 1980, pp. 56–64. See also Robert K. Elliott and John J. Willingham, *Management Fraud: Detection and Deterrence* (New York: Petrocelli Books, 1980).

[5]Marshall B. Clinard and Peter C. Yeager, *Corporate Crime* (New York: Free Press, 1980); and "Drive to Curb Kickbacks and Bribes by Business," *U.S. News & World Report,* September 4, 1978, pp. 41–44.

[6]"IBM Data Plot Tied to Hitachi and Mitsubishi," *Wall Street Journal,* June 23, 1982, p. 4.

[7]Archie Carroll, "Managerial Ethics: A Post-Watergate View," *Business Horizons,* April 1975, pp. 75–80; and "The Pressure to Compromise Personal Ethics," *Business Week,* January 31, 1977, p. 107. See also "Some Middle Managers Cut Corners to Achieve High Corporate Goals," *Wall Street Journal.* November 8, 1979, pp. 1, 19.

side, 90 percent supported a code of ethics for business and the teaching of ethics in business schools.

This pressure and organizational climate can influence the ethical 6
judgments of individual managers. What the manager finds unethical in another setting or before taking this job is more readily considered acceptable behavior once the job is taken. Two recent research studies question whether American executives have a sufficient sensitivity to ethical issues, and whether their work environment works against such a sensitivity. Public affairs officers in firms have the direct responsibility for dealing with a wide variety of stakeholders: customers, suppliers, local community, and shareholders. These officers are a principal conduit through which the firm is informed of new social concerns. Evidence shows that even though these public affairs officers spend more time with these various stakeholders, they tend to be poor listeners. In fact, according to this study, the more contact company officers have with external publics, the less sensitive they become to their concerns.[8]

Another study was in an ethically sensitive area: corporate politi- 7
cal activities. It was found that the more involvement a company officer had in these activities, the less likely he or she would be alert to ethical issues. The more involved the manager was, the more dulled became her or his conscience. There are many ethically debatable areas with regard to a firm's political activities, and this evidence shows that those who are most involved in these activities are precisely those who are less sensitive to the moral and ethical issues involved. The more involved manager is more likely to declare a debatable activity to be ethically acceptable and is also more likely to declare as gray an activity that fellow managers would declare ethically unacceptable.[9]

Laboratory research has shown that unethical behavior tends to 8
rise as the climate becomes more competitive, and it increases even more if such behavior is rewarded. However, a threat of punishment tends to deter unethical behavior. Whether a person acts ethically or unethically is also very strongly influenced by the individual's personal ethical values and by informal organizational policy.[10]

These instances of unethical behavior of managers point to the 9
need for (1) a sensitive and informed conscience, (2) the ability to make ethical judgments, and (3) a corporate climate that rewards

[8]Jeffery Sonnenfeld, "Executive Differences in Public Affairs Information Gathering," *Academy of Management Proceedings*, 1981, ed. Kae H. Chung, p. 353.

[9]Steven N. Brenner, "Corporate Political Actions and Attitudes," *Academy of Management Proceedings*, 1981, pp. 361–2.

[10]W. Harvey Hegarty and Henry P. Sims Jr., "Unethical Decision Behavior: An Overview of Three Experiments," *Academy of Management Proceedings*, 1979, p. 9.

ethical behavior and punishes unethical behavior. Technical education does not bring with it better ethics, as we have seen, for example in Nazi Germany. In fact, as society becomes more technical, complex, and interdependent, the need for ethics increases dramatically. When encounters are person to person, there exists the built-in sanction of having to live with the people one has lied to. In the large, complex organization, or when one deals with people over the telephone or via a computer, ethical sensitivities and decision-making abilities are far more important.

. . .

Ethical Theories

Ethical criteria and ethical models have been the subject of consider- 10
able thinking over the centuries. Of all the ethical systems, businesspeople feel most at home with utilitarian theory—and not surprisingly, as it traces its origins to Adam Smith, the father of both modern economics and utilitarian ethics. Jeremy Bentham[11] and John Stuart Mill[12] more precisely formulated utilitarianism a bit later. Utilitarianism evaluates behavior in terms of its consequences. That action which results in the greatest net gain for all parties is considered moral.

Rights theories focus on the entitlements of individual persons. 11
Immanuel Kant[13] (personal rights) and John Locke[14] (property rights) were the first to present developed theories of rights. Justice theories have a longer tradition, going back to Plato and Aristotle in the fifth century B.C.[15] Theoretical work in each of these traditions has continued to the present.[16] For an overview of these three theories—history, strengths and weaknesses, and when most useful—see Table A.

---

[11]Jeremy Bentham, *An Introduction to the Principles of Morals and Legislation* (1789) (New York: Hafner, 1948).

[12]John Stuart Mill, *Utilitarianism* (1863) (Indianapolis, Ind.: Bobbs-Merrill, 1957).

[13]Immanuel Kant, *The Metaphysical Elements of Justice* (1797), tr. J. Ladd (New York: Library of Liberal Arts, 1965).

[14]John Locke, *The Second Treatise of Government* (1690) (New York: Liberal Arts Press, 1952).

[15]Aristotle, *Ethics*, tr. J.A.K. Thomson (London: Penguin, 1953).

[16]For example, John Rawls, *A Theory of Justice* (Cambridge, Mass.: Belknap, 1971). See two books of readings: Thomas Donaldson and Patricia Werhane, *Ethical Issues in Business* (Englewood Cliffs, N.J.: Prentice-Hall, 1979); and Tom Beauchamp and Norman Bowie, *Ethical Theory and Business* (Englewood Cliffs, N.J.: Prentice-Hall, 1979).

TABLE A. ***Ethical Models for Business Decisions***

DEFINITION AND ORIGIN	STRENGTHS	WEAKNESSES	WHEN USED
UTILITARIANISM			
"The greatest good for the greatest number: Bentham (1748–1832), Adam Smith (1723–1790), David Ricardo (1772–1823)	1. Concepts, terminology, methods are easiest for businesspersons to work with; justifies a profit maximization system. 2. Promotes view of entire system of exchange beyond "this firm." 3. Encourages entrepreneurship, innovation, productivity.	1. Impossible to measure or quantify all important elements. 2. "Greatest good" can degenerate into self-interest. 3. Can result in abridging person's rights. 4. Can result in neglecting less powerful segments of society.	1. Use in all business decisions, and will be dominant criteria in 90%. 2. Version of model is implicitly used already, although scope is generally limited to "this firm."
THEORY OF JUSTICE			
Equitable distribution of society's benefits and burdens: Aristotle (384–322 B.C.), Rawls (1921–)	1. The "democratic" principle. 2. Does not allow a society to become status- or class-dominated. 3. Ensures that minorities, poor, handicapped receive opportunities and a fair share of output.	1. Can result in less risk, incentive, and innovation. 2. Encourages sense of "entitlement."	1. In product decisions usefulness to *all* in society. 2. In setting salaries for unskilled workers, executives. 3. In public policy decisions: to maintain a floor of living standards for all. 4. Use with, for example, performance appraisal, due process, distribution of rewards and punishments.
THEORY OF RIGHTS			
Individual's freedom is not to be violated: Locke (1635–1701)—property; Kant (1724–1804)—personal rights	1. Ensures respect for individual's property and personal freedom. 2. Parallels political "Bill of Rights."	1. Can encourage individualistic, selfish behavior.	1. Where individual's property or personal rights are in question. 2. Use with, for example, employee privacy, job tenure, work dangerous to person's health.

Utilitarianism

Utilitarianism judges that an action is right if it produces the 12
greatest utility, "the greatest good for the greatest number." It is very much like a cost-benefit analysis applied to all parties who would be touched by a particular decision: That action is right that produces the greatest net benefit, when all the costs and benefits to all the affected parties are taken into consideration. Although it would be convenient if these costs and benefits could be measured in some comparable unit, this is not always possible. Many important values (for example, human life and liberty) cannot be quantified. So it is sufficient to state the number and the magnitude of the costs and benefits as clearly and accurately as possible.

The utilitarian principle says that the right action is that which 13
produces the greatest net benefit over any other possible action. However, this does not mean that the best act is that which produces the greatest good for the person performing the action. Rather, it is the action that produces the greatest summed net good for all those who are affected by the action. Utilitarianism can handle some ethical cases quite well, especially those that are complex and affect many parties. Although the model and the methodology are clear, carrying out the calculations is often difficult. Taking into account so many affected parties, along with the extent to which the action touches them, can be a calculation nightmare.

Hence several shortcuts have been proposed that can reduce the 14
complexity of utilitarian calculations. Each shortcut involves a sacrifice of accuracy for ease of calculation. Among these shortcuts are (1) adherence to a simplified rule (for example, the Golden Rule, "Do unto others as you would have them do unto you"); (2) for ease of comparison, calculate costs and benefits in dollar terms; and (3) take into account only those directly affected by the action, putting aside indirect effects. In using the above decision-making strategies, an individual should be aware that they are simplifications and that some interests may not be sufficiently taken into consideration.

A noteworthy weakness of utilitarianism as an ethical norm is 15
that it can advocate, for example, abridging an individual's right to a job or even life, for the sake of the greater good of a larger number of people. This, and other difficulties, are discussed elsewhere.[17] One additional caution in using utilitarian rules is in order: It is considered

---

[17]Gerald F. Cavanagh, Dennis J. Moberg, and Manuel Velasquez, "The Ethics of Organizational Politics," *Academy of Management Review*, 6 (July 1981), 363–74; and the more complete treatments in Manuel Velasquez, *Business Ethics: Concepts and Cases* (Englewood Cliffs, N.J.: Prentice-Hall, 1982), pp. 46–58; and Richard T. De George, *Business Ethics* (New York: Macmillan, 1982), pp. 47–54.

unethical to opt for the benefit of narrower goals (for example, personal goals, career, or money) at the expense of the good of a larger number, such as a nation or a society. Utilitarian norms emphasize the good of the group; it is a large-scale ethical model. In this sort of calculation, an individual and what is due that individual may be underemphasized. Rights theory has been developed to give appropriate emphasis to the individual and the standing of that individual with peers and within society.

Rights of the Individual

A right is a person's entitlement to something.[18] Rights may flow 16
from the legal system, such as the U.S. constitutional rights of freedom of conscience or freedom of speech. The U.S. Bill of Rights and the United Nations Universal Declaration of Human Rights are classical examples of individual rights spelled out in some detail in documents. Legal rights, as well as others which may not be written into law, stem from the human dignity of the person. Moral rights have these characteristics: (1) They enable individuals to pursue their own interests, and (2) they impose correlative prohibitions and/or requirements on others. That is, every right has a corresponding duty. My right to freedom of conscience is supported by the prohibition of other individuals from unnecessarily limiting that freedom of conscience. From another perspective, my right to be paid for my work corresponds to a duty of mine to perform "a fair day's work for a fair day's pay." In the latter case, both the right and duty stem from the right to private property, which is a traditional pillar of American life and law. However, the right to private property is not absolute. A factory owner may be forced by law, as well as by morality, to spend money on pollution control or safety equipment. For a listing of selected rights and other ethical norms, see Table B.

Judging morality by reference to individual rights is quite differ- 17
ent from using utilitarian standards. Rights express the requirements of morality from the standpoint of the individual; rights protect the individual from the encroachment and demands of society or the state. Utilitarian standards promote society's benefit and are relatively insensitive to a single individual, except insofar as that individual's welfare affects the overall good of society.

A business contract establishes rights and duties that were not 18
there before: The right of the purchaser to receive what was agreed

[18]Velasquez, *Business Ethics,* p. 29. See also Thomas Donaldson, *Corporations and Morality* (Englewood Cliffs, N.J.: Prentice-Hall, 1982).

TABLE B. ***Some Selected Ethical Norms***

UTILITARIAN

1. *Organizational goals* should aim at *maximizing the satisfactions* of the organization's constituencies.
2. The members of an organization should attempt to attain its goals as *efficiently* as possible by consuming as few inputs as possible and by minimizing the external costs which organizational activities impose on others.
3. The employee should use *every effective means* to achieve the goals of the organization, and should neither jeopardize those goals nor enter situations in which personal interests conflict significantly with the goals.

RIGHTS

1. *Life and safety:* The individual has the right not to have her or his life or safety unknowingly and unnecessarily endangered.
2. *Truthfulness:* The individual has a right not to be intentionally deceived by another, especially on matters about which the individual has the right to know.
3. *Privacy:* The individual has the right to do whatever he or she chooses to do outside working hours and to control information about his or her private life.
4. *Freedom of conscience:* The individual has the right to refrain from carrying out any order that violates those commonly accepted moral or religious norms to which the person adheres.
5. *Free speech:* The individual has the right to criticize conscientiously and truthfully the ethics or legality of corporate actions so long as the criticism does not violate the rights of other individuals within the organization.
6. *Private property:* The individual has a right to hold private property, especially insofar as this right enables the individual and his or her family to be sheltered and to have the basic necessities of life.

JUSTICE

1. *Fair treatment:* Persons who are similar to each other in the relevant respects should be treated similarly; persons who differ in some respect relevant to the job they perform should be treated differently in proportion to the difference between them.
2. *Fair administration of rules:* Rules should be administered consistently, fairly, and impartially.
3. *Fair compensation:* Individuals should be compensated for the cost of their injuries by the party that is responsible for those injuries.
4. *Fair blame:* Individuals should not be held responsible for matters over which they have no control.
5. *Due process:* The individual has a right to a fair and impartial hearing when he or she believes that personal rights are being violated.

Source: Reprinted by permission of American Management Association from *Organizational Dynamics*, Autumn 1983. © 1983. American Management Association, New York. All rights reserved.

upon, and the right of the seller to be paid what was agreed. Formal written contracts and informal verbal agreements are essential to business transactions.

Immanuel Kant recognized that an emphasis on rights can lead 19
one to focus largely on what is due oneself. So he formulated what he called his "categorical imperatives." As the first of these, Kant said, "I ought never to act except in such a way that I can also will that my maxim should become a universal law." Another way of putting this

is: "An action is morally right for a person in a certain situation if and only if the person's reason for carrying out the action is a reason that he would be willing to have every person act on, in any similar situation."[19] As a measure of a difficult judgment, Kant asks if our reason for taking this action is the same reason that would allow others to do the same thing. Note that Kant is focusing on a person's motivation or intention, and not on the consequences of the action, as is true of utilitarianism.

Kant's second categorical imperative cautions us against using 20
other people as a means to our own ends: "Never treat humanity simply as a means, but always also as an end." An interpretation of the second imperative is: "An action is morally right for a person if and only if in performing the action the person does not use others merely as a means for advancing his or her own interests, but also both respects and develops their capacity to choose for themselves."[20] Capital, plant, and machines are all to be used to serve men and women's purposes. On the other hand, individual persons are not to be used merely as instruments for achieving one's interests. This rules out deception, manipulation, and exploitation of other people.

Justice

Justice requires all persons, and thus managers too, to be guided by 21
fairness, equity, and impartiality. Justice calls for evenhanded treatment of groups and individuals (1) in the distribution of the benefits and burdens of society, (2) in the administration of laws and regulations, and (3) in the imposition of sanctions and means of compensation for wrongs a person has suffered. An action or policy is just in comparison with the treatment accorded to others.

Standards of justice are generally considered to be more impor- 22
tant than utilitarian consideration of consequences. If a society is unjust to some group of its members (for example, apartheid treatment of blacks in South Africa), we generally consider that society unjust and condemn it, even if the results of the injustices bring about greater productivity. On the other hand, we seem to be willing to trade off some equity, if the results will bring about greater benefits for all.

Standards of justice are not as often in conflict with individual 23
rights as are utilitarian norms. This is not surprising, since justice is

---

[19]Immanuel Kant, *Groundwork of the Metaphysics of Morals*, tr. H. J. Paton (New York: Harper & Row, 1964), pp. 62–90. See also Velasquez, *Business Ethics*, pp. 66–69.

[20]Kant, *Groundwork;* Velasquez, *Business Ethics*, p. 68.

largely based on the moral rights of individuals. The moral right to be treated as a free and equal person, for example, undergirds the notion that benefits and burdens should be distributed equitably. Personal moral rights are so basic that they generally may not be traded off (for example, free consent, right to privacy, freedom of conscience, right to due process) to bring about a better distribution of benefits in a society. On the other hand, property rights may be abridged (for example, graduated income tax, tax on pollution) for the sake of a more fair distribution of benefits and burdens.

Distributive justice becomes important when there are not enough of society's goods to satisfy all needs or not enough people to bear the burdens. The question then becomes: What is a just distribution? The fundamental principle is that equals should be treated equally, and unequals treated in accord with their inequality. For example, few would argue that a new person who is hired for the same job as a senior worker with twenty years' experience should receive the same pay as the experienced worker. People performing work of greater responsibility or working more difficult hours would be eligible for greater pay. However, it is clear that pay differentials should be related to the work itself, not on some arbitrary bias of the employer. 24

Having said all of the above does not determine what is a fair distribution of society's benefits and burdens. In fact quite different notions of equity are generally proposed. A classic difference is the capitalist model (justice based on contribution) versus the socialist ("from each according to abilities, to each according to needs"). A more recent contribution to justice theory has been the work of John Rawls.[21] Rawls would have us construct the rules and laws of society as if we did not know what role we were to play in that society. We do not know if we would be rich or poor, male or female, African or European, manager or slave, handicapped or physically and mentally fit. He calls this the "veil of ignorance." The exercise is intended to try to rid ourselves of our status, national, and sexist biases. Under such circumstances each of us would try to design the rules of society to be of the greatest benefit to all, and not to undermine the position of any group. Thus Rawls proposes that people generally develop two principles: 25

1. Each person is to have an equal right to the most extensive liberty compatible with similar liberty for others.

[21]Rawls, *A Theory of Justice.*

2. Social and economic inequalities are to be arranged so that they are both reasonably expected to be to everyone's advantage and attached to positions and offices open to all.

The first principle is consonant with the American sense of liberty and thus is not controversial in the United States. The second principle is more egalitarian, and also more controversial. However, Rawls maintains that if people are honest behind the "veil of ignorance" they will opt for a system of justice that is most fair to all members of that society.

SOLVING ETHICAL DILEMMAS

Any human judgment is preceded by two steps: gathering data and analyzing the data. Before any ethically sensitive situation can be assessed, it is essential that all the relevant data be at hand. As an aid to analysis, the three classical norms—utility, rights, and justice—have been offered. For a schematic diagram of how ethical decision making can proceed, see Figure A. The diagram is simplified, but nevertheless it can be an aid in our handling of ethical problems. **26**

Let us apply our scheme to the case of an executive padding her expense account.[22] For our purposes, we will accept the limited data as provided in the case. Applying the utility criteria, we would judge that although padding the expense account satisfies the interests of the executive doing it, it does not optimize the concerns of others: shareholders, customers, more honest executives, and people in other firms in similar situations. It also adds to the expense of doing business. Hence, it seems that utility would not allow for such padding. The rights of individuals are not so involved here: The executive has no right to the extra money, although we might make the case that the shareholders' and customers' right to private property is being violated. With regard to justice, salary and commissions are the ordinary compensation for individuals. Expense accounts have a quite different purpose. **27**

In this instance, most managers responding to the case held that it was unethical for the executive to pad her expense account. John Rawls would maintain that any one of us would set the rules in this **28**

[22]Cavanagh, here, is referring to a case in which "an executive earning $30,000 a year has been padding his/her expense account by about $1,500 a year." In a survey of 1,700 "business executive readers of *Harvard Business Review*," 85 percent thought that the padding—or false reporting of expenses—was unethical.

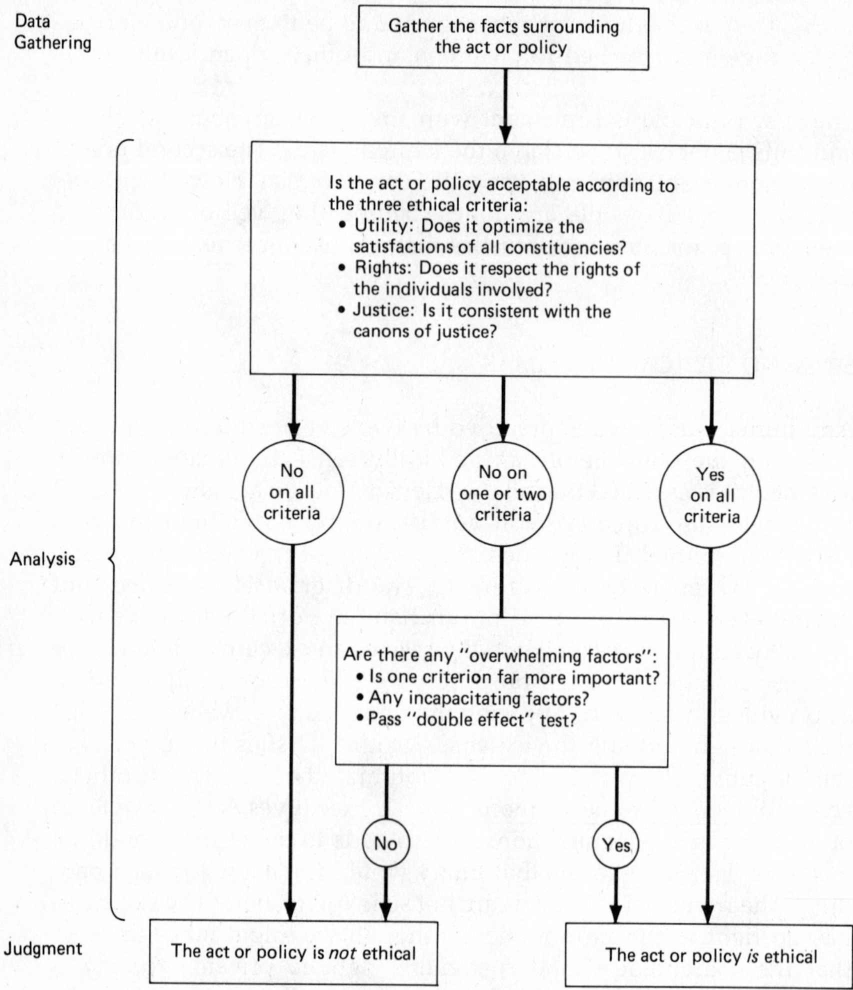

FIGURE A. ***Flow diagram of ethical decision making.***
Source: Reprinted by permission of American Management Association from *Organizational Dynamics,* Autumn 1983. © 1983. American Management Association, New York. All rights reserved.

fashion, given the fact that we would not know what role we ourselves would have in the society. Hence, we conclude that padding one's expense account is judged unethical on all three ethical norms, so it is clearly wrong. Notice that this agrees with the judgment of 73 percent of the executives who were asked.

On the other hand, the *Wall Street Journal* recently described an entrepreneur who sells blank official-looking receipts of fifty different plausible but fictitious restaurants. The individual can then fill out the receipts as he likes and can submit them to his firm for reimbursement. And he has the receipts to prove the purchase of the meal! What would we say of the ethics of selling such receipts? Of purchasing them and using them? 29

Model Aids Solution

Let us examine another case: 30

> Brian Curry, financial vice president of Digital Robotics Corporation, is about to retire and has been asked to recommend one of his two assistants for promotion to vice president. Curry knows that his recommendations will be acted upon. He also knows that, since both assistants are about the same age, the one not chosen will find future promotions unlikely. Debra Butler is the most qualified for the position. She is bright and outgoing and has better leadership ability. Moreover, her father is president of the largest customer of Digital, and Curry correctly reasons that they will more likely keep this business with Butler as an officer of Digital. On the other hand, Charles McNichols has been with the company longer, has worked seventy-hour weeks, and has pulled the company through some very difficult situations. He did this because he was told he was in line for the vice presidency. Nevertheless, Curry recommends Butler for the job.

Using our schema to examine this case, utility would conclude 31
that the selection of Debra Butler would optimize the satisfaction of top management, most of the workers, because she is a better leader, and shareholders and customers, for the same reason. The only cost is that to McNichols. Justice would conclude that because the promotional decision was made on relevant capabilities, it did not violate fair treatment. On the other hand, McNichols had been told that he would get the job, and worked extra hours because he thought the job would be his. He is being used in a fashion to which he did not consent. His rights are violated. Moreover, in being promised the job, and then having the promise broken, he is not being treated with fairness and equity.

Thus utility accepts the appointment of Butler as morally accept- 32
able, since there will be a net gain in satisfaction. However, because of the promise made earlier to McNichols and his resultant extended work weeks, his rights are being violated. We can then ask if there are

any "overwhelming factors" that ought to be taken into consideration (see Figure A, p. 538).

Overwhelming Factors

"Overwhelming factors" are data from the situation which may, in a given case, justify overriding one of the three ethical criteria: utility, rights, or justice. Overwhelming factors can be examined when there is a conflict in the conclusions drawn from the ethical norms. The first of the overwhelming factors are incapacitating factors. That is, if there are any elements that coerce an individual into a certain posture, then that individual is not held to be fully responsible. Managers at a H. J. Heinz plant felt great pressure from top management to show a profit. They could not do as well as was expected, so they began to juggle the books. While this meant cumulative overstatement of profits of $8.5 million, the managers who did the falsification would probably be judged less unethical than the top management that brought the unrelenting pressure to bear. Even though the act of falsifying the books was objectively unethical, the plant manager did not bear full responsibility because he was pressured by superiors.[23] 33

Second, the manager might not be able to utilize the criteria because she does not possess full information. She might think that another employee is embezzling from the bank. However, to report the employee to superiors might ruin the individual's reputation. So, even though stealing is a violation of justice, in this case there is not yet sufficient information to utilize the criteria. Finally, the manager may be sincerely uncertain of the criteria or their applicability in this particular case. 34

To return to the appointment of a financial vice president case: While utility would clearly call for recommending Debra Butler for the vice president's position, justice would call for considering McNichols' claim on the position more strongly. McNichols has worked harder, having considered this to be proportionate to the future promised reward. Moreover, since the position has been promised to him, fair treatment would call for some special consideration. Justice would probably say that, under these special circumstances, McNichols should get the position. 35

Because there is now a conflict between these two norms, it is necessary to see if any overwhelming factors should be taken into account. There seems to be little coercion involved, certainly no 36

[23]"Some Middle Managers Cut Corners to Achieve High Corporate Goals," *Wall Street Journal*, November 8, 1979, pp. 1, 19.

physical coercion. Curry made his decision freely. There might have been psychological coercion, however, if Debra Butler's father had mentioned the possible promotion to top management at Digital. Even without his mentioning it, the situation may still have caused psychological pressure for Curry.

The ultimate solution of this case would depend on a number of 37
factors: How much better a manager would Butler be than McNichols, and how would this affect the firm's performance and the jobs of others at Digital? Exactly what sort of promise was made to McNichols? Was it clear and unequivocal? If the promise was more in McNichols' mind, and if Butler's performance would be judged to be significantly better than McNichols', then Curry could ethically recommend Butler. However, some sort of compensation should be made to McNichols.

Another kind of overwhelming factor occurs when criteria come 38
to differing conclusions on the same case. The so-called "principle of double effect" can be useful here. When an act has both a good effect and a bad effect (for example, appointing Butler and not appointing McNichols), one may morally perform the act under three conditions: (1) One does not directly intend the bad effect (Curry is not trying to backstab or get back at McNichols); (2) the bad effect is not a means to the good end but is simply a side effect (the nonappointment of McNichols is not a means to Butler being appointed); and (3) the good effect sufficiently outweighs the bad (Butler's performance would be significantly superior to McNichols'). So this case passes the test of the double effect. Hence, in sum, Curry may ethically recommend Butler for the vice presidency.

Case of the Flammable Crib

Let us examine another case, this one on the issue of product safety 39
and quality:

> Assume you are president of a firm which manufactures baby cribs. You have the option of installing either of two pads: a less expensive one which meets what you feel to be too lenient federal safety requirements regarding flammability (a requirement which you are quite sure was established as a result of pressure from your industry) and one which is safe but somewhat more expensive. Assume that the safe pad will not bring a higher price for the crib.

Would using the flammable pad be unjust to purchasers? Initial- 40
ly, it would seem that there is no injustice here—all purchasers of baby cribs are being treated the same. A possible source of injustice, however, would be to the consumer, who is presuming that he is

purchasing a safe and not flammable baby crib. When examining rights, this becomes even clearer: The consumer presumes that his baby will be safe and that the product being sold has sufficient safeguards. The fact that the firm meets federal safety requirements does not settle the question, since the president is convinced that these are too lenient and were only set because of pressure from the industry. At stake are the lives of infants who might be burned. In fact, statistics tell us that some infants will be burned needlessly. As with sleepwear and toys, special precautions must be taken with infants and young children, since they cannot protect themselves. Although they don't smoke in bed, they nevertheless cannot put out a fire once it has begun from whatever source.

Applying the utilitarian norm demands weighing the costs and 41
benefits of the two pads to all parties. The cheaper pad would result in lower cost to the consumer and probably better enable the firm to meet the lower price of its competitors. The cost of the lower priced pad would be the cost of the infants who would be burned because the cheaper pad was used. On the other hand, the safer pad could be advertised as such, and it might establish the firm as a manufacturer of safe children's goods. Presuming that there is a significant difference in the flammability, and thus the number of children's lives saved, utility would probably call for installing the safer pad. Since there are no ethical criteria that would call for the installation of the cheaper pad, we can then judge that ethics would ask the president to call for the safer, even though more expensive, pad.

This judgment is also the judgment of corporate executives. In a 42
survey of chief executive officers, 94 percent would use the safe pad, even though it is more expensive.[24] Perhaps these executives are using a shortcut ethical test of a possible action: Would I do it if I knew that the decision was to be featured on this evening's TV news? Can my decision bear the sharp scrutiny of a probing reporter?

. . .

Ethics is a system of moral principles and the methods for applying 43
them; ethics thus provides the tools to make moral judgments. It encompasses the language, concepts, and models that enable an individual to effect moral decisions.

Mature ethical judgments are not always easy to make. The facts 44
of the case are not always clear-cut; the ethical criteria or principles to be used are not always agreed upon even by the experts themselves. Hence, ethics seems to most businesspeople, indeed to most Americans, to be subjective, amorphous, and ill-defined and thus not very useful. Just as with politics and religion, there is often more heat than

[24]"Business Executives and Moral Dilemmas." *Business and Society Review* (Spring 1975), p. 55.

light in discussion. This lack of confidence in ethics is unfortunate, since without some commonly agreed-upon ethical principles, it is everyone for him- or herself, and trust, which is basic to all business dealings, is undermined.

Review Questions

1. Why, in order to prevent the intrusion of government into business, must "each manager . . . possess a set of internalized and operative ethical criteria for decision making"?
2. Briefly define the ethical theories of utility, justice, and rights.
3. What is an "overwhelming factor" in the context of making a decision about ethics?
4. "What is the principle of "double effect" and how is it applied in the context of making a decision about ethics?

Discussion and Writing Suggestions

1. According to Cavanagh, between 59 and 70 percent of managers surveyed "feel pressured to compromise personal ethics to achieve corporate goals." Are you surprised? Why or why not? Develop your response into a brief essay.
2. Do you agree with Cavanagh's analysis of the Digital Robotics case, in which Debra Butler was recommended for vice president over Charles McNichols? Why? If you disagree, provide a rationale for your decision, as Cavanagh does for his.
3. How practical is it, in your view, to apply Cavanagh's flow diagram for making ethical decisions? How important is it for the conduct of ethical business that managers use *some* systematic model for making difficult decisions?

Whistleblowing

SISSELA BOK

At some point in your professional career, you may face a very particular and painful ethical dilemma: What would you do if you observed a colleague behaving in ways that you found irresponsible and potentially harmful to the public, financially or physically? Having made the discovery, you would inevitably consider several questions: Should you report the activities? To whom—someone inside your organization or outside? What would be the consequences to you, your company, and the person reported if you did "blow the whistle"? In the selection that follows, Sissela Bok discusses these and related matters. She defines whistleblowing as a "label for those who . . . make revelations meant to call attention to negligence, abuses, or dangers that threaten the public interest." The potential whistleblower faces extraordinary pressures, as you'll read in the Challenger case and in "Why Should My Conscience Bother Me?" Great harm can follow from a person's failing to blow the whistle (the public can be placed in danger); great harm can also follow from rashly or prematurely blowing the whistle (reputations can be needlessly damaged).

As did Gerald Cavanagh in his "Ethics in Business," Sissela Bok presents criteria useful in defining a problem (in this case, whistleblowing) and then offers sets of related questions that can help guide the process of decision making. As you read, take special note of Bok's three categories—dissent, breach of loyalty, and accusation—as well as the questions she associates with them.

Sissela Ann Bok was born in Stockholm, Sweden, in 1934. She attended the Sorbonne (1953–55); graduated George Washington University with an A.B. (1957) and M.A. (1958); and received a Ph.D. from Harvard University in 1970. Bok has been a member of many medical ethics committees and advisory boards, including those of the American Philosophical Association and the Massachusetts Task Force to Develop Regulations for Psychosurgery. She has edited and written several studies on medical and educational ethics, most notably: Lying: Moral Choice in Public and Private Life *(1978) and* Secrets *(1983), in which the present discussion of whistleblowing appears.*

REVELATION FROM WITHIN

> *All that pollution up at Mølledal—all that reeking waste from the mill—it's seeped into the pipes feeding from the pump-room; and the same damn poisonous slop's been draining out on the beach as well. . . . I've investigated the facts as scrupulously as possible . . . There's irrefutable proof of the presence of decayed organic matter in the water—millions of bacteria. It's positively injurious to health, for either internal or external use. Ah, what a blessing it is to feel that you've done some service for your home town and your fellow citizens.*
>
> —Dr. Thomas Stockman, in Henrik Ibsen,
> *An Enemy of the People*, Act 1

Such was Dr. Stockman's elation, in Ibsen's play, after having written 1
a report on the contamination of the town's newly installed mineral baths. As the spa's medical director, he took it for granted that everyone would be eager to learn why so many who had come to the baths for health purposes the previous summer had been taken ill; and he assumed that the board of directors and the taxpayers would gladly pay for the extensive repairs that he recommended. By the fifth act of the play, he had been labeled an "enemy of the people" at a public meeting, lost his position as the spa's medical director, and suffered through the stoning of his house by an angry crowd. But he held his ground: "Should I let myself be whipped from the field by public opinion and the solid majority and other such barbarities? No thank you!"[1]

"Whistleblower" is a recent label for those who, like Dr. Stock- 2
man, make revelations meant to call attention to negligence, abuses, or dangers that threaten the public interest. They sound an alarm based on their expertise or inside knowledge, often from within the very organization in which they work. With as much resonance as they can muster, they strive to breach secrecy, or else arouse an apathetic public to dangers everyone knows about but does not fully acknowledge.[2]

Few whistleblowers, however, share Dr. Stockman's initial belief 3
that it will be enough to make their message public, and that people who learn of the danger will hasten to counter it. Most know, rather, that their alarms pose a threat to anyone who benefits from the ongoing practice and that their own careers and livelihood may be at risk. The lawyer who breaches confidentiality in reporting bribery by corporate clients knows the risk, as does the nurse who reports on slovenly patient care in a hospital, the engineer who discloses safety defects in the braking systems of a fleet of new rapid-transit vehicles, or the industrial worker who speaks out about hazardous chemicals seeping into a playground near the factory dump.

. . . [The] concealment of negligence and abuses creates strong 4
tensions for insiders. They must confront questions of loyalty, conscience, and truthfulness, and personal concerns about careers and

[1]Excerpt from *An Enemy of the People* by Henrik Ibsen in Henrik Ibsen: *The Complete Major Prose Plays,* translated and edited by Rolf Fjelde. Copyright © 1965 by Rolf Fjelde. Reprinted by permission of New American Library, a division of Penguin Books USA, Inc.

[2]I draw, for this chapter, on my earlier essays on whistleblowing: "Whistleblowing and Professional Responsibilities," in Daniel Callahan and Sissela Bok, eds., *Ethics Teaching in Higher Education* (New York: Plenum Press, 1980), pp. 277–95 (reprinted, slightly altered, in *New York University Education Quarterly* 11 (Summer 1980):2–10; "Blowing the Whistle," in Joel Fleishman, Lance Liebman, and Mark Moore, eds., *Public Duties: The Moral Obligations of Officials* (Cambridge, Mass.: Harvard University Press, 1981), pp. 204–21.

peace of mind. What should they consider revealing? And which secrets must they at all costs bring to public attention?

Would-be whistleblowers also face conflicting pressures from 5
without. In many professions, the prevailing ethic requires above all else loyalty to colleagues and to clients; yet the formal codes of professional ethics stress responsibility to the public in cases of conflict with such loyalties. Thus the largest professional engineering society asks members to speak out against abuses threatening the safety, health, and welfare of the public.[3] A number of business firms have codes making similar requirements; and the United States Code of Ethics for government servants asks them to "expose corruption wherever uncovered" and to "put loyalty to the highest moral principles and to country above loyalty to persons, party, or Government department."[4] Regardless of such exhortations, would-be whistleblowers have reason to fear the results of carrying out the duty to reveal corruption and neglect. However strong this duty may seem in principle, they know that in practice, retaliation is likely. They fear for their careers and for their ability to support themselves and their families.

. . .

INDIVIDUAL MORAL CHOICE

What questions might individuals consider, as they wonder whether 6
to sound an alarm? How might they articulate the problem they see, and weigh its seriousness before deciding whether or not to reveal it? Can they make sure that their choice is the right one? And what about the choices confronting journalists or others asked to serve as intermediaries?

In thinking about these questions, it helps to keep in mind . . . 7
three elements . . . dissent, breach of loyalty, and accusation. They impose certain requirements: of judgment and accuracy in dissent, of exploring alternative ways to cope with improprieties that minimize the breach of loyalty, and of fairness in accusation. The judgment expressed by whistleblowers concerns a problem that should matter to the public. Certain outrages are so blatant, and certain dangers so great, that all who are in a position to warn of them have a *prima facie* obligation to do so. Conversely, other problems are so minor that to blow the whistle would be a disproportionate response. And still

[3]Institute of Electrical and Electronics Engineers, Code of Ethics for Engineers, art. 4, *IEEE Spectrum* 12 (February 1975):65.

[4]Code of Ethics for Government Service, passed by the U.S. House of Representatives in the 85th Congress, 1958, and applying to all government employees and office holders.

others are so hard to pin down that whistleblowing is premature. In between lie a great many of the problems troubling whistleblowers. Consider, for example, the following situation:

> An attorney for a large company manufacturing medical supplies begins to suspect that some of the machinery sold by the company to hospitals for use in kidney dialysis is unsafe, and that management has made attempts to influence federal regulatory personnel to overlook these deficiencies.
>
> The attorney brings these matters up with a junior executive, who assures her that he will look into the matter, and convey them to the chief executive if necessary. When she questions him a few weeks later, however, he tells her that all the problems have been taken care of, but offers no evidence, and seems irritated at her desire to learn exactly where the issues stand. She does not know how much further she can press her concern without jeopardizing her position in the firm.

The lawyer in this case has reason to be troubled, but does not yet 8
possess sufficient evidence to blow the whistle. She is far from being as sure of her case as was Ibsen's Dr. Stockman, who had received laboratory analyses of the water used in the town spa, or as the engineers in the BART[5] case, whose professional expertise allowed

[5]The San Francisco Bay Area Rapid Transit [BART] System opened in 1972. It was heralded as the first major breakthrough toward a safe, reliable, and sophisticated method of mass transportation. A public agency had been set up in 1952 to plan and carry out the project; and the task of developing its major new component, a fully automatic train control system, was allocated to Westinghouse.

In 1969, three of the engineers who worked on this system became increasingly concerned over its safety. They spotted problems independently, and spoke to their supervisors, but to no avail. They later said they might well have given up their effort to go farther had they not found out about one another. They made numerous efforts to speak to BART's management. But those in charge were already troubled by costs that had exceeded all projections, and by numerous unforseen delays. They were not disposed to investigate the charges that the control system might be unsafe. Each appeal by the three engineers failed.

Finally, the engineers interested a member of BART's board of trustees, who brought the matter up at a board meeting. Once again, the effort failed. But in March 1973, the three were fired once the complaint had been traced to them. When they wrote to ask why they had been dismissed, they received no answer.

Meanwhile, the BART system had begun to roll. The control system worked erratically, and at times dangerously. A month after the opening, one train overshot the last station and crashed into a parking lot for commuters. Claiming that some bugs still had to be worked out, BART began to use old-fashioned flagmen in order to avoid collisions.

The three engineers had turned, in 1972, to the California Society of Professional Engineers for support. The society, after investigating the complaint, agreed with their views, and reported to the California State legislature. It too had launched an investigation, and arrived at conclusions quite critical of BART's management.

The engineers filed a damage suit against BART in 1974, but settled out of court in 1975. They had difficulties finding new employment, and suffered considerable financial and emotional hardship in spite of their public vindication.

them to evaluate the risks of the faulty braking system. Dr. Stockman and the engineers would be justified in assuming that they had an obligation to draw attention to the dangers they saw, and that anyone who shared their knowledge would be wrong to remain silent or to suppress evidence of the danger. But if the attorney blew the whistle about her company's sales of machinery to hospitals merely on the basis of her suspicions, she would be doing so prematurely. At the same time, the risks to hospital patients from the machinery, should she prove correct in her suspicions, are sufficiently great so that she has good reason to seek help in looking into the problem, to feel complicitous if she chooses to do nothing, and to take action if she verifies her suspicions.

Her difficulty is shared by many who suspect, without being 9 sure, that their companies are concealing the defective or dangerous nature of their products—automobiles that are firetraps, for instance, or canned foods with carcinogenic additives. They may sense that merely to acknowledge what they don't know for sure is too often a weak excuse for inaction, but recognize also that the destructive power of adverse publicity can be great. If the warning turns out to have been inaccurate, it may take a long time to undo the damage to individuals and organizations. As a result, potential whistleblowers must first try to specify the degree to which there is genuine impropriety, and consider how imminent and how serious the threat is which they perceive.

If the facts turn out to warrant disclosure, and if the would-be 10 whistleblower has decided to act upon them in spite of the possibilities of reprisal, then how can the second element—breach of loyalty—be overcome or minimized? Here . . . the problem is one of which set of loyalties to uphold. Several professional codes of ethics, such as those of engineers and public servants, facilitate such a choice at least in theory, by requiring that loyalty to the public interest should override allegiance to colleagues, employers, or clients whenever there is a genuine conflict. Accordingly, those who have assumed a professional responsibility to serve the public interest—as had both Dr. Stockman in Ibsen's play and the engineers in the BART case—have a special obligation not to remain silent about dangers to the public.

Before deciding whether to speak out publicly, however, it is 11 important for them to consider whether the existing avenues for change within the organization have been sufficiently explored. By turning first to insiders for help, one can often uphold both sets of loyalties and settle the problem without going outside the organization. The engineers in the BART case clearly tried to resolve the problem they saw in this manner, and only reluctantly allowed it to come to public attention as a last resort. Dr. Stockman, on the other hand, acted much more impetuously and with little concern for discretion. Before the directors of the mineral baths had even received his report, he talked freely about it and welcomed a journalist's request to publicize the matter. While he had every reason to try to remedy the danger he had discovered, he was not justified in the methods he chose; on the contrary, they were singularly unlikely to bring about corrective action.

It *is* disloyal to colleagues and employers, as well as a waste of time for the public, to sound the loudest alarm first. Whistleblowing has to remain a last alternative because of its destructive side effects. It must be chosen only when other alternatives have been considered and rejected. They may be rejected if they simply do not apply to the problem at hand, or when there is not time to go through routine channels, or when the institution is so corrupt or coercive that steps will be taken to silence the whistleblower should he try the regular channels first. 12

What weight should an oath or a promise of silence have in the conflict of loyalties? There is no doubt that one sworn to silence is under a stronger obligation because of the oath he has taken, unless it was obtained under duress or through deceit, or else binds him to something in itself wrong or unlawful. In taking an oath, one assumes specific obligations beyond those assumed in accepting employment. But even such an oath can be overridden when the public interest at issue is sufficiently strong. The fact that one has promised silence is no excuse for complicity in covering up a crime or violating the public trust. 13

The third element in whistleblowing—accusation—is strongest whenever efforts to correct a problem without going outside the organization have failed, or seem likely to fail. Such an outcome is especially likely whenever those in charge take part in the questionable practices, or have too much at stake in maintaining them. The following story relates the difficulties one government employee experienced in trying to decide whether to go public with accusations against superiors in his agency: 14

> As a construction inspector for a federal agency, John Samuels (not his real name) had personal knowledge of shoddy and deficient construction practices by private contractors. He knew his superiors received free vacations and entertainment, had their homes remodeled, found jobs for their relatives—all courtesy of a private contractor. These superiors later approved a multimillion no-bid contract with the same "generous" firm.
>
> Samuels also had evidence that other firms were hiring nonunion laborers at a low wage while receiving substantially higher payments from the government for labor costs. A former superior, unaware of an office dictaphone, had incautiously instructed Samuels on how to accept bribes for overlooking sub-par performance.

> As he prepared to volunteer this information to various members of Congress, he became tense and uneasy. His family was scared and the fears were valid. It might cost Samuels thousands of dollars to protect his job. Those who had freely provided him with information would probably recant or withdraw their friendship. A number of people might object to his using a dictaphone to gather information. His agency would start covering up and vent its collective wrath upon him. As for reporters and writers, they would gather for a few days, then move on to the next story. He would be left without a job, with fewer friends, with massive battles looming, and without the financial means of fighting them. Samuels decided to remain silent.[6]

Samuels could be sure of his facts, and fairly sure that it would not help to explore avenues within the agency in trying to remedy the situation. But was the method he envisaged—of volunteering his information to members of Congress and to the press—the one most likely to do so, and to provide a fair hearing for those he was charging with corruption and crime? Could he have gone first to the police? If he had been concerned to proceed in the fairest possible manner, he should at least have considered alternative methods of investigating and reporting the abuses he had witnessed. 15

These abuses were clearly such as to warrant attention. At other times, potential whistleblowers must also ask themselves whether their message, however accurate, is one to which the public is entitled in the first place or whether it infringes on personal and private matters that no one should invade. Here, the very notion of what is in the public interest is at issue: allegations regarding an official's unusual sexual or religious practices may well appeal to the public's interest without therefore being relevant to "the public interest." Those who regard such private matters as threats to the public voice their own religious and political prejudices in the language of accusation. Such a danger is never stronger than when the accusation is delivered surreptitiously; the anonymous allegations made during the McCarthy period regarding political beliefs and associations often injured persons who did not even know their accusers or the exact nature of the charges. 16

In fairness to those criticized, openly accepted responsibility for blowing the whistle should therefore be preferred to the secret denunciation or the leaked rumor—the more so, the more derogatory and accusatory the information. What is openly stated can be more easily checked, its source's motives challenged, and the underlying information examined. Those under attack may otherwise be hard put to it to defend themselves against nameless adversaries. Often 17

[6]This case is adapted from Clark, "The Sound of Professional Suicide."

they do not even know that they are threatened until it is too late to respond.

. . .

Must the whistleblower who speaks out openly also resign? Only if staying on means being forced to participate in the objectionable activity, and thus to take on partial responsibility for its consequences. Otherwise, there should be no burden on whistleblowers to resign in voicing their alarm. In principle, at least, it is often their duty to speak out, and their positions ought not thereby to be at issue. In practice, however, they know that retaliation, forced departure, perhaps blacklisting, may be sufficient risks at times so that it may be wise to resign before sounding the alarm: to resign in protest, or to leave quietly, secure another post, and only then blow the whistle.[7] In each case, those who speak out can then do so with the authority and knowledge of insiders, but without their vulnerability. 18

It is not easy to weigh all these factors, nor to compensate for the degree of bias, rationalization, and denial that inevitably influences one's judgment. By speaking out, whistleblowers may spark a reexamination of these forces among colleagues and others who had ignored or learned to live with shoddy or corrupt practices. Because they have this power to dramatize moral conflict, would-be whistleblowers have a special responsibility to ask themselves about biases in deciding whether or not to speak out: a desire for self-defense in a difficult bureaucratic situation, perhaps, or unrealistic expectations regarding the likely effects of speaking out.[8] 19

As they weigh the reasons for sounding the alarm, or on the contrary for remaining silent, they may find it helpful to ask about the 20

[7]On resignation in protest, see Albert Hirschman, *Exit, Voice, and Loyalty* (Cambridge, Mass.: Harvard University Press, 1970); Brian Barry, in a review of Hirschman's book in *British Journal of Political Science* 4 (1974):79–104, has pointed out that "exit" and "voice" are not alternatives but independent variations that may occur separately or together. Both leaking and whistleblowing represent "voice." They can be undertaken while staying on at work, or before one's voluntary exit, or simultaneously with it, or after it; they can also have the consequence of involuntary or forced "exit" through dismissal or being "frozen out" even though retained at work. See also Edward Weisband and Thomas M. Franck, *Resignation in Protest* (New York: Viking Press, 1975); James Thomson, "Getting Out and Speaking Out," *Foreign Policy*, no. 13 (Winter 1973–1974), pp. 49–69; Joel L. Fleishman and Bruce L. Payne, *Ethical Dilemmas and the Education of Policymakers* (Hastings-on-Hudson, N.Y.: Hastings Center, 1980).

[8]If, for example, a government employee stands to make large profits from a book exposing the iniquities in his agency, there is danger that he might slant his report in order to cause more of a sensation. Sometimes a warning is so clearly justifiable and substantiated that it carries weight no matter what the motives of the speaker. But scandal can pay; and the whistleblower's motives ought ideally to be above suspicion, for his own sake as well as for the sake of the respect he desires for his warning. Personal gain from speaking out increases the need to check the accuracy of the speaker.

legitimacy of the rationale for collective secrecy in the particular problem they face. If they are wondering whether or not to blow the whistle on the unnecessary surgery they have witnessed, for example, or on the manufacture of unsafe machinery, what weight should they place on claims to professional confidentiality or corporate secrecy?

Reducing bias and error in moral choice often requires consultation, even open debate; such methods force us to articulate the arguments at stake and to challenge privately held assumptions. But choices about whether or not to blow the whistle present special problems for such consultation. On the one hand, once whistleblowers sound their alarm publicly, their judgment *will* be subjected to open scrutiny; they will have to articulate their reasons for speaking out and substantiate their charges. On the other hand, it will then be too late to retract their charges should they turn out to have been unfounded. 21

For those who are concerned about a situation within their organization, it is therefore preferable to seek advice *before* deciding either to go public or to remain silent. But the more corrupt the circumstances, the more dangerous it may be to consult colleagues, and the more likely it is that those responsible for the abuse or neglect will destroy the evidence linking them to it. And yet, with no one to consult, the would-be whistleblowers themselves may have a biased view of the state of affairs; they may see corruption and conspiracy where none exists, and choose not to consult others when in fact it would have been not only safe but advantageous to do so. 22

Given these difficulties, it is especially important to seek more general means of weighing the arguments for and against whistleblowing; to take them up in public debate and in teaching; and to consider changes in organizations, law, and work practices that could reduce the need for individuals to choose between blowing and "swallowing" the whistle.[9] 23

Review Questions

1. Define the term "whistleblower."
2. Bok states that whistleblowers face pressures both from within and from without. What are these pressures?
3. What are the dangers of unjustified whistleblowing?
4. According to Bok, a person does well to use *dissent, breach of loyalty,* and

[9]Alan Westin discusses "swallowing" the whistle in *Whistle Blowing!,* pp. 10–13. For a discussion of debate concerning whistleblowing, see Rosemary Chalk, "The Miner's Canary," *Bulletin of the Atomic Scientists* 38 (February 1982): 16–22.

accusation as criteria for helping to decide whether or not to blow the whistle. Specifically, what questions can help one make the decision? (Classify these questions according to the three criteria.)

Discussion and Writing Suggestions

1. Discuss the ways it is possible, even likely, that a whistleblower would find blowing the whistle on unethical behavior justifiable, whereas his or her colleagues would not.
2. Discuss or write a description of some incident in which you had trouble deciding whether or not you should "go public" with information. What were the tensions that led to indecision? How did you act—and why? Develop your response into a brief essay.
3. "It *is* disloyal to colleagues and employers, as well as a waste of time for the public, to sound the loudest alarm first. Whistleblowing has to remain the last alternative because of its destructive side effects." What examples can you think of that concern *irresponsible* whistleblowing? What damages resulted from the incident?
4. Do those being accused, those on whom the whistle is blown, have rights? What are they?

CASES FOR ANALYSIS AND DISCUSSION

Following, you'll find three cases for analysis and discussion, each of which will raise certain ethical dilemmas. In business schools around the country, the "case method" is an instructional technique of long standing. Whether the course be in finance, business law, management training, investment strategies, or business ethics, the rationale for presenting cases is the same. The "case," usually a narrative account, recreates a problem or a particular challenge in a business context. The case amounts to raw data that the student reviews in light of principles learned in class. The student is then asked to define problems and to recommend or evaluate courses of action, based on a clear method of analysis.

The cases that follow present ethical dilemmas that resulted from business dealings—real in "two" instances, hypothetical in one. As we've suggested, your job will be to read the cases, to define the problems, and to evaluate or recommend courses of action. What would you do in similar circumstances or if you were asked to advise those involved? What business decisions would follow from your recommendations? What would be the consequences of those decisions? These among other questions are fundamental to case-method instruction.

As you read, keep in mind the remarks of Gerald Cavanagh and Sissela Bok, who provide criteria that you can apply in defining problems and developing responses. Cavanagh and Bok offer you tools for analysis. Note that in one case (the Challenger *disaster), the authors assist you in raising questions. In the two others, you are essentially on your own.*

Case 1: Peter Green's First Day

Peter Green came home to his wife and new baby a dejected man. 1
What a contrast to the morning, when he had left the apartment full of enthusiasm to tackle his first customer in his new job at Scott Carpets. And what a customer! Peabody Rug was the largest carpet retailer in the area and accounted for 15% of the entire volume of Peter's territory. When Peabody introduced a Scott product, other retailers were quick to follow with orders. So when Bob Franklin, the owner of Peabody Rug, had called District Manager John Murphy expressing interest in "Carpet Supreme," Scott's newest commercial-duty home carpet, Peter knew that a $15,000–$20,000 order was a real probability, and no small show for his first sale. And it was important to do well at the start, for John Murphy had made no bones about his scorn for the new breed of salespeople at Scott Carpet.

Murphy was of the old school: in the business since his gradua- 2
tion from a local high school, he had fought his way through the stiffest retail competition in the nation to be District Manager of the area at age fifty-eight. Murphy knew his textiles, and he knew his competitors' textiles. He knew his customers, and he knew how well his competitors knew his customers. Formerly, when Scott Carpet had needed to fill sales positions, it had generally raided the competition for experienced personnel, put them on a straight commission, and thereby managed to increase sales and maintain its good reputation for service at the same time. When Murphy had been promoted eight years ago to the position of District Manager, he had passed on his sales territory to Harvey Katchorian, a sixty-year-old mill rep and son of an immigrant who had also spent his life in the carpet trade. Harvey had had no trouble keeping up his sales and had retired from the company the previous spring after forty-five years of successful service in the industry. Peter, in turn, was to take over Harvey's accounts, and Peter knew that John Murphy was not sure that his

original legacy to Harvey was being passed on to the best salesperson.

Peter was one of the new force of salespeople from Scott's Sales 3
Management Program. In 1976 top management had created a training program to compensate for the industry's dearth of younger salespeople with long-term management potential. Peter, a college graduate, had entered Scott's five-month training program immediately after college and was the first graduate of the program to be assigned to John Murphy's district. Murphy had made it known to top management from the start that he did not think the training program could compensate for on-the-job experience, and he was clearly withholding optimism about Peter's prospects as a salesperson despite Peter's fine performance during the training program.

Peter had been surprised, therefore, when Murphy volunteered 4
to accompany him on his first week of sales "to ease your transition into the territory." As they entered the office at Peabody Rug, Murphy had even seemed friendly and said reassuringly, "I think you'll get along with Bob. He's a great guy—knows the business and has been a good friend of mine for years."

Everything went smoothly. Bob liked the new line and appeared 5
ready to place a large order with Peter the following week, but he indicated that he would require some "help on the freight costs" before committing himself definitely. Peter was puzzled and unfamiliar with the procedure, but Murphy quickly stepped in and assured Bob that Peter would be able to work something out.

After the meeting, on their way back to Scott Carpets' district 6
office, Peter asked Murphy about freight costs. Murphy sarcastically explained the procedure: Because of its large volume, Peabody regularly "asked for a little help to cover shipping costs," and got it from all or most suppliers. Bob Franklin was simply issued a credit for defective merchandise. By claiming he had received second-quality goods, Bob was entitled to a 10%–25% discount. The discount on defective merchandise had been calculated by the company to equal roughly the cost of shipping the 500-lb. rolls back to the mill, and so it just about covered Bob's own freight costs. The practice had been going on so long that Bob demanded "freight assistance" as a matter of course before placing a large order. Obviously, the merchandise was not defective, but by making an official claim, the sales representative could set in gear the defective-merchandise compensation system. Murphy reiterated, as if to a two-year-old, the importance of a Peabody account to any sales rep, and shrugged off the freight assistance as part of doing business with such an influential firm.

Peter stared at Murphy. "Basically, what you're asking me to do, 7
Mr. Murphy, is to lie to the front office."

Murphy angrily replied, "Look, do you want to make it here or 8 not? If you do, you ought to know you need Peabody's business. I don't know what kind of fancy think they taught you at college, but where I come from you don't call your boss a liar."

From the time he was a child, Peter Green had been taught not to lie or steal. He believed these principles were absolute and that one should support one's beliefs at whatever personal cost. But during college the only even remote test of his principles was his strict adherence to the honor system in taking exams. 9

As he reviewed the conversation with Murphy, it seemed to Peter that there was no way to avoid losing the Peabody account, which would look bad on his own record as well as Murphy's—not to mention the loss in commissions for them both. He felt badly about getting into a tiff with Murphy on his first day out in the territory, and knew Murphy would feel betrayed if one of his salespeople purposely lost a major account. 10

The only out he could see, aside from quitting, was to play down the whole episode. Murphy had not actually *ordered* Peter to submit a claim for damaged goods (was he covering himself legally?), so Peter could technically ignore the conversation and simply not authorize a discount. He knew very well, however, that such a course was only superficially passive, and that in Murphy's opinion he would have lost the account on purpose. As Peter sipped halfheartedly at a martini, he thought bitterly to himself, "Boy, they sure didn't prepare me for this in Management Training. And I don't even know if this kind of thing goes on in the rest of Murphy's district, let alone in Scott's eleven other districts." 11

Case 2: Why Should My Conscience Bother Me?

KERMIT VANDIVIER[1]

The B. F. Goodrich Co. is what business magazines like to speak of as "a major American corporation." It has operations in a dozen states and as many foreign countries, and of these far-flung facilities, the Goodrich plant at Troy, Ohio, is not the most imposing. It is a small, one-story building, once used to manufacture airplanes. Set in the grassy flatlands of west-central Ohio, it employs only about six hun- 1

"Why Should My Conscience Bother Me?" by Kermit Vandivier from *In the Name of Profit,* by Robert Heilbroner, © 1972 by Doubleday, a division of Bantam, Doubleday, Dell Publishing Group, Inc. Reprinted by permission of the publisher.

[1]Reporter, *Daily News,* in Troy, Ohio.

dred people. Nevertheless, it is one of the three largest manufacturers of aircraft wheels and brakes, a leader in a most profitable industry. Goodrich wheels and brakes support such well-known planes as the F111, the C5A, the Boeing 727, the XB70 and many others. Its customers include almost every aircraft manufacturer in the world.

Contracts for aircraft wheels and brakes often run into millions of 2
dollars, and ordinarily a contract with a total value of less than $70,000, though welcome, would not create any special stir of joy in the hearts of Goodrich sales personnel. But purchase order P-23718, issued on June 18, 1967, by the LTV Aerospace Corporation, and ordering 202 brake assemblies for a new Air Force plane at a total price of $69,417, was received by Goodrich with considerable glee. And there was good reason. Some ten years previously, Goodrich had built a brake for LTV that was, to say the least, considerably less than a rousing success. The brake had not lived up to Goodrich's promises, and after experiencing considerable difficulty, LTV had written off Goodrich as a source of brakes. Since that time, Goodrich salesmen had been unable to sell so much as a shot of brake fluid to LTV. So in 1967, when LTV requested bids on wheels and brakes for the new A7D light attack aircraft it proposed to build for the Air Force, Goodrich submitted a bid that was absurdly low, so low that LTV could not, in all prudence, turn it down.

Goodrich had, in industry parlance, "bought into the business." 3
Not only did the company not expect to make a profit on the deal; it was prepared, if necessary, to lose money. For aircraft brakes are not something that can be ordered off the shelf. They are designed for a particular aircraft, and once an aircraft manufacturer buys a brake, he is forced to purchase all replacement parts from the brake manufacturer. The $70,000 that Goodrich would get for making the brake would be a drop in the bucket when compared with the cost of the linings and other parts the Air Force would have to buy from Goodrich during the lifetime of the aircraft. Furthermore, the company which manufactures brakes for one particular model of an aircraft quite naturally has the inside track to supply other brakes when the planes are updated and improved.

Thus, that first contract, regardless of the money involved, is very 4
important, and Goodrich, when it learned that it had been awarded the A7D contract, was determined that while it may have slammed the door on its own foot ten years before, this time, the second time around, things would be different. The word was soon circulated throughout the plant: "We can't bungle it this time. We've got to give them a good brake, regardless of the cost."

There was another factor which had undoubtedly influenced 5
LTV. All aircraft brakes made today are of the disk type, and the bid submitted by Goodrich called for a relatively small brake, one

containing four disks and weighing only 106 pounds. The weight of any aircraft part is extremely important. The lighter a part is, the heavier the plane's payload can be. The four-rotor, 106-pound brake promised by Goodrich was about as light as could be expected, and this undoubtedly had helped move LTV to award the contract to Goodrich.

The brake was designed by one of Goodrich's most capable engineers, John Warren. A tall, lanky blond and a graduate of Purdue, Warren had come from the Chrysler Corporation seven years before and had become adept at aircraft brake design. The happy-go-lucky manner he usually maintained belied a temper which exploded whenever anyone ventured to offer any criticism of his work, no matter how small. On these occasions, Warren would turn red in the face, often throwing or slamming something and then stalking from the scene. As his coworkers learned the consequences of criticizing him, they did so less and less readily, and when he submitted his preliminary design for the A7D brake, it was accepted without question. 6

Warren was named project engineer for the A7D, and he, in turn, assigned the task of producing the final production design to a newcomer to the Goodrich engineering stable, Searle Lawson. Just turned twenty-six, Lawson had been out of the Northrup Institute of Technology only one year when he came to Goodrich in January 1967. Like Warren, he had worked for a while in the automotive industry, but his engineering degree was in aeronautical and astronautical sciences, and when the opportunity came to enter his special field, via Goodrich, he took it. At the Troy plant, Lawson had been assigned to various "paper projects" to break him in, and after several months spent reviewing statistics and old brake designs, he was beginning to fret at the lack of challenge. When told he was being assigned to his first "real" project, he was elated and immediately plunged into his work. 7

The major portion of the design had already been completed by Warren, and major assemblies for the brake had already been ordered from Goodrich suppliers. Naturally, however, before Goodrich could start making the brakes on a production basis, much testing would have to be done. Lawson would have to determine the best materials to use for the linings and discover what minor adjustments in the design would have to be made. 8

Then, after the preliminary testing and after the brake was judged ready for production, one whole brake assembly would undergo a series of grueling, simulated braking stops and other severe trials called qualification tests. These tests are required by the military, which gives very detailed specifications on how they are to be conducted, the criteria for failure, and so on. They are performed in the 9

Goodrich plant's test laboratory, where huge machines called dynamometers can simulate the weight and speed of almost any aircraft. After the brakes pass the laboratory tests, they are approved for production, but before the brakes are accepted for use in military service, they must undergo further extensive flight tests.

Searle Lawson was well aware that much work had to be done 10
before the A7D brake could go into production, and he knew that LTV had set the last two weeks in June, 1968, as the starting dates for flight tests. So he decided to begin testing immediately. Goodrich's suppliers had not yet delivered the brake housing and other parts, but the brake disks had arrived, and using the housing from a brake similar in size and weight to the A7D brake, Lawson built a prototype. The prototype was installed in a test wheel and placed on one of the big dynamometers in the plant's test laboratory. The dynamometer was adjusted to simulate the weight of the A7D and Lawson began a series of tests, "landing" the wheel and brake at the A7D's landing speed, and braking it to a stop. The main purpose of these preliminary tests was to learn what temperatures would develop within the brake during the simulated stops and to evaluate the lining materials tentatively selected for use.

During a normal aircraft landing the temperatures inside the 11
brake may reach 1000 degrees, and occasionally a bit higher. During Lawson's first simulated landings, the temperature of his prototype brake reached 1500 degrees. The brake glowed a bright cherry-red and threw off incandescent particles of metal and lining material as the temperature reached its peak. After a few such stops, the brake was dismantled and the linings were found to be almost completely disintegrated. Lawson chalked this first failure up to chance and, ordering new lining materials, tried again.

The second attempt was a repeat of the first. The brake became 12
extremely hot, causing the lining materials to crumble into dust.

After the third such failure, Lawson, inexperienced though he 13
was, knew that the fault lay not in defective parts or unsuitable lining material but in the basic design of the brake itself. Ignoring Warren's original computations, Lawson made his own, and it didn't take him long to discover where the trouble lay—the brake was too small. There simply was not enough surface area on the disks to stop the aircraft without generating the excessive heat that caused the linings to fail.

The answer to the problem was obvious but far from simple—the 14
four-disk brake would have to be scrapped, and a new design, using five disks, would have to be developed. The implications were not lost on Lawson. Such a step would require the junking of all the four-disk-brake subassemblies, many of which had now begun to arrive from the various suppliers. It would also mean several weeks

of preliminary design and testing and many more weeks of waiting while the suppliers made and delivered the new subassemblies.

Yet, several weeks had already gone by since LTV's order had 15 arrived, and the date for delivery of the first production brakes for flight testing was only a few months away.

Although project engineer John Warren had more or less turned 16 the A7D over to Lawson, he knew of the difficulties Lawson had been experiencing. He had assured the young engineer that the problem revolved around getting the right kind of lining material. Once that was found, he said, the difficulties would end.

Despite the evidence of the abortive tests and Lawson's careful 17 computations, Warren rejected the suggestion that the four-disk brake was too light for the job. Warren knew that his superior had already told LTV, in rather glowing terms, that the preliminary tests on the A7D brake were very successful. Indeed, Warren's superiors weren't aware at this time of the troubles on the brake. It would have been difficult for Warren to admit not only that he had made a serious error in his calculations and original design but that his mistakes had been caught by a green kid, barely out of college.

Warren's reaction to a five-disk brake was not unexpected by 18 Lawson, and, seeing that the four-disk brake was not to be abandoned so easily, he took his calculations and dismal test results one step up the corporate ladder.

At Goodrich, the man who supervises the engineers working on 19 projects slated for production is called, predictably, the projects manager. The job was held by a short, chubby and bald man named Robert Sink. A man truly devoted to his work, Sink was as likely to be found at his desk at ten o'clock on Sunday night as ten o'clock on Monday morning. His outside interests consisted mainly of tinkering on a Model-A Ford and an occasional game of golf. Some fifteen years before, Sink had begun working at Goodrich as a lowly draftsman. Slowly, he worked his way up. Despite his geniality, Sink was neither respected nor liked by the majority of the engineers, and his appointment as their supervisor did not improve their feelings about him. They thought he had only gone to high school. It quite naturally rankled those who had gone through years of college and acquired impressive specialties such as thermodynamics and astronautics to be commanded by a man whom they considered their intellectual inferior. But, though Sink had no college training, he had something even more useful: a fine working knowledge of company politics.

Puffing upon a Meerschaum pipe, Sink listened gravely as young 20 Lawson confided his fears about the four-disk brake. Then he examined Lawson's calculations and the results of the abortive tests. Despite the fact that he was not a qualified engineer, in the strictest sense of the word, it must certainly have been obvious to Sink that

Lawson's calculations were correct and that a four-disk brake would never have worked on the A7D.

But other things of equal importance were also obvious. First, to concede that Lawson's calculations were correct would also mean conceding that Warren's calculations were incorrect. As projects manager, he not only was responsible for Warren's activities, but, in admitting that Warren had erred, he would have to admit that he had erred in trusting Warren's judgment. It also meant that, as projects manager, it would be he who would have to explain the whole messy situation to the Goodrich hierarchy, not only at Troy but possibly on the corporate level at Goodrich's Akron offices. And, having taken Warren's judgment of the four-disk brake at face value (he was forced to do this since, not being an engineer, he was unable to exercise any engineering judgment of his own), he had assured LTV, not once but several times, that about all there was left to do on the brake was pack it in a crate and ship it out the back door. 21

There's really no problem at all, he told Lawson. After all, Warren was an experienced engineer, and if he said the brake would work, it would work. Just keep on testing and probably, maybe even on the very next try, it'll work out just fine. 22

Lawson was far from convinced, but without the support of his superiors there was little he could do except keep on testing. By now, housings for the four-disk brake had begun to arrive at the plant, and Lawson was able to build up a production model of the brake and begin the formal qualification tests demanded by the military. 23

The first qualification attempts went exactly as the tests on the prototype had. Terrific heat developed within the brakes and, after a few, short, simulated stops, the linings crumbled. A new type of lining material was ordered and once again an attempt to qualify the brake was made. Again, failure. 24

On April 11, the day the thirteenth test was completed, I became personally involved in the A7D situation. 25

I had worked in the Goodrich test laboratory for five years, starting first as an instrumentation engineer, then later becoming a data analyst and technical writer. As part of my duties, I analyzed the reams and reams of instrumentation data that came from the many testing machines in the laboratory, then transcribed it to a more usable form for the engineering department. And when a new-type brake had successfully completed the required qualification tests, I would issue a formal qualification report. 26

Qualification reports were an accumulation of all the data and test logs compiled by the test technicians during the qualification tests, and were documentary proof that a brake had met all the requirements established by the military specifications and was therefore presumed safe for flight testing. Before actual flight tests were 27 conducted on a brake, qualification reports had to be delivered to the customer and to various government officials.

On April 11, I was looking over the data from the latest A7D test, and I noticed that many irregularities in testing methods had been noted on the test logs. 28

Technically, of course, there was nothing wrong with conducting tests in any manner desired, so long as the test was for research purposes only. But qualification test methods are clearly delineated by the military, and I knew that this test had been a formal qualification attempt. One particular notation on the test logs caught my eye. For some of the stops, the instrument which recorded the brake pressure had been deliberately miscalibrated so that, while the brake pressure used during the stops was recorded as 1000 psi (the maximum pressure that would be available on the A7D aircraft), the pressure had actually been 1100 psi! 29

I showed the test logs to the test lab supervisor, Ralph Gretzinger, who said he had learned from the technician who had miscalibrated the instrument that he had been asked to do so by Lawson. Lawson, said Gretzinger, readily admitted asking for the miscalibration, saying he had been told to do so by Sink. 30

I asked Gretzinger why anyone would want to miscalibrate the data-recording instruments. 31

"Why? I'll tell you why," he snorted. "That brake is a failure. It's way too small for the job, and they're not ever going to get it to work. They're getting desperate, and instead of scrapping the damned thing and starting over, they figure they can horse around down here in the lab and qualify it that way." 32

An expert engineer, Gretzinger had been responsible for several innovations in brake design. It was he who had invented the unique brake system used on the famous XB70. A graduate of Georgia Tech, he was a stickler for detail and he had some very firm ideas about honesty and ethics. "If you want to find out what's going on," said Gretzinger, "ask Lawson, he'll tell you." 33

Curious, I did ask Lawson the next time he came into the lab. He seemed eager to discuss the A7D and gave me the history of his months of frustrating efforts to get Warren and Sink to change the brake design. "I just can't believe this is really happening," said Lawson, shaking his head slowly. "This isn't engineering, at least not what I thought it would be. Back in school, I thought that when you were an engineer, you tried to do your best, no matter what it cost. But this is something else." 34

He sat across the desk from me, his chin propped in his hand. "Just wait," he warned. "You'll get a chance to see what I'm talking about. You're going to get in the act, too, because I've already had the word that we're going to make one more attempt to qualify the brake, 35 and that's it. Win or lose, we're going to issue a qualification report!"

I reminded him that a qualification report could only be issued after a brake had successfully met all military requirements, and therefore, unless the next qualification attempt was a success, no report would be issued. 36

"You'll find out," retorted Lawson. "I was already told that regardless of what the brake does on test, it's going to be qualified." He said he had been told in those exact words at a conference with Sink and Russell Van Horn. 37

This was the first indication that Sink had brought his boss, Van Horn, into the mess. Although Van Horn, as manager of the design engineering section, was responsible for the entire department, he was not necessarily familiar with all phases of every project, and it was not uncommon for those under him to exercise the what-he-doesn't-know-won't-hurt-him philosophy. If he was aware of the full extent of the A7D situation, it meant that matters had truly reached a desperate stage—that Sink had decided not only to call for help but was looking toward that moment when blame must be borne and, if possible, shared. 38

Also, if Van Horn had said, "Regardless what the brake does on test, it's going to be qualified," then it could only mean that, if necessary, a false qualification report would be issued! I discussed this possibility with Gretzinger, and he assured me that under no circumstances would such a report ever be issued. 39

"If they want a qualification report, we'll write them one, but we'll tell it just like it is," he declared emphatically. "No false data or false reports are going to come out of this lab." 40

On May 2, 1968, the fourteenth and final attempt to qualify the brake was begun. Although the same improper methods used to nurse the brake through the previous tests were employed, it soon became obvious that this too would end in failure. 41

When the tests were about half completed, Lawson asked if I would start preparing the various engineering curves and graphic displays which were normally incorporated in a qualification report. "It looks as though you'll be writing a qualification report shortly," he said. 42

I flatly refused to have anything to do with the matter and immediately told Gretzinger what I had been asked to do. He was furious and repeated his previous declaration that under no circumstances would any false data or other matter be issued from the lab. 43

"I'm going to get this settled right now, once and for all," he declared. "I'm going to see Line [Russell Line, manager of the Goodrich Technical Services Section, of which the test lab was a part] and find out just how far this thing is going to go!" He stormed out of the room. 44

In about an hour, he returned and called me to his desk. He sat 45
silently for a few moments, then muttered, half to himself, "I wonder what the hell they'd do if I just quit?" I didn't answer and I didn't ask him what he meant. I knew. He had been beaten down. He had reached the point when the decision had to be made. Defy them now while there was still time—or knuckle under, sell out.

"You know," he went on uncertainly, looking down at his desk, 46
"I've been an engineer for a long time, and I've always believed that ethics and integrity were every bit as important as theorems and formulas, and never once has anything happened to change my beliefs. Now this. . . . Hell, I've got two sons I've got to put through school and I just. . . ." His voice trailed off.

He sat for a few more minutes, then, looking over the top of his 47
glasses, said hoarsely, "Well, it looks like we're licked. The way it stands now, we're to go ahead and prepare the data and other things for the graphic presentation in the report, and when we're finished, someone upstairs will actually write the report.

"After all," he continued, "we're just drawing some curves, and 48
what happens to them after they leave here, well, we're not responsible for that."

He was trying to persuade himself that as long as we were 49
concerned with only one part of the puzzle and didn't see the completed picture, we really weren't doing anything wrong. He didn't believe what he was saying, and he knew I didn't believe it either. It was an embarrassing and shameful moment for both of us.

I wasn't at all satisfied with the situation and decided that I too 50
would discuss the matter with Russell Line, the senior executive in our section.

Tall, powerfully built, his teeth flashing white, his face tanned to 51
a coffee-brown by a daily stint with a sun lamp, Line looked and acted every inch the executive. He was a crossword-puzzle enthusiast and an ardent golfer, and though he had lived in Troy only a short time, he had been accepted into the Troy Country Club and made an official of the golf committee. He commanded great respect and had come to be well liked by those of us who worked under him.

He listened sympathetically while I explained how I felt about the 52
A7D situation, and when I had finished, he asked me what I wanted him to do about it. I said that as employees of the Goodrich Company we had a responsibility to protect the company and its reputation if at all possible. I said I was certain that officers on the corporate level would never knowingly allow such tactics as had been employed on the A7D.

"I agree with you," he remarked, "but I still want to know what 53
you want me to do about it."

I suggested that in all probability the chief engineer at the Troy 54
plant, H. C. "Bud" Sunderman, was unaware of the A7D problem and that he, Line, should tell him what was going on.

Line laughed, good-humoredly. "Sure, I could, but I'm not going 55
to. Bud probably already knows about this thing anyway, and if he doesn't, I'm sure not going to be the one to tell him."

"But why?" 56

"Because it's none of my business, and it's none of yours. I 57
learned a long time ago not to worry about things over which I had no control. I have no control over this."

I wasn't satisfied with this answer, and I asked him if his con- 58
science wouldn't bother him if, say, during flight tests on the brake, something should happen resulting in death or injury to the test pilot.

"Look," he said, becoming somewhat exasperated, "I just told 59
you I have no control over this thing. Why should my conscience bother me?"

His voice took on a quiet, soothing tone as he continued. "You're 60
just getting all upset over this thing for nothing. I just do as I'm told, and I'd advise you to do the same."

He had made his decision, and now I had to make mine. 61

I made no attempt to rationalize what I had been asked to do. It 62
made no difference who would falsify which part of the report or whether the actual falsification would be by misleading numbers or misleading words. Whether by acts of commission or omission, all of us who contributed to the fraud would be guilty. The only question left for me to decide was whether or not I would become a party to the fraud.

Before coming to Goodrich in 1963, I had held a variety of jobs, 63
each a little more pleasant, a little more rewarding than the last. At forty-two, with seven children, I had decided that the Goodrich Company would probably be my "home" for the rest of my working life. The job paid well, it was pleasant and challenging, and the future looked reasonably bright. My wife and I had bought a home and we were ready to settle down into a comfortable, middle-age, middle-class rut. If I refused to take part in the A7D fraud, I would have to either resign or be fired. The report would be written by someone anyway, but I would have the satisfaction of knowing I had had no part in the matter. But bills aren't paid with personal satisfaction, nor house payments with ethical principles. I made my decision.[2]

---

[2]Turn to page 607 for the author's concluding discussion on what happened in this case. Before reading that discussion, however, try to anticipate Vandivier's decision.

Case 3: The Challenger Disaster

RUSSELL P. BOISJOLY
ELLEN FOSTER CURTIS

INTRODUCTION

On January 28, 1986, the space shuttle *Challenger* exploded 73 seconds into its flight, killing the seven astronauts aboard. As the nation mourned the tragic loss of the crew members, the Rogers Commission was formed to investigate the causes of the disaster. (W. P. Rogers was the head of the congressional commission appointed by President Reagan in 1986 to investigate the *Challenger* accident.) The commission concluded that the explosion occurred due to seal failure in one of the solid rocket booster joints. Testimony given by Roger Boisjoly, senior scientist and acknowledged rocket seal expert, indicated that top management at NASA and Morton Thiokol, Inc. had been aware of problems with the O-ring seals, but agreed to launch against the recommendation of Boisjoly and other engineers. Biosjoly had alerted management to problems with the O-rings as early as January 1985, yet several shuttle launches prior to the *Challenger* had been approved without correcting the hazards. 1

The management process at NASA and Morton Thiokol the year prior to the launch, and Thiokol's postdisaster treatment of Boisjoly and his associates, demonstrate[s] a dramatic change in the corporate environment. Management's willingness to accept previously unacceptable risks increased, which contributed to a communications breakdown between technical experts, their supervisors, and top-level decision makers. This created conflicts about the corporate loyalty of the dissenting engineers, the welfare of the astronauts and the public, and the personal morality of the engineers, as well as the managers who made the launch decision and exacted retribution from the so-called whistle blowers. 2

The following case study focuses on Roger Boisjoly's attempt to prevent the *Challenger* launch, the scenario that resulted in the launch decision, and Boisjoly's quest to set the record straight despite enormous negative personal and professional consequences. A brief epilogue further analyzes some of the ethical questions raised throughout the case. 3

PREVIEW FOR DISASTER

4 On January 24, 1985, Roger Boisjoly, senior scientist at Morton Thiokol, watched the launch of Flight 51-C of the space shuttle program. He was at Cape Canaveral to inspect the solid rocket boosters from Flight 51-C following their recovery in the Atlantic Ocean and to conduct a training session at Kennedy Space Center (KSC) on the proper methods of inspecting the booster joints. While watching the launch, he noted that the temperature that day was much cooler than recorded at other launches, but was still much warmer than the 18 degree temperature encountered three days earlier when he arrived in Orlando. The unseasonably cold weather of the past several days had produced the worst citrus crop failures in Florida history.

5 When he inspected the solid rocket boosters several days later. Boisjoly discovered evidence that both the primary and secondary O-ring seals on a field joint had been compromised by hot combustion gases (that is, hot gas blow-by had occurred) which had also eroded part of the primary O-ring. This was the first time that a primary seal on a field joint had been penetrated. When he discovered the large amount of blackened grease between the primary and secondary seals, his concern heightened. The blackened grease was discovered over 60-degree and 110-degree arcs, respectively, on two of the seals, with the larger arc indicating greater hot gas blow-by. Postflight calculations indicated that the ambient temperature of the field joints at launch time was 53 degrees. This evidence, coupled with his recollection of the low temperature the day of the launch and the citrus crop damage caused by the cold spell, led to his conclusion that the severe hot gas blow-by may have been caused by, and related to, low temperature. After reporting these findings to his superiors. Boisjoly presented them to engineers and management at NASA's Marshall Space Flight Center (MSFC). As a result of his presentation at MSFC, Roger Boisjoly was asked to participate in the Flight Readiness Review (FRR) on February 12, 1985, for Flight 51-E which was scheduled for launch in April 1985. This FRR represents the first public association of low temperature with blow-by on a field joint, a condition that was considered an "acceptable risk" by Larry Mulloy, NASA's manager for the Booster Project, and other NASA officials.

6 Roger Boisjoly had twenty-five years of experience as an engineer in the aerospace industry. Among his many notable assignments were the performance of stress and deflection analysis on the flight control equipment of the Advanced Minuteman Missile at Autonetics and his service as a lead engineer on the lunar module of Apollo at Hamilton Standard. He moved to Utah in 1980 to take a position in the Applied Mechanics Department as a staff engineer at the Wasatch

Division of Morton Thiokol. He was considered the leading expert in the United States on O-rings and rocket joint seals and received plaudits for his work on the joint seal problems from Joe C. Kilminster, vice president of Space Booster Programs, Morton Thiokol (Kilminster, July 1985). His commitment to the company and the community was further demonstrated by his service as mayor of Willard, Utah, from 1982 to 1983.

The tough questioning he had received at the February 12 FRR convinced Boisjoly of the need for further evidence linking low temperature and hot gas blow-by. He worked closely with Arnie Thompson, supervisor of Rocket Motor Cases, who conducted subscale laboratory tests in March 1985, to further test the effects of temperature on O-ring resiliency. The bench tests that were performed provided powerful evidence to support Boisjoly's and Thompson's theory: Low temperatures greatly and adversely affected the ability of O-rings to create a seal on solid rocket booster joints. If temperature was too low (and they did not know what the threshold temperature would be), it was possible that neither the primary nor secondary O-rings would seal! 7

One month later the postflight inspection of Flight 51-B revealed that the primary seal of a booster nozzle joint did not make contact during its 2-minute flight. If this damage had occurred in a field joint, the secondary O-ring may have failed to seal, causing the loss of the flight. As a result, Boisjoly and his colleagues became increasingly concerned about shuttle safety. This evidence from the inspection of Flight 51-B was presented at the FRR for Flight 51-F on July 1, 1985; the key engineers and managers at NASA and Morton Thiokol were now aware of the critical O-ring problems and the influence of low temperature on the performance of the joint seals. 8

During July 1985, Boisjoly and his associates voiced their desire to devote more effort and resources to solving the problems of O-ring erosion. In his activity reports dated July 22 and 29, 1985, Boisjoly expressed considerable frustration with the lack of progress in this area, despite the fact that a Seal Erosion Task Force had been informally appointed on July 19. Finally, Boisjoly wrote the following memo, labeled "Company Private," to R. K. Lund, vice president of engineering for Morton Thiokol, to express the extreme urgency of his concerns. Here are some excerpts from that memo: 9

> This letter is written to insure that management is fully aware of the seriousness of the current O-Ring erosion problem. . . . The mistakenly accepted position on the joint problem was to fly without fear of failure . . . is now drastically changed as a result of the SRM 16A [Solid Rocket Motor] nozzle joint erosion which eroded a secondary O-Ring with the primary O-Ring never sealing. If the same scenario should occur in a field joint (and it could), then it is a jump ball as to the success or failure

> of the joint. . . . The result would be a catastrophe of the highest order—loss of human life.
>
> It is my honest and real fear that if we do not take immediate action to dedicate a team to solve the problem, with the field joint having the number one priority, then we stand in jeopardy of losing a flight along with all the launch pad facilities (Boisjoly, July 1985).

On August 20, 1985, R. K. Lund formally announced the formation of the Seal Erosion Task Team. The team consisted of five full-time engineers from the 2500 employed by Morton Thiokol on the Space Shuttle Program. The events of the next five months would demonstrate that management had not provided the resources necessary to carry out the enormous task of solving the seal erosion problem. 10

On October 3, 1985, the Seal Erosion Task Force met with Joe Kilminster to discuss the problems they were having in gaining organizational support necessary to solve the O-ring problems. Boisjoly later stated that Kilminster summarized the meeting as a "good bullshit session." Once again frustrated by bureaucratic inertia, Boisjoly wrote in his activity report dated October 4th: 11

> . . . NASA is sending an engineering representative to stay with us starting Oct. 14th. We feel that this is a direct result of their feeling that we (MTI) are not responding quickly enough to the seal problem. . . . Upper management apparently feels that the SRM program is ours for sure and the customer be damned (Boisjoly, October 1985).

Boisjoly was not alone in his expression of frustration. Bob Ebeling, department manager, Solid Rocket Motor Igniter and Final Assembly, and a member of the Seal Erosion Task Force, wrote in a memo to Allan McDonald, manager of the Solid Rocket Motor Project, "HELP! The seal task force is constantly being delayed by every possible means. . . . We wish we could get action by verbal request, but such is not the case. This is a red flag" (McConnell, 1987).

The October 30 launch of Flight 61-A of the *Challenger* provided the most convincing, and yet to some the most contestable, evidence to date that low temperature was directly related to hot gas blow-by. The left booster experienced hot gas blow-by in the center and aft field joints without any seal erosion. The ambient temperature of the field joints was estimated to be 75 degrees at launch time based on postflight calculations. Inspection of the booster joints revealed that the blow-by was less severe than that found on Flight 51-C because the seal grease was a grayish black color, rather than the jet black hue of Flight 51-C. The evidence was now consistent with the bench tests for joint resiliency conducted in March. The actual flight data revealed greater hot gas blow-by for the O-rings on Flight 51-C which 12 had an ambient temperature of 53 degrees than for Flight 61-A which had an ambient temperature of 75 degrees. Those who rejected this line of reasoning concluded that temperature must be irrelevant, since hot gas blow-by had occurred even at room temperature (75 degrees). This difference in interpretation would receive further attention on January 27, 1986.

During the next two-and-one-half months, little progress was made in obtaining a solution to the O-ring problems. Roger Boisjoly made the following entry into his log on January 13, 1986, "O-ring resiliency tests that were requested on September 24, 1985 are now scheduled for January 15, 1986." 13

THE DAY BEFORE THE DISASTER

At 10 a.m. on January 27, 1986, Arnie Thompson received a phone call from Boyd Brinton, Thiokol's manager of Project Engineering at MSFC, relaying the concerns of NASA's Larry Wear, also at MSFC, about the 18-degree temperature forecast for the launch of Flight 51-L, the *Challenger,* scheduled for the next day. This phone call precipitated a series of meetings within Morton Thiokol, at the Marshall Space Flight Center, and at the Kennedy Space Center, which culminated in a three-way telecon involving three teams of engineers and managers beginning at 8:15 p.m. EST. 14

Joe Kilminster, vice president, Space Booster Programs, of Morton Thiokol began the telecon by turning the presentation of the engineering charts over to Roger Boisjoly and Arnie Thompson. They presented thirteen charts which resulted in a recommendation against the launch of the *Challenger.* Boisjoly demonstrated their concerns with the performance of the O-rings in field joints during the initial phases of *Challenger's* flight with charts showing the effects of primary O-ring erosion, and its timing, on the ability to maintain a reliable secondary seal. The tremendous pressure and release of power from the rocket boosters create rotation in the joint such that the metal moves away from the O-rings so that they cannot maintain contact with the metal surfaces. If, at the same time, erosion occurs in the primary O-ring for any reason, then there is a reduced probability of maintaining a secondary seal. It is highly probable that as the ambient temperature drops, the primary O-ring will not seat; that there will be hot gas blow-by and erosion of the primary O-ring; and that a catastrophe will occur when the secondary O-ring fails to seal. 15

Bob Lund presented the final chart that included the Morton Thiokol recommendations that the ambient temperature including wind must be such that the seal temperature would be greater than 53 degrees to proceed with the launch. Since the overnight low was 16 predicted to be 18 degrees. Bob Lund recommended against launch on January 28, 1986, or until the seal temperature exceeded 53 degrees.

NASA's Larry Mulloy bypassed Bob Lund and directly asked Joe 17
Kilminster for his reaction. Kilminster stated that he supported the position of his engineers and he would not recommend launch below 53 degrees.

George Hardy of MSFC said he was "appalled at that 18
recommendation," according to Allan McDonald's testimony before the Rogers Commission. Nevertheless, Hardy would not recommend to launch if the contractor was against it. After Hardy's reaction, Stanley Reinartz, manager of Shuttle Project Office at MSFC, objected by pointing out that the solid rocket motors were qualified to operate between 40 and 90 degrees Fahrenheit.

Larry Mulloy, citing the data from Flight 61-A which indicated to 19
him that temperature was not a factor, strenuously objected to Morton Thiokol's recommendation. He suggested that Thiokol was attempting to establish new Launch Commit Criteria at 53 degrees and that they couldn't do that the night before a launch. In exasperation Mulloy asked, "My God, Thiokol, when do you want me to launch? Next April?" (McConnell, 1987). Although other NASA officials also objected to the association of temperature with O-ring erosion and hot gas blow-by, Roger Boisjoly was able to hold his ground and demonstrate with the use of his charts and pictures that there was indeed a relationship: The lower the temperature, the higher the probability of erosion and blow-by and the greater the likelihood of an accident. Finally, Joe Kilminster asked for a 5-minute caucus off-net.

According to Boisjoly's testimony before the Rogers Commission, 20
Jerry Mason, senior vice president of Wasatch Operations for Morton Thiokol, began the caucus by saying that "a management decision was necessary." Sensing that an attempt would be made to overturn the no-launch decision, Thompson took a pad of paper and tried to sketch out the problem with the joint, while Boisjoly laid out the photos of the compromised joints from Flights 51-C and 61-A. When they became convinced that no one was listening, they ceased their efforts. As Boisjoly would later testify, "There was not one positive pro-launch statement ever made by anybody" (Boisjoly, 1986).

According to Boisjoly, after he and Thompson made their last 21
attempts to stop the launch, Jerry Mason asked rhetorically, "Am I the only one who wants to fly?" Mason turned to Bob Lund and asked him to "take off his engineering hat and put on his management hat." The four managers held a brief discussion and voted unanimously to recommend *Challenger's* launch.

Joe Kilminster revised the initial engineering recommendations 22 so that they would support management's decision to launch. Of the nine rationales presented that evening, only one objectively could support the launch decision; although one other rationale could be considered a neutral statement of engineering fact, the other seven rationales were negative, antilaunch, statements. After hearing Kilminster's presentation, which was accepted without a single probing question, George Hardy asked him to sign the chart and telefax it to Kennedy Space Center and Marshall Space Flight Center. At 11 p.m. EST the teleconference ended.

Aside from the four senior Morton Thiokol executives present at 23 the teleconference, all others were excluded from the final decision. The process represented a radical shift from previous NASA policy. Until that moment, the burden of proof had always been on the engineers to prove beyond a doubt that it was safe to launch. NASA, with their objections to the original Thiokol recommendation against the launch, and Mason, with his request for a "management decision," shifted the burden of proof in the opposite direction. Morton Thiokol was expected to prove that launching *Challenger* would not be safe (Boisjoly, 1986).

The change in the decision so deeply upset Boisjoly that he 24 returned to his office and made the following journal entry: "I sincerely hope that this launch does not result in a catastrophe. I personally do not agree with some of the statements made in Joe Kilminster's written summary stating that SRM-25 is okay to fly" (Boisjoly, 1987).

THE DISASTER AND ITS AFTERMATH

On January 28, 1986, a reluctant Roger Boisjoly watched the launch of 25 the *Challenger*. As the vehicle cleared the tower, Bob Ebeling whispered, "We've just dodged a bullet." (The engineers who opposed the launch assumed that O-ring failure would result in an explosion almost immediately after engine ignition.) To continue in Boisjoly's words, "At approximately T + 60 seconds Bob told me he had just completed a prayer of thanks to the Lord for a successful launch. Just thirteen seconds later we both saw the horror of the destruction as the vehicle exploded" (Boisjoly, 1987).

Morton Thiokol formed a failure investigation team on January 26 31, 1986, to study the causes of the *Challenger* explosion. Roger Boisjoly and Arnie Thompson were part of the team that was sent to the MSFC in Huntsville, Alabama. Boisjoly's first inkling of a division between himself and management came on February 13, when he was informed that he was to testify before the Rogers Commission the next day. He had very little time to prepare for his testimony. Five days later, two commission members held a closed session with Kilminster, Boisjoly, and Thompson. During the interview Boisjoly gave his memos and activity reports to the commissioners. After that meeting, Kilminster chastised Thompson and Boisjoly for correcting his interpretation of the technical data. Their response was that they would continue to correct his version if it was technically incorrect.

Boisjoly's February 25 testimony before the commission, rebut- 27
ting the general manager's statement that the initial decision by the Thiokol participants against the launch was not unanimous, drove a wedge further between him and Morton Thiokol management. Boisjoly was flown to MSFC before he could hear the NASA testimony about the preflight telecon. The next day, he was removed from the failure investigation team and returned to Utah.

Beginning in April, Boisjoly began to believe that for the previous 28
month he had been used solely for public relations purposes. Although given the title of seal coordinator for the redesign effort, he was isolated from NASA and the seal redesign effort. His design information had been changed without his knowledge and presented without his feedback. On May 1, 1986, in a briefing preceding closed sessions before the Rogers Commission, Ed Garrison, president of Aerospace Operations for Morton Thiokol, chastised Boisjoly for "airing the company's dirty laundry" with the memos he had given the commission. The next day, Boisjoly testified about the change in his job assignment. Commission chairman Rogers criticized Thiokol management:

> . . . if it appears that you're punishing the two people or at least two of the people who are right about the decision and objected to the launch which ultimately resulted in criticism of Thiokol and then they're demoted or feel that they are being retaliated against, that is a very serious matter. It would seem to me, just speaking for myself, they should be promoted, not demoted or pushed aside (Rogers, 1986).

Boisjoly now sensed a major rift developing within the corpora- 29
tion. Some coworkers perceived that his testimony was damaging the company image. In an effort to clear the air, he and McDonald requested a private meeting with the company's three top executives, which was held on May 16, 1986. According to Boisjoly, management was unreceptive throughout the meeting. The CEO told McDonald and Boisjoly that the company "was doing just fine until Al and I testified about our job reassignments" (Boisjoly, 1987). McDonald and Boisjoly were nominally restored to their former assignments, but Boisjoly's position became untenable as time passed. On July 21,

1986, Roger Boisjoly requested an extended sick leave from Morton Thiokol.[1]

Is Business Bluffing Ethical?

ALBERT CARR

"Business ethics? It's a contradiction in terms." Some version of this joke often begins introductions to books on business ethics, whose authors are quick to argue that we must carefully examine the perception that business and ethics don't mix. For if they don't, we're obliged to accept all manner of abuses as legitimate or defensible (in which case, we wouldn't call them abuses) so long as businessmen and -women operate within the bounds of law. Recall the Ford Pinto case: An automobile manufacturer rushes a car to market, knowing that in some circumstances the car will prove dangerous to occupants. That car, nonetheless, meets existing federal safety standards. Is the manufacturer behaving unethically by not redesigning the car to reduce a known threat to consumers? If ethics and business don't mix, we answer one way; if they do, we answer another.

A classic in the literature of business ethics calls attention to this very issue. On publication in the January-February 1968 issue of the Harvard Business Review, *Albert Carr's "Is Business Bluffing Ethical?" generated heated debate. Carr claimed that business operates according to its* own *set of ethical principles, separate and distinct from those of religion. It is confusing and misplaced, he said, to apply standards of religious ethics to business. Many disagreed, and on this disagreement turns our response to the claim that businesses owe the public a show of good faith. Following Carr's article, you'll find "Showdown on 'Business Bluffing,' " a* Harvard Business Review *editor's summary of the reaction that Carr stirred.*

A respected businessman with whom I discussed the theme of this 1
article remarked with some heat, "You mean to say you're going to encourage men to bluff? Why, bluffing is nothing more than a form of lying! You're advising them to lie!"

---

[1]Turn to page 611 for the authors' concluding remarks. Before reading that discussion, try conducting your own analysis.

I agreed that the basis of private morality is a respect for truth and that the closer a businessman comes to truth, the more he deserves respect. At the same time, I suggested that most bluffing in business might be regarded simply as game strategy—much like bluffing in poker which does not reflect on the morality of the bluffer. 2

I quoted Henry Taylor, the British statesman who pointed out that "falsehood ceases to be falsehood when it is understood on all sides that the truth is not expected to be spoken"—an exact description of bluffing in poker, diplomacy, and business. I cited the analogy of the criminal court, where the criminal is not expected to tell the truth when he pleads "not guilty." Everyone from the judge down takes it for granted that the job of the defendant's attorney is to get his client off, not to reveal the truth; and this is considered ethical practice. I mentioned Representative Omar Burleson, the Democrat from Texas, who was quoted as saying, in regard to the ethics of Congress, "Ethics is a barrel of worms"—a pungent summing-up of the problem of deciding who is ethical in politics. I reminded my friend that millions of businessmen feel constrained every day to say *yes* to their bosses when they secretly believe *no* and that this is generally accepted as permissible strategy when the alternative might be the loss of a job. The essential point, I said, is that the ethics of business are game ethics, different from the ethics of religion. 3

He remained unconvinced. Referring to the company of which he is president, he declared: "Maybe that's good enough for some businessmen, but I can tell you that we pride ourselves on our ethics. In 30 years not one customer has ever questioned my word or asked to check our figures. We're loyal to our customers and fair to our suppliers. I regard my handshake on a deal as a contract. I've never entered into price-fixing schemes with my competitors. I've never allowed my salesmen to spread injurious rumors about other companies. Our union contract is the best in our industry. And, if I do say so myself, our ethical standards are of the highest!" 4

He really was saying, without saying it, that he was living up to the ethical standards of the business game—which are a far cry from those of private life. Like a gentlemanly poker player, he did not play in cahoots with others at the table, try to smear their reputations, or hold back chips he owed them. 5

But this same fine man, at the very time, was allowing one of his products to be advertised in a way that made it sound a great deal better than it actually was. Another item in his product line was notorious among dealers for its "built-in obsolescence." He was holding back from the market a much-improved product because he did not want it to interfere with sales of the inferior item it would have replaced. He had joined with certain of his competitors in hiring a 6 lobbyist to push a state legislature, by methods that he preferred not to know too much about, into amending a bill then being enacted.

In his view these things had nothing to do with ethics; they were 7
merely normal business practice. He himself undoubtedly avoided outright falsehood—never lied in so many words. But the entire organization that he ruled was deeply involved in numerous strategies of deception.

PRESSURE TO DECEIVE

Most executives from time to time are almost compelled, in the 8
interests of their companies or themselves, to practice some form of deception when negotiating with customers, dealers, labor unions, government officials, or even other departments of their companies. By conscious misstatements, concealment of pertinent facts, or exaggeration—in short, by bluffing—they seek to persuade others to agree with them. I think it is fair to say that if the individual executive refuses to bluff from time to time—if he feels obligated to tell the truth, the whole truth, and nothing but the truth—he is ignoring opportunities permitted under the rules and is at a heavy disadvantage in his business dealings.

But here and there a businessman is unable to reconcile himself to 9
the bluff in which he plays a part. His conscience, perhaps spurred by religious idealism, troubles him. He feels guilty; he may develop an ulcer or a nervous tic. Before any executive can make profitable use of the strategy of the bluff, he needs to make sure that in bluffing he will not lose self-respect or become emotionally disturbed. If he is to reconcile personal integrity and high standards of honesty with the practical requirements of business, he must feel that his bluffs are ethically justified. The justification rests on the fact that business, as practiced by individuals as well as by corporations, has the impersonal character of a game—a game that demands both special strategy and an understanding of its special ethics.

The game is played at all levels of corporate life, from the highest 10
to the lowest. At the very instant that a man decides to enter business, he may be forced into a game situation, as is shown by the recent experience of a Cornell honor graduate who applied for a job with a large company:

> This applicant was given a psychological test which included the statement, "Of the following magazines, check any that you have read either regularly or from time to time, and double-check those which interest you most. *Reader's Digest, Time, Fortune, Saturday Evening Post, The New Republic, Life, Look, Ramparts, Newsweek, Business Week, U.S. News & World Report, The Nation, Playboy, Esquire, Harper's, Sports Illustrated.*"

> His tastes in reading were broad, and at one time or another he had read almost all of these magazines. He was a subscriber to *The New Republic*, an enthusiast for *Ramparts*, and an avid student of the pictures in *Playboy*. He was not sure whether his interest in *Playboy* would be held against him, but he had a shrewd suspicion that if he confessed to an interest in *Ramparts* and *The New Republic*, he would be thought a liberal, a radical, or at least an intellectual, and his chances of getting the job, which he needed, would greatly diminish. He therefore checked five of the more conservative magazines. Apparently it was a sound decision, for he got the job.

He had made a game player's decision, consistent with business ethics. 11

A similar case is that of a magazine space salesman who, owing to a merger, suddenly found himself out of a job: 12

> This man was 58, and, in spite of a good record, his chance of getting a job elsewhere in a business where youth is favored in hiring practice was not good. He was a vigorous, healthy man, and only a considerable amount of gray in his hair suggested his age. Before beginning his job search he touched up his hair with a black dye to confine the gray to his temples. He knew that the truth about his age might well come out in time, but he calculated that he could deal with that situation when it arose. He and his wife decided that he could easily pass for 45, and he so stated his age on his resume.

This was a lie; yet within the accepted rules of the business game, no moral culpability attaches to it. 13

THE POKER ANALOGY

We can learn a good deal about the nature of business by comparing it with poker. While both have a large element of chance, in the long run the winner is the man who plays with steady skill. In both games ultimate victory requires intimate knowledge of the rules, insights into the psychology of the other players, a bold front, a considerable amount of self-discipline, and the ability to respond swiftly and effectively to opportunities provided by chance. 14

No one expects poker to be played on the ethical principles preached in churches. In poker it is right and proper to bluff a friend out of the rewards of being dealt a good hand. A player feels no more than a slight twinge of sympathy, if that, when—with nothing better than a single ace in his hand—he strips a heavy loser, who holds a pair, of the rest of his chips. It was up to the other fellow to protect 15 himself. In the words of an excellent poker player, former President Harry Truman, "If you can't stand the heat, get out of the kitchen." If one shows mercy to a loser in poker, it is a personal gesture, divorced from the rules of the game.

Poker has its special ethics, and here I am not referring to rules 16
against cheating. The man who keeps an ace up his sleeve or who marks the cards is more than unethical; he is a crook, and can be punished as such—kicked out of the game or, in the Old West, shot.

In contrast to the cheat, the unethical poker player is one who, 17
while abiding by the letter of the rules, finds ways to put the other players at an unfair disadvantage. Perhaps he unnerves them with loud talk. Or he tries to get them drunk. Or he plays in cahoots with someone else at the table. Ethical poker players frown on such tactics.

Poker's own brand of ethics is different from the ethical ideals of 18
civilized human relationships. The game calls for distrust of the other fellow. It ignores the claim of friendship. Cunning deception and concealment of one's strength and intentions, not kindness and openheartedness, are vital in poker. No one thinks any worse of poker on that account. And no one should think any worse of the game of business because its standards of right and wrong differ from the prevailing traditions of morality in our society.

DISCARD THE GOLDEN RULE

This view of business is especially worrisome to people without much 19
business experience. A minister of my acquaintance once protested that business cannot possibly function in our society unless it is based on the Judeo-Christian system of ethics. He told me:

> I know some businessmen have supplied call girls to customers, but there are always a few rotten apples in every barrel. That doesn't mean the rest of the fruit isn't sound. Surely the vast majority of businessmen are ethical. I myself am acquainted with many who adhere to strict codes of ethics based fundamentally on religious teachings. They contribute to good causes. They participate in community activities. They cooperate with other companies to improve working conditions in their industries. Certainly they are not indifferent to ethics.

That most businessmen are not indifferent to ethics in their private lives, everyone will agree. My point is that in their office lives they cease to be private citizens; they become game players who must be guided by a somewhat different set of ethical standards.

The point was forcefully made to me by a Midwestern executive 20
who has given a good deal of thought to the question:

> So long as a businessman complies with the laws of the land and avoids telling malicious lies, he's ethical. If the law as written gives a man a wide-open chance to make a killing, he'd be a fool not to take advantage of it. If he doesn't, somebody else will. There's no obligation on him to stop and consider who is going to get hurt. If the law says he can do it, that's all the justification he needs. There's nothing unethical about that. It's just plain business sense.

This executive (call him Robbins) took the stand that even industrial espionage, which is frowned on by some businessmen, ought not to be considered unethical. He recalled a recent meeting of the National Industrial Conference Board where an authority on marketing made a speech in which he deplored the employment of spies by business organizations. More and more companies, he pointed out, find it cheaper to penetrate the secrets of competitors with concealed cameras and microphones or by bribing employees than to set up costly research and design departments of their own. A whole branch of the electronics industy has grown up with this trend, he continued, providing equipment to make industrial espionage easier. 21

Disturbing? The marketing expert found it so. But when it came to a remedy, he could only appeal to "respect for the golden rule." Robbins thought this a confession of defeat, believing that the golden rule, for all its value as an ideal for society, is simply not feasible as a guide for business. A good part of the time the businessman is trying to do unto others as he hopes others will *not* do unto him. Robbins continued: 22

> Espionage of one kind or another has become so common in business that it's like taking a drink during Prohibition—it's not considered sinful. And we don't even have Prohibition where espionage is concerned; the law is very tolerant in this area. There's no more shame for a business that uses secret agents than there is for a nation. Bear in mind that there already is at least one large corporation—you can buy its stock over the counter—that makes millions by providing counterespionage service to industrial firms. Espionage in business is not an ethical problem; it's an established technique of business competition.

"WE DON'T MAKE THE LAWS"

Wherever we turn in business, we can perceive the sharp distinction between its ethical standards and those of the churches. Newspapers abound with sensational stories growing out of this distinction: 23

> We read one day that Senator Philip A. Hart of Michigan has attacked food processors for deceptive packaging of numerous products.

> The next day there is a Congressional to-do over Ralph Nader's book, *Unsafe at Any Speed,* which demonstrates that automobile companies for years have neglected the safety of car-owning families.
>
> Then another Senator, Lee Metcalf of Montana, and journalist Vic Reinemer show in their book, *Overcharge,* the methods by which utility companies elude regulating government bodies to extract unduly large payments from users of electricity.

These are merely dramatic instances of a prevailing condition; there is hardly a major industry at which a similar attack could not be aimed. Critics of business regard such behavior as unethical, but the companies concerned know that they are merely playing the business game. **24**

Among the most respected of our business institutions are the insurance companies. A group of insurance executives meeting recently in New England was startled when their guest speaker, social critic [now Senator from New York] Daniel Patrick Moynihan, roundly berated them for "unethical" practices. They had been guilty, Moynihan alleged, of using outdated actuarial tables to obtain unfairly high premiums. They habitually delayed the hearings of lawsuits against them in order to tire out the plaintiffs and win cheap settlements. In their employment policies they used ingenious devices to discriminate against certain minority groups. **25**

It was difficult for the audience to deny the validity of these charges. But these men were business game players. Their reaction to Moynihan's attack was much the same as that of the automobile manufacturers to Nader, of the utilities to Senator Metcalf, and of the food processors to Senator Hart. If the laws governing their businesses change, or if public opinion becomes clamorous, they will make the necessary adjustments. But morally they have in their view done nothing wrong. As long as they comply with the letter of the law, they are within their rights to operate their businesses as they see fit. **26**

The small business is in the same position as the great corporation in this respect. For example: **27**

> In 1967 a key manufacturer was accused of providing master keys for automobiles to mail-order customers, although it was obvious that some of the purchasers might be automobile thieves. His defense was plain and straightforward. If there was nothing in the law to prevent him from selling his keys to anyone who ordered them, it was not up to him to inquire as to his customers' motives. Why was it any worse, he insisted, for him to sell car keys by mail, than for mail-order houses to sell guns that might be used for murder? Until the law was changed, the key manufacturer could regard himself as being just as ethical as any other businessman by the rules of the business game.

Violations of the ethical ideals of society are common in business, but they are not necessarily violations of business principles. Each year the Federal Trade Commission orders hundreds of companies, many of them of the first magnitude, to "cease and desist" from practices which, judged by ordinary standards, are of questionable morality but which are stoutly defended by the companies concerned. 28

In one case, a firm manufacturing a well-known mouthwash was accused of using a cheap form of alcohol possibly deleterious to health. The company's chief executive, after testifying in Washington, made this comment privately: 29

> We broke no law. We're in a highly competitive industry. If we're going to stay in business, we have to look for profit wherever the law permits. We don't make the laws. We obey them. Then why do we have to put up with this "holier than thou" talk about ethics? It's sheer hypocrisy. We're not in business to promote ethics. Look at the cirgarette companies, for God's sake! If the ethics aren't embodied in the laws by the men who made them, you can't expect businessmen to fill the lack. Why, a sudden submission to Christian ethics by businessmen would bring about the greatest economic upheaval in history!

It may be noted that the government failed to prove its case against him. 30

CAST ILLUSIONS ASIDE

Talking about ethics by businessmen is often a thin decorative coating over the hard realities of the game: 31

> Once I listened to a speech by a young executive who pointed to a new industry code as proof that his company and its competitors were deeply aware of their responsibilities to society. It was a code of ethics, he said. The industry was going to police itself, to dissuade constituent companies from wrongdoing. His eyes shone with conviction and enthusiasm.
>
> The same day there was a meeting in a hotel room where the industry's top executives met with the "czar" who was to administer the new code, a man of high repute. No one who was present could doubt their common attitude. In their eyes the code was designed primarily to forestall a move by the federal government to impose stern restrictions on the industry. They felt that the code would hamper them a good deal less than new federal laws would. It was, in other words, conceived as a protection for the industry, not for the public.
>
> The young executive accepted the surface explanation of the code; these leaders, all experienced game players, did not deceive themselves for a moment about its purpose.

The illusion that business can afford to be guided by ethics as conceived in private life is often fostered by speeches and articles containing such phrases as, "It pays to be ethical," or, "Sound ethics is good business." Actually this is not an ethical position at all; it is a self-serving calculation in disguise. The speaker is really saying that in the long run a company can make more money if it does not antagonize competitors, suppliers, employees, and customers by squeezing them too hard. He is saying that oversharp policies reduce ultimate gains. That is true, but it has nothing to do with ethics. The underlying attitude is much like that in the familiar story of the shopkeeper who finds an extra $20 bill in the cash register, debates with himself the ethical problem—should he tell his partner?—and finally decides to share the money because the gesture will give him an edge over the s.o.b. the next time they quarrel. 32

I think it is fair to sum up the prevailing attitude of businessmen on ethics as follows: 33

We live in what is probably the most competitive of the world's civilized societies. Our customs encourage a high degree of aggression in the individual's striving for success. Business is our main area of competition, and it has been ritualized into a game of strategy. The basic rules of the game have been set by the government, which attempts to detect and punish business frauds. But as long as a company does not transgress the rules of the game set by law, it has the legal right to shape its strategy without reference to anything but its profits. If it takes a long-term view of its profits, it will preserve amicable relations, so far as possible, with those with whom it deals. A wise businessman will not seek advantage to the point where he generates dangerous hostility among employees, competitors, customers, government, or the public at large. But decisions in this area are, in the final test, decisions of strategy, not of ethics. 34

THE INDIVIDUAL AND THE GAME

An individual within a company often finds it difficult to adjust to the requirements of the business game. He tries to preserve his private ethical standards in situations that call for game strategy. When he is obliged to carry out the company policies that challenge his conception of himself as an ethical man, he suffers. 35

It disturbs him when he is ordered, for instance, to deny a raise to a man who deserves it, to fire an employee of long standing, to prepare advertising that he believes to be misleading, to conceal facts that he feels customers are entitled to know, to cheapen the quality of materials used in the manufacture of an established product, to sell as 36 new a product that he knows to be rebuilt, to exaggerate the curative powers of a medicinal preparation, or to coerce dealers.

There are some fortunate executives, who, by the nature of their work and circumstances, never have to face problems of this kind. But in one form or another the ethical dilemma is felt sooner or later by most businessmen. Possibly the dilemma is most painful not when the company forces the action on the executive but when he originates it himself—that is, when he has taken or is contemplating a step which is in his own interest but which runs counter to his early moral conditioning. To illustrate: 37

> The manager of an export department, eager to show rising sales, is pressed by a big customer to provide invoices, which, while containing no overt falsehood that would violate a U.S. law, are so worded that the customer may be able to evade certain taxes in his homeland.
>
> A company president finds that an aging executive, within a few years of retirement and his pension, is not as productive as formerly. Should he be kept on?
>
> The produce manager of a supermarket debates with himself whether to get rid of a lot of half-rotten tomatoes by including one, with its good side exposed, in every tomato sixpack.
>
> An accountant discovers that he has taken an improper deduction on his company's tax return and fears the consequences if he calls the matter to the president's attention, though he himself has done nothing illegal. Perhaps if he says nothing, no one will notice the error.
>
> A chief executive officer is asked by his directors to comment on a rumor that he owns stock in another company with which he has placed large orders. He could deny it, for the stock is in the name of his son-in-law and he has earlier formally instructed his son-in-law to sell the holding.

Temptations of this kind constantly arise in business. If an executive allows himself to be torn between a decision based on business considerations and one based on his private ethical code, he exposes himself to a grave psychological strain. 38

This is not to say that sound business strategy necessarily runs counter to ethical ideals. They may frequently coincide; and when they do, everyone is gratified. But the major tests of every move in business, as in all games of strategy, are legality and profit. A man who intends to be a winner in the business game must have a game player's attitude. 39

The business strategist's decisions must be as impersonal as those of a surgeon performing an operation—concentrating on objective and technique, and subordinating personal feelings. If the chief executive admits that his son-in-law owns the stock, it is because he stands to lose more if the fact comes out later than if he states it boldly and at once. If the supermarket manager orders the rotten tomatoes 40 to be discarded, he does so to avoid an increase in consumer complaints and a loss of good will. The company president decides not to fire the elderly executive in the belief that the negative reaction of other employees would in the long run cost the company more than it would lose in keeping him and paying his pension.

All sensible businessmen prefer to be truthful, but they seldom feel inclined to tell the *whole* truth. In the business game truth-telling usually has to be kept within narrow limits if trouble is to be avoided. The point was neatly made a long time ago (in 1888) by one of John D. Rockefeller's associates, Paul Babcock, to Standard Oil Company executives who were about to testify before a government investigating committee: "Parry every question with answers which, while perfectly truthful, are evasive of *bottom* facts." This was, is, and probably always will be regarded as wise and permissible business strategy. 41

FOR OFFICE USE ONLY

An executive's family life can easily be dislocated if he fails to make a sharp distinction between the ethical systems of the home and the office—or if his wife does not grasp that distinction. Many a businessman who has remarked to his wife "I had to let Jones go today" or "I had to admit to the boss that Jim has been goofing off lately," has been met with an indignant protest. "How could you do a thing like that? You know Jones is over 50 and will have a lot of trouble getting another job." Or, "You did that to Jim? With his wife ill and all the worry she's been having with the kids?" 42

If the executive insists that he had no choice because the profits of the company and his own security were involved, he may see a certain cool and ominous reappraisal in his wife's eyes. Many wives are not prepared to accept the fact that business operates with a special code of ethics. An illuminating illustration of this comes from a Southern sales executive who related a conversation he had had with his wife at a time when a hotly contested political campaign was being waged in their state: 43

> I made the mistake of telling her that I had had lunch with Colby, who gives me about half my business. Colby mentioned that his company had a stake in the election. Then he said, "By the way, I'm treasurer of the citizens' committee for Lang. I'm collecting contributions. Can I count on you for a hundred dollars?"
>
> Well, there I was. I was opposed to Lang, but I knew Colby. If he withdrew his business I could be in a bad spot. So I just smiled and wrote out a check then and there. He thanked me, and we started to talk about

his next order. Maybe he thought I shared his political views. I wasn't going to lose any sleep over it.

I should have had sense enough not to tell Mary about it. She hit the ceiling. She said she was disappointed in me. She said I hadn't acted like a man, that I should have stood up to Colby.

I said, "Look, it was an either-or situation. I had to do it or risk losing the business."

She came back at me with, "I don't believe it. You could have been honest with him. You could have said that you didn't feel you ought to contribute to a campaign for a man you weren't going to vote for. I'm sure he would have understood."

I said, "Mary, you're a wonderful woman, but you're way off the track. Do you know what would have happened if I had said that? Colby would have smiled and said, 'Oh, I didn't realize. Forget it.' But in his eyes from that moment I would be an oddball, maybe a bit of a radical. He would have listened to me talk about his order and would have promised to give it consideration. After that I wouldn't hear from him for a week. Then I would telephone and learn from his secretary that he wasn't yet ready to place the order. And in about a month I would hear through the grapevine that he was giving his business to another company. A month after that I'd be out of a job."

She was silent for a while. Then she said, "Tom, something is wrong with business when a man is forced to choose between his family's security and his moral obligation to himself. It's easy for me to say you should have stood up to him—but if you had, you might have felt you were betraying me and the kids. I'm sorry that you did it, Tom, but I can't blame you. Something is wrong with business!"

This wife saw the problem in terms of moral obligation as conceived in private life; her husband saw it as a matter of game strategy. As a player in a weak position, he felt that he could not afford to indulge an ethical sentiment that might have cost him his seat at the table. 44

PLAYING TO WIN

Some men might challenge the Colbys of business—might accept serious setbacks to their business careers rather than risk a feeling of moral cowardice. They merit our respect—but as private individuals, not businessmen. When the skillful player of the business game is compelled to submit to unfair pressure, he does not castigate himself for moral weakness. Instead, he strives to put himself into a strong position where he can defend himself against such pressures in the future without loss. 45

If a man plans to take a seat in the business game, he owes it to himself to master the principles by which the game is played, 46 including its special ethical outlook. He can then hardly fail to recognize than an occasional bluff may well be justified in terms of the game's ethics and warranted in terms of economic necessity. Once he clears his mind on this point, he is in a good position to match his strategy against that of the other players. He can then determine objectively whether a bluff in a given situation has a good chance of succeeding and can decide when and how to bluff, without a feeling of ethical transgression.

To be a winner, a man must play to win. This does not mean that 47
he must be ruthless, cruel, harsh, or treacherous. On the contrary, the better his reputation for integrity, honesty, and decency, the better his chances of victory will be in the long run. But from time to time every businessman, like every poker player, is offered a choice between certain loss or bluffing within the legal rules of the game. If he is not resigned to losing, if he wants to rise in his company and industry, then in such a crisis he will bluff—and bluff hard.

Every now and then one meets a successful businessman who 48
has conveniently forgotten the small or large deceptions that he practiced on his way to fortune. "God gave me my money," old John D. Rockefeller once piously told a Sunday school class. It would be a rare tycoon in our time who would risk the horse laugh with which such a remark would be greeted.

In the last third of the twentieth century even children are aware 49
that if a man has become prosperous in business, he has sometimes departed from the strict truth in order to overcome obstacles or has practiced the more subtle deceptions of the half-truth or the misleading omission. Whatever the form of the bluff, it is an integral part of the game, and the executive who does not master its techniques is not likely to accumulate much money or power.

Review Questions

1. Albert Carr's definition of the term "business ethics" is inconsistent with the term as defined by others in this chapter. How so?
2. Much of Carr's argument derives from what he calls "the poker analogy." Summarize this analogy.
3. According to Carr, decisions in business are governed by strategy, not ethics. Why are the two sometimes confused?
4. What are the consequences of an individual's being caught between a personal code of ethics and "a decision based on business considerations"?

Discussion and Writing Suggestions

1. By the third paragraph of the article, Carr directly states his essential point: " . . . the ethics of business are game ethics, different from the ethics of

religion." This is to say, the ethical considerations that help you to make decisions in your private life are different from the ones that guide business people in making decisions. Business has its own rules. Do you agree? Develop your answer into a brief essay.

2. Carr presents several examples of playing "within the accepted rules of the business game": lying about one's age in a job application; conducting industrial espionage; taking any action, even at the expense of others, if the law allows it. If you were running a business, to what extent would you endorse these behaviors?
3. "Cunning deception and concealment of one's strength and intentions, not kindness and openheartedness, are vital in poker"—and to the success of a business enterprise, implies Carr through his analogy. What's your response?
4. Do you accept Carr's final assertion that "whatever the form of the bluff, it is an integral part of the game, and the executive who does not master its techniques is not likely to accumulate much money or power"?
5. Carr states that "most executives from time to time are almost compelled, in the interests of their companies or themselves, to practice some sort of deception when negotiating with customers, dealers, labor unions, government officials, or even other departments of their companies." Check the accuracy of this assertion by interviewing one or more men or women involved in business life. Summarize Carr's thesis for them and ask for their reactions. Report on your findings.
6. In an analysis attempting to refute Carr's thesis and prove that business does *not* operate according to its own code of ethics, writers Joseph R. Desjardins and John J. McCall offer the following argument:

> Think of the Mafia and the elaborate code of conduct that guides behavior within this group. Following Carr's use of "ethics," we can call such rules "Mafia ethics." Now, could an argument similar to Carr's be constructed to show that Mafia hit squads are ethical? We might write a paper on the topic and call it "Is Mafia Murder Ethical?" Within the ethics of organized crime, such activity is accepted, is well-known by the participants, and is necessary for the successful operation of organized crime. Murder is, after all, part of the "rules of the game." To paraphrase the final sentence in Carr's final section on poker, "No one should think any the worse of the Mafia game because its standards of right and wrong differ from the prevailing traditions of morality in our society."
>
> Presumably, however, we all want to say that murder is morally wrong regardless of its role in the rules of the Mafia game. In fact, we would say that the entire game is immoral. We would, in other words, insist that the standards of morality be applied to the activities of organized crime and conclude that morality overrides the rules of the game.
>
> This example demonstrates what should happen when we remain clear about the two uses of "ethics." When "ethics" is taken to mean just any rules of conduct, it is easy to think that all "ethics" are equally valid when applied to their own activities and equally invalid when imported into other fields. However, when

ethics is understood as "morality," we normally do not hesitate to make ethical (moral) judgements about any serious human activity. (11–12)[1]

Discuss your reactions to this argument against Carr's thesis.

Showdown on "Business Bluffing"

TIMOTHY B. BLODGETT

"Few articles that [the Harvard Business Review] *has published have aroused a response as great and as vociferous as Albert Z. Carr's "Is Business Bluffing Ethical?" So begins the journal's* Special Report *on the reaction to Carr's assertion that a certain amount of deception is considered ethical in business. (Then) associate editor of HBR, Timothy B. Blodgett summarizes the response to Carr.*

This article presents a very realistic and accurate account of the standards used in business decisions, at least for those companies and individuals who are subject to competitive pressures and therefore feel that they must take every legally permissible advantage in order to survive and grow.

Fortunately, Mr. Carr's view does not appear to be the prevailing view, except, perhaps, along the few remaining frontiers of civilization, such as the upper Amazon.

These two quotations—the first from a letter written by Rawson L. Wood, Chairman of the Board of Arwood Corporation, Rockleigh, New Jersey, and the second from a letter by Leon P. Chemlen, who is on the marketing staff of Dynamics Research Corporation, Stoneham, Massachusetts—distill the contrasting reactions of HBR readers to Mr. Carr's article. 1

Of the many readers who responded, more than twice as many are critical of the article as are favorable to it. Many others seem uncertain or are noncommittal about Mr. Carr's position, devoting themselves mainly to discussion of the state of business ethics today. 2

[1]From *Contemporary Issues in Business Ethics* by Joseph R. Desjardins and John J. McCall. © 1985 by Wadsworth, Inc. Reprinted by permission of the publisher.

The tone of the letters ranges from enthusiastic to shocked. In- 3
terestingly, a couple of the most favorable letters have come from persons in the advertising business, an endeavor not noted for understatement about the virtues and powers of goods being marketed.

A few correspondents question HBR's motives in publishing the 4
article. One indignant writer gives this title to a lengthy dissertation: "Is the Article on Business Bluffing Ethical?" Another even questions the existence of "A. Z. Carr" and suggests that the Editors may have been playing an early April Fool's joke.

But most readers have been as serious and thoughtful in answer- 5
ing Mr. Carr as he was in presenting his view of the way things are.

"NO MEDALS FOR HONESTY"

Was Mr. Carr "telling it like it is" (in the current expression)? One 6
reader who thinks so is Richard O. Lundquist, an underwriter in Washington, D.C., with The Equitable Life Assurance Society of the United States. He cites this case:

"A young manager was upset because his boss had told a pro- 7
spective salesman, 'The minimum income a new man earned with us last year was $8,900.' That was about $2,000 from the truth. When the senior manager was questioned about this, he answered, 'Well, that's not important. We are just trying to attract him into the business.' "

Mr. Lundquist mentions two similar examples and then concludes: 8

"What is universal about these examples is that these managers, 9
each functioning on a different corporate level, are concerned with one thing—*getting the job done.* Most companies give numerous awards for achievement and accomplishment, for sales, for growth, for longevity and loyalty; but there are no medals in the business world for honesty, compassion, or truthfulness."

A person in church affairs discourses in similar vein, but offers a 10
different motive for such behavior. Morton O. Nace, Jr., Executive Director of the Episcopal Churchmen of the Diocese of Chicago, mentions a series of vocational seminars sponsored by his organization. He describes in this way some comments of more than 1,000 persons who have participated in them:

"The vocational seminars have shown that *self-preservation* and 11
self-indulgence are the real motivations behind the decisions that businessmen and women make—rather than their conscience! Our

evidence clearly supports the premise of Mr. Carr that it is a 'special game of business ethics' that governs the lives of most, if not all, businessmen. Salesmen have said, 'The important thing for me is to make my sales quota, and not whether I should tell the whole truth about a product.' Engineers have said, 'What can I do if my company's main concern is for greater profit instead of using the best materials and design?' Office workers have said, 'Why shouldn't I steal a little from the company? They owe me more than I make now anyhow!' And realtors have said, 'If I show my listing to a Negro, I'll be out of business. I'm not about to do that.' "

Another reader takes particular note of Mr. Carr's discussion of conflicts between personal ethical standards and "game strategy" in business. Bob L. Plunkett, Accounting and Office Manager of Tic Toc Markets, Inc., Costa Mesa, California, confides: 12

"When I first started telling my wife some of the decisions that I was making, she just couldn't understand how I could be so unsympathetic at the office and so kind at home. My answer to her has always been that we are playing a game just as I used to play football; some make the team and some don't. I have to see that the best players are on the team. It is unfortunate that it poses a problem for those that do not make the team, but that is the breaks of the game." 13

. . .

A MATTER OF "MUTUAL TRUST"

Many readers have given careful thought to refutation of Mr. Carr's contention that deception is an integral part of the business "game." I shall try to present their views fairly by quoting representative selections from letters. 14

Some readers take particular exception to Mr. Carr's claim that deception succeeds: 15

"All of us in business know that 'playing the game' yields only short-term rewards. We'll admit our faults, but we'll not endorse them as part of our philosophy. To do so would bring the house of business down on itself." (John Valiant, New Product Manager, William H. Rorer, Inc., Fort Washington, Pennsylvania) 16

"My own experience in dealing with hundreds of companies has led me to believe that sharp dealing or the slightest prevarication on the part of a businessman usually results in informal excommunication to the back alleys of the business world or to obscurity." (Mark Rollinson, President, Greater Washington Industrial Investments, Inc., Washington, D.C.) 17

"I think a better strategy in business is to work hard, be honest, 18
and be smarter than anyone else." (L. D. Barre, Vice President—Marketing, RTE Corporation, Waukesha, Wisconsin)

Warren R. Howard, Technical Director of Wall Industries, Inc., Bever- 19
ly, New Jersey, wonders where such practices would lead us:

"Should a quality control engineer falsify a certified test report 20
simply because he knows that his customer will not test a particular lot of material, and because he has slipped such 'out-of-spec' material through in the past? Should a manager shade the facts in his application for funds from top management in order to make his ROI forecast meet management's minimum requirements? Just where can we draw the limits when dishonesty is adopted as a game strategy? Is it proper to insist on strict integrity and honesty? Does it actually harm the mental and ethical life of the executive to tell the truth as a matter of rule?"

Mr. Carr cited as an accurate description of "bluffing" in business and 21
poker this utterance of a British statesman: "Falsehood ceases to be falsehood when it is understood on all sides that the truth is not expected to be spoken." This has moved Alan B. Potter, Vice President of the Dye Division (Dorval, Quebec) of Ciba Company Limited, to comment:

"But it is not at all the case that businessmen do not expect the 22
truth to be spoken. On the contrary, almost all day-to-day business is conducted verbally or on the basis of nonlegal documents. The economic system would collapse without mutual trust on a practically universal scale among business executives.

"Mr. Carr apparently assumes that 'not telling the whole truth' is 23
synonymous with 'telling a lie.' Businessmen know that it would be ridiculous to expect anything more than a straight answer to a straight question. Moreover, it is perfectly acceptable to withhold the truth by saying, 'I am sorry, I am not willing to discuss that subject.' There are many reasons of self-interest or discretion which would justify a refusal to answer any question, and businessmen do not expect that those reasons need be given."

Another recurrent theme in the letters is an insistence that business's 24
ethics cannot be separated from those of society. Typical is the response of J. Douglas McConnell, Marketing Economist at Stanford Research Institute and Lecturer at San Francisco State College:

"Mr. Carr's argument would be sound if business functioned in a 25
vacuum. Because business is an integral part of society, however, it will always be judged by societal criteria.

"It is inevitable that the ethics of business and those of society will always have a considerable degree of commonality. For one thing, business as a group is large and powerful in our society, and many of its values are accepted by society at large. Business's goal is to function at a profit, and to a considerable extent making money is also a value of society. 26

"Another point of commonality is that most people are members of several groups. The business executive is likely to be a veteran, a member of a school or college board, a member of a local church, or a committeeman for the Community Chest; and he and his family are also consumers. The norms of these other groups carry over to his business life to a greater or lesser extent. 27

"We live in a highly complex world, with diverse pressures and interests, where simple answers seldom fit simple questions such as 'Is business bluffing ethical?' Business's principal role is that of the wealth-generating group in society—and its ethics will always reflect this. However, the other groups in society—such as education, health services, religion, the military, government, and the consumer—will occasionally be in conflict with these ethics, and there will be (as there is now) pressure to bring business ethics more into conformity with those of society." 28

. . .

One of Mr. Carr's anecdotes particularly struck a chord and has produced some interesting comments. It concerns the Cornell honor graduate who applied for a job and was confronted with a list of magazines running the gamut from *The Reader's Digest* to *Ramparts*. Mr. Chemlen, whom I quoted at the beginning of this article, excuses the young man's deception in reporting his reading tastes: 29

"This is merely one of the more amusing and illogical aspects of the organizational dialectic and has precious little to do with ethics or poker. It is more akin to coming in out of the rain. Just as no one faults the matador for sidestepping the head-long thrust of his adversary, no one may fault the Cornell honor graduate for parrying the charge of the clumsy buffalo of bureaucracy." 30

But Mr. Potter, whom I also quoted earlier, sees grave implications in this anecdote: 31

"There is no evidence that the candidate would not have been given the job if he had answered truthfully. On the contrary, if the company included *Playboy* magazine in the list, it almost certainly meant it would appreciate truthfulness. In modern business we are desperately searching for intelligent liberals, radicals, and intellectuals. 32

"This story is the most unpleasant example of all. It clearly shows 33 how business can become corrupted when it is thought, erroneously, to reward corruption. What are we to think of this young man? How can he elevate business standards, believing as he does that he needed to lie before he could even be recruited?"

. . .

ABUSE OF FREEDOM?

Many readers (often on the assumption that Mr. Carr is an advocate of the behavior he described) venture serious forebodings about our democratic and capitalist system if the attitude of the game player should prevail. "The shoddy results of the poker god are beginning to show around the world," is the way Arthur D. Margison expresses it. 34

Mr. Margison, who is President of a Don Mills, Ontario, engineering firm, A. D. Margison and Associates Limited, is worried about the state of business ethics, as represented by the "bluffing" strategy, at a time when "'our way of life' is in competition with other systems." 35

Zeb V. Beck, Jr., Division Plant Manager in Charlotte, North Carolina, for the Southern Bell Telephone & Telegraph Company, conjures up the same specter: 36

"Of course there are conflicts that exist when our values oppose one another. However, the decisions we make on the basis of ethical values in these conflicts should far outweigh those based on 'profit,' social acceptability, or political expediency. Unless they do, there is practically nothing to distinguish us from the materialistic value system of the Communists." 37

Dr. Carlos W. Moreno, an industrial engineer in Cincinnati, Ohio, also concerns himself on a broad canvas with the effects of the notion that "whatever is not forbidden by law is acceptable." He comments: 38

"One basis of a free society is reliance on self-restriction. We have seen all too often, and as expected, that abuse of freedom has resulted in its restriction and in a more regulated life. 39

"The conclusion that follows is that if many people do not practice self-control, the pressure of society at large will bring about the regulation of every meaningful action, such as business, to the point that future history books might describe the nineteenth and twentieth centuries as a period in which one section of humanity had a chance to live in freedom, but proved to be too undeveloped for it." 40

James B. Dickson of Dickson Associates, employee relations counselors in Neenah, Wisconsin, is more optimistic: 41

"In the long run, deception cannot compete against quality. Fortunately, we are beginning to see the emergence of business organizations which recognize that people have had their bellyful of shoddy merchandise. (And shoddy merchandise is the inevitable byproduct of a business that operates on the ethic of bluffing.) 42

"The analogy of business and the poker game would be excellent except for the fact that business ultimately must rely on the consuming public. The public may not be interested in joining the poker game when it finds it can get full value from a business enterprise that puts its time and effort into developing a product worthy of people." 43

WHAT CAN BE DONE?

So if we have a problem—whether it can be defined in a broad frame of reference or only in the narrower one of business—what can we do about it? Graham R. Briggs, Executive Assistant to the First Vice President of Abex Corporation, New York City, offers this reflection: 44

"Business, like society, operates within a set of norms of acceptable behavior. A radical departure from these norms in either direction, toward idealism or toward complete immorality, spells trouble at least and ruin at worst. Moreover, it seems to me to be true that acceptable behavior in business includes much that would be unacceptable in one's personal life. 45

"However, Mr. Carr sidesteps the question of where an individual should draw the line between acceptable and immoral action. Every businessman is tempted to be just a little less moral than his competitors—not enough to be operating right outside the business 'moral code,' but enough to secure a competitive edge. 46

"Then how can the inevitable gradual decline of business morals to an eventual state of complete anarchy be prevented? The law is insufficient protection against this; it can cover only the most flagrant violations, it cannot change as quickly as circumstances nowadays require, and it is too easily circumvented by those who are quick-witted and prepared to take a risk. 47

"The only guard against a gradual decline in morals is the ideals of each businessman. All of us have (or if we do not, something is wrong with us) an ideal of how business should be conducted; how we would like to be able to behave, or, rather, how we wish we could rely on other businessmen to act. It is usually impossible to adhere to this ideal in practice, since we live in an imperfect world, but we should always have this ideal in mind, be prepared to make some sacrifices for its sake, and be conscious of what we are doing when we depart from it. 48

"Only in this way can we apply 'upward' pressure on business 49 morality, which, if practiced by a sufficient number of businessmen, will tend over time to raise the level of business values closer to the ideal. Most of us would like to be able to trust our fellow businessmen more than we can now. I see no other way of ever achieving this result."

. . .

I shall leave it to Mr. Wood, who opened this discussion, to close it: 50

"If business is to survive as an independent force in our society of free enterprise, it will have to accelerate its acceptance of social responsibilities. Because of the tremendous economic power of corporations in every industrial society, they cannot be allowed to use it without consideration of its effect on those outside the poker game. 51

"If the players in Mr. Carr's poker game shoot it out among themselves and thereby endanger the lives of the people living next door, someone is going to call the police and break up the game for good." 52

MR. CARR COMMENTS:

I was especially struck by the high charge of emotion, ranging from fury to enthusiasm, in the letters received by HBR, as well as in a number of letters and even phone calls that have come directly to me. It may be significant that, of the *company heads* responding, a large majority ruefully agree that the state of business ethics portrayed in the article was accurate. The letters strongly suggest that the men who have "made it" are more willing to face the realities of the problem than are those farther down the ladder. 53

I have the distinct impression that many of HBR's more outraged respondents (one or two even burst into vituperative verse!) have not yet fully sensed the nature of the strategic questions confronting the men responsible for the profitability and growth of their companies. 54

Perhaps I can assuage some of the pain the article seems to have caused by listing below the main criticisms leveled against it, and appending a few comments of my own. 55

"Business is too important to be regarded as a game." This misses the point of the article, which is that—whether or not business ought to be regarded and conducted as a game—it *is* so regarded and conducted by many of its practitioners, including executives of great importance and high reputation. A businessman is certainly entitled to refuse to employ game strategy himself, but he may be at a severe disadvantage if he does not recognize that it is being used by others. 56

"The comparison to poker is unfair and inaccurate." Like all useful 57

analogies, this one was intended to throw light on the subject, not to provide an exact parallel. The honorable poker player who, within the laws of the game, takes pleasure in outsmarting the other fellow has many a counterpart in the paneled offices of the corporate hierarchies. Again, it may be noted that there is no compulsion for any executive to mislead others, any more than there is for the poker player to bluff. The option is his; most players exercise it at one time or another.

"The article condones unethical practices." This complaint seems to me extraordinary. More than once, the article stresses the values of truth-telling and integrity in business, where, certainly, there are as many high-minded men as one will find in most walks of life. My point is that, given the prevailing ethical standards of business, an executive who accepts those standards and operates accordingly is guilty of nothing worse than conformity; he is merely playing the game according to the rules and the customs of society. 58

"A man cannot separate the ethics of his business life from the ethics of his home life." Over the long run, that is probably true. What happens is that, in too many instances, the ethical outlook of business comes to dominate in the home as well. Perhaps that accounts in part for the notorious instability of the middle-class home in our society, and the increasing revolt of the young against the corporate establishment. It may also explain why so many wives of businessmen have, like their husbands, been conscience-washed into undiscriminating acceptance of corporation policies. 59

"The article is one-sided and extreme in its description of what goes on in business." This I must deny. I regard the article as mild, objective, and, if anything, overdiscreet. If it had incorporated all the facts in my files, it would have curled HBR readers' hair. And I am talking now not about violations of law, but of decisions within the realm of business ethics—the so-called "gray area," where complexity so often provides the executive with a rationalization for doing what serves his interests. 60

"The article does not point out that if business fails to raise the moral level of its practices, it invites eventual reprisals from the public and the government." This thought was not within the scope of the article, but I could not agree with it more. As the article plainly conveys, sound long-range business strategy and ethical considerations are usually served by the same policy. 61

Discussion and Writing Suggestions

1. Choose two statements that particularly intrigued you from the excerpted letters that Blodgett quotes. Write your response to these statements, showing clearly your approval or disapproval.

2. Mr. Chemlen forgives the student Carr refers to—the one who lied about which magazines he preferred reading. Mr. Potter, in the paragraph that follows, does not. Whose view do you support, and why?

3. Dr. Carlos Moreno remarks that if businesspeople do not practice self-control, then the government will for them—through regulation. What is your view of the government's involvement in business affairs (for instance, in laws forbidding monopolies)? What would happen, in your view, if the government stopped requiring manufacturers to meet safety standards or pollution standards? What does your response to these questions reveal about your assumptions concerning ethics in business?

4. Mr. Graham Briggs states that "the law is insufficient protection against [the inevitable gradual decline of business morals to an eventual state of complete anarchy]." The law, he says, can only respond to "the most flagrant violations"; it can only respond after the fact, and it can be sidestepped by those who set their minds to it. Thus, Briggs concludes, "The only guard against a gradual decline in morals is the ideals of each businessman." Your response?

5. Having read both the original article and a sampling of the responses, sum up *your* responses to Carr's "Is Business Bluffing Ethical?" Develop your thoughts into an essay.

Babbitt

SINCLAIR LEWIS

Henry Sinclair Lewis—writer of poetry, plays, and more than twenty novels—was the first American to receive the Nobel Prize for literature. He is known for taking large themes important to the emerging, urban identity in America after World War I and, with sharp satirical treatment, exposing hypocrisies. In Main Street *(1920), Lewis explored the "virus" of village and small-town life that bred boredom and spiritual death; in* Arrowsmith *(1925), he probed conflicts between science and profit; in* Elmer Gantry *(1927), he savaged the pretensions of fundamentalist preachers; and in* Babbitt *(1922), Lewis exposed the petty, materialistic, conforming ways of the new business class. The novel is set in the fictional city of Zenith—the great, shining representative of American urban life. In George Babbitt, Sinclair Lewis gave the English language a new word. The* Random House Dictionary *defines a "babbitt" as "a self-satisfied person who conforms readily to conventional, middle-class ideas and ideals, especially of business and material success." Earlier novels on American business celebrated the tycoon spirit of railway magnates and industrial giants. In* Babbitt, *Lewis examined the life of one middle-class realtor who embraced the politics, the mores, and the country-club life that his culture had taught him to value and yet still found himself unhappy. The novel documents the growth and causes of George Babbitt's discontent.*

Sinclair Lewis was born in 1885 in the small town of Sauk Center, Minnesota (population 2,500). His mother, a schoolteacher, died when he was three; his father, a teacher-turned-country-doctor, soon remarried. The young Lewis showed more interest in reading and creative writing than in sports. He graduated from Yale in 1908 (having taken time off in his senior year to work on the Panama Canal). Lewis's first novel, Our Mister Wren, *was published in 1914. A year later, the* Saturday Evening Post *published the first of what was to be many of his short stories. Five unsuccessful novels followed before the writing of* Main Street *(1920) and* Babbitt *(1922), which secured Lewis's fame and fortune. He reached the height of his career in 1930 with the awarding of the Nobel Prize but in the years after suffered a decline, due in part to a recurring drinking problem. Lewis died in Rome, Italy, in 1951.*

In the excerpt to follow, you will read of a real estate transaction in George Babbitt's office. Consider the ethics as well as the legality of the transaction. Is Babbitt doing anything wrong by trying to maximize his and his client's profits?

His name was George F. Babbitt. He was forty-six years old now, in April, 1920, and he made nothing in particular, neither butter nor shoes nor poetry, but he was nimble in the calling of selling houses for more than people could afford to pay. 1

His large head was pink, his brown hair thin and dry. His face was babyish in slumber, despite his wrinkles and the red spectacle-dents on the slopes of his nose. He was not fat but he was exceedingly well fed; his cheeks were pads, and the unroughened hand which lay helpless upon the khaki-colored blanket was slightly puffy. He seemed prosperous, extremely married and unromantic; and altogether unromantic appeared this sleeping-porch, which looked on one sizable elm, two respectable grass-plots, a cement driveway, and a corrugated iron garage. Yet Babbitt was again dreaming of the fairy child, a dream more romantic than scarlet pagodas by a silver sea. 2

For years the fairy child had come to him. Where others saw but Georgie Babbitt, she discerned gallant youth. She waited for him, in the darkness beyond mysterious groves. When at last he could slip away from the crowded house he darted to her. His wife, his clamoring friends, sought to follow, but he escaped, the girl fleet beside 3 him, and they crouched together on a shadowy hillside. She was so slim, so white, so eager! She cried that he was gay[1] and valiant, that she would wait for him, that they would sail—

Rumble and bang of the milk-truck. 4

Babbitt moaned, turned over, struggled back toward his dream. 5
He could see only her face now, beyond misty waters. The furnace-man slammed the basement door. A dog barked in the next yard. As Babbitt sank blissfully into a dim warm tide, the paper-carrier went by whistling, and the rolled-up *Advocate* thumped the front door. Babbitt roused, his stomach constricted with alarm. As he relaxed, he was pierced by the familiar and irritating rattle of some one cranking a Ford: snap-ah-ah, snap-ah-ah, snap-ah-ah. Himself a pious motorist, Babbitt cranked with the unseen driver, with him waited through taut hours for the roar of the starting engine, with him agonized as the roar ceased and again began the infernal patient snap-ah-ah—a round, flat sound, a shivering cold-morning sound, a sound infuriating and inescapable. Not till the rising voice of the motor told him that the Ford was moving was he released from the panting tension. He glanced once at his favorite tree, elm twigs against the gold patina of sky, and fumbled for sleep as for a drug. He who had been a boy very credulous of life was no longer greatly interested in the possible and improbable adventures of each new day.

He escaped from reality till the alarm-clock rang, at seven-twenty. 6

. . .

His morning was not sharply marked into divisions. Interwoven 7
with correspondence and advertisement-writing were a thousand nervous details: calls from clerks who were incessantly and hopefully seeking five furnished rooms and bath at sixty dollars a month; advice to Mat Penniman on getting money out of tenants who had no money.

Babbitt's virtues as a real-estate broker—as the servant of society 8
in the department of finding homes for families and shops for distributors of food—were steadiness and diligence. He was conventionally honest, he kept his records of buyers and sellers complete, he had experience with leases and titles and an excellent memory for prices. His shoulders were broad enough, his voice deep enough, his relish of hearty humor strong enough, to establish him as one of the ruling caste of Good Fellows. Yet his eventual importance to mankind was perhaps lessened by his large and complacent ignorance of all architecture save the types of houses turned out by speculative builders; all landscape gardening save the use of curving roads, grass, and six ordinary shrubs; and all the commonest axioms of

[1]In 1922, the sense of the word is "Merry."

economics. He serenely believed that the one purpose of the real-estate business was to make money for George F. Babbitt. True, it was a good advertisement at Booster Club lunches, and all the varieties of Annual Banquets to which Good Fellows were invited, to speak sonorously of Unselfish Public Service, the Broker's Obligation to Keep Inviolate the Trust of His Clients, and a thing called Ethics, whose nature was confusing but if you had it you were a High-class Realtor and if you hadn't you were a shyster, a piker, and a fly-by-night. These virtues awakened Confidence, and enabled you to handle Bigger Propositions. But they didn't imply that you were to be impractical and refuse to take twice the value of a house if a buyer was such an idiot that he didn't jew you down on the asking-price.

Babbitt spoke well—and often—at these orgies of commercial 9
righteousness about the "realtor's function as a seer of the future development of the community, and as a prophetic engineer clearing the pathway for inevitable changes"—which meant that a real-estate broker could make money by guessing which way the town would grow. This guessing he called Vision.

In an address at the Boosters' Club he had admitted, "It is at once 10
the duty and the privilege of the realtor to know everything about his own city and its environs. Where a surgeon is a specialist on every vein and mysterious cell of the human body, and the engineer upon electricity in all its phases, or every bolt of some great bridge majestically arching o'er a mighty flood, the realtor must know his city, inch by inch, and all its faults and virtues."

Though he did know the market-price, inch by inch, of certain 11
districts of Zenith, he did not know whether the police force was too large or too small, or whether it was in alliance with gambling and prostitution. He knew the means of fire-proofing buildings and the relation of insurance-rates to fire-proofing, but he did not know how many firemen there were in the city, how they were trained and paid, or how complete their apparatus. He sang eloquently the advantages of proximity of school-buildings to rentable homes, but he did not know—he did not know that it was worth while to know—whether the city schoolrooms were properly heated, lighted, ventilated, furnished; he did not know how the teachers were chosen; and though he chanted "One of the boasts of Zenith is that we pay our teachers adequately," that was because he had read the statement in the *Advocate-Times*. Himself, he could not have given the average salary of teachers in Zenith or anywhere else.

He had heard it said that "conditions" in the County Jail and the 12
Zenith City Prison were not very "scientific"; he had, with indignation at the criticism of Zenith, skimmed through a report in which the notorious pessimist Seneca Doane, the radical lawyer, asserted that to throw boys and young girls into a bull-pen crammed with men

suffering from syphilis, delirium tremens, and insanity was not the perfect way of educating them. He had controverted the report by growling, "Folks that think a jail ought to be a bloomin' Hotel Thornleigh make me sick. If people don't like a jail, let 'em behave 'emselves and keep out of it. Besides, these reform cranks always exaggerate." That was the beginning and quite completely the end of his investigations into Zenith's charities and corrections; and as to the "vice districts" he brightly expressed it, "Those are things that no decent man monkeys with. Besides, smatter fact, I'll tell you confidentially: it's a protection to our daughters and to decent women to have a district where tough nuts can raise cain. Keeps 'em away from our own homes."

As to industrial conditions, however, Babbitt had thought a great 13
deal, and his opinions may be coördinated as follows:

"A good labor union is of value because it keeps out radical 14
unions, which would destroy property. No one ought to be forced to belong to a union, however. All labor agitators who try to force men to join a union should be hanged. In fact, just between ourselves, there oughtn't to be any unions allowed at all; and as it's the best way of fighting the unions, every business man ought to belong to an employers'-association and to the Chamber of Commerce. In union there is strength. So any selfish hog who doesn't join the Chamber of Commerce ought to be forced to."

In nothing—as the expert on whose advice families moved to new 15
neighborhoods to live there for a generation—was Babbitt more splendidly innocent than in the science of sanitation. He did not know a malaria-bearing mosquito from a bat; he knew nothing about tests of drinking water; and in the matters of plumbing and sewage he was as unlearned as he was voluble. He often referred to the excellence of the bathrooms in the houses he sold. He was fond of explaining why it was that no European ever bathed. Some one had told him, when he was twenty-two, that all cesspools were unhealthy, and he still denounced them. If a client impertinently wanted him to sell a house which had a cesspool, Babbitt always spoke about it—before accepting the house and selling it.

When he laid out the Glen Oriole acreage development, when he 16
ironed woodland and dipping meadow into a glenless, orioleless, sunburnt flat prickly with small boards displaying the names of imaginary streets, he righteously put in a complete sewage-system. It made him feel superior; it enabled him to sneer privily at the Martin Lumsen development, Avonlea, which had a cesspool; and it provided a chorus for the full-page advertisements in which he announced the beauty, convenience, cheapness, and supererogatory healthfulness of Glen Oriole. The only flaw was that the Glen Oriole sewers had insufficient outlet, so that waste remained in them, not

very agreeably, while the Avonlea cesspool was a Waring septic tank.

The whole of the Glen Oriole project was a suggestion that Babbitt, though he really did hate men recognized as swindlers, was not too unreasonably honest. Operators and buyers prefer that brokers should not be in competition with them as operators and buyers themselves, but attend to their clients' interests only. It was supposed that the Babbitt-Thompson Company were merely agents for Glen Oriole, serving the real owner, Jake Offutt, but the fact was that Babbitt and Thompson owned sixty-two per cent. of the Glen, the president and purchasing agent of the Zenith Street Traction Company owned twenty-eight per cent., and Jake Offutt (a gang-politician, a small manufacturer, a tobacco-chewing old farceur who enjoyed dirty politics, business diplomacy, and cheating at poker) had only ten per cent., which Babbitt and the Traction officials had given to him for "fixing" health inspectors and fire inspectors and a member of the State Transportation Commission. 17

But Babbitt was virtuous. He advocated, though he did not practise, the prohibition of alcohol; he praised, though he did not obey, the laws against motor-speeding; he paid his debts; he contributed to the church, the Red Cross, and the Y.M.C.A.; he followed the custom of his clan and cheated only as it was sanctified by precedent; and he never descended to trickery—though, as he explained to Paul Riesling: 18

"Course I don't mean to say that every ad I write is literally true or that I always believe everything I say when I give some buyer a good strong selling-spiel. You see—you see it's like this: In the first place, maybe the owner of the property exaggerated when he put it into my hands, and it certainly isn't my place to go proving my principal a liar! And then most folks are so darn crooked themselves that they expect a fellow to do a little lying, so if I was fool enough to never whoop the ante I'd get the credit for lying anyway! In self-defense I got to toot my own horn, like a lawyer defending a client—his bounden duty, ain't it, to bring out the poor dub's good points? Why, the Judge himself would bawl out a lawyer that didn't, even if they both knew the guy was guilty! But even so, I don't pad out the truth like Cecil Rountree or Thayer or the rest of these realtors. Fact, I think a fellow that's willing to deliberately up and profit by lying ought to be shot!" 19

Babbitt's value to his clients was rarely better shown than this morning, in the conference at eleven-thirty between himself, Conrad Lyte, and Archibald Purdy. 20

Conrad Lyte was a real-estate speculator. He was a nervous speculator. Before he gambled he consulted bankers, lawyers, architects, contracting builders, and all of their clerks and stenographers who were willing to be cornered and give him advice. He was a bold 21 entrepreneur, and he desired nothing more than complete safety in his investments, freedom from attention to details, and the thirty or forty per cent profit which, according to all authorities, a pioneer deserves for his risks and foresight. He was a stubby man with a cap-like mass of short gray curls and clothes which, no matter how well cut, seemed shaggy. Below his eyes were semicircular hollows, as though silver dollars had been pressed against them and had left an imprint.

Particulary and always Lyte consulted Babbitt, and trusted in his slow cautiousness. 22

Six months ago Babbitt had learned that one Archibald Purdy, a grocer in the indecisive residential district known as Linton, was talking of opening a butcher shop beside his grocery. Looking up the ownership of adjoining parcels of land, Babbitt found that Purdy owned his present shop but did not own the one available lot adjoining. He advised Conrad Lyte to purchase this lot, for eleven thousand dollars, though an appraisal on a basis of rents did not indicate its value as above nine thousand. The rents, declared Babbitt, were too low; and by waiting they could make Purdy come to their price. (This was Vision.) He had to bully Lyte into buying. His first act as agent for Lyte was to increase the rent of the battered store-building on the lot. The tenant said a number of rude things, but he paid. 23

Now, Purdy seemed ready to buy, and his delay was going to cost him ten thousand extra dollars—the reward paid by the community to Mr. Conrad Lyte for the virtue of employing a broker who had Vision and who understood Talking Points, Strategic Values, Key Situations, Underappraisals, and the Psychology of Salesmanship. 24

Lyte came to the conference exultantly. He was fond of Babbitt, this morning, and called him "old hoss." Purdy, the grocer, a long-nosed man and solemn, seemed to care less for Babbitt and for Vision, but Babbitt met him at the street door of the office and guided him toward the private room with affectionate little cries of "This way, Brother Purdy!" He took from the correspondence-file the entire box of cigars and forced them on his guests. He pushed their chairs two inches forward and three inches back, which gave an hospitable note, then leaned back in his desk-chair and looked plump and jolly. But he spoke to the weakling grocer with firmness. 25

"Well, Brother Purdy, we been having some pretty tempting offers from butchers and a slew of other folks for that lot next to your store, but I persuaded Brother Lyte that we ought to give you a shot at the property first. I said to Lyte, 'It'd be a rotten shame,' I said, 'if somebody went and opened a combination grocery and meat market right next door and ruined Purdy's nice little business.' Especially—" Babbitt leaned forward, and his voice was harsh, "—it would be hard luck if one of these cash-and-carry chain-stores got in there and 26 started cutting prices below cost till they got rid of competition and forced you to the wall!"

Purdy snatched his thin hands from his pockets, pulled up his trousers, thrust his hands back into his pockets, tilted in the heavy oak chair, and tried to look amused, as he struggled: 27

"Yes, they're bad competition. But I guess you don't realize the Pulling Power that Personality has in a neighborhood business." 28

The great Babbitt smiled. "That's so. Just as you feel, old man. We thought we'd give you first chance. All right then—" 29

"Now look here!" Purdy wailed. "I know f'r a fact that a piece of property 'bout same size, right near, sold for less 'n eighty-five hundred, 'twa'n't two years ago, and here you fellows are asking me twenty-four thousand dollars! Why, I'd have to mortgage—I wouldn't mind so much paying twelve thousand but—Why good God, Mr. Babbitt, you're asking more 'n twice its value! And threatening to ruin me if I don't take it!" 30

"Purdy, I don't like your way of talking! I don't like it one little bit! Supposing Lyte and I were stinking enough to want to ruin any fellow human, don't you suppose we know it's to our own selfish interest to have everybody in Zenith prosperous? But all this is beside the point. Tell you what we'll do: We'll come down to twenty-three thousand—five thousand down and the rest on mortgage—and if you want to wreck the old shack and rebuild, I guess I can get Lyte here to loosen up for a building-morgtage on good liberal terms. Heavens, man, we'd be glad to oblige you! We don't like these foreign grocery trusts any better 'n you do! But it isn't reasonable to expect us to sacrifice eleven thousand or more just for neighborliness, *is* it! How about it, Lyte? You willing to come down?" 31

By warmly taking Purdy's part, Babbitt persuaded the benevolent Mr. Lyte to reduce his price to twenty-one thousand dollars. At the right moment Babbitt snatched from a drawer the agreement he had had Miss McGoun type out a week ago and thrust it into Purdy's hands. He genially shook his fountain pen to make certain that it was flowing, handed it to Purdy, and approvingly watched him sign. 32

The work of the world was being done. Lyte had made something over nine thousand dollars, Babbitt had made a four-hundred-and-fifty dollar commission, Purdy had, by the sensitive mechanism of modern finance, been provided with a business-building, and soon the happy inhabitants of Linton would have meat lavished upon them at prices only a little higher than those down-town. 33

It had been a manly battle, but after it Babbitt drooped. This was the only really amusing contest he had been planning. There was nothing ahead save details of leases, appraisals, mortgages. 34

He muttered, "Makes me sick to think of Lyte carrying off most of the profit when I did all the work, the old skinflint! And—What else 35 have I got to do to-day? . . . Like to take a good long vacation. Motor trip. Something."

Discussion and Writing Suggestions

1. [I]t was a good advertisement . . . to speak sonorously of . . . a thing called Ethics, whose nature was confusing but if you had it you were a High-class Realtor and if you hadn't you were a shyster, a piker, and a fly-by-night. These virtues awakened Confidence, and enabled you to handle Bigger Propositions. But they didn't imply that you were to be impractical and refuse to take twice the value of a house if a buyer was such an idiot that he didn't [work] you down on the asking price.

Do you agree with Babbitt's code of ethics? That is, is it reasonable to you that a realtor would accept twice the value of a property if a buyer were foolish enough to offer it?

2. The grocer, Purdy, is an example of "an idiot" that doesn't work a realtor down on the asking price. (See the preceding question.) Accordingly, Babbitt and his client Conrad Lyte succeed in making a handsome profit—legally. What is your reaction to this "work of the world," as Lewis calls it?

3. In your experience, have you seen or heard of any business conducted in the manner of the Conrad Lyte–Purdy affair? Describe the important "players" in this transaction and then, either in narrative form or as lines in a miniplay, recount what happened.

4. Lewis presents a series of apparent contradictions in Babbitt's character, of which Babbitt seems oblivious. For instance, while Babbitt believes realtors should know every inch of their city so that they may then communicate valuable information to customers, he does not himself know much about the adequacy of the police or fire departments, or whether teachers are paid well. Cite other apparent contradictions in Babbitt's character.

5. *Babbitt* was written in 1922. To what extent do the subjects taken up here remain current in the discussion of business ethics seventy years later? Develop your answer into an essay.

6. Characterize the tone of Lewis's portrait of George Babbitt. What attitude does the narrator adopt toward the character? In answering this question, cite particular sentences in the excerpt and discuss the tone of each.

SYNTHESIS ACTIVITIES

1. Analyze an action taken or contemplated by a protagonist in any of the cases you've read in this chapter. The case could be one of the five offered for analysis and discussion: "Case of the Collapsed Mine," "Peter Green's First Day," "Why Should My Conscience Bother Me?" "The Challenger

Disaster," or "Babbitt." Or the case could have been included as part of an article read in the chapter. Analyze the case in one of three ways:

- Analyze the actions taken or contemplated based on Gerald Cavanagh's strategy for making ethical business decisions.
- Analyze the case based on criteria set out in Sissela Bok's article.
- Analyze the case following principles set out in Albert Carr's article.

A more ambitious effort: Analyze any one case on the basis of two or three sets of competing principles and then explain which analysis seems most satisfying—and why. Before your analysis, be sure that you've accurately summarized the principles you're about to apply. Structurally, you might lay out your paper in one of two ways: Introduce several criteria for analysis in one section of the paper and apply these criteria in another. Alternately, you could introduce *and* apply a single criterion in one section of the paper, do the same for another criterion in a second section, and so on, for as many criteria as you care to discuss.

2. Devise your own criteria for making ethical business decisions. As you devise these criteria, bear in mind that a decision maker in business must seek to balance financial needs with the rights of employees, consumers, and the community. Then, using your criteria, analyze one of the cases presented in this chapter.

3. Albert Carr argues that we should free decisions in business from the moral considerations that govern behavior in private life. Write a critique of Carr's position, drawing on Carr himself as well as on those who responded to his article in Blodgett. At some point in the critique, you will need to articulate *your* views on the role of ethics in business. You may find it helpful in the critique to refer to one or more of the ethical predicaments illustrated in the chapter's cases.

4. Whistleblowing figures prominently in at least three cases presented in this chapter. Analyze one or more of these cases in light of Sissela Bok's discussion on whistleblowing; then determine the comprehensiveness of Bok's criteria for helping people decide whether or not to blow the whistle on colleagues in the workplace. Essentially, this paper would be structured as a critique of Bok's article. (See Chapter 2 for an extended discussion of critique.)

5. Compare and contrast the presentation of George Babbitt's real estate transaction as a case for ethical analysis with one of the business school cases presented in the chapter. How are these presentations similar? How do they differ? Which case do you prefer—and why? (See pages 101–102 for advice on structuring the comparison and contrast synthesis.)

6. Prepare summaries of Gerald Cavanagh's method for making ethical

decisions in business and Albert Carr's position on the use of deception in business. Then present these summaries to a businessman or -woman. Interview this person after he or she has read the summaries and ask which of the views seems the more appealing—or more realistic—and why. In a paper, introduce the interview and the occasion for holding it; provide a partial transcript of the interview; and conclude with an analysis of the interviewee's remarks. What have you learned about ethics and business both from summarizing the articles and from conducting the interview?

Following are the concluding paragraphs to two of the case studies presented earlier.

Conclusion to "Why Should My Conscience Bother Me?"

64

. . . The next morning, I telephoned Lawson and told him I was ready to begin on the qualification report.

In a few minutes, he was at my desk, ready to begin. Before we started, I asked him, "Do you realize what we are going to do?" 65

"Yeah," he replied bitterly, "we're going to screw LTV. And speaking of screwing," he continued, "I know now how a whore feels, because that's exactly what I've become, an engineering whore. I've sold myself. It's all I can do to look at myself in the mirror when I shave. I make me sick." 66

I was surprised at his vehemence. It was obvious that he too had done his share of soul-searching and didn't like what he had found. Somehow, though, the air seemed clearer after his outburst, and we began working on the report. 67

I had written dozens of qualification reports, and I knew what a "good" one looked like. Resorting to the actual test data only on occasion, Lawson and I proceeded to prepare page after page of elaborate, detailed engineering curves, charts, and test logs, which purported to show what had happened during the formal qualification tests. Where temperatures were too high, we deliberately chopped them down a few hundred degrees, and where they were too low, we raised them to a value that would appear reasonable to the LTV and military engineers. Brake pressure, torque values, distances, times—everything of consequence was tailored to fit the occasion. 68

Occasionally, we would find that some test either hadn't been performed at all or had been conducted improperly. On those occasions, we "conducted" the test—successfully, of course—on paper. 69

For nearly a month we worked on the graphic presentation that would be a part of the report. Meanwhile, the fourteenth and final qualification attempt had been completed, and the brake, not unexpectedly, had failed again. 70

During that month, Lawson and I talked of little else except the enormity of what we were doing. The more involved we became in our work, the more apparent became our own culpability. We discussed such things as the Nuremberg trials and how they related to our guilt and complicity in the A7D situation. Lawson often expressed his opinion that the brake was downright dangerous and that, once on flight tests, "anything is liable to happen." 71

I saw his boss, John Warren, at least twice during that month and needled him about what we were doing. He didn't take the jibes too kindly but managed to laugh the situation off as "one of those things." One day I remarked that what we were doing amounted to fraud, and he pulled out an engineering handbook and turned to a section on laws as they related to the engineering profession. 72

He read the definition of fraud aloud, then said, "Well, technically I don't think what we're doing can be called fraud. I'll admit it's not right, but it's just one of those things. We're just kinda caught in the middle. About all I can tell you is, do like I'm doing. Make copies of everything and put them in your SYA file." 73

"What's an 'SYA' file?" I asked. 74

"That'a a 'save your ass' file." He laughed. 75

On June 5, 1968, the report was officially published and copies were delivered in person to the Air Force and LTV. Within a week, flight tests were begun at Edwards Air Force Base in California. Searle Lawson was sent to California as Goodrich's representative. Within approximately two weeks, he returned because some rather unusual incidents during the tests had caused them to be canceled. 76

His face was grim as he related stories of several near crashes during landings—caused by brake troubles. He told me about one incident in which, upon landing, one brake was literally welded together by the intense heat developed during the test stop. The wheel locked, and the plane skidded for nearly 1500 feet before coming to a halt. The plane was jacked up and the wheel removed. The fused parts within the brake had to be pried apart. 77

Lawson had returned to Troy from California that same day, and that evening, he and others of the Goodrich engineering department left for Dallas for a high-level conference with LTV. 78

That evening I left work early and went to see my attorney. After I told him the story, he advised that, while I was probably not actually guilty of fraud, I was certainly part of a conspiracy to defraud. He advised me to go to the Federal Bureau of Investigation and offered to 79 arrange an appointment. The following week he took me to the Dayton office of the FBI, and after I had been warned that I would not be immune from prosecution, I disclosed the A7D matter to one of the agents. The agent told me to say nothing about the episode to anyone and to report any further incident to him. He said he would forward the story to his superiors in Washington.

A few days later, Lawson returned from the conference in Dallas 80
and said that the Air Force, which had previously approved the qualification report, had suddenly rescinded that approval and was demanding to see some of the raw test data taken during the tests. I gathered that the FBI had passed the word.

Finally, early in October 1968, Lawson submitted his resignation, 81
to take effect on October 25. On October 18, I submitted my own resignation, to take effect on November 1. In my resignation, addressed to Russell Line, I cited the A7D report and stated: "As you are aware, this report contained numerous deliberate and willful misrepresentations which, according to legal counsel, constitute fraud and expose both myself and others to criminal charges of conspiracy to defraud. . . . The events of the past seven months have created an atmosphere of deceit and distrust in which it is impossible to work. . . ."

On October 25, I received a sharp summons to the office of Bud 82
Sunderman. As chief engineer at the Troy plant, Sunderman was responsible for the entire engineering division. Tall and graying, impeccably dressed at all times, he was capable of producing a dazzling smile or a hearty chuckle or immobilizing his face into marble hardness, as the occasion required.

I faced the marble hardness when I reached his office. He 83
motioned me to a chair. "I have your resignation here," he snapped, "and I must say you have made some rather shocking, I might even say irresponsible, charges. This is very serious."

Before I could reply, he was demanding an explanation. "I want 84
to know exactly what the fraud is in connection with the A7D and how you can dare accuse this company of such a thing!"

I started to tell some of the things that had happened during the 85
testing, but he shut me off saying, "There's nothing wrong with anything we've done here. You aren't aware of all the things that have been going on behind the scenes. If you had known the true situation, you would never have made these charges." He said that in view of my apparent "disloyalty" he had decided to accept my resignation "right now," and said it would be better for all concerned if I left the plant immediately. As I got up to leave he asked me if I intended to "carry this thing further."

I answered simply, "Yes," to which he replied, "Suit yourself." 86
Within twenty minutes, I had cleaned out my desk and left. Forty-

eight hours later, the B. F. Goodrich Company recalled the qualification report and the four-disk brake, announcing that it would replace the brake with a new, improved, five-disk brake at no cost to LTV.

Ten months later, on August 13, 1969, I was the chief government 87
witness at a hearing conducted before Senator William Proxmire's Economy in Government Subcommittee of the Congress's Joint Economic Committee. I related the A7D story to the committee, and my testimony was supported by Searle Lawson, who followed me to the witness stand. Air Force officers also testified, as well as a four-man team from the General Accounting Office, which had conducted an investigation of the A7D brake at the request of Senator Proxmire. Both Air Force and GAO investigators declared that the brake was dangerous and had not been tested properly.

Testifying for Goodrich was R. G. Jeter, vice-president and gener- 88
al counsel of the company, from the Akron headquarters. Representing the Troy plant was Robert Sink. These two denied any wrongdoing on the part of the Goodrich Company, despite expert testimony to the contrary by Air Force and GAO officials. Sink was quick to deny any connection with the writing of the report or of directing any falsifications, claiming to be on the West Coast at the time. John Warren was the man who supervised its writing, said Sink.

As for me, I was dismissed as a high-school graduate with no 89
technical training, while Sink testified that Lawson was a young, inexperienced engineer. "We tried to give him guidance," Sink testified, "but he preferred to have his own convictions."

About changing the data and figures in the report, Sink said: 90
"When you take data from several different sources, you have to rationalize among those data what is the true story. This is part of your engineering know-how." He admitted that changes had been made in the data, "but only to make them more consistent with the overall picture of the data that is available."

Jeter pooh-poohed the suggestion that anything improper oc- 91
curred, saying: "We have thirty-odd engineers at this plant . . . and I say to you that it is incredible that these men would stand idly by and see reports changed or falsified. . . . I mean you just do not have to do that working for anybody. . . . Just nobody does that."

The four-hour hearing adjourned with no real conclusion reached 92
by the committee. But, the following day the Department of Defense made sweeping changes in its inspection, testing and reporting procedures. A spokesman for the DOD said the changes were a result of the Goodrich episode.

The A7D is now in service, sporting a Goodrich-made five-disk 93
brake, a brake that works very well, I'm told. Business at the Goodrich plant is good. Lawson is now an engineer for LTV and has been

assigned to the A7D project. And I am now a newspaper reporter.

At this writing, those remaining at Goodrich are still secure in the 94
same positions, all except Russell Line and Robert Sink. Line has been rewarded with a promotion to production superintendent, a large step upward on the corporate ladder. As for Sink, he moved up into Line's old job.

Conclusion to "The Challenger Disaster"

EPILOGUE—ETHICAL ANALYSIS AND IMPLICATIONS

Roger Boisjoly's experience before, during, and after the *Challenger* 30
tragedy raises ethical questions which can be applied generally to other management situations. Some of those questions concern the moral obligations of engineers and managers, the link imposed by technology on the relationship between engineering and business ethics, and the issues of corporate loyalty and whistleblowing.

Most codes of ethics adopted by engineering professional societ- 31
ies agree with Cicero that "the engineer shall hold paramount the health, safety, and welfare of the public in the performance of his professional duties" (Broome, 1986). New technologies will tie the ethics of engineering more closely to business ethics as corporate tragedies force recognition that traditional ethical standards alone cannot answer the questions posed by a more complex world. Entrenched corporate cultures, failure of managers to ask hard questions, and ethical illiteracy make new technologies difficult to manage. The dangers present in technology are usually forewarned, as in the *Challenger* case, but managers apparently refuse to consider them or are not diligent enough in their efforts to recognize them. The following is one explanation for the occurrence of corporate tragedies:

> Most of us are unaware that we have the following unspoken compact with life: "The world is inherently orderly and predictable. It will behave as it always has; the worst will not happen to me." Imagine the shock to an individual or a corporation when something so terrible and unpredictable happens that it shatters our belief in the orderliness of the world" (Pastin, 1986)

Mark Pastin goes on to state "an accident or disaster differs from a 32
tragedy in that tragedy violates ground rules" (Pastin, 1986). In this sense, the *Challenger* explosion was a corporate and national tragedy:

NASA and Morton Thiokol violated a basic ground rule by shifting the burden of proof during the prelaunch teleconference. In making their "management decision" to launch, the executives indicated their belief that the worst could not happen and expressed a willingness to accept risks that they had previously considered unacceptable. One explanation for this "risk taking," given by Howard Schwartz, is that NASA began to view itself as the ideal organization that did not make mistakes. According to Schwartz, "The organization ideal is an image of perfection. It is, so to speak, an idea of God. God does not make mistakes. Having adopted the idea of NASA as the organization ideal it follows that the individual will believe that, if NASA has made a decision, that decision will be correct" (Schwartz, 1987). In his testimony before the Rogers Commission, Roger Boisjoly indicated the extent to which NASA procedure had changed: "This was a meeting (the night before the launch) where the determination was to launch, and it was up to us to prove beyond the shadow of a doubt that it was not safe to do so. This is the total reverse to what the position usually is in a preflight conversation or a flight readiness review" (Boisjoly, 1986). As Schwartz indicates: "If it was a human decision, engineering standards of risk should prevail in determining whether it is safe to launch. On the other hand, if the decision was a NASA decision, it is simply safe to launch, since NASA does not make mistakes" (Schwartz, 1987).

Roger Boisjoly's dilemma became more complicated after the 33
Challenger explosion. Boisjoly's repeated efforts to alert management to the problems facing the Seal Task Force, and his attempts to prevent the launch, illustrate his desire to effect changes within normal corporate channels, without violating the "rules." In doing so, he became the "loyal opposition." Thiokol management did not question his loyalty until the government hearings, when, in their eyes, he became a "whistle blower." At that critical juncture, Boisjoly, by testifying as he did, contradicted the company line and made documents available to the Rogers Commission. As discussed above, the personal cost to Boisjoly has been extremely high. His professional position, relationships, and health have suffered. Still, his belief in the moral imperative of his actions prompted him to make the following statement in a speech given to engineering students at Massachusetts Institute of Technology on January 7, 1987:

> I have been asked by some if I would testify again if I knew in advance of the potential consequences to me and my career. My answer is always an immediate "yes." I couldn't live with any self respect if I tailored my actions based upon the personal consequences as a result of my honorable actions (Boisjoly, 1987).

The case of Roger Boisjoly and the *Challenger* disaster illustrates the need for protection of individual employee rights, as well as the public safety. Currently, only twenty-one states have legislation protecting corporate and government whistleblowers. [Utah's law (Thiokol is located in Utah) protects public employees only.] The *Challenger* disaster has focused enough attention on the need to protect the rights of whistle blowers that on June 4, 1987, NASA announced a formal policy designed to protect individuals like Roger Boisjoly who have information that should be brought to the attention of top-level decision makers. The future struggle facing engineering managers will be the need to balance technological advancement with their moral obligations to the public, while fostering corporate loyalty and protecting individual employee rights. **34**

BIBLIOGRAPHY

Boisjoly, R. M. Applied Mechanics Memorandum to Robert K. Lund, Vice President, Engineering, Wasatch Division. Morton Thiokol, Inc. July 31, 1985.

———. Activity Report, SRM Seal Erosion Task Team Status. October 4, 1985.

———. *Testimony Before the Presidential Commission on Space Shuttle Challenger Accident*. Washington, D.C. February 25, 1986.

———. "Ethical Decisions: Morton Thiokol and the Shuttle Disaster." Speech given at Massachusetts Institute of Technology, January 7, 1987.

Broome, T. "The Slippery Ethics of Engineering." *Washington Post*, December 28, 1986, D3.

Kilminster, J. C. Memorandum (E000–FY86–003) to Robert Lund. Vice President, Engineering, Wasatch Division, Morton Thiokol, Inc. July 5, 1985.

McConnell, M. *Challenger, A Major Malfunction: A True Story of Politics, Greed, and the Wrong Stuff*. Garden City, N.J.: Doubleday and Company, Inc., 1987.

Pastin, M. *The Hard Problems of Management: Gaining the Ethics Edge*. San Francisco: Jossey-Bass, 1986.

Rogers, W. P. *Proceedings Before the Presidential Commission on the Space Shuttle Accident*. Washington, D.C. May 2, 1986.

Schwartz, H. S. "On the Psychodynamics of Organizational Disaster: The Case of the Space Shuttle Challenger." *The Columbia Journal of World Business*, Spring 1987.

AIDS: PUBLIC GOOD VS. PRIVATE RIGHTS

12

In November 1988, California citizens who entered the voting booth were faced with a decision on an initiative known as Proposition 102. According to the official summary by the state attorney general, Proposition 102 mandated the following measures:

> Requires doctors, blood blanks, and others, to report patients and blood donors, whom they reasonably believe to have been infected by or tested positive for AIDS virus, to local health officers. Restricts confidential testing. Requires reporting by persons infected or tested positive. Directs local health officers to notify reported person's spouse, sexual partners, and others possibly exposed. Repeals prohibition on use of AIDS virus tests for employability or insurability. Creates felony for persons with knowledge of infection or positive test to donate blood. Modifies fines and penalties for unauthorized disclosure of AIDS virus test results.

Advocates of Proposition 102 maintained that such strong measures were necessary to protect the general public—both those who had not yet been exposed to the AIDS (Acquired Immune Deficiency Syndrome) virus and those who may have unknowingly been exposed. Opponents of Proposition 102 charged that these measures were not only unworkable but constituted a gross violation of civil rights.

Proposition 102 and the arguments for and against it form the centerpiece of this chapter on AIDS. This controversial voter initiative (conceived by activist Paul Gann) crystallizes the debate that is fundamental not only to the question of how society should deal with AIDS but to such other issues as gun control, capital punishment, censorship, and even smoking in public places. That debate focuses on the following primary questions: What measures does the public have a right to take in protecting itself from a perceived threat? What individual rights are so important that they may not be infringed, even in the name of the public good? The debate also involves such secondary questions as: How real is the threat? How serious? What compromises are possible?

To take up one of these questions, few doubt that the threat of AIDS is real. Acquired immune deficiency syndrome is a new plague. As of mid-1990, about 130,000 cases of AIDS had been reported in the United States, and about 80,000 of these people had died. The Centers for Disease Control (CDC) estimates that 52,000 new cases will appear by 1991 and projects a cumulative death total of 453,000 by 1993. The World Health Organization estimates that 500,000 people in the world have AIDS (and that 5 to 10 million are infected with the AIDS virus), and that during the next decade, there will be 5.5 million new cases. According to Ronald Bayer, a professor of public health at the Columbia University School of Public Health, "AIDS might indeed dwarf the earlier epidemics of smallpox, typhoid, and the Black Death."

Since the threat is so real, what steps should public authorities take in combatting it? Should those who test positive for the AIDS virus be quarantined? If they are not quarantined, should they be publicly identified? Should health officers seek out those who have had sexual intercourse with identified AIDS carriers and notify them of their risk status? Should potential employers and insurers have the right to use AIDS testing to refuse employment or insurance to those who test positive? Should children with AIDS be permitted to attend school with other uninfected children? Just what are the chances of those not infected with AIDS catching the disease from those who are? These are some of the questions facing government officials and health officers now and for the foreseeable future.

One set of solutions to these questions was provided in June 1988 by the Presidential Commission on the Human Immunodeficiency Virus Epidemic. The commission recommended that the federal government ensure the privacy of those with AIDS but also advised that public health authorities begin notifying sexual partners of those so diagnosed, though without identifying the AIDS-carrier. The commission also recommended that AIDS (which they preferred to call "HIV infection") be considered a disability and that persons with AIDS, like persons with other disabilities, be protected from discrimination by employers and school officials.

In this chapter, we will provide for your consideration a number of other viewpoints on this issue. First, a pamphlet by the Abbott medical laboratories, "AIDS: The New Epidemic," provides a question-and-answer introduction to the basic facts about the disease. Next, we present a set of arguments for and against Proposition 102—"Proposition 102: Reporting Exposure to AIDS Virus." Following this, neurologist Richard Restak argues for the rights of society: "When a Plague Looms, Society Must Discriminate." The opposite point of view is taken by Christian ethicist James B. Nelson, who argues in "Blaming the Victim" that we should favor the rights of individuals, particularly when these individuals are likely to be members of oppressed minorities. In "The Moral Crusade," political scientist Dennis Altman shows how AIDS has worsened the existing problems of homophobia and racism because many people are inclined to view the disease as divine retribution. (As another writer in this chapter, John Tierney, explains, "In a recent *Times-Mirror* Gallup poll, 42.5 percent of Americans said AIDS might be a punishment from God for immoral behavior.")

In "Identify All the Carriers," *National Review* editor and columnist William F. Buckley comes up with a startling proposal to help combat the AIDS epidemic. Next, John Tierney, writing for *Rolling Stone,* considers the question in "Straight Talk" of how much risk AIDS poses to the heterosexual population—an important question, since the degree of heterosexual risk is directly proportional to the discriminatory legislation directed at persons with AIDS. Finally, in a moving short story, "The Way We Live Now," Susan Sontag dramatizes the effect of AIDS not only on the victim but also on the people around him.

AIDS: The New Epidemic

ABBOTT LABORATORIES

By the mid-1980s, AIDS was beginning to create a kind of hysteria, not only among those groups who were at high risk but also among the general public. Most people—while recognizing the deadly nature of AIDS—simply did not understand enough about the disease to know how much of a threat it posed to them or what they should do if they thought they were at risk. The federal government under President Ronald Reagan had seemed reluctant to get involved in public education about AIDS. But Reagan's surgeon general, C. Everett Koop, felt very strongly about the government's obligation to inform the public about AIDS; and in an unprecedented action, Koop and his staff in the U.S. Public Health Service wrote a pamphlet ("The Surgeon General's Report on Acquired Immune Deficiency Syndrome") that was sent to every household in the United States in late 1986. And other information was readily available to those who sought it. Doctors, health professionals, and organizations like the American Red Cross had produced numerous articles and pamphlets on AIDS. The following pamphlet was prepared by Abbott Laboratories, a worldwide health-care company headquartered in Illinois.

AIDS, an incurable illness resulting from deterioration of the human immune system, was first reported in the United States in 1981. In the beginning, many considered AIDS a "gay" disease because most of its victims were believed to be male homosexuals. However, the sudden appearance of AIDS and its rapid spread throughout the population created mystery for everyone, and deep concern in many communities. The fears created by a lack of knowledge in these early years promoted actions ranging from simply irrational to blatantly harmful. 1

In recent years, scientists have begun to solve the AIDS mystery. 2
We now know that untold thousands of people in some countries have been suffering from AIDS for many years. As knowledge grows, so does our ability to live safely and intelligently with AIDS in our society—to dispel our fears, but maintain our safety. You, too, should understand AIDS so that you can be cautious, but not fearful. While more will be learned in coming years, this pamphlet covers the current knowledge about AIDS in our society. By reading it, you can become more comfortable with the facts about AIDS and its related conditions and understand its possible impact on your life.

WHAT IS AIDS?

AIDS, Acquired Immune Deficiency Syndrome, weakens the body's 3
ability to fight off infection and disease. While other diseases can topple the body's defenses in a similar manner, AIDS is the only condition which is "acquired" as the result of exposure to an infectious agent. When this occurs, victims experience recurrent illnesses and infections. In addition, AIDS victims get unusual diseases which healthy individuals rarely experience.

The recurrent illnesses of AIDS take a continuous toll upon the 4
victims and are eventually fatal. More than 70 percent of all AIDS cases prove fatal within two years of diagnosis. While doctors are learning more about treating the infections which plague AIDS victims, little can be done to restore the body's immune system to normal.

HOW COMMON IS AIDS?

While still less common than most forms of cancer, the number of 5
AIDS cases continues to grow at a rapid rate. Since it was first reported, thousands of cases have been detected and almost every state has been affected. Most alarmingly, the number of reported cases doubles every nine to 15 months. As this trend continues, AIDS gains increasing recognition as an epidemic. Some officials estimate that as many as one million Americans may have been exposed to the AIDS virus. At this point, no one knows how many among those exposed will actually develop the disease.

WHAT CAUSES AIDS?

Scientists believe that a virus known as Human T-Lymphotropic 6
Virus, Type III causes AIDS. Abbreviated HTLV-III, the AIDS virus

shares characteristics with viruses linked to adult leukemia and lymphoma.

While much has been learned about the virus since its discovery in 1984, many questions remain. It appears that HTLV-III, like other viruses, may remain latent in the body without ever causing AIDS disease. Thus, a person may carry the virus for many years before it attacks his or her immune system. Also some individuals may never become ill from this virus. Currently, medical researchers estimate that five to 20 percent of infected persons will develop AIDS or AIDS-related conditions, but they don't know why some individuals are susceptible while others are not. 7

HOW IS THE HTLV-III VIRUS SPREAD?

HTLV-III, the AIDS virus, passes from person to person through the exchange of body fluids, particularly semen. Transmission occurs when body fluids are exchanged during intimate sexual contact, while sharing infected hypodermic needles, or upon receiving contaminated blood transfusions. Shared razors, toothbrushes, or other items contaminated with blood can also theoretically transmit the virus to subsequent users. Physicians believe that any body fluid could play a role in transmission of the virus during intimate contact. Currently, however, nothing indicates that transmission is possible through sneezing, touching, or other casual contact. 8

HOW IS AIDS ASSOCIATED WITH DONATING BLOOD AND RECEIVING BLOOD TRANSFUSIONS?

Before the transmission of AIDS was understood, the association of AIDS with blood transfusions created some fears about donating blood. In fact, no one can get AIDS while making a blood or plasma donation. Blood collection centers operate under a doctor's supervision and use only new, sterile equipment. Needles are used once and discarded, so that donors are never exposed to anyone else's blood. In short, donating blood is a safe activity that provides a much-needed service to the community. 9

Once donated, blood undergoes many tests and procedures to ensure that blood received by hospitalized patients is safe. In early 1985, blood banks in the United States began using a screening test for HTLV-III antibody. When verified, this test identifies donors who have been exposed to the AIDS virus. Although these individuals may appear perfectly healthy, it's possible their blood *may* contain the virus, and so it will not be used for transfusion purposes. 10

Individuals at risk for AIDS are urged *not* to donate blood. While some individuals in risk groups may wish to find out if they are positive for this antibody test, blood banks are not an appropriate place to seek this information. Such testing should be done through physicians or special clinics where pre- and post-test information and counseling and proper medical evaluation are available. 11

CAN THE HTLV-III TEST TELL IF A PERSON HAS AIDS?

No. A positive HTLV-III test does not mean that an individual has AIDS. The test detects antibodies which the body forms when exposed to the virus. These antibodies alone do not mean that a person has AIDS or will get AIDS in the future. 12

As with most diseases, the diagnosis of AIDS or related illnesses can only be made by a physician after careful examination, a full patient history, and certain laboratory tests—which may include the HTLV-III antibody test. Other tests are now under development for the diagnosis of a viral infection in humans, monitoring AIDS patients, and determining if an individual has developed immunity to the disease. 13

However, positive HTLV-III antibody test results cannot be disregarded. The presence of HTLV-III antibodies *has* been associated with active viral infections. This means that those with confirmed positive test results, even though apparently healthy, should take certain precautions for themselves and others. This includes avoiding activities which might infect others, as well as paying close attention to one's own health and lifestyle. 14

Individuals who think they might be at risk for AIDS should contact a physician or local public health department for referral to a specialist with experience in dealing with AIDS. 15

WHO GETS AIDS?

More than 90 percent of all AIDS victims belong to three high-risk groups: male homosexuals or bisexuals, intravenous drug abusers, and hemophiliacs. A small but increasing number of AIDS victims has been found outside these groups. These include recipients of blood transfusions, sexual partners of high-risk persons, children born to infected women, and sexually active heterosexuals. 16

Until recently, Haitian immigrants were considered a risk group, but researchers now believe these individuals contracted the disease through one of the activities mentioned above. 17

WHAT ARE THE SYMPTOMS OF AIDS?

During initial stages of the infection, most victims show no outward signs or symptoms. But after an incubation period of a few months to several years, the virus has been known to cause such symptoms as: 18

- Recurring fever and night sweating
- Shortness of breath and a dry cough not due to allergies or cigarette smoking
- Changes in illness patterns, either how often a person gets sick, how severely, or for how long
- Constant fatigue not caused by physical, emotional, or social reasons
- Diarrhea and loss of appetite
- Rapid weight loss for no apparent reason
- Swollen lymph glands in the armpits, groin, or neck

In later stages of AIDS, the victim's immune system is so weakened that normally mild or unusual diseases become life-threatening. The most common of these are Kaposi's sarcoma, a form of cancer that marks its victims with pink to purplish spots, and *Pneumocystis carinii* pneumonia, a virulent form of pneumonia. 19

IS THERE A CURE FOR AIDS?

No cure has yet been found for AIDS. A true cure would involve destroying the virus and revitalizing the damaged immune system. Several drugs which have been found to have some action against the AIDS virus are now being tested on a small number of patients. Medical researchers are also trying to develop a vaccine and new antiviral agents. 20

Currently, treatment for AIDS generally focuses on the secondary illnesses that invade the body and take advantage of the weakened immune system. Drugs, radiation, and surgery have all been used to combat these secondary illnesses. 21

WHAT SHOULD THOSE WITH AIDS DO TO AVOID EXPOSING OTHERS?

An individual with clear indications of AIDS-related diseases should take the following precautions to avoid spreading the virus to family members and close contacts. 22

- Do not donate blood.
- Avoid sex practices, such as open-mouthed kissing or oral or anal sex, in which body fluids are exchanged. Condoms may help prevent transmission of semen.
- Inform doctors, dentists, and other health professionals so they can protect themselves and provide you with proper care.
- Limit sexual contacts, and be honest with sexual partners about steps you are taking to prevent the spread of the virus.
- Don't share toothbrushes or razor blades.
- Women are advised to avoid or postpone pregnancy, since some infants have developed AIDS from their infected mothers.

WHAT CAN I DO TO PROTECT MYSELF FROM AIDS?

Since it appears that the disease can be transmitted through hetero- 23
sexual contact, even individuals in low-risk groups must exercise some caution. Limiting the number of sexual contacts and avoiding individuals who do not take this precaution will help reduce your exposure to all sexually transmitted diseases, including AIDS.

AIDS IS A SERIOUS PROBLEM

AIDS is a serious public health problem. Until a cure is discovered, 24
prevention is the only way to fight it. By knowing the facts about AIDS, taking personal precautions, and supporting efforts to find a cure, everyone can play an important part in the battle against AIDS.

You can get more information on AIDS by writing to the Office of 25
Public Affairs, U.S. Public Health Service, Room 721-H, 200 Independence Ave., S.W., Washington, D.C. 20201.

Review Questions

1. Everyone infected with the HTLV-III virus will eventually get AIDS or AIDS-related conditions. True or false? Explain.
2. How is AIDS transmitted?
3. Which individuals are at highest risk for AIDS?
4. What is currently being done to treat AIDS patients?

Discussion and Writing Suggestions

1. How useful do you believe pamphlets like this one are in preventing the spread of AIDS? What did you know about AIDS before having read it? What did you learn from the pamphlet?
2. Pamphlets like this are often created to correct common misconceptions that people have. Based on your own prior knowledge, as well as hints from the pamphlet itself, what are some of the most common misconceptions about AIDS?
3. The question-and-answer format used in this pamphlet has been found an effective device to explain a somewhat complex or intimidating subject. Choose another subject—perhaps one that you, yourself, have more knowledge about than the average person. Then, discuss this subject in question-and-answer format so that it will be clear to a general audience. The questions, of course, should focus on the most important aspects of this subject. (Essentially, they are subheadings that have been converted to questions).

Proposition 102: Reporting Exposure to AIDS Virus

During the past fifteen or so years, the citizen initiative (or referendum) has become an increasingly popular method of enacting legislation. Indeed, in his book Megatrends, *John Naisbett predicted that initiatives would eventually replace legislative action as the major source of our laws. That seems unlikely to happen anytime soon; still, the recent proliferation of initiatives in states throughout the Union has been a remarkable phenomenon of American democracy. Initiatives are born when one or more citizens draft a proposed law and then accumulate a sufficient number of signatures to get it on a ballot. If a majority votes for the initiative, it becomes law. Increasingly, citizens rely on initiatives when they are dissatisfied with legislatures that are unwilling or unable (perhaps because they are captives of various lobbies and special interests) to pass laws widely thought to be necessary—for instance, laws to protect consumers or to lower insurance rates. One of the most famous (or notorious) of initiatives was Proposition 13, voted into law in 1978 by California citizens outraged by rapidly spiraling property tax increases. (Proposition 13 froze property tax rates. The down side of its passage was that because of the loss of revenues, the state had to slash other services,*

"Reporting Initiative to AIDS Virus, Initiative Statute." from *California Ballot Pamphlet, General Election, 8 Nov. 1988.* Published by March Fong Eu, California Secretary of State.

such as funding for parks and subsidies to county libraries, some of which had to be closed down.)

California has always led the nation in ballot initiatives. In the November 1988 election, there were twelve propositions on the state ballot, ranging from funding for the hungry and homeless to levying an additional tax on cigarettes to be used for treatment of tobacco-related diseases. Among these initiatives, one of the more controversial was Proposition 102, which played on the public's fears of AIDS by calling for the required reporting to health authorities of individuals who test positive for the AIDS virus. This was not the first time California voters had been asked to vote on an AIDS initiative. Two years earlier, Proposition 64, sponsored by the Lyndon LaRouche organization, had called for the quarantining of AIDS patients and anyone else carrying the AIDS virus. (Proposition 64 was handily defeated.) And sharing the ballot with Proposition 102—originated by Paul Gann, a conservative businessman, who had also helped draft Proposition 13—was Proposition 96, which called for involuntary testing of certain persons believed to have spread the AIDS virus.

Notice the structure of Proposition 102, as it appeared in this informational pamphlet. (The proposed law itself is not included.) A brief summary is provided by the state attorney general, followed by a somewhat longer analysis by the legislative analyst; then, two sets of arguments are presented: Arguments in favor of, and against, Proposition 102 are each rebutted by counterarguments. Such a highly structured form of argument was developed as the fairest means of presenting issues to voters and of allowing them to make up their own minds.

(The outcome of the vote on Proposition 102 is indicated at the end of the Discussion and Writing Suggestions.)

OFFICIAL TITLE AND SUMMARY PREPARED BY THE ATTORNEY GENERAL

REPORTING EXPOSURE TO AIDS VIRUS. INITIATIVE. Requires doctors, blood banks, and others, to report patients and blood donors, whom they reasonably believe to have been infected by or tested positive for AIDS virus, to local health officers. Restricts confidential testing. Requires reporting by persons infected or tested positive. Directs local health officers to notify reported person's spouse, sexual partners, and others possibly exposed. Repeals prohibition on use of AIDS virus tests for employment or insurability. Creates felony for persons with knowledge of infection or positive test to donate blood. Modifies fines and penalties for unauthorized disclosure of AIDS virus test results. Summary of Legislative An- 1 alyst's estimate of net state and local government fiscal impact: Fiscal impact is unknown, possibly tens or hundreds of millions of dollars depending on costs of measures "reasonably necessary" to prevent spread of disease, number and types of cases investigated, testing criminal offenders, and public health care for those denied insurance or employment.

ANALYSIS BY THE LEGISLATIVE ANALYST

Background

Acquired immune deficiency syndrome (AIDS) is a disease that impairs the body's normal ability to resist serious diseases and infections. The disease is caused by a virus—the human immunodeficiency virus (HIV)—that is spread through intimate sexual contact or exposure to the blood of an infected person. At the time this analysis was prepared (June 1988), there was no readily available method to detect whether a person actually has HIV. An HIV antibody test does exist to detect whether a person has ever been infected with HIV and, as a result, has developed antibodies to it. A person infected with HIV may or may not develop AIDS after a period of years. There is no known cure for AIDS, which is ultimately fatal. 2

AIDS became a recognized disease in 1981. Since then about 14,000 persons in California have been diagnosed as having the disease, and about 8,000 of them have died. The State Department of Health Services estimates that possibly 500,000 persons in California are infected with HIV. The department estimates that by 1991 a total of approximately 50,000 AIDS cases will have been identified in the 10 years since AIDS became a recognized disease. 3

Health Officers' Authority to Prevent the Spread of Communicable Diseases. State law gives health officers broad authority to take actions they believe are necessary to protect the public health and to prevent the spread of communicable diseases such as tuberculosis and various venereal diseases, among others. The kind of action taken by health officers varies, depending on how easily the disease is spread from one person to another. For example, health officers may isolate or quarantine individuals infected with a communicable disease, or exclude them from certain jobs, if the health officer believes it is necessary in order to protect the health of others. Health officers may also investigate cases of communicable diseases in order to contact individuals who may have been exposed to a communicable disease. If a health officer carries out such an investigation, the law requires the infected person's identity to be kept confidential. 4

According to the State Department of Health Services, persons 5
who have AIDS and persons who are capable of spreading the HIV are subject to existing communicable disease laws. However, no health officer has ever taken any official action to require persons infected with HIV to be isolated or quarantined, because there is no medical evidence which demonstrates that HIV is spread by casual contact with an infected person. Many health officers, however, have initiated some limited investigation of cases.

Current Testing and Confidentiality Requirements Related to 6
AIDS and HIV Infection. In addition to the laws relating specifically to communicable diseases, there are also laws relating to AIDS and HIV infection. These laws prohibit involuntary HIV antibody testing and require that voluntary test results be kept confidential. These laws also prohibit the use of the HIV antibody test for purposes of determining insurability or employability. With limited exceptions, a person may not be tested for antibodies to HIV without his or her written consent. With few exceptions, no one, except physicians who have been authorized in writing by the person tested, may disclose the results of an HIV antibody test. Anyone making an unauthorized disclosure may be subject to civil penalties or, if the disclosure causes harm to the person tested, the person making the disclosure may be charged with a misdemeanor and punished by imprisonment or a fine, or both. In addition, no one can be compelled to identify an individual who has been tested for HIV antibodies in any criminal or other governmental proceeding, nor can public health records of HIV antibody test results be used in those proceedings.

Current Reporting Requirements for Persons with AIDS and 7
HIV Infection. Current law requires health care providers to report the names of persons with AIDS to local health officers. There are no requirements for reporting the names of persons who have tested positive for HIV infection. However, counties must report to the state the number of cases in which blood tests performed at certain facilities reveal that a person has been infected with HIV.

Existing Laws Governing Investigation of Persons with AIDS 8
and HIV Infection. Although health officers have the authority under existing law to investigate cases of AIDS and HIV infection to identify the sources of infection and persons to whom the infection may have been transmitted, current law does not require health officers to do so. Health officers may alert persons who potentially have been exposed to the virus if the infected person provides written consent to the health officer to do so. If the health officer contacts a person who

may have been exposed to the virus, the health officer must keep confidential the identity of the infected person.

Exposing Others to HIV. Current law does not impose specific 9
criminal penalties on persons who knowingly expose others to HIV. Current law makes no provision for testing of persons charged with crimes to determine whether they are infected with the HIV.

Proposal

This measure makes various changes to existing laws that affect 10
reporting, investigation, confidentiality, and penalties related to HIV infection. The measure also changes references in existing law from testing for HIV antibodies to testing for evidence of infection. The measure contains the following specific provisions:

Reporting and Investigation of HIV-Infected Persons. The mea- 11
sure requires health care providers to report the names of HIV-infected persons to local health officers and requires HIV-infected persons to report their own names and the names of their contacts to local health officers. It also directs local health officers (1) to immediately investigate cases of AIDS and HIV infection and (2) to take all measures "reasonably necessary" to prevent transmission of infection. The measure requires the State Department of Health Services to adopt regulations specifying procedures for case investigation and "reasonably necessary" methods for preventing transmission of HIV infection.

**Elimination of Restrictions on Using HIV Antibody Test Re- 12
sults.** The measure removes current restrictions on using HIV antibody test results for determining insurability or employability of individuals. It also allows use of HIV test results in criminal or civil actions against infected persons and provides that physicians and nurses cannot be held liable for damages resulting from their disclosure of test results to certain persons.

Testing Persons Charged with Crimes. The measure allows in- 13
voluntary HIV testing of persons charged with prostitution, certain sex crimes, or assault by means likely to produce great bodily injury. The state Department of Justice would be required to keep the test results on file and provide them to the courts, legal personnel, and law enforcement agencies upon request.

Criminal Penalties for Persons Who Knowingly Expose Others 14
to the HIV. Anyone who donates blood or engages in prostitution, knowing that he or she is infected with HIV, would be guilty of a felony, punishable by imprisonment in state prison for five, seven, or nine years. In addition, anyone who commits certain crimes (including rape, sexual battery, and assault by means likely to produce great bodily injury), knowing that he or she is infected with HIV, would be sentenced to three additional years in prison for each violation, in addition to the prison term imposed for the sex crime or assault.

Consent and Confidentiality Related to HIV Testing. The mea- 15
sure (1) eliminates the express requirement that consent for an HIV test be in writing and (2) prohibits physicians from being held criminally or civilly liable for disclosing test results without consent to (a) persons who may have been infected by the test subject, such as sexual partners, and (b) other medical personnel involved in treating the test subject. The measure also reduces fines and penalties for violation of provisions requiring that test results be kept confidential.

Protective Clothing. The measure prohibits any employer from 16
inhibiting or interfering with an employee's decision to wear any type of protective clothing, such as gloves or a mask, the employee believes necessary to protect against HIV infection, unless the clothing interferes with the employee's ability to perform his or her job.

Biological Hazard Labels. The measure requires health facilities 17
and clinics to place biological hazard labels on all items soiled by, or containing body fluids of, persons who are HIV-infected.

Compliance with the Measure. Failure to comply with specified 18
provisions of the measure or State Department of Health Services regulations implementing these provisions would be a misdemeanor, punishable by imprisonment in a county jail or a fine or both.

Fiscal Effect

The measure has three potentially major, and a variety of minor or 19
unknown, fiscal effects:

1. *Reporting and Investigation of Cases.* The fiscal impact of this 20
provision could vary greatly depending on the number of persons who test positive for HIV infection, the number of cases investigated, the costs of investigating cases, and the types of measures deter-

mined to be reasonably necessary to prevent transmission of infection. The costs are potentially in the tens of millions of dollars annually. Costs could significantly exceed this amount if additional measures beyond tracing of contacts, such as widespread testing, are determined to be "reasonably necessary" to prevent the spread of the disease.

2. *Elimination of Restrictions on Using Test Results.* The costs of this 21
provision to government health care programs ultimately could be in the tens to hundreds of millions of dollars annually if insurance companies institute HIV testing programs to eliminate or reduce their costs related to AIDS. This is because the annual costs of AIDS care in California will grow substantially over time. Currently, a majority of this care is funded by insurance companies. Allowing insurance companies to deny coverage based on HIV tests could shift a significant portion of these costs to public programs.

Potential costs resulting from employer testing programs are un- 22
known. If a substantial number of people lose their jobs as a result of HIV testing, there could be substantial unemployment compensation and other costs.

3. *Testing of Criminal Offenders.* The fiscal impact of this provision 23
is unknown, but could vary greatly, depending on how it is implemented. If all persons charged with prostitution, sex crimes, or assault by means likely to produce great bodily injury are ordered to submit to blood testing under the measure, the costs to local governments could range up to several hundred thousand dollars annually. However, because the measure does not require HIV testing of all offenders but merely permits it, the costs of this provision could be considerably less.

Minor or Unknown Fiscal Effects. The following provisions 24
would have minor or unknown fiscal effect:

- Imposing additional penalties for persons who knowingly expose others to HIV through sex crimes, certain assaults, or donation of blood
- Changing existing restrictions on disclosure and reporting of HIV test results
- Requiring clinics and health facilities to label items soiled by HIV-infected persons

Summary of Fiscal Effect. In summary, the fiscal impact of this 25
measure is unknown. It could be as high as tens or hundreds of millions of dollars, depending on (1) the types of measures determined to be "reasonably necessary" to prevent further spread of the disease, (2) the costs for investigating HIV cases, (3) the extent of

actions by insurance companies and employers to exclude persons who are HIV-infected, and (4) the number of criminal offenders who would be required to submit to a blood test.

ARGUMENT IN FAVOR OF PROPOSITION 102

Do you believe that infection by the AIDS virus should be treated like 26
any other communicable disease and reported to the health department?

PROPOSITION 102 is specifically designed to stop the spread of 27
AIDS. It does this by requiring confidential reporting to public health authorities.

Although AIDS is treatable, there is no cure—yet. But we *can* stop 28
it from spreading.

Currently, doctors are required to confidentially report to public 29
health authorities cases of venereal disease, such as syphilis. But, if a doctor were to report all who are infected with the AIDS virus, he would be subject to a $10,000 fine and/or up to a year imprisonment.

In short, *UNDER CURRENT LAW, IF A DOCTOR TREATS AIDS* 30
INFECTION LIKE HE WOULD ANY OTHER DISEASE, HE WOULD COMMIT A CRIME.

Under PROPOSITION 102, persons found to be infected with the 31
AIDS virus would be interviewed by the health department so that others with whom they have had sexual contact or shared drug needles can be *confidentially* counseled.

PROPOSITION 102 does *not* call for the quarantine of people with 32
AIDS.

While AIDS is not *curable,* it is *preventable,* which is why it is so 33
important to have the health department contact those who have been unknowingly exposed as well as those who have been unknowingly exposing others.

Current AIDS-related public health laws have been politically 34
motivated and simply don't work.

One fact says it all: THE OVERWHELMING MAJORITY OF 35
THOSE INFECTED BY THE AIDS VIRUS ARE UNAWARE OF THEIR CONDITION OR THE POTENTIAL THREAT THEY MAY POSE TO OTHERS.

For many decades, our public health officers have been con- 36
fidentially *testing, tracing* and *counseling* those with communicable diseases. THE SYSTEM WORKS.

Has "contact tracing" driven people "underground," away from 37
treatment? Of course not. Experience in Colorado with similar laws has shown that many more people have undergone voluntary testing than here in California.

Persons who believe that they may have been exposed to any disease have been able to turn to the public health department in complete reliance upon the time-honored system of confidentiality. 38

PROPOSITION 102 *will* enhance confidentiality by expanding the legal definition of the AIDS test. 39

PROPOSITION 102 *will not* give your employer the right to test you for AIDS without your consent. 40

Health and life insurance premiums will likely increase as a result of the AIDS epidemic. PROPOSITION 102 will help keep the cost of insurance down. 41

With AIDS, the only way to save a life is to prevent infection. That's what PROPOSITION 102 is all about. 42

PROPOSITION 102 is both reasonable and effective. 43

It will help stop the spread of a killer disease while respecting the confidentiality of those affected. It will *save lives* while providing *early* detection for countless thousands of victims. That's why thousands of California physicians support PROPOSITION 102. 44

VOTE "YES" ON PROPOSITION 102. 45

It's *GOOD MEDICINE.* 46

WARREN L. BOSTICK, M.D.
Former President, California Medical Association
Former Dean of the College of Medicine, University of California, Irvine
Former President, American Society of Clinical Pathologists

LAWRENCE J. McNAMEE, M.D.
President, California Physicians for a Logical AIDS Response
Member, Los Angeles County Medical Association Committee on AIDS

PAUL GANN
President, People's Advocate, Inc.

REBUTTAL TO ARGUMENT IN FAVOR OF PROPOSITION 102

Proposition 102 isn't "good medicine." It's a public health nightmare and fiscal disaster. 47

Don't be fooled by the proponents' "medical" arguments. The California Medical Association, California Nurses Association and Health Officers' Association strongly oppose Proposition 102 as being counterproductive to the medical fight against AIDS. 48

The argument for Proposition 102 is based on the simpleminded idea that AIDS is "like any other communicable disease." But all diseases aren't alike, and public health officials have special strategies for dealing with each of them. Proposition 102 would destroy important policies designed by health experts to stop the spread of AIDS. 49

The argument for Proposition 102 is packed with mistruths. 50

Proposition 102 wouldn't "enhance confidentiality"—it actually 51 repeals California's AIDS confidentiality law. Anonymous AIDS testing has been highly successful in reducing the rate of new infections in high-risk communities. Proposition 102 would reverse this important progress.

Proposition 102 wouldn't keep insurance costs down. It would 52
shift millions of dollars of health care costs to the taxpayers.

Proposition 102 wouldn't prevent employers from forcing their 53
employees to be tested—it repeals the law which prevents involuntary testing.

Proposition 102 would drive potentially infected individuals away 54
from voluntary testing which is linked to counseling to educate them about how not to spread AIDS.

Proposition 102 would cost California taxpayers hundreds of mil- 55
lions of dollars and would only make the epidemic worse.

Vital research, treatment and education programs on AIDS would 56
be closed down, endangering the lives of all Californians.

Vote NO on Proposition 102! 57

LEO McCARTHY
Lieutenant Governor

LAURENS P. WHITE, M.D.
President, California Medical Association

ROBERT J. MELTON, M.D., M.P.H.
President, Health Officers' Association of California

ARGUMENT AGAINST PROPOSITION 102

AIDS is a serious public health crisis. It should not be a political 58
football.

Twice before, Californians have overwhelmingly rejected a mis- 59
guided initiative on AIDS that was proposed by a politician with no medical expertise. We must do so again.

Proposition 102 must be defeated for the health and safety of all 60
Californians.

This initiative would cripple the efforts of physicians, researchers 61
and public health officials to halt the spread of AIDS. It would only make the epidemic worse.

Proposition 102 is as extreme and irrational as the AIDS Quar- 62
antine Initiative (Propositions 64 and 69), which voters defeated by margins of two to one. In fact, the proponent of Proposition 102 was the only major public official to support the Quarantine Initiative.

Like the AIDS Quarantine Initiative, Proposition 102 could cost 63
California taxpayers hundreds of millions of dollars to enforce—money that would be far better spent on legitimate needs, including

the prevention and treatment of AIDS. Worse yet, this initiative could cost many Californians their lives by creating a climate of fear that undermines research to find a vaccine and cure for AIDS.

Like the AIDS Quarantine Initiative, Proposition 102 would 64
strongly discourage people from getting tested for AIDS because they could lose their jobs, homes or health care. Thus more people will unknowingly transmit the virus to others and more infected blood will be donated to blood banks. Fewer volunteers will participate in vital research studies and fewer infected people will receive the early treatment which could save their lives.

Proposition 102 is *NOT* about the reporting of AIDS cases. The 65
law already requires that this be done. Rather, this initiative would require the public reporting of all persons who have positive AIDS antibody tests, tests which aren't even always accurate.

Public health officials agree that voluntary, anonymous AIDS 66
testing is one of the single greatest factors contributing to the reduction of new infections in high-risk communities. Proposition 102 would take away from medical professionals this vital tool to control the epidemic.

Like the AIDS Quarantine Initiative, Proposition 102 could force 67
thousands of Californians out of their jobs in our schools and food service industries. It could throw many students out of school. None of them are any threat to the public health because medical science has proven that AIDS is not casually contagious

Like the AIDS Quarantine Initiative, Proposition 102 would create 68
disruption and division in our workplaces, all for no legitimate public health purpose.

Like the AIDS Quarantine Initiative, Proposition 102 would au- 69
thorize widespread "witch hunts" and invasions of the privacy of Californians. The lives of even those who are perfectly healthy could be ruined by misguided people making irresponsible charges.

Proposition 102 is a punitive, political approach to AIDS that is 70
totally at odds with modern medicine and science.

Join us once again in supporting a sane, effective AIDS policy. 71
Send the message again that California voters want medical solutions to AIDS, not politics.

Vote NO on Proposition 102. 72

LAURENS P. WHITE, M.D.
President, California Medical Association

MARILYN RODGERS
President, California Nurses Association

TOM BRADLEY
Mayor, City of Los Angeles

REBUTTAL TO ARGUMENT AGAINST PROPOSITION 102

Quarantine is not necessary to stop the spread of AIDS. That's why 73
PROPOSITION 102 says "nothing contained in this section shall be
construed to require the use of quarantine or isolation."

The record is clear. 74

PROPOSITION 102 *is not* an AIDS quarantine initiative. To sug- 75
gest otherwise only adds to the fear and confusion experienced by the
victims of this terrible disease. Haven't they suffered enough?

The purpose of reporting and contact tracing is to let those who 76
are infected know that they pose a risk to others.

Current law calls for reporting of AIDS patients because that is 77
good public health policy. But there are hundreds of thousands of
others who carry the AIDS virus, *and are contagious,* but have not
developed the advanced disease, yet.

Doesn't it make sense for doctors to report these cases, too? 78

Confidential contact tracing is a fair and effective way to balance 79
the rights of victims with the rights of the public. That's why the
nation's largest medical association has recommended that all states
do it.

Opponents to PROPOSITION 102 say that contact tracing will 80
lead to "witch hunts? We say it's time to stop peddling such fear and
panic.

California's present AIDS policy was proposed by the current 81
mayor of San Francisco, a "politician without medical expertise."

It is a *miserable* failure. 82

PROPOSITION 102 was developed by doctors practicing in com- 83
munities throughout California. It represents doctors doing what
they do best—*saving lives.*

VOTE "YES" ON PROPOSITION 102. 84

LARIMORE CUMMINS, M. D.
Chairman, Santa Cruz County Medical Society AIDS Task Force
Former President, Santa Cruz County Medical Society

WILLIAM E. DANNEMEYER
United States Congressman, California

LAWRENCE J. McNAMEE, M.D.
President, California Physicians for a Logical AIDS Response
Member, Los Angeles County Medical Association Committee on AIDS

Review Questions

1. What are the main provisions of Proposition 102?
2. Cite some of the chief differences between current law and the proposed law.

3. How much money would Proposition 102 have cost the state of California?
4. What do the advocates of Proposition 102 mean when they say, "THE SYSTEM WORKS"?
5. Opponents of Proposition 102 argue that this proposition is "NOT about the reporting of AIDS cases" but rather "persons who have positive AIDS antibody tests." What's the difference?

Discussion and Writing Suggestions

1. This selection actually consists of six separate pieces of writing on Proposition 102. Discuss the logic behind the organization (and relative lengths) of these six pieces of writing. For example, what is the relationship between the "Official Title and Summary Prepared by the Attorney General" section and the other five sections? Between the "Official Title and Summary" and the "Analysis by the Legislative Analyst"?
2. Summarize the debate over Proposition 102 by writing a multiparagraph essay that incorporates the ideas of those favoring the proposal and those opposed to it. You may choose to organize your essay either by a pro-con (or con-pro) pattern or by taking up one issue at a time (for example, required reporting, confidentiality, use of test results, blood donor provisions) and summarizing the pro and con positions on that issue.
3. Based on the arguments you have just read, how might you have voted? Explain the reasons for your vote. To extend this assignment, conduct a special classroom "ballot" and explain why other students voted the way they did. You may want to conduct interviews with some of the "voters."
4. A major point of those favoring Proposition 102 is that AIDS should be treated like any other communicable disease (such as syphilis or typhus), both of which require reporting of confirmed cases by public health authorities. Is this argument convincing to you? Why or why not?
5. Advocates of Proposition 102 believe that "*Confidential* contact tracing [of those who may be infected wth the AIDS virus] is a fair and effective way to balance the rights of victims with the rights of the public." Develop an essay whose thesis is the previous statement, or a negative version of it (i.e., " . . . is *not* a fair and effective way . . .").

   Before developing your response, place yourself both in the position of the "victim" (i.e., the person testing positive for AIDS) and the position of the "public" (i.e., one who has had sexual contact with a person who had tested positive for the AIDS antibody). Does Proposition 102 represent a reasonable "balance" of interests, or does it threaten to overbalance the rights of the victim? Explain.
6. Draft your own initiative for AIDS testing, which takes all the arguments and objections into account.

Postscript: Proposition 102 was defeated, 66 percent to 34 percent.

When a Plague Looms, Society Must Discriminate

RICHARD RESTAK

Do victims of AIDS have the same civil rights as other citizens? That is, perhaps, the main question fueling the controversy over the treatment of persons with AIDS. The lines drawn in this controversy generally set the rights of AIDS victims on one side and the rights of society on the other. To change the metaphor a bit, consider the two sides on opposite ends of a seesaw. Should the two sides be balanced, or should one side overbalance the other? The proponents of Proposition 102 thought that the rights of AIDS victims had overbalanced the rights of society, and they proposed measures they believed would tilt the balance more favorably for society. Opponents argued (successfully) that Proposition 102 would unnecessarily underbalance the rights of AIDS victims by invading privacy, violating confidentiality, and imposing unnecessary restrictions on employability and insurability.

In the following passage, Richard Restak contributes to the debate by arguing that society's rights must take precedence over the rights of persons with AIDS. Restak believes that AIDS is not a civil rights issue but a medical issue. He maintains that until we know more about how AIDS is transmitted, it would be irreponsible not to take measures to protect society at large—even though these measures require some discrimination against AIDS victims.

Restak (b. 1942) practices neurology and psychiatry in Washington, D.C., and has lectured at Georgetown University and many other educational institutions. A member of the clinical faculty at St. Elizabeth's Hospital, Restak has also lectured at government agencies, including the Department of State, the CIA, and the National Aeronautics and Space Agency. He has written numerous articles; and his books include Premediated Man: Bioethics and the Control of Future Human Life *(1975),* The Brain: The Last Frontier *(1979), and* The Self Seekers *(1982).*

Paradoxically, the truly humanitarian position in the face of an AIDS plague is that we not identify with the victims and instead cast our lot with what in earlier times was dubbed the "common good." 1

More than 1 million Americans may have been infected with the AIDS virus. And the 13,000 Americans with confirmed cases of the disease, whose number is doubling every year, should be treated 2

"When a Plague Looms, Society Must Discriminate" by Richard Restak. Originally appeared in *The Washington Post,* September 1985. Reprinted by permission of the author.

with the care and compassion due to anyone who is ill with a so-far incurable and invariably fatal disease. This shouldn't be confused, however, with a refusal to make painful, sometimes anguishing but nonetheless necessary distinctions in the interest of diminishing the likelihood that this awful disease will spread further.

Plagues are not new. They have been encountered in every age 3 and among every nationality: syphilis among the Spanish, bubonic plague among the French, tuberculosis among the Eskimos, polio among Americans.

A NEW RESPONSE

What is new are efforts by medically unsophisticated politicians and 4 attorneys to dictate policy in regard to an illness that has the potential for wreaking a devastation such as has not been encountered on this planet in hundreds of years.

Also different is the response that, in some quarters, is being 5 suggested: Accept the AIDS victim into our schools, place little or no restrictions on employment or housing. The AIDS victims' "rights" in these areas, we are told, should take precedence over the incompletely determined potential for these victims to spread this dread illness.

What some are describing as "discrimination" and "segregation" 6 has a long history in medicine. Quarantines have been effective in beating outbreaks of scarlet fever, smallpox and typhoid in this century. Indeed, by protecting the healthy from the ill we follow a long-established, sensible and ultimately compassionate course. Throughout history true humanitarianism has traditionally involved the compassionate but firm segregation of those afflicted with communicable diseases. Through such a policy diseases have been contained.

Only sentimentalists refuse to make any distinction between the 7 victims of a scourge and those not yet afflicted. Scientists still are unsure why the AIDS virus targets the white blood cells that are the one indispensable element of the body's immune system. But the threat of AIDS demands from us all a discrimination based on our instinct for survival against a peril that, if not controlled, can destroy this society. This is a discrimination that recognizes that caution is in order when knowledge is incomplete. This argument is not a counsel against good medical care or proper concern for AIDS victims. Nor is it a suggestion that we curtail any "civil right" that doesn't potentially imperil the lives of others.

CIVIL RIGHTS

The humanitarian response to AIDS is exactly the opposite of a humanitarian response to sexism or racism: In the presence of considerable ignorance about the causes and effects of the syndrome, the benefit of the doubt should not be given to the victim of AIDS. This is not a civil-rights issue; it is a medical issue. To take a position that the AIDS virus must be eradicted is not to make judgments on morals or life styles. It is to say that the AIDS virus has no civil rights. 8

On Aug. 14 the Los Angeles City Council unanimously approved an ordinance making it illegal to discriminate against AIDS patients in regard to jobs, housing and health care. "We have an opportunity to set an example for the whole nation, to protect those people who suffer from AIDS against insidious discrimination," said the councilman who introduced the measure. . . . 9

Councilman Ernani Bernardi said the ordinance was meant to educate the public to "prevent hysteria." 10

Preventing hysteria is good. But doctors have not yet made up their minds on the degree of contact required for the disease to be spread from one person to another. 11

Consider, for example, the varied and patently contradictory measures put into effect across the country in response to the recent discovery that the AIDS virus can be isolated from a victim's tears. 12

At Boston University, when an AIDS patient is examined, "We are not using the applanation tonometer (a device that tests for glaucoma) because we don't feel we can adequately sterilize it," said the chairman of the department of ophthalmology. 13

The Massachusetts Eye and Ear Infirmary specialists plan to "review our technique." Translation: We're not sure yet what we're going to do. 14

In San Francisco, the chief of the eye service routinely sterilizes his optic instruments with merthiolate, which "as far as I know" kills the AIDS virus. 15

The AIDS virus has been isolated from blood, semen, serum, saliva, urine and tears. If the virus exists in these fluids, wisdom dictates that we assume it can also be transmitted by these routes. 16

It seems reasonable, therefore, that AIDS victims should not donate blood or blood products, should not contribute to semen banks, should not donate tissues or organs to organs banks, should not work as dental or medical technicians and probably should not be employed as food handlers. 17

While the Los Angeles ordinance exempts blood banks and sperm banks, it's prepared to exert the full power of the law against 18 nonconformists who exclude AIDS sufferers from employment in restaurants, hotels, barber shops and dental offices.

According to the new law, then, a person afflicted with AIDS may, if he is properly trained, work as a dental hygienist. He may clean your teeth. He may clean your teeth even if he has a paper cut on one of his fingers of which he is barely aware. This despite the fact that the AIDS virus can be transmitted from bloodstream to bloodstream. 19

The battle lines that are presently forming in regard to the admission of AIDS victims into our nation's schools are similarly disturbing. "This is the test case for the nation," says attorney Charles Vaughn, who represents 13-year-old AIDS victim Ryan White, who has been refused admission to his local school in Kokomo, Ind.* "What happens here will set the trends across the country." (In America there are about 180 children, not all of school age, diagnosed as having AIDS.) 20

To those such as Vaughn who see this issue in civil liberties terms, the plight of Ryan White represents simply another instance of prejudice and discrimination that should be opposed with all of the vigor that has marked the efforts against racism and sexism in the past. In support of their position, they point to the recent directive of the CDC that AIDS cases be evaluated on an individual basis in order to determine whether or not a child should be admitted to school. 21

CDC spokesmen and other AIDS authorities, including Dr. Arye Rubenstein, who treats the largest group of children with AIDS, may be correct in stating that there is "overwhelming evidence that AIDS is not a highly contagious disease." However, in a combined interview, they gave the following responses to an interviewer's questions: 22

Q. Suppose my child got into a fight with an AIDS victim and both began to bleed? 23

A. That kind of fight with a possible exchange of body fluids would arouse some concern about transmission of the virus. 24

Q. What if my child is in a classroom with an AIDS victim who threw up or had diarrhea? 25

A. Such events would be a matter of concern. In its guidelines, the CDC said that AIDS victims who cannot control body secretions should be kept out of ordinary classrooms. 26

Q. Suppose a child with AIDS bit my child? 27

A. Again, a bite would arouse concern. 28

*Ryan White died in May 1990.

Any grade-school teacher can attest that "body-fluid contamination" in the form of scratching, throwing up, diarrhea, biting and spitting are everyday fare within a normal schoolroom. That's why infectious diseases like the flu spread through schools like flash fires. It is difficult to imagine how the CDC or anyone else is going to make individual determinations under such circumstances. 29

What if future research shows that AIDS can be caught in ways other than those already identified? Isn't it more sensible to forgo premature steps against "discrimination" and await scientific developments? 30

A TRUE PLAGUE

AIDS is not about civil rights, political power or "alternative life styles." It's a disease, a true plague that already, in the words of infectious-disease expert Dr. John Seale, writing in the August issue of Britain's *Journal of the Royal Society of Medicine,* is capable of producing "a lethal pandemic throughout the crowded cities and villages of the Third World of a magnitude unparalleled in human history." 31

Further, this disease is only partially understood, is untreatable, and is invariably fatal. For these reasons alone, caution would seem to be in order when it comes to exposing the public to those suffering from this illness. 32

But in addition, the incubation period is sufficiently lengthy to cast doubt on any proclamations, no matter how seemingly authoritative, in regard to the transmissibility of the illness: "The virus may be transmitted from an infected person many years before the onset of clinical manifestations," according to Dr. George Lundberg, editor of the *Journal of the American Medical Association.* "Latency of many years may occur between transmission, infection and clinically manifest disease." 33

Truly authoritative statements regarding AIDS cannot be made. "The eventual mortality following infection . . . cannot be ascertained by direct observation till those recently infected have been followed well into the 21st century," according to Seale. 34

Given these realities, lawyers and legislators should ponder long and hard whether they wish, by means of legal maneuvering, to create situations—child AIDS victims in the schools, adult AIDS victims working in medical or dental offices and other health-care facilities—in which those afflicted are in a position to pass this virus on to the general public. 35

The most pressing issue is to arrive at an understanding of all of 36 the ways in which the AIDS virus spreads. But until we do that, political posturing, sloganeering, hollow reassurances and the inappropriate application of legal remedies to a medical problem can only make matters worse and potentially imperil us all.

Review Questions

1. What kind of conflict does Restak set up in the first paragraph?
2. For what purpose does Restak mention victims of scarlet fever, smallpox, and typhoid?
3. Why does Restak maintain that the state of our knowledge about AIDS is a crucial factor for society in deciding whether or not to pass antidiscrimination legislation?

Discussion and Writing Suggestions

1. In paragraph 8 Restak asserts: "In the presence of considerable ignorance about the causes and effects of the syndrome, the benefit of the doubt should not be given to the victim of AIDS. This is not a civil-rights issue; it is a medical issue." Based on your knowledge of AIDS thus far, to what extent do you agree with Restak?
2. Restak asserts that "political posturing, hollow reassurances and the inappropriate application of legal remedies to a medical problem can only make matters worse and potentially imperil us all." In other words, by bending over backwards to protect the rights of AIDS victims, we may increase the chances of ourselves or our children getting AIDS. Your response?
3. Most literature on AIDS suggests that the disease cannot be spread through casual contact. For example, the Abbott Laboratories pamphlet, while conceding that "[s]hared razors, toothbrushes and other items contaminated with blood can . . . theoretically transmit the [AIDS] virus to subsequent users," and that "any body fluid could play a role in transmission of the virus during intimate contact," also states that "nothing . . . indicates that transmission is possible through sneezing, touching, or other casual contact." And the surgeon general's report on AIDS asserts:

   > There is no known risk of non-sexual infection in most of the situations we encounter in our daily lives. We know that family members living with individuals who have the AIDS virus do not become infected except through sexual contact. There is no evidence of transmission (spread) of AIDS virus by everyday contact even though these family members shared food, towels, cups, razors, even toothbrushes, and kissed each other.

   Restak, however, after surveying responses from various medical facilities (paragraphs 13–15), maintains that the risks of nonsexual transmission of the AIDS virus *may* be great enough so that people with AIDS should be denied the right to employment in restaurants, hotels, barbershops, and dental offices. And in paragraphs 20–29, Restak suggests that AIDS patients who are children should not be permitted to attend the same schools as other children.

Write a multiparagraph essay (perhaps in the form of an editorial) in which you assess these conflicting views on the transmission of the AIDS virus. Are steps against discrimination "premature" and unwise, as Restak suggests? Should we restrict the employment rights of AIDS victims? Should we not permit children with AIDS to attend schools with other children? To help make your assessment, try to place yourself in the various positions of people directly affected by such issues: the parent of a healthy schoolchild, the parent of a schoolchild with AIDS, a dental technician at an office where people with AIDS are treated, a customer at a restaurant where people with AIDS work in the kitchen, a lawyer specializing in civil liberties cases, and so on.

4. Write a critique of Restak's article, drawing on your responses to some of the questions above.

Blaming the Victim

JAMES B. NELSON

While Restak believes that the rights of society take precedence over the rights of people with AIDS, James B. Nelson asserts unapologetically that we should "presume in favor of oppressed minorities." In the following article, Nelson focuses on the homophobia and racism at the heart of many of society's policies and attitudes on AIDS. Agreeing that it is legitimate to strive for a balance between the social good and individual rights, Nelson suggests five principles that should be applied to the policy dilemmas created by AIDS. As you read Nelson's article, compare and contrast his approach to Restak's—as well as to the arguments made by the proponents and opponents of Proposition 102.

James B. Nelson (b. 1930) is professor of Christian ethics at United Theological Seminary of the Twin Cities (Minneapolis and St. Paul, Minnesota). Among his books are Human Medicine: Ethical Perspectives on New Medical Issues *(1973),* Rediscovering the Person in Medical Care *(1976), and* Between Two Gardens: Reflections of Sexuality and Religious Experience *(1983).*

It is increasingly clear that this is an epidemic of extraordinarily serious proportions. If the rate of *infection* has slowed slightly in some areas, the dramatic increases in actual *cases* of AIDS will certainly continue for the foreseeable future. The number of persons in high risk groups exposed to the virus, more over, has increased dramatically. (In San Francisco, the 1980 estimate for gay and bisexual males exposed to the AIDS virus [HTLV-III] was 8 percent; in 1986 the estimate is 80 percent.) In spite of occasional hopeful reports, it is unrealistic to expect either a vaccine or a cure in the near future. Thus, the main hope for containing the epidemic in the next several years will continue to lie mainly in the screening of all donated blood, and in education toward modifying high-risk sexual practices and intravenous drug abuse. 1

We now know that the hysteria over casual transmission has been virtually groundless. Overwhelming data now make it clear that the chances for contracting the virus through nonsexual contact [are] almost negligible. According to Dr. Merle A. Sande, a leading AIDS specialist at San Francisco General Hospital, writing in the February 6 *New England Journal of Medicine,* "It is now time for members of the medical profession, armed with this knowledge, to take a more active and influential role in quelling the hysteria over casual transmission of AIDS. We need to support public and medical officials who oppose universal screening, quarantine, the exclusion of students from classrooms, and the removal of employees, including health care workers, from the work place." 2

The hysteria continues, nevertheless. In AIDS, the fears which surround those two most anxiety-ridden dimensions of human life—sexuality and death—powerfully join together. Add to this the irrational fear of homosexuality in a particularly homophobic society, and there is the prescription for trouble. 3

One of the puzzling and difficult things about the present epidemic is the conjunction of two facts: (1) AIDS as such is *not* "a gay disease"; (2) however, in the U.S. it is strongly associated with gay and bisexual males. (National figures indicate 73 percent; when the New York–Newark area—where high drug incidence accounts for more than half of the cases—is removed from the statistical summary, gay and bisexual males constitute something over 90 percent of the AIDS cases nationally.) And the epidemic crisis—of which, tragically, we are seeing only the beginning—is enormously complicated and magnified by homophobia. White racism is a serious companion complication, given the Haitian/African AIDS connections and the fact that intravenous drug abusers involve a disporportionate number of people of color. The focus of this article on homophobia should in no way blind us to the racism issue. 4

AIDS has become one of history's classic examples of "blaming 5
the victim." The logic seems to go like this: Homosexuality is a freely chosen orientation; because it is both immoral and an illness, one illness leads to another. Further, the logic suggests, since sexual orientation is a perfectly appropriate way of categorizing the essence of human beings, it is perfectly appropriate to treat AIDS as "a homosexual disease"—in spite of the fact that there are no "heterosexual diseases." Thus, a medical diagnosis becomes a moral diagnosis, and vice versa. . . .

PUBLIC AND PRIVATE RIGHTS

In certain ways, the public policy issues now surrounding AIDS 6
seem, on the surface, to be a classic case of individual rights versus the social good. The individual rights at stake are at least of two major types: the right to adequate health care and the right to privacy. Both have been widely affirmed, if not always honored in practice, for all members of our society.

The right to adequate health care for persons with AIDS has been 7
seriously compromised by the slowness of response by many in medicine and government. It is difficult to avoid the conclusion that those at high risk for AIDS did not seem as significant as the populations affected by previous epidemics. Even as medicine has gradually mobilized to cope with this disease, adequate health care in many hospitals is still compromised by fearful staff members who distance themselves from AIDS patients in a variety of ways—in spite of the scientific evidence against casual transmission.

Still another right-to-care issue looms ahead of us. In a society 8
which largely blames the victim for having this disease, will resource allocation for patient care be adequate as numbers and costs dramatically mount?

In ethics and public policy generally, considerations of social 9
good are always relevant and important. Sometimes the social good does indeed demand that individual rights be modified or even curtailed. But those cases should always demand special care and justification. Such has not been the case in regard to persons with AIDS. It is difficult to argue that the nature of medicine's response to AIDS has been justified because large numbers of others have higher health priorities. Likewise, it is difficult to argue that the withdrawal of hospital personnel from patients with AIDS can be justified by the social good of larger numbers of other patients.

The right to privacy shows a similar story. One instance of this 10
right is that of sexual expression between consenting adults. Regard-

ing gays, this right is legally established in only some jurisdictions. The presence of sodomy statutes and the absence of effective civil rights laws in many other areas [testify] to the spottiness of legal protection. In any event, the closing of gay bathhouses in certain cities raises a troublesome and rather complex issue of privacy rights. Though bathhouses are patronized by only a minority of the gay population, their closing represents questionable discrimination against persons who have already borne an undue burden of social prejudice. Empirically, there is evidence that sexual activity in many bathhouses has changed to lower-risk expressions and that frequently these establishments have functioned as educational sites for safer sex practices. Thus, the positive results of these closings are not unambiguously clear. Quite possibly, shutting them may even be counterproductive, not only removing locations for safer sex education for some of the most high risk persons of the high risk group, but also contributing to a climate of alienation which inhibits cooperation with public health efforts. The bathhouse closings frequently have been portrayed as obviously justified by the wider social good. But the case is more complex than that.

Another challenge to privacy rights, potentially much more far- 11
reaching in its impact, is the issue of confidentiality. Who has the right to the names of those who receive an HTLV-III positive blood test? Only the affected individuals? Their sex partners? Employers? Insurance companies? Offices of the city, state, and federal government? The military? It is important to remember that a positive blood test only means *exposure* to the HTLV-III virus. It does not indicate that the individual has or will ever get AIDS. It is also no secret that many groups seriously want possession of this information. Some have already pressed blood-testing centers for such data. When an insurance company argues its right to know on grounds of its own financial self-interest, for example, that argument is still predictably clothed in language of the common good.

If we start from the other end, the social good, important con- 12
siderations also arise. The health of the whole is a legitimate concern of any society. Thus, questions of mass screening, of protecting the blood supply, of protecting health care personnel, of notifying recipients of blood from donors now found to have the virus, of protecting school children, of allocating medical resources in the face of draining expenditures—all are legitimate issues, though in the AIDS crisis they have frequently been compounded by ignorance and fear.

Are there any procedural principles that can bring some clarifica- 13
tion to these hard issues of policy? The following are starters. They will not automatically resolve policy problems. But they—and undoubtedly other principles which should be added—might help to bring some needed perspectives to the policy dilemmas.

1. *Do not separate individual rights and social good from each other.* In the vision of the good community, a foretaste of the Commonwealth of God, there can be no such division. A utilitarian cost-benefit analysis, so frequently employed in policy decisions, always risks the violation of this principle. At best such utilitarian calculus will maximize the fundamental issues of society at large. It seldom offers protection for the rights of minorities. Thus, to those who propose that we quarantine all persons with AIDS, let the question be asked: In addition to the fundamental violation of civil liberties this would involve, what would such a policy do to the whole fabric of society? In addition to the enormous personal costs to those affected, what would be the social costs if resources were spent on quarantine? What might be the costs to everyone's liberty? Do we want to live in such a society? 14

Note that questions such as these involve both individual rights and social good. That is utterly appropriate, and the bias is in the direction of a "no quarantine" judgment. But now, what if the question is not that of quarantining *all* persons with AIDS, but rather just *one?* The man who insists upon continuing his work of male prostitution after a positive diagnosis? The case is not fictional. The decision is difficult. The lesson, I believe, is that no rule is absolute, even a no-quarantine rule. But, however the difficult cases are decided, neither the social good nor individual rights ought to be considered or emphasized apart from each other. 15

2. *Consciously test each policy proposal for elements of homophobia, and racism as well.* Because of these elements, this epidemic is different from any other we have faced. For example, a false-but-powerful contagion theory has long operated concerning sexual orientation ("If we allow gay and lesbian teachers into our elementary schools, our children will 'catch it' "). Now, in spite of clear medical information to the contrary, such contagion fears unconsciously and strongly lap over into AIDS issues ("Don't let that child with AIDS into my child's school"). The insidious and distorting power of homophobic fears needs constant reminder and vigilance. 16

3. *Presume in favor of oppressed minorities.* "God's preferential option for the oppressed" is one of liberation theology's important recoveries from the prophetic biblical tradition. Such a perspective leads to a certain burden-of-proof mentality in assessing policies. There is a presumption in favor of those who are most likely to be hurt. They have already been discriminated against by social structures and practices. Thus, in formulating policies relating to AIDS for cities, state health departments, hospitals, and community agencies, it is extraordinarily important that members of AIDS high-risk groups be strongly represented and carefully heard in all deliberations. 17

4. *Ensure as much self-control as possible by those most directly affected* 18

in the execution of policies. The policy of "contact notification" is a case in point. Gay and bisexual men realistically fear possession by the State of sexual contact names. On the other hand, public health officials (also with some realism) fear that if sexual contact notification is left entirely to the individual's own motivation and sense of responsibility, in some cases it will not happen. But a public agency might contract with a private organization (gay-controlled and gay-trusted) to undertake followup tracing and notifying of sexual contacts. Granted, legal problems would have to be ironed out in this arrangement, but they are not insuperable. The benefits are worth it. The trust and cooperation of the gay community is absolutely essential if this and other measures are to work.

5. *Avoid moralizing the issue at hand.* "Moralizing" means the 19
tendency to sacrifice larger issues of justice and well-being in favor of controlling certain behaviors of which one does not approve. Some people are offended by frank "safer sex" education. But only that educational approach which is sufficiently explicit and erotically appealing may be effective. Yes, some people are offended by the image of sex in the bathhouse. But, as argued above, closing bathhouses may actually be counterproductive in modifying high-risk sexual behaviors, in addition to being a questionable violation of personal rights. Or—to shift the focus to another, if small, high-risk group—some may be offended by the public provision of free sanitary needles to I.V. drug users. But the withholding of needles will scarcely modify the drug practice. Their provision might significantly slow this source of AIDS transmission.

THE CHURCH'S CREATIVE REPENTANCE

We who call ourselves Christian bear major responsibility for the 20
problems created by the AIDS crisis. Over the centuries we have given considerable religious sanction to homophobia. We have been the major institutional legitimizer of compulsory heterosexuality—and the punisher of those who did not conform to that heterosexual norm. Our *metanoia,* our creative repentance, calls us to constructive responses to the current tragedy.

To date, with the notable exceptions of some gay-lesbian min- 21
istries—the Universal Fellowship of Metropolitan Community Churches, and a few scattered urban mainline churches—the response of most church bodies has been hesitant and tardy. Some of the needs are clear: Like any other problem of human suffering and social complexity, the AIDS situation calls for acts of compassion, sensitivity, levelheadedness, and informed public advocacy. A good place to begin is education and communication about the disease and

the needs of those most affected, especially in cooperation with members of the high risk groups themselves. Further, direct acts of caring, service, and compassion are obviously needed, in volunteers for home care, hospitals, hospices, and for support for other care-givers.

Sensitive pastoral care and counseling for those directly affected 22
by the disease are urgent needs. These pastoral needs extend to the families of persons with AIDS. For some, the diagnosis of the disease will also reveal for the first time a son's, brother's, or husband's sexual orientation. If public policies and agencies are to be mobilized more fully, enormous tasks of advocacy need to be undertaken.

Review Questions

1. Why has public reaction to AIDS involved large elements of homophobia and racism, according to Nelson?
2. How does the syndrome of "blaming the victim" apply to AIDS?
3. What are two primary individual rights to which people with AIDS are entitled, according to Nelson?
4. Why does the church bear considerable responsibility for the problems created by the AIDS crisis?

Discussion and Writing Suggestions

1. Nelson is opposed to the closing of gay bathhouses, maintaining that such closings are not necessary for the public good and may even be counter-productive. To what extent do you agree with him?
2. In paragraph 14, Nelson poses a number of questions we should ask ourselves when considering the issue of individual rights versus social good, as it relates to AIDS. He asks, [W]hat would such a policy [of quarantining AIDS victims] do to the whole fabric of society? In addition to the enormous personal costs to those affected, what would be the social costs if resources were spent on quarantine? What might be the costs to everyone's liberty? Do we want to live in such a society?

   In a multiparagraph essay, respond to some of these questions, based on your own understanding of AIDS and your own personal ethics. Consider, also, the question Nelson raises (paragraph 15) of quarantining *one* individual—"the man who insists upon continuing his work of male prostitution after a positive diagnosis."
3. Weigh Nelson's recommendation that we "presume in favor of oppressed minorities" with Restak's belief that the public good outweighs the rights of people with AIDS. Summarize both positions and explain why you believe one is preferable to the other.
4. In paragraph 19, Nelson raises a matter that has caused considerable controversy—the distribution of free, sanitary needles by public health

authorities to intravenous drug abusers. (New York City had such a program in effect.) The rationale for distribution of needles is that it would help prevent the spread of AIDS. Opponents argue that such a policy would give the appearance that the state sanctions drug abuse. In a multiparagraph essay, discuss your views on this matter.

5. Write a critique of Nelson's article, drawing on your responses to some of the questions above.

The Moral Crusade

DENNIS ALTMAN

As Nelson suggests, some of the public attitudes and policies concerning AIDS are based on homophobic attitudes. These attitudes are difficult to combat because they are often based on religious fundamentalist ideas: antigay people will quote the Bible, for instance, to "prove" that God condemns homosexuality and, therefore, so should everybody else. Even among heterosexuals who are not particularly religious, the feeling is often strong that homosexuality is "unnatural" (as is anything different from the majority-ordained norm), and that if this unnatural behavior leads to fearsome consequences, then the perpetrators have been fittingly punished. (In some cases, heterosexuals feel called upon to exact punishment themselves.) In the following selection, Dennis Altman explores the "moral crusade" associated with AIDS, citing various ways in which this crusade manifests itself in public policy.

Dennis Altman (b. 1943), who describes himself as a "libertarian socialist," is a professor of political science at La Trobe University, Australia, and has lectured in the United States at the University of California, Santa Cruz. He has also worked as a news commentator and drama critic for the Australian Broadcasting Commission. Altman is the author of Homosexual: Oppression and Liberation *(1971),* Coming Out in the Seventies *(1979),* Rehearsals for Change *(1980), and* The Homosexualization of America *(1982). The following selection is excerpted from his 1986 book* AIDS in the Mind of America. *Altman has remarked of himself, "My involvement with Gay Liberation, both in the States and in Australia, has made me conscious of the complex nature of repression in contemporary liberal societies, and will undoubtably continue to influence my writings."*

Medicine and religion might seem quite distinct to us who live, despite the efforts of the religious right, in a largely secular age, but they have common origins and even after a century of "modern" medicine (often dated from the nineteenth-century work of Pasteur, Roux and Koch on microorganisms) it is all too easy for doctors unable to explain a disease scientifically to fall back on mysticism. There is a long tradition of explaining illness in terms of God's wrath; the Papal Bull of 1348 saw the Black Death as "the pestilence with which God is afflicting the Christian people" (while the doctors of the time explained it as being due to the triple conjunction of Saturn, Jupiter and Mars in the fortieth degree of Aquarius on March 20, 1345).[1] One wonders if current immunological theories will seem as odd several centuries hence. 1

Six centuries later, God is still perceived as wreaking punishment in much the same way. Perhaps the most extraordinary example of this in regard to AIDS came in an editorial by Dr. James Fletcher which appeared in the *Southern Medical Journal,* an official publication of the Southern Medical Association, in which biblical and scientific sources are melded to claim: 2

> A logical conclusion is that AIDS is a self-inflicted disorder for the majority of those who suffer from it. For again, without placing reproach upon certain Haitians or hemophiliacs, we see homosexual men reaping not only expected consequences of sexual promiscuity, suffering even as promiscuous heterosexuals the usual venereal diseases, but other unusual consequences as well.
>
> Perhaps, then, homosexuality is not "alternative" behavior at all, but as the ancient wisdom of the Bible states, most certainly pathologic. Indeed from an empirical medical perspective alone current scientific observation seems to require the conclusion that homosexuality is a pathologic condition.[2]

One wonders if the students at the Medical College of Georgia, in Augusta, where Dr. Fletcher teaches, might not get a more scientifically respectable education from medieval astrologers.

The AIDS epidemic in the United States coincided with the politicization of religious fundamentalism that began in the late 1970s and was expressed most clearly in the growth of groups like the Moral Majority. This coincidence was more than accidental; the spread of AIDS was linked to changes in sexual and social life which 3

[1]Barbara Tuchman, *A Distant Mirror: The Calamitous Fourteenth Century* (New York: Knopf, 1978), pp. 103–4.

[2]James Fletcher, "Homosexuality: Kick and Kickback," *Southern Medical Journal,* Feb. 1984, p. 149.

in turn were part of a general shift in mores which created anxiety among those who saw their traditional values under siege and were attracted to the certainties of the religious right. It is hardly surprising—though it may make one wonder about Christian charity—that the spokespersons for the new right, already prone to cite the acceptance of homosexuality as a sign of the current degeneracy, were quick to seize upon AIDS as fodder for their argument.

4 Perhaps because most people are not very receptive to attacks on those who are ill and dying, the new right has made use of AIDS less wholeheartedly than one might have expected. Indeed, Jerry Falwell, whose Moral Majority is one of the best-known components of the new right, has denied saying that "AIDS is the wrath of God upon homosexuals," although many reporters claim to have heard him.

5 Certainly Falwell has invoked AIDS a number of times, most strongly in July 1983, when he used the analogy of brucellosis to advocate the quarantine of homosexuals, acknowledging that this was unlikely because "homosexuals constitute a potent voting bloc and cows do not." He went on to advocate the closing of gay bathhouses and back-room bars, punishment for gays who donated blood and "firm guidelines" for those in contact with high-risk groups.[3] These views were taken up again in mid-1985, when Falwell launched a new campaign "to fight the spread of the deadly AIDS disease."[4] Falwell's views were to be echoed by a number of others, and not only in the United States; in Australia the leader of the local Festival of Light echoed the call for quarantine. In the United States an organization called the American Family Association sought support for a petition to the Surgeon General, Dr. Everett Koop, himself a sympathizer of the new right:[5]

> Dear Family Member:
>
> Since AIDS is transmitted primarily by perverse homosexuals your name on my national petition to quarantine all homosexual establishments is crucial to your family's health and security. . . . If you want your family's health and security protected, these AIDS-carrying homosexuals must be quarantined immediately. . . . These disease-carrying deviants wander the streets unconcerned, possibly making you their next victims. What else can you expect from sex-crazed degenerates but selfishness?[6]

---

[3]See *The New York Native,* Aug. 1, 1983.

[4]Letter reprinted in *The New York Native,* July 15, 1985.

[5]Koop later alienated himself from the new right by his new thinking on AIDS and other public health matters [Behrens & Rosen].

[6]Quoted by Cindy Patton, "Illness as Weapon," *Gay Community News,* June 30, 1984.

Subsequent mailings from the Moral Majority also advocated excluding homosexuals from food handling.

6 Other religious-right groups made similar proposals. In the summer of 1983 a group called the Pro-Family Christian Coalition sought to prohibit the Reno Gay Rodeo from taking place, claiming it would cause a health crisis and using, once again, the argument that "close contact" could be contagious. A full-page advertisement in Nevada's papers was headed "AIDS Alert," but the agenda of the group was a broader homophobia; one of the group—a minister—was quoted as saying: "I think we should do what the Bible says and cut their throats." After considerable press controversy and a large public forum the local county commission refused to act against the rodeo.[7]

7 Some religious zealots have sought to "convert" homosexuals—both to Christianity and to heterosexuality—by playing on the fear of AIDS, and in one case a group entered the AIDS ward in San Francisco General Hospital under the guise of delivering toiletries and began to "witness" (i.e., proselytize).[8] Most involved in the work of sexual conversion is a New York–based group known as Aesthetic Realists, who claim to possess a "cure" for homosexuality and who invaded a panel on AIDS at a meeting of the New York Academy of Sciences in 1983 to promote their philosophies.[9]

8 Moralistic attacks inspired by AIDS have clear implications for the behavior of governments. In debates over decriminalizing homosexual behavior—still a crime in almost half the American states, in Israel, in New Zealand and in several Australian states—or in arguments over including homosexuals within the ambit of anti-discrimination laws, AIDS is increasingly invoked. Anti-gay doctors were paraded before the Virginia House of Delegates in 1984 to oppose the repeal of the state's anti-sodomy law, and in Duluth, Minnesota, voters repealed a human rights law in which fear of AIDS was an issue.[10] When the Australian state of New South Wales decriminalized homosexuality in 1984, a Liberal Party front-bencher attacked homosexuals as responsible for AIDS, adding: "I hope they do not find a cure for it."[11] AIDS was invoked in a ferocious campaign spearheaded by the New Zealand Salvation Army in 1985 to prevent that country decriminalizing homosexuality.

---

[7]See Allen White, "Reno Rodeo Will Go On," *Bay Area Reporter,* July 28, 1983.

[8]Allen White, "Fundamentalists Make Hay Out of AIDS Dead and Dying," *Bay Area Reporter,* March 29, 1984.

[9]See Bob Nelson, "New York Groups Counter AIDS Hysteria," *Gay Community News,* Dec. 31, 1984.

[10]*The Advocate,* March 20, 1984; "Viewpoint," *Bay Area Reporter,* Sept. 20, 1984.

[11]*The Star* (Sydney) (editorial), May 31, 1984.

9 The best examples of the confluence of religious, medical and political stigmatization due to AIDS occurred in Texas, where the "Dallas Doctors against AIDS" have invoked the disease to sponsor legislation that would overturn a 1982 District Court decision (*Baker* v. *Wade*) which declared the state's anti-sodomy law unconstitutional because it infringed the right to privacy. (At the same time the Amarillo district attorney invoked AIDS in an unsuccessful argument against the decision before a U.S. Court of Appeals.) Using both medical and religious evidence, and equally careless with both, the group has been active in lobbying against gay rights. (They also supported a move to ban the gay student group of Texas A. and M. University.) In the campaign that led up to a referendum in Houston in January 1985 on the city's policy of non-discrimination against gays in employment, the threat of AIDS was frequently invoked: "The medical problems associated with homosexuality," began one pamphlet, "impact on us all. Since the diseases of one segment of society are often transmitted to others, it is in the collective interest to inhabit as disease-free a society as is possible."[12] The anti-gay position was upheld by a large majority, and AIDS clearly played a role.[13]

10 Prejudice against homosexuals sparked by AIDS ranges from the trivial, such as Joan Collins' attacks on homosexual "moral laxity,"[14] to the serious, as in reports of violence in which AIDS is the spark:

> They were chasing the gays with sticks and stones and shouting "unclean." Hate was in their voices. Their eyes were bloodshot. They were about 20 of them, all teenagers. They were macho and they were drunk.
>
> "Faggots got AIDS. Faggots got AIDS," they screamed, hitting gay men and lesbian women on the shoulders and legs with sticks.
>
> A big hulk of a kid with slow eyes threw a rock at a lesbian.
>
> "You're diseased," he said.
>
> It was a scene of gang brutality out of the movie *Clockwork Orange.*
>
> It happened in San Francisco, in bucolic Sigmund Stern Grove, on a Sunday afternoon last summer when a homophobic rat pack attacked a picnic sponsored by the gay Catholic group Dignity.[15]

In another incident in San Francisco the AIDS Foundation received an anxious call from someone who had helped beat up a man with AIDS—and was worried about his chances of infection. Other reports suggest a marked increase in anti-gay violence since AIDS.[16]

---

[12]Jo Baker, "Houston to Vote on Gay Rights Issues," *The Advocate,* Sept. 4, 1984.

[13]See "Houston Voters Reject Gay Rights 4–1," *Update,* Jan. 23, 1985.

[14]Nathan Fain, "Yet Another Injured Foot," *The Advocate,* April 17, 1984.

[15]Warren Hinckle, "Cop Makes It Safer for Gays," *San Francisco Chronicle,* Oct. 1, 1984.

[16]See Peter Freiberg, "Antigay Violence," *The Advocate,* Dec. 22, 1983.

Review Questions

1. How does Altman link the growth of the Moral Majority and other fundamentalist groups with the AIDS epidemic?
2. What are the chief ways in which religious fundamentalists and antigay activists have attempted to express their views on AIDS?

Discussion and Writing Suggestions

1. Write a letter to Dr. James Fletcher, responding to his editorial in the *Southern Medical Journal.* Or write a letter to the American Family Association, whose petition to Dr. Everett Koop Altman quotes in paragraph 5.
2. To what extent would you classify Restak's article ("When a Plague Looms, Society Must Discriminate") as an example of the "Moral Crusade" of which Altman writes? Explain.
3. Write about an event in your own life (or the life of someone you know) in which you were accused of being immoral, when, as far as you were concerned, there was no moral aspect to your behavior. (A trivial example: You were accused of being a "bad" child because you wouldn't eat your spinach.) Discuss the matter both from the point of view of yourself and the person making the accusation. Conclude with a reconsideration of how (if at all) you might have avoided—or answered—the accusation.
4. Altman discusses many examples of intolerance. How might it be possible to deal with, or counteract, such intolerance? In a multiparagraph essay, suggest several ways of doing so and explain how they might work. Are some groups or people more amenable to changing their views than others? Is it likely that one could change the mind of someone like Jerry Falwell?
5. Altman's footnotes indicate the considerable number of sources on which he drew. Select five to seven of his sources and summarize the information he used from each source.

Identify All the Carriers

WILLIAM F. BUCKLEY

The AIDS debate, by its very nature, is highly controversial. Some of the extremes in this controversy have been noted by Dennis Altman in "The Moral Crusade" (in which one minister [!] is quoted as saying of

---

homosexuals: "I think we should do what the Bible says and cut their throats"). Leaving out this lunatic fringe, one of the more controversial proposals on the AIDS crisis has come from a man who prides himself on outraging his critics, William F. Buckley, Jr.

Buckley (b. 1925) is probably America's best-known and most influential conservative writer. A graduate of Yale University (his first book, published in 1951, was an attack on Yale, entitled God and Man at Yale: The Superstitions of "Academic Freedom"*), he founded and continues to edit* The National Review, *a bi-weekly bible of conservative thought. In 1965, he ran as the Conservative party candidate for mayor of New York City (and was resoundingly defeated). Among his numerous political books are* Up from Liberalism *(1959),* The Unmaking of a Mayor *(1965), and* United Nations Journal: A Delegate's Odyssey *(1974). He has also produced several books on sailing and eight espionage novels. His syndicated column, "On the Right," appears three times a week. He also hosts a weekly television interview show, "Firing Line." Even those who abhor Buckley's ideas admire his energy, his wit, and his flair. One critic remarked that "Buckley excels in the use of language, the sparkling epigram, and biting sarcasm that penetrates to the heart of a matter."*

However, for those who have not previously encountered it, Buckley's prose may be a bit difficult. A brief summary may be helpful. At the outset of this editorial, Buckley refers to the two sides in the AIDS debate—the sides we have used as reference points thoughout this chapter: those who believe that in combatting AIDS the civil liberties of individuals should be primary (School A) and those who believe that the public welfare should be primary (School B). After summarizing the positions of both sides, he adopts a question-and-answer format—the questioner representing School A; the answerer, School B. School B then offers a series of suggestions for dealing with the AIDS crisis. It is the final suggestion that caused an uproar.

I have read and listened, and I think now that I can convincingly crystallize the thoughts chasing about in the minds of, first, those whose concern with AIDS victims is based primarily on a concern for them and for the maintenance of the most rigid standards of civil liberties and personal privacy, and, second, those whose anxiety to protect the public impels them to give subordinate attention to the civil amenities of those who suffer from AIDS and primary attention to the safety of those who do not. 1

Arguments used by both sides are sometimes utilitarian, sometimes moral, sometimes a little of each—and almost always a little elusive. Most readers will locate their own inclinations and priorities somewhere other than in the polar positions here put forward by design. 2

School A suspects, in the array of arguments of School B, a venture in ethical opportunism. Look, they say, we have made enormous headway in the matter of civil rights for all, dislodging the straight-laced from mummified positions they inherited through eclectic superstitions ranging from the Bible's to Freud's. A generation ago, homosexuals lived mostly in the closet. Nowadays they take over cities and parade on Halloween and demand equal rights for themselves qua homosexuals, not merely as apparently disinterested civil libertarians. 3

Along comes AIDS, School A continues, and even though it is well known that the virus can be communicated by infected needles, known also that heterosexuals can transmit the virus, still it is both a fact and the popular perception that AIDS is the special curse of the homosexual, transmitted through anal sex between males. And if you look hard, you will discern that little smirk on the face of the man oh-so-concerned about public health. He is looking for ways to safeguard the public, sure, but he is by no means reluctant, in the course of doing so, to sound an invidious tocsin whose clamor is a call to undo all the understanding so painfully cultivated over a generation by those who have fought for the privacy of their bedroom. What School B is really complaining about is the extension of civil rights to homosexuals. 4

School A will not say all that in words quite so jut-jawed, but it plainly feels that no laws or regulations should be passed that have the effect of identifying the AIDS carrier. It isn't, School A concedes, as if AIDS were transmitted via public drinking fountains. But any attempt to segregate the AIDS carrier is primarily an act of moral ostracism. 5

School B does in fact tend to disapprove forcefully of homosexuality, but tends to approach the problem of AIDS empirically. It argues that acquired immune deficiency syndrome is potentially the most serious epidemic to have shown its face in this century. Summarizing currently accepted statistics, the *Economist* recently raised the possibility "that the AIDS virus will have killed more than 250,000 Americans in eight years' time." Moreover, if the epidemic extended to that point, it would burst through existing boundaries. There would then be "no guarantee that the disease will remain largely confined to groups at special risk, such as homosexuals, hemophiliacs and people who inject drugs intravenously. If AIDS were to spread through the general population, it would become a catastrophe." Accordingly, School B says, we face a utilitarian imperative, and this requires absolutely nothing less than the identification of the million-odd people who, the doctors estimate, are carriers. 6

How? 7

Well, the military has taken the first concrete step. Two million 8 soldiers will be given the blood test, and those who have AIDS will be discreetly discharged.

Discreetly, you say! 9

Hold on. I'm coming to that. You have the military making the first massive move designed to identify AIDS sufferers—and, bear in mind, an AIDS carrier today is an AIDS carrier on the day of his death, which day, depending on the viral strain, will be two years from now or when he is threescore and 10. The next logical step would be to require of anyone who seeks a marriage license that he present himself not only with a Wassermann test but also an AIDS test. 10

But if he has AIDS, should he then be free to marry? 11

Only after the intended spouse is advised that her intended husband has AIDS, and agrees to sterilization. We know already of children born with the disease, transmitted by the mother, who contracted it from the father. 12

What then would School B suggest for those who are not in the military and who do not set out to get a marriage license? Universal testing? 13

Yes, in stages. But in rapid stages. The next logical enforcer is the insurance company. Blue Cross, for instance, can reasonably require of those who wish to join it a physical examination that requires tests. Almost every American, making his way from infancy to maturity, needs to pass by one or another institutional turnstile. Here the lady will spring out, her right hand on a needle, her left on a computer, to capture a blood specimen. 14

Is it then proposed by School B that AIDS carriers should be publicly identified as such? 15

The evidence is not completely in as to the communicability of the disease. But while much has been said that is reassuring, the moment has not yet come when men and women of science are unanimously agreed that AIDS cannot be casually communicated. Let us be patient on that score, pending any tilt in the evidence: If the news is progressively reassuring, public identification would not be neccessary. If it turns in the other direction and AIDS develops among, say, children who have merely roughhoused with other children who suffer from AIDS, then more drastic segregation measures would be called for. 16

But if the time has not come, and may never come, for public identification, what then of private identification? 17

Everyone detected with AIDS should be tatooed in the upper forearm, to protect common-needle users, and on the buttocks, to prevent the victimization of other homosexuals. 18

You have got to be kidding! That's exactly what we suspected all along! You are calling for the return of the Scarlet Letter, but only for homosexuals! 19

Answer: The Scarlet Letter was designed to stimulate public obloquy. The AIDS tattoo is designed for private protection. And the whole point of this is that we are not talking about a kidding matter. Our society is generally threatened, and in order to fight AIDS, we need the civil equivalent of universal military training. 20

Review Questions

1. What is the difference between School A and School B?
2. In paragraph 4, the following statement—written in Buckleyese—appears: "And if you look hard, you will discern that little smirk on the face of the man oh-so-concerned about public health. He is looking for ways to safeguard the public, sure, but he is by no means reluctant, in the course of doing so, to sound an individual tocsin whose clamor is a call to undo all the understanding so painfully cultivated over a generation by those who have fought for the privacy of the bedroom." Paraphrase this statement in plain English.
3. In addition to the tatooing of people who test positive for AIDS, what other steps does Buckley advocate?

Discussion and Writing Suggestions

1. Among the selections reprinted so far in this chapter, which ones do you believe are in Buckley's School A? School B? Cite particular statements in those selections that appear to confirm your judgment. (For example, have you seen the argument Buckley makes in paragraph 16 elsewhere in this chapter?) Of what school is Buckley himself? How do you know? Cite specific statements.
2. Write a letter to Buckley, responding to his suggestion that persons determined to have AIDS should be tatooed. Take into account both the anonymous questioner's immediate response (paragraph 19) and Buckley's rejoinder (paragraph 20).

Postscript

To no one's surprise, Buckley's proposal generated considerable controversy. Buckley himself, while not backing off an inch, took note of the reaction in a column in his *National Review:*

> What about requiring anyone who has AIDS to be tattooed, discreetly, to protect against nonchalant spreading of the disease? I ventilated that thought recently and have got angry denunciations from the people one would least expect, namely gays (they so identified themselves, in most cases, over the phone). But they would be the principal beneficiaries of such a social contrivance, even as pedestrians are the principal beneficiaries of reins on drunk drivers. One or two calls were so thoughtless as to compare the tattooing of AIDS carriers to the tattooing

practiced by Hitler, the obvious distinction being that Hitler was advancing the cause of genocide, whereas the other proposal seeks to advance the longevity of uninfected gays.[1]

And in an editorial entitled "Stigmatizing the Victim," *The Nation* distastefully noted Buckley's proposal, along with an even more extreme one calling for a "Star of David" concept of "mandatory and overt identification" of AIDS victims. The editorial concluded:

> Perhaps pink triangles would better make the historical point. [In Nazi Germany, Jews were required to publically identify themselves by wearing yellow Stars of David.] Add that to the plans for homosexual concentration camps recommended not only by the La Rouchies, but also by responsible physicians and respectable politicians, and a final solution[2] does not seem out of the question.[3]

Straight Talk

JOHN TIERNEY

AIDS is a disease that primarily affects homosexuals and intravenous drug abusers. Statistics indicate, however, not only that AIDS is spreading at an alarming rate but also that it is spreading into the general (i.e., heterosexual) population. As a result, AIDS hysteria has also spread among heterosexuals, particularly among those whose life-style involves casual sex with a variety of partners. And to a great extent, it is this hysteria that is responsible for the increasing homophobia that seeks laws or regulations restricting or revoking the civil rights of gays.

*But how serious a threat is AIDS to the general population? Just how reliable are those statistics purporting to show that heterosexuals can contract the AIDS virus almost as easily as homosexuals? And how crucial is it for "straights" to modify their sexual behavior in an attempt to avoid AIDS? These are some of the questions that John Tierney attempts to answer in the following article. (*Note: *The title is a pun. Be advised also that the author explicitly discusses sexual practices, which you may find offensive.)*

[1]*National Review* 25 Apr. 1986:26–27.

[2]The "final solution" was the name the Nazis gave to their program for exterminating the Jews.

[3]From editorial "Stigmatizing the Victim" in *The Nation,* April 12, 1986

Tierney is a freelance reporter. This article originally appeared in Rolling Stone *on November 17, 1988.*

SNOOPING FOR THE BREAKOUT

One April morning in 1630, as the Black Plague was starting to ravage Milan, the town's inhabitants woke up to find mysterious spots on their doors. The citizenry turned to astrologers and other seers, who were currently in high repute—after all, they had seen a comet two years earlier and correctly predicted that a plague was on the way. This time their conclusions were even more alarming: the spots had been daubed by Satan, a.k.a. the Demon of the Pestilence. Apparently not satisfied with a random epidemic, the Demon wanted to poison *all* of Milan. 1

People became terrified of touching anything or anyone. Suspected accomplices of Satan were tortured on the rack and executed. A man announced in the marketplace that he had gone for a ride in the Demon's chariot. Satan, a dark-skinned, longhaired figure with fire flashing from his black eyes, took the old man to a palace in Milan filled with chattering skeletons, a senate of ghosts monitoring the epidemic, a black rock gushing poisoned water into the ground and lots of pestiferous salve to daub on doors. The old man's tale was quickly confirmed by scores of others. They, too, had seen the Demon of the Pestilence and heard the chariot, louder than thunder, rumbling through the streets at midnight. 2

I started thinking about the seers and the Demon when Masters and Johnson announced this year that the AIDS virus could lurk on toilet seats. Perhaps this was unfair of me. Masters and Johnson could turn out to be right about AIDS spreading rampantly, among heterosexuals, and in any case they weren't the first to terrify the American populace. That distinction probably belongs to *Life* magazine's cover: NOW NO ONE IS SAFE FROM AIDS. It ran in the summer of 1985, a time when it was easy to believe the doomsayers—after all, they had been right several years earlier in predicting that this strange new virus would cause a horrific plague among homosexual men and drug addicts. Now researchers had seen signs of a new peril: the AIDS virus was beginning to poison the rest of the population. 3

This "rapidly spreading" epidemic, said Secretary of Health and Human Services Otis R. Bowen, could make the Black Plague "pale by comparison." Alarming reports came in about AIDS in African heterosexuals and Floridian mosquitoes. The virus was sighted in saliva and teardrops. It was reported to be breaking out from the 4 known risk groups to heterosexual soldiers, to prostitutes and to the singles-bar habitués chronicled in *Crisis: Heterosexual Behavior in the Age of AIDS,* the book by William H. Masters, Virginia E. Johnson and Robert C. Kolodny. Another noted sex therapist, Helen Singer Kaplan, wrote a book, *The Real Truth About Women and AIDS,* warning that condoms weren't foolproof, French kissing was a risk, and the smart woman should consider alternatives. "Dry humping," Kaplan noted, "is *ultrasafe.* If you are careful you can press together in the nude. But, again watch out! This can be very exciting! Do not let yourself be tempted to go beyond the bounds of safety!"

And so spread the highly contagious AIDS Angst. A Gallup Poll 5
last year found that fifty-one percent of Americans think AIDS will become epidemic in the general population. Victims have been driven out of schools, hospitals, neighborhoods, jobs. This year a politician in New York City helped shut down an AIDS counseling center because he claimed the patients might infect children at an elementary school—two blocks away. Almost half the American teenagers surveyed by the federal government were unwilling to share a classroom with an AIDS patient. In the recent national ROLLING STONE survey of Americans aged eighteen to forty-four, nearly half the respondents said they avoid contact with homosexuals for fear of AIDS.

Dispatches from the singles scene now wax on monogamy, citing 6
authorities like the bartender in Philadelphia who has observed a sharp decrease in cars left overnight in the parking lot—people are going home alone. In the ROLLING STONE survey, forty-four percent of the single people said AIDS had caused them to change their lifestyle, typically by refraining from casual sex. My own unscientific survey has found that 100 percent of married people now take smug pleasure in announcing, "Thank *God* I'm not single these days."

But has anyone actually seen the AIDS Demon? Is there evidence 7
for the dread Heterosexual Breakout? The answer depends on which statistics and reports you prefer to heed. You can conclude that it's only prudent to be worried, or you can decide that the seers are self-serving alarmists. I can't make your choice for you, but I can tell you what I decided after looking at the statistics and seeing how the numbers were gathered. I undertook the search partly as a theoretical exercise, to examine how Americans choose their risks and when they decide to panic. Mainly, though, I was interested in the two practical questions of the day for a heterosexual who doesn't inject anything into his veins. Am I going to die from this virus? Do I really need to use a condom?

THE KOJAK OF AIDS

Anastasia Lekatsas remembers one man as the turning point, the case that set her on the way to becoming America's most dogged snooping street detective of AIDS. It was in 1984, when the epidemic was three years old and researchers were anxiously looking for the first signs of the Heterosexual Breakout. New York City, with a quarter of the nation's AIDS cases and a large population of bisexual men and heterosexual drug users, seemed the most logical place for it, and at Bellevue Hospital there was an NIR case: an AIDS patient classified as No Identified Risk, because he didn't fit any of the categories (homosexual or bisexual men, intravenous drug abusers, hemophiliacs, recipients of blood transfusions, persons from Haiti or Africa or sex partners of anyone in a risk group). 8

The patient was a middle-aged Hispanic maintenance worker, a widower with children. Lekatsas, then thirty-four, a Greek immigrant with a thin, aquiline face and intense dark eyes, was the coordinator of investigations for the AIDS Surveillance Unit of the New York City Department of Health. She went to the man's hospital room and shut the door behind her. This is how Lekatsas recalls the conversation at his bedside: 9

"I have this terrible problem," she began. 10

"What's your problem?" he said. 11

"I've come here to make you feel bad." 12

"What do you mean?" 13

"You told your doctor that you got infected by having sex with female prostitutes, and I don't believe you." 14

"Why not?" 15

"I don't think you can get it that way." 16

Silence from the man. 17

"Do you think," Lekatsas asked, "that one of those prostitutes might have actually been a man?" 18

"No." 19

"It's really important that you share the truth with me." 20

"Why?" 21

"Does the nurse's aide bring your food to your bed?" 22

"Yes." 23

"Does your doctor come in to see you?" 24

"Yes." 25

"The reason those people aren't afraid to come near you is that we think we understand the way this is transmitted. That's why my research is important. Now, do you think one of those prostitutes could have been a man?" 26

"I don't think so." 27

"Look, I'm not going to share this information with your doctor. 28
It's just a number at the health department. Do you think one of those prostitutes could have been a man?"

"I don't remember." 29

"Why don't you close your eyes—you don't have to look at me. 30
I'm not here to make a judgment. And I'm not going to think you're a homosexual if you've had sex with a man one time. Do you think one of those prostitutes could have been a man?"

The man closed his eyes, said yes and started to cry. Then he 31
spent two hours telling how a woman had taken advantage of him after his wife's death and how in his bitterness he had started snorting cocaine at social clubs and ended up having sex with men. Lekatsas started crying too, and she didn't bother going through the sixteen-page questionnaire she had brought. This NIR case was solved.

"I discovered a couple of crucial things that afternoon about 32
getting people to admit they're lying," Lekatsas says. "One is that you have to try to give them a reason to tell you the truth. The other is that you have to free up the person. You have to give them a chance to say that it happened once, or that it might have been a man in drag. I don't believe anyone who ever confessed to me that he had a one-time blow job from a man really did have only that one blow job. But you can't say to him, 'Come on now, you were anal receptive, weren't you?' You can't take away all his cards."

This is not the way that most scientists gather statistics, which is a 33
crucial point to remember when considering *any* research on AIDS. Those alarming stories about non–drug-using heterosexuals getting AIDS, those statistics quoted so authoritatively in newspapers—utlimately, they're based on what people chose to tell health officials. It would be more accurate to say "alleged non–drug-using heterosexuals." Researchers have become more conscientious about interviewing and reinterviewing subjects in AIDS studies, but many still rely on the kind of questionnaire that would never have induced that man in Bellevue to confess his bisexuality.

"They use the questionnaires because it's easier," Lekatsas says. 34
"You can go down the list and not really confront the person with these painful issues—you can withdraw into the questionnaire. But it's not the way to get the truth. In my experience, only once did someone really get something from a questionnaire. There was a young guy from the navy, and his doctor reported that he was a heterosexual. So we sent a worker over, and the guy said no to the questions about homosexuality or bisexuality, and the worker kept going through the form. There was a question, "What percentage of

the time during sex did you or your partner insert a fist in the rectum?' He answered, 'Fifty percent.' I think he didn't realize that heterosexuals don't do that. So we kept investigating, and eventually we found out that he was homosexual."

Because it's simpler to lie when asked a yes-or-no question ("Have you ever had sex with a man?"), Lekatsas and her fellow investigators used open-ended questions ("Tell me about your sex life") or an indirect approach ("When was the last time you had sex with a man?"). When the questions didn't work, it was time for detective work. Lekatsas would ask the patient for permission to speak to relatives, friends or employers. 35

"There's always *somebody* who knows the truth," she says. "The trick is being motivated to find that someone. You have to pick up on anything that seems suspicious—someone's mannerisms, what they're evasive about, any clue. I went to visit one patient who claimed he'd gotten infected by giving mouth-to-mouth resuscitation to a Haitian. This man had just immigrated from Poland, but he wasn't living in a Polish neighborhood like other new immigrants. He was wearing pink socks, and there was a wok in his apartment. I know it sounds irrational, but I thought this all just didn't add up. Why would someone just arrived from Poland own a wok? Why would he live so far from the other immigrants? He claimed he was living alone, but I suspected someone else lived there, probably a man. He never admitted that, but he did finally say that he'd had homosexual experiences. 36

"I interviewed another man in the hospital. He's fifty-seven years old and married. His hair's dyed, he's very trim and fit, and he tells me that he exercises on his balcony in the morning. He says that he hasn't had sex with his wife in seven years because he's impotent. And he's lying in bed, obsessively looking down and rearranging the sheets—and the only thing I can figure is that he's checking to see if he has an erection. 37

"I said, 'Didn't it bother you that you were impotent?' He said, 'No, I'm an old man.' To me this was a lie—here's a guy completely attentive to himself, dyeing his hair, exercising every morning. He wouldn't admit anything to me, but I sent in a young gay caseworker later, and he admitted not only that he'd had sex with men, but that he was anal receptive." 38

The investigations often went on after the patient's death. Lekatsas solved one case three years after a man had died claiming that he'd been infected at work by handling the garbage of AIDS victims. Lekatsas tracked down the widow, who stood by the story and said she didn't know where any of her husband's relatives or friends were. Lekatsas suspected the widow was afraid of losing her pension 39 if she said anything. "I just begged and begged her until she told me the name of a friend of her husband." This friend was evasive in phone call after phone call but eventually provided the address of the victim's mother. Lekatsas paid her a visit in the Bronx.

"It was such a sad situation," Lekatsas recalls. "Here she'd lost her son, and I was bothering her, and I felt awful. I apologized and tried to be as discreet as I could. 'Do you have any idea how your son could have gotten this infection?' I asked. The mother was much calmer than I was. She just looked at me and said matter-of-factly, 'Well, he shot drugs.' " 40

. . .

SHOULD DR. KAPLAN'S HUSBAND WEAR A CONDOM?

> You are twenty-seven years old, and you have just broken up with your boyfriend. You are lonely and looking for a new romance. You are sharing a summer house at the shore with a bunch of friends, and your roommate brings her handsome, curly-haired, sensitive, brilliant cousin who has just graduated from Harvard Law School out for the weekend. He is attracted to you; you are attracted to him. It is a beautiful starry night. Everyone else who is sharing the house is married or engaged and paired up. 41
>
> Now what? 42

This scenario is in Helen Singer Kaplan's book *The Real Truth About Women and AIDS*. Kaplan, whose career has been devoted to helping people enjoy sex (she runs a sexuality program at the New York Hospital–Cornell Medical Center), has a discouraging answer for the young woman, not to mention the curly-haired lawyer: "Three years ago, you might have gone to bed with him. Now you really can't." 43

What exactly can this couple do? "Dry sex," as Kaplan calls it. She thinks that even a strictly heterosexual man is a risk if he's had a few other partners recently, so it's better not to have intercourse with him—even if he wears a condom—and it's not completely safe to do any wet kissing, either, until the man is tested for AIDS. And if the man passes the AIDS test, he's still not completely safe, because it can take six months after infection for the AIDS virus to be detectable. So during the first six months of courtship, until the man is retested, Kaplan suggests either using a condom or continuing with dry sex. A more specific tip—which Kaplan recommended in *Newsweek*—is for the couple to watch erotic movies with their clothes on. 44

Starry nights and dry sex. It didn't sound quite fair to young lovers, so I called Kaplan. 45

"I feel sorry for kids today," she said. "But casual sex is dangerous. How would this woman know that this lawyer from Harvard didn't have a gay experience three weeks earlier?" 46

"Well," I said, "what about a married woman? Say, someone living in New York, where there's a high rate of AIDS infection. Should she have her husband tested or make him wear a condom? 47

"Of course not, unless she has reason to suspect he's had other partners." 48

"But how does she know he didn't have a gay experience three weeks earlier? Or that he didn't visit a New York prostitute with AIDS? It's not something he's likely to tell her." 49

"Yes, but it doesn't make sense for every married woman to insist her husband wear a condom because a few married men are bisexual." 50

I reminded Kaplan that she herself has warned there seemed to be a surprisingly high number of secretly bisexual men. At first Kaplan argued that a woman would have some intuition about a husband's extracurricular activities. But as we talked, she reassessed her position. 51

"You know, you're absolutely right," she finally said. "In my book, I didn't pay enough attention to dishonesty in monogamous relationships. In the next edition, I may change that. Maybe married women should be more alert." 52

"How about yourself?" I asked. "You live in New York. Would you worry about your husband or make him wear a condom?" 53

"Oh, I *know* about him," she said. "He's strictly monogamous and doesn't like needles. A husband might sleep with someone he met at a party—but there aren't that many women out there with AIDS, and the chances of a man getting it that way are very small." 54

Now, I have no reason whatsoever to suspect her husband of infidelity, and I agree that the odds of his having AIDS are minuscule. But are the odds much lower than for the roommate's curly-haired cousin from Harvard? You could argue that the young single Bostonian is more likely to be bisexual, but then you could also argue that an older married New Yorker is more likely to have visited a male or female prostitute with AIDS. You might conclude that the young lawyer is still a higher risk but that if he wears a condom—and the married man doesn't—then there might not be much difference in the overall risk to their partners. 55

No one, obviously, knows the exact relative risks. But then why is Helen Singer Kaplan so quick to advise the young woman to abstain altogether and so certain she herself doesn't even need to consider the protection of a condom? Why did her book neglect the risks from secretly bisexual husbands (who have been shown to infect their 56 wives) but explicitly warn single women about the dangers of wet kissing (which has never been demonstrated to infect anyone)?

The answer lies in the burgeoning literature of the new scientific field of risk analysis. And the answer is that risk perception is a profoundly irrational, idiosyncratic process, whether it's done by Helen Singer Kaplan or Trisha on Eleventh Avenue. It takes psychologists, not statisticians, to explain why Americans worry about dying from airplane crashes, nuclear meltdowns, shark attacks—and then get in a car and refuse to buckle a seat belt most of the time. One explanation is that people get a skewed image of death from the media's emphasis on the sensational—the few hundred Americans killed yearly in airline crashes get more press than the 46,000 who die on the roads. Another explanation is that people feel they have control over their risk when they're driving. This feeling may be an illusion—people tend to overrate their driving skills (surveys show that the average American rates himself as a better-than-average driver), and no amount of skill will save you in many accidents. But at least a driver can feel that he's making choices about safety. For most people, the risk of driving seems preferable to the much, much lower risk of living next to a nuclear-power plant, because someone else is imposing that nuclear plant on them. 57

Above all, people hate risks that are new or unfamiliar. A perfect example of this attitude showed up recently in New Jersey, where outraged citizens prevented the disposal of some low-level radioactive waste (from a factory that made luminescent paint for watch dials) in an abandoned quarry. This threat was infinitesimal compared with something that researchers happened to be studying at the same time: the radioactive radon gas emanating from natural rock formations into many New Jersey homes. Researchers found that breathing the air in some New Jersey homes was equivalent to smoking three or four packs of cigarettes a day—yet even after the residents were told, most of them didn't plan to do anything about it. The rocks under their homes were a risk they could live with: something natural, something that had been around forever. But don't put any "unnatural" new poisons in a quarry down the road. 58

AIDS brings out all these biases in weird ways. It's practically a litmus test of a person's attitude about risk (and sex, of course). From one perspective, you can look at AIDS as a "natural" and familiar risk—it's something you get from sex, an activity that has been around forever and that you've engaged in countless times without being killed. So you can regard it as the equivalent of a traffic accident: something that despite all the warnings, you don't really believe will happen to you. Helen Singer Kaplan has been having sex with her husband for years, and Trisha has been working on Eleventh Avenue for years—they're still alive, so it's easy for both to assume 59 that their activity is safe. It's also easy to believe that you have some control over this risk. You can tell yourself, for instance, that you'd know if your partner was dangerous. Or you might convince yourself that you can protect yourself from being infected if you take a shower after sex—a belief that researchers have actually heard from gay men who continue going to bathhouses where perhaps half the men are AIDS carriers.

60 But in some, AIDS can hit all the panic buttons. It's a mysterious new risk that gets a disproportionate share of publicity—the 40,000 Americans killed by the AIDS epidemic have gotten more press than the 200,000 people killed by cirrhosis of the liver during this period, or the 6 million killed by heart disease. It can also seem to be a risk beyond your personal control. Thus people who smoke cigarettes will get absurdly hysterical about working or studying near an AIDS victim—they don't mind killing themselves with tobacco, but they refuse to have any imagined danger imposed on them by someone else.

61 And that someone else is likely to have done something that much of society considers unnatural. Homosexuality, drug abuse, promiscuity—just what Mom warned you not to do, which makes the consequences seem especially unacceptable. In a recent Times Mirror Gallup Poll, 42.5 percent of Americans said AIDS might be a punishment from God for immoral behavior. This happened to be the same explanation that the Milanese gave for the Black Plague of 1630, and it made the righteous citizens all the more hysterical when they heard rumors of the Demon of the Pestilence. They were ready to believe that Satan was spreading pestiferous salve on everyone's door, because the rumor confirmed their feeling that the plague was a punishment for the wickedness of certain inhabitants. The cry from Milan's pulpits during the year of the Demon was not dissimilar to the warnings today: Stop sinning.

62 It seems odd to hear the cries for restraint coming from sex therapists like Kaplan or Masters and Johnson—and it's been suggested that this is their form of repentance for helping to foster the sexual revolution. But I think they merely reflect biases that affect the risk perception of most researchers and health officials dealing with AIDS. One obvious bias stems from the fact that many researchers spend their days seeing AIDS victims and mortality statistics; like people who watch plane crashes on the evening news, they're liable to worry about a relatively rare event because they personally see it happen so often.

63 Researchers and health officials also have a professional bias to be pessimistic. If the Heterosexual Breakout never materializes, the false alarms will be forgotten (or they'll even be credited with averting the crisis); but if the Breakout does happen, anybody who advised het-

erosexuals not to worry is going to have serious career problems. It's tempting for officials to take the outlook of Mathilde Krim of the American Foundation for AIDS Research, one of the more pessimistic prophets of AIDS. "Given that we're dealing with a deadly disease that could cause enormous disruption in society," she says, "it is justifiable to assume that the worst scenario is the right one. If we're mistaken, we'll have a few hospital beds too many and we can congratulate ourselves."

Unfortunately, however, a few extra hospital beds are not the 64
only cost of being too pessimistic. One cost is borne by AIDS victims: no matter how often officials insist that casual contact poses no risk, as long as the public is terrified of getting AIDS, there's going to be homophobia and mindless prejudice toward the disease's victims. Another cost is borne by the nonvictims: the fear that seems to be causing millions of people to avoid or fret through one of life's more exquisite moments. Call it the Lost Starry Nights Factor.

Your own risk perception of AIDS will depend, ultimately, on 65
how important those nights are to you. But you should at least try to put the risk in perspective, and the best source is a study by epidemiologists at the University of California at San Francisco medical school. Based on the studies of heterosexual couples in which one partner is infected, Norman Hearst and Stephen B. Hulley assume that the chance of woman getting the virus from an infected partner during one session of vaginal intercourse is 1 in 500—if the man is not wearing a condom. (The risk of a man getting the virus from an infected woman would probably be less.) These odds are lower than your risk of being killed in a car accident sometime in your life (which is about 1 in 50), but there aren't many other activities this risky.

If the infected man wears a condom, Hearst and Hulley estimate 66
the risk of transmission is 1 in 5000. You have about the same chance of being killed in a car accident during the next year.

Now suppose your partner tells you he's not infected. And sup- 67
pose he's in a risk group. The AIDS virus seems to be carried by between five and fifty percent of the people in risk groups, so your odds of getting AIDS in one sexual encounter, without a condom, range from 1 in 1000 (the chance that a motorcyclist will have a fatal accident during one year) to 1 in 10,000 (the chance of dying if you fly 100,000 miles). If a condom is used, the odds drop to a range between 1 in 10,000 and 1 in 100,000 (the chance of dying on a round-trip flight from Los Angeles to London).

If your partner isn't in one of the risk groups, your odds of being 68
infected in one sexual encounter, even without a condom, drop to 1 in 5 million—the same chance of your dying in a thirty-mile car trip or of being struck by lightning during the next five months. And if your

partner isn't in a risk group and you use a condom, your odds of getting infected are 1 in 50 million. You have about the same chance of dying during the next three months by being hit by an airplane falling out of the sky.

Finally, for those afraid to touch or work with or live near AIDS victims, the odds of getting AIDS from toilet seats or any other casual contact are roughly the same as the odds of Chicago being leveled by a giant asteroid: no one can rule out the possibility, but no one has yet observed it happen, either. 69

These are just educated guesses. There may be more people infected out there than anyone realizes, and it may be that Hearst and Hulley's assumption about the efficiency of AIDS transmission—a 1-in-500 chance without a condom—is too low in some cases, especially if a partner is at the highly infectious stage. The risk of transmission is certainly increased if either partner has genital ulcers or abrasions, and other factors may also encourage transmission: taking oral contraceptives (which can weaken the lining of the cervix), being uncircumcised (the foreskin tissue may be a potential entry point for the virus), having sex without enough lubrication (which can cause abrasions) or during menstruation (when the woman's blood vessels are apparently more vulnerable to the entry of the virus). Given all these qualifications and uncertainties, Hearst and Hulley's odds may be way off. But they're the only odds we've got for now. 70

So what do the odds mean? To me, a middle-class heterosexual male in America, the message is, Relax. When it comes to risk perception, I part company with many of the AIDS experts. I don't mean to suggest that heterosexuals should stop caring about AIDS—as a public catastrophe, it obviously requires their attention, their dollars and their compassion for the victims. I just mean that I don't see it as much of a personal problem. 71

I definitely wouldn't worry about getting the virus from casual contact and probably not from kissing or oral sex, either. I wouldn't have a one-night stand with someone I suspected to be in a high-risk group, such as a needle sharer, and I would plan to use a condom with someone I didn't know well—maybe also with someone I did know well, but mainly to avoid other diseases and to reassure my partner. And I wouldn't feel suicidal if I didn't use a condom. I'd choose a condom with a spermicide containing nonoxynol-9 and encourage my partner to use this chemical as well (it's in vaginal sponges and many spermicidal foams and jellies). Nonoxynol's effectiveness against the AIDS virus is unproven—it can definitely kill an isolated AIDS virus of the sort found in semen, saliva and other secretions, but it doesn't kill the viruses that are hidden inside cells in blood or semen, and these cells are believed to be the major way the 72 disease is spread. Nevertheless, using nonoxynol-9 is worthwhile simply because it protects against other venereal diseases, like herpes, chlamydia, syphilis and gonorrhea, which are more contagious than AIDS.

If I weren't in a monogamous relationship, I would get myself 73
tested for AIDS occasionally—partly because I wouldn't want to spread the virus and partly to put any future partner's mind at ease. I'd probably encourage a steady partner to be tested. But I wouldn't demand a test result before sleeping with someone—which is to say, I wouldn't confine myself to dry sex on a starry night. And if I had to choose between never wearing a condom and never wearing a seat belt, I would keep the seat belt on.

If I were a heterosexual woman, I imagine I would be more 74
cautious. The risks would be greater of meeting a partner with the virus (because more men carry it), and it seems to pass more easily from men to women than vice versa. I imagine I'd be more selective and more insistent on condoms. I certainly wouldn't have casual anal intercourse. But above all, I would try to remind myself that getting this virus is not one of the major worries of my life. There are many likelier ways to die.

I am not—repeat, not—trying to advise anyone else how to be- 75
have sexually. I can't decide what risks anyone else should tolerate. Nor can I guarantee that the epidemic isn't going to suddenly change and start spreading wildly among heterosexuals. But then, neither can I guarantee that someone will not spread pestiferous salve on your door tomorrow morning. I can only tell you that despite all the horrors wrought by AIDS, despite the prophecies of general doom, in most streets of heterosexual America there have been no confirmed sightings of the Demon of the Pestilence. Once again, the Demon seems to be mainly in ourselves.

Review Questions

1. What is the main purpose of Tierney's article? At what point does he make this purpose clear?
2. What was the significance of Anastasia Lekatsas's conversation with the Hispanic AIDS patient? Why does this conversation cast doubt on the reliability of statistics on AIDS?
3. What is the chief danger Tierney sees in the unwarranted hysteria about AIDS among the general population?
4. How does Tierney use statistics to downplay the risk of hetereosexuals being infected with AIDS?

Discussion and Writing Suggestions

1. Tierney begins his article with a historical anecdote about Satan in seventeenth-century Milan (and makes two further references to it later in the article). What is the purpose of this horrific tale?
2. To what extent does it strike you that Lekatsas is invading the privacy of the people she investigates? To what extent do you believe such invasion of privacy is justified?
3. Tierney concludes that AIDS does not pose much of a personal problem for heterosexuals. "Relax," he advises. " . . . There are many likelier ways to die." To what extent are you reassured by his arguments? How do these arguments stack up against the arguments of others—for instance, of Restak?
4. What does Tierney mean by his final sentence; "Once again, the Demon seems to be mainly in ourselves"? How is the idea represented by this sentence related to his overall thesis?
5. In paragraph 57, Tierney discusses the often irrational manner in which Americans assess the various risks they encounter. Thus, they fear living in the vicinity of a nuclear power plant but refuse to buckle their seat belts when traveling in cars. (No Americans have died as a result of nuclear power plant accidents, but tens of thousands have died because they failed to wear seat belts.) In a multiparagraph essay, discuss several cases of this kind of irrationality that you have encountered (perhaps even that you indulge in) and try to account for such illogicalities and inconsistencies.

The Way We Live Now

SUSAN SONTAG

Faced with the threat of a spreading AIDS epidemic, how do we balance the sometimes conflicting demands of the public welfare and the rights of people with AIDS? This is the central question we have explored in the previous selections in this unit, and it is a crucial question; but we have so far given little attention to the equally crucial personal dimension of AIDS: How does this deadly disease affect those who contract it, and how does it affect their loved ones? These painful matters are the focus of the following story by Susan Sontag.

"The Way We Live Now" by Susan Sontag. Originally appeared in *The New Yorker,* 1986. Reprinted by permission of Wylie, Aitken & Stone, Inc.

Sontag (b. 1933) is a critic, essayist, novelist, short-story writer, screenwriter, and film director. Her influential critical works include Against Interpretation, and Other Essays *(1966),* On Photography *(1977), and* Illness as Metaphor *(1978), inspired by a near fatal case of cancer in the early 1970s. One critic described* Illness as Metaphor *as "a critical analysis of conceptualizing illness and of using the vocabulary of illness to articulate our feelings about other crises, economic, political, and military." Sontag's two novels are* The Benefactor *(1963) and* Death Kit *(1967). Of her collection of short stories,* I, etcetera *(1978),* Ms. *reviewer Laurie Stone wrote, "[Sontag] is not so much interested in abstract ideas and experimental styles as she is in revealing human character. . . . Sontag is focused simply (artfully) on the dear, idiosyncratic, alienating behavior of human beings." This observation also applies to "The Way We Live Now," a story that first appeared in* The New Yorker *and that was selected by editors Anne Beattie and Shannon Ravenal as one of the* Best American Short Stories 1987.

Since this story is told somewhat unconventionally, some introduction to its chief narrative devices may be helpful. "The Way We Live Now" traces the life of a person (never named) who contracts AIDS (the disease is also unnamed) from shortly after he first becomes sick to the final stages of the disease. It is told from the point of view of his numerous friends, and much of it is reported as hearsay from one or another of these friends, or as conversation between them. (No quotation marks are used, however—which may take some getting used to.) Each new paragraph focuses on several additional dimensions of AIDS and its effects both on the victim and on those around him. The point of view is apparently objective (i.e., third person), but this surface objectivity actually is a mosaic consisting of numerous subjective points of view. Perhaps the most difficult aspect of the story, initially, will be its long, frequently run-on sentences. These sentences are so long because they often involve several points of view. After you get used to this unusual style, though, you will probably not find the story difficult (it is not in the least obscure). Indeed, you may find, as we have, that it is particularly moving and insightful, and that by forcing us to view the unnamed protagonist and his situation from so many viewpoints, Sontag generates a sense of immediacy and emotional involvement that would be otherwise difficult to achieve.

At first he was just losing weight, he felt only a little ill, Max said to Ellen, and he didn't call for an appointment with his doctor, according to Greg, because he was managing to keep on working at more or less the same rhythm, but he did stop smoking, Tanya pointed out, which suggests he was frightened, but also that he wanted, even more than he knew, to be healthy, or healthier, or maybe just to gain back a few pounds, said Orson, for he told her, Tanya went on, that 1 he expected to be climbing the walls (isn't that what people say?) and found, to his surprise, that he didn't miss cigarettes at all and reveled in the sensation of his lungs' being ache-free for the first time in years. But did he have a good doctor, Stephen wanted to know, since it would have been crazy not to go for a checkup after the pressure was off and he was back from the conference in Helsinki, even if by then he was feeling better. And he said, to Frank, that he would go, even though he was indeed frightened, as he admitted to Jan, but who wouldn't be frightened now, though, odd as that might seem, he hadn't been worrying until recently, he avowed to Quentin, it was only in the last six months that he had the metallic taste of panic in his mouth, because becoming seriously ill was something that happened to other people, a normal delusion, he observed to Paolo, if one was thirty-eight and had never had a serious illness; he wasn't, as Jan confirmed, a hypochondriac. Of course, it was hard not to worry, everyone was worried, but it wouldn't do to panic, because, as Max pointed out to Quentin, there wasn't anything one could do except wait and hope, wait and start being careful, be careful, and hope. And even if one did prove to be ill, one shouldn't give up, they had new treatments that promised an arrest of the disease's inexorable course, research was progressing. It seemed that everyone was in touch with everyone else several times a week, checking in, I've never spent so many hours at a time on the phone, Stephen said to Kate, and when I'm exhausted after the two or three calls made to me, giving me the latest, instead of switching off the phone to give myself a respite I tap out the number of another friend or acquaintance, to pass on the news. I'm not sure I can afford to think so much about it, Ellen said, and I suspect my own motives, there's something morbid I'm getting used to, getting excited by, this must be like what people felt in London during the Blitz. As far as I know, I'm not at risk, but you never know, said Aileen. This thing is totally unprecedented, said Frank. But don't you think he ought to see a doctor, Stephen insisted. Listen, said Orson, you can't force people to take care of themselves, and what makes you think the worst, he could be just run down, people still do get ordinary illnesses, awful ones, why are you assuming it has to be *that*. But all I want to be sure, said Stephen, is that he understands the options, because most people don't, that's why they won't see a doctor or have the test, they think there's nothing one can do. But is there anything one can do, he said to Tanya (according to Greg), I mean what do I gain if I go to the doctor; if I'm really ill, he's reported to have said, I'll find out soon enough.

And when he was in the hospital, his spirits seemed to lighten, 2
according to Donny. He seemed more cheerful than he had been in

the last months, Ursula said, and the bad news seemed to come almost as a relief, according to Ira, as a truly unexpected blow, according to Quentin, but you'd hardly expect him to have said the same thing to all his friends, because his relation to Ira was so different from his relation to Quentin (this according to Quentin, who was proud of their friendship), and perhaps he thought Quentin wouldn't be undone by seeing him weep, but Ira insisted that couldn't be the reason he behaved so differently with each, and that maybe he was feeling less shocked, mobilizing his strength to fight for his life, at the moment he saw Ira but overcome by feelings of hopelessness when Quentin arrived with flowers, because anyway the flowers threw him into a bad mood, as Quentin told Kate, since the hospital room was choked with flowers, you couldn't have crammed another flower into that room, but surely you're exaggerating, Katie said, smiling, everybody likes flowers. Well, who wouldn't exaggerate at a time like this, Quentin said sharply. Don't you think *this* is an exaggeration. Of course I do, said Kate gently, I was only teasing, I mean I didn't mean to tease. I know that, Quentin said, with tears in his eyes, and Kate hugged him and said well, when I go this evening I guess I won't bring flowers, what does he want, and Quentin said, according to Max, what he likes best is chocolate. Is there anything else, asked Kate, I mean like chocolate but not chocolate. Licorice, said Quentin, blowing his nose. And besides that. Aren't *you* exaggerating now, Quentin said, smiling. Right, said Kate, so if I want to bring him a whole raft of stuff, besides chocolate and licorice, what else. Jelly beans, Quentin said.

He didn't want to be alone, according to Paolo, and lots of people 3
came in the first week, and the Jamaican nurse said there were other patients on the floor who would be glad to have the surplus flowers, and people weren't afraid to visit, it wasn't like the old days, as Kate pointed out to Aileen, they're not even segregated in the hospital anymore, as Hilda observed, there's nothing on the door of his room warning visitors of the possibility of contagion, as there was a few years ago; in fact, he's in a double room and, as he told Orson, the old guy on the far side of the curtain (who's clearly on the way out, said Stephen) doesn't even have the disease, so, as Kate went on, you really should go and see him, he'd be happy to see you, he likes having people visit, you aren't not going because you're afraid, are you. Of course not, Aileen said, but I don't know what to say, I think I'll feel awkward, which he's bound to notice, and that will make him feel worse, so I won't be doing him any good, will I. But he won't notice anything, Kate said, patting Aileen's hand, it's not like that, it's not the way you imagine, he's not judging people or wondering about their motives, he's just happy to see his friends. But I never

was really a friend of his, Aileen said, you're a friend, he's always liked you, you told me he talks about Nora with you, I know he likes me, he's even attracted to me, but he respects you. But, according to Wesley, the reason Aileen was so stingy with her visits was that she could never have him to herself, there were always others there already and by the time they left still others had arrived, she'd been in love with him for years, and I can understand, said Donny, that Aileen should feel bitter that if there could have been a woman friend he did more than occasionally bed, a woman he really loved, and my God, Victor said, who had known him in those years, he was crazy about Nora, what a heart-rending couple they were, two surly angels, then it couldn't have been she.

And when some of the friends, the ones who came every day, 4
waylaid the doctor in the corridor, Stephen was the one who asked the most informed questions, who'd been keeping up not just with the stories that appeared several times a week in the *Times* (which Greg confessed to have stopped reading, unable to stand it anymore) but with articles in the medical journals published here and in England and France, and who knew socially one of the principal doctors in Paris who was doing some much-publicized research on the disease, but his doctor said little more than that the pneumonia was not life-threatening, the fever was subsiding, of course he was still weak but he was responding well to the antibiotics, that he'd have to complete his stay in the hospital, which entailed a minimum of twenty-one days on the IV, before she could start him on the new drug, for she was optimistic about the possibility of getting him into the protocol; and when Victor said that if he had so much trouble eating (he'd say to everyone when they coaxed him to eat some of the hospital meals, that food didn't taste right, that he had a funny metallic taste in his mouth) it couldn't be good that friends were bringing him all that chocolate, the doctor just smiled and said that in these cases the patient's morale was also an important factor, and if chocolate made him feel better she saw no harm in it, which worried Stephen, as Stephen said later to Donny, because they wanted to believe in the promises and taboos of today's high-tech medicine but here this reassuringly curt and silver-haired specialist in the disease, someone quoted frequently in the papers, was talking like some oldfangled country GP who tells the family that tea with honey or chicken soup may do as much for the patient as penicillin, which might mean, as Max said, that they were just going through the motions of treating him, that they were not sure about what to do, or rather, as Xavier interjected, that they didn't know what the hell they were doing, that the truth, the real truth, as Hilda said, upping the ante, was that they didn't, the doctors, really have any hope.

Oh, no, said Lewis, I can't stand it, wait a minute, I can't believe it, 5
are you sure, I mean are they sure, have they done all the tests, it's getting so when the phone rings I'm scared to answer because I think it will be someone telling me someone else is ill; but did Lewis really not know until yesterday, Robert said testily, I find that hard to believe, everybody is talking about it, it seems impossible that someone wouldn't have called Lewis; and perhaps Lewis did know, was for some reason pretending not to know already, because, Jan recalled, didn't Lewis say something months ago to Greg, and not only to Greg, about his not looking well, losing weight, and being worried about him and wishing he'd see a doctor, so it couldn't come as a total surprise. Well, everybody is worried about everybody now, said Betsy, that seems to be the way we live, the way we live now. And, after all, they were once very close, doesn't Lewis still have the keys to his apartment, you know the way you let someone keep the keys after you've broken up, only a little because you hope the person might just saunter in, drunk or high, late some evening, but mainly because it's wise to have a few sets of keys strewn around town, if you live alone, at the top of a former commercial building that, pretentious as it is, will never acquire a doorman or even a resident superintendent, someone whom you can call on for keys late one night if you find you've lost yours or have locked yourself out. Who else has keys, Tanya inquired, I was thinking somebody might drop by tomorrow before coming to the hospital and bring some treasures, because the other day, Ira said, he was complaining about how dreary the hospital room was, and how it was like being locked up in a motel room, which got everybody started telling funny stories about motel rooms they'd known, and at Ursula's story, about the Luxury Budget Inn in Schenectady, there was an uproar of laughter around his bed, while he watched them in silence, eyes bright with fever, all the while, as Victor recalled, gobbling that damned chocolate. But, according to Jan, whom Lewis's keys enabled to tour the swank of his bachelor lair with an eye to bringing over some art consolation to brighten up the hospital room, the Byzantine icon wasn't on the wall over his bed, and that was a puzzle until Orson remembered that he'd recounted without seeming upset (this disputed by Greg) that the boy he'd recently gotten rid of had stolen it, along with four of the *maki-e* lacquer boxes, as if these were objects as easy to sell on the street as a TV or a stereo. But he's always been very generous, Kate said quietly, and though he loves beautiful things isn't really attached to them, to things, as Orson said, which is unusual in a collector, as Frank commented, and when Kate shuddered and tears sprang to her eyes and Orson inquired anxiously if he, Orson, had said something wrong, she pointed out that they'd begun talking about him in a retrospective mode, summing up what he was like, what made them

fond of him, as if he were finished, completed, already a part of the past.

Perhaps he was getting tired of having so many visitors, said Robert, who was, as Ellen couldn't help mentioning, someone who had come only twice and was probably looking for a reason not to be in regular attendance, but there could be no doubt, according to Ursula, that his spirits had dipped, not that there was any discouraging news from the doctors, and he seemed now to prefer being alone a few hours of the day; and he told Donny that he'd begun keeping a diary for the first time in his life, because he wanted to record the course of his mental reactions to this astonishing turn of events, to do something parallel to what the doctors were doing, who came every morning and conferred at his bedside about his body, and that perhaps it wasn't so important what he wrote in it, which amounted, as he said wryly to Quentin, to little more than the usual banalities about terror and amazement that this was happening to him, to him also, plus the usual remorseful assessments of his past life, his pardonable superficialities, capped by resolves to live better, more deeply, more in touch with his work and his friends, and not to care so passionately about what people thought of him, interspersed with admonitions to himself that in this situation his will to live counted more than anything else and that if he really wanted to live, and trusted life, and liked himself well enough (down, ol' debbil Thanatos!), he *would* live, he would be an exception; but perhaps all this, as Quentin ruminated, talking on the phone to Kate, wasn't the point, the point was that by the very keeping of the diary he was accumulating something to reread one day, slyly staking out his claim to a future time, in which the diary would be an object, a relic, in which he might not actually reread it, because he would want to have put this ordeal behind him, but the diary would be there in the drawer of his stupendous Majorelle desk, and he could already, he did actually say to Quentin one late sunny afternoon, propped up in the hospital bed, with the stain of chocolate framing one corner of a heartbreaking smile, see himself in the penthouse, the October sun streaming through those clear windows instead of this streaked one, and the diary, the pathetic diary, safe inside the drawer. 6

It doesn't matter about the treatment's side effects, Stephen said (when talking to Max), I don't know why you're so worried about that, every strong treatment has some dangerous side effects, it's inevitable, you mean otherwise the treatment wouldn't be effective, Hilda interjected, and anyway, Stephen went on doggedly, just because there *are* side effects it doesn't mean he has to get them, or all of them, each one, or even some of them. That's just a list of all the 7 possible things that could go wrong, because the doctors have to cover themselves, so they make up a worst-case scenario, but isn't what's happening to him, and to so many other people, Tanya interrupted, a worst-case scenario, a catastrophe no one could have imagined, it's too cruel, and isn't everything a side effect, quipped Ira, even *we* are all side effects, but we're not bad side effects, Frank said, he likes having his friends around, and we're helping each other, too; because his illness sticks us all in the same glue, mused Xavier, and, whatever the jealousies and grievances from the past that have made us wary and cranky with each other, when something like this happens (the sky is falling, the sky is falling!) you understand what's really important. I agree, Chicken Little, he is reported to have said. But don't you think, Quentin observed to Max, that being as close to him as we are, making time to drop by the hospital every day, is a way of our trying to define ourselves more firmly and irrevocably as the well, those who aren't ill, who aren't going to fall ill, as if what's happened to him couldn't happen to us, when in fact the chances are that before long one of us will end up where he is, which is probably what he felt when he was one of the cohort visiting Zack in the spring (you never knew Zack, did you?), and, according to Clarice, Zack's widow, he didn't come very often, he said he hated hospitals, and didn't feel he was doing Zack any good, that Zack would see on his face how uncomfortable he was. Oh, he was one of those, Aileen said. A coward. Like me.

And after he was sent home from the hospital, and Quentin had 8
volunteered to move in and was cooking meals and taking telephone messages and keeping the mother in Mississippi informed, well, mainly keeping her from flying to New York and heaping her grief on her son and confusing the household routine with her oppressive ministrations, he was able to work an hour or two in his study, on days he didn't insist on going out, for a meal or a movie, which tired him. He seemed optimistic, Kate thought, his appetite was good, and what he said, Orson reported, was that he agreed when Stephen advised him that the main thing was to keep in shape, he was a fighter, right, he wouldn't be who he was if he weren't, and was he ready for the big fight, Stephen asked rhetorically (as Max told it to Donny), and he said you bet, and Stephen added it could be a lot worse, you could have gotten the disease two years ago, but now so many scientists are working on it, the American team and the French team, everyone bucking for that Nobel Prize a few years down the road, that all you have to do is stay healthy for another year or two and then there will be good treatment, real treatment. Yes, he said, Stephen said, my timing is good. And Betsy, who had been climbing on and rolling off macrobiotic diets for a decade, came up with a

Japanese specialist she wanted him to see but thank God, Donny reported, he'd had the sense to refuse, but he did agree to see Victor's visualization therapist, although what could one possibly visualize, said Hilda, when the point of visualizing disease was to see it as an entity with contours, borders, here rather than there, something limited, something you were the host of, in the sense that you could disinvite the disease, while this was so total; or would be, Max said. But the main thing, said Greg, was to see that he didn't go the macrobiotic route, which might be harmless for plump Betsy but could only be devastating for him, lean as he's always been, with all the cigarettes and other appetite-suppressing chemicals he'd been welcoming into his body for years; and now was hardly the time, as Stephen pointed out, to be worried about cleaning up his act, and eliminating the chemical additives and other pollutants that we're all blithely or not so blithely feasting on, blithely since we're healthy, healthy as we can be; so far, Ira said. Meat and potatoes is what I'd be happy to see him eating, Ursula said wistfully. And spaghetti and clam sauce, Greg added. And thick cholesterol-rich omelets with smoked mozzarella, suggested Yvonne, who had flown from London for the weekend to see him. Chocolate cake, said Frank. Maybe not chocolate cake, Ursula said, he's already eating so much chocolate.

And when, not right away but still only three weeks later, he was 9
accepted into the protocol for the new drug, which took considerable behind-the-scenes lobbying with the doctors, he talked less about being ill, according to Donny, which seemed like a good sign, Kate felt, a sign that he was not feeling like a victim, feeling not that he *had* a disease but, rather, was living *with* a disease (that was the right cliché, wasn't it?), a more hospitable arrangement, said Jan, a kind of cohabitation which implied that it was something temporary, that it could be terminated, but terminated how, said Hilda, and when you say hospitable, Jan, I hear hospital. And it was encouraging, Stephen insisted, that from the start, at least from the time he was finally persuaded to make the telephone call to his doctor, he was willing to say the name of the disease, pronounce it often and easily, as if it were just another word, like boy or gallery or cigarette or money or deal, as in no big deal, Paolo interjected, because, as Stephen continued, to utter the name is a sign of health, a sign that one has accepted being who one is, mortal, vulnerable, not exempt, not an exception after all, it's a sign that one is willing, truly willing, to fight for one's life. And we must say the name, too, and often, Tanya added, we mustn't lag behind him in honesty, or let him feel that, the effort of honesty having been made, it's something done with and he can go on to other things. One is so much better prepared to help him, Wesley replied. In a way he's fortunate, said Yvonne, who had taken

care of a problem at the New York store and was flying back to London this evening, sure, fortunate, said Wesley, no one is shunning him, Yvonne went on, no one's afraid to hug him or kiss him lightly on the mouth, in London we are, as usual, a few years behind you, people I know, people who would seem to be not even remotely at risk, are just terrified, but I'm impressed by how cool and rational you all are; you find us cool, asked Quentin. But I have to say, he's reported to have said, I'm terrified, I find it very hard to read (and you know how he loves to read, said Greg; yes, reading is his television, said Paolo) or to think, but I don't feel hysterical. I feel quite hysterical, Lewis said to Yvonne. But you're able to *do* something for him, that's wonderful, how I wish I could stay longer, Yvonne answered, it's rather beautiful, I can't help thinking, this utopia of friendship you've assembled around him (this pathetic utopia, said Kate), so that the disease, Yvonne concluded, is not, anymore, out there. Yes, don't you think we're more at home here, with him, with the disease, said Tanya, because the imagined disease is so much worse than the reality of him, whom we all love, each in our fashion, having it. I know for me his getting it has quite demystified the disease, said Jan, I don't feel afraid, spooked, as I did before he became ill, when it was only news about remote acquaintances, whom I never saw again after they became ill. But you know you're not going to come down with the disease, Quentin said, to which Ellen replied, on her behalf, that's not the point, and possibly untrue, my gynecologist says that everyone is at risk, everyone who has a sexual life, because sexuality is a chain that links each of us to many others, unknown others, and now the great chain of being has become a chain of death as well. It's not the same for you, Quentin insisted, it's not the same for you as it is for me or Lewis or Frank or Paolo or Max, I'm more and more frightened, and I have every reason to be. I don't think about whether I'm at risk or not, said Hilda, I know that I was afraid to know someone with the disease, afraid of what I'd see, what I'd feel, and after the first day I came to the hospital I felt so relieved. I'll never feel that way, that fear, again; he doesn't seem different from me. He's not, Quentin said.

According to Lewis, he talked more often about those who visited 10
more often, which is natural, said Betsy, I think he's even keeping a tally. And among those who came or checked in by phone every day, the inner circle as it were, those who were getting more points, there was still a further competition, which was what was getting on Betsy's nerves, she confessed to Jan; there's always that vulgar jockeying for position around the bedside of the gravely ill, and though we all feel suffused with virtue at our loyalty to him (speak for yourself, said Jan), to the extent that we're carving time out of every

day, or almost every day, though some of us are dropping out, as Xavier pointed out, aren't we getting at least as much out of this as he is. Are we, said Jan. We're rivals for a sign from him of special pleasure over a visit, each stretching for the brass ring of his favor, wanting to feel the most wanted, the true nearest and dearest, which is inevitable with someone who doesn't have a spouse and children or an official in-house lover, hierarchies that no one would dare contest, Betsy went on, so we are the family he's founded, without meaning to, without official titles and ranks (we, we, snarled Quentin); and is it so clear, though some of us, Lewis and Quentin and Tanya and Paolo, among others, are ex-lovers and all of us more or less than friends, which one of us he prefers, Victor said (now it's us, raged Quentin), because sometimes I think he looks forward more to seeing Aileen, who has visited only three times, twice at the hospital and once since he's been home, than he does you or me; but, according to Tanya, after being very disappointed that Aileen hadn't come, now he was angry, while, according to Xavier, he was not really hurt but touchingly passive, accepting Aileen's absence as something he somehow deserved. But he's happy to have people around, said Lewis; he says when he doesn't have company he gets very sleepy, he sleeps (according to Quentin), and then perks up when someone arrives, it's important that he not feel ever alone. But, said Victor, there's one person he hasn't heard from, whom he'd probably like to hear from more than most of us; but she didn't just vanish, even right after she broke away from him, and he knows exactly where she lives now, said Kate, he told me he put in a call to her last Christmas Eve, and she said it's nice to hear from you and Merry Christmas, and he was shattered, according to Orson, and furious and disdainful, according to Ellen (what do you expect of her, said Wesley, she was burned out), but Kate wondered if maybe he hadn't phoned Nora in the middle of a sleepless night, what's the time difference, and Quentin said no, I don't think so, I think he wouldn't want her to know.

And when he was feeling even better and had regained the pounds 11
he'd shed right away in the hospital, though the refrigerator started to fill up with organic wheat germ and grapefruit and skimmed milk (he's worried about his cholesterol count, Stephen lamented), and told Quentin he could manage by himself now, and did, he started asking everyone who visited how he looked, and everyone said he looked great, so much better than a few weeks ago, which didn't jibe with what anyone had told him at that time; but then it was getting harder and harder to know how he looked, to answer such a question honestly when among themselves they wanted to be honest, both for honesty's sake and (as Donny thought) to prepare for the worst,

because he'd been looking like *this* for so long, at least it seemed so long, that it was as if he'd always been like this, how did he look before, but it was only a few months, and those words, pale and wan looking and fragile, hadn't they always applied? And one Thursday Ellen, meeting Lewis at the door of the building, said, as they rode up together in the elevator, how is he *really?* But you see how he is, Lewis said tartly, he's fine, he's perfectly healthy, and Ellen understood that of course Lewis didn't think he was perfectly healthy but that he wasn't worse, and that was true, but wasn't it, well, almost heartless to talk like that. Seems inoffensive to me, Quentin said, but I know what you mean, I remember once talking to Frank, somebody, after all, who has volunteered to do five hours a week of office work at the Crisis Center (I know, said Ellen), and Frank was going on about this guy, diagnosed almost a year ago, and so much further along, who'd been complaining to Frank on the phone about the indifference of some doctor, and had gotten quite abusive about the doctor, and Frank was saying there was no reason to be so upset, the implication being that *he,* Frank, wouldn't behave so irrationally, and I said, barely able to control my scorn, but Frank, Frank, he has every reason to be upset, he's dying, and Frank said, said according to Quentin, oh, I don't like to think about it that way.

And it was while he was still home, recuperating, getting his weekly 12
treatment, still not able to do much work, he complained, but, according to Quentin, up and about most of the time and turning up at the office several days a week, that bad news came about two remote acquaintances, one in Houston and one in Paris, news that was intercepted by Quentin on the ground that it could only depress him, but Stephen contended that it was wrong to lie to him, it was so important for him to live in the truth; that had been one of his first victories, that he was candid, that he was even willing to crack jokes about the disease, but Ellen said it wasn't good to give him this end-of-the-world feeling, too many people were getting ill, it was becoming such a common destiny that maybe some of the will to fight for his life would be drained out of him if it seemed to be as natural as, well, death. Oh, Hilda said, who didn't know personally either the one in Houston or the one in Paris, but knew *of* the one in Paris, a pianist who specialized in twentieth-century Czech and Polish music, I have his records, he's such a valuable person, and, when Kate glared at her, continued defensively, I know every life is equally sacred, but that *is* a thought, another thought, I mean, all these valuable people who aren't going to have their normal four score as it is now, these people aren't going to be replaced, and it's such a loss to the culture. But this isn't going to go on forever, Wesley said, it can't,

they're bound to come up with something (they, they, muttered Stephen), but did you ever think, Greg said, that if some people don't die, I mean even if they can keep them alive (they, they, muttered Kate), they continue to be carriers, and that means, if you have a conscience, that you can never make love, make love fully, as you'd been wont—wantonly, Ira said—to do. But it's better than dying, said Frank. And in all his talk about the future, when he allowed himself to be hopeful, according to Quentin, he never mentioned the prospect that even if he didn't die, if he were so fortunate as to be among the first generation of the disease's survivors, never mentioned, Kate confirmed, that whatever happened it was over, the way he had lived until now, but, according to Ira, he did think about it, the end of bravado, the end of folly, the end of trusting life, the end of taking life for granted, and of treating life as something that, samurai-like, he thought himself ready to throw away lightly, impudently; and Kate recalled, sighing, a brief exchange she'd insisted on having as long as two years ago, huddling on a banquette covered with steel-gray industrial carpet on an upper level of The Prophet and toking up for their next foray onto the dance floor: she'd said hesitantly, for it felt foolish asking a prince of debauchery to, well, take it easy, and she wasn't keen on playing big sister, a role, as Hilda confirmed, he inspired in many women, are you being careful, honey, you know what I mean. And he replied, Kate went on, no, I'm not, listen, I can't, I just can't, sex is too important to me, always has been (he started talking like that, according to Victor, after Nora left him), and if I get it, well, I get it. But he wouldn't talk like that now, would he, said Greg; he must feel awfully foolish now, said Betsy, like someone who went on smoking, saying I can't give up cigarettes, but when the bad X-ray is taken even the most besotted nicotine addict can stop on a dime. But sex isn't like cigarettes, is it, said Frank, and, besides, what good does it do to remember that he was reckless, said Lewis angrily, the appalling thing is that you just have to be unlucky once, and wouldn't he feel even worse if he'd stopped three years ago and had come down with it anyway, since one of the most terrifying features of the disease is that you don't know when you contracted it, it could have been ten years ago, because surely this disease has existed for years and years, long before it was recognized; that is, named. Who knows how long (I think a lot about that, said Max) and who knows (I know what you're going to say, Stephen interrupted) how many are going to get it.

I'm feeling fine, he's reported to have said whenever someone asked 13
him how he was, which was almost always the first question anyone asked. Or: I'm feeling better, how are you? But he said other things, too. I'm playing leapfrog with myself, he is reported to have said,

according to Victor. And: There must be a way to get something positive out of this situation, he's reported to have said to Kate. How American of him, said Paolo. Well, said Betsy, you know the old American adage: When you've got a lemon, make lemonade. The one thing I'm sure I couldn't take, Jan said he said to her, is becoming disfigured, but Stephen hastened to point out the disease doesn't take that form very often anymore, its profile is mutating, and, in conversation with Ellen, wheeled up words like blood-brain barrier; I never thought there was a barrier *there,* said Jan. But he mustn't know about Max, Ellen said, that would really depress him, please don't tell him, he'll have to know, Quentin said grimly, and he'll be furious not to have been told. But there's time for that, when they take Max off the respirator, said Ellen; but isn't it incredible, Frank said, Max was fine, not feeling ill at all, and then to wake up with a fever of a hundred and five, unable to breathe, but that's the way it often starts, with absolutely no warning, Stephen said, the disease has so many forms. And when, after another week had gone by, he asked Quentin where Max was, he didn't question Quentin's account of a spree in the Bahamas, but then the number of people who visited regularly was thinning out, partly because the old feuds that had been put aside through the first hospitalization and the return home had resurfaced, and the flickering enmity between Lewis and Frank exploded, even though Kate did her best to mediate between them, and also because he himself had done something to loosen the bonds of love that united the friends around him, by seeming to take them all for granted, as if it were perfectly normal for so many people to carve out so much time and attention for him, visit him every few days, talk about him incessantly on the phone with each other; but, according to Paolo, it wasn't that he was less grateful, it was just something he was getting used to, the visits. It had become, with time, a more ordinary kind of situation, a kind of ongoing party, first at the hospital and now since he was home, barely on his feet again, it being clear, said Robert, that I'm on the B list; but Kate said, that's absurd, there's no list; and Victor said, but there is, only it's not he, it's Quentin who's drawing it up. He wants to see us, we're helping him, we have to do it the way he wants, he fell down yesterday on the way to the bathroom, he mustn't be told about Max (but he already knew, according to Donny), it's getting worse.

When I was home, he is reported to have said, I was afraid to sleep, 14
as I was dropping off each night it felt like just that, as if I were falling down a black hole, to sleep felt like giving in to death, I slept every night with the light on; but here, in the hospital, I'm less afraid. And to Quentin he said, one morning, the fear rips through me, it tears me open; and, to Ira, it presses me together, squeezes me toward myself.

Fear gives everything its hue, its high. I feel so, I don't know how to say it, exalted, he said to Quentin. Calamity is an amazing high, too. Sometimes I feel *so* well, so powerful, it's as if I could jump out of my skin. Am I going crazy, or what? Is it all this attention and coddling I'm getting from everybody, like a child's dream of being loved? Is it the drugs? I know it sounds crazy but sometimes I think this is a *fantastic* experience, he said shyly; but there was also the bad taste in the mouth, the pressure in the head and at the back of the neck, the red, bleeding gums, the painful, if pink-lobed, breathing, and his ivory pallor, color of white chocolate. Among those who wept when told over the phone that he was back in the hospital were Kate and Stephen (who'd been called by Quentin), and Ellen, Victor, Aileen, and Lewis (who were called by Kate), and Xavier and Ursula (who were called by Stephen). Among those who didn't weep were Hilda, who said that she'd just learned that her seventy-five-year-old aunt was dying of the disease, which she'd contracted from a transfusion given during her successful double bypass of five years ago, and Frank and Donny and Betsy, but this didn't mean, according to Tanya, that they weren't moved and appalled, and Quentin thought they might not be coming soon to the hospital but would send presents; the room, he was in a private room this time, was filling up with flowers, and plants, and books, and tapes. The high tide of barely suppressed acrimony of the last weeks at home subsided into the routines of hospital visiting, though more than a few resented Quentin's having charge of the visiting book (but it was Quentin who had the idea, Lewis pointed out); now, to insure a steady stream of visitors, preferably no more than two at a time (this, the rule in all hospitals, wasn't enforced here, at least on this floor; whether out of kindness or inefficiency, no one could decide), Quentin had to be called first, to get one's time slot, there was no more casual dropping by. And his mother could no longer be prevented from taking a plane and installing herself in a hotel near the hospital; but he seemed to mind her daily presence less than expected, Quentin said; said Ellen it's we who mind, do you suppose she'll stay long. It was easier to be generous with each other visiting him here in the hospital, as Donny pointed out, than at home, where one minded never being alone with him; coming here, in our twos and twos, there's no doubt about what our role is, how we should be, collective, funny, distracting, undemanding, light, it's important to be light, for in all this dread there is gaiety, too, as the poet said, said Kate. (His eyes, his glittering eyes, said Lewis.) His eyes looked dull, extinguished, Wesley said to Xavier, but Betsy said his face, not just his eyes, looked soulful, warm; whatever is there, said Kate, I've never been so aware of his eyes; and Stephen said, I'm afraid of what my eyes show, the way I watch him, with too much intensity, or a phony kind of casualness, said Victor. And, unlike at home, he was cleanshaven each morning, at whatever hour they visited him; his curly hair was always combed; but he complained that the nurses had changed since he was here the last time, and that he didn't like the change, he wanted everyone to be the same. The room was furnished now with some of his personal effects (odd word for one's things, said Ellen), and Tanya brought drawings and a letter from her nine-year-old dyslexic son, who was writing now, since she'd purchased a computer; and Donny brought champagne and some helium balloons, which were anchored to the foot of his bed; tell me about something that's going on, he said, waking up from a nap to find Donny and Kate at the side of his bed, beaming at him; tell me a story, he said wistfully, said Donny, who couldn't think of anything to say; *you're* the story, Kate said. And Xavier brought an eighteenth-century Guatemalan wooden statue of Saint Sebastian with upcast eyes and open mouth, and when Tanya said what's that, a tribute to eros past, Xavier said where I come from Sebastian is venerated as a protector against pestilence. Pestilence symbolized by arrows? Symbolized by arrows. All people remember is the body of a beautiful youth bound to a tree, pierced by arrows (of which he always seems oblivious, Tanya interjected), people forget that the story continues, Xavier continued, that when the Christian women came to bury the martyr they found him still alive and nursed him back to health. And he said, according to Stephen, I didn't know Saint Sebastian didn't die. It's undeniable, isn't it, said Kate on the phone to Stephen, the fascination of the dying. It makes me ashamed. We're learning how to die, said Hilda, I'm not ready to learn, said Aileen; and Lewis, who was coming straight from the other hospital, the hospital where Max was still being kept in ICU, met Tanya getting out of the elevator on the tenth floor, and as they walked together down the shiny corridor past the open doors, averting their eyes from the other patients sunk in their beds, with tubes in their noses, irradiated by the bluish light from the television sets, the thing I can't bear to think about, Tanya said to Lewis, is someone dying with the TV on.

He has that strange, unnerving detachment now, said Ellen, that's 15
what upsets me, even though it makes it easier to be with him. Sometimes he was querulous. I can't stand them coming in here taking my blood every morning, what are they doing with all that blood, he is reported to have said; but where was his anger, Jan wondered. Mostly he was lovely to be with, always saying how are *you*, how are you feeling. He's so sweet now, said Aileen. He's so nice, said Tanya. (Nice, nice, groaned Paolo.) At first he was very ill, but he was rallying, according to Stephen's best information, there

was no fear of his not recovering this time, and the doctor spoke of his being discharged from the hospital in another ten days if all went well, and the mother was persuaded to fly back to Mississippi, and Quentin was readying the penthouse for his return. And he was still writing his diary, not showing it to anyone, though Tanya, first to arrive one late-winter morning, and finding him dozing, peeked, and was horrified, according to Greg, not by anything she read but by a progressive change in his handwriting: in the recent pages, it was becoming spidery, less legible, and some lines of script wandered and tilted about the page. I was thinking, Ursula said to Quentin, that the difference between a story and a painting or photograph is that in a story you can write, He's still alive. But in a painting or a photo you can't show "still." You can just show him being alive. He's still alive, Stephen said.

Discussion and Writing Suggestions

1. Summarize this story in conventional narrative fashion. Explain who the protagonist is and whatever you know about him, apart from his having AIDS. Who are his most important friends and lovers? Describe their personalities, on the basis of the evidence. (For instance, what qualities distinguish Quentin? Aileen?) What is their relationship to him and to each other? What happens to him as the weeks go by? What changes do you observe in him? What happens to his friends? How does the story end? What does it all mean?
2. Does this story have a message or thesis? If so, what is it? If there is nothing so clear-cut as a message, what do you think Sontag was trying to accomplish by writing this story? (Does the title provide any clue?)
3. Based on your reading of Sontag's story, what are the most notable reactions that AIDS generates in its victims? In the victim's friends and loved ones? Structure your response in terms of the progress of the disease, devoting a paragraph or so to each type of reaction. (Note that the reactions and responses shift subtly as the weeks go by.)
4. Why do you think Sontag decided to tell this story in such an unusual manner—the long, run-on sentences, the numerous points of view, the refusal to give us any clear, objective view of the protagonist, unmediated by his friend's descriptions? How did you respond to this story and to its style? What did you like best about it? Least? Structure your response in the form of a critique.
5. Frequently, in reading fiction, we derive insights into ourselves, into the people around us, and into how to live our own lives. What insights do you draw from "The Way We Live Now"? In a multiparagraph essay, cite some of the passages that were the most meaningful to you and explain why they were meaningful.

SYNTHESIS ACTIVITIES

1. Imagine that you are an editorial writer for a major California newspaper, such as the *Los Angeles Times,* the *Sacramento Bee,* or the *San Francisco Chronicle.* Proposition 102 has just qualified for the ballot. Your job is to write an editorial supporting or opposing this proposition.

   After deciding what position you are going to take (assume that you have discussed your position with other members of the editorial staff and that you are in basic agreement), consider what arguments you will use to support your position. Draw on not only arguments made by the proponents and opponents of this Proposition 102 but also on some of the writers in this chapter including Restak, Altman, and Tierney.

   You will probably want to begin with a clear statement of your (and the newspaper's) position. Then you should summarize the chief measures that would be enacted into law by the passage of Proposition 102. Proceed with a discussion of three or four of the major arguments for or against the proposition. Focus not only on the question of whether or not Proposition 102 is reasonable and fair but also whether or not it is practical.

2. In late 1988, a promiscuous, bisexual carrier of the AIDS virus infected three women (one of them, pregnant) in Halifax, Nova Scotia. A warrant was issued for the man's arrest, but he disappeared. Authorities were divided on how to handle the case. Some thought that it should be handled as a criminal matter and that the man should be charged with criminal negligence causing bodily harm. It might be difficult to prove criminal intent, however (the man's mental functioning might have been impaired by the AIDS virus). The alternative would be to handle the case as a civil matter—which would enable the authorities to quarantine the man, as an endangerment to public health. AIDS-support groups have consistently opposed quarantine, as a gross violation of civil rights, insisting that such cases be handled through the courts, where the rights of individuals are better protected.

   Imagine that you are the magistrate who must recommend action, and further imagine that the fugitive has been apprehended and brought before you. Consider whether to charge the man with criminal negligence or to order his quarantine. Write a ruling, basing your ruling on some of the arguments made by writers in this chapter. (You may, within reason, create specific details about this man and his actions that would serve to justify your ruling.)

   You should probably begin with a summary of the chief facts of the case and then proceed with a discussion of the advantages and disadvantages of criminal charges and quarantine. (You may wish to draw on such sources as Restak, Nelson, and Buckley, here.) Finally, indicate your decision and your reasons for making such a decision.

3. Explain which reading in this chapter has made the greatest positive impression on you and which reading you most disagreed with. (Leave out of your consideration the first and last pieces in this chapter; the Abbott Labs pamphlet and the Sontag story are special cases.) What criteria are most important in making both your positive and negative selections? Do the readings you have chosen have any relationship to one another? How do the beliefs expressed in these two readings coincide with your own beliefs—not only about AIDS but about broader questions of public good and individual rights?

   You may wish to handle this assignment as a related pair of critiques. Keep in mind, however, that you are less concerned with the overall quality and validity of the readings (though this may be important) than with your own personal reactions to what the authors have to say.

4. The conflict between the public good and individual rights is not, of course, limited to the AIDS epidemic. We see numerous examples of such conflicts in both our public and our personal lives. For example, the debate on gun control turns on whether or not the rights of gun owners outweigh the right of the public to be protected against the unlawful use of guns. In a previous generation, the debate on the military draft turned on whether or not the public good—as defined by the government—should require young men to give up their personal liberties for a specified period of time—perhaps to fight wars of which the young men disapproved. In our personal lives, our families may be considered microcosms of the general public. Our parents impose restrictions on our personal liberties for the good of the family; so, for instance, we have to do chores when we'd rather be with our friends. (By the same token, the public good of the family also requires the parents to restrict their own liberties!)

   Select a public or a personal issue that involves a conflict between the public good (as defined by authority figures, of course) and individual civil rights. (You may select one of the examples mentioned above.) Weigh the conflicting rights involved in this issue, using specific examples. Then, explain which side should predominate, in your view. Indicate whatever exceptions you believe are appropriate. (For example, some who believe that individual rights should generally predominate in the AIDS issue make an exception for people who willfully endanger their fellow citizens—as in the Halifax case described in Question 2 above.)

5. You are a staff writer at *Newsweek* magazine preparing a story on the debate over the civil rights of persons with AIDS. Your intent is to remain (for the most part) neutral, while summarizing the key positions of both sides in the debate. Draw on some of the sources in this chapter—including the general introduction and the headnotes, if appropriate—to write your story.

Review recent issues of *Newsweek* or *Time* to see how they handle stories like this one. Frequently, you will find, they begin with an anecdote that illustrates the conflicts inherent in the issue. Then they will lay out both sides in the debate. Sometimes, also, they indicate which side they believe has the stronger case—and you may do the same. But for the most part, compose this essay as a description, rather than an argument.

6. In 1989 attorney Michael Kirby, writing on the AIDS crisis, declared, "[T]here is no human right to spread a deadly virus, whether knowingly or recklessly. The right to the protection of life is primary. But it must be achieved with the protection of other relevant rights, such as the right to privacy, the right to marry and found a family, the right to work and the right to freedom from inhuman or degrading treatment." Here again is the "seesaw" we have discussed earlier in the chapter—the attempt to balance the rights of the public with the rights of the individual. Richard Restak might disagree with Kirby's statement. But try to find your own balance.

   Draft an AIDS law that you believe achieves a balance between protecting the rights of the public and protecting the rights of the AIDS victim. Deal with some of the same matters covered in Proposition 102: reporting, confidentiality, tracing of sexual contacts, discrimination in employment and insurability, penalties for knowingly exposing others to the AIDS virus. In a brief section following your law, explain why you think it achieves an ideal balance. How does it take into account the concerns of both sides in the AIDS debate? How would Restak feel about it? How about Nelson and Altman? (Some practical points to consider: How expensive would it be to implement this law? Could penalties be enforced?)

7. Consider the larger issues of the AIDS debate: public good versus individual rights. Can these be defined? What constitutes the public good? What do citizens have a right to expect from their government—and from their fellow citizens? Should society guarantee certain protections to its citizens? If so, how can these guaranteed protections coexist with individual rights? Recall the classic case of the person yelling "Fire!" in a crowded theater. Can he claim that his freedom of speech is being violated if he is prosecuted for endangering the safety of the other theatergoers? What about the right to smoke? To what extent does the right to breathe smoke-free air conflict with the right of an individual to light up a cigarette, if he or she so desires?

   Draft a section of the Constitution for a model society that tries to come to grips with this difficult issue. Begin it, as follows:

   And in those cases when an individual's rights conflict with the public good, the following principles should apply:

Assume that the "public good" means the rights of the citizenry as a whole. Keep in mind that some issues are more serious than others: AIDS, for example, is a matter of life or death; in other cases (someone playing loud music at 3:00 A.M., for example), the consequences of violating one another's rights are less critical on both sides). So while keeping particular examples in mind, keep your law flexible enough to accommodate a variety of situations.

BARTLEBY: WHY DOES HE PREFER NOT TO?

13

Although *Moby Dick* is Herman Melville's greatest and most famous creation, his later "Bartleby, the Scrivener: A Story of Wall Street" is probably the work that continues to exert the greatest fascination for modern readers. "Bartleby" has become Melville's most anthologized piece; it has been the subject of volumes of criticism, two operas (one with libretto by playwright Edward Albee), and several films. The story first appeared in two parts in the November and December 1853 issues of *Putnam's Magazine* and three years later was included by Melville in a collection of stories called *The Piazza Tales* (1856).

During the 1840s, Melville had been a popular writer; novels like *Typee* (1846) and its sequel *Omoo,* with their romantic stories of native life in the Pacific Islands (life that Melville had witnessed firsthand), had enthralled contemporary readers. With the publication of *Moby Dick* (1851), however, readers discovered a new, darker side of Melville; and many did not like what they saw. The author's popularity waned, not to recover during his lifetime. "Bartleby" won some favorable reviews, but on the whole, *The Piazza Tales,* along with most of Melville's other later work, failed with the public. Not until the hundredth anniversary of his birth, in 1919, did scholars and critics begin taking a fresh look at Melville's works. Since that time, his reputation has risen steadily, and he is now generally considered the greatest American novelist and short-story writer of the nineteenth century.

What is the attraction of "Bartleby"? The title of one collection of essays on the story—"Bartleby, the Inscrutable"—suggests the answer. On one level, "Bartleby" is easy to read. The action is plain enough; the characters are vividly drawn; unlike many stories and plays with deep allegorical or symbolic meanings, "Bartleby" is rich in realistic detail; the story's language is by no means complex or obscure—and yet . . . and yet . . . it seems impossible to account rationally for the behavior of the central character. And since it is impossible to account for Bartleby's behavior rationally, most readers have concluded either that there is an irrational reason or that the story is not to be taken realistically at all but rather symbolically. As one critic, Leo Marx, has observed, "The unique quality of this tale . . . resides in its ability to say almost nothing on its placid and inscrutable surface, and yet so powerfully to suggest that a great deal is being said." Melville himself was surely aware that his story would give readers this kind of problem, which is probably why he felt compelled to add an epilogue that would provide a "rational" explanation. Many critics have found, however, either that the epilogue is unsatisfactory or that it raises as many questions as it tries to answer.

As critic Thomas Inge has remarked, "The story will yield a meaning from practically any conceivable critical approach—biographical, philosophical, historical, sociological, or formalistic—and nearly all of them have been applied in the past forty years." In this chapter, you will have the opportunity to put your own mind to the fascinating (and perhaps exasperating) puzzle of "Bartleby." After reading the story itself, you will study five critical responses, each approaching it from a different perspective. The titles of the articles indicate these various critical perspectives: "Bartleby Is a Schizophrenic," "Bartleby Is Christ," "Bartleby Is Marx's Alienated Worker," "Bartleby Is Melville," and "Bartleby Is a Woman."

Some of these approaches are contradictory; some are complementary. After reading them, you may be just as mystified as you were before. How, you may ask, can professional critics view the same text in such different ways? It's a good question. But the fact that critics disagree does not necessarily mean that any of them (or all but one of them) are wrong or misguided—or that literary criticism is useless. It means only that critics, each bringing his or her individual perspective to bear, view the text in different ways. (For example, film critics Siskel and Ebert frequently view a particular movie in different ways—which leads one to vote thumbs up, the other, thumbs down.) As you read these commentaries, bear in mind that the purpose of literary criticism is not necessarily to provide the final answers to the questions inevitably surrounding a rich and suggestive literary work. It is rather to provide a kind of dialogue, a conversation, among various readers of a work, a dialogue from which other writers may derive enlightenment and even enjoyment. Then, it is your turn to contribute to the dialogue—either by agreeing or disagreeing with one or more of the previous readers or by offering a distinctive viewpoint of your own.

Bartleby, the Scrivener

HERMAN MELVILLE

Herman Melville was born in New York City in 1819 to a prosperous family. His father, of Scotch-Irish descent, was an importer; his mother was of a distinguished Dutch family; his grandfather had been a general in the Revolutionary War. When Melville was eleven, his father went

"Bartleby the Scrivener" by Herman Melville. 1853.

bankrupt, then died two years later. Melville and his mother moved to Albany, New York, where he worked as a store clerk and a bank messenger; later, he went to Pittsfield, Massachusetts, and for a short time taught school. In 1839, he began a series of voyages, as a merchant seaman. His first trip, to Liverpool, England, gave him material for his novel Redburn *(1849). In 1841, he signed on the whaler* Acushnet *for a South Seas voyage. The following year, unable to tolerate sea life any more, he deserted his ship at Nukuheva in the Marquesas Islands and lived for a month among a cannibal tribe. His South Sea experiences gave him the material for his popular novels* Typee *(1846) and* Omoo *(1847). After several more voyages, a job as a warehouse clerk in Hawaii, and a fourteen-month tour of duty on the U.S. Navy frigate* United States, *Melville returned to civilian life, settled in New York City, and began his literary career.*

His early novels were very successful. But with Mardi *(1849), Melville began attempting more serious and allegorical themes, and the public lost interest in his work. He temporarily returned to adventure novels, with* Redburn *and* White Jacket *(1850), the latter based on his experiences on the* United States. *During this period, Melville joined a New York literary group and became a friend and neighbor of Nathaniel Hawthorne. Melville's next novel,* Moby Dick *(1851), is dedicated to Hawthorne. Now generally considered the greatest American novel,* Moby Dick *was a failure during Melville's lifetime, as were his next two novels,* Pierre *(1852) and* Israel Potter *(1855).*

In 1847, Melville married Elizabeth Shaw of Massachusetts. Three years later, the Melvilles moved to a farm in Pittsfield, Massachusetts, where they lived for the next thirteen years. During this time, Melville wrote articles and short stories for Putnam's Magazine *and* Harper's.

"Bartelby, the Scrivener" was published in Putnam's *in 1853 and collected (along with "Benito Cereno") into his* Piazza Tales *in 1856. Melville's last novel published during his lifetime was* The Confidence Man *(1857), set on a Mississippi River steamboat. Like his other works since 1850,* The Confidence Man *brought him no success and no income.*

In 1856 Melville suffered a nervous breakdown. After returning from a tour of the Holy Land the following year, he attempted to support himself and his wife through lectures. Now considerably in debt and in poor health, Melville was forced to sell the farm at Pittsfield, moved back to New York City, and worked as a customs clerk until his retirement in 1885. The last few years of his life were devoted to writing poetry, which he collected into several privately published volumes. When he died, in 1891, he left behind not only a considerable quantity of poetry but also the short novel Billy Budd, *a story about a good man destroyed by an evil one, which was not published until 1924. The revival of interest in Melville's work began on the centennial of his birth, 1919.*

I am a rather elderly man. The nature of my avocations for the last thirty years has brought me into more than ordinary contact with what would seem an interesting and somewhat singular set of men, of whom as yet nothing that I know of has ever been written:—I mean the law-copyists or scriveners. I have known very many of them, professionally and privately, and if I pleased, could relate divers histories, at which good-natured gentlemen might smile, and sentimental souls might weep. But I waive the biographies of all other scriveners for a few passages in the life of Bartleby, who was a scrivener the strangest I ever saw or heard of. While of other law-copyists I might write the complete life, of Bartleby nothing of that sort can be done. I believe that no materials exist for a full and satisfactory biography of this man. It is an irreparable loss to literature. Bartleby was one of those beings of whom nothing is ascertainable, except from the original sources, and in his case those are very small. What my own astonished eyes saw of Bartleby, *that* is all I know of him, except, indeed, one vague report which will appear in the sequel. 1

Ere introducing the scrivener, as he first appeared to me, it is fit I make some mention of myself, my *employées,* my business, my chambers, and general surroundings; because some such description is indispensable to an adequate understanding of the chief character about to be presented. 2

Imprimis: I am a man who, from his youth upwards, has been filled with a profound conviction that the easiest way of life is the best. Hence, though I belong to a profession proverbially energetic and nervous, even to turbulence, at times, yet nothing of that sort have I ever suffered to invade my peace. I am one of those unambitious lawyers who never addresses a jury, or in any way draws down public applause; but in the cool tranquillity of a snug retreat, do a snug business among rich men's bonds and mortgages and title-deeds. All who know me, consider me an eminently *safe* man. The late John Jacob Astor, a personage little given to poetic enthusiasm, had no hesitation in pronouncing my first grand point to be prudence; my next, method. I do not speak it in vanity, but simply record the fact, that I was not unemployed in my profession by the late John Jacob Astor; a name which, I admit, I love to repeat, for it hath a rounded and orbicular sound to it, and rings like unto bullion. I will freely add that I was not insensible to the late John Jacob Astor's good opinion. 3

Some time prior to the period at which this little history begins, my avocations had been largely increased. The good old office, now extinct in the State of New York, of a Master in Chancery, had been conferred upon me. It was not a very arduous office, but very pleasantly remunerative. I seldom lose my temper; much more 4 seldom indulge in dangerous indignation at wrongs and outrages; but I must be permitted to be rash here and declare, that I consider the sudden and violent abrogation of the office of Master in Chancery, by the new Constitution, as a—premature act; inasmuch as I had counted upon a life-lease of the profits, whereas I only received those of a few short years. But this is by the way.

My chambers were up stairs at No.——Wall Street. At one end 5
they looked upon the white wall of the interior of a spacious skylight shaft, penetrating the building from top to bottom. This view might have been considered rather tame than otherwise, deficient in what landscape painters call "life." But if so, the view from the other end of my chambers offered, at least, a contrast, if nothing more. In that direction my windows commanded an unobstructed view of a lofty brick wall, black by age and everlasting shade; which wall required no spyglass to bring out its lurking beauties, but for the benefit of all near-sighted spectators, was pushed up to within ten feet of my window panes. Owing to the great height of the surrounding buildings, and my chambers being on the second floor, the interval between this wall and mine not a little resembled a huge square cistern.

At the period just preceding the advent of Bartleby, I had two 6
persons as copyists in my employment, and a promising lad as an office-boy. First, Turkey; second, Nippers; third, Ginger Nut. These may seem names the like of which are not usually found in the Directory. In truth they were nicknames, mutually conferred upon each other by my three clerks, and were deemed expressive of their respective persons or characters. Turkey was a short, pursy Englishman of about my own age, that is, somewhere not far from sixty. In the morning, one might say, his face was of a fine florid hue, but after twelve o'clock, meridian—his dinner hour—it blazed like a grate full of Christmas coals; and continued blazing—but, as it were, with a gradual wane—till 6 o'clock, P.M. or thereabouts, after which I saw no more of the proprietor of the face, which gaining its meridian with the sun, seemed to set with it, to rise, culminate, and decline the following day, with the like regularity and undiminished glory. There are many singular coincidences I have known in the course of my life, not the least among which was the fact, that exactly when Turkey displayed his fullest beams from his red and radiant countenance, just then, too, at that critical moment began the daily period when I considered his business capacities as seriously disturbed for the remainder of the twenty-four hours. Not that he was absolutely idle, or averse to business then; far from it. The difficulty was, he was apt to be altogether too energetic. There was a strange, inflamed, flurried, flighty recklessness of activity about him. He would be incautious in dipping his pen into his inkstand. All his blots upon my documents were dropped there after twelve oclock, meridian. Indeed, not only

would he be reckless and sadly given to making blots in the afternoon, but some days he went further, and was rather noisy. At such times, too, his face flamed with augmented blazonry, as if cannel coal had been heaped on anthracite. He made an unpleasant racket with his chair; spilled his sand-box; in mending his pens, impatiently split them all to pieces, and threw them on the floor in a sudden passion; stood up and leaned over his table, boxing his papers about in a most indecorous manner, very sad to behold in an elderly man like him. Nevertheless, as he was in many ways a most valuable person to me, and all the time before twelve o'clock, meridian, was the quickest, steadiest creature too, accomplishing a great deal of work in a style not easy to be matched—for these reasons, I was willing to overlook his eccentricities, though indeed, occasionally, I remonstrated with him. I did this very gently, however, because, though the civilest, nay, the blandest and most reverential of men in the morning, yet in the afternoon he was disposed, upon provocation, to be slightly rash with his tongue, in fact, insolent. Now, valuing his morning services as I did, and resolved not to lose them; yet, at the same time made uncomfortable by his inflamed ways after twelve o'clock; and being a man of peace, unwilling by my admonitions to call forth unseemly retorts from him; I took upon me, one Saturday noon (he was always worse on Saturdays), to hint to him, very kindly, that perhaps now that he was growing old, it might be well to abridge his labors; in short, he need not come to my chambers after twelve o'clock, but, dinner over, had best go home to his lodgings and rest himself till tea-time. But no; he insisted upon his afternoon devotions. His countenance became intolerably fervid, as he oratorically assured me—gesticulating with a long ruler at the other end of the room—that if his services in the morning were useful, how indispensable, then, in the afternoon?

"With submission, sir," said Turkey on this occasion, "I consider myself your right-hand man. In the morning I but marshal and deploy my columns; but in the afternoon I put myself at their head, and gallantly charge the foe, thus!"—and he made a violent thrust with the ruler. 7

"But the blots, Turkey," intimated I. 8

"True,—but, with submission, sir, behold these hairs! I am getting old. Surely, sir, a blot or two of a warm afternoon is not to be severely urged against gray hairs. Old age—even if it blot the page—is honorable. With submission, sir, we *both* are getting old." 9

This appeal to my fellow-feeling was hardly to be resisted. At all events, I saw that go he would not. So I made up my mind to let him stay, resolving, nevertheless, to see to it, that during the afternoon he had to do with my less important papers. 10

Nippers, the second on my list, was a whiskered, sallow, and, 11 upon the whole, rather piratical-looking young man of about five and twenty. I always deemed him the victim of two evil powers—ambition and indigestion. The ambition was evinced by a certain impatience of the duties of a mere copyist, an unwarrantable usurpation of strictly professional affairs, such as the original drawing up of legal documents. The indigestion seemed betokened in an occasional nervous testiness and grinning irritability, causing the teeth to audibly grind together over mistakes committed in copying; unnecessary maledictions, hissed, rather than spoken, in the heat of business; and especially by a continual discontent with the height of the table where he worked. Though of a very ingenious mechanical turn. Nippers could never get this table to suit him. He put chips under it, blocks of various sorts, bits of pasteboard, and at last went so far as to attempt an exquisite adjustment by final pieces of folded blotting-paper. But no invention would answer. If, for the sake of easing his back, he brought the table lid at a sharp angle well up towards his chin, and wrote there like a man using the steep roof of a Dutch house for his desk:—then he declared that it stopped the circulation in his arms. If now he lowered the table to his waistbands, and stooped over it in writing, then there was a sore aching in his back. In short, the truth of the matter was, Nippers knew not what he wanted. Or, if he wanted any thing, it was to be rid of a scrivener's table altogether. Among the manifestations of his diseased ambition was a fondness he had for receiving visits from certain ambiguous-looking fellows in seedy coats, whom he called his clients. Indeed I was aware that not only was he, at times, considerable of a ward-politician, but he occasionally did a little business at the Justices' courts, and was not unknown on the steps of the Tombs. I have good reason to believe, however, that one individual who called upon him at my chambers, and who, with a grand air, he insisted was his client, was no other than a dun, and the alleged title-deed, a bill. But with all his failings, and the annoyances he caused me, Nippers, like his compatriot Turkey, was a very useful man to me; wrote a neat, swift hand; and, when he chose, was not deficient in a gentlemanly sort of deportment. Added to this, he always dressed in a gentlemanly sort of way: and so, incidentally, reflected credit upon my chambers. Whereas with respect to Turkey, I had much ado to keep him from being a reproach to me. His clothes were apt to look oily and smell of eating-houses. He wore his pantaloons very loose and baggy in summer. His coats were execrable; his hat not to be handled. But while the hat was a thing of indifference to me, inasmuch as his natural civility and deference, as a dependent Englishman, always led him to doff it the moment he entered the room, yet his coat was another matter. Concerning his coats, I reasoned with him; but with no effect. The truth was, I suppose, that a man with so small an income, could not afford to sport such a lustrous face and a lustrous coat at one and the same time. As Nippers once observed, Turkey's money went chiefly for red ink. One winter day I presented Turkey with a highly-respectable looking coat of my own, a padded gray coat, of a most comfortable warmth, and which buttoned straight up from the knee to the neck. I thought Turkey would appreciate the favor, and abate his rashness and obstreperousness of afternoons. But no. I verily believe that buttoning himself up in so downy and blanket-like a coat had a pernicious effect upon him; upon the same principle that too much oats are bad for horses. In fact, precisely as a rash, restive horse is said to feel his oats, so Turkey felt his coat. It made him insolent. He was a man whom prosperity harmed.

Though concerning the self-indulgent habits of Turkey I had my 12
own private surmises, yet touching Nippers I was well persuaded that whatever might be his faults in other respects, he was, at least, a temperate young man. But indeed, nature herself seemed to have been his vintner, and at his birth charged him so thoroughly with an irritable, brandy-like disposition, that all subsequent potations were needless. When I consider how, amid the stillness of my chambers, Nippers would sometimes impatiently rise from his seat, and stooping over his table, spread his arms wide apart, seize the whole desk, and move it, and jerk it, with a grim, grinding motion on the floor, as if the table were a perverse voluntary agent, intent on thwarting and vexing him; I plainly perceive that for Nippers, brandy and water were altogether superfluous.

It was fortunate for me that, owing to its peculiar cause— 13
indigestion—the irritability and consequent nervousness of Nippers, were mainly observable in the morning, while in the afternoon he was comparatively mild. So that Turkey's paroxysms only coming on about twelve o'clock, I never had to do with their eccentricities at one time. Their fits relieved each other like guards. When Nippers' was on, Turkey's was off; and *vice versa.* This was a good natural arrangement under the circumstances.

Ginger Nut, the third on my list, was a lad some twelve years old. 14
His father was a carman, ambitious of seeing his son on the bench instead of a cart, before he died. So he sent him to my office as student at law, errand boy, and cleaner and sweeper, at the rate of one dollar a week. He had a little desk to himself, but he did not use it much. Upon inspection, the drawer exhibited a great array of the shells of various sorts of nuts. Indeed, to this quick-witted youth the whole noble science of the law was contained in a nutshell. Not the least among the employments of Ginger Nut, as well as one which he discharged with the most alacrity, was his duty as cake and apple purveyor for Turkey and Nippers. Copying law papers being proverbially a dry, husky sort of business, my two scriveners were fain to

moisten their mouths very often with Spitzenbergs to be had at the numerous stalls nigh the Custom House and Post Office. Also, they sent Ginger Nut very frequently for that peculiar cake—small, flat, round, and very spicy—after which he had been named by them. Of a cold morning when business was but dull, Turkey would gobble up scores of these cakes, as if they were mere wafers—indeed they sell them at the rate of six or eight for a penny—the scrape of his pen blending with the crunching of the crisp particles in his mouth. Of all the fiery afternoon blunders and flurried rashnesses of Turkey, was his once moistening a ginger-cake between his lips, and clapping it on to a mortgage for a seal. I came within an ace of dismissing him then. But he mollified me by making an oriental bow, and saying—"With submission, sir, it was generous of me to find you in stationery on my own account."

Now my original business—that of a conveyancer and title hunt- 15
er, and drawer-up of recondite documents of all sorts—was considerably increased by receiving the master's office. There was now great work for scriveners. Not only must I push the clerks already with me, but I must have additional help. In answer to my advertisement, a motionless young man one morning stood upon my office threshold, the door being open, for it was summer. I can see that figure now—pallidly neat, pitiably respectable, incurably forlorn! It was Bartleby.

After a few words touching his qualifications, I engaged him, 16
glad to have among my corps of copyists a man of so singularly sedate an aspect, which I thought might operate beneficially upon the flighty temper of Turkey, and the fiery one of Nippers.

I should have stated before that ground glass folding-doors di- 17
vided my premises into two parts, one of which was occupied by my scriveners, the other by myself. According to my humor I threw open these doors, or closed them. I resolved to assign Bartleby a corner by the folding-doors, but on my side of them, so as to have this quiet man within easy call, in case any trifling thing was to be done. I placed his desk close up to a small side-window in that part of the room, a window which originally had afforded a lateral view of certain grimy backyards and bricks, but which, owing to subsequent erections, commanded at present no view at all, though it gave some light. Within three feet of the panes was a wall, and the light came down from far above, between two lofty buildings, as from a very small opening in a dome. Still further to a satisfactory arrangement, I procured a high green folding screen, which might entirely isolate Bartleby from my sight, though not remove him from my voice. And thus, in a manner, privacy and society were conjoined.

At first Bartleby did an extraordinary quantity of writing. As if 18
long famishing for something to copy, he seemed to gorge himself on my documents. There was no pause for digestion. He ran a day and

night line, copying by sunlight and by candlelight. I should have been quite delighted with his application, had he been cheerfully industrious. But he wrote on silently, palely, mechanically.

It is, of course, an indispensable part of a scrivener's business to 19
verify the accuracy of his copy, word by word. Where there are two or more scriveners in an office, they assist each other in this examination, one reading from the copy, the older holding the original. It is a very dull, wearisome, and lethargic affair. I can readily imagine that to some sanguine temperaments it would be altogether intolerable. For example, I cannot credit that the mettlesome poet Byron would have contentedly sat down with Bartleby to examine a law document of, say, five hundred pages, closely written in a crimpy hand.

Now and then, in the haste of business, it had been my habit to 20
assist in comparing some brief document myself, calling Turkey or Nippers for this purpose. One object I had in placing Bartleby so handy to me behind the screen, was to avail myself of his services on such trivial occasions. It was on the third day, I think, of his being with me, and before any necessity had arisen for having his own writing examined, that, being much hurried to complete a small affair I had in hand, I abruptly called to Bartleby. In my haste and natural expectancy of instant compliance, I sat with my head bent over the original on my desk, and my right hand sideways, and somewhat nervously extended with the copy, so that immediately upon emerging from his retreat, Bartleby might snatch it and proceed to business without the least delay.

In this very attitude did I sit when I called to him, rapidly stating 21
what it was I wanted him to do—namely, to examine a small paper with me. Imagine my surprise, nay, my consternation, when without moving from his privacy, Bartleby, in a singularly mild, firm voice, replied, "I would prefer not to."

I sat awhile in perfect silence, rallying my stunned faculties. 22
Immediately it occurred to me that my ears had deceived me, or Bartleby had entirely misunderstood my meaning. I repeated my request in the clearest tone I could assume. But in quite as clear a one came the previous reply, "I would prefer not to."

"Prefer not to," echoed I, rising in high excitement, and crossing 23
the room with a stride. "What do you mean? Are you moon-struck? I want you to help me compare this sheet here—take it," and I thrust it towards him.

"I would prefer not to," said he. 24

I looked at him steadfastly, His face was leanly composed; his 25
gray eye dimly calm. Not a wrinkle of agitation rippled him. Had there been the least uneasiness, anger, impatience or impertinence in his manner; in other words, had there been anything ordinarily human about him, doubtless I should have violently dismissed him

from the premises. But as it was, I should have as soon thought of turning my pale plaster-of-paris bust of Cicero out-of-doors. I stood gazing at him awhile, as he went on with his own writing, and then reseated myself at my desk. This is very strange, thought I. What had one best do? But my business hurried me. I concluded to forget the matter for the present, reserving it for my future leisure. So calling Nippers from the other room, the paper was speedily examined.

A few days after this, Bartleby concluded four lengthy documents, being quadruplicates of a week's testimony taken before me in my High Court of Chancery. It became necessary to examine them. It was an important suit, and great accuracy was imperative. Having all things arranged I called Turkey, Nippers and Ginger Nut from the next room, meaning to place the four copies in the hands of my four clerks, while I should read from the original. Accordingly Turkey, Nippers and Ginger Nut had taken their seats in a row, each with his document in hand, when I called to Bartleby to join this interesting group. 26

"Bartleby! quick, I am waiting." 27

I heard a slow scrape of his chair legs on the uncarpeted floor, and soon he appeared standing at the entrance of his hermitage. 28

"What is wanted?" said he mildly. 29

"The copies, the copies," said I hurriedly. "We are going to examine them. There"—and I held towards him the fourth quadruplicate. 30

"I would prefer not to," he said, and gently disappeared behind the screen. 31

For a few moments I was turned into a pillar of salt, standing at the head of my seated column of clerks. Recovering myself, I advanced towards the screen, and demanded the reason for such extraordinary conduct. 32

"*Why* do you refuse?" 33

"I would prefer not to." 34

With any other man I should have flown outright into a dreadful passion, scorned all further words, and thrust him ignominiously from my presence. But there was something about Bartleby that not only strangely disarmed me, but in a wonderful manner touched and disconcerted me. I began to reason with him. 35

"These are your own copies we are about to examine. It is labor saving to you, because one examination will answer for your four papers. It is common usage. Every copyist is bound to help examine his copy. Is it not so? Will you not speak? Answer!" 36

"I prefer not to," he replied in a flute-like tone. It seemed to me that while I had been addressing him, he carefully revolved every statement that I made; fully comprehended the meaning; could not 37 gainsay the irresistible conclusion; but, at the same time, some paramount consideration prevailed with him to reply as he did.

"You are decided, then, not to comply with my request—a re- 38
quest made according to common usage and common sense?"

He briefly gave me to understand that on that point my judgment 39
was sound. Yes: his decision was irreversible.

It is not seldom the case that when a man is browbeaten in some 40
unprecedented and violently unreasonable way, he begins to stagger in his own plainest faith. He begins, as it were, vaguely to surmise that, wonderful as it may be, all the justice and all the reason is on the other side. Accordingly, if any disinterested persons are present, he turns to them for some reinforcement for his own faltering mind.

"Turkey," said I, "what do you think of this? Am I not right?" 41

"With submission, sir," said Turkey, with his blandest tone, "I 42
think that you are."

"Nippers," said I, "what do *you* think of it?" 43

"I think I should kick him out of the office." 44

(The reader of nice perceptions will here perceive that, it being 45
morning, Turkey's answer is couched in polite and tranquil terms, but Nippers replies in ill-tempered ones. Or, to repeat a previous sentence, Nipper's ugly mood was on duty, and Turkey's off.)

"Ginger Nut," said I, willing to enlist the smallest suffrage in my 46
behalf, "what do *you* think of it?"

"I think, sir he's a little *luny*," replied Ginger Nut, with a grin. 47

"You hear what they say," said I, turning towards the screen, 48
"come forth and do your duty."

But he vouchsafed no reply. I pondered a moment in sore per- 49
plexity. But once more business hurried me. I determined again to postpone the consideration of this dilemma to my future leisure. With a little trouble we made out to examine the papers without Bartleby, though at every page or two, Turkey deferentially dropped his opinion that this proceeding was quite out of the common; while Nippers, twitching in his chair with a dyspeptic nervousness, ground out between his set teeth occasional hissing maledictions against the stubborn oaf behind the screen. And for his (Nippers's) part, this was the first and the last time he would do another man's business without pay.

Meanwhile Bartleby sat in his hermitage, oblivious to everything 50
but his own peculiar business there.

Some days passed, the scrivener being employed upon another 51
lengthy work. His late remarkable conduct led me to regard his ways narrowly. I observed that he never went to dinner; indeed that he never went anywhere. As yet I had never of my personal knowledge known him to be outside of my office. He was a perpetual sentry in

the corner. At about eleven o'clock though, in the morning, I noticed that Ginger Nut would advance toward the opening in Bartleby's screen, as if silently beckoned thither by a gesture invisible to me where I sat. The boy would then leave the office jingling a few pence, and reappear with a handful of ginger-nuts which he delivered in the hermitage, receiving two of the cakes for his trouble.

He lives, then, on ginger-nuts, thought I; never eats a dinner, 52
properly speaking; he must be a vegetarian then; but no; he never eats even vegetables, he eats nothing but ginger-nuts. My mind then ran on in reveries concerning the probable effects upon the human constitution of living entirely on ginger-nuts. Ginger-nuts are so called because they contain ginger as one of their peculiar constituents, and the final flavoring one. Now what was ginger? A hot, spicy thing. Was Bartleby hot and spicy? Not at all. Ginger, then, had no effect upon Bartleby. Probably he preferred it should have none.

Nothing so aggravates an earnest person as a passive resistance. 53
If the individual so resisted be of a not inhumane temper, and the resisting one perfectly harmless in his passivity; then, in the better moods of the former, he will endeavor charitably to construe to his imagination what proves impossible to be solved by his judgment. Even so, for the most part, I regarded Bartleby and his ways. Poor fellow! thought I, he means no mischief; it is plain he intends no insolence; his aspect sufficiently evinces that his eccentricities are involuntary. He is useful to me. I can get along with him. If I turn him away, the chances are he will fall in with some less indulgent employer, and then he will be rudely treated, and perhaps driven forth miserably to starve. Yes. Here I can cheaply purchase a delicious self-approval. To befriend Bartleby; to humor him in his strange wilfulness, will cost me little or nothing, while I lay up in my soul what will eventually prove a sweet morsel for my conscience. But this mood was not invariable with me. The passiveness of Bartleby sometimes irritated me. I felt strangely goaded on to encounter him in new opposition, to elicit some angry spark from him answerable to my own. But indeed I might as well have essayed to strike fire with my knuckles against a bit of Windsor soap. But one afternoon the evil impulse in me mastered me, and the following little scene ensued:

"Bartleby," said I, "when those papers are all copied, I will 54
compare them with you."

"I would prefer not to." 55

"How? Surely you do not mean to persist in that mulish vagary?" 56

No answer. 57

I threw open the folding-doors near by, and turning upon Turkey 58
and Nippers, exclaimed in an excited manner—

59 "He says, a second time, he won't examine his papers. What do you think of it, Turkey?"

60 It was afternoon, be it remembered. Turkey sat glowing like a brass boiler, his bald head steaming, his hands reeling among his blotted papers.

61 "Think of it?" roared Turkey; "I think I'll just step behind his screen, and black his eyes for him!"

62 So saying, Turkey rose to his feet and threw his arms into a puglistic position. He was hurrying away to make good his promise, when I detained him, alarmed at the effect of incautiously rousing Turkey's combativeness after dinner.

63 "Sit down, Turkey," said I, "and hear what Nippers has to say. What do you think of it, Nippers? Would I not be justified in immediately dismissing Bartleby?"

64 "Excuse me, that is for you to decide, sir. I think his conduct quite unusual, and indeed unjust, as regards Turkey and myself. But it may only be a passing whim."

65 "Ah," exclaimed I, "you have strangely changed your mind then—you speak very gently of him now."

66 "All beer," cried Turkey; "gentleness is effects of beer—Nippers and I dined together today. You see how gentle *I* am, sir. Shall I go and black his eyes?"

67 "You refer to Bartleby, I suppose. No, not today, Turkey," I replied; "pray, put up your fists."

68 I closed the doors, and again advanced towards Bartleby. I felt additional incentives tempting me to my fate. I burned to be rebelled against again. I remembered that Bartleby never left the office.

69 "Bartleby," said I, "Ginger Nut is away; just step round to the Post Office, won't you? (it was but a three minutes' walk,) and see if there is anything for me."

70 "I would prefer not to."

71 "You *will* not?"

72 "I *prefer* not."

73 I staggered to my desk, and sat there in a deep study. My blind inveteracy returned. Was there any other thing in which I could procure myself to be ignominiously repulsed by this lean, penniless wight?—my hired clerk? What added thing is there, perfectly reasonable, that he will be sure to refuse to do?

74 "Bartleby!"

75 No answer.

76 "Bartleby," in a louder tone.

77 No answer.

78 "Bartleby," I roared.

Like a very ghost, agreeably to the laws of magical invocation, at 79
the third summons, he appeared at the entrance of his hermitage.

"Go to the next room, and tell Nippers to come to me." 80

"I prefer not to," he respectfully and slowly said, and mildly 81
disappeared.

"Very good, Bartleby," said I, in a quiet sort of serenely severe 82
self-possessed tone, intimating the unalterable purpose of some terrible retribution very close at hand. At the moment I half intended something of the kind. But upon the whole, as it was drawing towards my dinner-hour, I thought it best to put on my hat and walk home for the day, suffering much from perplexity and distress of mind.

Shall I acknowledge it? The conclusion of this whole business 83
was, that it soon became a fixed fact of my chambers, that a pale young scrivener, by the name of Bartleby, had a desk there; that he copied for me at the usual rate of four cents a folio (one hundred words); but he was permanently exempt from examining the work done by him, that duty being transferred to Turkey and Nippers, one of compliment doubtless to their superior acuteness; moreover, said Bartleby was never on any account to be dispatched on the most trivial errand of any sort; and that even if entreated to take upon him such a matter, it was generally understood that he would prefer not to—in other words, that he would refuse point-blank.

As days passed on, I became considerably reconciled to Bartleby. 84
His steadiness, his freedom from all dissipation, his incessant industry (except when he chose to throw himself into a standing revery behind his screen), his great stillness, his unalterableness of demeanor under all circumstances, made him a valuable acquisition. One prime thing was this,—*he was always there;*—first in the morning, continually through the day, and the last at night. I had a singular confidence in his honesty. I felt my most precious papers perfectly safe in his hands. Sometimes to be sure I could not, for the very soul of me, avoid falling into sudden spasmodic passions with him. For it was exceeding difficult to bear in mind all the time those strange peculiarities, privileges, and unheard of exemptions, forming the tacit stipulations on Bartleby's part under which he remained in my office. Now and then, in the eagerness of dispatching pressing business, I would inadvertently summon Bartleby, in a short, rapid tone, to put his finger, say, on the incipient tie of a bit of red tape with which I was about compressing some papers. Of course, from behind the screen the usual answer, "I prefer not to," was sure to come; and then, how could a human creature with the common infirmities of our nature, refrain from bitterly exclaiming upon such perverseness—such unreasonableness? However, every added repulse

of this sort which I received only tended to lessen the probability of my repeating the inadvertence.

Here it must be said, that according to the custom of most legal 85
gentlemen occupying chambers in densely-populated law buildings, there were several keys to my door. One was kept by a woman residing in the attic, which person weekly scrubbed and daily swept and dusted my apartments. Another was kept by Turkey for convenience sake. The third I sometimes carried in my own pocket. The fourth I knew not who had.

Now, one Sunday morning I happened to go to Trinity Church, 86
to hear a celebrated preacher, and finding myself rather early on the ground, I thought I would walk round to my chambers for a while. Luckily I had my key with me; but upon applying it to the lock, I found it resisted by something inserted from the inside. Quite surprised, I called out; when to my consternation a key was turned from within; and thrusting his lean visage at me, and holding the door ajar, the apparition of Bartleby appeared, in his shirt sleeves, and otherwise in a strangely tattered dishabille, saying quietly that he was sorry, but he was deeply engaged just then, and—preferred not admitting me at present. In a brief word or two, he moreover added, that perhaps I had better walk round the block two or three times, and by that time he would probably have concluded his affairs.

Now, the utterly unsurmised appearance of Bartleby, tenanting 87
my law-chambers of a Sunday morning, with his cadaverously gentlemanly *nonchalance,* yet withal firm and self-possessed, had such a strange effect upon me, that incontinently I slunk away from my own door, and did as desired. But not without sundry twinges of impotent rebellion against the mild effrontery of this unaccountable scrivener. Indeed, it was his wonderful mildness, chiefly, which not only disarmed me, but unmanned me, as it were. For I consider that one, for the time, is sort of unmanned when he tranquilly permits his hired clerk to dictate to him, and order him away from his own premises. Furthermore, I was full of uneasiness as to what Bartleby could possibly be doing in my office in his shirt sleeves, and in an otherwise dismantled condition of a Sunday morning. Was anything amiss going on? Nay, that was out of the question. It was not to be thought of for a moment that Bartleby was an immoral person. But what could he be doing there?—copying? Nay again, whatever might be his eccentricities, Bartleby was an eminently decorous person. He would be the last man to sit down to his desk in any state approaching to nudity. Besides, it was Sunday; and there was something about Bartleby that forbade the supposition that he would by any secular occupation violate the proprieties of the day.

Nevertheless, my mind was not pacified; and full of a restless 88 curiosity, at last I returned to the door. Without hindrance I inserted my key, opened it, and entered. Bartleby was not to be seen. I looked round anxiously, peeped behind his screen; but it was very plain that he was gone. Upon more closely examining the place, I surmised that for an indefinite period Bartleby must have ate, dressed, and slept in my office, and that too without plate, mirror, or bed. The cushioned seat of a ricketty old sofa in one corner bore the faint impress of a lean, reclining form. Rolled away under his desk, I found a blanket under the empty grate, a blacking box and brush; on a chair, a tin basin, with soap and a ragged towel; in a newspaper a few crumbs of ginger-nuts and a morsel of cheese. Yes, thought I, it is evident enough that Bartleby has been making his home here, keeping bachelor's hall all by himself. Immediately then the thought came sweeping across me. What miserable friendlessness and loneliness are here revealed! His poverty is great; but his solitude, how horrible! Think of it. Of a Sunday, Wall Street is deserted as Petra; and every night of every day it is an emptiness. This building too, which of weekdays hums with industry and life, at nightfall echoes with sheer vacancy, and all through Sunday is forlorn. And here Bartleby makes his home; sole spectator of a solitude which he has seen all populous—a sort of innocent and transformed Marius brooding among the ruins of Carthage!

For the first time in my life a feeling of overpowering stinging 89
melancholy seized me. Before, I had never experienced aught but a not-unpleasing sadness. The bond of a common humanity now drew me irresistibly to gloom. A fraternal melancholy! For both I and Bartleby were sons of Adam. I remembered the bright silks and sparkling faces I had seen that day, in gala trim, swan-like sailing down the Mississippi of Broadway; and I contrasted them with the pallid copyist, and thought to myself, Ah, happiness courts the light, so we deem the world is gay; but misery hides aloof, so we deem that misery there is none. These sad fancyings—chimeras, doubtless, of a sick and silly brain—led on to other and more special thoughts, concerning the eccentricities of Bartleby. Presentiments of strange discoveries hovered round me. The scrivener's pale form appeared to me laid out, among uncaring strangers, in its shivering winding sheet.

Suddenly I was attracted by Bartleby's closed desk, the key in 90
open sight left in the lock.

I mean no mischief, seek the gratification of no heartless curios- 91
ity, thought I; besides, the desk is mine, and its contents too, so I will make bold to look within. Everything was methodically arranged, the papers smoothly placed. The pigeonholes were deep, and removing the files of documents, I groped into their recesses. Presently I felt something there, and dragged it out. It was an old

bandanna handkerchief, heavy and knotted. I opened it, and saw it was a savings' bank.

I now recalled all the quiet mysteries which I had noted in the man. I remembered that he never spoke but to answer; that though at intervals he had considerable time to himself, yet I had never seen him reading—no, not even a newspaper; that for long periods he would stand looking out, at his pale window behind the screen, upon the dead brick wall; I was quite sure he never visited any refectory or eating house; while his pale face clearly indicated that he never drank beer like Turkey, or tea and coffee even, like other men; that he never went anywhere in particular that I could learn; never went out for a walk, unless indeed that was the case at present; that he had declined telling who he was, or whence he came, or whether he had any relatives in the world; that though so thin and pale, he never complained of ill health. And more than all, I remembered a certain unconscious air of pallid—how shall I call it?—of pallid haughtiness, say, or rather an austere reserve about him, which had positively awed me into my tame compliance with his eccentricities, when I had feared to ask him to do the slightest incidental thing for me, even though I might know, from his long-continued motionlessness, that behind his screen he must be standing in one of those dead-wall reveries of his. 92

Revolving all these things, and coupling them with the recently discovered fact that he made my office his constant abiding place and home, and not forgetful of his morbid moodiness; revolving all these things, a prudential feeling began to steal over me. My first emotions had been those of pure melancholy and sincerest pity; but just in proportion as the forlornness of Bartleby grew and grew to my imagination, did that same melancholy merge into fear, that pity into repulsion. So true it is, and so terrible too, that up to a certain point the thought or sight of misery enlists our best affections; but, in certain special cases, beyond that point it does not. They err who would assert that invariably this is owing to the inherent selfishness of the human heart. It rather proceeds from a certain hopelessness of remedying excessive and organic ill. To a sensitive being, pity is not seldom pain. And when at last it is perceived that such pity cannot lead to effectual succor, common sense bids the soul be rid of it. What I saw that morning persuaded me that the scrivener was the victim of innate and incurable disorder. I might give alms to his body; but his body did not pain him; it was his soul that suffered, and his soul I could not reach. 93

I did not accomplish the purpose of going to Trinity Church that morning. Somehow, the things I had seen disqualified me for the time from churchgoing. I walked homeward, thinking what I would do with Bartleby. Finally, I resolved upon this;—I would put certain 94 calm questions to him the next morning, touching his history, &c., and if he declined to answer them openly and unreservedly (and I supposed he would prefer not), then to give him a twenty-dollar bill over and above whatever I might owe him, and tell him his services were no longer required; but that if in any other way I could assist him, I would be happy to do so, especially if he desired to return to his native place, wherever that might be, I would willingly help to defray the expenses. Moreover, if, after reaching home, he found himself at any time in want of aid, a letter from him would be sure of a reply.

The next morning came. 95

"Bartleby," said I, gently calling to him behind his screen. 96

No reply. 97

"Bartleby," said I, in a still gentler tone, "come here; I am not 98
going to ask you to do anything you would prefer not to do—I simply wish to speak to you."

Upon this he noiselessly slid into view. 99

"Will you tell me, Bartleby, where you were born?" 100

"I would prefer not to." 101

"Will you tell me *anything* about yourself?" 102

"I would prefer not to." 103

"But what reasonable objection can you have to speak to me? I 104
feel friendly towards you."

He did not look at me while I spoke, but kept his glance fixed 105
upon my bust of Cicero, which as I then sat, was directly behind me, some six inches above my head.

"What is your answer, Bartleby?" said I, after waiting a consider- 106
able time for a reply, during which his countenance remained immovable, only there was the faintest conceivable tremor of the white attenuated mouth.

"At present I prefer to give no answer," he said, and retired into 107
his hermitage.

It was rather weak in me I confess, but his manner on this 108
occasion nettled me. Not only did there seem to lurk in it a certain calm disdain, but his perverseness seemed ungrateful, considering the undeniable good usuage and indulgence he had received from me.

Again I sat ruminating what I should do. Mortified as I was at his 109
behavior, and resolved as I had been to dismiss him when I entered my office, nevertheless I strangely felt something superstitious knocking at my heart, and forbidding me to carry out my purpose, and denouncing me for a villain if I dared to breathe one bitter word against this forlornest of mankind. At last, familiarly drawing my chair behind his screen, I sat down and said: "Bartleby, never mind then about revealing your history; but let me entreat you, as a friend,

to comply as far as may be with the usages of this office. Say now you
will help to examine papers tomorrow or next day: in short, say now
that in a day or two you will begin to be a little reasonable:—say so,
Bartleby."

"At present I would prefer not to be a little reasonable," was his 110
mildly cadaverous reply.

Just then the folding-doors opened, and Nippers approached. He 111
seemed suffering from an unusually bad night's rest, induced by
severer indigestion than common. He overheard those final words of
Bartleby.

"*Prefer not,* eh?" gritted Nippers—"I'd *prefer* him, if I were you, 112
sir," addressing me—"I'd *prefer* him; I'd give him preferences, the
stubborn mule! What is it, sir, pray, that he *prefers* not to do now?"

Bartleby moved not a limb. 113

"Mr. Nippers," said I. "I'd prefer that you would withdraw for 114
the present."

Somehow, of late I had got into the way of involuntarily using 115
this word "prefer" upon all sorts of not exactly suitable occasions.
And I trembled to think that my contact with the scrivener had
already and seriously affected me in a mental way. And what further
and deeper aberration might it not yet produce? This apprehension
had not been without efficacy in determining me to summary means.

As Nippers, looking very sour and sulky, was departing, Turkey 116
blandly and deferentially approached.

"With submission, sir," said he, "yesterday I was thinking about 117
Bartleby here, and I think that if he would but prefer to take a quart of
good ale every day, it would do much towards mending him and
enabling him to assist in examining his papers."

"So you have got the word too," said I, slightly excited. 118

"With submission, what word, sir?" asked Turkey, respectfully 119
crowding himself into the contracted space behind the screen, and by
so doing making me jostle the scrivener. "What word, sir?"

"I would prefer to be left alone here," said Bartleby, as if offended 120
at being mobbed in his privacy.

"*That's* the word, Turkey," said I—"*that's* it." 121

"Oh, *prefer?* oh yes—queer word. I never use it myself. But, sir, as 122
I was saying, if he would but prefer—"

"Turkey," interrupted I, "you will please withdraw." 123

"Oh certainly, sir, if you prefer that I should." 124

As he opened the folding-door to retire, Nippers at his desk 125
caught a glimpse of me, and asked whether I would prefer to have a
certain paper copied on blue paper or white. He did not in the least
roguishly accent the word *prefer.* It was plain that it involuntarily
rolled from his tongue. I thought to myself, surely I must get rid of a
demented man, who already has in some degree turned the tongues,

if not the heads of myself and clerks. But I thought it prudent not to break the dismission at once.

The next day I noticed that Bartleby did nothing but stand at his window in his dead-wall revery. Upon asking him why he did not write, he said that he had decided upon doing no more writing. 126

"Why, how now? what next?" exclaimed I, "do no more writing?" 127

"No more." 128

"And what is the reason?" 129

"Do you not see the reason for yourself," he indifferently replied. 130

I looked steadfastly at him, and perceived that his eyes looked dull and glazed. Instantly it occurred to me, that his unexampled diligence in copying by his dim window for the first few weeks of his stay with me might have temporarily impaired his vision. 131

I was touched. I said something in condolence with him. I hinted that of course he did wisely in abstaining from writing for a while; and urged him to embrace that opportunity of taking wholesome exercise in the open air. This, however, he did not do. A few days after this, my other clerks being absent, and being in a great hurry to dispatch certain letters by the mail, I thought that, having nothing else earthly to do, Bartleby would surely be less inflexible than usual, and carry these letters to the post office. But he blankly declined. So, much to my inconvenience, I went myself. 132

Still added days went by. Whether Bartleby's eyes improved or not, I could not say. To all appearance, I thought they did. But when I asked him if they did, he vouchsafed no answer. At all events, he would do no copying. At last, in reply to my urgings, he informed me that he had permanently given up copying. 133

"What!" exclaimed I; "suppose your eyes should get entirely well—better than ever before—would you not copy then?" 134

"I have given up copying," he answered, and slid aside. 135

He remained, as ever, a fixture in my chamber. Nay—if that were possible—he became still more of a fixture than before. What was to be done? He would do nothing in the office: why should he stay there? In plain fact, he had now become a millstone to me, not only useless as a necklace, but afflictive to bear. Yet I was sorry for him. I speak less than truth when I say that, on his own account, he occasioned me uneasiness. If he would but have named a single relative or friend, I would instantly have written, and urged their taking the poor fellow away to some convenient retreat. But he seemed alone, absolutely alone in the universe. A bit of wreck in the mid-Atlantic. At length, necessities connected with my business tyrannized over all other considerations. Decently as I could, I told Bartleby that in six days' time he must unconditionally leave the office. I warned him to take measures, in the interval, for procuring some other abode. I offered to assist him in this endeavor, if he 136 himself would but take the first step towards a removal. "And when you finally quit me, Bartleby," added I, "I shall see that you go not away entirely unprovided. Six days from this hour, remember."

At the expiration of that period, I peeped behind the screen, and lo! Bartleby was there. 137

I buttoned up my coat, balanced myself; advanced slowly towards him, touched his shoulder, and said, "The time has come; you must quit this place; I am sorry for you; here is money; but you must go." 138

"I would prefer not," he replied, with his back still towards me. 139

"You *must*." 140

He remained silent. 141

Now I had an unbounded confidence in this man's common honesty. He had frequently restored to me sixpences and shillings carelessly dropped upon the floor, for I am apt to be very reckless in such shirt-button affairs. The proceeding then which followed will not be deemed extraordinary. 142

"Bartleby," said I, "I owe you twelve dollars on account; here are thirty-two; the odd twenty are yours.—Will you take it?" and I handed the bills towards him. 143

But he made no motion. 144

"I will leave them here then," putting them under a weight on the table. Then taking my hat and cane and going to the door I tranquilly turned and added—"After you have removed your things from these offices, Bartleby, you will of course lock the door—since everyone is now gone for the day but you—and if you please, slip your key underneath the mat, so that I may have it in the morning. I shall not see you again; so good-bye to you. If hereafter in your new place of abode I can be of any service to you, do not fail to advise me by letter. Good-bye, Bartleby, and fare you well." 145

But he answered not a word; like the last column of some ruined temple, he remained standing mute and solitary in the middle of the otherwise deserted room. 146

As I walked home in a pensive mood, my vanity got the better of my pity. I could not but highly plume myself on my masterly management in getting rid of Bartleby. Masterly I call it, and such it must appear to any dispassionate thinker. The beauty of my procedure seemed to consist in its perfect quietness. There was no vulgar bullying, no bravado of any sort, no choleric hectoring, and striding to and fro across the apartment, jerking out vehement commands for Bartleby to bundle himself off with his beggarly traps. Nothing of the kind. Without loudly bidding Bartleby depart—as an inferior genius might have done—I *assumed* the ground that depart he must; and upon that assumption built all I had to say. The more I thought over my procedure, the more I was charmed with it. Nevertheless, next 147 morning, upon awakening, I had my doubts,—I had somehow slept off the fumes of vanity. One of the coolest and wisest hours a man has is just after he awakes in the morning. My procedure seemed as sagacious as ever,—but only in theory. How it would prove in practice—there was the rub. It was truly a beautiful thought to have assumed Bartleby's departure; but, after all, that assumption was simply my own, and none of Bartleby's. The great point was, not whether I had assumed that he would quit me, but whether he would prefer so to do. He was more a man of preferences than assumptions.

After breakfast, I walked downtown, arguing the probabilities *pro* 148
and *con*. One moment I thought it would prove a miserable failure, and Bartleby would be found all alive at my office as usual; the next moment it seemed certain that I should see his chair empty. And so I kept veering about. At the corner of Broadway and Canal Street, I saw quite an excited group of people standing in earnest conversation.

"I'll take odds he doesn't," said a voice as I passed. 149

'Doesn't go?—done!" said I, "put up your money." 150

I was instinctively putting my hand in my pocket to produce my 151
own, when I remembered that this was an election day. The words I had overheard bore no reference to Bartleby, but to the success or non-success of some candidate for the mayoralty. In my intent frame of mind, I had, as it were, imagined that all Broadway shared in my excitement, and were debating the same question with me. I passed on, very thankful that the uproar of the street screened my momentary absent-mindedness.

As I had intended, I was earlier than usual at my office door. I 152
stood listening for a moment. All was still. He must be gone. I tried the knob. The door was locked. Yes, my procedure had worked to a charm; he indeed must be vanished. Yet a certain melancholy mixed with this: I was almost sorry for my brilliant success. I was fumbling under the door mat for the key, which Bartleby was to have left there for me, when accidentally my knee knocked against a panel, producing a summoning sound, and in response a voice came to me from within—"Not yet; I am occupied."

It was Bartleby. 153

I was thunderstruck. For an instant I stood like the man who, 154
pipe in mouth, was killed one cloudless afternoon long ago in Virginia, by summer lightning; at his own warm open window he was killed, and remained leaning out there upon the dreamy afternoon, till some one touched him, when he fell.

"Not gone!" I murmured at last. But again obeying that wondrous 155
ascendancy which the inscrutable scrivener had over me, and from which ascendancy, for all my chafing, I could not completely escape, I slowly went downstairs and out into the street, and while walking

round the block, considered what I should next do in this unheard-of perplexity. Turn the man out by an actual thrusting I could not; to drive him away by calling him hard names would not do; calling in the police was an unpleasant idea; and yet, permit him to enjoy his cadaverous triumph over me,—this too I could not think of. What was to be done? or, if nothing could be done, was there anything further that I could *assume* in the matter? Yes, as before I had prospectively assumed that Bartleby would depart, so now I might retrospectively assume that departed he was. In the legitimate carrying out of this assumption, I might enter my office in a great hurry, and pretending not to see Bartleby at all, walk straight against him as if he were air. Such a proceeding would in a singular degree have the appearance of a homethrust. It was hardly possible that Bartleby could withstand such an application of the doctrine of assumptions. But upon second thoughts the success of the plan seemed rather dubious. I resolved to argue the matter over with him again.

"Bartleby," said I, entering the office, with a quietly severe ex- 156
pression, "I am seriously displeased. I am pained, Bartleby. I had thought better of you. I had imagined you of such a gentlemanly organization, that in any delicate dilemma a slight hint would suffice—in short, an assumption. But it appears I am deceived. Why," I added, unaffectedly starting, "you have not even touched that money yet," pointing to it, just where I had left it the evening previous.

He answered nothing. 157

"Will you, or will you not, quit me?" I now demanded in a 158
sudden passion, advancing close to him.

"I would prefer *not* to quit you," he replied, gently emphasizing 159
the *not*.

"What earthly right have you to stay here? Do you pay any rent? 160
Do you pay my taxes? Or is this property yours?"

He answered nothing. 161

"Are you ready to go on and write now? Are your eyes recov- 162
ered? Could you copy a small paper for me this morning? or help examine a few lines? or step round to the post office? In a word, will you do anything at all, to give a coloring to your refusal to depart the premises?"

He silently retired into his hermitage. 163

I was now in such a state of nervous resentment that I thought it 164
but prudent to check myself at present from further demonstrations. Bartleby and I were alone. I remembered the tragedy of the unfortunate Adams and the still more unfortunate Colt in the solitary office of the latter; and how poor Colt, being dreadfully incensed by Adams, and imprudently permitting himself to get wildly excited, was at unawares hurried into his fatal act—an act which certainly no man could possibly deplore more than the actor himself. Often it had

occurred to me in my ponderings upon the subject, that had that altercation taken place in the public street, or at a private residence, it would not have terminated as it did. It was the circumstance of being alone in a solitary office, up stairs, of a building entirely unhallowed by humanizing domestic associations—an uncarpeted office, doubtless, of a dusty, haggard sort of appearance;—this it must have been, which greatly helped to enhance the irritable desperation of the hapless Colt.

But when this old Adam of resentment rose in me and tempted 165
me concerning Bartleby, I grappled him and threw him. How? Why, simply by recalling the divine injunction: "A new commandment give I unto you, that ye love one another." Yes, this it was that saved me. Aside from higher considerations, charity often operates as a vastly wise and prudent principle—a great safeguard to its possessor. Men have committed murder for jealousy's sake, and anger's sake, and hatred's sake, and selfishness' sake, and spiritual pride's sake; but no man that ever I heard of, ever committed a diabolical murder for sweet charity's sake. Mere self-interest, then, if no better motive can be enlisted, should, especially with high-tempered men, prompt all beings to charity and philanthropy. At any rate, upon the occasion in question, I strove to drown my exasperated feelings towards the scrivener by benevolently construing his conduct. Poor fellow, poor fellow! thought I, he don't mean anything; and besides, he has seen hard times, and ought to be indulged.

I endeavored also immediately to occupy myself, and at the same 166
time to comfort my despondency. I tried to fancy that in the course of the morning, at such time as might prove agreeable to him, Bartleby, of his own free accord, would emerge from his hermitage, and take up some decided line of march in the direction of the door. But no. Half-past twelve o'clock came; Turkey began to glow in the face, overturn his inkstand, and become generally obstreperpous; Nippers abated down into quietude and courtesy; Ginger Nut munched his noon apple; and Bartleby remained standing at his window in one of his profoundest dead-wall reveries. Will it be credited? Ought I to acknowledge it? That afternoon I left the office without saying one further word to him.

Some days now passed, during which, at leisure intervals I 167
looked a little into "Edwards on the Will," and "Priestley on Necessity." Under the circumstances, those books induced a salutary feeling. Gradually I slid into the persuasion that these troubles of mine touching the scrivener, had been all predestinated from eternity, and Bartleby was billeted upon me for some mysterious purpose of an all-wise Providence, which it was not for a mere mortal like me to fathom. Yes, Bartleby, stay there behind your screen, thought I; I shall persecute you no more; you are harmless and noiseless as any of

these old chairs; in short, I never feel so private as when I know you are here. At least I see it, I feel it; I penetrate to the predestinated purpose of my life. I am content. Others may have loftier parts to enact; but my mission in this world, Bartleby, is to furnish you with office-room for such period as you may see fit to remain.

I believe that this wise and blessed frame of mind would have 168
continued with me, had it not been for the unsolicited and uncharitable remarks obtruded upon me by my professional friends who visited the rooms. But thus it often is, that the constant friction of illiberal minds wears out at last the best resolves of the more generous. Though to be sure, when I reflected upon it, it was not strange that people entering my office should be struck by the peculiar aspect of the unaccountable Bartleby, and so be tempted to throw out some sinister observations concerning him. Sometimes an attorney having business with me, and calling at my office, and finding no one but the scrivener there, would undertake to obtain some sort of precise information from him touching my whereabouts; but without heeding his idle talk, Bartleby would remain standing immovable in the middle of the room. So after contemplating him in that position for a time, the attorney would depart, no wiser than he came.

Also, when a Reference was going on, and the room full of 169
lawyers and witnesses and business was driving fast; some deeply occupied legal gentleman present, seeing Bartleby wholly unemployed, would request him to run round to his (the legal gentleman's) office and fetch some papers for him. Thereupon Bartleby would tranquilly decline, and yet remain idle as before. Then the lawyer would give a great stare, and turn to me. And what could I say? At last I was made aware that all through the circle of my professional acquaintance, a whisper of wonder was running round, having reference to the strange creature I kept at my office. This worried me very much. And as the idea came upon me of his possibly turning out a long-lived man, and keep occupying my chambers, and denying my authority; and perplexing my visitors; and scandalizing my professional reputation; and casting a general gloom over the premises; keeping soul and body together to the last upon his savings (for doubtless he spent but half a dime a day), and in the end perhaps outlive me, and claim possession of my office by right of his perpetual occupancy: as all these dark anticipations crowded upon me more and more, and my friends continually intruded their relentless remarks upon the apparition in my room; a great change was wrought in me. I resolved to gather all my faculties together, and forever rid me of this intolerable incubus.

Ere revolving any complicated project, however, adapted to this 170
end, I first simply suggested to Bartleby the propriety of his permanent departure. In a calm and serious tone, I commended the idea

to his careful and mature consideration. But having taken three days to meditate upon it, he apprised me that his original determination remained the same; in short, that he still preferred to abide with me.

What shall I do? I now said to myself, buttoning up my coat to the 171
last button. What shall I do? what ought I to do? what does conscience say I *should* do with this man, or rather ghost. Rid myself of him, I must; go, he shall. But how? You will not thrust him, the poor, pale, passive mortal,—you will not thrust such a helpless creature out of your door? you will not dishonor yourself by such cruelty? No, I will not, I cannot do that. Rather would I let him live and die here, and then mason up his remains in the wall. What then will you do? For all your coaxing, he will not budge. Bribes he leaves under your own paperweight on your table; in short, it is quite plain that he prefers to cling to you.

Then something severe, something unusual must be done. What! 172
surely you will not have him collared by a constable, and commit his innocent pallor to the common jail? And upon what ground could you procure such a thing to be done?—a vagrant, is he? What! he a vagrant, a wanderer, who refuses to budge? It is because he will *not* be a vagrant, then, that you seek to count him *as* a vagrant. That is too absurd. No visible means of support: there I have him. Wrong again: for indubitably he *does* support himself, and that is the only unanswerable proof that any man can show of his possessing the means so to do. No more then. Since he will not quit me, I must quit him. I will change my offices; I will move elsewhere; and give him fair notice, that if I find him on my new premises I will then proceed against him as a common trespasser.

Acting accordingly, next day I thus addressed him: "I find these 173
chambers too far from the City Hall; the air is unwholesome. In a word, I propose to remove my offices next week, and shall no longer require your services. I tell you this now, in order that you may seek another place."

He made no reply, and nothing more was said. 174

On the appointed day I engaged carts and men, proceeded to my 175
chambers, and having but little furniture, everything was removed in a few hours. Throughout, the scrivener remained standing behind the screen, which I directed to be removed the last thing. It was withdrawn; and being folded up like a huge folio, left him the motionless occupant of a naked room. I stood in the entry watching him a moment, while something from within me upbraided me.

I re-entered, with my hand in my pocket—and—and my heart in 176
my mouth.

"Good-bye, Bartleby; I am going—good-bye, and God some way 177
bless you; and take that," slipping something in his hand. But it

dropped upon the floor, and then,—strange to say—I tore myself from him whom I had so longed to be rid of.

Established in my new quarters, for a day or two I kept the door locked, and started at every footfall in the passages. When I returned to my rooms after any little absence, I would pause at the threshold for an instant, and attentively listen, ere applying my key. But these fears were needless. Bartleby never came nigh me. 178

I thought all was going well, when a perturbed-looking stranger visited me, inquiring whether I was the person who had recently occupied rooms at No.——Wall Street. 179

Full of forebodings, I replied that I was. 180

"Then sir," said the stranger, who proved a lawyer, "you are responsible for the man you left there. He refuses to do any copying; he refuses to do anything; he says he prefers not to; and he refuses to quit the premises." 181

"I am very sorry, sir," said I, with assumed tranquility, but an inward tremor, "but, really, the man you allude to is nothing to me—he is no relation or apprentice of mine, that you should hold me responsible for him." 182

"In mercy's name, who is he?" 183

"I certainly cannot inform you. I know nothing about him. Formerly I employed him as a copyist; but he has done nothing for me now for some time past." 184

"I shall settle him then,—good morning, sir." 185

Several days passed, and I heard nothing more; and though I often felt a charitable prompting to call at the place and see poor Bartleby, yet a certain squeamishness of I know not what withheld me. 186

All is over with him, by this time, thought I at last, when through another week no further intelligence reached me. But coming to my room the day after, I found several persons waiting at my door in a high state of nervous excitement. 187

"That's the man—here he comes," cried the foremost one, whom I recognized as the lawyer who had previously called upon me alone. 188

"You must take him away, sir, at once," cried a portly person among them, advancing upon me, and whom I knew to be the landlord of No.——Wall Street. "These gentlemen, my tenants, cannot stand it any longer; Mr. B——" pointing to the lawyer, "has turned him out of his room, and he now persists in haunting the building generally, sitting upon the banisters of the stairs by day, and sleeping in the entry by night. Everybody is concerned; clients are leaving the offices; some fears are entertained of a mob; something you must do, and that without delay." 189

Aghast at this torrent, I fell back before it, and would fain have 190 locked myself in my new quarters. In vain I persisted that Bartleby was nothing to me—no more than to anyone else. In vain:—I was the last person known to have anything to do with him, and they held me to the terrible account. Fearful then of being exposed in the papers (as one person present obscurely threatened) I considered the matter, and at length said, that if the lawyer would give me a confidential interview with the scrivener, in his (the lawyer's) own room, I would that afternoon strive my best to rid them of the nuisance they complained of.

Going upstairs to my old haunt, there was Bartleby silently sitting 191
upon the banister at the landing.

"What are you doing here, Bartleby?" said I. 192

"Sitting upon the banister," he mildly replied. 193

I motioned him into the lawyer's room, who then left us. 194

"Bartleby," said I, "are you aware that you are the cause of great 195
tribulation to me, by persisting in occupying the entry after being dismissed from the office?"

No answer. 196

"Now one of two things must take place. Either you must do 197
something, or something must be done to you. Now what sort of business would you like to engage in? Would you like to re-engage in copying for someone?"

"No; I would prefer not to make any change." 198

"Would you like a clerkship in a drygoods store?" 199

"There is too much confinement about that. No, I would not like a 200
clerkship; but I am not particular.

"Too much confinement," I cried, "why you keep yourself con- 201
fined all the time!"

"I would prefer not to take a clerkship," he rejoined, as if to settle 202
that little item at once.

"How would a bartender's business suit you? There is no trying 203
of the eyesight in that."

"I would not like it at all; though, as I said before, I am not 204
particular."

His unwonted wordiness inspirited me. I returned to the charge. 205

"Well then, would you like to travel through the country collect- 206
ing bills for the merchants? That would improve your health."

"No, I would prefer to be doing something else." 207

"How then would going as a companion to Europe, to entertain 208
some young gentleman with your conversation,—how would that suit you?"

"Not at all. It does not strike me that there is anything definite 209
about that. I like to be stationary. But I am not particular."

"Stationary you shall be then," I cried, now losing all patience, 210
and for the first time in all my exasperating connection with him fairly

flying into a passion. "If you do not go away from these premises before night, I shall feel bound—indeed I *am* bound—to—to—to quit the premises myself!" I rather absurdly concluded, knowing not with what possible threat to try to frighten his immobility into compliance. Despairing of all further efforts, I was precipitately leaving him, when a final thought occurred to me—one which had not been wholly unindulged before.

"Bartleby," said I, in the kindest tone I could assume under such 211
exciting circumstances, "will you go home with me now—not to my office, but my dwelling—and remain there till we can conclude upon some convenient arrangement for you at our leisure? Come, let us start now, right away."

"No: at present I would prefer not to make any change at all." 212

I answered nothing; but effectually dodging everyone by the 213
suddenness and rapidity of my flight, rushed from the building, ran up Wall Street toward Broadway, and jumping into the first omnibus was soon removed from pursuit. As soon as tranquility returned I distinctly perceived that I had now done all that I possibly could, both in respect to the demands of the landlord and his tenants, and with regard to my own desire and sense of duty, to benefit Bartleby, and shield him from rude persecution. I now strove to be entirely carefree and quiescent; and my conscience justified me in the attempt; though indeed it was not so successful as I could have wished. So fearful was I of being again hunted out by the incensed landlord and his exasperated tenants, that, surrendering my business to Nippers, for a few days I drove about the upper part of the town and through the suburbs, in my rockaway; crossed over to Jersey City and Hoboken, and paid fugitive visits to Manhattanville and Astoria. In fact I almost lived in my rockaway for the time.

When again I entered my office, lo, a note from the landlord lay 214
upon the desk. I opened it with trembling hands. It informed me that the writer had sent to the police, and had Bartleby removed to the Tombs as a vagrant. Moreover, since I knew more about him than anyone else, he wished me to appear at that place, and make a suitable statement of the facts. These tidings had a conflicting effect upon me. At first I was indignant; but at last almost approved. The landlord's energetic, summary disposition had led him to adopt a procedure which I do not think I would have decided upon myself; and yet as a last resort, under such peculiar circumstances, it seemed the only plan.

As I afterwards learned, the poor scrivener, when told that he 215
must be conducted to the Tombs, offered not the slightest obstacle, but in his pale unmoving way, silently acquiesced.

Some of the compassionate and curious bystanders joined the 216
party; and headed by one of the constables arm in arm with Bartleby,

the silent procession filed its way through all the noise, and heat, and joy of the roaring thoroughfares at noon.

The same day I received the note I went to the Tombs, or to speak more properly, the Halls of Justice. Seeking the right officer, I stated the purpose of my call, and was informed that the individual I described was indeed within. I then assured the functionary that Bartleby was a perfectly honest man, and greatly to be compassionated, however unaccountably eccentric. I narrated all I knew, and closed by suggesting the idea of letting him remain in as indulgent confinement as possible till something less harsh might be done—though indeed I hardly knew what. At all events, if nothing else could be decided upon, the alms-house must receive him. I then begged to have an interview. 217

Being under no disgraceful charge, and quite serene and harmless in all his ways, they had permitted him freely to wander about the prison, and especially in the inclosed grass-platted yards thereof. And so I found him there, standing all alone in the quietest of the yards, his face towards a high wall, while all around, from the narrow slits of the jail windows, I thought I saw peering out upon him the eyes of murderers and thieves. 218

"Bartleby!" 219

"I know you," he said, without looking round,—"and I want nothing to say to you." 220

"It was not I that brought you here, Bartleby," said I, keenly pained at his implied suspicion. "And to you, this should not be so vile a place. Nothing reproachful attaches to you by being here. And see, it is not so sad a place as one might think. Look, there is the sky, and here is the grass." 221

"I know where I am," he replied, but would say nothing more, and so I left him. 222

As I entered the corridor again, a broad meat-like man, in an apron, accosted me, and jerking his thumb over his shoulder said—"Is that your friend?" 223

"Yes." 224

"Does he want to starve? If he does, let him live on the prison fare, that's all. 225

"Who are you?" asked I, not knowing what to make of such an unofficially-speaking person in such a place. 226

"I am the grub-man. Such gentlemen as have friends here, hire me to provide them with something good to eat." 227

"Is this so?" said I, turning to the turnkey. 228

He said it was. 229

"Well then," said I, slipping some silver into the grub-man's hands (for so they called him). "I want you to give particular attention 230 to my friend there; let him have the best dinner you can get. And you must be as polite to him as possible."

"Introduce me, will you?" said the grub-man, looking at me with an expression which seemed to say he was all impatience for an opportunity to give a specimen of his breeding. 231

Thinking it would prove of benefit to the scrivener, I acquiesced; and asking the grub-man his name, went up with him to Bartleby. 232

"Bartleby, this is Mr. Cutlets; you will find him very useful to you." 233

"Your sarvant, sir, your sarvant," said the grub-man, making a low salutation behind his apron. "Hope you find it pleasant here, sir;—spacious grounds—cool apartments, sir—hope you'll stay with us some time—try to make it agreeable. May Mrs. Cutlets and I have the pleasure of your company to dinner, sir, in Mrs. Cutlets' private room?" 234

"I prefer not to dine today," said Bartleby, turning away. "It would disagree with me; I am unused to dinners." So saying he slowly moved to the other side of the inclosure, and took up a position fronting the dead-wall. 235

"How's this?" said the grub-man, addressing me with a stare of astonishment. "He's odd, ain't he?" 236

"I think he is a little deranged," said I, sadly.
237

"Deranged? deranged is it? Well now, upon my word, I thought that friend of yourn was a gentleman forger; they are always pale and genteel-like, them forgers. I can't help pity 'em—can't help it, sir. Did you know Monroe Edwards?" he added touchingly, and paused. Then, laying his hand pityingly on my shoulder, sighed, "He died of consumption at Sing Sing. So you weren't acquainted with Monroe?" 238

"No, I was never socially acquainted with any forgers. But I cannot stop longer. Look to my friend yonder. You will not lose by it. I will see you again." 239

Some few days after this, I again obtained admission to the Tombs, and went through the corridors in quest of Bartleby; but without finding him. 240

"I saw him coming from his cell not long ago," said a turnkey, "may be he's gone to loiter in the yards." 241

So I went in that direction.
242

"Are you looking for the silent man?" said another turnkey passing me. "Yonder he lies—sleeping in the yard there. 'Tis not twenty minutes since I saw him lie down." 243

The yard was entirely quiet. It was not accessible to the common prisoners. The surrounding walls, of amazing thickness, kept off all sounds behind them. The Egyptian character of the masonry weighed upon me with its gloom. But a soft imprisoned turf grew under foot. 244

The heart of the eternal pyramids, it seemed, wherein, by some strange magic, through the clefts, grass seed, dropped by birds, had sprung.

Strangely huddled at the base of the wall, his knees drawn up, 245
and lying on his side, his head touching the cold stones, I saw the wasted Bartleby. But nothing stirred. I paused; then went close up to him; stooped over, and saw that his dim eyes were open; otherwise he seemed profoundly sleeping. Something prompted me to touch him. I felt his hand, when a tingling shiver ran up my arm and down my spine to my feet.

The round face of the grub-man peered upon me now. "His 246
dinner is ready. Won't he dine today, either? Or does he live without dining?"

"Lives without dining," said I, and closed the eyes. 247

"Eh!—He's asleep, ain't he?" 248

"With kings and counsellors," murmured I. 249

There would seem little need for proceeding further in this his- 250
tory. Imagination will readily supply the meager recital of poor Bartleby's interment. But ere parting with the reader, let me say, that if this little narrative has sufficiently interested him, to awaken curiosity as to who Bartleby was, and what manner of life he led prior to the present narrator's making his acquaintance, I can only reply, that in such curiosity I fully share, but am wholly unable to gratify it. Yet here I hardly know whether I should divulge one little item of rumor, which came to my ear a few months after the scrivener's decease. Upon what basis it rested, I could never ascertain; and hence, how true it is I cannot now tell. But inasmuch as ths vague report has not been without a certain strange suggestive interest to me, however sad, it may prove the same with some others; and so I will briefly mention it. The report was this: that Bartleby had been a subordinate clerk in the Dead Letter Office at Washington, from which he had been suddenly removed by a change in the administration. When I think over this rumor, I cannot adequately express the emotions which seize me. Dead letters! does it not sound like dead men? Conceive a man by nature and misfortune prone to a pallid hopelessness, can any business seem more fitted to heighten it than that of continually handling these dead letters, and assorting them for the flames? For by the cartload they are annually burned. Sometimes from out the folded paper the pale clerk takes a ring:—the finger it was meant for, perhaps, molders in the grave; a banknote sent in swiftest charity:—he whom it would relieve, nor eats nor hungers any more; pardon for those who died despairing; hope for those who died unhoping; good tidings for those who died stifled by unrelieved calamities. On errands of life, these letters speed to death.

Ah Bartleby! Ah humanity! 251

Discussion and Writing Suggestions

1. Assess the narrator. Do you find him good-natured, tolerant, and generous, or smug and self-satisfied? (Or something in-between?) How does your view of the narrator affect the meaning of the story?
2. What is the significance of the setting of the story—Wall Street and the city? What is the significance of the physical layout of the office? What is the significance of the type of work done in the lawyer's office? What is the significance of where Bartleby sits in the office? Of the folding screen? Of his staring out the window at the wall?
3. What conclusions can you draw from the other employees—Turkey, Nippers, and Ginger Nut? In what way do they contribute to the meaning of the story? What is the significance of their eccentric behavior?
4. The central question: What is the significance of Bartleby's refusal to perform his duties? Is Bartleby a symbol? If so, of what? In a multiparagraph essay, discuss your thoughts on this subject.
5. Evaluate the narrator's behavior as he attempts to deal with Bartleby's refusal to work. Does he handle the situation well, from beginning to end? Was he too tolerant? Not tolerant enough? Was he too concerned with what other people thought? What *should* he have done? Discuss your response in a multiparagraph essay.
6. What is the significance of the prison? Of Bartleby's death?
7. Assess the two paragraphs that constitute the epilogue. Some critics have found them essential to the meaning of the story. Others have found them anticlimactic and literal-minded, detracting from the symbolic aspect of "Bartleby." What do you think?
8. Melville's story has generated a myriad of interpretations: psychological, religious, economic, social, autobiographical, literary. Before reading any of the criticism, in what area or areas do you believe the key to "Bartleby" is most likely to be found? Write a paragraph or two explaining which of those approaches you believe is most likely to yield a satisfactory answer to the problem of "Bartleby."

Bartleby Is a Schizophrenic

MORRIS BEJA

After reading "Bartleby," many readers might conclude, along with Ginger Nut, that "he's a little luny.*" After all, whenever people do anything inexplicable (to us), it's natural enough to write them off as*

Reprinted from *The Massachusetts Review*,

crazy. Of course, we no longer use words like "loony" and "crazy" in polite company. If the behavior in question goes beyond simple illogicality or pigheadedness (like refusing to take an umbrella out into the rain), we would probably draw on some of the current terminology for mental illness to account for it. Of these terms, "schizophrenia" is probably the most familiar to the general public; it covers a range of psychic disorders, often characterized by delusions, withdrawal from reality, and disintegration of the personality—all of which, of course, result in outwardly illogical (though inwardly logical) behavior. In the article below, Morris Beja, a literary critic, considers the question of whether or not Bartleby is schizophrenic, drawing parallels between the character's behavior and similar behavior of actual persons diagnosed as schizophrenic. As you read Beja's article, ask yourself how plausibly he makes his case.

Morris Beja, born in 1935, educated at the City College of New York, Columbia University, and Cornell University, has taught literature since 1961 at the Ohio State University. He has edited a casebook on Virginia Woolf's To the Lighthouse *(1970),* Psychological Fiction *(1971), and a selection of critical essays on James Joyce's* The Dubliners *(1973). He has also written numerous articles on modern literature, short stories, and book reviews. The following article first appeared under the title "Bartleby and Schizophrenia" in the* Massachusetts Review *(1978).*

History and Development of Symptoms. The patient, a young apprentice in Chartered Accountancy, was admitted to hospital in January 1958, at the age of 23 years. . . . On leaving school at 17 he embarked on a career of his own choosing, that of chartered accountancy with a City firm. For the first five years his performance was beyond reproach. . . .

. . . The initial change was a general slowing up and impairment in efficiency in carrying out all his usual activities, both at work in the office and at home. . . .

. . . When setting out for work . . . he began to stop and stand still at street corners, aimlessly looking about for 5–10 min. A few weeks later, he stopped going to work altogether, and thereafter, for a period of one year, he remained at home and did not leave the house except on one occasion for a few hours only. . . .

He preferred to stay up very late at nights. . . . In general he preferred to remain upright and would each day stand rigidly in the same spot for periods varying from 1 to 3 hours. . . .

. . . Movement by the patient was associated with visual perceptual distortion of the environment which he described at various times as "a flatness," "a flat streak of colour," "a painting," "a wall." . . .

. . . "I can do something about what I see. For example I could turn round and look at this blank wall. But I can't do anything about sounds.

> . . ." [James Chapman, et al., "Clinical Research in Schizophrenia—The Psychotherapeutic Approach"][1]

Although we are twice told what the patient described in this case history "preferred" to do, readers familiar with Herman Melville's "Bartleby, the Scrivener: A Story of Wall Street" will probably be most struck by all that he would prefer not to. Yet while few readers would deny the similarities—some of them, indeed, almost uncanny—between Bartleby and the schizophrenic described above, many critics nevertheless resist any application of "clinical" terms to Bartleby. Sometimes they do so out of a general distaste for treating imaginative artifacts as "people." But even readers who do not recognize the legitimacy of such an absolute restriction will remember the admonition by the lawyer (who tells us all we know about Bartleby) that "no materials exist, for a full and satisfactory biography of this man." And they will realize, in any case, that too easy an application of clinical terms can be reductive; if Bartlebys are much more common in the world than we usually acknowledge, it is not merely because people with schizophrenic symptoms are so common. Yet if we refrain from the assumption that the victim of schizophrenia is Other, an awareness of psychological contexts should help rather than impair us. The mistake is to take an either/or approach: either "Bartleby" is a psychological study, or it is a socio-economic one, or a metaphysical one, or an existential one, or an autobiographical one, and so on. 1

A clinical analysis of Bartleby would probably identify him as at least schizoid, probably schizophrenic. "Schizoid" refers to a non-psychotic personality disorder in which key traits are withdrawal, introversion, aloofness, difficulty in recognizing or relating to "reality," and an acute over-sensitivity coupled with an inability to express ordinary hostility or aggressive feelings. But we may feel that even the term schizoid does not do justice to the depths of Bartleby's disturbance. "I think, sir, he's a little *luny*" (paragraph 47), says Ginger Nut with the brutality of innocence; his comment comes fairly early in the story; by the end it would probably seem to most people to err on the side of understatement. 2

We learn little about Bartleby's "case history"—though enough to feel that his parallels with the patient described in the passages quoted at the start of this essay are not gratuitous. If there is any doubt, let me indulge in a citation of another case study, that of "A. J.": 3

> After leaving school . . . the patient obtained many odd jobs. . . . He did not hold any one job longer than several weeks; neither was he regular in

[1]*British Journal of Medical Psychology*, 32 (1959), rpt. in Don E. Dulany, Jr., et al., eds., *Contributions to Modern Psychology* (New York: Oxford University Press, 1963), pp. 391–97.

> performing his duties in the several occupations. He finally became altogether unemployable and stayed home.
>
> His behavior became more seclusive and he gradually withdrew from community life. When people visited the house he would run out of the room and hide under the bed. He would sit with his head bowed most of the time. Sometimes he would refuse to dine with the rest of the family and would wait until they were through. . . . On some occasions he made rather strange remarks to his mother; e.g., "I am automatic." . . .
>
> A visiting social worker finally persuaded the mother to bring A. to the local mental hygiene clinic for an examination. It took some time to get him out of the worker's car and persuade him to enter the clinic building. He seated himself under the stairs near the waiting room, facing the wall. . . .[2]

"And so I found him there, standing all alone in the quietest of the yards, his face towards a high wall . . ." ("Bartleby," paragraph 218).

If Bartleby is indeed psychotic, his disorder is probably the most 4
common of all psychoses: schizophrenia. More specifically, I believe, he displays the symptoms and behavior patterns of "schizophrenia, catatonic type, withdrawn."[3] He is detached, withdrawn, immobile, excessively silent, yet given to remarks or associations that do not make sense to others, depressed, at least outwardly apathetic and refraining from all display of ordinary emotion, possibly autistic, and compulsively prone to repetitive acts or phrases ("I would prefer not to").

The trait that leads one to specify "catatonic type" is of course one 5
of Bartleby's most notable characteristics: "his great stillness," his "long-continued motionlessness" (paragraphs 84, 92). Of Bartleby's first appearance, the lawyer says: "In answer to my advertisement, a motionless young man one morning stood upon my office threshold, the door being open, for it was summer" (paragraph 15). Melville has carefully arranged this appearance so that we are not told that Bar-

---

[2]Albert I. Rabin, "Schizophrenia, Simple Form," in Arthur Burton and Robert E. Harris, eds., *Case Histories in Clinical and Abnormal Psychology* (New York: Harper and Brothers, 1947), p. 26.

[3]Although a number of commentators have applied the term "schizophrenic" to Bartleby, few have been much more specific than that or have pursued the implications of the term in its clinical sense. See, e.g., Newton Arvin, *Herman Melville* (New York: William Sloane, 1950), p. 243; Richard Chase, *Herman Melville: A Critical Study* (New York: Macmillan, 1949), p. 143; Henry A. Murray, "Bartleby and I," in Howard P. Vincent, ed., *Melville Annual 1965, A Symposium: Bartleby the Scrivener* (Kent, Ohio: Kent State University Press, 1966), p. 9. Kingsley Widmer in *The Ways of Nihilism: A Study of Herman Melville's Short Novels* (Los Angeles: California State Colleges, 1970), p. 112, is skeptical of this "uncertain clinical category": I hope my study will make it seem more useful. For a briefer statement of the specific grounds for associating Bartleby with the category of schizophrenia I cite, see my *Psychological Fiction* (Glenview, Ill.: Scott, Foresman, 1971), p. 203.

tleby walked into, or even entered, the lawyer's office: he is there, immobile. We see this feature develop, but even our first glimpse of him shows that he has been immobile at the best of times. On the first occasion of Bartleby's use of his enigmatic phrase, "without moving from his privacy, Bartleby, in a singularly mild, firm voice, replied, 'I would prefer not to' " (paragraph 21), his mildness and immobility conveying the fact that what he is doing is not so much an act as a form of inaction. From that point on "he never went to dinner; indeed . . . he never went anywhere" (paragraph 51). Eventually the lawyer is forced to move, since Bartleby will not: as the scrivener says in a rare burst of volubility, "I like to be stationary" (paragraph 209). Finally, told that he must be taken to the Tombs, Bartleby "offered not the slightest obstacle, but, in his pale, unmoving way, silently acquiesced" (paragraph 215).

Such quotations can perhaps help to recall for the reader the 6
emotional experience of reading "Bartleby"—an experience which reading such case histories as those I have cited (moving as they may be in themselves) cannot begin to match. We are concerned here with a truly powerful work of art, and the psychological terms which seem "applicable" to Bartleby *in themselves* clarify very little. Indeed, when their purposes are distorted in order to provide us with handy labels, they end by perverting our response to the story—and may even become aids in developing relatively painless ways of dealing with (that is, dismissing) Bartleby's painful case. Clearly, terms like "schizophrenia, catatonic type, withdrawn," however accurate, do little more than identify symptoms. To understand Bartleby in any real way—to "come to terms" with him in any but a superficial sense—we would have to go beyond them and attempt to get at what a therapist, again, would call the *etiology* of Bartleby's . . . "incurable disorder." That is not easy, of course: "it was his soul that suffered, and his soul I could not reach" (paragraph 93).

Recent psychological thought may help; specifically, I would like 7
to explore Bartleby's plight in light of the work of R. D. Laing. Probably the most forceful aspect of Laing's approach has been his refusal to regard schizophrenics, for example, as "them," and the rest of us as "us." In our context, resisting the temptation to distinguish in any facile manner between the normal lawyer and the schizophrenic Bartleby reinforces the critical interpretations which see the two men as "doubles" of one another.[4] But although those interpretations have

[4]See, for example: Mordecai Marcus, "Melville's Bartleby as a Psychological Double," *College English,* 23 (February 1962), 365–68; Widmer, *Ways of Nihilism,* pp. 112 ff.; Robert Rogers, *A Psychoanalytic Study of the Double in Literature* (Detroit: Wayne State University Press, 1970), pp. 67–70; C. F. Keppler, *The Literature of the Second Self* (Tucson: University of Arizona Press, 1972), pp. 115–20.

sometimes been enlightening, they have strongly stressed what the scrivener and his behavior reveal to us about the lawyer, not what we learn about Bartleby. Of course, many critics (nowadays, perhaps most) do in fact claim that the story is the lawyer's more than it is Bartleby's, and many others implicitly assume it. But that does not tie in with my own experience of Melville's story; for me and—as far as I have been able to tell from my conversations with friends, colleagues, and students—for most people, the center of interest remains Bartleby. And if that is so, then we want to know how he may have come to his present pass—and indeed where he is. We want to know what is "wrong" with him, and not just what his being the lawyer's double reveals about the lawyer.

In Laing's terms—indeed his most famous ones—both the lawyer 8
the Bartleby are men with divided selves: cut off from others and from the world, but also self-divided, dissociated.[5] Laing believes (and is of course far from alone in doing so) that "no one can begin to think, feel or act now except from the starting point of his or her own alienation."[6] In their different ways both Bartleby and the lawyer try to avoid the necessity to "begin to think, feel or act." Bartleby's mode of avoidance leads the world to call him "luny"; the lawyer's mode—he is, after all, an "eminently *safe* man" (paragraph 3)—leads the world to give him the title of Master in Chancery. Clearly, then, there are vast differences in the outward success of their two situations, but it is nevertheless essential to recognize some basic similarities in their modes of being-in-the-world. For "what we call 'normal' is a product of repression, denial, splitting, projection, introjection and other forms of destructive action on experience. . . . It is radically estranged from the structure of being" (*Experience*, p. 27).

Insofar as we may sense a fundamental accuracy in that view, we 9
may come to look upon Bartleby's mode of adaptation as a pathetic attempt to make himself *truly* "sane." As Laing puts it, "the madness that we encounter in 'patients' is a gross travesty, a mockery, a grotesque caricature of what the natural healing of that estranged integration we call sanity might be" (*Experience*, p. 144). These remarks, though general, are surely suggestive in regard to Bartleby; more specific is a passage reminiscent of Plato's Allegory of the Cave. Laing is discussing the degree to which we—those of us who are

[5]R. D. Laing, *The Divided Self: An Existential Study in Sanity and Madness* (1959; rpt. Harmondsworth: Penguin, 1965).

[6]*The Politics of Experience* (1967; rpt. New York: Ballantine, 1968), p. [12], hereafter abbr. to *Experience* in textual references. In a study guide on "Bartleby" designed for students, Daniel R. Buerger astutely reprints some excerpts from *The Politics of Experience*, although he does not discuss their relevance: see *Melville's "Bartleby the Scrivener" and the Problem of Perception* (New York: Harper and Row, 1974), pp. 32–36.

"normal"—are "out of touch" with "the inner space and time of consciousness":

> The situation I am suggesting is precisely as though we all had almost total lack of any knowledge whatever of what we call the outer world. What would happen if some of us then started to see, hear, touch, smell, taste things? We would hardly be more confused than the person who first has vague intimations of, and then moves into, inner space and time. This is where the person labeled catatonic has often gone. He is not at all here: he is all there. (p. 127)

The essential point to recognize about Bartleby's behavior is that from his perspective it is not silly, or inappropriate, or "absurd," but relevant, rational, proper, and "preferable"—indeed inevitable. For him, what we call schizophrenia becomes a refuge—the awful result of a desperate attempt to avoid insanity. In other words, it is a *tactic.* According to Laing, *"without exception"* the "behavior that gets labeled schizophrenic is *a special strategy that a person invents in order to live in an unlivable situation"* (pp. 114–15). Of course, words like "tactic" and "strategy" should not be confused with the pejorative sense in which a cynic might use them to refer to malingering, gold-bricking patients who are seen as simply "trying to get attention": the devices of people like Bartleby are desperate ones, resorted to at great cost. 10

The fact that such behavior seems the only *rational* choice to people in Bartleby's sort of plight is too often unrecognized, even by professional therapists. Of the patient described at the start of this essay, the writers of the case study remark that "he had no insight," as shown by his persistence "in the view that his behaviour was justifiable and could be logically explained" ("Clinical Research," p. 393). To a layman, such terminology seems to lend support to Laing's attacks on the myopia of so many psychiatrists in their relationship to their patients. *Of course* this patient views his behavior as justifiable, and to be sure that behavior *could* "be logically explained"; in effect he asks, like Bartleby, "Do you not see the reason for yourself?" ("Bartleby," paragraph 130)—a question we might expect from a therapist as much as from a patient. The patient described as having "no insight" is quoted: "Although you are one integral thing, there are certain things you can do without. For example an amputated leg. You can remove some part of you and you still remain yourself. My body is not quite separate but not quite integral either" ("Clinical Research," p. 398). Laing, in discussing the anxieties of dissociation from one's own body—the fears of the "unembodied self"—also recognizes that "there is a sense of course, in which such an attitude could be the height of wisdom": "when, for example, Socrates maintains that no harm can possibly be done to a good man. In this case, 'he' and his 'body' were dissociated" (*Divided Self,* p. 68). 11

At one point in Melville's story, the lawyer begs Bartleby to "begin to be a little reasonable": " 'At present I would prefer not to be a little reasonable,' was his mildly cadaverous reply" (paragraph 110). Such a remark makes him seem somehow simultaneously inside himself and outside himself, as if he were both a patient and a therapist calling attention to the patient's behavior. And, as always, Bartleby's words suggest that his behavior is a volitional response to his situation, consciously—even provocatively—made. To Bartleby, moreover, it is the preferable, appropriate response, whether "reasonable" or not. The lawyer of course cannot comprehend "such perverseness—such unreasonableness" (paragraph 84). When he demands of Bartleby, "What earthly right have you to stay here? Do you pay any rent? Do you pay my taxes? Or is this property yours?" the scrivener is silent: "He answered nothing" (paragraphs 160–61). Inevitably—for the questions are irrelevant. From Bartleby's perspective, his right to remain is not earthly. It lies not in taxes and property, but in something other, or something internal: in mind, or in soul. 12

I hope my comments do not make it seem as if I am embracing some sort of sentimental or excessively "romantic" view of either Bartleby or schizophrenic patients. I am especially wary of this danger because I am not certain that it is one that Laing himself always avoids, in his desire to convey the ways in which what we call mental disease may be health, and the ways in which "breakdowns" may in fact be or become "breakthroughs." As Robert Coles put it during a panel discussion on Laing, it is misleading to overlook the "terror . . . that some people on this earth feel": "I suspect there is a difference between us and the mad patients and I suspect that we don't know it quite as well as the mad patients do."[7] Or as Bartleby replies to the lawyer's attempts to comfort him in the Tombs, "I know where I am" (paragraph 222). We may be tempted to romanticize Bartleby as an existential hero (certainly many critics are), a prophet better off in his sane madness than the rest of us in our mad sanity; but Bartleby knows where he is. 13

Still, if Bartleby's refrain of "I would prefer not to" is a sign of anguished mental illness, it is also his forceful psychic response to existence on this earth. As Laing (like of course other psychologists before him) has been wise enough to perceive, the enigmatic statements of patients "are psychotic, not because they may not be 'true' but because they are cryptic: they are often quite impossible to fathom without the patient decoding them for us" (*Divided Self*, p. 192). But 14

[7]"R. D. Laing and Anti-Psychiatry: A Symposium," in Robert Boyers and Robert Orrill, eds., *R. D. Laing and Anti-Psychiatry* (New York: Perennial Library, 1971), pp. 223–24.

Bartleby would prefer not to. So when we ask, with the perplexed lawyer, "what is the reason" for Bartleby's behavior, and the scrivener replies, as we have seen, "Do you not see the reason for yourself?" few of us will confidently respond that yes, to be sure we do, certainly.

15 Nevertheless, out of an urge to dive rather than be eminently safe, I would like to suggest that Bartleby is a victim of what Laing calls "ontological insecurity"—which in its "preliminary form" entails "partial loss of the synthetic unity of self, concurrently with partial loss of relatedness with the other," while in its "ultimate form" we have "the hypothetical end-state of *chaotic nonentity,* total loss of relatedness with self and other."[8] We are always "between being and non-being," and faced with the fear of the latter—or, for that matter, of the former—we may resort to whatever measures of security we can find. Laing quotes a patient, not his own: "The only thing I was sure of was being a 'catatonic, paranoid and schizophrenic.' I had seen that written on my chart. That at least had substance and gave me an identity and personality" (*Divided Self,* p. 173). That remark is reminiscent of Dostoevsky's study in existential paranoia, the underground man: "Question: What is he? Answer: A sluggard; how very pleasant it would have been to hear that of oneself! It would mean that I was positively defined, it would mean that there was something to say about me."[9] A patient closer to Bartleby, however, is one described in both *The Divided Self* and *Self and Others*—Peter, "a young man who was preoccupied with guilt *because* he occupied a place in the world, even in a physical sense":

> A peculiar aspect of his childhood was that his presence in the world was largely ignored. . . . He had been physically cared for in that he had been well fed and kept warm, and underwent no physical separation from his parents during his earlier years. Yet he had been consistently treated as though he did not 'really' exist. . . . He believed that to make his presence felt he would have to go to such extremes that no one would want to have anything to do with him, and thus he came to make the central enterprise of his life to be nobody. (*Self and Others,* pp. 137–38)

Such a "solution" is no help at all—though perfectly reasonable from the perspectives of a Peter and a Bartleby, who seem to share an awareness of what is happening to (of what they are doing to) themselves. Laing quotes Tillich: "Neurosis is the way of avoiding

[8]R. D. Laing, *Self and Others,* 2nd ed. (Harmondsworth: Penguin, 1969), p. 51.

[9]*Notes from the Underground,* trans. Constance Garnett, rev. Avrahm Yarmolinsky, in *Three Short Novels of Dostoevsky* (New York: Anchor Books, 1960), p. 194.

non-being by avoiding being."[10] Just as schizophrenia can be the result of a desperate attempt to avoid insanity, so Bartleby's retreat from being may result from an attempt to escape from non-being.

It seems to me that Bartleby is especially relevant to the last of 16
Laing's "three forms of anxiety encountered by the ontologically insecure person: engulfment, implosion, petrification" (*Divided Self*, p. 43). *Petrification* entails a retreat into stasis or even catatonia which is one of those modes of self-preservation by which we are accomplices in our self-destruction. One may so dread being "petrified," "turning, or being turned, from a live person into a dead thing, into a stone" (p. 46), that the terror brings about what is feared. Laing tells of a young woman who dreamed that her parents had turned into stone, and who afterward herself fell "into a state which was remarkably similar to the physical petrification of her family that she had dreamt about"; and then he makes an important observation which strikes me as extremely suggestive in regard to Bartleby:

> It seems to be a general law that at some point those very dangers most dreaded can themselves be encompassed to forestall their actual occurrence. Thus, to forgo one's autonomy becomes the means of secretly safeguarding it; to play possum, to feign death, becomes a means of preserving one's aliveness. . . . To turn oneself into a stone becomes a way of not being turned into a stone by someone else. (p. 51)

When one is turned into a stone by someone who ignores one's identity or autonomy, or who regards one as a "thing," "an *it*," one is "depersonalized"—and, as Laing observes, "depersonalization is a technique that is universally used as a means of dealing with the other when he becomes too tiresome or disturbing" (p. 46).

Certainly it is easy enough to show that Bartleby is regarded and 17
treated as an inorganic object, a thing, even by the fundamentally kind and impressively patient lawyer:

> Had there been the least uneasiness, anger, impatience or impertinence in his manner; in other words, had there been anything ordinarily human about him, doubtless I should have violently dismissed him from the premises. But as it was, I should have as soon thought of turning my pale plaster-of-paris bust of Cicero out of doors. (paragraph 25)

He also compares Bartleby to "a bit of Windsor soap" (paragraph 53), or "the last column of some ruined temple" (paragraph 146), and describes him as "a fixture in my chamber" (paragraph 136). Even at

[10]*Divided Self*, p. 111. Cf. Paul Tillich, *The Courage to Be* (New Haven: Yale University Press, 1952), p. 66.

one of his most sympathetic moments, when he recognizes the "predestinated purpose" of his life to be that of providing Bartleby with "office-room," the lawyer expresses himself in similar imagery: "I shall persecute you no more; you are harmless and noiseless as any of these old chairs" (paragraph 167). Surely at least one of the sources for Bartleby's having become a "thing" is that he has been looked upon and treated as one.

But Laing provides still further hints indicating the sources be- 18
hind Bartleby's petrification. We have already touched upon the paradoxical possibility that Bartleby has adopted petrification as a form of self-protection. Unfortunately, like so many psychological defenses, petrification is not merely futile but more destructive than what it is supposed to provide a defense against—notably, the world: "If the whole of the individual's being cannot be defended, the individual retracts his lines of defence until he withdraws within a central citadel. He is prepared to write off everything he is, except his 'self.' But the tragic paradox is that the more the self is defended in this way, the more it is destroyed" (*Divided Self,* p. 77).

Alternatively, the self may be protected or defended by means of 19
its denial: this will be seen, however, as a repudiation of the "false self." The "false self" is the "personality" that one has in the outer world, which relates with that world and is observed by others, but which is divorced from one's "true," "inner," "unembodied" self. In Laing's observations on the development of "the false-self system," we may trace as well Bartleby's development as Melville's story proceeds: "The observable behaviour that is the expression of the false self is often perfectly normal. We see a model child, an ideal husband, an industrious clerk. This façade, however, usually becomes more and more stereotyped, and in the stereotype bizarre characteristics develop" (*Divided Self,* p. 99). Finally, "if the individual delegates all transactions between himself and the other to a system within his being which is not 'him,' then the world is experienced as unreal, and all that belongs to this system is felt to be false, futile, and meaningless" (p. 80). While the false-self system becomes more "extensive" and "autonomous," it also "becomes 'harassed' by compulsive behaviour fragments," and "all that belongs to it becomes more and more dead, unreal, false, mechanical" (p. 144). In the meantime, the inner self remains "transcendent, unembodied, and thus never to be grasped, pinpointed, trapped, possessed" (pp. 94–95). Given such distinctions, when the false self is repudiated, there may be nothing left.

Moreover, dividing the self in such a way not only entails dis- 20
sociation from and within oneself, but inevitably leads as well to dissociation from others. In repudiating the false self—the self after all that relates to others, however "falsely"—one repudiates all

contact with other people. Bartleby obviously does that, yet even as he does so his dissociation from others takes a form that surely reveals an appeal to the lawyer for some mode of contact.

But the lawyer, however sincerely he tries, cannot seem sufficiently to help Bartleby, whose increasingly disconcerting behavior seems to be a way of getting back at him in some awful manner. Indeed, this attack apparently takes the form, as it often does in mental patients, of imitation of the person seen as the persecutor or aggressor. At the start of Melville's story we are introduced to the lawyer as "a man who, from his youth upwards, has been filled with a profound conviction that the easiest way of life is the best. Hence, though I belong to a profession proverbially energetic and nervous, even to turbulence, at times, yet nothing of that sort have I ever suffered to invade my peace." He tells us that he is "one of those unambitious lawyers who never address a jury," preferring "the cool tranquillity of a snug retreat" (paragraph 3). In other words, he is a person who would prefer not to do anything very active. Even his later attempts to get rid of Bartleby can hardly be taken seriously, and perhaps they more than anything else display his deep tendency toward inaction and passivity. 21

In that context, Bartleby's behavior comes to seem an increasingly grotesque parody of the man to whom he has attached himself. 22

> There is a tendency for the false self to assume *more and more of the characteristics of the person upon whom its compliance is based*. . . . The *hatred of the impersonation* becomes evident when the impersonation begins to turn into a *caricature*.
>
> The impersonation of the other by the false self is not entirely the same as its compliance with the will of the other, for it may be directly counter to the other's will. (*Divided Self,* p. 100)

This "concealed indictment" of the impersonated other "reaches its most extreme form" in such manifestations as the "echolalia [repetition of words or phrases], and flexibilitas cerea [inert flexibility] of the catatonic" (p. 102). The indictment is less concealed in Bartleby's case when, in the Tombs near the end of the story, he says to the lawyer, "I know you . . . and I want nothing to say to you" (paragraph 220).

Although it has become commonplace to be condescending toward or even contemptuous of the lawyer, Bartleby's quiet indictment becomes all the more devastating in its effect upon us when we realize that the lawyer is more patient, more generous, and more self-aware than most of us would be. (Or than we are: if, say, we are teachers—as I am—how many of us have responded so admirably and so personally to the students who appear in our offices and reveal in obscure ways that they are, or potentially are, Bartlebys?) Yet even the lawyer fails. 23

An indictment of the lawyer is a mode of accusation against the 24
world he represents, just as withdrawing from others entails withdrawing from that world. People trapped in a "double bind"[11] or an otherwise impossible, unlivable situation may—as in the notable instance of prisoners in concentration camps—abandon the world and the aspects of one's supposed self that are most "in" the world. In the brutal parlance of everyday life, Bartleby dissociates himself from the outer world because he can no longer take it.

The ultimate form of withdrawal from the world is death. Bart- 25
leby seems all along to desire death—in existential terms, to be choosing non-being over being—even as, in a paradoxical but relentlessly logical way, his retreat into a death-like state of immobility may also reflect his *fear* of death: we have seen Laing quote Tillich on neurosis as "the way of avoiding non-being by avoiding being" (*Divided Self,* p. 111). Of Peter—whom he quotes as having once said, "I've been sort of dead in a way. I cut myself off from other people and became shut up in myself. And I can see that you become dead in a way when you do this" (p. 133)—Laing writes that he had "set about trying to reduce his whole being to non-being; he set about as systematically as he could to become nothing. Under the conviction that he was nobody, that he was nothing, he was driven by a terrible sense of honesty to *be* nothing" (p. 131). If Bartleby shares that terrible honesty, its most pressing manifestation is probably his refrain of "I would prefer not to." At first to be sure it refers merely to proofreading, but as time goes on its reference becomes more and more encompassing until in the end it becomes all-inclusive—until, indeed, it refers to all of life and living. For poor Bartleby would prefer not to.

Discussing the dilemma of the person "in an alienated untenable 26
position," Laing says that as soon as he "realizes that he is in a box, he can try to get out of it. But since to *them* [others] the box is *the whole world,* to get out of the box is tantamount to stepping off the end of the world, a thing that no one who loves him could sit by and let happen" (*Self and Others,* p. 41). Good intentions can be murderous, or simply ineffective: when on the second occasion of Bartleby's refusal to read copy and his statement that he "would prefer not to," the lawyer finds himself "not only strangely disarmed" but "in a

[11]This term originated in an attempt to explore the etiology of schizophrenia: see Gregory Bateson, et al., "Toward a Theory of Schizophrenia," *Behavioral Science,* 1 (October 1956), 251–64; the authors state that a person in a double bind may, for example, "try to detach his interest from the external world and concentrate on his own internal processes and, therefore, give the appearance of being a withdrawn, perhaps mute, individual"—which "is another way of saying that . . . he may defend himself in ways which have been described as paranoid, hebephrenic, or catatonic" (p. 256).

wonderful manner, touched and disconcerted," he tells us: "I began to reason with him" ("Bartleby," paragraph 35).

That is all well and good, but not likely to work. Later, the lawyer is wiser, and he recognizes that it is Bartleby's "soul that suffered, and his soul I could not reach" (paragraph 93). Indeed, the first task in helping a person with Bartleby's problems is no doubt to *reach* that person. The *"sense of identity requires the existence of another by whom one is known"* (*Divided Self,* p. 139). Even that, however, is not enough, as the lawyer realizes still later, "recalling the divine injunction: 'A new commandment give I unto you, that ye love one another' " ("Bartleby," paragraph 165). Obeying that call involves a complete breakdown in the normal relationship between employer and employee, just as Laing calls for the complete breakdown in the traditional relationship between psychotherapist and patient: "The main agent in uniting the patient, in allowing the pieces to come together and cohere, is the physician's love, a love that recognizes the patient's total being, and accepts it, with no strings attached" (*Divided Self,* p. 165). 27

Only an inordinately cynical reading of Melville's story will fail to recognize that the lawyer does come to experience genuine love for the scrivener. "Ah, Bartleby! Ah, humanity!" ends his narration: this from the man who, as we have seen, has earlier felt the absence of "anything ordinarily human" in his employee. But his love never attains—perhaps it rarely if ever can attain—the absolute totality apparently demanded or needed by Bartleby. As a result, the lawyer does not succeed in thrusting through the wall that Bartleby has set up—the wall that Bartleby has become. As Bartleby lives and ends his life facing walls, we may keep in mind Laing's quotation—in the context of a warning in regard to the danger of the "tendency to *become what one perceives*"—of a patient, Julie: "That chair . . . that wall. I could be that wall. It's a terrible thing for a girl to be a wall" (*Divided Self,* p. 198). Or for a young man, too. 28

Discussion and Writing Suggestions

1. Beja writes, at the end of paragraph 1: "The mistake [in interpreting "Bartleby"] is to take an either/or approach: either "Bartleby" is a psychological study, or it is a socio-economic one, or a metaphysical one, or an existential one, or an autobiographical one, and so on." What are the implications of this statement for the interpretation of "Bartleby"—or any other literary work? What happens if we do make such a "mistake"?

2. In what way—according to the thought of R. D. Laing—might Bartleby's behavior be considered sane, even healthy? Does this interpretation of Bartleby's behavior make sense to you?

3. In paragraph 6, Beja remarks that when the purposes of psychological terms "are distorted in order to provide us with handy labels, they end by perverting our response to the story—and may even become aids in developing relatively painless ways of dealing with (that is, dismissing) Bartleby's painful case." How could psychological terms (like "schizophrenia," "catatonic," etc.) pervert our response to "Bartleby"? How could they help us to dismiss his "painful case"?

4. Using Laing's terminology, Beja suggests that Bartleby has suffered "partial loss of the synthetic unity of self, concurrently with partial loss of relatedness with the other." What do you think this means? Does it help account for Bartleby's speech and actions—his combination of logic and illogic, his inability to relate rationally to the narrator and the other characters?

5. How does Laing's process of "petrification" apply to Bartleby? Do the quotations from the text of "Bartleby" that Beja offers in paragraph 17 persuade you that such a process is indeed happening to Bartleby?

6. In paragraph 19, Beja discusses the concept of the "false self." Do you have a "false self"? What is its purpose? How does your "real" or "inner self" feel about your "false self"? Do you agree that Bartleby's repudiation of his false self accounts for his apparently illogical behavior toward others? In a multiparagraph essay, explore some of these questions.

7. At the end of his essay, Beja suggests that had the lawyer loved Bartleby more, he might have been able to prevent the scrivener's demise and might even have reversed his withdrawal from the world. But he fails to penetrate the wall Bartleby has erected—indeed, the wall that Bartleby has become. Is this a fair conclusion? Explain. (For a further exploration of the issues raised by this question, see Patricia Barber's essay—"Bartleby Is a Woman"—at the end of this chapter.)

8. Write a critique of Beja's essay. Draw on your responses to some of the questions posed above, but focus also on the question of whether or not you think literary characters can or should be (psycho)analyzed in this way.

Bartleby Is Christ

H. BRUCE FRANKLIN

If a story does not make sense literally, perhaps it makes sense figuratively. Perhaps the characters and their situations are not to be interpreted

---

Reprinted from *The Wake of the Gods: Melville's Mythology* by H. Bruce Franklin with the permission of the publishers, Stanford University Press © 1963 by the Board of Trustees of the Leland Stanford Junior University.

realistically, not to be taken at face value. If not, then just how are *they to be taken? One significant approach to literary criticism is religious—and more specifically, Christian—interpretation. Using such an approach, we would consider the characters in a work, and their situations, not literally but rather as acting out allegories of Christian belief. With certain works, of course—works like Milton's* Paradise Lost *and Bunyan's* Pilgrim's Progress*—the validity of such an approach may be taken for granted. With other works, the validity of a Christian interpretation may be open to serious question. (In his classic parody* The Pooh Perplex, *a collection of imaginary critiques of Milne's* Winnie the Pooh, *Frederick Crews poked fun at various schools of inappropriately applied literary criticism.)*

Does "Bartleby" make sense when viewed as a Christian allegory—with Bartleby himself as the Christ figure? In the following article, H. Bruce Franklin suggests that it does make sense. In fact, Franklin broadens the Christian interpretation to suggest that "Bartleby" may also have connections to Hindu myth. Ask yourself whether or not "Bartleby," viewed through Franklin's eyes, becomes plausibly explicable. Does the work become more rich, more meaningful, than it was before? Does it make more sense to consider Bartleby as a figure in a Christian allegory than as a clinical dramatization of a schizophrenic? Keep in mind that accepting one interpretation does not necessarily *mean rejecting all others. So don't be afraid of being "simplistic" or "reductive." And don't worry, either, about whether or not it is likely that Melville* intended *such an interpretation. Once he has written the story and left it to us, Melville and his intention become (in a sense) irrelevant.*

H. Bruce Franklin was born in 1934 in Brooklyn, New York, and educated at Amherst and Stanford universities. He began his career as a tugboat deckhand and mate in New York Harbor, going on to teach literature at Johns Hopkins and Stanford. His radical political views, particularly on the war in Vietnam, caused him to become the only tenured professor ever to be fired from Stanford (1972). Unemployed for three years, he subsequently accepted an appointment at Rutgers University, where, since 1980, he has been distinguished professor of English. Noted for his thoroughly documented research, Franklin is the author of numerous articles and books, including The Wake of the Gods: Melville's Mythology *(1971), editions of Melville, Hawthorne, and Stalin;* Back Where You Came From: A Life in the Death of the Empire *(1975), a political autobiography; and* The Victim as Criminal and Artist: Literature from the American Prison *(1978); several works on science fiction; and several more on education. The following passage is the opening section ("Bartleby: The Ascetic's Advent") of Chapter 5 of* The Wake of the Gods.

There are essentially three ethics available to man—action in and of 1
the world, action in the world for other-worldly reasons, and nonaction, that is, withdrawal from the world. We might call the extreme of the first the ethic of Wall Street, the extreme of the second the ethic of Christ, and the extreme of the third the ethic of the Eastern monk. Wall Street's ethic seeks the world as an end; Christ's ethic prescribes certain behavior in this world to get to a better world; the Eastern monk's ethic seeks to escape all worlds. *Bartleby* is a world in which these three ethics directly confront one another.

To read *Bartleby* well, we must first realize that we can never 2
know who or what Bartleby is, but that we are continually asked to guess who or what he might be. We must see that he may be anything from a mere bit of human flotsam to a conscious and forceful rejecter of the world to an incarnation of God. When we see the first possibility we realize the full pathos of the story; when we see the last possibility we realize that the story is a grotesque joke and a parabolic tragedy.

But of course the possibility that Bartleby may be the very least of 3
men does not necessarily contradict the possibility that Bartleby may be an embodiment of God. For as Christ explains in Matthew 25, the least of men (particularly when he appears as a stranger) is the physical representative and representation of Christ. Upon this identification depend the Christian ethic, the next world to which Christ sends every man, and the central meanings of *Bartleby:*

> 34 Then shall the King say unto them on his right hand, Come, ye blessed of my Father, inherit the kingdom prepared for you from the foundation of the world:
>
> 35 For I was ahungered, and ye gave me meat: I was thirsty, and ye gave me drink: I was a stranger, and ye took me in:
>
> 36 Naked, and ye clothed me: I was sick, and ye visited me: I was in prison, and ye came unto me.
>
> 37 Then shall the righteous answer him, saying, Lord, when saw we thee ahungered, and fed thee? or thirsty, and gave thee drink?
>
> 38 When saw we thee a stranger, and took thee in? or naked, and clothed thee?
>
> 39 Or when saw we thee sick, or in prison, and came unto thee?
>
> 40 And the King shall answer and say unto them, Verily I say unto you, Inasmuch as ye have done it unto one of the least of these my brethren, ye have done it unto me.
>
> 41 Then shall he say also unto them on the left hand, Depart from me, ye cursed, into everlasting fire, prepared for the devil and his angels:
>
> 42 For I was ahungered, and ye gave me no meat: I was thirsty, and ye gave me no drink:

43 I was a stranger, and ye took me not in: naked, and ye clothed me
not: sick, and in prison, and ye visited me not.
44 Then shall they also answer him, saying, Lord, when saw we thee
ahungered, or athirst, or a stranger, or naked, or sick, or in prison, and
did not minister unto thee?
45 Then shall he answer them, saying, Verily I say unto you, Inasmuch as ye did it not to one of the least of these, ye did it not to me.

Christ is here saying that the individual comes to God and attains his salvation when he shows complete charity to a stranger, and he rejects God and calls for his damnation whenever he refuses complete charity to *one* stranger, even "the least of these." As the story of Bartleby unfolds, it becomes increasingly apparent that it is in part a testing of this message of Christ. The narrator's soul depends from his actions toward Bartleby, a mysterious, poor, lonely, sick stranger who ends his life in prison. Can the narrator, the man of our world, act in terms of Christ's ethics? The answer is yes and no. The narrator fulfills the letter of Christ's injunction point by point: he offers money to the stranger so that he may eat and drink; he takes him in, finally offering him not only his office but also his home; when he sees that he is sick, he attempts to minister to him; he, alone of all mankind, visits and befriends the stranger in prison. But he hardly fulfills the spirit of Christ's message: his money is carefully doled out; he tries to evict the stranger, offers his home only after betraying him, and then immediately flees from him in the time of his greatest need; it is his demands on the stranger which have made him sick; he visits the stranger in prison only once while he is alive, thus leaving him alone for several days before and after his visit, thus leaving him to die entirely alone. At the heart of both the tragedy and the comedy lies the narrator's view of the drama, a view which sees all but all in the wrong terms: "To befriend Bartleby; to humor him in his strange wilfulness, will cost me little or nothing, while I lay up in my soul what will eventually prove a sweet morsel for my conscience." (paragraph 53)

According to Christ's words in Matthew 25, it would make no 4
difference to the narrator's salvation whether Bartleby is the Saviour incarnate or merely the least of his brethren. And certainly reading *Bartleby* with Matthew 25 in mind defines the central issues, no matter who Bartleby is. But the story repeatedly suggests that Bartleby may not be merely the least of Christ's brethren but may in fact be the Saviour himself. Again I wish to emphasize that we are certainly not justified in simply taking Bartleby to be an incarnation or reincarnation of Christ (except in the terms of Matthew 25). But if we do not entertain the possibility that Bartleby is Christ, although we still see most of the tragedy, we miss a great deal of the comedy. Bartleby's

story is the story of the advent, the betrayal, and torment of a mysterious and innocent being; this is a tragic story no matter who the being is. These events carefully and pointedly re-enact the story of Christ, and there is nothing funny about this. Nor is there anything inherently funny about the fact that for all we know Bartleby may be God incarnate. The central joke of the story is that although the narrator comes close to seeing this possibility without ever seeing what he sees, his language continually recognizes and defines the possibility that Bartleby may be Christ. The narrator's own words define his own tragedy as cosmic and comic.

The narrator tells us that he is an "eminently *safe* man," an "unambitious" lawyer who, "in the cool tranquillity of a snug retreat," does "a snug business among rich men's bonds and mortgages and title-deeds." He tells of receiving the "good old office" of "Master in Chancery," which greatly enlarges his business. This is the time which he significantly labels "the period just preceding the advent of Bartleby." After mentioning this office only once, he digresses for several pages. When he next mentions it, he calls it simply—and significantly—"the master's office." This joke introduces the pointedly ambiguous description of the advent of Bartleby: 5

> Now my original business . . . was considerably increased by receiving the master's office. There was now great work for scriveners. Not only must I push the clerks already with me, but I must have additional help.
>
> In answer to my advertisement, a motionless young man one morning stood upon my office threshold, the door being open, for it was summer. I can see that figure now—pallidly neat, pitiably respectable, incurably forlorn! It was Bartleby. (paragraph 15)

So Bartleby is a being who answers the narrator's call for "additional help" at a time of "great work for scriveners." The narrator responds by placing "this quiet man within easy call, in case any trifling thing was to be done."

Bartleby at first does an "extraordinary" amount of work, but, "on the third day," begins to answer "I would prefer not to" to the narrator's petty orders. Who is this being? The narrator can only tell us that "Bartleby was one of those beings of whom nothing is ascertainable, except from the original sources, and, in his case, those are very small." 6

As Bartleby, by merely standing, sitting, and lying still, step by step withdraws from the world, the narrator follows him, leaving behind, bit by bit, his worldly values. Slowly the narrator's compassion for Bartleby and his sense of brotherhood with him emerge, and as they emerge we see more and more clearly that the drama involves the salvation of both Bartleby—the poor, lonely stranger—and the 7 narrator—the "safe" man who in many ways represents our world. As this drama becomes clear, the narrator's language becomes more and more grotesquely ironic.

At the beginning of his withdrawal, Bartleby is only saved from being "violently dismissed" because the narrator cannot find "anything ordinarily human about him." In the next stage of his withdrawal, Bartleby stands at the entrance of his "hermitage" and "mildly" asks "What is wanted?" When the narrator "hurriedly" demands that he proofread the copies, Bartleby answers that he "would prefer not to," and the narrator tells us that "for a few moments I was turned into a pillar of salt." 8

The narrator, as boss of the office, plays god. What he does not realize, but what his language makes clear, is that he may be playing this role with God himself. The narrator tells us that he "again advanced towards Bartleby" because "I felt additional incentives tempting me to my fate." "Sometimes, to be sure, I could not, for the very soul of me," he ironically admits, "avoid falling into sudden spasmodic passions with him." 9

The narrator even discovers "something superstitious knocking at my heart, and forbidding me to carry out my purpose . . . if I dared to breathe one bitter word against this forlornest of mankind." At this point we need hardly remember Matthew 25 or that Melville referred to Christ as the Man of Sorrows to see why the narrator should look to his salvation instead of his safety. But when the narrator surmises that Bartleby has "nothing else earthly to do," he blandly asks him to carry some letters to the post office. 10

The narrator then realizes that Bartleby is "absolutely alone in the universe," but his response to this cosmic loneliness is to tell Bartleby that "in six days' time he must unconditionally leave the office." On the appointed day, the narrator tries to dismiss Bartleby with words that become grotesquely ludicrous if they are seen as an inversion of the true roles of these two beings: "If, hereafter, in your new place of abode, I can be of any service to you, do not fail to advise me by letter." Perhaps the narrator has already received in very clear letters all the advice he needs, a description of what service Bartleby might be to him in his new place of abode, and what his own place of abode will be if he rejects the advice and denies the man. (But perhaps, as the last few paragraphs of the story hint, Matthew 25 and its entire context is now the Dead Letter Office.) 11

Shortly after saying these words, the narrator discovers that this very day is "an election day." Still, "a sudden passion"—the very thing which the narrator's words had recognized as endangering his "very soul"—makes him demand that Bartleby leave him. The scrivener gently replies, "I would prefer *not* to quit you." The narrator 12 reminds Bartleby ironically that he has no "earthly right" to stay; Bartleby "answered nothing" and "silently retired into his hermitage."

This infuriates the narrator; as he says, the "old Adam of resentment rose in me and tempted me concerning Bartleby." But on this election day the narrator saves himself for the time being "simply by recalling the divine injunction: 'A new commandment give I unto you, that ye love one another.' " "Yes," he says, "this it was that saved me." But the narrator fails to grasp what he has seen; he defines this love "as a vastly wise and prudent principle"; "mere self-interest" becomes his most clearly perceived motive to "charity." 13

After some days pass in which he has had a chance to consult "Edwards on the Will" and "Priestley on Necessity," the narrator has his most complete revelation of his own drama: 14

> Gradually I slid into the persuasion that these troubles of mine, touching the scrivener, had been all predestinated from eternity, and Bartleby was billeted upon me for some mysterious purpose of an all-wise Providence, which it was not for a mere mortal like me to fathom. Yes, Bartleby, stay there behind your screen, thought I; I shall persecute you no more; you are harmless and noiseless as any of these old chairs; in short, I never feel so private as when I know you are here. At last I see it, I feel it; I penetrate to the predestinated purpose of my life. I am content. Others may have loftier parts to enact; but my mission in this world, Bartleby, is to furnish you with office-room for such period as you may see fit to remain. (paragraph 167)

According to Christ's own words in Matthew 25, the narrator is absolutely right; he has finally seen his mission in the world.

But the narrator's resolution of his dilemma is short-lived. It withers quickly under the "uncharitable remarks obtruded upon" him by his "professional friends." He confesses that the whispers of his professional acquaintance "worried me very much." When he then thinks of the possibility of Bartleby's "denying my authority," outliving him, and claiming "possession of my office by right of his perpetual occupancy," the narrator resolves to "forever rid me of this intolerable incubus." Even then, after he informs Bartleby that he must leave, and after Bartleby takes "three days to meditate upon it," he learns that Bartleby "still preferred to abide with" him, that "he prefers to cling to" him. This sets the stage for the narrator's denial of Bartleby, for he decides that "since he will not quit me, I must quit him." 15

To hear the full significance of his three denials of Bartleby, we must hear the loud echoes of Peter's three denials of Christ. Matthew 26: 16

> 70 But he denied before them all, saying, I know not what thou sayest.
> 72 And again he denied with an oath, I do not know the man.
> 74 Then began he to curse and to swear, saying, I know not the man.

Even closer are Peter's words in Mark 14:71: "I know not this man of whom ye speak."

The first denial: 17

> "Then, sir," said the stranger, who proved a lawyer, "you are responsible for the man you left there." . . .
>
> "I am very sorry, sir," said I, with assumed tranquillity, but an inward tremor, "but, really, the man you allude to is nothing to me." (paragraphs 181–82)

The second denial: 18

> "In mercy's name, who is he?"
>
> "I certainly cannot inform you. I know nothing about him." (paragraphs 183–84)

The third denial: 19

> In vain I persisted that Bartleby was nothing to me—no more than to any one else. (paragraph 190)

After the narrator's three denials of Bartleby, he belatedly makes his most charitable gesture toward him, offering, "in the kindest tone I could assume under such exciting circumstances," to permit him to come to his home. But Bartleby answers, "No: at present I would prefer not to make any change at all." The narrator leaves; the new landlord has the police remove Bartleby to the Tombs. The narrator then learns of Bartleby's procession to his Golgotha:

> As I afterwards learned, the poor scrivener, when told that he must be conducted to the Tombs, offered not the slightest obstacle, but, in his pale, unmoving way, silently acquiesced.
>
> Some of the compassionate and curious bystanders joined the party; and headed by one of the constables arm in arm with Bartleby, the silent procession filed its way through all the noise, and heat, and joy of the roaring thoroughfares at noon. (paragraphs 215–16)

"Quite serene and harmless in all his ways," Bartleby is, like Christ, "numbered with the transgressors" (Mark 15:28). The world places him in prison where, amidst "murderers and thieves," he completes his withdrawal from the world.

When the narrator more or less meets the last condition laid down in Matthew 25—visiting the stranger in prison—all his charity is shown to be too little and too late. Before Bartleby leaves the world he says to the narrator, "I know you," and adds, without looking at him, "and I want nothing to say to you." At this point we can hear new ironies in the narrator's attempt to dismiss Bartleby: "If, hereafter, in your new place of abode, I can be of any service to you, do not fail to advise me by letter." Thus, when the narrator retells the rumor of Bartleby's having worked in the Dead Letter Office, he describes in part himself, in part Bartleby, and in part the scriptural letters which spell the hope of salvation. "The master's office" has become the Dead Letter Office. 20

> Dead letters! does it not sound like dead men? . . . pardon for those who died despairing; hope for those who died unhoping; good tidings for those who died stifled by unrelieved calamities. On errands of life, these letters speed to death.
>
> Ah, Bartleby! Ah, humanity! (paragraphs 250–51)

But all this is only half the story. For if the narrator is weighed and found wanting, what then of Bartleby himself? At least the narrator at times can show compassion, sympathy, and charity. Indeed, he at times much more than transcends the worldly ethics with which he starts and to which he tends to backslide. (One must bear in mind while evaluating the narrator's behavior that he is continually defending himself from two possible accusations—that he is too hard-hearted and that he is too soft-hearted.) Although he begins by strictly following horological time, he conforms more and more closely to chronometrical time. And he is after all certainly the most charitable character in the story. What time does Bartleby follow, and, finally, how charitable is he? Or is it possible to account for the actions of a being who is almost by definition enigmatic? 21

Because "Bartleby was one of those beings of whom nothing is ascertainable, except from the original sources, and, in his case, those are very small," he is almost as difficult to judge as to identify. But whether he is finally a god incarnate as a man or only a man playing the role of a crucified god, his behavior fits a pattern which implies an ethic. 22

If, as the Plotinus Plinlimmon pamphlet asserts in *Pierre*, chronometrical time is an impossibility for man, if man is left with the choice in the world between following chronometrical time and being destroyed or following horological time and being contemptible, if, then, no action in the world can be at the same time safe and worthy of salvation, what is there left for man to do? One answer is that man can try to live out of the world, can withdraw from the world 23 altogether. This is the answer which forms the counterpoint with worldly ethics in both *Bartleby* and *Benito Cereno,* each of which dramatizes a particular and different kind of monasticism.

Bartleby's monkish withdrawal from the world has been de- 24
scribed by Saburo Yamaya and Walter Sutton as essentially Buddhistic in nature. Yamaya shows the connections between Buddhist Quietism and the stone imagery of both *Pierre* and *Bartleby,* citing as one of Melville's sources this passage from Bayle's *Dictionary:*

> The great lords and the most illustrious persons suffered themselves to be so infatuated with the [Buddhist] Quietism, that they believed insensibility to be the way to perfection and beatitude and that the nearer a man came to the nature of a block or *a stone,* the greater progress he made, the more he was like the first principle, into which he was to return.

Sutton quite accurately perceives (apparently without reference to Yamaya) that Bartleby, in achieving "the complete withdrawal of the hunger artist," has attained what "in Buddhist terms . . . is Nirvana, extinction, or nothingness," and he suggests that at this point in his life Melville was unconsciously approaching Buddhism. But Melville was probably quite aware that Bartleby's behavior conforms very closely to a kind of Oriental asceticism which Thomas Maurice had spent about fifty pages describing.

The Oriental ascetic who most closely resembles Bartleby is the 25
Saniassi, a Hindu rather than a Buddhist. It seems probable that once again Maurice's *Indian Antiquities* served as a direct source for Melville's fiction. Maurice describes in detail the systematic withdrawal from the world practiced by the Saniassi, and many details have a surprising—and grotesquely humorous—correspondence to the systematic withdrawal from the world practiced by Bartleby. For instance, in the fifth stage the Saniassi "eats only one particular kind of food during the day and night, but as often as he pleases." Bartleby "lives, then, on ginger-nuts . . . never eats a dinner, properly speaking; he must be a vegetarian, then, but no; he never eats even vegetables, he eats nothing but ginger-nuts." "During the last three days," the Saniassi "neither eats nor drinks." During Bartleby's last few days, he prefers not to eat.

The fact that external details of Bartleby's withdrawal closely 26
parallel some of the external details of the Saniassi's withdrawal is not nearly so significant as this fact: Bartleby's behavior seems to be the very essence of Maurice's description of the Saniassi's behavior. In fact, Maurice's general description and judgment of the Saniassi often seems to be a precise description and judgment of Bartleby.

Most striking are the very things which Maurice claims are 27 peculiar to the Saniassi. He observes that one of the principal ways in which the Saniassi is distinguished from the Yogi is "by the calm, the silent, dignity with which he suffers the series of complicated evils through which he is ordained to toil." The Saniassi "can only be fed by the charity of others"; "he must himself make no exertion, nor feel any solicitude for existence upon this contaminated orb." The Saniassis' design "is to detach their thoughts from all concern about sublunary objects; to be indifferent to hunger and thirst; to be insensible to shame and reproach."

Perhaps most important to the judgment of Bartleby is the Saniassis' "incessant efforts . . . to stifle every ebullition of human passion, and live upon earth as if they were already, and in reality, disembodied." This may at once help account for Bartleby's appearing as a "ghost" or as "cadaverous" to the narrator and explain what ethical time he follows, for "it is the boast of the Saniassi to sacrifice every human feeling and passion at the shrine of devotion." Like Bartleby, the Saniassi "is no more to be soothed by the suggestions of *adulation* in its most pleasing form, than he is to be terrified by the loudest clamours of *reproach*. . . . By long habits of indifference, he becomes inanimate as a piece of wood or stone; and, though he mechanically respires the vital air, he is to all the purposes of active life *defunct*." 28

"Bartleby" is, then, in part the story of a man of the world who receives "the master's office"; who advertises for help; who is thereupon visited by a strange being who in an "extraordinary" way at first does all that is asked of him; who treats this strange being with contempt; who nevertheless receives from this being what seems to be his purpose in life; who betrays this being; and who watches and describes the systematic withdrawal of this being. It is also in part the story of this strange being, who replays much of the role of Christ while behaving like an Hindu ascetic, and who ends by extinguishing himself and making dead letters of the scripture which describes his prototype. 29

Discussion and Writing Suggestions

1. Franklin equates Peter's three denials of Christ with the narrator's three denials of Bartleby. To what extent do you accept this equation? Has the narrator betrayed Bartleby? (If so, what else should he have done?)
2. In paragraph 3 Franklin asserts, "As the story of Bartleby unfolds, it becomes increasingly apparent that it is in part a testing of the message of Christ." The reader is invited to see Bartleby as a representation of the "stranger" of Christ's story in Matthew 25, quoted above. To what extent do you agree that such an approach is the key to Melville's story? Has Franklin argued convincingly? Discuss your response in the form of a

critique of Franklin's essay. Before drafting your response, consider some of the following questions and draw on your responses in your critique.

3. Franklin maintains that "Bartleby" is both tragic and comic. In what does the comedy consist? What is the role of the narrator in the "comedy"?
4. In what way can the narrator's dismissal of Bartleby from his office be seen as an ironic, even ludicrous reversal? (You may need to look up the meaning of "irony.")
5. Which section of "Bartleby" does Franklin see as central to his interpretation? Do you agree that this section carries the significance Franklin believes it does?
6. In the final section of this passage, Franklin suggests that Bartleby can also be compared to the Hindu ascetic Saniassi, in terms of his withdrawal and detachment from the world and from his own emotions and physical needs. Does this interpretation seem more plausible or less than the equation of Bartleby with Christ (or one who represents Christ)?

Bartleby Is Marx's Alienated Worker

LOUISE K. BARNETT

Considerably more common—and influential among literary scholars—than Christian interpretations of literature are Marxist interpretations. Marxist critics are particularly interested in the social and economic environment portrayed in literary works. Examining the living and working conditions of the protagonist and other characters, these critics speculate on how these conditions affect their behavior and their feelings—indeed, on how these conditions affect the very nature of the work in question: its theme, its tone, its structure, its central conflict. For these critics, this central conflict is frequently the same conflict underlying orthodox Marxist thought itself—the class struggle. Thus, the exploitation of working-class characters by the bourgoisie becomes one way to account for the fates of the characters in a particular work. As with Christian interpretations, the plausibility of Marxist interpretations often depends on the work being analyzed. The novels of Charles Dickens, for example (e.g., Oliver Twist, Great Expectations*), can certainly be illuminated by such analysis. And one does not have to be a Marxist to appreciate the power of this particular approach as a critical tool—not only for literature but for social and economic analysis, in general. (In fact, it is now a commonplace that Marxism is considerably more effective*

"Bartleby as Alienated Worker" (Retitled: "Bartleby Is Marx's Alienated Worker") by Louise Barnett from pp. 379–85 in *Studies in Short Fiction* 11:4 (Autumn 1953).

as an analytical tool than as a blueprint for social reform or for government itself.)

In the following essay, Louise K. Barnett uses Marxist analysis to account for Bartleby's apparently illogical behavior. Read her essay with the same general question in mind as for the previous analyses: How satisfactorily does this analysis account for Bartleby's behavior? How well does it illuminate the work for you?

Louise K. Barnett teaches literature at Rutgers University. She has written articles on American prose fiction; is the author of two books, The Ignoble Savage: American Literary Racism, 1790–1890 *(1976) and* Swift's Poetic Worlds *(1981); and is the coeditor of* New World Journeys: Contemporary Italian Writers and the Experience of America *(1978). The following article first appeared under the title "Bartleby as Alienated Worker" in* Studies in Short Fiction.

A decade after Karl Marx first described the worker's alienation in a capitalistic society, his contemporary, Herman Melville, independently created the perfect exemplum of this condition in his tale of "Bartleby, the Scrivener."[1] Although critics have seen Bartleby in a number of interesting and even heroic guises,[2] I believe that he is a figure of another sort: the alienated worker who, realizing that his work is meaningless and without a future, can only protest his humanity by a negative assertion. Defined only by his job, and becoming increasingly dissociated from it, Bartleby sums up the worker's plight. Given a system committed to profits, the only alternative to working under such demeaning conditions is death. 1

1

According to Marx, the worker experiences alienation for the following reasons: "First, that the work is *external* to the worker, that it is not a part of his nature, that consequently he does not fulfil himself in his work but denies himself, has a feeling of misery, not of well-being, does not develop freely a physical and mental energy, but is physically exhausted and mentally debased. . . . Finally, the alienated 2

[1]Marx's *Economic and Philosophical Manuscripts of 1844* were not published until 1932; the tale of "Bartleby the Scrivener" first appeared in *Putnam's Monthly Magazine* (December, 1853).

[2]Literally dozens of critics have identified Bartleby with Melville or with artists in general. For a thorough review of "Bartleby" criticism through 1965 see Donald M. Fiene, "A Bibliography of Criticism of 'Bartleby, the Scrivener,' " *The Melville Annual*, 1965; *A Symposium: Bartleby, the Scrivener*, ed. Howard P. Vincent (Kent, Ohio; Kent University Press, 1966), pp. 140–190. Bartleby as Thoreau is discussed by Egbert S. Oliver, "A Second Look at 'Bartleby,' " *College English*, 6 (1944–1945), 434–439.

character of work for the worker appears in the fact that it is not his work but work for someone else, that in work he does not belong to himself but to another person."[3] All three of the scriveners employed in the lawyer-narrator's office illustrate the aspects of alienation that Marx delineates, but only Bartleby comes to understand the situation and reject it.

That the conditions of labor in the law office are undesirable, 3
likely to produce a feeling of misery rather than well being, is amply confirmed by the narrator. Describing the general surroundings—which, as he rightly notes, have some bearing on the story of Bartleby—he reveals satisfaction in the dehumanized but functional environment. The windows, for example, let in light but present no distracting vistas, only varieties of wall. Placing Bartleby's desk close to one of these viewless openings is part of the narrator's "satisfactory arrangement" for the new employee. Another detail is the use of a folding screen to remove Bartleby from sight while keeping him within easy call, in case any trifling thing was to be done."[4] The narrator is pleased with this way of achieving privacy and society at the same time, but what for him is the best of both these worlds is clearly the worst for Bartleby. Conveniently placed to answer his employer's summons with alacrity, he must inhabit a circumscribed and isolated cell whose lack of outlook mirrors the lack of prospects of his menial occupation.

In his solitary confinement[5] Bartleby works *mechanically,* an adjec- 4
tive well suited to the tedious copying which comprises the chief part of his job. The other duty of a scrivener, verification, is "very dull, wearisome, and lethargic" (paragraph 19). According to the lawyer such labor would be intolerable to anyone of sanguine temperament or mettle—to almost any human being, we might assume.

Although the narrator has described himself as an easy-going 5
man in a traditionally hard-driving profession, his description of himself and of office business undercuts this self-characterization. John Jacob Astor is referred to with approval three times in as many sentences; indeed, the narrator confesses that he loves to repeat the

[3]*Economic and Philosophical Manuscripts of 1844* in *Karl Marx Selected Writings in Sociology and Social Philosophy,* ed. T. B. Bottomore and Maximilien Rubel, trans. T. B. Bottomore (New York: McGraw-Hill, 1964), pp. 169–70.

[4]Herman Melville, *Piazza Tales,* ed. Egbert S. Oliver (New York, 1948), p. 23.

[5]We should keep in mind that by the arrangement which he describes, the narrator isolates Bartleby before the copyist "chooses" isolation.

name because "it rings like unto bullion" (paragraph 3).[6] The making of money is the only discernible motive in the lawyer's account of his practice, from his usual traffic in rich men's documents to the remunerative office of Master in Chancery. If a certain indolence is suggested by the lawyer's report of his efforts, it is not characteristic of what he demands from his employees, who are often expected to work at top speed. The account of Bartleby's first refusal to read copy reveals this climate of pressure: "Being much hurried to complete a small affair I had in hand, I abruptly called to Bartleby. In my haste and natural expectancy of instant compliance, I sat with my head bent over the original on my desk, and my right hand sideways, and somewhat nervously extended with the copy, so that, immediately upon emerging from his retreat, Bartleby might snatch it and proceed to business without the least delay" (paragraph 20). The course of office events is punctuated by words like *speedily, quick, hurriedly, fast.*

In his attitude toward his employees, the narrator is a typically 6
enlightened master[7] who realizes that self-interest will be served by a charitable indulgence. When his scriveners assert their individuality and unconsciously rebel against their dehumanized labors, he tolerates the resulting eccentric behavior because it is still profitable to his business to do so. For all their idiosyncrasies, the other scriveners are an easily managed lot who neither challenge the employer's authority as Bartleby does nor support Bartleby in his disobedience.[8] When Turkey offends the lawyer by sealing a mortgage with a ginger nut, he avoids dismissal by the exaggerated obeisance of "an oriental bow" and a speech beginning with his usual placatory formula: "With submission, sir."

As seen through the lawyer's eyes from an amused, paternalistic 7
height, Turkey and Nippers are only caricatures—ludicrously nicknamed bundles of eccentricities. A keener observer might perceive that the montonous work itself engenders their antics, but the narrator makes only a superficial connection between the conditions of employment and the various foibles of his scriveners. All have hopes of more prestigious and less menial work: Turkey describes himself as

[6]As William Bysshe Stein comments: "John Jacob Astor, the high priest of financial duplicity, incarnates the ruling ethic of callous self-intersest." ("Bartleby: the Christian Conscience," *The Melville Annual*, 1965, p. 104).

[7]The lawyer's becoming "Master in Chancery" has led to the advertisement for additional help that Bartleby answers.

[8]As Leo Marx has noted, in acquiring the habit of using the word *prefer*, the other employees assume the form but not the substance of Bartleby's rebellion. ["Melville's Parable of the Walls," *Sewance Review*, 61 (1953), 620–621.]

the lawyer's right hand man; Nippers is guilty of "an unwarrantable usurpation of strictly professional affairs" (paragraph 11); and the office boy, Ginger Nut, has been placed in the law office because of his working class father's desire that he rise in life. In the narrator's view these aspirations are only delusions of grandeur. He notices Nippers' endless adjusting of his table, but interprets this as simply a manifestation of indigestion—an affliction vaguely coupled in the narrator's mind with "diseased ambition." The response of Turkey to the gift of his employer's hand-me-down coat is similarly regarded as an example of that scrivener's failure to know his inferior place in the scheme of things: "I thought Turkey would appreciate the favour, and abate his rashness and obstreperousness of afternoons. But no; I verily believe that buttoning himself up in so downy and blanket-like a coat had a pernicious effect upon him—upon the same principle that too much oats are bad for horses. In fact, precisely as a rash, restive horse is said to feel his oats, so Turkey felt his coat. It made him insolent. He was a man whom prosperity harmed" (paragraph 11).[9] Even Ginger Nut, whose youthful apprenticeship might auger possibility, seems little likely to escape his humble origin and present job. As the lawyer comments: "He had a little desk to himself, but he did not use it much. Upon inspection, the drawer exhibited a great array of the shells of various sorts of nuts" (paragraph 14).

Physically as well as mentally, the scriveners illustrate Marx's diagnosis of malaise. Turkey's inflamed face witnesses his over-indulgence; Nippers is given to teeth grinding and nervous attacks; Bartleby is pale and thin. Nursing their vain expectations, Turkey and Nippers take what solace they can in cakes and ale and fits of temper. Bartleby chooses not to continue working. 8

The lawyer's possessive attitude towards the entire world of his law office exemplifies still another Marxian contention: that a factor contributing to the alienated character of work is its belonging not to the worker, but to another person. Giving Turkey a coat, the lawyer thinks to control his behavior completely; disobeyed by Bartleby, he feels the shameful anomaly of being stymied by a man who should be his creature: "Was there any other thing in which I could procure myself to be ignominiously repulsed by this lean, penniless wight?—my hired clerk?" (paragraph 73)[10] Later, he justifies his unlocking of Bartleby's desk, and consequent infringement of his privacy, by his 9

[9]Cf. Karl Marx, p. 168: "The proletarian, just like a horse, need only receive so much as enables him to work."

[10]The lawyer's chagrin is based on class distinctions as well as on the boss-worker relationship. Bartleby is a "lean, penniless wight," i.e., a nobody, while the lawyer is a man of substance and position.

own proprietary right: "The desk is mine, and its contents, too, so I will make bold to look within" (paragraph 91). Bartleby's family and past, however, are locked within a place that the narrator cannot violate. The scrivener absolutely refuses to respond to any of the narrator's overtures, and thus provokes his employer's exasperation. In the latter's opinion the lowly copyist's life ought to be accessible for his employer's convenience.

The narrator's belief in the sanctity of his property is further 10
demonstrated when Bartleby maintains his intransigence. Finding the scrivener still on the premises after receiving an ultimatum to leave, the narrator, in an appropriate simile, compares himself to a man killed by lightning "at his own warm open window"—where presumably he should enjoy security. A similar sense of injured property rights informs the series of questions that he puts to Bartleby: "What earthly right have you to stay here? Do you pay any rent? Do you pay my taxes? Or is this property yours?" (paragraph 160). Unable to free himself from the exigencies of ownership, the narrator temporarily reconciles himself to Bartleby's continued presence by transforming the scrivener into a piece of his property: "I shall persecute you no more; you are harmless and noiseless as any of these old chairs" (paragraph 167). Finally, the thought that Bartleby might outlive him and establish the right of occupancy to the office is one of the "dark anticipations" that decide the lawyer to take action against the scrivener.

2

When Bartleby comes to the narrator's office, he appears to be a 11
model employee—quiet, neat, and devoted to copying. Significantly, his first resistance to the lawyer's will is a refusal to perform the most tedious of the scrivener's duties, examination of copy. The astounded employer, too hurried to go into the matter fully, eventually decides that the business ethic of buying cheap and selling dear will apply to this peculiar case: "Here I can cheaply purchase a delicious self-approval. To befriend Bartleby; to humour him in his strange wilfulness, will cost me little or nothing, while I lay up in my soul what will eventually prove a sweet morsel for my conscience" (paragraph 53). Moreover, Bartleby is still useful: while the other malleable scriveners examine copy, he can continue to write and thus earn the narrator's indulgence.

Later, when Bartleby refuses to do any work at all, he exhibits the 12
mental and physical exhaustion characteristic of Marx's alienated worker. "His eyes looked dull and glazed" (paragraph 131), which the narrator interprets as temporary eyestrain rather than an

enduring physical and spiritual anguish. Now the employer's charity is truly tested, for there is no longer any material profit to be made from the recalcitrant scrivener.

Bartleby as neither profit nor loss can be tolerated, but when business begins to suffer, the narrator acts—radically, if not decisively. Rather than confront his inhumanity by taking violent measures, he moves his office, denies responsibility for Bartleby to the new tenant—even when implored "in mercy's name"—and only reassumes the problem under threat of adverse publicity. Then, in their most extensive conversation of the story, Bartleby cryptically explains himself to the narrator. In preferring not to follow any of the unskilled occupations which the lawyer suggests, but at the same time affirming that he is not particular, Bartleby articulates the worker's dilemma. He is willing to do any meaningful work, but none of the jobs enumerated would be any improvement over the body- and mind-destroying labor he has just given up. Uncomprehending, and desperate to rid himself of a nuisance, the narrator now offers to install Bartleby temporarily in his own home, so that the process of money-making can continue without interruption.[11] Whether or not genuine humanity could now rehabilitate the alienated worker is a useless conjecture: the profit system cannot accommodate it, and Bartleby must necessarily reject an offer so redolent of self-interest. 13

After this failure to move Bartleby, the lawyer, true to his commercial values, experiences relief *first* at the thought of having done all he could vis-à-vis the other parties of his class: the landlord and lawyer tenants who had been insisting on his responsibility for Bartleby. Concern for the scrivener takes second place. The narrator's next action is similarly prompted not by the proddings of conscience over Bartleby's now certain eviction but by fear of further bother: "So fearful was I of being again hunted out by the incensed landlord and his exasperated tenants, that, surrendering my business to Nippers, for a few days, I drove about the upper part of the town and through the suburbs. . . ." (paragraph 213). When Bartleby is safely behind bars, continuing the dead-wall revery he pursued in the law office, the narrator can patronize him once more and encourage him to make the best of it: " 'And see, it is not so sad a place as one might think. Look, there is the sky, and here is the grass' " (paragraph 221). Bartleby will not be deluded into seeing his situation falsely, however. He knows that the natural world is equally constrained in the Tombs and on Wall Street; the man-made wall is omnipresent. Knowing as he does their respective positions, and the lawyer's real un- 14

[11]The same tone of peremptory command that informed the narrator's office speech to Bartleby is evident in this supposedly benevolent offer: "'Come, let us start now, right away' " (paragraph 211).

willingness to blur the distinction between their roles, Bartleby repudiates the narrator firmly: " 'I know you, he said, without looking round—'and I want nothing to say to you' " (ibid.).[12] When, on his last visit, the narrator reaches out to touch Bartleby—his first attempt at physical contact—the effort is once more too little and too late. His benediction over the dead scrivener, that he sleeps "with kings and counsellors," is an ironic acknowledgment of the common humanity of all men, an idea subordinated to considerations of class and position in his treatment of the enigmatic Bartleby.[13]

The narrator's epilogue is of a piece with his imperceptive evaluation of Bartleby throughout—a failure to see which is unconsciously motivated by self-protection. Wishing to view Bartleby as a man doomed "by nature and misfortune"[14] rather than by the commercial values that have given himself a comfortable existence, the narrator finds Bartleby's past occupation symbolically fitting. The final exclamation, linking Bartleby and humanity, is a way of merging the individual into the vast human tide for which he need take no responsibility. 15

3

To see Bartleby as victim of and protest against the numbing world of capitalistic profit and alienated labor suggested by the story's subtitle, "A Story of Wall Street," is not to insist upon a reductive economic meaning or to deny that other symbolic dimensions are necessarily untenable. The alienated worker can also be the alienated writer; alienation from work—the necessary labor by which most of us live—is the key in Marx's thinking to alienation from self and society as well. 16

Discussion and Writing Suggestions

1. Barnett announces her thesis in the first paragraph: "Defined only by his job, and becoming increasingly alienated from it, Bartleby sums up the worker's plight. Given a system committed to profits, the only alternative

---

[12]Liane Norman, "Bartleby and the Reader," *New England Quarterly*, 44 (1971), 38, similarly interprets this to mean: "I know your freedom and prosperity and I want nothing to do with them. They did not permit me to choose."

[13]The narrator has felt the attraction of Bartleby as *doppelgänger* early on but has never wanted to place "the bond of a common humanity" (paragraph 89) above business considerations.

[14]Similar statements about Bartleby earlier in the story have the same function of relieving the narrator of responsibility: whatever he does, Bartleby is fated to hopelessness and the narrator thus escapes blame.

to working under such demeaning conditions is death." To what extent do you agree with such an interpretation of "Bartleby"?

2. Do you agree that Marx's description of alienated labor quoted by Barnett in paragraph 2 applies to the kind of work done in the lawyer's office? Explain.
3. Explain how Barnett attacks the lawyer as an exploitative capitalist, with typical capitalist attitudes and behavior patterns? Do you agree with this assessment of the narrator?
4. Barnett attributes the other scriveners' (Turkey's, Nipper's, Ginger Nut's) eccentricities and nervous habits to their alienation from their jobs. How plausible do you find this explanation?
5. At one point in "Bartleby," the narrator says, "I shall persecute you no more; you are harmless and noiseless as any of these old chairs." Beja interprets this to indicate the final stage in Bartleby's "petrification"—a metamorphosis he undergoes as a defense against the world (Beja, paragraph 17). To Barnett, this same statement is evidence of the narrator's transformation of Bartleby "into a piece of his property" (paragraph 10). Which interpretation is more plausible? How far apart are these interpretations?
6. Barnett interprets Bartleby's refusal to consider any of the "unskilled occupations" suggested by the lawyer as the basic worker's dilemma: "He is willing to do any meaningful work, but none of the jobs enumerated would be any improvement over the body- and mind-destroying labor he has just given up." Do you think this is true? Would Bartleby be likely to accept more "meaningful" work?
7. To Franklin, the narrator's failure to better serve Bartleby is a failure of love and charity. To Barnett, it is a surrender to the profit motive. Beja acknowledges that Bartleby's final withdrawal is a rejection of the world that the lawyer represents but does not further characterize that world; for the most part, he does not blame the lawyer. What is your own view of the responsibility of the lawyer (and his world) for Bartleby's withdrawal and death?
8. Write a critique of Barnett's essay, drawing on your responses to some of the questions above.

Bartleby Is Melville

LEO MARX

Readers are frequently baffled as to how to account for an apparently illogical and meaningless sequence of events in a story and for the

"Melville's Parable of the Walls" (Retitled: "Bartleby Is Melville") by Leo Marx from *Sewanee Review* 61 (Autumn 1953). Reprinted by permission of the University of the South.

eccentric and unlikely characters therein. They quickly become unbaffled, however, when informed that the story is autobiographical, that the protagonist is the author himself, that the other characters are based on (or composites of) real people that the author has known, and that the situations are events (to various degrees reshaped or even allegorized) that actually happened to the author.

Does such an approach work for Bartleby? Is Bartleby Melville's allegorized portrait of himself? Is Bartleby's behavior Melville's allegorized account of what happened to a once-appreciated American man of letters? In the following essay (one of the most well-known and influential articles on "Bartleby"), Leo Marx carefully explains why he believes this to be the case. Again, keep in mind that one interpretation does not necessarily exclude others. The fact that Bartleby may be a fictional relation of Melville himself does not mean, for example, that you cannot also *apply Marxist analysis to the characters and the action.*

Born in New York City in 1919, and educated at Harvard and Amherst universities, Leo Marx has taught literature at Harvard, the University of Minnesota, Amherst, MIT, and the University of Nottingham in England. He is the author of The Machine in the Garden: Technology and the Pastoral Ideal in America *(1964) and the editor of books on Whitman and Thoreau. This article first appeared under the title "Melville's Parable of the Walls" in* Sewannee Review *(Aug. 1953).*

Dead,
25. Of a wall . . .: Unbroken, unrelieved by breaks or interruptions; absolutely uniform and continuous.

—*New English Dictionary*

In the spring of 1851, while still at work on *Moby Dick*, Herman 1
Melville wrote his celebrated "dollars damn me" letter to Hawthorne:

> In a week or so, I go to New York, to bury myself in a third-story room, and work and slave on my "Whale" while it is driving through the press. *That* is the only way I can finish it now—I am so pulled hither and thither by circumstances. The calm, the coolness, the silent grass-growing mood in which a man *ought* always to compose,—that, I fear, can seldom be mine. Dollars damn me. . . . My dear Sir, a presentiment is on me,—I shall at last be worn out and perish. . . . What I feel most moved to write, that is banned,—it will not pay. Yet, altogether, write the *other* way I cannot.

He went on and wrote the "Whale" as he felt moved to write it; the public was apathetic and most critics were cool. Nevertheless Melville stubbornly refused to return to the *other* way, to his more successful earlier modes, the South Sea romance and the travel narrative. In 1852 he published *Pierre*, a novel even more certain not to be popular.

And this time the critics were vehemently hostile. Then, the following year, Melville turned to shorter fiction. "Bartleby, the Scrivener," the first of his stories, dealt with a problem unmistakably like the one Melville had described to Hawthorne.

There are excellent reasons for reading "Bartleby" as a parable having to do with Melville's own fate as a writer. To begin with, the story *is* about a kind of writer, a "copyist" in a Wall Street lawyer's office. Furthermore, the copyist is a man who obstinately refuses to go on doing the sort of writing demanded of him. Under the circumstances there can be little doubt about the connection between Bartleby's dilemma and Melville's own. Although some critics have noted the autobiographical relevance of this facet of the story, a close examination of the parable reveals a more detailed parallel with Melville's situation than has been suggested.[1] In fact the theme itself can be described in a way which at once establishes a more precise relation. "Bartleby" is not only about a writer who refuses to conform to the demands of society, but it is, more relevantly, about a writer who foresakes conventional modes because of an irresistible preoccupation with the most baffling philosophical questions. This shift of Bartleby's attention is the symbolic equivalent of Melville's own shift of interest between *Typee* and *Moby Dick*. And it is significant that Melville's story, read in this light, does not by any means proclaim the desirability of the change. It was written in a time of deep hopelessness, and as I shall attempt to show, it reflects Melville's doubts about the value of his recent work. 2

Indeed, if I am correct about what this parable means, it has immense importance, for it provides the most explicit and mercilessly self-critical statement of his own dilemma that Melville has left us. Perhaps it is because "Bartleby" reveals so much of his situation that Melville took such extraordinary pains to mask its meaning. This may explain why he chose to rely upon symbols which derive from his earlier work, and to handle them with so light a touch that only the reader who comes to the story after an immersion in the other novels can be expected to see how much is being said here. Whatever Melville's motive may have been, I believe it may legitimately be accounted a grave defect of the parable that we must go back to *Typee* and *Moby Dick* and *Pierre* for the clues to its meaning. It is as if 3

[1]The most interesting interpretations of the story are those of Richard Chase and Newton Arvin. Chase stresses the social implications of the parable in his *Herman Melville, A Critical Study* (New York, 1949), pp. 143–149. Arvin describes "Bartleby" as a "wonderfully intuitive study in what would now be called schizophrenia . . ." in his *Herman Melville* (New York, 1950), pp. 240–242. Neither Chase nor Arvin makes a detailed analysis of the symbolism of the walls. E. S. Oliver has written of the tale as embodying Thoreau's political ideas in "A Second Look at 'Bartleby'," *College English* (May, 1945), pp. 431–439.

Melville had decided that the only adequate test of a reader's qualifications for sharing so damaging a self-revelation was a thorough reading of his own work.

I

"Bartleby, the Scrivener" is a parable about a particular kind of writer's relations to a particular kind of society. The subtitle, "A Story of Wall Street," provides the first clue about the nature of the society. It is a commercial society, dominated by a concern with property and finance. Most of the action takes place in Wall Street. But the designation has a further meaning: as Melville describes the street it literally becomes a walled street. The walls are the controlling symbols of the story, and in fact it may be said that this is a parable of walls, the walls which hem in the meditative artist and for that matter every reflective man. Melville also explicitly tells us that certain prosaic facts are "indispensable" to an understanding of the story. These facts fall into two categories: first, details concerning the personality and profession of the narrator, the center of consciousness in this tale, and more important, the actual floor-plan of his chambers. 4

The narrator is a Wall Street lawyer. One can easily surmise that at this unhappy turning point in his life Melville was fascinated by the problem of seeing what his sort of writer looked like to a representative American. For his narrator he therefore chose, as he did in "Benito Cereno," which belongs to the same period, a man of middling status with a propensity for getting along with people, but a man of distinctly limited perception. Speaking in lucid, matter-of-fact language, this observer of Bartleby's strange behavior describes himself as comfortable, methodical and prudent. He has prospered; he unabashedly tells of the praise with which John Jacob Astor has spoken of him. Naturally, he is a conservative, or as he says, an "eminently *safe*" man, proud of his snug traffic in rich men's bonds, mortgages and deeds. As he tells the story we are made to feel his mildness, his good humor, his satisfaction with himself and his way of life. He is the sort who prefers the remunerative though avowedly obsolete sinecure of the Mastership of Chancery, which has just been bestowed upon him when the action starts, to the exciting notoriety of the courtroom. He wants only to be left alone; nothing disturbs his complacency until Bartleby appears. As a spokesman for the society he is well chosen; he stands at its center and performs a critical role, unravelling and retying the invisible cords of property and equity which intertwine in Wall Street and bind the social system. 5

The lawyer describes his chambers with great care, and only when the plan of the office is clearly in mind can we find the key to 6 the parable. Although the chambers are on the second floor, the surrounding buildings rise above them, and as a result only very limited vistas are presented to those inside the office. At each end the windows look out upon a wall. One of the walls, which is part of a sky-light shaft, is *white.* It provides the best light available, but even from the windows which open upon the white wall the sky is invisible. No direct rays of the sun penetrate the legal sanctum. The wall at the other end gives us what seems at first to be a sharply contrasting view of the outside world. It is a lofty brick structure within ten feet of the lawyer's window. It stands in an everlasting shade and is *black* with age; the space it encloses reminds the lawyer of a huge black cistern. But we are not encouraged to take this extreme black and white, earthward and skyward contrast at face value (readers of *Moby Dick* will recall how illusory colors can be), for the lawyer tells us that the two "views," in spite of their colors, have something very important in common: they are equally "deficient in what landscape painters call 'life'." The difference in color is less important than the fact that what we see through each window is only a wall.

This is all we are told about the arrangement of the chambers 7
until Bartleby is hired. When the lawyer is appointed Master in Chancery he requires the services of another copyist. He places an advertisement, Bartleby appears, and the lawyer hastily checks his qualifications and hires him. Clearly the lawyer cares little about Bartleby's previous experience; the kind of writer wanted in Wall Street need merely be one of the great interchangeable white-collar labor force. It is true that Bartleby seems to him peculiarly pitiable and forlorn, but on the other hand the lawyer is favorably impressed by his neat, respectable appearance. So sedate does he seem that the boss decides to place Bartleby's desk close to his own. This is his first mistake; he thinks it will be useful to have so quiet and apparently tractable a man within easy call. He does not understand Bartleby then or at any point until their difficult relationship ends.

When Bartleby arrives we discover that there is also a kind of wall 8
inside the office. It consists of the ground-glass folding-doors which separate the lawyer's desk, and now Bartleby's, from the desks of the other employees, the copyists and the office boy. Unlike the walls outside the windows, however, this is a social barrier men can cross, and the lawyer makes a point of telling us that he opens and shuts these doors according to *his* humor. Even when they are shut, it should be noted, the ground glass provides at least an illusion of penetrability quite different from the opaqueness of the walls outside.

So far we have been told of only two possible views of the 9
external world which are to be had from the office, one black and the other white. It is fitting that the coming of a writer like Bartleby is what makes us aware of another view, one neither black nor white,

but a quite distinct third view which is now added to the topography of the Wall Street microcosm.

> I placed his desk close up to a small side-window in that part of the room [a corner near the folding-doors]—a window which orginally had afforded a lateral view of certain grimy back yards and bricks, but which, owing to subsequent erections, commanded at present no view at all, though it gave some light. Within three feet of the panes was a wall, and the light came down from far above, between two lofty buildings, as from a very small opening in a dome. Still further to a satisfactory arrangement, I procured a high green folding screen, which might entirely isolate Bartleby from my sight, though not remove him from my voice. And thus, in a manner, privacy and society were conjoined.

Notice that of all the people in the office Bartleby is to be in the best possible position to make a close scrutiny of a wall. His is only three feet away. And although the narrator mentions that the new writer's window offers "no view at all," we recall that he has, paradoxically, used the word "view" a moment before to describe the walled vista to be had through the other windows. Actually every window in the office looks out upon some sort of wall; the important difference between Bartleby and the others is that he is closest to a wall. Another notable difference is implied by the lawyer's failure to specify the color of Bartleby's wall. Apparently it is almost colorless, or blank. This also enhances the new man's ability to scrutinize and know the wall which limits his vision; he does not have to contend with the illusion of blackness or whiteness. Only Bartleby faces the stark problem of perception presented by the walls. For him external reality thus takes on some of the character it had for Ishmael, who knew that color did not reside in objects, and therefore saw beyond the deceptive whiteness of the whale to "a colorless, all-color of atheism." As we shall see, only the nature of the wall with which the enigmatic Bartleby is confronted can account for his strange behavior later.

What follows (and it is necessary to remember that all the impressions we receive are the lawyer's) takes place in three consecutive movements: Bartleby's gradually stiffening resistance to the Wall Street routine, then a series of attempts by the lawyer to enforce the scrivener's conformity, and finally, society's punishment of the recalcitrant writer. 10

During the first movement Bartleby holds the initiative. After he is hired he seems content to remain in the quasi-isolation provided by the "protective" *green* screen and to work silently and industriously. This screen, too, is a kind of wall, and its color, as will become apparent, means a great deal. Although Bartleby seems pleased with it and places great reliance upon it, the screen is an extremely ineffectual wall. It is the flimsiest of all the walls in and out of the office; 11

it has most in common with the ground glass door—both are "folding," that is, susceptible to human manipulation.

Bartleby likes his job, and in fact at first seems the exemplar of the writer wanted by Wall Street. Like Melville himself in the years between *Typee* and *Pierre,* he is an ardent and indefatigable worker; Bartleby impresses the lawyer with probably having "been long famished for something to copy." He copies by sun-light and candle-light, and his employer, although he does detect a curiously silent and mechanical quality in Bartleby's behavior, is well satisfied. 12

The first sign of trouble is Bartleby's refusal to "check copy." It is customary for the scriveners to help each other in this dull task, but when Bartleby is first asked to do it, to everyone's astonishment, he simply says that he prefers not to. From the lawyer's point of view "to verify the accuracy of his copy" is an indispensable part of the writer's job. But evidently Bartleby is the sort of writer who is little concerned with the detailed accuracy of his work, or in any case he does not share the lawyer's standards of accuracy. This passage is troublesome because the words "verify accuracy" seem to suggest a latter-day conception of "realism." For Melville to imply that what the public wanted of him in 1853 was a kind of "realism" is not plausible on historical grounds. But if we recall the nature of the "originals" which the lawyer wants impeccably copied the incident makes sense. These documents are mortgages and title-deeds, and they incorporate the official version of social (property) relations as they exist at the time. It occurs to the lawyer that "the mettlesome poet, Byron" would not have acceded to such a demand either. And like the revolutionary poet, Bartleby apparently cares nothing for "common usage" or "common sense"—a lawyer's way of saying that this writer does not want his work to embody a faithful copy of human relations as they are conceived in the Street. 13

After this we hear over and over again the reiterated refrain of Bartleby's nay-saying. To every request that he do something other than copy he replies with his deceptively mild, "I would prefer not to." He adamantly refuses to verify the accuracy of copy, or to run errands, or to do anything but write. But it is not until much later that the good-natured lawyer begins to grasp the seriousness of his employee's passive resistance. A number of things hinder his perception. For one thing he admits that he is put off by the writer's impassive mask (he expresses himself only in his work); this and the fact that there seems nothing "ordinarily human" about him saves Bartleby from being fired on the spot. Then, too, his business preoccupations constantly "hurry" the lawyer away from considering what to do about Bartleby. He has more important things to think 14 about; and since the scrivener unobtrusively goes on working in his green hermitage, the lawyer continues to regard him as a "valuable acquisition."

On this typically pragmatic basis the narrator has become recon- 15
ciled to Bartleby until, one Sunday, when most people are in church, he decides to stop at his office. Beforehand he tells us that there are several keys to this Wall Street world, four in fact, and that he himself has one, one of the other copyists has another, and the scrub woman has the third. (Apparently the representative of each social stratum has its own key.) But there is a fourth key he cannot account for. When he arrives at the office, expecting it to be deserted, he finds to his amazement that Bartleby is there. (If this suggests, however, that Bartleby holds the missing key, it is merely an intimation, for we are never actually provided with explicit evidence that he does, a detail which serves to underline Melville's misgivings about Bartleby's conduct throughout the story.) After waiting until Bartleby has a chance to leave, the lawyer enters and soon discovers that the scrivener has become a permanent resident of his Wall Street chambers, that he sleeps and eats as well as works there.

At this strange discovery the narrator feels mixed emotions. On 16
the one hand the effrontery, the vaguely felt sense that his rights are being subverted, angers him. He thinks his actual identity, manifestly inseparable from his property rights, is threatened. "For I consider that one . . . is somehow unmanned when he tranquilly permits his hired clerk to dictate to him, and order him away from his own premises." But at the same time the lawyer feels pity at the thought of this man inhabiting the silent desert that is Wall Street on Sunday. Such abject friendlessness and loneliness draws him, by the bond of common humanity, to sympathize with the horrible solitude of the writer. So horrible is this solitude that it provokes in his mind a premonitory image of the scrivener's "pale form . . . laid out, among uncaring strangers, in its shivering winding sheet." He is reminded of the many "quiet mysteries" of the man, and of the "long periods he would stand looking out, at his pale window behind the screen, upon the *dead brick wall*." The lawyer now is aware that death is somehow an important constituent of that no-color wall which comprises Bartleby's view of reality. After this we hear several times of the forlorn writer immobilized in a "*dead*-wall revery." He is obsessed by the wall of death which stands between him and a more ample reality than he finds in Wall Street.

The puzzled lawyer now concludes that Bartleby is the victim of 17
an "innate" or "incurable" disorder; he decides to question him, and if that reveals nothing useful, to dismiss him. But his efforts to make

Bartleby talk about himself fail. Communication between the writer and the rest of Wall Street society has almost completely broken down. The next day the lawyer notices that Bartleby now remains permanently fixed in a "dead-wall revery." He questions the writer, who calmly announces that he has given up all writing. "And what is the reason?" asks the lawyer. "Do you not see the reason for yourself?" Bartleby enigmatically replies. The lawyer looks, and the only clue he finds is the dull and glazed look of Bartleby's eyes. It occurs to him that the writer's "unexampled diligence" in copying may have had this effect upon his eyes, particularly since he has been working near the dim window. (The light surely is very bad, since the wall is only three feet away.) If the lawyer is correct in assuming that the scrivener's vision has been "temporarily impaired" (Bartleby never admits it himself) then it is the proximity of the colorless dead-wall which has incapacitated him. As a writer he has become paralyzed by trying to work in the shadow of the philosophic problems represented by the wall. From now on Bartleby does nothing but stand and gaze at the impenetrable wall.

Here Melville might seem to be abandoning the equivalence he 18
has established between Bartleby's history and his own. Until he chooses to have Bartleby stop writing and stare at the wall the parallel between his career as a writer and Bartleby's is transparently close. The period immediately following the scrivener's arrival at the office, when he works with such exemplary diligence and apparent satisfaction, clearly corresponds to the years after Melville's return to America, when he so industriously devoted himself to his first novels. And Bartleby's intransigence ("I prefer not to") corresponds to Melville's refusal ("Yet . . . write the other way I cannot.") to write another *Omoo,* or, in his own words, another "beggarly 'Redburn.' " Bartleby's switch from copying what he is told to copy to staring at the wall is therefore, presumably, the emblematic counterpart to that stage in Melville's career when he shifted from writing best-selling romances to a preoccupation with the philosophic themes which dominate *Mardi, Moby Dick* and *Pierre.* But the question is, can we accept Bartleby's merely passive staring at the blank wall as in any sense a parallel to the state of mind in which Melville wrote the later novels?

The answer, if we recall who is telling the story, is Yes. This is the 19
lawyer's story, and in his eyes, as in the eyes of Melville's critics and the public, this stage of his career *is* artistically barren; his turn to metaphysical themes *is* in fact the equivalent of ceasing to write. In the judgment of his contemporaries Melville's later novels are no more meaningful than Bartleby's absurd habit of staring at the dead-wall. Writing from the point of view of the Wall Street lawyer,

Melville accepts the popular estimate of his work and of his life.[2] The scrivener's trance-like stare is the surrealistic device with which Melville leads us into the nightmare world where he sees himself as his countrymen do. It is a world evoked by terror, and particularly the fear that he may have allowed himself to get disastrously out of touch with actuality. Here the writer's refusal to produce what the public wants is a ludicrous mystery. He loses all capacity to convey ideas. He becomes a prisoner of his own consciousness. "Bartleby the Scrivener" is an imaginative projection of that premonition of exhaustion and death which Melville had described to Hawthorne.

To return to the story. With his decision to stop copying the first, or "Bartleby," movement ends. For him writing is the only conceivable kind of action, and during the rest of his life he is therefore incapable of action or, for that matter, of making any choice except that of utter passivity. When he ceases to write he begins to die. He remains a fixture in the lawyer's chamber, and it is the lawyer who now must take the initiative. Although the lawyer is touched by the miserable spectacle of the inert writer, he is a practical man, and he soon takes steps to rid himself of the useless fellow. 20

He threatens Bartleby, but the writer cannot be frightened. He tries to bribe him, but money holds no appeal for Bartleby. Finally he conceives what he thinks to be a "masterly" plan; he will simply convey to the idle writer that he "assumes" Bartleby, now that he has ceased to be productive, will vacate the premises. But when he returns to the office after having communicated this assumption, which he characteristically thinks is universally acceptable, he finds Bartleby still at his window. This "doctrine of assumptions," as he calls it, fails because he and the writer patently share no assumptions whatsoever about either human behavior or the nature of reality. However, if Bartleby refuses to accept the premises upon which the Wall Street world operates, he also refuses to leave. We later see that the only escape available to Bartleby is by way of prison or death. 21

Bartleby stays on, and then an extraordinary thing happens. After yet another abortive attempt to communicate with the inarticulate scrivener the narrator finds himself in such a state of nervous indignation that he is suddenly afraid he may murder Bartleby. The fear recalls to his mind the Christian doctrine of charity, though 22

[2]It is not unreasonable to speculate that Melville's capacity for entertaining this negative view of his work is in fact a symptom of his own doubts about it. Was there some truth to the view that he was merely talking to himself? He may have asked himself this question at the time, and it must be admitted that this fear, at least in the case of *Pierre* and *Mardi,* is not without basis in fact.

he still tends, as Melville's Confidence Man does later, to interpret the doctrine according to self-interest: it pays to be charitable. However, this partial return to a Christain view leads him on toward metaphysical speculation, and it is here that he finds the help he needs. After reading Jonathan Edwards on the will and Joseph Priestly on necessity, both Christian determinists (though one is a Calvinist and the other on the road to Unitarianism), he becomes completely reconciled to his relationship with Bartleby. He infers from these theologians that it is his fate to furnish Bartleby with the means of subsistence. This excursion in Protestant theology teaches him a kind of resignation; he decides to accept the inexplicable situation without further effort to understand or alleviate the poor scrivener's suffering.

At this point we have reached a stasis and the second, or "law- 23
yer's" movement ends. He accepts his relation to Bartleby as "some purpose of an allwise Providence." As a Christian he can tolerate the obstinate writer although he cannot help him. And it is an ironic commentary upon this fatalistic explanation of what has happened that the lawyer's own activities from now on are to be explicitly directed not, insofar as the evidence of the story can be taken as complete, by any supernatural force, but rather by the Wall Street society itself. Now it seems that it is the nature of the social order which determines Bartleby's fate. (The subtitle should be recalled; it is after all Wall Street's story too.) For the lawyer admits that were it not for his professional friends and clients he would have condoned Bartleby's presence indefinitely. But the sepulchral figure of the scrivener hovering in the background of business conferences causes understandable uneasiness among the men of the Street. Businessmen are perplexed and disturbed by writers, particularly writers who don't write. When they ask Bartleby to fetch a paper and he silently declines, they are offended. Recognizing that his reputation must suffer, the lawyer again decides that the situation is intolerable. He now sees that the mere presence of a writer who does not accept Wall Street assumptions has a dangerously inhibiting effect upon business. Bartleby seems to cast a gloom over the office, and more disturbing, his attitude implies a denial of all authority. Now, more clearly than before, the lawyer is aware that Bartleby jeopardizes the sacred right of private property itself, for the insubordinate writer in the end may "outlive" him and so "claim possession . . . [of his office] by right of perpetual occupancy" (a wonderful touch!). If this happens, of course, Bartleby's unorthodox assumptions rather than the lawyer's will eventually dominate the world of Wall Street. The lawyer's friends, by "relentless remarks," bring great pressure to bear upon him, and henceforth the lawyer is in effect an instrument of the great power of social custom, which forces him to take action against the non-conforming writer.

When persuasion fails another time, the only new strategem which the lawyer can conceive is to change offices. This he does, and in the process removes the portable green screen which has provided what little defense Bartleby has had against his environment. The inanimate writer is left "the motionless occupant of a naked room." However, it soon becomes clear to the lawyer that it is not so easy to abdicate his responsibility. Soon he receives a visit from a stranger who reports that the scrivener still inhabits the old building. The lawyer refuses to do anything further. But a few days later several excited persons, including his former landlord, confront him with the news that Bartleby not only continues to haunt the building, but that the whole structure of Wall Street society is in danger of being undermined. By this time Bartleby's rebellion has taken on an explicitly revolutionary character: "Everyone is concerned," the landlord tells the lawyer, "clients are leaving the offices; some fears are entertained of a mob. . . ." 24

Fear of exposure in the public press now moves the lawyer to seek a final interview with the squatter. This time he offers Bartleby a series of new jobs. To each offer the scrivener says no, although in every case he asserts that he is "not particular" about what he does; that is, all the jobs are equally distasteful to him. Desperate because of his inability to frighten Bartleby's "immobility into compliance," the lawyer is driven to make a truly charitable offer; he asks the abject copyist to come home with him. (The problem of dealing with the writer gradually brings out the best in this complacent American.) But Bartleby does not want charity; he prefers to stay where he is. 25

Then the narrator actually escapes. He leaves the city, and when he returns there is word that the police have removed Bartleby to the Tombs as a vagrant. (He learns that even physical compulsion was unable to shake the writer's impressive composure, and that he had silently obeyed the orders of the police.) There is an official request for the lawyer to appear and make a statement of the facts. He feels a mixture of indignation and approval at the news. At the prison he finds Bartleby standing alone in the "inclosed grass-platted yards" silently facing a high wall. Renewing his efforts to get through to the writer, all the lawyer can elicit is a cryptic "I know where I am." A moment later Bartleby turns away and again takes up a position "fronting the dead-wall." The wall, with its deathlike character, completely engages Bartleby. Whether "free" or imprisoned he has no concern for anything but the omnipresent and impenetrable wall. Taking the last resort of the "normal" man, the lawyer concludes that Bartleby is out of his mind. 26

A few days pass and the lawyer returns to the Tombs only to find that they have become, for Bartleby, literally a tomb. He discovers the 27 wasted figure of the writer huddled up at the base of a wall, dead, but with his dim eyes open.

In a brief epilogue the lawyer gives us a final clue to Bartleby's story. He hears a vague report which he asserts has a "certain suggestive interest"; it is that Bartleby had been a subordinate clerk in the Dead Letter Office at Washington. There is some reason to believe, in other words, that Bartleby's destiny, his appointed vocation in this society, had been that of a writer who handled communications for which there were no recipients—PERSON UNKNOWN AT THIS ADDRESS. The story ends with the lawyer's heartfelt exclamation of pity for Bartleby and humankind. 28

II

What did Melville think of Bartleby? The lawyer's notion that Bartleby was insane is of course not to be taken at face value. For when the scrivener says that he knows where he is we can only believe that he does, and the central irony is that there was scarcely a difference, so far as the writer's freedom was concerned, between the prison and Wall Street. In Wall Street Bartleby did not read or write or talk or go anywhere or eat any dinners (he refuses to eat them in prison too) or, for that matter, do anything which normally would distinguish the free man from the prisoner in solitary confinement. And, of course, the office in which he had worked was enclosed by walls. How was this to be distinguished from the place where he died? 29

> The yard was entirely quiet. It was not accessible to the common prisoners. The surrounding walls, of amazing thickness, kept off all sounds behind them. The Egyptian character of the masonry weighed upon me with its gloom. But a soft imprisoned turf grew under foot. The heart of the eternal pyramids, it seemed, wherein, by some strange magic, through the clefts, grass-seed, dropped by the birds, had sprung. (paragraph 244)

At first glance the most striking difference between the Wall Street office and the prison is that here in prison there are four walls, while only three had been visible from the lawyer's windows. On reflection, however, we recall that the side of the office containing the door, which offered a kind of freedom to the others, was in effect a fourth wall for Bartleby. He had refused to walk through it. The plain inference is that he acknowledged no distinction between the lawyer's chambers and the world outside; his problem was not to be solved by leaving the office, or by leaving Wall Street; indeed, from Bartleby's point of view, Wall Street *was* America. The difference between Wall Street and the Tombs was an illusion of the lawyer's, 30 not Bartleby's. In the prison yard, for example, the lawyer is disturbed because he thinks he sees, through the slits of the jail windows, the "eyes of murderers and thieves" peering at the dying Bartleby. (He has all along been persuaded of the writer's incorruptible honesty.) But the writer knows where he is, and he offers no objection to being among thieves. Such minor distinctions do not interest him. For him the important thing is that he still fronts the same dead-wall which has always impinged upon his consciousness, and upon the mind of man since the beginning of time. (Notice the archaic Egyptain character of the prison wall.) Bartleby has come as close to the wall as any man can hope to do. He finds that it is absolutely impassable, and that it is not, as the Ahabs of the world would like to think, merely a pasteboard mask through which man can strike. The masonry is of "amazing thickness."

Then why has Bartleby allowed the wall to paralyze him? The 31
others in the office are not disturbed by the walls; in spite of the poor light they are able to do their work. Is it possible that Bartleby's suffering is, to some extent, self-inflicted? that it is symptomatic of the perhaps morbid fear of annihilation manifested in his preoccupation with the dead-wall? Melville gives us reason to suspect as much. For Bartleby has come to regard the walls as permanent, immovable parts of the structure of things, comparable to man's inability to surmount the limitations of his sense perceptions, or comparable to death itself. He has forgotten to take account of the fact that these particular walls which surround the office are, after all, man-made. They are products of society, but he has imputed eternality to them. In his disturbed mind metaphysical problems which seem to be timeless concomitants of the condition of man and problems created by the social order are inextricably joined, joined in the symbol of the wall.

And yet, even if we grant that Bartleby's tortured imagination has 32
had a part in creating his dead-wall, Melville has not ignored society's share of responsibility for the writer's fate. There is a sense in which Bartleby's state of mind may be understood as a response to the hostile world of Wall Street. Melville has given us a fact of the utmost importance: the window through which Bartleby had stared at the wall had "originally . . . afforded a lateral view of certain grimy backyards and bricks, but . . . owing to subsequent erections, commanded at present no view at all, though it gave some light" (paragraph 17). Melville's insinuation is that the wall, whatever its symbolic significance for Bartleby, actually served as an impediment to (or substitute for?) the writer's vision of the world around him. This is perhaps the most awesome moment in Melville's cold self-examination. The whole fable consists of a surgical probing of Bartleby's motives, and here he questions the value, for a novelist, of those

metaphysical themes which dominate his later work. What made Bartleby turn to the wall? There is the unmistakable hint that such themes (fixing his attention on "subsequent erections") had had the effect of shielding from view the sordid social scene ("grimy backyards and bricks") with which Melville, for example, had been more directly concerned in earlier novels such as *Redburn* or *White Jacket.* At this point we are apparently being asked to consider whether Bartleby's obsession was perhaps a palliative, a defense against social experience which had become more than he could stand. To this extent the nature of the Wall Street society has contributed to Bartleby's fate. What is important here, however, is that Melville does not exonerate the writer by placing all the onus upon society. Bartleby has made a fatal mistake.

Melville's analysis of Bartleby's predicament may be appallingly 33
detached, but it is by no means unsympathetic. When he develops the contrast between a man like Bartleby and the typical American writers of his age there is no doubt where his sympathies lie. The other copyists in the office accept their status as wage earners. The relations between them are tinged by competitiveness—even their names, "Nippers" and "Turkey," suggest "nip and tuck." Nevertheless they are not completely satisfactory employees; they are "useful" to the lawyer only half of the time. During half of each day each writer is industrious and respectful and compliant; during the other half he tends to be recalcitrant and even mildly rebellious. But fortunately for their employer these half-men are never aggressive at the same time, and so he easily dominates them, he compels them to do the sort of writing he wants, and has them "verify the accuracy" of their work according to his standards. When Bartleby's resistance begins they characteristically waver between him and the lawyer. Half the time, in their "submissive" moods ("submission" is their favorite word as "prefer" is Bartleby's), they stand with the employer and are incensed against Bartleby, particularly when his resistance inconveniences *them;* the rest of the time they mildly approve of his behavior, since it expresses their own ineffectual impulses toward independence. Such are the writers the society selects and, though not too lavishly, rewards.

One of Melville's finest touches is the way he has these compliant 34
and representative scriveners, though they never actually enlist in Bartleby's cause, begin to echo his "prefer" without being aware of its source. So does the lawyer. "Prefer" is the nucleus of Bartleby's refrain, "I prefer not to," and it embodies the very essence of his power. It simply means "choice," but it is backed up, as it clearly is not in the case of the other copyists, by will. And it is in the strength of his will that the crucial difference between Bartleby and other writers lies. When Nippers and Turkey use the word "prefer" it

is only because they are unconsciously imitating the manner, the surface vocabulary of the truly independent writer; they say "prefer," but in the course of the parable they never make any real choices. In their mouths "prefer" actually is indistinguishable from "submission"; only in Bartleby's does it stand for a genuine act of will. In fact writers like Nippers and Turkey are incapable of action, a trait carefully reserved for Bartleby, the lawyer, and the social system itself (acting through various agencies, the lawyers' clients, the landlord, and the police). Bartleby represents the only real, if ultimately ineffective, threat to society; his experience gives some support to Henry Thoreau's view that one lone intransigent man can shake the foundations of our institutions.

But he can only shake them, and in the end the practical consequence of Bartleby's rebellion is that society has eliminated an enemy. 35 The lawyer's premonition was true; he finally sees Bartleby in death. Again the story insinuates the most severe self-criticism. For the nearly lifeless Bartleby, attracted neither by the skyward tending white wall, nor the cistern-like black wall, had fixed his eyes on the "dead" wall. This wall of death which surrounds us, and which Melville's heroes so desperately needed to pierce, has much in common with the deadly White Whale. Even Ahab, who first spoke of the whale as a "pasteboard mask" through which man might strike, sensed this, and he significantly shifted images in the middle of his celebrated quarter-deck reply to Starbuck:

> All visible objects, man, are but as pasteboard masks. . . . If man will strike, strike through the mask! How can the prisoner reach outside except by thrusting through the wall? To me, the white whale is that wall, shoved near to me.

Like the whale, the wall will destroy the man who tries too obstinately to penetrate it. Bartleby had become so obsessed by the problem of the dead-wall that his removal to prison hardly changed his condition, or, for that matter, the state of his being; even in the walled street he had allowed his life to become suffused by death.

The detachment with which Melville views Bartleby's situation is 36 perhaps the most striking thing about the fable. He gives us a powerful and unequivocal case against Wall Street society for its treatment of the writer, yet he avoids the temptation of finding in social evil a sentimental sanction for everything his hero thinks and does. True, the society has been indifferent to Bartleby's needs and aspirations; it has demanded of him a kind of writing he prefers not to do; and, most serious of all, it has impaired his vision by forcing him to work in the shadow of its walls. Certainly society shares the responsibility for Bartleby's fate. But Melville will not go all the way with those who find in the guilt of society an excuse for the writer's every hallucination. To understand what led to Bartleby's behavior is not to condone it. Melville refuses to ignore the painful fact that even if society shares the blame for Bartleby's delusion, it was nevertheless a delusion. What ultimately killed this writer was not the walls themselves, but the fact that he confused the walls built by men with the wall of human mortality.

III

Is this, then, as F. O. Matthiessen has written, "a tragedy of utter negation"? If it is not it is because there is a clear if muted note of affirmation here which must not be ignored. In the end, in prison, we are made to feel that the action has somehow taken us closer to the mysterious source of positive values in Melville's universe. "And see," says the lawyer to Bartleby in the prison yard, "it is not so sad a place as one might think. Look, there is the sky, and here is the grass." To the lawyer the presence of the grass in the Tombs is as wonderful as its presence in the heart of eternal pyramids where "by some strange magic through the clefts, grass-seed, dropped by birds, had sprung." The saving power attributed to the green grass is the clue to Melville's affirmation.[3] 37

The green of the grass signifies everything that the walls, whether black or white or blank, do not. Most men who inhabit Wall Street merely accept the walls for what they are—man-made structures which compartmentalize experience. To Bartleby, however, they are abstract emblems of all the impediments to man's realization of his place in the universe. Only the lawyer sees that the outstanding characteristic of the walls, whether regarded as material objects or as symbols, is that they are "deficient in . . . 'life.' " Green, on the other hand, *is* life. The color green is the key to a cluster of images of 38

[3]Recall that two years before, in the letter to Hawthorne which I quoted at the beginning of this essay, Melville had contrasted the unhappy circumstances under which he wrote *Moby Dick* to "the silent grass-growing mood in which a man *ought* always to compose." Later in the same letter he described his own development in the identical image which comes to the mind of the lawyer in "Bartleby":

> I am like one of those seeds taken out of the Egyptian Pyramids, which, after being three thousand years a seed and nothing but a seed, being planted in English soil, it developed itself, grew to greenness, and then fell to the mould.

The fact that this same constellation of images reappears in "Bartleby" in conjunction with the same theme (the contrast between two kinds of writing) seems to me conclusive evidence of the relation between the parable and the "dollars damn me" letter.

fecundity which recurs in Melville's work beginning with *Typee*. It is the color which dominates that tropical primitive isle. It is the color of growth and of all pastoral experience. Indeed the imminent disappearance of our agrarian society is an important motive for Ishmael's signing on the Pequod. "Are the green fields gone?" he asks as *Moby Dick* begins. And later he says, in describing the ecstacy of squeezing sperm: "I declare to you that for the time I lived as in a musky meadow." So he gives a green tint to his redeeming vision of "attainable felicity," a felicity which he says resides in the country, the wife, the heart, the bed—wherever, that is, men may know the magical life-giving force in the world. And *Pierre*, published the year before "Bartleby," also begins with a vision of a green paradise. There Melville makes his meaning explicit. He compares a certain green paint made of verdigris with the "democratic element [which] operates as subtile acid among us, forever producing new things by corroding the old. . . ."

> Now in general nothing can be more significant of decay than the idea of corrosion; yet on the other hand, nothing can more vividly suggest luxuriance of life than the idea of green as a color; for green is the peculiar signet of all-fertile Nature herself.

By some curious quirk of the human situation, Bartleby's un- 39
compromising resistance, which takes him to prison, also takes him a step closer to the green of animal faith. Melville deftly introduces this note of hope by having the lawyer compare the grass in the prison yard to the mystery of the grass within the pyramids. In time greenness, the lawyer suggests, may penetrate the most massive of walls. Indeed green seems virtually inherent in time itself, a somehow eternal property of man's universe. And in a Wall Street society it is (paradoxically) most accessible to the scrivener when he finds himself in prison and at the verge of death. Why? If Bartleby's suicidal obsession has taken him closer to grass and sky, are we to understand that it has had consequences both heartening and meaningful? Is Melville implying, in spite of all the reasons he has given us for being skeptical of Bartleby's motives, that an understanding of his fate may show us the way to a genuine affirmation? Before attempting to answer these questions, it is appropriate to note here how remarkable a fusion of manner and content Melville has achieved. While the questions are never explicitly asked, they are most carefully insinuated. The unique quality of this tale, in fact, resides in its ability to say almost nothing on its placid and inscrutable surface, and yet so powerfully to suggest that a great deal is being said. This quality of style is a perfect embodiment of the theme itself: concealed beneath

the apparently meaningless if not mad behavior of Bartleby is a message of utmost significance to all men.

While the presence of the grass at Bartleby's death scene is the 40
clue to Melville's affirmation, the affirmation can only exist outside of the scrivener's mind. Green now means nothing to him. In the Wall Street world he had known, the green fields *were* gone; he was able to see neither grass nor sky from the walled-in windows. The only green that remained was the artificial green painted upon his flimsy screen, the screen behind which he did his diligent early work. But the screen proved a chimerical means of protection. Again Melville seems to be pointing the most accusing questions at himself. Had not his early novels contained a strong ingredient of primitivism? Had he not in effect relied upon the values implicit in the *Typee* experience (values which reappeared in the image of the inaccessible "insular Tahiti" in *Moby Dick*) as his shelter from the new America? Was this pastoral commitment of any real worth as a defense against a Wall Street society? The story of Bartleby and his green screen, like the letter to Hawthorne (dollars damn me!), denies that it was. In this fable, artificial or man-made green, used as a shield in a Wall Street office, merely abets self-delusion. As for the other green, the natural green of the grass in the prison yard, it is clear that Bartleby never apprehended its meaning. For one thing, a color could hardly have meant anything to him at that stage. His skepticism had taken him beyond any trust in the evidence of his senses; there is no reason to believe that green was for him any less illusory a color than the black or white of the walls. We know, moreover, that when he died Bartleby was still searching: he died with his eyes open.

It is not the writer but the lawyer, the complacent representative 41
American, who is aware of the grass and to whom, therefore, the meaning is finally granted. If there is any hope indicated, it is hope for his, not Bartleby's, salvation. Recall that everything we understand of the scrivener's fate has come to us by way of the lawyer's consciousness. From the first the situation of the writer has been working upon the narrator's latent sensibility, gradually drawing upon his capacity for sympathy, his recognition of the bond between his desperate employee and the rest of mankind. And Bartleby's death elicits a cry of compassion from this man who had once grasped so little of the writer's problem. "Ah, Bartleby! Ah, humanity!" are his (and Melville's) last words. They contain the final revelation. Such deeply felt and spontaneous sympathy is the nearest equivalent to the green of the grass within reach of man. It is an expression of human brotherhood as persistent, as magical as the leaves of grass. Charity is the force which may enable men to meet the challenge of death, whose many manifestations, real and imagined, annihilated the valiant Bartleby.

The final words of the fable are of a piece with Melville's undeviating aloofness from his hero: they at once acknowledge Bartleby's courage and repudiate his delusion. If such a man as the lawyer is ultimately capable of this discernment, then how wrong Bartleby was in permitting the wall to become the exclusive object of his concern! The lawyer can be saved. But the scrivener, like Ahab, or one of Hawthorne's genuises, has made the fatal error of turning his back on mankind. He has failed to see that there were in fact no impenetrable walls between the lawyer and himself. The only walls which had separated them were the folding (manipulatable) glass doors, and the green screen. Bartleby is wrong, but wrong or not, he is a hero; much as Ahab's mad quest was the necessary occasion for Ishmael's salvation, this writer's annihilation is the necessary occasion for Everyman's perception. 42

Among the countless imaginative statements of the artist's problems in modern literature, "Bartleby" is exceptional in its sympathy and hope for the average man, and in the severity of its treatment of the artist. This is particularly remarkable when we consider the seriousness of the rebuffs Melville had so recently been given by his contemporaries. But nothing, he is saying, may be allowed to relieve the writer of his obligations to mankind. If he forgets humanity, as Bartleby did, his art will die, and so will he. The lawyer, realizing this, at the last moment couples Bartleby's name with that of humanity itself. The fate of the artist is inseparable from that of all men. The eerie story of Bartleby is a compassionate rebuke to the self-absorption of the artist, and so a plea that he devote himself to keeping strong his bonds with the rest of mankind. Today, exactly a century after it was written, "Bartleby the Scrivener" is a counterstatement to the large and ever-growing canon of "ordealist" interpretations of the situation of the modern writer. 43

Discussion and Writing Suggestions

1. Marx's main purpose is to show that for Melville "Bartleby" is (at least partially) an autobiographical work: specifically, that it is "about a writer who refuses to conform to the demands of society . . . a writer who forsakes conventional modes because of an irresistible preoccupation with the most baffling philosophical questions" (paragraph 2). How well do you think that Marx has succeeded in this purpose? Do you find any difficulties with his argument? For example, at the beginning of his essay, Marx calls a copyist "a kind of writer." If the reader does not accept this premise, then Marx's whole argument—that Bartleby is "a kind of" Melville—crumbles to pieces. Do you accept it?
2. To Marx, the world of Wall Street in "Bartleby" is a symbol of the world of conventional American literature. Bartleby's refusal to keep copying

documents is analogous to Melville's refusal to keep writing the same kind of commercially successful fiction he had written earlier. (Melville does, in fact, implicitly compare Bartleby to Byron.) Marx also suggests that Bartleby's unaccountable staring at the wall is a symbol of the way Melville's readers might have viewed his difficult later novels. To what extent do you accept these analogies?

3. Marx claims that "only the nature of the wall with which the enigmatic Bartleby is confronted can account for his strange behavior later" (paragraph 9). Write a paper in which you consider the ways that walls function as symbols in "Bartleby." Consider the various types of walls: the colorless wall outside the lawyer's window, the green folding screen inside the office, the "deathlike" prison wall.
4. Is it possible to accept some of Marx's conclusions without accepting others? Even if you don't accept the idea that "Bartleby" is an autobiographical work, is it still possible for this essay to throw light on Melville's story and his life? For example, might it throw light on Melville's self-doubt about the value of his later fiction? Explain.
5. In Marx's scheme of things, what or who is symbolized by the narrator, Turkey, and Nippers? What is the significance of the latter two's beginning to adopt Bartleby's favorite word—"prefer"?
6. What does Marx mean when he says (in paragraph 36) that "[w]hat ultimately killed [Bartleby] was not the walls themselves, but the fact that he confused the walls built by men with the wall of human mortality"?
7. What is the significance of the color green in "Bartleby"?
8. If you have read *Moby Dick,* explain how Bartleby is like Ahab.
9. One of the problems of interpreting "Bartleby" is to decide how to assess the narrator. Should he be condemned for not sufficiently supporting Bartleby, even for hastening his death? (Franklin and Barnett appear to suggest that he should be.) Or did the narrator do all that could reasonably be expected? How does Marx feel about this issue? (A key to responding to this question is to see how critics treat the narrator's final cry, "Ah, Bartleby! Ah, humanity!")
10. Write a critique of Marx's essay, drawing on your responses to some of the questions above.

Bartleby Is a Woman

PATRICIA BARBER

The title of the following article suggests that the author is applying a feminist analysis to "Bartleby." But Barber is not concerned in this

Reprinted from *The Authority of Experience: Essays in Feminist Criticism* edited by Arlyn Diamond and Lee R. Edwards (Amherst: University of Massachusetts Press, 1977) *critique with the exploitation of women by men, nor with the empowerment of women. Rather, she suggests that there are hidden elements in "Bartleby" that become more clearly revealed if we temporarily suppose that Bartleby is a woman, rather than a man. (Barber is not suggesting that Bartleby really is a woman, as, for instance, some critics have suggested that Shakespeare's Hamlet was a woman.) She is suggesting that "Bartleby," viewed thus, is a love story.*

Because of its unusual thesis, Barber's analysis may be even more difficult for you to accept than some of the possibly farfetched suppositions in the preceding articles. Nevertheless, try to suspend your disbelief as you read this article; accept (for the moment) the premise, and see whether or not "Bartleby" appears in a new light. If so, does the action of the story now make greater sense than it did when you first read it? Does the analysis help persuade you that at least one dimension of "Bartleby" that you may have ignored previously is the dimension of human relationships—if not of love, itself?

Patricia Barber is a short-story writer and filmmaker, with a special interest in American Studies. This article first appeared under the title "What If Bartleby Were a Woman?" In The Authority of Experience: Essays in Feminist Criticism *(1977).*

Except in one respect, Herman Melville's "Bartleby, the Scrivener: A Story of Wall-Street" (1853) is an oddly timely story not only in its theme of office alienation but also in its setting. The lawyer of today—like the story's narrator—might well have offices on New York's Wall Street; he might well have recalcitrant help, he might well be familiar with the still barbaric city jail, the Tombs; he might well have windows looking only onto blank walls. But today's lawyer would not have men doing his copying for him: by historical circumstance the male scrivener has given way to that office commonplace, the female typist. 1

At first thought this recognition seems merely nice, a device, perhaps, for reminding undergraduates, especially women, that the oppressiveness of the office world is still with us, that one of them could be a Bartleby. Then, if one plays further with the idea of Bartleby as a woman, the sex-changed story seems to contain the makings of a farce. A Hollywood treatment might involve an unconsciously sexy young thing who moves right into the office of a middle-aged, but eligible lawyer, hangs her undies across the window, makes his clients wonder what is going on, and coolly refuses to do the least bit of work. And at the end they would marry, or at least fall into bed. 2

But let us not succumb to the Hollywood version entirely—which could not, after all, encompass the suicide that closes the scrivener's story—but rather consider seriously the story of a female Bartleby. In 3 fact, how would a dignified gentleman like the lawyer of Melville's story respond to a woman who "prefers not to," who refuses, say, to make coffee, or answer the phone, or talk pleasantly to her boss's clients, or do anything other than merely copy documents? And, more drastically, who sets up housekeeping there in the office behind no more than an opaque glass screen, then refuses to do even her copying, and finally refuses to leave?

Is it even legitimate to ask these questions when, in fact, Melville 4
did not write a story about a man and his secretary? To change the sex of a centrally placed character in a story might seem to amount to an act of critical violence. If Hamlet—to take one example—has been played *by* a woman, he has never, so far as I know, been played *as* a woman, and the very idea is a staggering one. What would happen if Ulysses or Oedipus or the Redcrosse Knight or—to jump space and time—Ahab or Huck Finn or any male Hemingway hero became women? What if Eve were a man? The gender of a character would seem to be a given with which a critic cannot tamper, unless, however, we understand the tampering as a heuristic device.

If a female Ulysses or Ahab seems only an impossible joke, this 5
"joke" may serve to point up the separate boundaries we have imposed around our expectations regarding men and women. We might better understand, for one thing, to what a vast extent people's genders have determined their social roles. In considering, say, the absurdity of a sex-changed love story, Cleopatra or Jane Eyre as men, for example, we might realize how largely one's gender and resulting social role determine the emotional life. One might try to imagine Faustus as a woman and if that seems impossible, go on to consider how gender may affect the style and intensity of a person's intellectual life.[1]

[1]We note here the rise of an idea that the differences between the sexes really matter very little, that psychologically we are all androgynous. Although so far as I know there is no evidence either to support or to refute this theory, the wish for it is strong, and strong, I think, for at least five reasons. First of all, most of the ideas about how women's minds differ from men's—they are not so logical, are prone to "hysteria"—are insulting to women and contrary to commonly observed fact. Second, we now generally believe in the principles of equal social and economic opportunity, and to say that men and women are importantly different from one another may seem to argue that real equality of opportunities is impossible. In the third place, it is a common literary experience especially for feminist readers to notice that our literature is male-dominated, that female characters rarely attain the status of complex heroes, that they have a range of personalities and potentialities far more limited than in reality, and are rarely models of, say, courage, intelligence, and forthrightness: in order, then, to take literature seriously one has to believe that the supposedly "masculine" or "feminine" traits can be possessed by both sexes, so that the female reader may legitimately identify with Oedipus as well as Antigone, Antony as well as Cleopatra, Ahab as well as Hester Prynne. In the fourth place, we commonly believe in the importance of

(*continued*)

It might also happen—as I suggest it does with "Bartleby"—that changing the sex of a character would not turn the story into a joke. The change might suggest new possibilities of human experience, create, in a sense, new role models. Or we might recognize how we do sometimes participate in certain situations in the same way, particularly in those situations arising from social roles which either are open equally to men and women or else—as with Bartleby's job—have become over time open to the other sex. For the critic, the technique of the sex-change might help to expose elements in a literary work which previously were obscure. Our conventional expectations regarding sexual behavior create a kind of critical myopia in us: we do not perceive what we do not expect to find, and thus we may miss seeing, to take Bartleby and the lawyer as an example, the intensity of feeling of one person for another of the same sex. 6

I would like therefore to present a synopsis of the story of Miss Bartleby in order to show both the insight Melville's story has into the contemporary relationship of a male boss with his female employee, and also the way the sex-changed story reveals that "Bartleby, the Scrivener" is a story of failed love, a love the lawyer conceals by adopting a rhetorical tone of genial detachment toward his experience. To "write" Miss Bartleby's story I have done no more to Melville's version than change 'man' to 'woman' or 'lady,' alter the pronouns, and add the title to Bartleby's name. For brevity's sake I have ignored the other office help in the story: in a fuller version of Miss Bartleby's story the three other quirky scriveners would also, I feel, be women, the "girls" in the office. 7

The story opens with the lawyer explaining to the reader that in all his many years of law practice he never met with so strange a copyist as Miss Bartleby. He describes his comfortable professional circumstances at the time he hired this woman and then returns to her story: "In answer to my advertisement, a motionless young 8

---

empathy for good human relations and if one is to believe that we are all able to experience and understand the concerns of both men and women, one is tempted to explain this ability with an idea that we all share in an androgynous universality of human experience. In the fifth place, there are many people who feel restricted by their own gender, who wish they could do and experience the things the other sex does, who, in short, wish they were androgynous and thus evolve a theory of psychological androgyny to make at least part of their wish come true. Still, given that androgyny is a rare phenomenon physiologically, and that it is infrequent in the social realm in that few social roles are equally open to both sexes, it is difficult to see how it could exist psychologically either, however strong the wish for androgyny might be. On the other hand, there seems reason to believe that if people struggle so that the social structure changes to permit women and men to share equally in a wider variety of roles, then perhaps a kind of psychological androgyny will come into being—for there is no principle in psychology which states that changes in psychological human nature are impossible.

woman one morning stood upon my office threshold, the door being open, for it was summer. I can see that figure now—pallidly neat, pitiably respectable, incurably forlorn! It was Miss Bartleby." He tells how she worked without stopping, how she "seemed to gorge herself on my documents." "I should have been quite delighted with her application," he says, "had she been cheerfully industrious. But she wrote on silently, palely, mechanically." Up to this point Miss Bartleby is a mysterious, Jamesian figure. She is a young woman with some secret sorrow that makes her seem, both in her lack of vitality and her desperate industriousness, old before her time. As the lawyer relates the story in retrospect, we learn that at first he was not sensitive to Miss Bartleby's troubled soul.

One day, however, he was seated at his desk in that archetypal 9
posture of the busy boss: his head was bent over his papers, his hand extended waiting to be relieved of the document in its grasp. Without looking up he calls out to Miss Bartleby to proofread the document with him: "Imagine my surprise, nay, my consternation, when without moving from her privacy, Miss Bartleby, in a singularly mild, firm voice, replied, 'I would prefer not to.'" He is silenced for a moment, finally repeats the question, and again hears her say that she would prefer not to. He gets up "in high excitement," asks if she is "moonstruck" and insists that she help him. For a third time she answers, " 'I would prefer not to.' " Annoying as it is, Miss Bartleby's extraordinary refusal to do anything but simply copy documents intrigues him. He begins watching her closely, not sure what action to take, but to his every request for an office task other than silent copying, she answers that she would prefer not to.

He is not, however, at first totally dismayed by Miss Bartleby's 10
terms: "Her steadiness, her freedom from all dissipation, her incessant industry (except when she chose to throw herself into a standing revery behind her screen), her great stillness, her unalterableness of demeanor under all circumstances, made her a valuable acquisition. One prime thing was this—*she was always there*—first in the morning, continually through the day, and last at night." His satisfaction with these Protestant-ethic virtues of his "acquisition" is shaken shortly thereafter when he happens by his office one Sunday morning before church. He is startled to find the office door locked from inside and Miss Bartleby there. She comes to the door "in a strangely tattered deshabille" and coolly tells him to go away for a while and then come back. Astounded, he does so and begins wondering why she is there, quickly dismissing the idea that anything "amiss" was going on.

When he returns to his office, she has gone, and he discovers that 11
she has made the office into her living quarters. He looks through her desk and finds a bandanna with her money knotted in it. In good

lawyer-fashion he then methodically counts the evidence regarding her mysterious life: he recalls that she never initiates conversation, never reads, that "for long periods she would stand looking out, at her pale window behind her screen, upon a dead brick wall," that she never goes out to eat or to walk or for any other reason, that she never said who she was or where she came from, that she never complains of ill health. He recalls in particular "a certain unconscious air of pallid—how shall I call it?—of pallid haughtiness, say, or rather an austere reserve about her," a reserve which awes him. He then reaches the conclusion that she "was the victim of innate and incurable disorder. I might give alms to her body; but her body did not pain her; it was her soul that suffered, and her soul I could not reach."

He decides to give her another chance at self-explanation, and 12
this time will try direct interrogation. Several times he asks if she will give him some information, but to each request she replies that she would prefer not to. Despite these refusals, the lawyer cannot yet bring himself to do as he had planned—to fire her. The next day Miss Bartleby informs him that she will do no more writing. When he asks why, she stares at the wall: " 'Do you not see the reason for yourself?' she indifferently replied." He does not see any reason, although he does notice, when he looks closely at her, that her eyes are dull and glazed. He decides that she must have strained her vision by writing in a poor light, and assumes that in a few days she will be back at work.

But after a few days she tells him she has given up copying for 13
good. His anxiety mounts: he wishes he could write to her relatives and ask that they take her away "to some convenient retreat." But he knows of no relatives and she seems to him alone—"absolutely alone in the universe. A bit of wreck in the mid-Atlantic." He finally tells her she must go in six days time. But six days later she is still there. Again he tells her to leave and tries to give her some extra money, but still she stays. Finally he resorts to stern fatherly reproval and tells her that she must either do some work or get out. But still she silently refuses.

Miss Bartleby's impassive response drives the usually temperate 14
lawyer to thoughts of murder. Shocked by his own passion, he struggles to maintain a charitable view. But gradually he becomes worried about what his clients and fellow lawyers must be thinking about the strange silent creature in his office. The thought of what her presence might do to his professional reputation finally resolves him to rid himself forever of "this intolerable incubus."

Knowing that Miss Bartleby will not leave of her own accord, he 15
decides that it will actually be simpler if he leaves her. He rents a new office for himself, says goodbye to Miss Bartleby, and then "strange

to say—I tore myself from whom I longed to be rid of." Though he is surprised that he was reluctant to leave her, he is relieved to find that she does not follow him. But the new tenants of his office find that they are now stuck with her. She sleeps, it seems, in the entry and sits all day on the banisters of the stairs.

The lawyer tries once more to persuade her to leave, but when he proposes several different jobs he might find her she is quite uninterested. Finally he asks her if she will come home with him "not to my office, but to my dwelling," and there they will work out "some convenient arrangement." She refuses and the lawyer is so dismayed by the whole situation that he leaves town and for the next few days does nothing but drive around out in the countryside, avoiding his office altogether. When he finally returns, he finds a note saying that the police have taken Miss Bartleby to the Tombs as a vagrant. 16

He goes down to the jail to see her. She is allowed to go outside in the prison yard, since her offense is so trivial and her manner so mild. Feeling guilty now, he tries to defend himself: " 'It was not I that brought you here, Miss Bartleby,' said I, keenly pained at her implied suspicion. 'And to you, this should not be so vile a place. Nothing reproachful attaches to you by being here. And see, it is not so sad a place as one might think. Look, there is the sky, and here is the grass.' 'I know where I am,' she replied, but would say nothing more, and so I left her." He arranges for her to get some decent food, but she refuses to eat. The next time he comes to see her, a few days later, he finds her lying next to the stone wall out in the courtyard. She is dead, and he closes her eyes. The lawyer notes that he later heard that she had once been a clerk in the Dead Letter Office in Washington, an occupation he finds fitting to "a woman by nature and misfortune prone to a pallid hopelessness." And he concludes his tale, "Ah, Miss Bartleby! Ah, humanity!" 17

Melville's story clearly, I think, loses none of its power when Bartleby becomes a woman, a woman who refuses with such a dignified—but suicidal—emphasis. We have an all too plausible portrait of a young woman of great, if pathological, dignity who refuses to accommodate herself to a sterile world of meaningless office work. Her copying tasks offer no means of self-expression or creativity; she can declare her existence only by her passive but determined resistance. Her dignity does not permit either fist-shaking rebellion or the petty carelessness and insolence of the rightfully resentful office employee. For reasons we do not know, her outside life offers no compensating satisfactions, and even though her inner malaise is great, the failure of her office life to offer any relief at all is a devastating commentary on our modern office-bound existence. 18

Although no feminist would advocate suicide as an appropriate method of protesting one's working condition, still those conditions of office life are a part of what feminist agitation is all about. The lawyer in this story is no Simon Legree, but he still might be called a Mr. Shelby, the kindest of all possible slaveholders, a tactful, polite, patient boss, as decent a boss as one might expect to find; by any ordinary standard he goes out of his way to accommodate Miss Bartleby. We note that at first she seems to him a "valuable acquisition," hard-working, uncomplaining, quiet, like a machine that never causes trouble, the ideal office worker. "One prime thing," he says, "*she was always there*"—like a faithful servant or slave. At least a part of the lawyer's good feeling for her, then, rises from this initial view of her as a useful acquisition or piece of property, an attitude any worker might resent. 19

It is when she stops doing her work and thus ceases to be a useful acquisition to him that he vaguely realizes by his inability to fire her immediately that he has become attached to her not just because she did his copying for him, but because her loneliness and mysterious sorrow as well as her persistent refusal to leave him express her need—and his need—for human connection. He would like to help her, but his sense of what the employer-employee relationship *should* be—no work, no wages—prevents him from letting Miss Bartleby use a part of the office as a refuge. And in any case, I suggest, he would like their relationship to be more than that: when as a last resort he asks her to come home with him, he does so not only to get her out of the office, but also, one feels, as a way of expressing his own loneliness in a situation where his only relationships are with clients or office workers, relationships necessarily limited by being basically exploitative. 20

This story about a boss and his secretary speaks perceptively to the difficulties of making satisfying relationships in an office context.[2] In a state of despair a person who is valued only for her machine-like abilities—copying documents—rebels: she refuses, as so many would 21

[2]There is a whole profession of business consultants devoted to these very difficulties of making human relationships in an office context. Their clients are businesses or other bureaucratic organizations who want to keep employees happy mainly in order to increase productivity or improve quality control. While earlier theories about employee satisfaction held that salary, physical working conditions, and good personal relations with supervisors and fellow workers were the main factors, a new school of "behavioralists" believe that these so-called "hygiene" factors only *prevent* dissatisfaction; in order to have actual satisfaction the work itself has to be challenging, creative, lead to new challenges, and in general give the worker a feeling of fulfilling his or her individual potential. See Frederick Herzberg, *Work and the Nature of Man* (Cleveland: World, 1966); see also Clayton Reesor, "What the Behavioral Scientists Are Up To," *Machine Design*, October 5, 1972, pp. 96–101.

like to do but being more realistic than Miss Bartleby, do not do, and thereby expresses the hollowness of that situation in which both employers and employees suffer, but the employees, I think, suffer the most. This theme inheres in both Melville's story of the male scrivener and the sex-changed version, but since such a large part of the lower-grade office employees are now women—and their bosses men—the economic exploitation has taken sexist overtones, and by making Bartleby a woman we reveal how Melville's story explores a situation the author could not have known about.

Changing Bartleby to a woman not only serves as a device for bringing the story closer to a contemporary condition of life but also works to reveal an otherwise hidden erotic quality in the original. One of the striking aspects about the sex-changed story is how gracefully it works: the story, one can say, in fact hardly changes, surprising as this seems in view of the radical change to Bartleby. There are, I think, two reasons why Miss Bartleby's story is so similar to Mr. Bartleby's. In the first place the story is not really so much about Bartleby as it is about the lawyer who narrates the story, about passive, affluent complacency shaken by passive, irrational refusal. We never, after all, really do find out what makes Bartleby act as he does, even though we recognize the psychological realism of that suicidal refusal. Instead, as we identify with the lawyer's quiet reasonableness, the story evokes our sense of pity and helplessness in the confrontation with this isolato. That we do not really know Bartleby, that he hardly develops beyond the cadaverous figure staring at the dead brick wall, leads to the second reason why his sexual gender makes so little difference to the story. 22

Bartleby, whether male or female, is, by the nature of his mysterious ailment, so devitalized, so unerotic, that he becomes for us essentially sexless. This awful sexlessness and seeming absence of any erotic drive are most clearly apparent in the Miss Bartleby version. Let us take the scene where the lawyer unexpectedly encounters her one morning in, as he puts it, "deshabille." The staid man is taken aback both by her undress and her cool behavior, her "wonderful mildness" which "not only disarmed me, but unmanned me, as it were." Naturally enough he wonders what she is up to, half-dressed there in his office. The lawyer's tension here has an obvious erotic element not obvious in the male Bartleby story and hints at the possibility of the office farce. That possibility is cut short, however, not so much by the lawyer's propriety as by Miss Bartleby's stubborn opposition to any sort of social intercourse, an opposition which, in view of her loneliness, seems startling and abnormal. 23

Clearly, however, Miss Bartleby intrigues the lawyer, partly by her mystery and solitude, partly by that dignified passivity which he semi-consciously recognizes in himself, and also by the very strength 24 of her defiant stance. That strength has, I think, a distinctly erotic aspect. Here is a woman who in cold and silent anger has pushed her past life away, is pushing her present life away because it is beneath her dignity, and apparently is trying to confront only what is essential, a task few risk. The blank wall she stares at is a *tabula rasa,* Locke's image of the mind prior to experience, the mind at the beginning, the starting-point of knowledge. She is a woman who is alone: perhaps more obviously than a man alone would be, a man like the original Bartleby, she is a figure of pathos, a figure whose solitary state seems to call out for human contact, sexual bonding.

Part of the lawyer's frustration with Bartleby has to do with 25
Bartleby's inaccessibility in his loneliness. As the lawyer narrates the story in meticulous detail, recalling whole conversations, lengthy sequences of thought, nuances of complex feelings, we understand that his experience with Bartleby was a significant one. From the time he first saw Bartleby at his office door the young man made a sharp impression on him, one that stays with him—"I can see that figure now. . . ." In the sex-changed story we cannot help but read this distinct recollection as the first hint of erotic interest on the lawyer's part. This reading is then reinforced when the lawyer tells how closely he observed the girl's working habits and living arrangements, and becomes strong when he tells us that her "austere reserve" had "positively awed" him into a "tame compliance" with her ways. Miss Bartleby may not be a likely object of erotic interest, but the point is that she is young and female and does live and undress and go to bed right there in the office, activities which can only be sexually provocative. In any case this lawyer does not apparently have ordinary tastes: he is not married though well along in years, himself leads a safe, austere life, and his interest in the other office workers amounts to little more than bemusement. And he is lonely.

As Miss Bartleby more and more withdraws from ordinary office 26
activity, she forces the lawyer to regard her as not just another girl in the office but rather as a special human being. As the lawyer does so, his interest in her intensifies so that when he finally moves out he realizes he does not entirely want to leave her. When he then reaches the point of asking her to come home with him, we cannot help hearing an echo of what is usually a seductive invitation: the lawyer is thoroughly frustrated, finds himself most uncharacteristically "fairly flying into a passion," and is about to walk out "when a final thought occurred to me—one which had not been wholly unindulged before," that is, asking her to come "not to my office, but to my dwelling." We realize here that the lawyer has thought before of asking her to come home with him, and however proper the man is, the wish for a more domestic, a more erotic connection is apparent. When Miss Bartleby coldly refuses, this middle-aged man rushes from the building, runs

up the hill on Wall Street toward Broadway, and jumps onto the first passing bus to escape the whole situation. The unusual energy he exhibits plus what follows—heading for the country to spend several days driving aimlessly around—suggest that to him her refusal was an emphatic rejection of him in every respect, including the sexual, a rejection enraging and even somewhat deranging.

The scenes of the lawyer with Bartleby at the Tombs are plainly 27
tender ones, but when Bartleby is a woman the lawyer's tenderness takes on a romantic quality. He tells us that he saw the "wasted" Miss Bartleby "huddled at the base of the wall, her knees drawn up, and lying on her side, her head touching the cold stones," and that when he felt her hand, "a tingling-shiver ran up my arms and down my spine to my feet" and he realized she was dead. The man at the jail asked if she was asleep and the lawyer murmured, " 'With kings and counselors,' " thus quoting *Job* and playing wishfully on his own occupation as a counselor-at-law. The lawyer, then, gives the effect of being a lover at the graveside, the figure of his loved one making him shiver and invoking in him thoughts of her afterlife.

If little of this erotic quality seems apparent in the tale of the male 28
Bartleby, there are, I think, two explanations—one, that the lawyer's propriety and language tend to lead us away from seeing that element, and two, the more important, that we simply do not expect to find a man having an erotic feeling for another man, no matter how familiar we are with Melville's scene of Ishmael and Queequeg in bed.

To take up the first explanation, let us consider the passage 29
midway through the story where the lawyer describes his feelings for Bartleby. For the first time in his life, he says, he was overpowered by "a stinging melancholy" when he contemplated Bartleby's small, lonely life in the office: "The bond of a common humanity now drew me irresistibly to gloom. A fraternal melancholy! For both I and Bartleby were sons of Adam." This talk of a fraternal bond, of a bond between two men, or between men in general, is the jarring note in the sex-changed story, for a fraternal bond would seem to preclude an attachment to a woman, an erotic attachment. The lawyer here seems to see himself and Bartleby in a rather rarified way, as two among all those cast out from Eden, bound, perhaps, by a sort of spiritual loss. If we recognize, however, that this elevated rhetoric is associated with an emotion as rare—for him—and as sharp as a "stinging melancholy," we can see that the lawyer is responding not merely to a vague, generalized sense of humanity but rather to a specific one-to-one relationship. The exalted rhetoric here, along with the frequent use of juristical terms and the heavy use of the passive voice, all serve as the lawyer's linguistic defenses against what would be a too painful understanding of the depth of his own feeling. And

because he tells us at the outset what an "eminently *safe* man" he is, how tame his emotions are, we tend to feel he is incapable of strong feelings.

If the lawyer's language and propriety conceal the intensity of his feeling for Bartleby, it is also true that this feeling is concealed by our own unreadiness to see it. We only dimly feel the strength of the lawyer's feeling for Bartleby, in part simply because we do not expect such a respectable, middle-aged type to have such feelings, feelings that are basically homosexual. Our conventional attitude which does not expect to find erotic impulses between "normal" mature people of the same sex is, of course, a denial of the facts. In turn, the effect of this denial is to prevent us from understanding the roots and power of "fraternal" feelings and from understanding that these feelings are the basis of a necessary sense of common human bondage regardless of sexual gender. 30

The point here is that this element of fraternal passion in the lawyer is nowhere so clearly exposed as when we imagine Bartleby as a woman and therefore a more "appropriate" object of an erotic impulse. By imagining the story of Miss Bartleby, we realize that the story of the lawyer and Bartleby—for all its oddity, dry humor, and stuffy rhetoric—is essentially a love story, a story about a man who is confined in an office setting that forbids intimacy and who comes to love a person he cannot save. Melville's story of human loneliness and ineffectual compassion does not, I think, become merely an office farce. 31

Discussion and Writing Suggestions

1. To what extent do you accept Barber's main premise: that making Bartleby a woman enables us to throw light on aspects of Melville's story—and particularly on the narrator—that otherwise would remain dark? (Barber suggests other advantages gained by turning Bartleby into a woman in paragraph 6.) Do you think Barber has succeeded in her purpose? Why or why not?
2. Do you agree with Barber when she says (in paragraph 18) that "Melville's story . . . loses none of its power when Bartleby becomes a woman"? Or does the supposition remain merely a joke?
3. In what way(s) does Barber's analysis of "Bartleby" resemble Louise K. Barnett's? Consider especially the judgment of the narrator and the kind of work performed in his office.
4. To what extent do you agree with Barber's contention (paragraph 22) that "the story is not really so much about Bartleby as it is about the lawyer who narrates the story, about passive, affluent complacency shaken by passive, irrational refusal"?
5. Barber explores at some length what she calls "a hidden erotic quality in

the original [story]." Do you find her analysis—particularly of the lawyer's erotic attraction to Bartleby—convincing? If not, then how do *you* account for the lawyer's behavior after Bartleby rejects his offer to come home with him? (As Barber writes, he leaves "for the country to spend several days driving aimlessly around—suggest[ing] that to him her refusal was an emphatic rejection of him in every respect, including sexual, a rejection enraging and even somewhat deranging.")

6. To most readers, the lawyer's tenderness for Bartleby appears to be "a vague generalized sense of humanity" rather than "a specific one-to-one relationship." But, as Barber points out (paragraph 29), appearances are deceptive: "The exalted rhetoric here, along with the frequent use of . . . the passive voice, all serve as the lawyer's linguistic defenses against what would be a too painful understanding of the depth of his own feeling." Comment.

7. Barber concludes, "By imagining the story of Miss Bartleby, we realize that the story of the lawyer and Bartleby—for all its oddity, dry humor, and stuffy rhetoric—is essentially a love story, a story about a man who is confined in an office setting that forbids intimacy and who comes to love a person he cannot save." Forget Barber's supposition that Bartleby is a woman. Does this interpretation of Melville's story make sense to you? Why or why not? Write your response in the form of a critique.

SYNTHESIS ACTIVITIES

1. Write a summary essay on the range of critical approaches to Melville's "Bartleby."

   This assignment calls basically for a series of interconnected summaries. You will need to categorize the approaches you find: for instance, the clinical approach, the religious approach, and so on; or perhaps approaches that assume Bartleby is a real person, approaches that assume he is a symbol, and so on. If you have only one example in each category, summarize each essay, emphasizing in your summary those elements that show how the article falls into that category. If there are two or more examples in each category, emphasize those common elements of the examples that allow them to be placed in the same category.

2. Of the five critical approaches to "Bartleby," which one or two do you find the most plausible? Why? Which do you find most thought-provoking? Which do you find most outlandish? Explain.

   First, select the quality or qualities on which you will focus (plausibility, outlandishness, etc.). Then select the one or two articles that evoke these qualities. Finally (before writing your paper), identify two or three features of, or examples from, each article (some features may be general; some, specific) that have impressed you the most, either positively or negatively.

In the process, you should probably draw contrasts with other articles, while keeping the emphasis on your one or two main selections. Write your response in the form of a critique.

3. Compare and contrast two or more critical approaches to various *motifs* or *characters* in "Bartleby" (e.g., the narrator, the office, Bartleby's refusal to work, the jail, the epilogue). Which seem to throw the most light on Melville's meaning?

You may want to review the material on comparison-contrast syntheses in Chapter 3. You may decide to organize by article (discuss the approaches to the motifs or characters in one article, then the other[s]), or you may decide to organize by elements, discussing how two or more authors deal with one element, then another, and so on. Of course, some other logic of organization may suggest itself; feel free to follow your own best hunches.

4. One of the central critical issues of "Bartleby" is how we as readers should respond to (a) Bartleby; (b) the narrator; (c) the physical setting; (d) the type of work done in the office. For example, is Bartleby being treated satirically? Should we regard him as a kind of warning? Is the narrator being held up for our approval or our scorn? What do the critics say about some of these matters? What is your opinion?

One method of organization is suggested by the question itself; you may wish to treat, in turn, (a), (b), (c), and (d), above, in this or some other order. Don't feel obliged to treat all of these elements; on the other hand, you may want to add some of your own. You may also wish to add or substitute other questions that focus on your—or the critics'—reactions to the various elements of "Bartleby."

5. Compare and contrast Louise K. Barnett's essay on "Bartleby Is Marx's Alienated Worker" and Patricia Barber's on "Bartleby Is a Woman." How are the critical approaches and conclusions similar? How are they different?

As in the second question above, you could organize your comparison-contrast essay in one of two ways: (1) organize by source: summarize the key elements of each essay, in turn, and then compare and contrast their approaches; (2) organize by criterion. Thus, how does each article treat the office (and Wall Street) environment? How does each treat interpersonal relationships? And so on.

6. How is it possible for the same story to generate so many widely varying interpretations? One answer is that the critics are operating under widely varying assumptions about which elements of both life and literature are most important (or, at least, are of greatest interest). Thus, the Marxist (and in some ways, the feminist) tends to view both life and literature in terms of class struggle, in terms of the exploitation of one class by another. Reexamine several of the critics in this chapter and show how their varying critical *assumptions* about what kinds of things are significant can account for their divergent approaches to "Bartleby." (Consider, along the way, your *own* assumptions about human behavior, human relationships, the relationship between individuals and society, and the relationship between writers of fiction, the worlds they inhabit, and their literary creations.)

The suggested subtopics in the sentence above offer one organizational basis for your paper. Select several of these subtopics (or add or substitute several of your own) and for each, show how two or more critics rely on differing critical assumptions in dealing with them. Or, organize by critical approach (or author) and show how, for each approach, distinctive assumptions generate distinctive conclusions about the nature of the work under consideration. Whichever approach you select, don't forget to discuss your *own* assumptions as a factor in your response both to Melville's story and to the various critical responses.